THE THEORY
AND
PRACTICE OF
GROUP
PSYCHOTHERAPY

Books by the Same Author

Every Day Gets a Little Closer: A Twice-Told Therapy
(with Ginny Elkin)

Encounter Groups: First Facts
(with Morton A. Lieberman and Matthew B. Miles)

Existential Psychotherapy

Inpatient Group Psychotherapy

THE THEORY AND PRACTICE OF GROUP PSYCHOTHERAPY

THIRD EDITION

IRVIN D. YALOM

Basic Books, Inc., Publishers

NEW YORK

Library of Congress Cataloging in Publication Data

Yalom, Irvin D., 1931–
   The theory and practice of group psychotherapy.

   Bibliography: p. 539
   Includes index.
   1. Group psychotherapy. I. Title.
RC488.Y3 1985   616.89'152   85-47566
ISBN 0-465-08447-8

To my mother,

RUTH YALOM,

and to the memory of my father,

BENJAMIN YALOM

CONTENTS

vii

PREFACE

Since group therapy was first introduced in the 1940s, it has undergone a series of adaptations to meet the changing face of clinical practice. As new clinical syndromes, settings, and theoretical approaches have emerged (and sometimes vanished), so too have corresponding variants of group therapy. The multiplicity of forms is so evident today that it is best not to speak of group therapy but of the many group therapies. Chronic aftercare groups, cancer support groups, eating disorders groups, rap groups for Vietnam war veterans, groups for patients with myocardial infarct, paraplegia, diabetic blindness, renal failure—all of these are forms of group therapy. A group of chronically or acutely hospitalized psychiatric patients is also group therapy; and so, too, is a group of relatively well functioning individuals with neurotic or characterological disorders meeting in a psychotherapist's private office.

The number of group therapies is swollen even more by the presence of distant cousins—groups that are almost or sometimes therapy groups, such as encounter groups, personal growth groups, T-groups, interpersonal skills training groups, family therapy groups, marital couple groups, and numerous self-help groups like Alcoholics Anonymous and Recovery Incorporated. Some of these are designated therapy groups, while others straddle the blurred border between personal growth and therapy (see chapter 16 for a full discussion of this topic).

How, then, to write a single group therapy book that addresses all these group therapies? The strategy I chose fifteen years ago when I wrote the first edition of this book seems sound to me still. I attempted to introduce order by separating "front" from "core" in each of the group therapies. The front consists of the trappings, the form, the techniques, the specialized language, and the aura surrounding each of the schools of therapy; the core consists of those aspects of the experience that are intrinsic to the therapeutic process—that is, the bare-boned mechanisms of change.

Disregard the "front," consider only the actual mechanism of effecting change in the patient, and we will find that these mechanisms of change are limited in number and remarkably similar across groups. Therapy groups with similar goals which appear totally different in external form may rely on identical mechanisms of change. In the first and second editions of this book, I, influenced by the positivistic zeitgeist surrounding the developing psychotherapies, referred to these mechanisms of change as "curative factors." The passing years have taught us that psychotherapy effects growth or change but that "cure" is an illusion. It is time, now, to heed the dictates of moderation: hence, in this edition, I have rechristened the "curative factors" as "therapeutic factors."

The therapeutic factors constitute the central organizing principle of this book. I begin with a detailed discussion of eleven therapeutic factors and from there proceed to describe a psychotherapeutic approach based on these factors. There are so many group therapies that it is not possible to address each one separately. I have chosen, as my prototypic model, one particular type of therapy group—the outpatient psychotherapy group with its ambitious goals of both symptomatic relief and characterological change. I selected this group because I believe it to be the most common and the most representative therapy group. The work of this type of group entails considerable support, risk taking, interaction and analysis of that interaction. The therapeutic strategies and techniques required to lead such a group are complex; but once the student masters them and understands, as well, how to modify basic technique to fit specialized therapy situations (see chapter 14), then he or she is in a position to fashion a group therapy to meet any clinical situation.

The great majority of my readers are clinicians, and I intend this text to be of immediate clinical relevance. I also believe, however, that it is imperative that clinicians remain conversant with the world of research and, accordingly, I review and rely heavily upon relevant clinical and basic social and psychological research. While searching through library stacks during the writing of this book, I often browsed in antiquated psychiatric texts. How unsettling it is to realize that the devotees of therapy through venesection, starvation, purgation, and trephining were obviously clinicians of high intelligence, dedication, and integrity! The same may be said of the last generation of therapists who advocated hydrotherapy, rest cures, leucotomy, and insulin coma. Their texts are as well written, their optimism as unbridled, and their reported results as impressive as those of the practitioners of the modern age.

Many other patient-care fields have left us far behind because they have applied the principles of the scientific method. Without a rigorous research base, the psychotherapists of today who are enthusiastic about current treatment modes are tragically similar to the hydrotherapists of yesterday. Without the utilization of scientific rigor to test basic principles and relative treatment efficacies, the field remains at the mercy of passing fashions. Therefore, whenever possible, I have attempted to base my approach upon hard relevant research and to call attention to areas in which further research seems especially necessary and feasible. Some areas (for example, preparation for group therapy or group dropouts) have been successfully studied, while others (for example, "working through" or countertransference) have been virtually untouched by research. Naturally the relevant chapters reflect this distribution of research emphasis: some chapters may appear, to clinicians, to stress research too heavily, while other chapters may appear, to research-minded colleagues, to lack rigor.

It is unrealistic to expect research to effect a rapid major change in the practice of psychotherapy. Complex systems of therapy with adherents who have spent many years in training and apprenticeship will change slowly and only in the face of very substantial evidence. Furthermore, front-line therapists faced with suffering patients obviously cannot wait for science. In addition, there is yet another consideration: unlike the physical sciences, many aspects of psychotherapy defy quantification. Psychotherapy is both art and science; research findings may ultimately shape the broad contours of practice, but the human encounter at the center of therapy will always be a deeply subjective, nonquantifiable experience.

It was with some reluctance that I undertook the considerable task of revising this text. For the most part, I remain satisfied with the theoretical foundations and the technical approach to group therapy as delineated in the second edition. Yet age spares few books, and the second edition was beginning to show its seams. At my last reading, it seemed awash with dated or anachronistic allusions. Much of the language, especially gender referents, seemed outmoded: it took no note, for example, that at least half, probably more, of contemporary group leaders were women. Furthermore, much content needed updating: the field has changed, new types of groups have sprung up, others have passed away; nine years of clinical and research literature needed to be reviewed and assimilated into the text. Furthermore, since the last edition, I had led approximately two thousand group meetings, and my notes were bulging with new clinical observations and illustrations.

The first four chapters present the therapeutic factors. The first chapter discusses seven: instillation of hope, universality, imparting information, altruism, the corrective recapitulation of the primary family group, development of socializing techniques, and imitative behavior. Chapters 2 and 3 discuss the factors that are of primary importance in the long-term interactional group: interpersonal learning and cohesiveness. Chapter 4 discusses catharsis and existential factors and addresses the comparative importance and the interdependence of the therapeutic factors. It surveys the considerable research on therapeutic factors conducted in the past nine years.

The next two chapters address the work of the therapist. Chapter 5 discusses the tasks of the group therapist—especially those of shaping a therapeutic group culture and of harnessing the group interaction for therapeutic benefit. I emphasize, in chapter 6, that the therapist must both activate the here-and-now (that is, plunge the group into its own experience) and illuminate the meaning of the here-and-now experience. Chapter 7 explicates the role of the therapist; the discussion pivots around two fundamental issues: transference and transparency.

Chapters 8 through 14 present a chronological view of the therapy group and emphasize group phenomena and the therapist's techniques that are relevant to each stage. I have revised chapters 8 and 9 (on patient selection and group composition) to make them more clinically useful: most of the considerable research conducted in these areas has not proven relevant to clinical practice. Chapter 10 discusses the practical realities of beginning a group and includes much new material on the preparation of the patient for group therapy. Chapter 11 addresses the early stages of the therapy group and includes new material on dealing with the therapy dropout. Chapter 12 deals with phenomena encountered in the mature phase of the group therapy work: subgrouping, conflict, self-disclosure, and termination. To the discussion of problem patients in chapter 13, I have added new sections on narcissistic and borderline patients. Chapter 14, on specialized techniques of the therapist, contains additional material on concurrent individual and group therapy, on co-therapy, and on the use of the written summary in group therapy.

Chapter 15, on the specialized therapy group, is a new chapter which addresses the many new groups that have emerged to deal with specialized clinical syndromes or specialized clinical situations. This chapter presents the principles that the therapist must use to fashion a specialized group and to modify traditional group therapy technique. These principles are illustrated by an in-depth description of the most common (and challenging) specialized therapy group—that on the acute psychiatric inpatient ward.

Chapter 16, on the encounter group, presented the single greatest challenge for this revision. Because the encounter group *qua* encounter group has so largely faded from the scene, I considered deleting the chapter entirely. However, several factors, such as the historical and research value of encounter groups as well as the fact that more people than ever are attending groups that use encounter group technology, if under a different nomenclature, have persuaded me to retain this chapter but to shorten and adapt it to contemporary group therapy practice.

Chapter 17, on the training of group therapists, has been altered to reflect the changing patterns and requirements in the education of student practitioners.

Excessively overweight volumes tend to gravitate to the "reference book" shelves. In the hope that this book avoid that fate, I have resisted lengthening it. Since much new material and an entire new chapter have been added, I have had the painful task of cutting older sections. (I left my writing desk daily with fingers stained by the blood of many condemned second-edition sentences.) I also removed descriptions and critiques of research method from the text and placed them in the notes at the end of the book. Even so, this edition is 5 percent longer than the last.

I am grateful to Stanford University for providing the academic freedom and the research accoutrements necessary to accomplish this work. To Jerome Frank, my thanks for having introduced me to group therapy and for having offered a model of integrity, curiosity, and dedication. I thank the many teachers who have offered advice for this revision. Phoebe Hoss, of Basic Books, provided valuable editorial assistance. The emotional and intellectual support of my wife, Marilyn, and the formidable industry and incomparable good cheer of my secretary, Bea Mitchell, sustained me throughout this work.

THE THEORY
AND
PRACTICE OF
GROUP
PSYCHOTHERAPY

1

THE THERAPEUTIC
FACTORS IN
GROUP THERAPY

How does group therapy help patients? If we can answer this seemingly naïve question with some measure of precision and certainty, we shall have at our disposal a central organizing principle by which to approach the most vexing and controversial problems of psychotherapy. Once identified, the crucial aspects of the change process will constitute a rational basis upon which the therapist may base tactics and strategy.

I suggest that therapeutic change is an enormously complex process and occurs through an intricate interplay of various guided human experiences, which I shall refer to as "therapeutic factors." There is considerable advantage in approaching the complex through the simple, the total phenomenon through its basic component processes; and, accordingly, I shall begin by describing and discussing these elemental factors.

From my viewpoint, natural lines of cleavage divide the therapeutic experience into eleven primary factors:

1. Instillation of hope,
2. Universality,
3. Imparting of information,
4. Altruism,
5. The corrective recapitulation of the primary family group,
6. Development of socializing techniques,
7. Imitative behavior,
8. Interpersonal learning,
9. Group cohesiveness,

3

10. Catharsis,
11. Existential factors.

In the rest of this chapter, I shall discuss the first seven factors. I consider interpersonal learning and group cohesiveness so important and complex that I have treated them separately in the next two chapters. Existential factors are discussed in chapter 4, where they are best understood in the context of other material presented there. Catharsis is intricately interwoven with other therapeutic factors and will also be discussed in chapter 4. Keep in mind that, though I discuss these factors singly, the discriminations are arbitrary and, to a large extent, the factors are interdependent: they neither occur nor function separately.

Moreover, these factors may represent different parts of the change process; some factors refer to actual mechanisms of change, whereas others may be more accurately described as conditions for change. Though the same therapeutic factors operate in every type of therapy group, their interplay and differential importance can vary widely from group to group. Furthermore, patients in the same group may be benefited by widely differing clusters of therapeutic factors. At its core, therapy is a deeply human experience, and, consequently, there are an infinite number of pathways through the therapeutic process. (I discuss all of these issues more fully in chapter 4.)

The inventory of therapeutic factors I propose issues from my clinical experience, from the experience of other therapists, from the views of the successfully treated group patient, and from relevant systematic research. None of these sources of conviction is beyond doubt, however; neither group members nor group leaders are entirely objective, and our research methodology is both crude and often inapplicable.

From the group therapists we obtain a variegated and internally inconsistent inventory of therapeutic factors (see chapter 4). Therapists are by no means disinterested or unbiased observers. They have invested considerable time and energy in mastering a certain therapeutic approach, and their answers will be largely determined by their particular school of conviction. Even among therapists who share the same ideology and speak the same language, there may be no consensus about why patients improve. In research on encounter groups, my colleagues and I learned that many successful group leaders attributed their success to factors that were quite irrelevant to the therapy process: for example, the "hot seat" technique, or nonverbal exercises, or the direct impact of a therapist's own person (see chapter 16).[1] But that does not surprise us; the history of psychotherapy abounds in healers

4

who were effective, but not for the reasons they supposed. At other times we therapists throw up our hands in bewilderment. Who has not had a patient who made vast improvement for reasons entirely obscure to us?

From the group therapy patients at the end of a course of treatment we can obtain data concerning those therapeutic factors that they consider most and least helpful; or, during therapy, they can supply evaluations of the significant aspects of each group meeting. For these purposes an interview or a variety of data-collecting approaches may be employed. Yet we know the patients' evaluations will be subjective. Will they not, perhaps, focus primarily on superficial factors and neglect some profound healing forces which may be beyond their awareness? Will their responses not be influenced by a variety of factors difficult to control? For example, their views may be distorted by the nature of their relationship to the therapist or to the group. (One team of researchers demonstrated that when patients were interviewed four years after the conclusion of therapy, they were far more apt to comment on unhelpful or harmful aspects of their group experience than when interviewed immediately at its termination.)[2]

Research has also shown, for example, that the therapeutic factors valued by patients may differ greatly from the factors cited by their therapists or by group observers.[3] Furthermore, many factors influence the patient's evaluation of the therapeutic factors: for example, the length of time in treatment and the level of a patient's functioning,[4] the type of group (that is, whether outpatient, inpatient, day hospital, brief therapy),[5] the age and the diagnosis of a patient,[6] and the ideology of the group leader.[7] Another factor that complicates the search for common therapeutic factors is the extent to which different group patients perceive and experience the same event in different ways.[8] Any given experience may be important or helpful to some members and inconsequential or even harmful to others.

Despite these limitations, patient reports are a rich and relatively untapped source of information. After all, it is *their* experience, theirs alone, and the further we move from the patient's experience, the more inferential are our conclusions. To be sure, there are aspects of the process of change that operate outside of a patient's awareness, but it does not follow that we should disregard what patients *do* say. It is my experience that the richness and the accuracy of a patient's report is largely determined by the mode of inquiry. The more the questioner can enter into the experiential world of the patient, the more lucid and meaningful does the report of the therapy experience become. To the degree that the therapist is able to suppress personal bias, he or she becomes the ideal questioner: the therapist is trusted and, more than anyone else, understands the inner world of the patient.

In addition to therapists' views and patients' reports, there is yet a third important method of evaluating the therapeutic factors: the systematic research approach. The most common research strategy is to correlate a series of in-therapy variables with ultimate patient outcome in therapy. By discovering which variables are significantly related to successful outcome, one can establish a reasonable base from which to begin to delineate the therapeutic factors. However, the research approach is not beyond reproach. There are many inherent problems: the measurement of outcome is itself a methodological morass, and the selection and measurement of the in-therapy variables are equally problematic. (Generally the accuracy of the measurement is directly proportional to the triviality of the variable. It is easy, for example, to measure the number of words spoken by each patient but extraordinarily difficult to measure the meaningfulness of insight.)

I have drawn from all these methods to derive the therapeutic factors discussed in this book. I do not present these factors as definitive; rather, I offer them as provisional guidelines which may be tested and perhaps expanded by other clinical researchers. For my part, I am satisfied that they derive from the best available evidence and constitute the basis of an effective approach to therapy.

Instillation of Hope

The instillation and maintenance of hope is crucial in all of the psychotherapies: not only is hope required to keep the patient in therapy so that other therapeutic factors may take effect, but faith in a treatment mode can in itself be therapeutically effective. Several research inquiries have demonstrated that high expectation of help before therapy is significantly correlated with positive therapy outcome.[9] Consider also the massive data documenting the efficacy of faith healing and placebo treatment—therapies mediated entirely through hope and conviction.

Therapy groups invariably contain individuals who are at different points along a coping-collapse continuum. Patients have continual contact with group members who have improved in the group and often encounter patients who have had problems very similar to their own and have coped with them more effectively. I have often heard patients

6

remark at the end of their therapy how important it was for them to have observed the improvement of others. Group therapists should by no means be above exploiting this factor by periodically calling attention to the improvement that members have made. If I receive, let us say, Christmas cards from members who have recently terminated the group, I shamelessly share with the current group all the positive changes they describe. Therapy group members themselves often proffer spontaneous testimonials when new, skeptical members enter the group.

Research substantiates that it is also vitally important that therapists believe in themselves and in the efficacy of their group.[10] I sincerely believe that I am able to help every motivated patient who is willing to work in the group for at least six months. In my initial individual meetings with patients, I share this conviction with them and attempt to imbue them with my optimism.

Many of the self-help groups that have emerged in the past decade (for example, Compassionate Friends [bereaved parents], THEOS [widows], or Mended Heart [heart surgery patients]) place heavy emphasis on the instillation of hope.[11] A major part of Recovery, Inc., and Alcoholics Anonymous meetings is dedicated to testimonials. Recovery, Inc., members give accounts of potentially stressful incidents in which they avoided tension by the application of Recovery, Inc., methods. Successful Alcoholics Anonymous members tell their stories of downfall and salvation at each meeting. One of the great strengths of Alcoholics Anonymous is the fact that the leaders are all ex-alcoholics—living inspirations to the others. Many substance-abuse treatment programs mobilize hope in patients by using recovered drug addicts as group leaders. The members develop a strong conviction that they can be best understood by someone who has trod the same path as they and who has found the way back.

Universality

Many patients enter therapy with the disquieting thought that they are unique in their wretchedness, that they alone have certain frightening or unacceptable problems, thoughts, impulses, and fantasies. There is a core of truth in this notion, since many patients have had an unusual constellation of life stresses and are periodically flooded by material that is usually unconscious. A patient's sense of uniqueness is often heightened by social isolation; because of interpersonal difficulties, opportunities for frank and candid consensual validation in an intimate relationship are often not available to patients. In the therapy group, especially in the early stages, the disconfirmation of a patient's feelings of uniqueness is a powerful source of relief. After hearing other members disclose concerns similar to their own, patients report feeling more in touch with the world and describe the process as a "welcome to the human race" experience. Simply put, the phenomenon finds expression in the cliché, "We're all in the same boat," or perhaps more cynically, "Misery loves company."

There is no human deed or thought that is fully outside the experience of other people. I have heard group members reveal such acts as incest, burglary, embezzlement, murder, attempted suicide, and fantasies of an even more desperate nature; invariably, I have observed other group members reach out and embrace these very acts as within the realm of their own possibilities. Long ago Freud noted that the staunchest taboos (against patricide and incest) were constructed precisely because these very impulses are part of the human being's deepest nature.

Nor is this form of aid limited to group therapy. Universality plays a role in individual therapy also, although in that format less of an opportunity for consensual validation exists. Once I reviewed with a patient his 600-hour experience in individual analysis with another therapist. When I inquired about his recollection of the most significant event in his therapy, he recalled an incident when he was profoundly distressed about his feelings toward his mother. Despite strong concurrent positive sentiments, he was beset with death wishes for her so that he might inherit a sizable estate. His analyst, at one point, commented simply, "That seems to be the way we're built." That artless statement offered considerable relief and furthermore enabled the patient to explore his ambivalence in great depth.

Despite the complexity of human problems, certain common denominators are clearly evident; and the members of a therapy group are not long in perceiving their similarities. An example is illustrative: for many years I asked members* of T-groups (see chapter 16) to engage in a "top secret" task. The group members are asked to write, anonymously, on a slip of paper their top secret—the one thing they would be most disinclined to share with the group.† The secrets prove to be

---

*Nonpatients—primarily medical students, psychiatric residents, nurses, psychiatric technicians, and Peace Corps volunteers.

†There are several methods of employing this data in the work of the group. One technique that has proved effective is to collect the anonymous secrets and redistribute

8

startlingly similar, with a couple of major themes predominating. The most common secret is a deep conviction of basic inadequacy—a feeling that if others really knew the person, they would discover his or her incompetence and see through his or her intellectual bluff. Next in frequency is a deep sense of interpersonal alienation. Individuals report that they do not or cannot really care for or love another person. The third most frequent category is some variety of sexual secret, often a dread of homosexual inclinations. These chief concerns, in nonpatients, are qualitatively the same in individuals seeking professional help, who become labeled as patients. Almost invariably, patients experience deep concern about their sense of worth and their ability to relate to others.

Some specialized groups composed of individuals for whom secrecy has been an especially important and isolating factor place a particularly great emphasis on universality. For example, short-term structured groups for bulimic patients build into their protocol a strong requirement for self-disclosure, especially disclosure about attitudes toward body image and detailed accounts of each patient's eating and purging practices. With rare exceptions, patients express great relief at discovering that they are not alone and that others share the same dilemmas and life experiences.[12]

Universality, like the other therapeutic factors, cannot be appreciated separately. As patients perceive their similarity to others and share their deepest concerns, they benefit further from the accompanying catharsis and from ultimate acceptance (see chapter 3 on group cohesiveness) by other members.

Imparting Information

Under the general rubric of imparting information, I include didactic instruction about mental health, mental illness, and general psychodynamics given by the therapists, as well as advice, suggestions, or direct guidance about life problems offered either by the therapist or by other patients. Generally, when therapists or patients retrospectively examine their experience in interactional group therapy, they do not highly value didactic information or advice.

---

them to the members, each one receiving another's secret. Each member is then asked to read the secret aloud and to reveal how he or she would feel if harboring such a secret. This method usually proves to be a valuable demonstration of universality, empathy, and the ability of others to understand.

DIDACTIC INSTRUCTION

Most patients, at the conclusion of successful interactional group therapy, have learned a great deal about psychic functioning, the meaning of symptoms, interpersonal and group dynamics, and the process of psychotherapy. However, the educational process is implicit; most group therapists do not offer explicit didactic instruction in interactional group therapy. There are, however, some group therapy approaches in which formal instruction is an important part of the program. For example, Maxwell Jones, in his early work with large groups, devoted three hours a week to lectures which instructed patients about the structure and function of the central nervous system and the relevance of this material to psychiatric symptoms and disability.[13] J. W. Klapman developed a form of didactic group therapy for outpatients in which he used formal lectures and textbook assignments.[14] L. C. Marsh also organized groups of patients into classes and created a classroom atmosphere by means of lectures, homework, and grading procedures.[15]

Recovery, Inc., is basically organized along didactic lines.[16] This self-help organization was founded in 1937 by the late Abraham Low and, in 1985, had over one thousand operating groups with a regular attendance of over 10,000 individuals. The membership is completely voluntary and includes individuals complaining of any psychological problem. The leaders spring from the membership; and though there is no formal professional guidance, the conduct of the meetings has been highly structured by Dr. Low; parts of his textbook, *Mental Health Through Will Training*, are read aloud and discussed at every meeting.[17] Psychological illness is explained on the basis of a few simple principles which are memorized by the members: for example, the neurotic symptom is distressing but not dangerous; tension intensifies and sustains the symptom and should be avoided; the use of free will is the solution to the nervous patient's dilemmas.

Many other self-help groups strongly emphasize the imparting of information. Groups such as Parents Anonymous, Gamblers Anonymous, Make Today Count (for cancer patients), Parents Without Partners, and Mended Hearts (cardiac surgery patients) encourage the exchange of information among members and often invite experts to address the group.[18]

The recent group therapy literature abounds with descriptions of specialized groups for patients who have some specific disorder or face some definitive life crisis (for example, obesity,[19] adjustment after divorce,[20] chronic pain,[21] sexual dysfunction,[22] rape victims,[23] epilepsy,[24] myocardial infarction,[25] hemodialysis.[26] These groups build in a didactic component and offer explicit instruction about the nature of a patient's illness or life situation. For example, the leaders of a group for primiparous mothers instruct the members about the physiological basis of the physical and psychological changes the latter are undergoing and about the actual mechanics of labor and delivery. The leaders offer anticipatory guidance by helping the members verbalize their fears and then addressing their irrational beliefs systematically by rational, informational means.

D. I. Malamud and S. Machover report an innovative approach organized on a didactic base.[27] They organized "workshops in self-understanding," consisting of approximately twenty patients drawn from a psychiatric clinic waiting list. The workshop aimed to prepare patients for group psychotherapy and consisted of fifteen two-hour sessions which were carefully planned to clarify important reasons for psychological dysfunction as well as methods of self-exploration. The technique was not only successful in preparing patients for further treatment but proved to be effective therapy: at the conclusion of the workshop, many patients felt sufficiently enough improved that no further treatment was required.

My colleagues and I have used an analogous type of anticipatory guidance for psychiatric patients about to enter a frightening situation —the psychotherapy group.[28] By predicting patients' fears, by providing them with a cognitive structure, we helped them to cope more effectively with the initial "culture shock." (This procedure is described in detail in chapter 10.)

Didactic instruction has thus been employed in a variety of fashions in group therapy: to transfer information, to structure the group, to explain the process of illness. Often such instruction functions as the initial binding force in the group until other therapeutic factors become operative. In part, however, explanation and clarification function as effective therapeutic agents in their own right. Human beings have always abhorred uncertainty and through the ages have sought to order the universe by providing explanations, primarily religious or scientific. The explanation of a phenomenon is the first step toward its control. If a volcanic eruption is caused by a displeased volcanic god, then at least there is hope of pleasing and eventually controlling the god. Frieda Fromm-Reichman underscores the role of uncertainty in the production of anxiety.[29] She points out that being aware that one is not one's own helmsman, that one's perceptions and behavior are controlled by irrational forces, is in itself an important source of anxiety. Jerome Frank, in a study of Americans' reactions to an unfamiliar South Pacific disease (schistosomiasis), demonstrates that secondary anxiety stemming from uncertainty often creates more havoc than the primary disease.[30] Similarly with psychiatric patients: fear and anxiety that stem from uncertainty of the source, meaning, and seriousness of psychiatric symptoms may so compound the total dysphoria that effective exploration becomes vastly more difficult. Thus, didactic instruction, through its provision of structure and explanation, has intrinsic value and deserves a place in our repertoire of therapeutic instruments. (See chapter 5 for a more complete discussion of this issue.)

DIRECT ADVICE

Unlike explicit didactic instruction from the therapist, direct advice from the members occurs without exception in every therapy group. In dynamic interactional therapy groups, it is invariably part of the early life of the group and occurs with such regularity that it can be used to estimate the age of the group. If I observe or hear a tape of a group in which the patients with some regularity say, "I think you ought to . . ." or, "What you should do is . . ." or, "Why don't you . . . ," then I can be reasonably certain either that the group is young or that it is an older group facing some difficulty that has either impeded its development or effected temporary regression. Despite the fact that advice giving is common in early interactional group therapy, I can recall few instances when a specific suggestion concerning some problem was of direct benefit to any patient. Indirectly, however, advice giving serves a purpose; the process, rather than the content of the advice, may be beneficial, since it implies and conveys mutual interest and caring. In other words, what is important is implicit in the very offering of advice. It is seen by the patient as a gift.

Advice-giving or advice-seeking behavior is often an important clue in the elucidation of interpersonal pathology. The patient who, for example, continuously pulls advice and suggestions from others, only to reject it ultimately and frustrate others, is well known to group therapists as the "help-rejecting complainer" or the "yes . . . but" patient (see chapter 13).[31] Other patients may bid for attention and nurturance by asking for suggestions about a problem that either is insoluble or has already been solved. Other patients soak up advice with an unquenchable thirst yet never reciprocate to others equally needy. Some group members are so intent on preserving a high status role in the group or a facade of cool self-sufficiency that they never ask directly for help; some are effusive in their gratitude; others never acknowledge the gift but take it home, like a bone, to gnaw on privately.

Other types of group, noninteractionally focused, make explicit and effective use of direct suggestions and guidance. For example, behavior-shaping groups, discharge groups (preparing patients for discharge from a hospital), Recovery, Inc., and Alcoholics Anonymous all proffer considerable direct advice. Discharge groups may discuss the events of a patient's trial home visit and offer suggestions for alternative behavior. Alcoholics Anonymous makes use of guidance and slogans: for example, patients are asked to remain abstinent for only the next twenty-four hours, one day at a time. Recovery, Inc., teaches members how to "spot symptoms," how to "erase and retrace," how to "rehearse and reverse," how to apply will power effectively. Researchers studied a behavior-shaping group of male sex offenders and noted not only that advice was common but that it came in several forms: the least effective form of advice was a direct suggestion; the most effective were more systematic operationalized instructions or alternative suggestions about how to achieve a desired goal.[32]

Altruism

There is an old Hasidic story of a rabbi who had a conversation with the Lord about Heaven and Hell. "I will show you Hell," said the Lord, and led the rabbi into a room in the middle of which was a very big round table. The people sitting at it were famished and desperate. In the middle of the table there was an enormous pot of stew, more than enough for everyone. The smell of the stew was delicious and made the rabbi's mouth water. The people around the table were holding spoons with very long handles. Each person found that it was just possible to reach the pot to take a spoonful of the stew, but because the handle of the spoon was longer than anyone's arm, no one could get the food into his mouth. The rabbi saw that their suffering was indeed terrible. "Now I will show you Heaven," said the Lord, and they went into another room, exactly the same as the first. There was the same big round table and the same enormous pot of stew. The people, as before, were equipped with the same long-handled spoons—but here they were well nourished and plump, laughing and talking. At first the rabbi could not understand. "It is simple, but it requires a certain skill," said the Lord. "You see, they have learned to feed each other."

In therapy groups, too, patients receive through giving, not only as part of the reciprocal giving-receiving sequence but also from the intrinsic act of giving. Psychiatric patients beginning therapy are demoralized and possess a deep sense of having nothing of value to offer others. They have long considered themselves as burdens, and the experience of finding that they can be of importance to others is refreshing and boosts self-esteem.

And, of course, patients are enormously helpful to one another in the group therapeutic process. They offer support, reassurance, suggestions, and insight and share similar problems with one another. Not infrequently a patient will listen and absorb observations from another member far more readily than from the group therapist. To many patients, the therapist remains the paid professional; but the other members can be counted upon for spontaneous and truthful reactions and feedback. A patient looking back over the course of therapy invariably credits other members as having been important in his or her improvement—if not for deliberate support and advice, then at least for having been there and permitted the patient to gain self-knowledge through their relationship.

Nor has this therapeutic factor been absent from other psychotherapeutic systems. In primitive cultures, for example, a troubled person is often given the task of preparing a feast or performing some type of service for the community.[33] Altruism plays an important part in the healing process at Catholic shrines such as at Lourdes, where the sick pray not only for themselves but for one another. Warden Duffy of San Quentin Prison is reputed to have claimed that the best way to help a man is to let him help you. People need to feel they are needed. I have known ex-alcoholics who have continued their A.A. contacts for years after they achieved complete sobriety; one worker told me that he had related the story of his downfall and subsequent reclamation at least a thousand times.

This source of help is at first not appreciated. Many patients resist the suggestion of group therapy with the question, "How can the blind lead the blind?" Or, "What can I possibly get from others as confused as I? We'll end up pulling one another down." Such resistance to entering the group is best worked through by exploring a patient's critical self-evaluation. Generally, a patient who deplores the prospect of getting help from other patients is really saying, "I have nothing of value to offer anyone."

There is another, more subtle benefit inherent in the altruistic act. Many patients are immersed in a morbid self-absorption, which takes the form of obsessive introspection or a teeth-gritting effort to "actualize" oneself. But self-actualization or meaning in life can never be attained via deliberate, self-conscious pursuit. I agree with Victor Frank that these qualities ensue but cannot be successfully pursued: that they are always derivative phenomena which appear on our experiential landscape when we have transcended ourselves, when we have forgotten ourselves in absorption in someone (or something) outside of ourselves.[34] The therapy group implicitly teaches its members that lesson and provides a new counter-solipsistic perspective.

The Corrective Recapitulation of the Primary Family Group

Without exception, patients enter group therapy with the history of a highly unsatisfactory experience in their first and most important group —the primary family. The group resembles a family in many aspects, and many groups are led by a male-female therapy team in a deliberate effort to simulate the parental configuration as closely as possible. Depending upon a patient's assumptive world (shaped to a large degree by early family experience), one interacts with leaders and other members as one may have once interacted with parents and siblings.

There are an infinite variety of patterns: helpless dependence upon the leaders, whom one imbues with unrealistic knowledge and power; blind defiance of the leaders who are thought to block autonomous growth or to strip members of their individuality; an attempt to split the co-therapists and to incite disagreements or rivalry between the two; bitter competition with other members in an effort to accumulate units of attention and caring from the therapists; a search for allies among the other patients in an effort to topple the therapists; or neglect of one's own interests in a seemingly selfless effort to appease or provide for other members.

Obviously, similar phenomena occur in individual therapy. The difference, however, is that the group provides a vastly greater number and array of recapitulative possibilities. In one of my groups, a patient who had been silently pouting for a couple of meetings bemoaned the fact that she was not in one-to-one therapy. The group could not satisfy her needs, and she found herself unable to speak in the meeting, whereas she knew she could speak freely of herself in a private conversation with the therapist or with any one of the members. When pressed, the patient disclosed her anger that, in a recent meeting, another member had been welcomed warmly upon returning from a vacation. She, too, had recently returned from a vacation, but had not had a similarly warm reception from the group. Furthermore, another patient was praised for offering an important interpretation to a member, whereas she had made a similar statement weeks ago which had gone unnoticed. For some time, too, she had noticed her growing resentment at sharing the group time; she was impatient while waiting for the floor and angry when attention was shifted away from her. All of these experiences obviously had a long history and were deeply rooted in her early relationships with her siblings. Together, they did not constitute a valid criticism for the group therapeutic mode. Quite the contrary: the group format was particularly valuable for her, as it is for many narcissistic patients, since it allowed both her envy and her cravings for attention to surface. In individual therapy these particular conflicts emerge belatedly, if at all; the therapist is always there; the patient is expected to take all the time; there is no other person with whom one must share the therapist or the therapy hour.

What is important, though, is not only that early familial conflicts are relived but that they are relived correctively. Growth-inhibiting relationships must not be permitted to freeze into the rigid, impenetrable system that characterizes many family structures. Instead, fixed roles must be constantly explored and challenged; and ground rules for investigating relationships and testing new behavior must be constantly encouraged. For many patients, then, working out problems with therapists and other members is also working through unfinished business from long ago. (How explicit the working in the past need be is a complex and controversial issue, which I shall address in chapter 5.)

Development of Socializing Techniques

Social learning—the development of basic social skills—is a therapeutic factor that operates in all therapy groups, although the nature of the skills taught and the explicitness of the process vary greatly depending upon the type of group therapy. In some groups—for example, groups preparing long-term hospitalized patients for discharge, or adolescent groups—there may be explicit emphasis on the development of social skills. Role playing may be employed where patients learn to approach prospective employers for a job or adolescent boys learn to invite a girl to a dance.

In dynamic group therapy with ground rules encouraging open feedback, patients may obtain considerable information about maladaptive social behavior. A patient may, for example, learn about a disconcerting tendency to avoid looking at the person with whom he or she is conversing; or about others' impressions of his or her haughty, regal attitude; or about a variety of other social habits which, unbeknownst to the patient, have been undermining his or her social relationships. For individuals lacking intimate relationships, the group often represents the first opportunity for accurate interpersonal feedback. One patient, for example, who obsessively included endless, minute, irrelevant details in his social conversation realized that he did so for the first time in group therapy. For years he had been aware only that other people either avoided or curtailed social contact with him. Obviously, therapy involves far more than the simple recognition and deliberate alteration of social behavior; but, as I shall show in chapter 3, these gains are more than fringe benefits and are often exceedingly instrumental in the initial phases of therapeutic change.

Frequently the senior members of the therapy group acquire highly sophisticated social skills: they are attuned to process (see chapter 6); they have learned how to be helpfully responsive to others; they have acquired methods of conflict resolution; they are less likely to be judgmental and more capable of experiencing and expressing accurate empathy. These skills cannot but help to serve these patients well in future social interactions.

Imitative Behavior

Pipe-smoking therapists often beget pipe-smoking patients. Patients during individual psychotherapy may sit, walk, talk, and even think like their therapists. In groups the imitative process is more diffuse, as patients may model themselves upon aspects of the other group members as well as of the therapist. The importance of imitative behavior in the therapeutic process is difficult to gauge, but social psychological research suggests that therapists may have underestimated its importance. A. Bandura, who has long claimed that social learning cannot be adequately explained on the basis of direct reinforcement, has experimentally demonstrated that imitation is an effective therapeutic force.[35] For example, he has successfully treated a large number of individuals with snake phobias by asking them to observe their therapist handle a snake. In group therapy it is not uncommon for a patient to benefit by observing the therapy of another patient with a similar problem constellation—a phenomenon generally referred to as "vicarious" or "spectator" therapy.[36] Even if specific imitative behavior is short-lived, it may function to help the individual "unfreeze" by experimenting with new behavior. In fact, it is not uncommon for patients throughout therapy to try on, as it were, bits and pieces of other people and then relinquish them as ill fitting. This process may have solid therapeutic impact; finding out what we are not is progress toward finding out what we are.

2

INTERPERSONAL

LEARNING

Interpersonal learning, as I define it, is a broad and complex therapeutic factor representing both the group therapy analogue of such therapeutic factors in individual therapy as insight, working through the transference, and the corrective emotional experience, as well as processes unique to the group setting. To define the concept of interpersonal learning and to describe the mechanism whereby it mediates therapeutic change in the individual, I shall first need to discuss three other concepts:

1. The importance of interpersonal relationships,
2. The corrective emotional experience,
3. The group as social microcosm.

The Importance of Interpersonal Relationships

From whatever perspective we study human society, we find that interpersonal relations play a crucial role. Whether we scan humanity's broad evolutionary history or scrutinize the development of the single individual, we are at all times obliged to consider the human being in the matrix of his or her interpersonal relationships. There is convincing data from the study of primitive human cultures and nonhuman primates that humans have always lived in groups that have been characterized by intense and persistent relationships among members. Interpersonal behavior has been clearly adaptive in an evolutionary sense: without intense, positive, reciprocal interpersonal bonds, both individual and species survival would not have been possible. John Bowlby, from his studies of the early mother-child relationship, concludes also that attachment behavior is built into us.[1] If mother and infant are separated, both experience marked anxiety concomitant with their search for the lost object. If the separation is prolonged, the consequences will be proportionately profound. W. Goldschmidt, on the basis of an exhaustive review of the ethnographic evidence, states:

> Man is by nature committed to social existence, and is therefore inevitably involved in the dilemma between serving his own interests and recognizing those of the group to which he belongs. Insofar as this dilemma can be resolved it is resolved by the fact that man's self-interest can best be served through his commitment to his fellows. . . . Need for positive affect means that each person craves response from his human environment. It may be viewed as a hunger, not unlike that for food, but more generalized. Under varying conditions it may be expressed as a desire for contact, for recognition and acceptance, for approval, for esteem, or for mastery. . . . As we examine human behavior, we find that persons not only universally live in social systems, which is to say they are drawn together, but also universally act in such ways as to attain the approval of their fellow men.[2]

Similarly, ninety years ago, William James said,

> We are not only gregarious animals liking to be in sight of our fellows, but we have an innate propensity to get ourselves noticed, and noticed favorably, by our kind. No more fiendish punishment could be devised, were such a thing physically possible, than that one should be turned loose in society and remain absolutely unnoticed by all the members thereof.[3]

Indeed, James's speculations have been substantiated time and again by contemporary research that documents the pain and the adverse consequences of loneliness. There is, for example, persuasive evidence that the rate for virtually every major cause of death is significantly higher for the lonely—the single, the divorced, and the widowed.[4]

All modern schools of dynamic psychotherapy are interpersonally based and rest upon Harry Stack Sullivan's systematic interpersonal theory of psychiatry. Although we are all Sullivanians at heart, new generations of therapists rarely read Sullivan. For one thing, his language is often obscure; furthermore, his work has been so seminal and so pervasively influential that his contributions often seem overly familiar or obvious. (I do, however, recommend the reader to primary sources[5] or to some lucid expositions of his work.[6]) Sullivan's formulations are exceedingly helpful for understanding the group therapeutic process and, although a comprehensive discussion of his interpersonal theory is obviously beyond the scope of this book, I shall describe a few key concepts. Sullivan contends that the personality is almost entirely the product of interaction with other significant human beings. The need to be closely related to others is as basic as any biological need and is, in the light of the prolonged period of helpless infancy, equally necessary to survival. The developing child, in the quest for security, tends to stress those traits and aspects of the self that meet with approval, and will squelch or deny those that meet with disapproval. Eventually the individual develops a concept of the self (self-dynamism) based on these perceived appraisals of significant others.

The self may be said to be made up of reflected appraisals. If these were chiefly derogatory, as in the case of an unwanted child who was never loved, of a child who has fallen into the hands of foster parents who have no real interest in him as a child; as I say, if the self-dynamism is made up of experience which is chiefly derogatory, it will facilitate hostile, disparaging appraisals of other people and it will entertain disparaging and hostile appraisals of itself.[7]

Sullivan used the term *parataxic distortions* to describe the individual's proclivity to distort his or her perceptions of others. A parataxic distortion occurs in an interpersonal situation when one person relates to another not on the basis of the realistic attributes of the other, but wholly or chiefly on the basis of a personification existing chiefly in the former's own fantasy. Parataxic distortion is similar to the concept of transference but broader in scope: it refers not only to the therapeutic but to all interpersonal relationships; it includes not only the simple transferring of attitudes from real-life figures but also the distortion of interpersonal reality in response to intrapersonal needs.*

Interpersonal distortions tend to be self-perpetuating. For example, an individual with a derogatory, debased self-image may, through selective inattention or projection, incorrectly perceive another to be a harsh, rejecting figure. Moreover, the process compounds itself because that individual may then gradually develop mannerisms and behavioral traits—for example, servility, defensive antagonism, or scorn—that eventually will cause others to become, in fact, harsh and rejecting. The term *self-fulfilling prophecy* has been applied to this phenomenon.

Parataxic distortions, in Sullivan's view, are modifiable primarily through consensual validation, through comparing one's interpersonal evaluations with those of others. This brings us to Sullivan's view of the therapeutic process: "Psychiatry is the study of processes that involve or go on between people."[8] Mental disorder, psychiatric symp-

---

*Although their origins differ, transference and parataxic distortion may be considered operationally identical. Many therapists today use the term *transference* to refer to all interpersonal distortions rather than confining its use to the patient-therapist relationship (see chapter 7).

tomatology in all of its varied manifestations, is translated into interpersonal terms and treated accordingly. "Mental disorder as a term refers to interpersonal processes either inadequate to the situation in which the persons are integrated, or excessively complex because of illusionary persons also integrated into the situations. It implies sometimes a greater ineffectiveness of the behavior by which the person is conceived to be pursuing the satisfactions that he requires."[9] Accordingly, psychiatric treatment should be directed toward the correction of interpersonal distortions, thus enabling the individual to lead a more abundant life, to participate collaboratively with others, to obtain interpersonal satisfactions in the context of realistic, mutually satisfying interpersonal relationships. "One achieves mental health to the extent that one becomes aware of one's interpersonal relationships."[10] Psychiatric cure is the "expanding of the self to such final effect that the patient as known to himself is much the same person as the patient behaving to others."[11]

Thus, therapy is broadly interpersonal, both in its goals and in its means. The therapeutic goals of group therapy patients, somewhere between the third and the sixth months of therapy, often undergo a shift. Their initial goal, relief of suffering, is modified and eventually replaced by new goals, usually interpersonal in nature. Goals may change from wanting relief from anxiety or depression to wanting to learn to communicate with others, to be more trusting and honest with others, to learn to love.

The goal shift from relief of suffering to change in interpersonal functioning is an essential early step in the dynamic therapeutic process. The therapist cannot, for example, treat depression *per se:* "depression" offers no therapeutic handhold, no rationale for examining interpersonal relationships which, as I hope to demonstrate, is the key to the therapeutic power of the therapy group. It is necessary, first, to translate depression into interpersonal terms and then to treat the underlying interpersonal pathology. Thus, the therapist translates "depression" into its interpersonal issues—for example, passive-dependency, isolation, obsequiousness, inability to express anger, hypersensitivity to separation—and then addresses those interpersonal issues in therapy.

Sullivan's statement of the overall process and goals of therapy is deeply consistent with those of interactional group therapy. However, the emphasis on the patient's understanding of the past, of the genetic development of those maladaptive interpersonal stances, may be less crucial in group therapy than in the individual setting where Sullivan worked (see chapter 6).

The theory of interpersonal relationships is presently so much an integral part of the fabric of psychiatric thought that it needs no further underscoring. People need people—for initial and continued survival, for socialization, for the pursuit of satisfaction. No one—neither the dying, nor the outcast, nor the mighty—transcends the need for human contact.

For many years, I led groups of patients who all had some advanced form of cancer. I was repeatedly struck by the realization that, in the face of death, we dread not so much nonbeing or nothingness but the accompanying utter loneliness. The dying patient's concerns are not infrequently interpersonal. One is distressed at being abandoned, even shunned, by the world of the living. One patient, for example, had planned to give a large evening social function and learned that very morning that her cancer, heretofore believed contained, had metastasized. She kept the information secret and gave the party, all the while dwelling on the horrible thought that the pain from her disease would be so unbearable that she would become less human and, finally, unacceptable to others.

I agree with Elisabeth Kübler-Ross that the question is not whether to tell the patient but how to tell the patient openly and honestly. The patient is always informed covertly that he or she is dying by the demeanor, by the shrinking away, of the living.[12]

Dying often separates one from those to whom one is closest. One protects or cheers friends by an airy facade. Dying patients avoid morbid talk to such an extent that a wide gulf is created between them and the "living." Physicians often keep patients with far advanced cancer at a considerable psychological distance, probably to avoid dread of their own death and their sense of guilt, limitation, and futility. There is, after all, nothing more they can do. Yet from the patient's standpoint, this is the time when one needs the physician the most—not for technical aid but for sheer human presence. What the patient needs is contact, to be able to touch others, to voice concerns openly, to be reminded that he or she is not only "apart from" but also "a part of."

The outcasts—those individuals often thought to be so inured to rejection that their interpersonal needs have become heavily calloused—they, too, have compelling social needs. An experience in a prison provided me with a forceful reminder of the ubiquitous nature of this human need.

An untrained psychiatric technician requested consultation with his therapy group composed of twelve inmates. The members of the group were all hardened recidivists, whose offenses ranged from aggressive sexual violation of a minor to murder. The group, he complained, was sluggish and persisted in focusing on extraneous extragroup material. I agreed to observe his group and suggested that first he obtain some sociometric information by asking each member privately to rank-order everyone in their group for "general popularity." (I had hoped that the discussion of this task would induce the group to turn its attention upon itself.) Although we had planned to discuss these results before the next group session, unexpected circumstances forced us to cancel our pre-session consultation.

During the next group meeting, the therapist, enthusiastic but professionally inexperienced and insensitive to interpersonal needs, decided that he would simply read out the results of the popularity poll. The group members began the meeting in a somewhat agitated manner and, clearly frightened and threatened, soon made it explicit that they did not wish to know the results of the poll. Several members spoke so vehemently of the possible devastation of learning that they might appear at the bottom of the list that the therapist quickly and permanently abandoned his plan of reading aloud the list. I suggested an alternative plan: each member was asked to indicate whose vote he cared about most in the group, and to explain his choice. This device, also, was too threatening, and only one third of the members ventured a choice. Nevertheless, the group shifted to an interactional level and developed a degree of tension, involvement, and exhilaration previously unknown. These human beings had received the ultimate message of rejection from society at large; they were imprisoned, segregated, and explicitly labeled as outcasts. To the casual observer, these men, of all people, seemed calloused, hardened, and indifferent to the subtleties of interpersonal approval and disapproval; yet they cared, and cared deeply.

The need for acceptance and intercourse with others is no different among people at the opposing pole of human fortunes—those who occupy the ultimate realms of power, renown, or wealth. I once worked for three years with an enormously wealthy patient. The major issues revolved about the wedge that money created between herself and others. Did anyone value her for herself rather than her money? Was she continually being exploited by others? To whom could she complain of the burdens of a twenty-million-dollar fortune? If she kept her identity or her wealth a secret from others, she felt like a fraud. How could she possibly give others appropriate gifts without their feeling disappointed or awed? There is no need to belabor the point; the loneliness of the very great is common knowledge. (These experiences are, incidentally, not irrelevant to the group therapist; in chapter 7, I will discuss the loneliness inherent in the role of group leader.)

Every group therapist has, I am sure, encountered patients who profess indifference to or detachment from the group. They proclaim: "I don't care what they say or think or feel about me; they're nothing to me; I have no respect for the other members," or words to that effect. My experience has been that if I can keep such patients in the group long enough, another aspect inevitably surfaces. They are concerned at a very deep level about the group. They may dream about the group, feel great anxiety before meetings, feel too shaken after meetings to drive home or to sleep that night. One patient who maintained her indifferent posture for many months was once invited to ask the group her secret question, the one question she would like most of all to place before the group. To everyone's astonishment, her question was, "How can you put up with me?" People do not long feel indifferent toward others in a group. Patients do not quit the therapy group because of boredom. Believe scorn, contempt, fear, discouragement, shame, panic, hatred—believe any of these, but never believe indifference!

In summary, then, I have reviewed some aspects of personality development, mature functioning, psychopathology, and psychiatric treatment from the point of view of interpersonal theory. Many of the issues that I have raised have a vital bearing on the therapeutic process in group therapy: the concept that mental illness emanates from disturbed interpersonal relationships, the role of consensual validation in the modification of interpersonal distortions, the definition of the therapeutic process as an adaptive modification of interpersonal relationships, and the enduring nature and potency of the human being's social needs. Let us now turn to the corrective emotional experience, the second of the three concepts necessary to understand the therapeutic factor of interpersonal learning.

The Corrective Emotional Experience

In 1946, Franz Alexander, when describing the mechanism of psychoanalytic cure, introduced the concept of the "corrective emotional experience." The basic principle of treatment, he stated, is "to expose the patient, under more favorable circumstances, to emotional situations that he could not handle in the past. The patient, in order to be helped, must undergo a corrective emotional experience suitable to repair the traumatic influence of previous experience."[13] Alexander insisted that intellectual insight alone is insufficient: there must be an emotional component and systematic reality testing as well. The patient, while affectively interacting with the analyst in a distorted fashion because of transference (or parataxic distortion), gradually must become aware of the fact that "these reactions are not suited to the analyst's reactions, not only because he (the analyst) is objective, but also because he is what he is, a person in his own right. They are not suited to the situation between patient and therapist, and they are equally unsuited to the patient's current interpersonal relationships in his daily life."[14]

These basic principles of individual therapy—the importance of the emotional experience in therapy and the patient's discovery through reality testing, of the inappropriateness of his or her interpersonal reactions—are equally crucial to group therapy. In fact, the group setting offers far more opportunities for the generation of corrective emotional experiences; in the individual setting, the corrective emotional experience, valuable as it is, may be hard to come by because of the insularity and unreality of the patient-therapist relationship. (In fact, Alexander suggested that the analyst may have to be an actor and to play a role in order to create the desired emotional atmosphere.[15])

No such role playing or simulation is necessary in the therapy group, which contains a host of inbuilt tensions: for example, sibling rivalry, competition for the leaders' attention, competition for the group's attention, the struggle for dominance and status, sexual tensions, parataxic distortions, differences in background and values among the members. But tensions are not sufficient: they have to be transformed into a corrective emotional experience. For that to occur two conditions are required: the members must experience the group as sufficiently safe and supportive so that they may permit these differences to emerge, and there must be sufficient feedback and honesty of expression to permit effective reality testing.

Over many years of clinical work, I have made it a practice to interview patients after they have completed group therapy. I always inquire about some single critical incident, some turning point or the most helpful single event in therapy. Although the single critical incident is not synonymous with *therapeutic factor*, clearly the two are not unrelated and much may be learned from an examination of single important events. My patients almost invariably select an incident that is highly laden emotionally and involves some other group member, rarely the therapist.

The most common type of incident my patients report—as well as patients described by J. Frank and E. Ascher[16]—involves the patient's suddenly expressing strong feelings of anger or hatred toward another member. In each instance, communication was maintained, the storm was weathered, and the patient experienced a sense of liberation from inner restraints as well as an enhanced ability to explore more deeply his or her interpersonal relationships.

The common characteristics of these critical incidents were:

1. The patient expressed strong negative affect.
2. This expression was a unique or novel experience for the patient.
3. The feared catastrophe did not occur; no one left or died, the roof did not collapse.
4. Reality testing ensued. The patient realized either that the affect expressed was inappropriate in intensity or direction, or that prior avoidance of affect expression was irrational. He or she may or may not have gained some insight: that is, the reasons accounting either for the inappropriate affect or for his or her prior avoidance of affect experience or expression.
5. The patient was enabled to interact more freely and to explore his or her interpersonal relationships more deeply.

The second most common type of critical incident described by my patients also involved strong affect—but, in these instances, positive affect. For example, a schizoid patient ran after and comforted a distressed patient who had bolted out of the group room; later he spoke of how profoundly he was affected by learning that he could care for and help someone else. Others similarly spoke of discovering their "aliveness" or of feeling "in touch with" themselves. These incidents had in common the following characteristics:

1. The patient expressed strong positive affect—an unusual occurrence.
2. The feared catastrophe did not occur—neither derision, rejection, engulfment, nor the destruction of others.
3. The patient discovered a previously unknown part of the self and thus was enabled to relate to others in a new fashion.

The third most common category of critical incident was similar to the second. Patients recalled an incident, usually involving self-disclosure, which plunged them into greater involvement with the group. For example, a previously withdrawn reticent patient who had missed a couple of meetings disclosed to the group how desperately he wanted to hear the group members say that they had missed him during his absence. Others, too, in one fashion or another openly asked the group for help.

To summarize, the corrective emotional experience in group therapy has several components:

1. A strong expression of emotion which is interpersonally directed and is a risk taken by the patient;
2. A group supportive enough to permit this risk taking;
3. Reality testing which allows the patient to examine the incident with the aid of consensual validation from the other members;
4. A recognition of the inappropriateness of certain interpersonal feelings and behavior or of the inappropriateness of certain avoided interpersonal behavior;
5. The ultimate facilitation of the individual's ability to interact with others more deeply and honestly.

This dual nature of the therapeutic process is of elemental significance, and I shall return to it again and again in this text. Therapy is *an emotional and a corrective* experience. We must experience something strongly; but we must also, through our faculty of reason, understand the implications of that emotional experience. This formulation has direct relevance to the concept of the here-and-now—a key concept of group therapy which I shall discuss in depth in chapter 6. For the present, I shall state only the basic premise: to the degree that the therapy group focuses on the here-and-now, it increases in power and effectiveness. But if the here-and-now focus (that is, a focus on what is happening in this room in the immediate present) is to be therapeutic, it must be two-pronged: the group members must experience one another with as much spontaneity and honesty as possible, and *they must also reflect upon that experience.* The self-reflective loop is crucial if the experience is to become therapeutic. As we shall see in the discussion of the therapist's task, most groups have little difficulty in entering the emotional stream of the here-and-now; it is the therapist's job to keep directing the group toward the self-reflective aspect of that process.

The mistaken assumption that a strong emotional experience is in itself a sufficient force for change is seductive as well as venerable. Modern psychotherapy was conceived in that very error: the first description of dynamic psychotherapy (Freud and Breuer's 1895 book on hysteria)[17] described a method of cathartic treatment based on the conviction that hysteria is caused by a traumatic event to which the individual has never fully responded emotionally. Since illness was supposed to be caused by strangulated affect, treatment thus consisted of giving a voice to the stillborn emotion. It was not long before Freud recognized that emotional expression, though necessary, was not a sufficient condition for change. Freud's discarded ideas, tossed carelessly away, have refused to die and have been the seed for a continuous skein of fringe therapeutic ideologies.The Viennese *fin de siècle* cathartic treatment lives today through the approaches of primal scream, bioenergetics, structural integration, and many group leaders' sole emphasis on intensive emotional catharsis.

My colleagues and I conducted an intensive investigation of the process and outcome of many of the encounter techniques popular in the 1970's (see chapter 16 for a description of this research), and our findings provide much support for the dual emotional-intellectual components of the psychotherapeutic process.[18]

We explored, in a number of ways, the relationship between each member's experience in the group and his or her outcome. For example, we asked the members to reflect, retrospectively, on those aspects of the group experience that they deemed most pertinent to their change. We also asked them during the course of the group (at the end of each meeting) to describe the event of that meeting which had the most personal significance. When we correlated the type of event with outcome, we obtained surprising results which disconfirmed many of the current stereotypes about the prime ingredients of the successful encounter group experience. Although emotional experiences (expression and experiencing of strong affect, self-disclosure, giving and receiving feedback) were considered extremely important, they did not distinguish successful from unsuccessful group members. In other words, the members who were unchanged or even had a destructive experience were as likely as successful members to value highly the emotional incidents of the group.

What types of experiences did differentiate the successful from the unsuccessful members? There was clear evidence that a cognitive component was essential; the successful members either acquired information or personal insight. That these findings occurred in groups led by leaders who did not attach much importance to the intellectual component speaks strongly for its being part of the core, and not the facade, of the change process.[19]

The Group as Social Microcosm

A freely interactive group, with few structural restrictions, will, in time, develop into a social microcosm of the participant members. Given enough time, every patient will begin to be himself or herself: one will interact with the group members as one interacts with others in one's social sphere, will create in the group the same interpersonal universe one has always inhabited. In other words, patients will begin to display their maladaptive interpersonal behavior in the group; there is no need for them to describe their pathology: they will sooner or later act it out before the group members' eyes.

This concept is of paramount importance in group therapy and constitutes a keystone upon which the entire approach to group therapy rests. It is widely accepted by clinicians, although each therapist's perception and interpretation of group events and descriptive language are determined by his or her school of conviction. Freudians may see patients manifesting their oral, sadistic, or masochistic needs in their relationship to other members; object relations theorists may focus on splitting, projective identification, idealization, mirroring, devaluation; correctional workers may see "conning," exploitative behavior; certain social psychologists may see manifold bids for dominance, affection, or inclusion; Adlerians may speak more of compensatory behavior and are likely to observe birth-order behavior (youngest sister, older brother, and so on); students of Karen Horney may see the detached, resigned person putting his energies into acting noncommittal and indifferent, or the arrogant-vindictive person struggling to prove him or herself right by proving others wrong.[20]

The important point is that, regardless of the type of conceptual spectacles worn by the therapist-observer, each member's interpersonal style will eventually appear in his or her transactions in the group. Some styles have greater inherent possibilities for interpersonal friction and will manifest themselves in the group more rapidly than others. Individuals who are, for example, angry, vindictive, harshly judgmental, self-effacing, or grandly coquettish will generate considerable interpersonal static early in the group. Their maladaptive social patterns will seem clear far earlier than those of individuals equally or more severely troubled who may, for example, subtly exploit others or achieve intimacy to a point but then, becoming frightened, disengage themselves. The initial business of a group usually consists of dealing with the members whose pathology is most interpersonally blatant. Some interpersonal styles become crystal clear from a single transaction; others, from a single group meeting; while others require months of observation to understand. The development of the ability to identify and put to therapeutic advantage maladaptive interpersonal behavior as seen in the social microcosm of the small group is one of the chief tasks of a training program for group psychotherapists. Some clinical examples may make these principles more graphic.[21]

The Grand Dame

• Valerie, a twenty-seven-year-old musician, sought therapy with me primarily because of severe marital discord of several years' standing. She had had considerable, unrewarding, individual and hypnotic uncovering therapy. Her husband, she reported, was an alcoholic who was reluctant to engage her socially, intellectually, or sexually. Now the group could have, as some groups do, investigated her marriage interminably. They might have taken a complete history of the courtship, of the evolution of the discord, of her husband's pathology, of her reasons for marrying him, of her role in the conflict; they might have given advice for new behavior, trial or permanent separation—but all would have been in vain. This approach not only disregards the unique potential of therapy groups but is also based on the highly questionable premise that a patient's account of a marriage is even reasonably accurate. Groups that function in this manner not only fail to help the particular protagonist but also suffer demoralization because a problem-solving, historical group therapy approach is so ineffective.

Valerie's group behavior was flamboyant. First, there was her grand entrance, always five or ten minutes late. Bedecked in flamboyant, ever-different garb, she swept in, sometimes throwing kisses, and immediately began talking, oblivious to whether some other member was in the midst of a sentence or, indeed, of a word. Here was narcissism in the raw! Her world view was so solipsistic that she did not consider that life could have been going on in the group before her arrival.

After a very few group meetings, Valerie began to give gifts in the group: to an obese female member, a copy of a new diet; to a female with strabismus, the name of a good ophthalmologist; to a male homosexual patient, a subscription to *Field and Stream* magazine (to masculinize him); to a twenty-four-year-old virginal male, an introduction to a divorcée friend of hers. Gradually it became apparent that the gifts were not duty free. For example, she intruded in the relationship between the male member and her divorcée friend by serving gratuitously as a third-party go-between, and thus exerted considerable control over both individuals.

Her efforts to dominate soon colored all of her interactions in the group. I became a challenge to her, and she made various efforts to control me. By chance, I saw her sister in consultation and referred her to a competent therapist, a clinical psychologist. In the group Valerie congratulated me for the "brilliant tactic" of sending her sister to a psychologist; I "must have divined her deep-seated aversion for physicians." Similarly, on another occasion, I made a comment to her, and she responded, "How perceptive you were to have noticed my hands trembling." Now, in fact, I had not divined her sister's alleged aversion for physicians, but had simply referred her to the best therapist I knew; nor had I noted Valerie's hands trembling. The trap was set: if I silently accepted her tribute, then I entered into ambiguous collusion with Valerie; on the other hand, if I admitted that I had not been sensitive either to the trembling of the hands or to the sister's aversion, then in a sense I had also been bested. In such situations, the therapist does well to concentrate instead on the process and to comment on the nature and the meaning of the entrapment. (I shall have a great deal more to say about relevant therapist technique in chapter 6.)

Valerie vied with me in many other ways. Intuitive and intellectually gifted, she became the group expert on dream and fantasy interpretation. On one occasion she saw me between group sessions to ask whether she could use my name to take a book out of the medical library. On one level the request was reasonable: the book (on music therapy) was related to her profession; furthermore, she, having no university affiliation, was not permitted to use the library. However, in the context of the group process, the request was complex in that she was testing limits, and its granting would have meant to her and the rest of the group that she did occupy a "special place" vis à vis me and the other members. I clarified these considerations to her and suggested further discussion in the next session. Following this perceived rebuttal, however, she called the three male members at home and, after swearing them to secrecy, arranged to see them, and engaged in sexual relations with two. She failed with the third, a homosexual, only after a mighty attempt.

The following meeting was horrific. It was extraordinarily tense, unproductive, and demonstrated the axiom (to be discussed later) that *if something important in the group is actively avoided, then nothing else of import is talked about either.* Two days later Valerie, overcome with anxiety and guilt, asked for an individual session with me and made a full "confession." It was agreed that the whole matter should be discussed in the next group meeting.

This meeting was opened by Valerie, who said, "This is confession day! Go ahead, Charles!" and then later, "Your turn, Louis." The men performed as she bade them and, later in the meeting, received from her a critical evaluation of their sexual performance. Later, Valerie "accidentally" let her estranged husband know of this event, and soon he sent threatening messages to the men in the group, who then decided they could no longer trust her and thereupon voted her out of the group—the only such occasion I have known. (She continued her therapy by joining another group.) The saga does not end here, but perhaps I have gone far enough to illustrate the concept of the group as social microcosm.

To summarize, Valerie clearly displayed her interpersonal pathology in the group. Her narcissism, her need for adulation, her need to control, her sadistic relationship with men—the entire tragic behavioral scroll—unrolled in the here-and-now of therapy. Finally, she began to receive crucial feedback as the men, for example, talked of their deep humiliation and anger at having to "jump through a hoop" for her and at having received "grades" for their sexual performance. They began to reflect: "No wonder your husband avoids you!"; "Who wants to sleep with his mother?" and so on. The female patients and I shared the men's feelings about the tremendously destructive course of Valerie's behavior—destructive for the group as well as for herself. Most important of all, she had to deal with this fact: she had joined a group of troubled individuals who were anxious to help each other and whom she grew to like and respect; yet, in the course of one year, she had so poisoned her environment that, against her conscious wishes, she became a pariah, an outcast from a group that had had the potential of being very helpful to her. Facing and working through these issues in subsequent therapy, in part, enabled her to change and to employ much of her considerable potential constructively in her later relationships and endeavors.

The Man Who Liked Robin Hood

Ron, a forty-eight-year-old attorney, separated from his wife, entered therapy because of depression, anxiety, and intense feelings of loneliness. His relationships with both men and women were highly problematic. He yearned for a close male friend but had not had one since high school. His current relationships with men assumed one of two forms: either he and the other man related in a highly competitive antagonistic fashion, or he assumed an exceedingly dominant role and soon found the relationship empty and dull.

His relationships with women had always followed a predictable sequence: instant attraction, a flourish of passion, a rapid withering. His love for his wife had withered many years ago, and he was currently in the midst of a painful divorce.

Ron was intelligent and articulate and immediately assumed a position of dominance and influence in the group. He offered a continuous stream of useful and thoughtful observations to the other members, yet kept his own pain and his own needs well concealed. He requested nothing and accepted nothing from me or my co-therapist. Each time I set out to interact personally with Ron, I felt myself bracing for battle. His antagonistic resistance was so great that for months my major interaction with him consisted of repeatedly requesting him to examine his reluctance to experience me as someone who could offer help. "Ron," I asked often, "let's understand what's happening. You have many areas of unhappiness in your life. I'm an experienced therapist, and you come to me for help. You come regularly, you never miss a meeting, you pay me for my services, yet you systematically prevent me from helping. Either you so hide your pain that I find little to offer you, or when I do extend some help, you reject it in one fashion or another. Reason dictates that we should be allies, working together to help you. How does it come about that we are adversaries?"

Ron's relationship with the other group members was characterized by his insistence on seeing them outside the group. He systematically arranged for some extra-group activity with each of the members. He was a pilot and took some members flying, others sailing, others to lavish dinners; gave legal advice to some and became romantically involved with Irene, one of the female members; and (the final straw) invited my co-therapist, a female psychiatric resident, for a skiing weekend. Furthermore, he refused to examine his behavior or to discuss these extra-group meetings in the group, even though he and the other members of the group realized that such unexamined, undiscussed extra-group meetings generally sabotage therapy (see chapter 12).

After one meeting when enormous pressure had been placed on him to examine the meaning of the extra-group invitations, especially the invitation to my co-therapist, he left the session confused and shaken. On the way home, Ron suddenly remembered that, throughout his childhood, his favorite story had been Robin Hood. Following

34

an impulse, he drove directly to the children's section of the nearest public library to read the story once again. Suddenly the meaning of his behavior made sense to him. What had always fascinated and delighted him about the Robin Hood legend was the rescuing of individuals, especially women, from tyrants. That motif had played a powerful role in his interior life beginning first with the Oedipal struggles in his own family. He had started a successful legal partnership by first working for someone else and then setting up a competitive firm by enticing his ex-boss's employees to work for him. He had often been most attracted to women who were the property of some other powerful man. Even motives for marrying were blurred: he could not distinguish between the love for his wife and the desire to rescue her from a tyrannical father.

The first stage of interpersonal learning is *pathology display*. Ron's characteristic modes of relating to both men and women unfolded vividly in the microcosm of the group. His major interpersonal motif was to struggle with and to vanquish other men. He competed openly and, because of his intelligence and his great verbal skills, soon procured the dominant role in the group. He then began to mobilize the other members in the final conspiracy—the unseating of the therapist. He formed close alliances through extra-group meetings and through placing other members in his debt by offering favors. Next he proceeded to capture my women—first Irene, the most attractive member, and then my student co-therapist.

Not only was Ron's interpersonal pathology displayed in the group, but so also were the adverse, self-defeating consequences of his interpersonal behavior. His struggles with men resulted in the undermining of the very reason he had come to therapy: to obtain help. In fact, the competitive struggle was so powerful that any help I extended him was experienced not as help but as a defeat.

Furthermore, the microcosm of the group revealed the consequences of his actions upon the texture of his relationship with his peers. Soon the other members became aware that Ron did not really relate to them. He only appeared to relate but, in actuality, was using them as a mode of relating to me, the powerful and feared male in the group. The others soon felt used, felt the absence of a genuine desire in Ron to know them, and gradually began to distance themselves from him. Only after Ron was able to understand and to alter the intense and distorted modes of relating to me, was he able to turn to and relate in good faith to the other members of the group.

"Those Damn Men"

Robin, forty-six years old and thrice divorced, entered the group because of anxiety and severe functional gastrointestinal distress. Her major interpersonal issue was her tormented self-destructive relationship with her current boyfriend. In fact, throughout her life she had encountered a long series of men (father, brothers, bosses, lovers, and husbands) who had abused her both physically and psychologically. Her accounts of the abuse that she had suffered, and suffered still, at the hands of men were harrowing and persuasive.

The group could do little to help her aside from applying balm to her wounds and listening empathically to her accounts of continuing mistreatment by her current boss and boyfriend. Then one day an unusual incident occurred, which graphically illuminated her dynamics.

She called me one morning in great distress. She had had an extremely unsettling altercation with her boyfriend and felt panicky and suicidal. She pleaded for an immediate session; she could not possibly wait for the next group meeting, which was still four days off. Although it was considerably inconvenient, I rearranged my appointments that afternoon and scheduled time to meet her. Approximately thirty minutes before our meeting, she called and left word with my secretary that she would not be coming in after all.

In the next group meeting, I inquired what had happened, and Robin stated that she had decided to cancel the emergency session because she was feeling slightly better by the afternoon, and that she knew my rule that I would see a patient only one time in an emergency during the whole course of group therapy. She therefore thought it might be best to save that time until some future point when she might be even more in crisis.

I found her response bewildering. I had never made such a rule; it would be unthinkable for me to refuse to see someone who was in real crisis. Nor did any of the other members of the group recall my having issued such a dictum. But Robin stuck to her guns: she insisted that she had heard me say that, and was not shaken either by my denial that I had ever stated such a rule or by the unanimous consensus of the other group members. The discussion became circular, defensive, and acrimonious.

This incident, unfolding in the social microcosm of the group, was highly informative and allowed us to obtain an important perspective on Robin's responsibility for some of her problematic relationships with men. Up until that point, the group had had to rely entirely on her portrayal of these relationships. Robin's accounts were convincing, and the group had come to accept her vision of herself as victim of all those damn men out there. An examination of the group incident indicated that Robin had distorted her perceptions of at least one important man in her life—the therapist. Moreover, and this is extremely important, she had distorted the incident in a highly predictable fashion: she experienced me as far more uncaring, insensitive, and authoritarian than I really was.

This was new data. Moreover, it was extremely accurate data—data that was displayed before the eyes of all the members. For the first time, the group began to question the accuracy of Robin's accounts of her relationships with men. Undoubtedly, she accurately portrayed her feelings, but it became apparent that there were parataxic distortions at work: because of her expectations of men and her highly conflicted relationships with them, she misperceived their actions toward her.

But there was more yet to be learned from the social microcosm. An important piece of data was the tone of the discussion: the defensiveness, the irritation, the anger. I became aware that I, too, was irritated: I was irritated at the thankless inconvenience I had suffered by changing my entire schedule to schedule the emergency session with Robin. I was further irritated by her insistence that I had proclaimed a certain insensitive rule when I (and the rest of the group) was certain that I had not. I fell into a reverie in which I asked myself, "What would it be like to live with Robin all the time instead of an hour and a half a week?" If there were many such incidents, I could imagine myself often becoming angry, exasperated, and uncaring toward her. This is a particularly clear example of the concept of the self-fulfilling prophecy described on page 21. Robin predicted that men would behave to her in a certain way and then, unconsciously, operated so as to bring this prediction to pass.

Men Who Could Not Feel

Allen, a thirty-year-old unmarried scientist, sought therapy for a single, sharply delineated problem: "I want to be able to feel sexually stimulated by a woman." Intrigued by this conundrum, the group searched for the answer. They investigated his early life, sexual habits, fantasies, and finally, baffled, turned away. As life in the group continued, Allen, a regular attender, seemed impassive and insensitive to his own and others' pain. On one occasion, for example, a member in great distress announced in sobs that she was illegitimately pregnant and was planning to have an abortion. During her account she also mentioned that she had had a bad marijuana trip. Allen, seemingly unmoved by her tears, persisted in questioning her intellectually about marijuana effects and was puzzled when the group turned on him because of his insensitivity. So many similar incidents occurred that the group came to expect no emotions from him. When he was directly queried about his feelings, he responded as if he had been addressed in Sanskrit or Aramaic. After some months the group formulated a new answer to his oft-repeated question, "Why can't I have sexual feelings toward a woman?" They asked him to consider instead why he couldn't *have any feeling* toward man or woman.

Changes in his behavior occurred very gradually and were mediated via an investigation of his autonomic expressions of affect. The group wondered about his frequent facial flushing; he described his gastric tightness during emotional episodes in the group. On one occasion a very volatile girl in the group called him a "god-damned robot," said that she couldn't relate to a "psychologically deaf and dead" individual, and threatened to leave the group. Allen again remained impassive, stating that he wasn't going to "get down to her level." However, the next week he told the group that after the meeting he had gone home and cried like a baby. When he looked back at the course of his therapy, this seemed to be a turning point, and gradually he was able to feel and express sorrow, fear, and anger with others. His role within the group changed from that of tolerated mascot to that of accepted compeer.

In another group Ed, a forty-seven-year-old engineer, sought therapy because of loneliness and his inability to find a suitable mate. He had no male friends and unsatisfying short-lived relationships with women whom he did not respect and who invariably rejected him. Ed had good social skills and a lively sense of humor and was initially highly valued by other members. However, as time went on and as members deepened their relationship with one another, Ed was left behind until his experience in the group resembled closely his social life outside the group. The most obvious aspect of his behavior was his limited and offensive approach to women. His gaze was primarily directed toward their breasts or crotch; his attention was in voyeuristic fashion directed toward their sexual life; his suggested solutions were typically simplistic and sexual in nature. The men in the group were considered unwelcome competitors, and he ignored them; for months he did not initiate a single transaction with a man.

He could not appreciate attachments and for the most part considered people interchangeable. For example, one woman described her obsessive fantasy, whenever her boyfriend was late, that he would be killed in an automobile accident. Ed's response was to assure her that she was young and attractive and would have little trouble finding another man of at least equal quality. He was always puzzled that the members were troubled by the temporary absence of one of the co-therapists or, later, at the impending permanent departure of a therapist. Doubtless, he suggested, there was, even among the students, a therapist of equal competence. (In fact, he had seen in the hall a bosomy psychologist, whom he would welcome as therapist.)

He put it most succinctly when he described his M.D.R. (minimum daily requirement) for affection; in time it became clear to the group that the identity of the M.D.R. supplier was less relevant than the dependability and regularity of flow.

Thus, the first phase of the group therapy process evolved: Ed's typical interpersonal behavior was displayed in the group. He did not relate to others but used others as equipment, as objects to supply his life needs. Soon he had recreated in the group his habitual, lonely, interpersonal universe: he became extremely isolated in the group; the men reciprocated his total indifference; the women were not stimulated by the prospect of serving as his M.D.R. Those whom he especially craved were repulsed by his narrowly sexualized attentions.

The Dynamic Interaction between the Person and the Group Environment

There is a rich and subtle interplay between the group member and the group environment. Each member at once shapes and responds to his or her social microcosm. The more spontaneous interaction there is, the more varied will be the environment and the greater the likelihood that problematic issues will, for all the members, be touched upon.

• For example, Andrew, a young borderline patient, entered the group because of a disabling depression and a subjective state of disintegration. His symptoms were intensified by a threatened breakup of the small commune in which he lived. Andrew regularly experienced great anxiety when he was left alone. He had long been sensitized to the breakup of nuclear units; for years he had felt it was his task to keep his explosive family together. He had long nurtured a fantasy that his wedding would result in a reunion and permanent reconciliation of the various factions among his relations.

In the group, Andrew, sometimes for weeks on end, would work smoothly and comfortably on important but minor conflict areas. Periodically, certain events in the group would fan his major, but smoldering, concerns into full anxious conflagration. Often he became very upset when a member was absent. At the end of therapy, looking back, he recalled feeling so stunned at the absence of anyone that he frequently found himself unable to participate for the entire session. When a member thought about termination, Andrew was similarly concerned and could be counted upon to exert maximal pressure upon the member to continue in the group regardless of the best interests of the member. When members subgrouped and arranged contacts outside of the group meeting, Andrew became anxious at the threat to the integrity of the group. He longed for sameness and safety but, in fact, it was the very appearance of unsettling vicissitudes which made it possible for his major conflict areas to become exposed and to enter the stream of the therapeutic work.

Not only does the small group provide a social microcosm in which the maladaptive behavior of members is clearly displayed but also it becomes a laboratory in which is demonstrated, often with great clarity, the dynamics of the behavior. The therapist sees not only the behavior but also the events triggering it and sometimes, more importantly, the responses of others.

• Leonard, for example, entered the group with a major problem of procrastination. Procrastination was considered both a problem and an explanation. It "explained" his failures both professionally and socially; it "explained" his discouragement, depression, and alcoholism. And yet it was an explanation that obscured meaningful explanation. In the group we became well acquainted with Leonard's procrastination. It served as his supreme mode of resistance to therapy when all other resistance had failed. When members worked hard with Leonard, and when it appeared that part of his neurotic character was about to be uprooted, he found ways to delay the group work. "I don't want to be upset by the group today. This new job is make or break for me. I'm just hanging on by my fingernails. Don't rock the boat. After the last meeting I had my first drink in months," and so on. The variations were many, but the theme was consistent.

One day Leonard announced a major step, one for which he had long labored: he had quit his job and obtained a new one as a teacher. Only one step remained—getting a teaching certificate, a matter of filling out an application requiring approximately two hours' labor. And yet he could not do it! He delayed until the time had practically expired and, with only one day remaining, informed the group about the deadline and lamented the cruelty of his personal demon—procrastination. Everyone in the group, including the therapists, experienced a strong desire to sit Leonard down, possibly even in one's lap, place a pen between his fingers, and guide his hand along the application form. And one patient, the most mothering member of the group, did exactly that: she took him home, fed him, and schoolmarmed him through the application form.

As we began to review what had happened, we could now see his procrastination for what it was: a plaintive, anachronistic plea for a lost mother. Many things fell into place: Leonard's depressions (another type of plea for love, an even more desperate one), his alcoholism, and compulsive overeating.

The major point, I believe, is sufficiently clear: if the group is so conducted that the members can behave in an unguarded, unself-conscious manner, they will, most vividly, present their pathology to the group. Furthermore, in the *in vivo* drama of the group meeting, the trained observer has a unique opportunity to understand the dynamics of each patient's behavior.

Recognition of Behavioral Patterns in the Social Microcosm

Note that in the incident involving Leonard, the vital clue was the emotional response of members and leaders to him. These emotional responses are valid and indispensable data: they should not be overlooked or underestimated. The therapist or other group members may feel angry toward a member, or exploited, or sucked dry, or steamrollered, or intimidated, or bored, or tearful, or any of the infinite number of ways one person can feel toward another. These feelings represent data—a bit of the truth about the other person—and should be taken seriously. If the feelings elicited in others are highly discordant with the feelings that the patient would like to engender in others, or if the feelings aroused, though desired, obviously, as in the example of Leonard, inhibit growth, then therein lies an important part of the patient's problem. It is to this phenomenon that the therapist should direct attention.

There are many complications inherent in this thesis. The most obvious is that a strong emotional response is often due to pathology not in the subject but in the respondent. If, for example, a self-confident, assertive male evokes strong feelings of intense envy or bitter resentment or homosexual panic in another man, we can hardly conclude that the response is reflective of the former's pathology. So the therapist looks for confirmatory evidence, for consensual validation (the reactions of other members), for repetitive patterns over a period of time. Most of all the therapist relies upon the most valuable evidence—his or her own emotional responses.

Therapists are well advised to take seriously the responses of all patients, even those who are highly disturbed. Even the most exaggerated irrational responses contain a core of reality. Furthermore, the disturbed patient may be a valuable, accurate source of feedback at other times (no individual is highly conflicted in *every* area). Lastly, an idiosyncratic response contains much information about the respondent.

This latter point is important and constitutes a basic axiom for the group therapist. Not infrequently members of a group respond very differently to the same stimuli. Each of the seven members may observe and respond differently to a group incident. Since the incident is identical for all members, there is only one explanation for the differing responses: there are seven different inner worlds. Thus, analysis of these differing responses is a *via regia* into the inner worlds of the group members. For example, everyone in the group may be exposed to the same person, a controlling monopolistic person, such as the flamboyant Valerie. The members, according to their inner worlds, respond very differently to such a person, ranging from obsequious acquiescence, to impotent fury, to effective confrontation. Or again, consider certain structural aspects of the group meeting: members have markedly differing responses to sharing the group or the therapist's attention, to disclosing themselves, to asking for help or helping others. Nowhere are such differences more apparent than in the transference phenomenon: the same therapist will be experienced, by different members, as warm, cold, rejecting, or accepting.

Not infrequently the concept of the social microcosm is challenged by patients. One may claim that, though one behaves in a certain manner in this group, it is atypical behavior, not at all representative of one's normal behavior. Or that this group is unusual and perceives one inaccurately. Or even that group therapy is not real; it is an artificial, contrived experience which distorts rather than reflects one's real behavior. To the neophyte therapist, these arguments may seem formidable, even persuasive, but they are in fact truth-distorting. In one sense, the group *is* artificial: members do not choose their friends from the group; they are not central to one another; they do not live, work, or eat together; they meet together in a professional's office for ninety minutes once or twice a week; the end of their relationship is built into the social contract at the very beginning.

• When faced with these considerations, I often think of Earl and Marguerite, two patients in a group long ago. Earl had been a member of the group for four months when Marguerite was introduced. They both blushed to see one another in the group room since, by chance, they had only a month previously gone on a Sierra Club camping trip together for a night and been "intimate." Neither wanted to be in the group with the other. To Earl, Marguerite was a foolish, empty girl, a "mindless piece of ass," as he was to put it later in the group. To Marguerite, Earl was a dull nonentity, someone whose penis she had once used as a means of retaliation against her husband. They worked together in the group once a week for about a year. During that time, they came to know one another intimately in the full sense of the word; they shared their deepest feelings; they weathered fierce, vicious battles; they helped each other through suicidal depressions; and, on more than one occasion, they wept for each other. Which was the real world, and which the artificial?

Paradoxically, the group can be far more real than the world out there. There are no social, prestige, or sexual games in the group; members go through vital life experiences together; the reality-distorting facades are doffed as members try hard to be honest with one another. How many times have I heard a group member say, "This is the first time I have ever told this to anyone"? These are not strangers. Quite the contrary: these are individuals likely to know one another deeply and fully. Psychological reality is not equivalent to physical reality. Psychologically, group members spend infinitely more time together than the one or two meetings a week when they physically occupy the same professionally sponsored room.

Overview

Let me now return to the primary task of this chapter: to define and describe the therapeutic factor of interpersonal learning. All the necessary premises have been posited and described in this discussion of:

1. The importance of interpersonal relationships;
2. The corrective emotional experience;
3. The group as a social microcosm.

43

If these principles are organized into a logical sequence, the mechanism of interpersonal learning as a therapeutic factor becomes more evident:

1. Psychiatric symptomatology emanates from disturbed interpersonal relationships. The task of psychotherapy is to help the patient learn how to develop distortion-free, gratifying interpersonal relationships.

2. The psychotherapy group, provided its development is unhampered by severe structural restrictions, evolves into a social microcosm, a miniaturized representation of each patient's social universe.

3. The group members, through consensual validation and self-observation, become aware of significant aspects of their interpersonal behavior: their strengths, their limitations, their parataxic distortions, and their maladaptive behavior which elicits unwanted responses from other people. The patient, who in the past often has had a series of disastrous relationships and has subsequently suffered rejection, has failed to learn from these experiences because others, sensing the person's general insecurity and abiding by the rules of etiquette governing normal social interaction, have not communicated the reasons for rejecting him or her. Therefore, the patient has never learned to discriminate between objectionable aspects of his or her behavior and a self-concept as a totally unacceptable person. The therapy group, with its encouragement of accurate feedback, makes such discrimination possible.

4. A regular interpersonal sequence occurs:
    a. Pathology display—the member displays his or her behavior.
    b. Through feedback and self-observation, one
        (1) Becomes a better observer of one's behavior;
        (2) Appreciates the impact of that behavior upon
            (a) The feelings of others;
            (b) The opinions that others have of one;
            (c) The opinion one has of oneself.

5. The patient who has become fully aware of this sequence also becomes aware of personal responsibility for it: each individual is the author of his or her own interpersonal world.

6. The individual who fully accepts personal responsibility for that interpersonal world may then begin to grapple with the corollary of this discovery: the creator of a world is the only one able to alter it.

7. The depth and meaningfulness of this awareness is directly proportional to the amount of affect associated with the sequence. The more real and the more emotional an experience, the more potent is its impact; the more objectified and intellectualized the experience, the less effective is the learning.

8. As a result of this awareness, the patient gradually changes by risking new ways of being with others. The likelihood that change will occur is a function of:
    a. The patient's motivation for change and the amount of personal discomfort and dissatisfaction with current modes of behavior;

    b. The patient's involvement in the group—that is, how much the patient allows the group to matter;

    c. The rigidity of the patient's character structure and interpersonal style.

9. The change in behavior may generate a new cycle of interpersonal learning via self-observation and feedback from other members. Furthermore, the patient appreciates that some feared calamity, which had hitherto prevented such behavior, has been irrational; this new behavior has not resulted in such calamities as death, destruction, abandonment, derision, or engulfment.

10. The social microcosm concept is bi-directional: not only does outside behavior become manifest in the group, but behavior learned in the group is eventually carried over into the patient's social environment and alterations appear in his or her interpersonal behavior outside the group.

11. Gradually an *adaptive spiral* is set into motion, at first inside and then outside the group. As one's interpersonal distortions diminish, one's ability to form rewarding relationships is enhanced. Social anxiety decreases; self-esteem rises; there is less need for self-concealment; others respond positively to this behavior and show more approval and acceptance of the patient, which further increases self-esteem and enhances further change. Eventually the adaptive spiral achieves such autonomy and efficacy that professional therapy is no longer necessary.

Each of these steps requires specific facilitation by the therapist. Different sets of therapist behavior are needed: offering specific feedback, encouraging self-observation, clarifying the concept of responsibility, encouraging risk taking, disconfirming fantasied calamitous consequences, reinforcement of transfer of learning, and so on. Each of these tasks and techniques will be fully discussed in chapters 5 and 6.

Transference and Insight

Before concluding the examination of interpersonal learning as a mediator of change, I wish to call attention to two concepts which deserve further discussion. Transference and insight play too central a role in most formulations of the therapeutic process to be passed over lightly. I rely heavily on both of these concepts in my therapeutic work and do not mean to slight them. What I have done in this chapter is to embed them both into the factor of interpersonal learning.

Transference is a specific form of interpersonal perceptual distortion. In individual psychotherapy, the recognition and the working through of this distortion is of paramount importance. In group therapy, working through interpersonal distortions is, as we have seen, of no less importance; however, the range and variety of distortions is considerably greater. Working through distortion in the relationship to the therapist now becomes only one of a series of distortions to be examined by the patient.

For many patients, perhaps for the majority, it is the most important relationship to work through since the therapist is the living personification of parental images, of teachers, of authority, of established tradition. But most patients need to explore other interpersonal issues: competitive strivings with their peers; conflicts in the areas of assertion, of intimacy, of sexuality, of giving, of greed, of envy. Considerable research emphasizes the importance many members place on working through relationships with other members rather than with the leader.[22] For example, one team of researchers asked members, in a twelve-month follow-up of a short-term crisis group, to indicate the source of the help each had received. "Forty-two percent felt that the group members and not the therapist had been helpful, and 28 percent responded that both had been of aid.[23] Only 5 percent stated that the therapist alone was a major contributor to change. This corpus of research has important implications for the technique of the group therapist: rather than simply working directly on their relationship with patients, therapists must endeavor to facilitate the development and working-through of interactions among members. I shall have much more to say about these issues in chapters 6 and 7.

Insight defies precise description; it is not a unitary concept. I prefer to employ it in the general sense of "sighting inward": a process encompassing clarification, explanation, and derepression. Insight occurs when one discovers something important about oneself—about one's behavior, one's motivational system, or one's unconscious.

In the group therapy process, patients may obtain insight on at least four different levels:

1. Patients may gain a more objective perspective on their interpersonal presentation. They may for the first time learn how they are seen by other people: as tense, warm, aloof, seductive, bitter, arrogant, pompous, obsequious, and so on.
2. Patients may gain some understanding into their more complex patterns of behavior with other people. Does the patient exploit, reject, court constant admiration, seduce and then withdraw, relentlessly compete, plead for love, or relate only to the therapist or to the men or the women members?
3. The third level may be termed *motivational insight*. Patients may learn *why* they do what they do to and with other people. Aloof, detached patients may understand what they fear so much about intimacy. Competitive, vindictive, controlling patients may identify their need to be taken

care of, to be nurtured. Seductive-rejecting individuals may learn how their hostility corrupts their relationships. A common form of insight is the discovery that one behaves in certain ways because of the belief that different behavior would bring about some catastrophe: one might be humiliated, scorned, destroyed, abandoned, engulfed, or rejected, or one might even become uncontrollably destructive oneself.

4. A fourth level of insight, *genetic insight*, attempts to help patients understand how they got to be the way they are. Through an exploration of personal developmental history, the patient understands the genesis of present patterns of behavior. The theoretical framework and the language in which the genetic explanation is couched are, of course, largely dependent on the therapist's school of conviction.

These four levels have been listed in the order of degree of inference. An unfortunate and longstanding conceptual error has resulted, in part, from the tendency to equate a "superficial-deep" sequence with this "degree of inference" sequence. Furthermore, *deep* has become equated with *profound* or *good*, and *superficial* with *bad, obvious*, or *inconsequential*. Psychoanalysts have disseminated the belief that the more profound the therapist, the deeper the interpretation (from a genetic perspective), then the more complete the treatment. *There is, however, not a shred of evidence to support this contention.* We have all encountered patients who have achieved considerable genetic insight based on some accepted theory of child development—be it that of Freud, Klein, Winnicott, and so on—and yet have made no therapeutic progress. On the other hand, it is commonplace for significant clinical change to occur in the absence of genetic insight. Nor is there a demonstrated relationship between the acquisition of genetic insight and the persistence of change. In fact, there is considerable question even about the validity of our most revered assumptions about the relationship between types of early experience and adult behavior and character structure.[24]

A fuller discussion of causality would take us too far afield from interpersonal learning, but I shall return in depth to the issue in chapters 5 and 6. For now it is sufficient to emphasize that what is important is that insight occur—insight in its generic, not its genetic, sense. There is, in my view, little question that intellectual understanding lubricates the machinery of change. It seems that, in group therapy, we need to disengage the concept of "deep" or "profound" intellectual understanding from temporal considerations: something that is deeply felt or has deep meaning and deep significance for a patient may or, as is usually the case, may not be related to attempts to understand the early genesis of behavior.

3

GROUP COHESIVENESS

Beginning with the hypothesis that cohesiveness in group therapy is the analogue of "relationship" in individual therapy, this chapter deals with the available evidence for group cohesiveness as a therapeutic factor and the various pathways through which group cohesiveness exerts a therapeutic influence.

Over the past twenty years, a vast number of controlled studies of psychotherapy outcome have been performed. Competent, comprehensive reviews of the entire research evidence persuasively demonstrate that, over all, psychotherapy is an effective endeavor: patients who receive psychotherapy are benefited therefrom.[1] One particularly rigorous review of 475 controlled studies concludes that "the average person who receives psychotherapy is better off at the end of it than 80% of the persons who do not."[2] (The same review, incidentally, concluded that the outcome from group therapy was virtually identical to that of individual therapy.)

Another comprehensive review considers that the effectiveness of group therapy is "established," and suggests that researchers direct their efforts toward the question, What are the necessary conditions for effective psychotherapy?[3] After all, not all psychotherapy is successful. In fact, there is considerable evidence that treatment may be "for better or for worse"; that, though most therapists help their patients, some therapists make them worse.[4] Why? What makes for successful therapy? Although many factors are involved, a *sine qua non* in effective therapy outcome is a proper therapeutic relationship. The best research evidence available overwhelmingly supports the conclusion that successful therapy is mediated by a relationship between therapist and patient that is characterized by trust, warmth, empathic understanding, and acceptance.[5]

Furthermore, it has long been established that the quality of the relationship is independent of the individual therapist's school of conviction. Experienced and effective clinicians from different schools (Adlerian, Freudian, nondirective, gestalt, transactional analytic, encounter) resemble one another (and differ from nonexperts in their own school) in their conception of the ideal therapeutic relationship and in the nature of the relationship they themselves establish with their patients.[6] It has also been demonstrated that the warm, cohesive quality of the relationship is no less important in the more mechanical, behavioral, or systems-oriented forms of psychotherapy.[7]

The nature of the relationship has proven to be so critical in individual psychotherapy that we are compelled to ask whether relationship plays an equally critical role in group psychotherapy. It is obvious that the group therapy analogue of the patient-therapist relationship in individual therapy is a broader concept: it must encompass *the patient's relationship not only to the group therapist but to the other group members and to the group as a whole.* At the risk of courting semantic confusion, I shall refer to all these factors under the term *group cohesiveness.*

Cohesiveness is a widely researched basic property of groups. Several hundred research articles exploring cohesiveness have been written, many with widely varying definitions. In general, however, there is agreement that groups differ from one another in the amount of "groupness" present. Those with a greater sense of solidarity or "we-ness" value the group more highly and will defend it against internal and external threats; voluntary attendance, participation, mutual help, defense of the group standards are all greater than in groups with less *esprit de corps.*

There are many methods of measuring cohesiveness, and a precise definition depends upon the method employed. In this book cohesiveness is broadly defined as "the resultant of all the forces acting on all the members to remain in the group"[8] or more simply "the attractiveness of a group for its members."[9] There is also a difference between total group cohesiveness and individual member cohesiveness (or, more strictly, the individual's attraction to the group).[10] The two, of course, are interdependent, and group cohesiveness is often computed by summing the individual members' level of attraction to the group; nevertheless, we must keep in mind that group members are differentially attracted to their group. At times I shall refer to the therapy-facilitating effects of cohesiveness on the total group, while at other times to the effects on an individual member's own process of therapy of his or her attraction to the group.

Keep in mind, too, that cohesiveness is not a static, once-achieved forever-held property of a group; instead, the amount of cohesiveness fluctuates during the life of the group.[11]

Before leaving the matter of definition, it is well to remember that group cohesiveness is not *per se* a therapeutic factor but is instead a necessary precondition for effective therapy. When, in individual therapy, we say that "it is the relationship that heals," we do *not* mean that love or loving acceptance is enough; we mean that an ideal therapist-patient relationship creates conditions in which the necessary self-disclosure and intrapersonal and interpersonal exploration may unfold. In group therapy, similarly, group cohesiveness enhances the development of other important phenomena. Cohesiveness is not, for example, synonymous with intermember acceptance and understanding but is interdependent with these factors. Cohesiveness is both determinant and effect of intermember acceptance: the members of a highly cohesive therapy group will be more accepting of one another than will the members of a noncohesive group; groups with members who show high mutual understanding and acceptance are, by definition, cohesive.

The Importance of Group Cohesiveness

Although I have discussed the therapeutic factors separately, they are, to a great degree, interdependent. Catharsis and universality, for example, are part processes. It is not the sheer process of ventilation that is important; it is not only the discovery of others' problems similar to one's own, and the ensuing disconfirmation of one's wretched uniqueness, that is important; it is the affective sharing of one's inner world, and *then* the acceptance by others, that seems of paramount importance. To be accepted by others brings into question one's belief that one is basically repugnant, unacceptable, or unlovable. Provided one adheres to the group's procedural norms, the group will accept an individual regardless of his or her past life experiences, transgressions, or social failings. Deviant life styles, history of prostitution, sexual perversion, heinous criminal offenses, all can be accepted by the therapy group, provided norms of generosity and inclusiveness are established early in the group.

Frequently, psychiatric patients have had few opportunities for active sharing and acceptance in intimate relationships because of disturbed interpersonal skills. Furthermore, their conviction about the abhorrence of their impulses and fantasies has made interpersonal sharing even more difficult. I have known many isolated patients for whom the group represented their only deeply human contact. After only a few sessions, they have a deeper sense of being "at home" in the group than anywhere else. They may remember the sense of belonging and the basic acceptance years afterward, when most other recollections of the group have faded from memory. As one successful patient, looking back over two and a half years of therapy, put it, "The most important thing in it was just having a group there, people that I could always talk to, that wouldn't walk out on me. There was so much caring and hating and loving in the group and I was a part of it. I'm better now and have my own life, but it's sad to think that the group's not there any more."

Patients may internalize the group. "It's as though the group is sitting on my shoulder, watching me. I'm forever asking, 'What would the group say about this or that?' " Often therapeutic changes persist and are consolidated because the members are disinclined to let the group down.[12]

Group membership, acceptance, and approval are of the utmost importance in the individual's developmental sequence. The importance of belonging to childhood peer groups, adolescent cliques, fraternities, the proper social "in" group can hardly be overestimated. There seems to be nothing of greater importance for the adolescent, for example, than to be included and accepted in some social group, and nothing more devastating than exclusion. Consider in the United States the "blackball" suicides following exclusion from fraternities; or in the West Indies, the bone-pointing voodoo deaths, mediated by total exclusion from the community, which regards the outcast as dead from the time the voodoo spell is cast. Most psychiatric patients have an impoverished group history; never before have they been a valuable, integral, participating member of a group. For these patients, the sheer successful negotiation of a group experience may in itself be curative.

We rely on others not only for approval and acceptance but also for continual validation of our important value systems. *When Prophecy Fails* is a study of a religious cult that had predicted the end of the world.[13] When the doomsday passed without incident, the cult reacted, not with a crisis of doubt, but by increasing its proselytizing efforts; doubt in the belief system of the group apparently required a greater degree of interpersonal validation.

Thus, in a number of ways, members of a therapy group come to mean a great deal to one another. The therapy group, at first perceived as an artificial group which does not count, may in fact come to count very much. I have known groups to experience together severe depressions, psychoses, marriage, divorce, abortions, suicide, career shifts, sharing of innermost thoughts, and incest (sexual activity among the group members). I have seen a group mourn the death of one of its members and another group physically carry one of its members to the hospital. Relationships are often cemented by moving or hazardous adventures. How many relationships in life are so richly layered?

EVIDENCE

Research evidence for the importance of group cohesiveness in the therapeutic process is rudimentary compared with the research documenting the importance of relationship in individual psychotherapy. Nevertheless, there are a few relevant studies in the group therapy and in the experiential group literature. (See chapter 16 for a discussion of experiential [encounter] groups and for the justification of applying research on these groups to the group therapeutic process.) The reader who is less interested in research methodology may proceed directly to the next section (page 56).

H. Dickoff and M. Lakin, in a study of former group psychotherapy patients, found that, from the patients' point of view, group cohesiveness is of major therapeutic value.[14] These investigators transcribed and categorized patients' explanations of the therapeutic factors in their group experience, and found that "more than half of the former patients indicated that the primary mode of help in group therapy is through mutual support." Those patients who perceived their group as cohesive attended more sessions, experienced more social contact with other members, and judged the group as having offered a therapeutic mode. Those patients who reported themselves improved were significantly more likely to have:

1. Felt accepted by the other members;
2. Perceived similarity of some kind among group patients;
3. Made specific references to particular individuals when queried about their group experience.

The authors concluded that group cohesiveness is in itself of therapeutic value and is essential for perpetuation of the group.

In 1970, I reported a study in which successful group therapy patients were asked to look back over their group therapy experience and to rate, in order of effectiveness, the series of therapeutic factors I describe in this book.[15] In the past decade a number of studies have employed an analagous design and generated considerable data about patients' views of what aspects of group therapy have been most useful. I shall examine these results in depth in the next chapter; for now, it is sufficient to note that there is powerful consensus that patients regard group cohesiveness as an extremely important determinant of successful group therapy. R. Cabral, J. Best, and A. Paton studied two long-term therapy groups over a six-month period.[16] Trained observers rated the process of each group session by scoring each member along five variables: acceptance, activity, desensitivity, abreaction, and improvement. Weekly self-ratings were also obtained from each member. The results indicated that, from the perspective of both research raters and group members, acceptance was the only variable powerfully related to improvement.

F. T. Kapp et al. arrived at similar conclusions after a study of forty-seven patients who had been in one of twelve psychotherapy groups for a mean duration of thirteen months.[17] These investigators administered a questionnaire designed to measure self-perceived personality change and the individual's assessment of the degree of cohesiveness among the members of the group. They found that self-perceived personality change correlated significantly both with the members' feelings of involvement in the group and their assessment of total group cohesiveness.

J. Jones studied 130 patients who responded to questionnaires on a student mental health service.[18] These patients had attended one of thirty therapy groups offered in a university mental health service. Each group met forty hours (twenty two-hour sessions) over a five-month period. Over all, the respondents stated that the most positive aspect of their group experience was the feeling of security and acceptance they experienced in the group. The author correlated the amount of cohesiveness (a nineteen-item self-administered scale) with the degree of self-reported improvement, and reported a significant positive correlation on an individual and a group level: that is, a member who is positively attracted to the group will more likely experience positive change; a group that receives high cohesion scores from its members is more likely to generate a higher number of patients who improve than are groups scoring low on cohesion.

My colleagues and I evaluated the outcome at the end of a year of all the patients (N = 40) who had started therapy in five outpatient groups.[19] Outcome was then correlated with a host of variables that had been measured in the first three months of therapy. Positive outcome in therapy significantly correlated with only two predictor variables— "group cohesiveness"* and "general popularity."† That is, patients who were most attracted to the group (high cohesiveness), and who were rated as more popular by the other group members at the sixth and the twelfth weeks, had a better therapy outcome at the fiftieth week. The popularity finding, which in this study correlated even more positively with outcome than did cohesiveness, is, as I shall discuss shortly, relevant to group cohesiveness and sheds light upon the mechanism through which group cohesiveness mediates change.

I. Falloon studied fifty-one patients who attended ten sessions of behavioral group therapy.[20] He found that attraction to the group correlated significantly with improved self-esteem and inversely correlated with the group dropout rate.

J. Flowers, C. Booraem, and K. Hartman studied sixteen patients in ten therapy groups with two-hour sessions.[21] Research raters determined the amount of improvement on major problems. The researchers concluded that more patients evidenced greater improvement in high-cohesive (measured by members' self-rating) than in low-cohesive meetings. They also determined that patients were more likely to disclose details of major problems in highly cohesive meetings.

A rigorously designed study by J. B. Clark and S. A. Culbert demonstrates a significant relationship between the quality of intermember relationships and outcome in a T-group of eleven subjects who met

---

*Cohesiveness was measured by a post-group questionnaire filled out by each patient at the seventh and at the twelfth meetings, and consisting of eleven questions (each answered on a five-point defined scale):
1. How often do you think your group should meet?
2. How well do you like the group you are in?
3. If most of the members of your group decided to dissolve the group by leaving, would you like an opportunity to dissuade them?
4. Do you feel that working with the group you are in will enable you to attain most of your goals in therapy?
5. If you could replace members of your group with other "ideal group members," how many would you exchange (exclusive of group therapists)?
6. To what degree do you feel that you are included by the group in the group's activities?
7. How do you feel about your participation in, and contribution to, the group work?
8. What do you feel about the length of the group meeting?
9. How do you feel about the group therapist(s)?
10. Are you ashamed of being in group therapy?
11. Compared with other therapy groups, how well would you imagine your group works together?
†Popularity was measured sociometrically: each member, at the sixth and twelfth meetings, was asked to rank-order all the group members for general popularity.

twice a week for a total of sixty-four hours.[22] These investigators correlated outcome for the group members with intermember relationships.[23] Their results demonstrated that the members who entered into the most two-person mutually therapeutic relationships showed the most improvement during the course of the group. Furthermore, the perceived relationship with the group leader was unrelated to the extent of change. The authors conclude that the quality of the member-member relationship is a prime determinant of individual change in the group experience.

A large study of 210 subjects in eighteen encounter groups, encompassing ten ideological schools (gestalt, transactional analysis, N.T.L. T-groups, Synanon, personal growth, Esalen, psychoanalytic, marathon, psychodrama, encounter tape) was conducted by M. A. Lieberman, I. D. Yalom and M. Miles.[24] (See chapter 16 for a detailed discussion of this project.) Cohesiveness was assessed in several ways and correlated with outcome.[25] The results indicated that attraction to the group is indeed a powerful determinant of outcome. All methods of determining cohesiveness demonstrated a positive correlation between cohesiveness and outcome. A patient who experienced little sense of belongingness or attraction to the group, even when measured early in the course of the sessions, was unlikely to benefit from the group and, in fact, was likely to have a negative outcome. Furthermore, the *groups* with the higher overall levels of cohesiveness had a significantly higher total outcome than groups with low cohesiveness.

SUMMARY

I have cited evidence that patients in group therapy consider group cohesiveness to be a prime mode of help in their therapy experience. Patients value the acceptance they receive from the group. Self-perceived therapy outcome is positively correlated to attraction to the group. Highly cohesive groups have an overall higher outcome. Individuals with positive outcome have had more mutually satisfying relationships with other members. Highly cohesive groups have greater levels of self-disclosure. Positive patient outcome is correlated also to group popularity, a variable closely related to group support and acceptance. These findings taken together strongly support the contention that group cohesiveness is an important determinant of positive therapeutic outcome.

There is, in addition to this direct evidence, considerable indirect evidence stemming from research with other types of groups. A plethora of studies demonstrates that in laboratory task groups, increased group cohesiveness produces many results that may be considered as intervening therapy outcome factors. For example, group cohesiveness results in better group attendance, greater participation of members, greater influenceability of the members, and many other effects. I shall consider these findings in detail shortly, as I attempt to determine the mechanism by which cohesiveness fosters therapeutic change.

Mechanism of Action

INTRODUCTION

For the remainder of this chapter, I shall discuss the various ways in which cohesiveness produces change in group patients. How do group acceptance, group support, and intermember trust and acceptance help troubled individuals? Surely there is more to it than simple support or acceptance; therapists learn early in their careers that love is not enough. Although the quality of the relationship is crucial, therapy consists of more than relating warmly and honestly to the patient. The relationship creates favorable conditions for setting into motion other processes. What other processes? And how are they important?

Perhaps no one has thought more deeply about the therapeutic relationship than Carl Rogers. Let us start our investigation by examining his views about the mode of action of the therapeutic relationship in individual therapy. In his most systematic description of the process of therapy, Rogers states that when the conditions of an ideal therapist-patient relationship exist, a characteristic process is set into motion:

The patient is increasingly free in expressing his feelings.

He begins to test reality and to become more discriminatory in his feelings and perceptions of his environment, his self, other persons, and his experiences.

He increasingly becomes aware of the incongruity between his experiences and his concept of self.

He also becomes aware of feelings which have been previously denied or distorted in awareness.

His concept of self, which now includes previously distorted or denied aspects, becomes more congruent with his experience.

He becomes increasingly able to experience, without threat, the therapist's unconditional positive regard and to feel an unconditional positive self-regard.

He increasingly experiences himself as the focus of evaluation of the nature and worth of an object or experience.

He reacts to experience less in terms of his perception of others' evaluation of him and more in terms of its effectiveness in enhancing his own development.[26]

Central to Rogers's views is his formulation of an "actualizing tendency," an inherent tendency of the organism to expand and to develop itself. The therapist in individual and in group therapy functions as a facilitator and must help create conditions favorable for self-expansion. The first task of the individual is self-exploration: the examination of feelings and experiences previously denied awareness. This task is a ubiquitous stage in dynamic psychotherapy. Karen Horney, for example, emphasizes the individual's need for self-knowledge and self-realization, stating that the task of the therapist is to remove obstacles in the path of these autonomous processes.[27] There is experimental evidence that good rapport in individual therapy and cohesiveness in group therapy enable the individual to gain greater self-awareness. For example, C. Truax,[28] studying forty-five hospitalized patients in three heterogeneous groups, demonstrated that patients in cohesive groups were significantly more inclined to engage in deep and extensive self-exploration (measured by the Rogers-Rablen scale[29]).

After many years of research into the process of individual therapy, Rogers became interested in the group experience as a therapeutic medium; and although his views of the important growth-potentiating factors in groups are similar to his views of those in the individual relationship, he has commented upon additional powerful factors inherent in the group setting. He underscores, for example, that acceptance and understanding among members may carry greater power and meaning than acceptance by a therapist. Other group members, after all, do not have to care, or understand; they're not paid for it, it's not their "job."[30] This peer acceptance occurs regularly in childhood but not for many of our patients, who find validation by other group members a vital experience. In the affluence of modern American society, we have moved up the hierarchy of needs[31] from survival needs to emotional ones. The contemporary human being, steeped in abundance, turns to the question, With whom can I be personal? With the breakup of the extended nuclear family and the isolation of contemporary life, the problem becomes considerable. The intimacy developed in a group may be seen as a counterforce in a culture "which appears to be bent upon dehumanizing human relationships."[32] The deeply felt human experience in the group may be of great value to the patient, Rogers believes; even if there is no visible carryover, no external change in behavior, one may still experience a more human, richer part of oneself and have this as an internal reference point.

Group members' acceptance of one another, though crucial in the group therapeutic process, may be slow to develop. Acceptance by others and self-acceptance are mutually dependent; not only is self-acceptance basically dependent on acceptance by others, but acceptance of others is fully possible only after one can accept oneself. The members of a therapy group may experience considerable self-contempt and a deep contempt for others. A manifestation of this feeling may be seen in the patient's initial refusal to join "a group of nuts" or reluctance to become closely involved in the group for fear of being sucked into a maelstrom of misery. The importance of self-acceptance for the acceptance of others has been demonstrated in research by I. Rubin,[33] who studied fifty individuals before and after an intensive live-in two-week T-group laboratory and found that an increase in self-acceptance was significantly correlated with increased acceptance of others. These results are consonant with Fromm's statement many years ago that only after being able to love oneself is one able to love others.

Although I have not yet used the term, I have begun to discuss *self-esteem,* a core concept in any approach to personality change. In my experience, all individuals seeking assistance from a mental health professional have in common two paramount difficulties: (1) establishing and maintaining meaningful interpersonal relationships and (2) maintaining a sense of personal worth (self-esteem). It is hard to discuss these two interdependent areas as separate entities but, since I have in the preceding chapter dwelled more heavily on the establishment of interpersonal relationships, I shall now concentrate on self-esteem.

Self-esteem (one's evaluation of one's identity) and public esteem (the group's evaluation of the worth of that aspect of a person's identity germane to that particular group) are highly interdependent.[34] Self-esteem refers to ones conception of what one is really worth, and is indissolubly linked to a person's experiences in social relationships. Recall Sullivan's statement, "The self may be said to be made up of reflected appraisals."[35] The beliefs one has developed, while growing up, about the attitudes of others toward oneself come to determine how one regards and values oneself. Depending upon the congruence of particular life experiences, one internalizes certain relationships and then relies upon these internalized relationships for some stable measure of self-worth. But, in addition to the internal picture of self-worth, one is, to a greater or lesser degree, always concerned and influenced by public esteem—the personal evaluation provided by the groups to which one belongs.

The influence of the group's public esteem on an individual and the individual's inclination to use the group's frame of reference depends on several factors: how important one feels the group to be; the frequency and specificity of the group's communications to one about that public esteem; and the salience to the individual of the traits in question. (Presumably, in therapy groups, the salience is very great, indeed, since these traits are close to a person's core identity.) In other words, the more the group matters to one, the more one subscribes to the group values, the more one will be inclined to agree with the group judgment.[36]

The last point has much clinical relevance. The more attracted one is to the group, the more one respects the judgment of the group, the more one will attend to and take seriously any discrepancy between one's public esteem and one's self-esteem. A discrepancy between the two will create a state of dissonance for that individual, and one will initiate activity to remove the dissonance.

Let us suppose this discrepancy veers to the negative side: that is, the group's evaluation of the individual is less than the individual's self-evaluation. How, then, can one resolve the discrepancy? One recourse is to misperceive, deny, or distort the group's evaluation of one's public esteem. In a therapy group, this development generates a vicious circle. One's public esteem is low because of one's failure to participate in the group task (which in a therapy group consists of active exploration of one's self and one's relationships to others). Any increase in defensiveness and communicational problems will only further lower public esteem. Eventually, the group's communication to the individual will break through unless he or she uses near-psychotic mechanisms to distort reality.

Another more common method of dealing with the discrepancy is to devalue the group. One may emphasize, for example, that the group is artificial or composed of highly disturbed individuals, and then compare it unfavorably with some anchor group (for example, a social or an occupational group) which might evaluate one differently. Members who follow the sequence, characteristic of the group history of "group deviants" described in chapter 8, usually end by dropping out of the group.

A final and therapeutic method of resolving the discrepancy is for the individual to attempt to raise his or her public esteem by changing those traits and attitudes that have been criticized by the group. This method of resolution is more likely if the individual is highly attracted to the group and if the discrepancy between low public esteem and higher self-esteem is not too great. Is this final approach—the use of group pressure to change individual behavior or attitudes—a form of social engineering? Is it not mechanical? Does it not neglect deeper levels of integration? Indeed, group therapy does employ behavioral principles; psychotherapy is, in all variants, basically a form of learning. Even the most nondirective therapists use, at an unconscious level, operant conditioning techniques: they signal desirable conduct or attitudes to patients through explicit statements or through more subtle signs.[37] However, this process does not suggest that we assume an explicit behavioral, mechanistic view of the patient. Aversive or operant conditioning of behavior and attitudes is, in my opinion, neither feasible nor effective when approached as an isolated technique.* In fact, as I have repeatedly stressed, all the therapeutic factors are intricately interdependent and must be appreciated as part of a complex spiraling process. Behavior and attitudinal change, regardless of origin, begets other changes. The group changes its evaluation of the patient; one feels more satisfied with oneself in the group and with the group itself; and the adaptive spiral described in the previous chapter is initiated.

A far more common occurrence in a psychotherapy group is a discrepancy in the opposite direction: the group evaluates one more highly than one evaluates oneself. Once again, the patient, in a state of dissonance, will attempt to resolve the discrepancy. One mode might be to lower one's public esteem further by revealing personal inadequacies. However, in therapy groups, this behavior has the paradoxical effect of raising public esteem still more, since disclosure of inadequacies is a cherished group norm and further enhances acceptance by the group. The most desirable therapeutic scenario occurs when the patient re-examines and alters his or her low level of self-esteem. An illustrative clinical vignette may flesh out this bare-boned formulation:

*Although lasting patient improvement is often reported following a removal, by behavioral therapy techniques, of some disabling complaint, closer inspection of the process inevitably reveals that important interpersonal relationships have been affected. Either the therapist-patient relationship has been more meaningful than the therapist realized; or some important changes, initiated by the symptomatic relief, have occurred in the patient's social relationships which have served to reinforce and maintain the patient's improvement.

• Mariatta, a thirty-four-year-old housewife with an emotionally impoverished background, sought therapy because of anxiety and guilt stemming from a series of extramarital affairs. Her self-esteem was exceedingly low; she was self-derogatory about her physical appearance, her intelligence, and her functioning as a mother and a wife. She had received some solace from her religious affiliation, though she had never considered herself good enough to socialize with the "church people" in her community. She had married a man whom she considered repugnant but nonetheless a good man and certainly good enough for her. Only in her sexual affairs, and particularly in an arrangement in which she had sexual relationships with several men at once, did she seem to come alive. Only here did she feel attractive, desirable, and able to give something of herself which seemed of value to others. However, this behavior clashed with her religious convictions and resulted in considerable anxiety and further self-derogation.

Viewing the group as a social microcosm, the therapist soon noted characteristic trends in Mariatta's group behavior. She related to the other members around sexual issues; and for many hours, the group struggled with all the exciting ramifications of her sexual dilemma. At all other times in the group, however, she disengaged and offered nothing. She related to the group as she did to her social environment. Though she could belong to the group, she could not really relate to the other members: the only thing of real interest she could offer was her genitals.

Her course of therapy consisted, in large part, of the gradual reexamination and eventual disconfirmation of her belief that she had little of value to offer. As she began to respond to others, to offer warmth and support, to exchange problems and feelings, she found herself increasingly valued by other members. The discrepancy between her public esteem and her self-esteem widened to a point where she was forced into a more realistic and positive view of herself. Her behavior changed to such a point that meaningful nonsexual relationships in and out of the group were possible, and these, in turn, further enhanced her self-esteem, thereby generating an adaptive spiral.

SELF-ESTEEM, PUBLIC ESTEEM, AND THERAPEUTIC CHANGE: EVIDENCE

Group therapy research has not specifically investigated the relationship between public esteem and shifts in self-esteem. However, there

are some interesting data on group popularity—a variable closely synonymous with public esteem.* A study of forty group therapy patients,
described on page 54, demonstrated that patients "elected" by the
other members as most popular at the sixth and twelfth weeks of therapy had significantly better therapy outcomes than the other group
members at the end of one year.[38] Thus, it seems that patients who have
high public esteem early in the course of a group are destined to have
a better therapy outcome.

To understand this phenomenon, the investigators studied the determinants of popularity. What factors seemed responsible for the attainment of popularity in therapy groups? Three variables, which did not
themselves correlate with outcome, correlated significantly with popularity, namely:

1. Previous self-disclosure.[39]
2. Interpersonal compatibility.[40] Individuals who had (perhaps fortuitously)
   those interpersonal needs that happen to blend well with those of the other
   group members become popular in the group.
3. Other sociometric measures; group members who were often chosen as
   leisure companions or work committee colleagues became popular in the
   group.

A clinical study of the most popular and least popular members revealed that members, in their selection of popular patients, placed a
premium on youth, education, intelligence, and the ability to be introspective. The popular patients all filled the leadership vacuum that
occurred early in the group when the therapist declined to assume the
traditional leader role.

The most unpopular patients were markedly rigid, moralistic, nonintrospective, and least involved in the group task. Some were blatantly
deviant in their groups. They attacked the group and quickly became
group isolates. Others who were more schizoid were frightened of the
group process; they remained on the periphery and never entered the
interactional wavelength of the group.

The Lieberman, Yalom, and Miles encounter group study corroborated these conclusions.[41] The sociometric data (asking members to
rank-order one another on several variables) revealed that members

*D. Lundgren and D. Miller reported a relevant study on nonpatients in a Bethel
T-group (see chapter 16).[42] They found that self-esteem decreased when public esteem
(measured by sociometrics) decreased. They also discovered that the more a group member underestimated his or her public esteem, the more acceptable he or she was to the
other members; in other words, the ability to face one's deficiencies or even to judge
oneself a little harshly increased one's public esteem. Humility, within limits, is far more
adaptable than arrogance.

who were most influential were also those who engaged in behavior closely in harmony with encounter group values (risk taking, spontaneity, openness, self-disclosure, expressivity, group facilitation and support). These influential members had a significantly higher outcome. These findings corroborate persuasive evidence from social psychological small-group research which demonstrates that the members adhering most closely to group norms attain positions of popularity and influence.[43]

To summarize: members who are popular and influential in therapy groups have a higher likelihood of changing. They attain popularity and influence in the group by virtue of these behaviors: active participation, self-disclosure, self-exploration, emotional expression, nondefensiveness, leadership, interest in others, and support of the group.

It is important to note that the individual who adheres to the group norms is not only rewarded by increased public esteem, but also reaps other dividends. The behavior required by the group norms will serve one in good stead in relationships outside the group. In other words, the social skills the individual uses in the group to attain popularity are reinforced by the popularity one achieves, and these very same skills are likely to help one deal more effectively with interpersonal problems outside the group. Thus, increased popularity in the group acts therapeutically in two ways: by augmenting self-esteem and by reinforcing adaptive social skills.

GROUP COHESIVENESS AND GROUP ATTENDANCE

Continuation in the group is obviously a necessary, though not sufficient, prerequisite for successful treatment. Several studies indicate that patients who terminate early in the course of group therapy receive little benefit.[44] Over fifty patients who dropped out of therapy groups within the first twelve meetings reported that they did so because of some stress encountered in the group. They were neither satisfied with their therapy experience nor did they improve; indeed, many of these patients felt worse.[45] Patients remaining in the group for at least several months, however, had a high likelihood (85 percent in one study) of profiting from therapy.[46]

The greater the patient's attraction to the group, the more inclined one will be to continue membership in therapy groups[47] as well as in encounter, laboratory, and task groups.[48] For example, D. C. Sagi and his colleagues found a significant correlation between attendance and group cohesiveness in twenty-three college student organizations.[49] Yalom and K. Rand studied cohesiveness among forty members of five therapy groups and found that the least cohesive members terminated within the first twelve meetings.[50] In another study Yalom et al. found that the members with the highest cohesiveness scores at the sixth and at the twelfth meetings attended significantly more meetings during the year.[51]

The Lieberman, Yalom, and Miles encounter group study discovered a high correlation between low cohesiveness and eventual dropping out from the group.[52] The dropouts did not have a sense of belongingness and most often dropped out because they felt rejected or attacked by the group.

The relationship between cohesiveness and maintenance of membership has implications for the total group as well. Not only do the least cohesive members terminate membership and fail to benefit from therapy, but noncohesive groups with high patient turnover prove to be less therapeutic for the remaining members as well.

Stability of membership is a necessary condition for effective long-term interactional group therapy. Most therapy groups go through an early phase of instability, as some members drop out and replacements are added. Thereafter, the groups often enter into a long, stable phase in which much of the solid work of therapy occurs. Some groups seem to enter this phase of stability early, while others never achieve it. Dropouts at times beget other dropouts, some patients terminating soon after the departure of a key member. In a group therapy follow-up study, patients often spontaneously underscored the importance of membership stability.[53]

In chapter 15, I will discuss the issue of cohesiveness in groups led in clinical settings that preclude a stable long-term membership. For example, drop-in crisis groups or groups on an acute inpatient ward rarely have consistent membership even for two consecutive meetings. In these clinical situations, therapists must radically alter their perspectives on the life development of the group. I believe, for example, that the appropriate life span for the acute inpatient group is a *single* session. The therapist must strive to be efficient, to offer effective help to as many patients as possible during each single session: there will be no meeting of that group the following day because, in all likelihood, the membership will have altered. Thus, the therapist must foster cohesiveness and attend to dropouts each session, since acutely disturbed patients not infrequently choose to leave (either physically or psychologically) before the end of the session.

GROUP COHESIVENESS AND THE EXPRESSION OF HOSTILITY

It would be a mistake to equate cohesiveness with comfort. Although cohesive groups may show greater acceptance, intimacy, and understanding, there is evidence that they also permit greater development and expression of hostility and conflict.

Unless hostility is openly expressed, persistent and impenetrable hostile attitudes may develop to hamper effective interpersonal learning. Hostility that is unexpressed simply smolders within, only to seep out in many indirect ways, none of which facilitates the group therapeutic process. It is not easy to continue communicating honestly with someone you dislike. The temptation to avoid the other and to break off communication is very great; and yet when channels of communication are closed, so too are any hopes for conflict resolution, for personal growth and attitude change.

This is as true on a megagroup—even a national—level as on the dyadic. Consider the experimental evidence offered by M. Sherif in his famed Robbers' Cave experiment.[54] A camp of eleven-year-old, well-adjusted boys was divided at the outset into two groups that were placed in competition with each other in a series of hotly contested events. Soon each group developed considerable cohesiveness and internal organization as well as a deep sense of hostility toward the other group. Any meaningful communication between the two groups became impossible. If, for example, they were placed in physical proximity in the dining hall, the group boundaries remained impermeable, and the members merely exchanged taunts, insults, and spitballs.*

In the therapy process, communication must not be ruptured; the adversaries must continue to work together in a meaningful way, to take responsibility for their statements, and to be willing to go beyond name calling. This is, of course, a major difference between therapy groups and social groups, in which conflicts often result in the permanent rupture of relationships. Patients' descriptions of the critical incident in therapy (see chapter 2) often involve an episode in which they

---

*The communications block between the members of the two groups was finally relieved only by instilling cohesion and allegiance in a single large group. Some superordinate goals were created to disrupt the small group boundaries and force the boys to work together in a single large group. For example, a truck carrying food for an overnight hike stalled in a ditch and could be rescued only by cooperative efforts of all the boys; a highly desirable movie could be rented only by the pooled contributions of the entire camp; the water supply was cut off and similarly could be restored only by the cooperative efforts of all campers. What is needed for the resolution of terrestrial hostility, then, is an urgently felt worldwide crisis that only meganational cooperation can avert: for example, atmospheric pollution, a nuclear crisis, or, best of all, an invasion by extraterrestrials.

expressed strong negative affect. However, in each instance the patient was able to weather the storm, to continue relating (often in a more gratifying manner) to the other member.

Underlying these events is the condition of cohesiveness. The group and the members must mean enough to each other that they will be willing to bear the discomfort of working through a conflict. Cohesive groups are, in a sense, like families with much internecine warfare but nonetheless a powerful sense of loyalty.

Several research studies demonstrate that cohesiveness is positively correlated with risk taking and intensive interaction.[55] Thus, cohesiveness is not synonymous with love or with a continuous stream of supportive, positive statements. Cohesive groups are groups that are able to embrace conflict and to derive constructive benefit therefrom. Obviously at times of conflict, cohesiveness scales that emphasize warmth, comfort, and support will temporarily gyrate; thus, many researchers have developed deep reservations about cohesiveness as a precise, stable, measurable, unidimensional variable.[56]

Once the conditions are such that conflict can be constructively dealt with in the group, therapy is enhanced in many ways. I already mentioned the importance of catharsis, of risk taking, of gradually exploring previously avoided or unknown parts of oneself and recognizing that the anticipated dreaded catastrophe is chimerical. It is also important for many patients to have the experience of weathering an attack. In the process, as Frank suggests, one may become better acquainted with the reasons for one's position and learn to withstand pressure from others.[57] Conflict may also enhance self-disclosure, as each opponent tends to reveal more and more to clarify his or her position. As members are able to go beyond the mere statement of position, as they begin to understand the other's experiential world, past and present, and view the other's position from his or her frame of reference, they may begin to understand that the other's point of view may be as appropriate for him as their own is for themselves. The coming to grips with, working through, and eventual resolution of extreme dislike or hatred of another person is an experience of great therapeutic power.

• A clinical illustration demonstrates many of these points. Susan, a forty-six-year-old, very proper school principal, and Jean, a twenty-one-year-old high school dropout, became locked into a vicious struggle. Susan despised Jean because of her libertine life style and what she imagined to be sloth and promiscuity. Jean was enraged by Susan's judgmentalism, her sanctimoniousness, her embittered spinsterhood, her closed posture to the world. Fortunately, both women were deeply committed members of the group. (Fortuitous circumstances played a part here. Jean had been a core member of the group for a year and then married and went abroad for three months. Just at that time Susan became a member and, during Jean's absence, became heavily involved in the group.)

Both had had considerable past difficulty in expressing and dealing with anger. Over a four-month period they interacted heavily, at times in pitched battles (for example, when Susan erupted sanctimoniously upon learning that Jean was obtaining illegal food stamps, and when Jean learned of Susan's virginity and ventured the opinion that she was a curiosity, a mid-Victorian relic). Much good group work was done; they learned a great deal about each other and eventually realized the cruelty of their mutual judgmentalism. Finally, they could both understand how much each meant for the other on both a personal and a symbolic level. Jean desperately wanted Susan's approval; Susan deeply envied Jean for the freedom she had never permitted herself. In the working-through process, both fully experienced their rage; they encountered and then accepted previously unknown parts of themselves; they ultimately developed an empathetic understanding and then an acceptance of one another. Neither could possibly have tolerated the extreme discomfort of the conflict were it not for the strong cohesion that, despite the pain, bound them to the group.

Not only are cohesive groups more able to express hostility among members, but there is evidence that they are also more able to express hostility toward the leader.* Regardless of the personal style or skill of the group leader, the therapy group will nonetheless come, often within the first dozen meetings, to experience some degree of hostility and resentment toward him or her. (See chapter 11 for a full discussion of this issue.) Leaders do not fulfill members' fantasied expectations, do not care enough, do not direct enough, and do not offer immediate relief. If the group members avoid their feelings of disappointment or

---

*A study by A. Pepitone and P. Reichling[58] offers experimental corroboration. Paid college student volunteers were divided into thirteen high- and thirteen low-cohesion laboratory task groups. Cohesion was created in the usual experimental manner: members of high-cohesive groups were told before their first meeting that their group had been composed of individuals who had been carefully matched from psychological questionnaires to ensure maximum compatibility. The members of low-cohesive groups were given the opposite treatment and were told the matching was unsuccessful and that they would probably not get along together. The groups, while waiting for the experiment to begin, were systematically insulted by a member of the research team. After he had left, the members of the high cohesive groups were significantly more able to express open and intense hostility about the authority figure. M. E. Wright obtained similar findings in research on nursery school groups.[59]

anger, several harmful consequences may ensue. The group members may attack a convenient scapegoat—either another member or some institution like "psychiatry" or "doctors"; they may suppress the anger only to experience a smoldering irritation within themselves or within the group as a whole; they may, in short, begin to establish norms discouraging open expression of feelings.

The group that is able to express negative feelings toward the therapist almost invariably is strengthened by the experience. It is an excellent exercise in direct communication and provides an important learning experience: that is, that one may express hostility directly without some ensuing irreparable calamity. It is far preferable that the therapist, the true object of the anger, be confronted than some member in the group upon whom the anger is displaced. Furthermore, the therapist, let us pray, is far better able to withstand confrontation than is some scapegoat in the group. The entire process is self-reinforcing; a concerted attack on the leader that is handled in a nondefensive, non-retaliatory fashion and serves to increase cohesiveness still further.

GROUP COHESIVENESS AND OTHER THERAPY-RELEVANT VARIABLES

Research has demonstrated in laboratory groups and dyads that group cohesiveness has many other important consequences.[60] Many of these have obvious relevance to the group therapeutic process; for example, it has been shown that the members of a cohesive group, in contrast to the members of a noncohesive group, will:

1. Try harder to influence other group members;[61]
2. Be more open to influence by the other members;[62]
3. Be more willing to listen to others[63] and more accepting of others;[64]
4. Experience greater security and relief from tension in the group;[65]
5. Participate more readily in meetings;[66]
6. Self-disclose more;[67]
7. Protect the group norms and, for example, exert more pressure on individuals deviating from the norms;[68]
8. Be less susceptible to disruption as a group when a member terminates membership.[69]*

*These findings stem from experimentally composed groups and situations. As an illustration of the methodology used in these studies, consider an experiment by S. Schachter, who organized groups of paid volunteers to discuss a social problem—the correctional treatment of a juvenile delinquent with a long history of recidivism.[70] In the manner described previously, several groups of low and high cohesiveness were formed, and paid confederates were introduced into each group who deliberately assumed an extreme position on the topic under discussion. The content of the discussion, sociometric

Summary

By definition, cohesiveness refers to the attraction that members have for their group and for the other members. The members of a cohesive group are accepting of one another, supportive, and inclined to form meaningful relationships in the group. Cohesiveness seems to be a significant factor in successful group therapy outcome. In conditions of acceptance and understanding, patients will be more inclined to express and explore themselves, to become aware of and integrate hitherto unacceptable aspects of self, and to relate more deeply to others. Self-esteem is greatly influenced by the patient's role in a cohesive group. The social behavior required for members to be esteemed by the group is socially adaptive to the individual out of the group.

In addition, highly cohesive groups are more stable groups with better attendance and less turnover. Evidence was presented to indicate that this stability is vital to successful therapy: early termination precludes benefit for the involved patient and impedes the progress of the rest of the group as well. Cohesiveness favors self-disclosure, risk taking, and the constructive expression of conflict in the group—phenomena that facilitate successful therapy.

What we have yet to consider are the determinants of cohesiveness. What are the sources of high and low cohesiveness? What does the therapist do to facilitate the development of a highly cohesive group? These important issues will be discussed in the chapters dealing with the group therapist's tasks and techniques.

---

data, and other post-group questionnaires were then analyzed to determine, for example, the intensity of the efforts of the group to influence the deviant and the degree of rejection of the deviant.

4

THE THERAPEUTIC FACTORS:

AN INTEGRATION

The inquiry into the therapeutic factors in group therapy began with the rationale that the delineation of these factors would lead to the development of systematic guidelines for the tactics and strategy of the therapist. The compendium of therapeutic factors presented in chapter 1 is, I believe, comprehensive but is yet not in a form that has great clinical applicability. For one thing, the factors have, for the sake of clarity, been considered as separate entities when in fact they are intricately interdependent.

I have taken the therapy process apart to examine it and am now obliged to put it back together again. One question I will consider in this chapter is: How do the therapeutic factors operate when they are viewed not separately but as part of a dynamic process? A second issue to be considered is the comparative potency of the therapeutic factors. Obviously, not all are of equal value. However, an absolute rank-ordering of therapeutic factors is not possible. Many contingencies must be considered. The importance of various therapeutic factors depends upon the type of group therapy practiced. Groups with differing clinical populations and therapeutic goals (for example, long-term outpatient groups, inpatient groups, partial hospitalization groups, behavioral shaping groups) may emphasize different clusters of therapeutic factors (see pages 104–107). Some therapeutic factors are important at one stage of a group, whereas others predominate at another (see pages 107–108). Even within the same group, different patients benefit from different therapeutic factors; patients may relate to the pool of group therapeutic resources as to a cafeteria: depending upon their needs, their social skills, their character structure, they make their "selection" of thera-peutic factors (see pages 110–11).

Lastly, some factors are not always independent mechanisms of change but are instead conditions for change; for example, in chap-ter 1, I describe how instillation of hope may serve largely to prevent early discouragement and to keep patients in the group until other, more potent forces for change come into play. Cohesiveness, the sheer experience of being a valued member of a group, may, for some pa-tients, be the major vehicle of change; for others, cohesiveness is impor-tant in that it provides the safety and support that allows one to explore oneself, to request interpersonal feedback, and to experiment with new behavior.

Our efforts to evaluate and integrate the therapeutic factors will, to some extent, always remain conjectural. There is little truly definitive research demonstrating the efficacy of any of the therapeutic factors and even less research bearing on the question of their comparative value or their interrelation. Nor may we ever expect to attain a high degree of certainty. I do not speak from a position of investigative nihilism but instead argue that the nature of our data is so rich, complex, and highly subjective that, to a large degree, it makes scientific method-ology inapplicable.

Some attempts have been made to translate the subjective therapeu-tic factors into measurable objective phenomena and then to use these measures as independent variables in outcome studies. Yet enormous difficulties are encountered in such research. The methodological prob-lems are formidable: as a general rule, the accuracy with which varia-bles can be measured is directly proportional to their triviality. A recent comprehensive review of such empirical studies produces only a hand-ful of studies with acceptable research design, and these have only limited clinical relevance.[1] For example, four studies attempt to quan-tify and evaluate insight by comparing "insight" groups with other approaches, such as assertiveness training groups or "interaction here-and-now" groups (as though such interactional groups offered no in-sight).[2] The researchers measured insight by counting the number of a therapist's insight-providing comments or by observers' ratings of a leader's insight orientation. Such a design fails to take into account crucial aspects of the experience of insight: for example, how *accu-rate* was the insight? How well timed? What was a patient's state of readiness to accept insight? What was the nature of a patient's relation-ship with the therapist (if adversarial, the patient is apt to reject any

71

interpretation; if dependent, the patient may—but not necessarily—ingest, without discrimination, all interpretations).

Thus, I fear that empirical psychotherapy research will never provide the certainty we crave, and we must learn to live effectively with uncertainty. We must listen to what patients tell us; we must consider the best available evidence from research and from intelligent clinical observation; and ultimately, we must evolve a reasoned therapy which offers the great flexibility needed to cope with the infinite range of human problems.

Comparative Value of the Therapeutic Factors: The Patient's View

How do patients evaluate the various therapeutic factors? Which factors do they regard as most salient to their improvement in therapy? In previous editions of this book, it was possible to review in a leisurely fashion the research bearing on this question: I discussed the two existing studies which explicitly explored the patient's subjective appraisal of the therapeutic factors, and then proceeded to describe in detail the results of a 1970 research project in which my colleagues and I administered to twenty successful group therapy patients a therapeutic factor questionnaire designed to compare the importance of the twelve therapeutic factors I described in chapter 1. Now things have changed. In the past decade, many studies have researched (or reviewed) the patient's view of the therapeutic factors (several of these studies have also obtained therapist's ratings of therapeutic factors).[3] This burst of research provides rich data and enables one to draw conclusions with far more conviction about therapeutic factors. But my task of reviewing and synthesizing the literature is far more difficult. Since the researchers (with only a few exceptions)[4] use the therapeutic factors and the research instrument (or some modification thereof) I described in my 1970 research, I shall, after describing the two early projects, describe that research in detail and then incorporate into my discussion the findings from the new research on therapeutic factors.

B. Berzon, C. Pious, and R. Parson studied eighteen members of two outpatient, time-limited therapy groups which met for fifteen sessions.[5] After each meeting the patients filled out a questionnaire in which they described the incident that they considered the most personally important. Two hundred and seventy-nine incidents were obtained and then sorted by three judges into nine categories, which were, in order of frequency:

1. Increased awareness of emotional dynamics—a broad category in which the subject "was helped to acquire new knowledge about himself, his strength and weakness, his pattern of interpersonal relating, his motivations, etc.";
2. Recognizing similarity to others;
3. Feeling positive regard, acceptance, sympathy for others;
4. Seeing self as seen by others;
5. Expressing self congruently, articulately, or assertively in the group;
6. Witnessing honesty, courage, openness, or expressions of emotionality in others;
7. Feeling responded to by others;
8. Feeling warmth and closeness generally in the group;
9. Ventilating emotions.

The authors noted that the main therapeutic mechanisms were reported to reside in the interaction among group members; few of the reports involved the therapists. Interpersonal feedback enabled the patients to restructure their self-image and to validate the universality of problems.

H. Dickoff and M. Lakin studied twenty-eight former members of two outpatient groups run by one psychiatrist.[6] The patients attended an average of eleven group sessions. In a semistructured interview the patients' retrospective views about the therapeutic factors in group therapy were discussed. Responses were taped, transcribed, and sorted by two judges into these categories, constructed *a priori* as they emerged from the data:

1. Support (reduction of isolation, universality, sharing problems, learning to express oneself);
2. Suppression (including catharsis);
3. Tools for action (understanding problems, insight of interpersonal and intrapersonal nature).

The results demonstrated that social support was experienced by the patients as the chief therapeutic mode. From the patients' point of view, group cohesiveness was seen not only as necessary for perpetuation of the group but as in itself of great therapeutic value. The "tools for action" category was considered by far the least important by the patients; however, there was a significant correlation between high verbal I.Q. and the selection of this category.

These two small studies deal with only the early stages of group therapy (less than fifteen meetings); yet their findings are consistent with many studies that followed.

I. Yalom, J. Tinklenberg, and M. Gilula studied the therapeutic factors in twenty successful long-term group therapy patients.[7] The investigators asked twenty group therapists to select their most successful patients. These therapists led groups of middle-class outpatients who had neurotic or characterologic problems. These subjects had been in therapy a minimum of eight months and had recently terminated or were about to terminate group therapy.[8] The range of duration of therapy was eight months to twenty-two months; the mean duration was sixteen months. All twenty subjects completed a therapeutic factor Q-sort and were interviewed by the team of three investigators.

Twelve categories of therapeutic factors were constructed from the sources outlined throughout this book,* and five items describing each category were written, making a total of sixty items, which are listed in table 4.1. Each item was typed on a 3 × 5 card; the patient was given the stack of random cards and asked to place a specified number of cards into seven piles labeled in the following manner:

1. Most helpful to me in the group (2 cards)
2. Extremely helpful (6 cards)
3. Very helpful (12 cards)
4. Helpful (20 cards)
5. Barely helpful (12 cards)
6. Less helpful (6 cards)
7. Least helpful to me in the group (2 cards).[9]

---

*The list of sixty therapeutic factor items passed through several versions and was circulated among many senior group therapists for suggestions, additions, or deletions. Some of the items are nearly identical, but it was necessary methodologically to have the same number of items representing each category. The twelve categories are: altruism; group cohesiveness; universality; interpersonal learning, "input"; interpersonal learning, "output"; guidance; catharsis; identification; family re-enactment; self-understanding; instillation of hope; existential factors. They are not quite identical to those described in this book; we attempted, unsuccessfully, to divide interpersonal learning into two parts —input and output. One category, "self-understanding," was included to permit examination of the importance of derepression and genetic insight. The therapeutic factor Q-sort was meant to be an exploratory instrument constructed, as I described, *a priori* on the basis of clinical intuition (my own and that of other experienced clinicians); it was not posited as a finely calibrated research instrument. It has been used in so much subsequent research that much discussion has arisen about construct validity and test-retest reliability. By and large, test-retest reliability has proven to be good; factor analytic studies have yielded varied results: some studies showing only fair, others good, item to individual scale correlations.[10] The most comprehensive factor analytic study provided fourteen item clusters that bore considerable resemblance to my twelve original therapeutic factor categories.[11]

Following the Q-sort, which took approximately thirty to for[ty] minutes, each patient was interviewed for an hour by the three in[ves]tigators. Their reasons for their choice of the most and least helpf[ul] items were reviewed, and a series of other areas relevant to therapeutic factors was discussed (for example, other, nonprofessional therapeutic influences in the patients' lives, critical events in therapy, goal changes, timing of improvement, therapeutic factors in their own words).

RESULTS

A sixty-item, seven-pile Q-sort for twenty subjects makes for complex data. Perhaps the clearest way to consider the results is a simple rank ordering of the sixty items.* Turn again to the list of sixty items (table 4.1). The number after each item represents its rank order. Thus, item 48 ("discovering and accepting previously unknown or unacceptable parts of myself") was considered the most important therapeutic factor by the consensus of patients; item 38 ("adopting mannerisms or the style of another group member") the least important; and so on. ("T" denotes a tie.)

The ten items deemed most helpful to the patients were (in the order of importance):

48. Discovering and accepting previously unknown or unacceptable parts of myself.
35. Being able to say what was bothering me instead of holding it in.
18. Other members honestly telling me what they think of me.
34. Learning how to express my feelings.
16. The group's teaching me about the type of impression I make on others.
32. Expressing negative and/or positive feelings toward another member.
60. Learning that I must take ultimate responsibility for the way I live my life no matter how much guidance and support I get from others.
17. Learning how I come across to others.
37. Seeing that others could reveal embarrassing things and take other risks and benefit from it helped me to do the same.
22. Feeling more trustful of groups and of other people.

Note that seven of the first eight items represent some form of catharsis or of insight. I again use "insight" in the broadest sense; the items, for the most part, reflect the first level of insight (gaining an objective perspective of one's interpersonal behavior) described in chapter 2. This remarkable finding lends considerable weight to the principle, also described in chapter 2, *that therapy is a dual process consisting of*

*Arrived at by ranking the sum of the twenty pile placements for each item.

75

TABLE 4.1

Therapeutic Factors
Rankings of the Sixty Individual Items

		RANK ORDER (THE LOWER THE RANK ORDER, THE HIGHER THE ITEM IS VALUED BY THE PATIENT)
1. Altruism	1. Helping others has given me more self-respect.	40 T*
	2. Putting others' needs ahead of mine.	52 T
	3. Forgetting myself and thinking of helping others.	37 T
	4. Giving part of myself to others.	17
	5. Helping others and being important in their lives.	33 T
2. Group Cohesiveness	6. Belonging to and being accepted by a group.	16
	7. Continued close contact with other people.	20 T
	8. Revealing embarrassing things about myself and still being accepted by the group.	11 T
	9. Feeling alone no longer.	37 T
	10. Belonging to a group of people who understood and accepted me.	20 T
3. Universality	11. Learning I'm not the only one with my type of problem; "We're all in the same boat."	45 T
	12. Seeing that I was just as well off as others.	25 T
	13. Learning that others have some of the same "bad" thoughts and feelings I do.	40 T
	14. Learning that others had parents and backgrounds as unhappy or mixed up as mine.	31 T
	15. Learning that I'm not very different from other people gave me a "welcome to the human race" feeling.	33 T

*"T" denotes a tie.

TABLE 4.1 *(continued)*

		RANK ORDER (THE LOWER THE RANK ORDER, THE HIGHER THE ITEM IS VALUED BY THE PATIENT)
4. Interpersonal Learning— Input	16. The group's teaching me about the type of impression I make on others.	5 T
	17. Learning how I come across to others.	8
	18. Other members honestly telling me what they think of me.	3
	19. Group members pointing out some of my habits or mannerisms that annoy other people.	18 T
	20. Learning that I sometimes confuse people by not saying what I really think.	13 T
5. Interpersonal Learning— Output	21. Improving my skills in getting along with people.	25 T
	22. Feeling more trustful of groups and of other people.	10
	23. Learning about the way I related to the other group members.	13 T
	24. The group's giving me an opportunity to learn to approach others.	27 T
	25. Working out my difficulties with one particular member in the group.	33 T
6. Guidance	26. The doctor's suggesting or advising something for me to do.	27 T
	27. Group members suggesting or advising something for me to do.	55
	28. Group members telling me what to do.	56
	29. Someone in the group giving definite suggestions about a life problem.	48 T
	30. Group members advising me to behave differently with an important person in my life.	52 T

TABLE 4.1 *(continued)*

		RANK ORDER (THE LOWER THE RANK ORDER, THE HIGHER THE ITEM IS VALUED BY THE PATIENT)
7. Catharsis	31. Getting things off my chest.	31 T
	32. Expressing negative and/or positive feelings toward another member.	5 T
	33. Expressing negative and/or positive feelings toward the group leader.	18 T
	34. Learning how to express my feelings.	4
	35. Being able to say what was bothering me instead of holding it in.	2
8. Identification	36. Trying to be like someone in the group who was better adjusted than I.	58
	37. Seeing that others could reveal embarrassing things and take other risks and benefit from it helped me to do the same.	8
	38. Adopting mannerisms or the style of another group member.	59
	39. Admiring and behaving like my therapist.	57
	40. Finding someone in the group I could pattern myself after.	60
9. Family Re-enactment	41. Being in the group was, in a sense, like reliving and understanding my life in the family in which I grew up.	51
	42. Being in the group somehow helped me to understand old hang-ups that I had in the past with my parents, brothers, sisters, or other important people.	30

TABLE 4.1 *(continued)*

		RANK ORDER (THE LOWER THE RANK ORDER, THE HIGHER THE ITEM IS VALUED BY THE PATIENT)
Family Re-enactment *(continued)*	43. Being in the group was, in a sense, like being in a family, only this time a more accepting and understanding family.	44
	44. Being in the group somehow helped me to understand how I grew up in my family.	45 T
	45. The group was something like my family—some members or the therapists being like my parents and others being like my relatives. Through the group experience I understand my past relationships with my parents and relatives (brothers, sisters, etc.).	48 T
10. Self-Understanding	46. Learning that I have likes or dislikes for a person for reasons which may have little to do with the person and more to do with my hang-ups or experiences with other people in my past.	15
	47. Learning why I think and feel the way I do (that is, learning some of the causes and sources of my problems).	11 T
	48. Discovering and accepting previously unknown or unacceptable parts of myself.	1
	49. Learning that I react to some people or situations unrealistically (with feelings that somehow belong to earlier periods in my life).	20 T
	50. Learning that how I feel and behave today is related to my childhood and development (there are reasons in my early life why I am as I am).	50

TABLE 4.1 *(continued)*

		RANK ORDER (THE LOWER THE RANK ORDER, THE HIGHER THE ITEM IS VALUED BY THE PATIENT)
11. Instillation of Hope	51. Seeing others getting better was inspiring to me.	42 T
	52. Knowing others had solved problems similar to mine.	37 T
	53. Seeing that others had solved problems similar to mine.	33 T
	54. Seeing that other group members improved encouraged me.	27 T
	55. Knowing that the group had helped others with problems like mine encouraged me.	45 T
12. Existential Factors	56. Recognizing that life is at times unfair and unjust.	54
	57. Recognizing that ultimately there is no escape from some of life's pain and from death.	42 T
	58. Recognizing that no matter how close I get to other people, I must still face life alone.	23 T
	59. Facing the basic issues of my life and death, and thus living my life more honestly and being less caught up in trivialities.	23 T
	60. Learning that I must take ultimate responsibility for the way I live my life no matter how much guidance and support I get from others.	5 T

emotional experience and of reflection upon that experience. More about this later.

The administration of scoring of a sixty-item Q–sort is so laborious that most researchers have subsequently used an abbreviated version —generally one that asks a patient to rank the twelve therapeutic factor categories (rather than sixty individual items). However, two studies replicate the sixty-item Q-sort study and report remarkably similar findings. S. Freedman and J. Hurley studied twenty-eight subjects in three fifty-one-hour sensitivity-training groups on four college cam-

TABLE 4.2

Most Valued Therapeutic Factors: Outpatient Groups

STUDY	POPULATION	FACTORS VALUED MOST HIGHLY
Yalom, et al., 1968[a]	Outpatients N = 20	Interpersonal learning (input) Catharsis Cohesiveness Self-understanding
Weiner, 1974[b]	Outpatients, short- and long-term N = 19	Interpersonal learning (input + output) Cohesiveness Self-understanding Catharsis
Rohrbaugh and Bartels, 1975[c]	9 therapy groups 4 personal growth groups N = 72	Catharis Cohesiveness Interpersonal learning (input) Self-understanding
Butler and Fuhriman, 1980[d]	Community mental health center outpatients N = 68	Self-understanding Universality Interpersonal Learning (input) Catharsis
Mower, 1980[e]	Community counseling service clients N = 25	Interpersonal learning (input) Self-understanding Universality Catharsis
Flora-Tostado, 1981[f]	Community mental health center outpatients N = 42	Catharsis Self-understanding Hope Universality
Butler and Fuhriman, 1983[g]	Community mental health center outpatients N = 91	Self-understanding Catharsis Universality Cohesiveness
Long and Cope, 1980[h]	Residential treatment center for felons N = 12	Catharsis Cohesiveness Interpersonal learning (input) Interpersonal learning (output)
Leszcz, Yalom, and Norden, 1985[i]	Private practice outpatient groups N = 34	Interpersonal learning Self-understanding Catharsis Vicarious learning

a. I. Yalom, J. Tinklenberg, and M. Gilula, "Curative Factors in Group Therapy," unpublished study, 1968.
b. M. Weiner, "Genetic versus Interpersonal Insight," *International Journal of Group Psychotherapy* 24 (1974): 230–37.
c. M. Rohrbaugh and B. Bartels, "Participants' Perceptions of 'Curative Factors' in Therapy and Growth Groups," *Small Group Behavior* 6 (4 [November 1975]): 430–56.
d. T. Butler and A. Fuhriman, "Patient Perspective on the Curative Process: A Comparison of Day Treatment and Outpatient Psychotherapy Groups," *Small Group Behavior* 11 (4 [November 1980]): 371–88.
e. R. K. Mower (1980), cited in T. Butler and A. Fuhriman, "Level of Functioning and Length of Time in Treatment: Variables Influencing Patients' Therapeutic Experience in Group Therapy," *International Journal of Group Psychotherapy* 33 (1983): 484–504.
f. J. Flora-Tostado, "Patient and Therapist Agreement of Curative Factors in Group Psychotherapy," *Dissertation Abstracts International* 42 (01 [July 1981]): 371-B.
g. T. Butler and A. Fuhriman, "Level of Functioning and Length of Time in Treatment: Variables Influencing Patients' Therapeutic Experience in Group Therapy," *International Journal of Group Psychotherapy* 33 (1983): 21–37.
h. L. Long and C. Cope, "Curative Factors in a Male Felony Offender Group," *Small Group Behavior* 11 (1980): 389–98.
i. M. Leszcz, I. Yalom, and M. Norden, "The Value of Inpatient Group Psychotherapy and Therapeutic Process: Patient's Perceptions," *International Journal of Group Psychotherapy*, in press, 1985.

puses.[12] Seven of the ten items selected as most helpful by these subjects were among the ten I have just listed. Their subjects placed three new items (21, 23, 24) into the top ten. These items (see table 4.1) are all interpersonal output items, and it is entirely consistent that members of a sensitivity group which explicitly focused on modifying interpersonal behavior should value these items.

B. Corder and two colleagues studied sixteen adolescents from four different groups in different clinical settings, both outpatient and inpatient.[13] They did not highly value the adults' top chosen item (insight), but their next four highest items were identical to those the adults had chosen. Over all, adolescents valued the therapeutic factors of universality and cohesiveness more highly than did adults.

If we turn our attention away from the individual items and onto the twelve general categories,* we see that they rank in order of importance:

1. Interpersonal input,
2. Catharsis,
3. Cohesiveness,
4. Self-understanding,
5. Interpersonal output,
6. Existential factors,
7. Universality,
8. Instillation of hope,
9. Altruism,
10. Family re-enactment,
11. Guidance,
12. Identification.†

Seven other studies describe the therapeutic factors selected by group therapy outpatients,[14] and table 4.2 depicts the four most commonly chosen therapeutic factors. Note the considerable consistency: catharsis, self-understanding, and interpersonal input head the list and are followed by cohesiveness and universality. The same trio of "most helpful" therapeutic factors (interpersonal input, self-understanding, and catharsis) has been reported by the four projects studying personal growth groups (see table 4.3).

Which therapeutic factors are *least* valued? All of the therapy group

---

*The twelve categories are used only for analysis and interpretation. The patients, of course, were unaware of these categories and dealt only with the sixty random items. The rank of each category was obtained by summing the mean rank of the five items (as rated by twenty patients).

†In considering these results, we must keep in mind that the subject's task was a forced sort, which means that the least chosen items are not necessarily unimportant but are, instead, less important relative to the others.

TABLE 4.3

Most Valued Therapeutic Factors: Personal Growth (T-group)
Members

STUDY	POPULATION	FACTORS VALUED MOST HIGHLY
Lieberman, Yalom, and Miles, 1973[a]	Personal growth groups, university setting N = 170	Interpersonal learning (input) Universality Guidance Self-understanding
Freedman and Hurley, 1979[b]	Personal growth groups, university setting N = 20	No rank order Interpersonal learning (input) Catharsis
Mower, 1980[c]	Personal growth groups, university setting N = 31	Interpersonal learning (input) Self-understanding Altruism Cohesiveness
Freedman and Hurley, 1980[d]	Personal growth, university setting N = 28	Interpersonal learning (output) Interpersonal learning (input) Catharsis Self-understanding

a. M. Lieberman, I. Yalom, and M. Miles, *Encounter Groups: First Facts* (New York: Basic Books, 1973).
b. Sharai Freedman and John Hurley, "Maslow's Needs: individuals' Perceptions of Helpful Factors in Growth Groups," *Small Group Behavior* 10 (1979): 355–67.
c. R. K. Mower (1980), cited by T. Butler and A. Fuhriman, "Level of Functioning and Length of Time in Treatment: Variables Influencing Patients' Therapeutic Experience in Group Therapy," *International Journal of Group Psychotherapy* 33 (1983): 484–504.
d. S. Freedman and J. Hurley, "Perceptions of Helpfulness and Behavior in Groups," *Group* 4 (1980): 51–58.

and personal growth group research studies report the same results: family re-enactment, guidance, and identification. These results all suggest that the real core of the therapeutic process in these therapy groups is an affectively charged, self-reflective interpersonal interaction. The basic concepts I discussed in chapter 2—the importance of the corrective emotional experience, and the concept that the therapeutic here-and-now focus consists of an experiencing and a cognitive component—are thus supported by the available research evidence. Rather than discuss these research results further, I shall instead incorporate them in a broader discussion of questions posited at the beginning of this chapter; that is, the interrelationships of the therapeutic factors and their comparative potency.

Keep in mind throughout this discussion that these research findings pertain to a specific type of therapy group: an interactionally based group with the ambitious goals of symptom relief and behavioral and characterological change. Other groups with different goals may capitalize upon a different cluster of therapeutic factors. Later in this chapter I will present some research on inpatient groups that demonstrate that very point.

CATHARSIS

Catharsis has always assumed an important role in the therapeutic process, though the rationale behind its use has varied considerably. For centuries, patients have been purged to cleanse themselves of excessive bile, evil spirits, and infectious toxins. Since Breuer and Freud's 1895 treatise on the treatment of hysteria, many therapists have attempted to help patients rid themselves of suppressed, choked affect. What Freud and subsequently all dynamic psychotherapists (except, as I have discussed, certain revivalist cults such as primal screamers) have learned is that catharsis is not enough. After all, we have emotional experiences, sometimes very intense ones, all our lives without ensuing change.

The data support this conclusion. Although the research into the patient's appraisal of the therapeutic factors reveals the importance of catharsis, the research also suggests important qualifications. The Lieberman, Yalom, and Miles study starkly illustrates the limitations of catharsis *per se*. [15] The authors asked 210 members of a thirty-hour encounter group to describe the most significant incident that occurred in the course of the group. Experiencing and expressing feelings (both positive and negative) was very frequently selected. Yet this critical incident was not related to positive outcome: incidents of catharsis were as likely to be selected by members with poor outcomes as by those with good outcomes. Catharsis was not unrelated to outcome; it was necessary but, in itself, not sufficient. Members who selected *only* catharsis were, in fact, somewhat more likely to have a negative experience in the group. The high learners characteristically showed a profile of catharsis *plus* some form of cognitive learning.

In the Q-sort therapeutic factor studies, the two items that are ranked most highly, and that on factor analytic studies are most characteristic of the catharsis category, are numbers 34 ("Learning how to express my ～ings") and 35 ("Being able to say what was bothering me").[16] Both ～～～ems convey a sense of something other than the sheer act of ventilation or abreaction. They connote, instead, a sense of liberation, of acquiring skills for the future. The other frequently chosen catharsis item—"Expressing negative and/or positive feelings toward another member" (32)—indicates the role of catharsis in the ongoing interpersonal process. The item that most conveys a pure sense of ventilation —"Getting things off my chest" (31)—was not frequently chosen.

Interviews with the patients to investigate the reasons for their selection of items confirmed this view. Catharsis is part of an interpersonal process; no one ever obtains enduring benefit from ventilating feelings in an empty closet. Furthermore, as I discussed in chapter 3, catharsis is intricately related to cohesiveness. Catharsis is more helpful once supportive group bonds have formed. S. Freedman and J. Hurley show that catharsis is more valued late rather than early in the course of the group.[17] Conversely, strong expression of emotion enhances the development of cohesiveness: members who express strong feelings toward one another and work honestly with these feelings will develop close mutual bonds.

In summary, then, the open expression of affect is without question vital to the group therapeutic process; in its absence a group would degenerate into a sterile academic exercise. Yet it is only a part process and must be complemented by other factors.

One last point. The intensity of emotional expression is highly relative and must be appreciated not from the leader's perspective but from that of each member's experiential world. A seemingly muted expression of emotion may, for a highly constricted individual, represent an event of considerable intensity.

SELF-UNDERSTANDING

The therapeutic factor Q-sort also underscores the important role that the intellectual component plays in the therapeutic process. Of the twelve categories, the two pertaining to self-understanding (interpersonal input and self-understanding) are both ranked very highly in all the research investigations.

Interpersonal input refers to the individual's learning how he or she is perceived by other people. It is the crucial first step in the therapeutic sequence of the therapeutic factor of interpersonal learning and was discussed at some length in chapter 2.

The category of *self-understanding* is more problematic. It was constructed to permit investigation of the importance of derepression and of the intellectual understanding of the relationship between past and present ("genetic insight"). When we examine the five items of this category (table 4.1), it is clear that the category is an inconsistent one containing several very different elements. There is poor correlation among items, some being very heavily valued, and some underchosen. Item 48—"Discovering and accepting previously unknown parts or unacceptable parts of myself"—is the most valued single item of all the sixty. Two items (46 and 47) that refer to understanding causes of problems and to recognizing the existence of parataxic distortion are also highly valued. The item (50) most explicitly referring to genetic insight is considered of little value by group therapy patients.*

When we interviewed patients to learn more about the meaning of their choices, we found that the most popular item —"discovering and accepting previously unknown or unacceptable parts of myself" (48)— had a very specific implication to them. More often than not, they discovered *positive* areas of themselves—the ability to care for another, to relate closely to others, to experience compassion. There is an important lesson to be learned here. Too often psychotherapy, especially in naïve, popularized, or 1920 conceptualizations, is viewed as a detective search, as a digging or a stripping away. Rogers, Horney, Maslow, and our patients as well remind us that therapy is also exploration horizontally and upward; digging or excavation may uncover our riches and treasures as well as shameful, fearful, or primitive aspects of ourselves. Abraham Maslow states that "uncovering psychotherapy *increases* love, courage, creativity and curiosity while it *reduces* fear and hostility. This kind of therapy does not create something from nothing; the implication is that it uncovers what was there in the first place."[18]

Thus, one way that self-understanding promotes change is in encouraging individuals to recognize, to integrate, and to give free expression to previously dissociated parts of themselves. When we deny or stifle parts of ourselves, we pay a heavy price: we feel a deep amorphous sense of restriction; we are "on guard"; we are often troubled and puzzled by inner, yet alien, impulses demanding expression. When we can reclaim these split-off parts, we experience a wholeness and a deep sense of liberation.

So far, so good. But what of the other components of the intellectual task? For example, how does the highly ranked item "learning why I think and feel the way I do" (47) result in therapeutic change?

---

*Rohrbaugh and Bartels replicated the therapeutic factor Q-sort study and, on the basis of a factor analysis, subdivided insight into two categories: "self-understanding" and "genetic (parataxic) insight."[19] Their sample of seventy-two patients ranked "self-understanding" fourth (of fourteen factors) and "genetic insight," eighth.

First, we must recognize that there is an urgent need for intellectual understanding in the psychotherapeutic enterprise—a need that comes from both patient and therapist. Our search for understanding is deeply rooted. Maslow, in a treatise on motivation, posited that the human being has cognitive needs that are as basic as the needs for safety, love, and self-esteem.[20] Monkeys in a solid enclosure will do considerable work for the privilege of being able to look through a window at the laboratory outside; furthermore, they will work hard and persistently to solve puzzles without any reward except the satisfactions inherent in the puzzle solving itself. Most children are dangerously curious; in fact, we grow concerned if a child lacks curiosity about the environment. Considerable observational and experimental evidence indicates that psychologically healthy individuals are positively attracted to the mysterious and unexplained.[21]

So patients automatically search for understanding, and therapists who always prize the intellectual pursuit join them. Often, it all seems so natural that we lose sight of the *raison d'être* of therapy. After all, the object of therapy is change, not self-understanding. Or is it? Or are the two synonymous? Or does any and every type of self-understanding lead automatically to change? Or is the quest for self-understanding simply an interesting, appealing, reasonable exercise for patients and therapists, serving, like mortar, to keep the two joined together while something else—most likely "relationship"—occurs, which is the real mutative force in therapy?

It is far easier to pose these questions than to answer them. I shall present some preliminary arguments here; and then in chapter 6, after developing some material on the interpretative task and techniques of the therapist, I shall attempt to present a coherent thesis.

If we examine the motives behind our curiosity and our proclivity to explore our environment, we shed some light on the process of change. These motives include *effectance* (our desire for mastery and power), *safety* (our desire to render the unexplained harmless through understanding), and *pure cognizance* (our desire for knowledge and exploration for its own sake).[22]

The worried householder who explores a mysterious and frightening noise in his home; the young student who, for the first time, looks through a microscope and experiences the exhilaration of understanding the structure of an insect wing; the medieval alchemist or the New World explorer probing uncharted and proscribed regions—all receive their respective rewards: safety, a sense of personal keenness and satisfaction, and mastery in the guise of knowledge or wealth.

87

Of these motives, the one least relevant for the change process is pure cognizance. There is little question that knowledge for its own sake has always propelled the human being; the lure of the forbidden is an extraordinarily popular and ubiquitous motif in folk literature from the story of Adam and Eve to the saga of Peeping Tom. It is no surprise, then, that the desire to know enters the psychotherapeutic arena; yet there is little evidence that understanding for its own sake results in change.

But the desire for safety and for mastery play an important and obvious role in psychotherapy. They are, of course, as R. W. White has ably discussed, closely intertwined.[23] The unexplained and, especially, the fearful unexplained cannot be tolerated for long; all cultures, either through a scientific or a religious explanation, attempt to make sense of chaotic and threatening situations—situations residing in the physical and social environment as well as in the nature of existence itself.

In the psychotherapeutic situation, information decreases anxiety by removing ambiguity. There is considerable research evidence to document this observation. To cite one well-known experiment: A. S. Dibner exposed forty psychiatric patients to a psychiatric interview after dividing them into two experimental conditions.[24] Half were prepared for the interview and given cues about how they should, in a general way, conduct themselves; whereas the other half were given no such cues (a high-ambiguity situation). The results demonstrated that the subjects in the high-ambiguity situation experienced, during the interview, far greater anxiety (as measured by several subjective, objective, and physiological techniques). The converse is, incidentally, also true: anxiety increases ambiguity by distorting perceptual acuteness. Anxious subjects show disturbed organization of visual perception; they are less capable of perceiving and organizing visual cues shown tachistoscopically[25] and are distinctly slower in completing and recognizing incomplete pictures in a controlled experimental setting. Unless one is able to order the world cognitively, one may experience anxiety which, if severe, interferes with the perceptual apparatus. Thus, anxiety begets anxiety; the ensuing perplexity and overt or subliminal awareness of perceptual distortion becomes itself a potent secondary source of anxiety.[26]

In psychotherapy, patients are enormously reassured by the belief that their chaotic inner world, their suffering, and their tortuous interpersonal relationships are all explicable and thereby governable. Therapists, too, are made less anxious if, when confronted with great suffering and voluminous, chaotic material, they can believe in a set of principles that will permit an ordered explanation. Frequently, therapists will cling tenaciously to a particular system in the face of considerable contradictory evidence; sometimes, in the case of researcher-clinicians, it is even evidence that has issued from their own investigations. A belief system is valuable also in that it enables the therapist to preserve equanimity in the face of considerable affect. Analysts working with an adult who expresses powerful and primitive emotions, for example, maintain their bearings by believing that the patient has regressed to the experiential world and expressive patterns of the infant.

Maslow goes beyond safety, anxiety reduction, and mastery in his explanation of the mutative effects of knowledge. He views psychiatric illness as a knowledge-deficiency disease. "I am convinced that knowledge and action are frequently synonymous, identical in the Socratic fashion. Where we know fully and completely, suitable action follows automatically and reflexively. Choices are then made without conflict, with full spontaneity."[27] Thus, Maslow would support the moral philosophic contention that if we know the good, we will always act for the good; presumably, it follows that if we know what is ultimately good for us, we will act in our own best interests.

There is little, so far, that is controversial. Self-knowledge permits us to integrate all parts of ourselves, decreases ambiguity, permits a sense of effectance and mastery, and allows us to act in concert with our own best interests. An explanatory scheme also permits generalization and transfer of learning from the therapy setting to new situations in the outside world.

The great controversies arise when we discuss not the process or the purpose or the effects of explanation but the *content* of explanation. As I shall hope to make clear in chapter 6, I think these controversies are irrelevant. When we focus on change rather than on self-understanding as our ultimate goal, we cannot but conclude that an explanation is correct if it leads to change. The final common result of all our intellectual efforts in therapy is change; each clarifying, explanatory, or interpretive act of the therapist is ultimately designed to exert leverage on the patient's will to change. More on this later.

IMITATIVE BEHAVIOR (IDENTIFICATION)

Group therapy patients rate imitative behavior as one of the least helpful of the twelve therapeutic factors. However, in retrospect, the five items in this category seem to have tapped only a limited sector of this therapeutic mode (see table 4.1). They failed to distinguish between mere mimicry, which apparently has only a restricted value for patients, and the acquisition of general modes of behavior, which may have considerable value. To patients, conscious mimicry is an especially unpopular concept as a therapeutic mode since it suggests a relinquishing of individuality—a basic fear of many group patients. On the other hand, patients may acquire from others a general strategy which may be used in different situations. Patients begin to approach problems by considering, not necessarily on a conscious level, what some other member or the therapist would think or do in the same situation. For example, D. Rosenthal has demonstrated that successful patients adopt the complex value system of the therapist.[28] Initially imitative behavior is, in part, an attempt to gain approval; however, it does not end there. The more intact patients retain their reality testing and flexibility and perceive that change in their behavior results in greater acceptance by others. This increased acceptance can then act to change one's self-concept and self-esteem in the manner described in chapter 3, and an adaptive spiral is instigated.

It is also possible for an individual to identify with aspects of two or more other people, resulting in an amalgam. Although parts of others are imitated, the amalgam represents a creative synthesis, a highly innovative individualistic identity.

What of spectator therapy? Is it not possible that patients may learn much from observing the solutions arrived at by others who have similar problems? I have no doubt that such learning occurs in the therapy group. Every experienced group therapist has at least one story of a patient who came regularly to the group for months on end, was extremely inactive, and finally terminated therapy much improved and grateful for all the help he or she derived from the group.

Spectator therapy may be even more important in the short-term encounter group. In the Lieberman, Yalom, and Miles study the "significant incident" data indicated that the members undergoing the most change profited considerably from incidents in which they were entirely passive observers but nonetheless acquired some cognitive input (self-understanding, knowledge about the laws of human interaction, and so on).[29]

Patients learn not only from observing the substantive work of others who are like them, but also from watching the *process* of others working. In that sense, imitative behavior is a transitional therapeutic factor which permits patients subsequently to engage more fully in other aspects of therapy. Proof of this is to be found in the fact that one of the five imitative behavior items was rated by the patients as the eighth (of sixty) most important therapeutic factor: "Seeing that others could reveal embarrassing things and take other risks and benefit from it helped me to do the same" (37).

FAMILY RE-ENACTMENT

Family re-enactment—or the corrective recapitulation of the primary family experience—a therapeutic factor highly valued by many therapists, is not generally considered helpful by group patients.

The fact that this factor is not cited often by patients, though, should not surprise us since it operates at a different level of awareness from such explicit factors as catharsis or universality. Family re-enactment becomes more a part of the general horizon against which the group is experienced. Few therapists will deny that the primary family of each group member is an omnipresent specter which relentlessly haunts the group therapy room. The patient's experience in his other primary family obviously will, to a great degree, determine the nature of his or her parataxic distortions, the role the patient assumes in the group, his or her attitudes toward the group leaders, and so on. In other words, there is every reason to believe that early primary family experience influences the nature of each member's therapy group experience and imbues it with power.

There is little doubt in my mind that the therapy group reincarnates the primary family; the group can be a time machine which flings patients back several decades and evokes deeply etched ancient memories and ancient feelings. In my last meeting with a group before departing for a sabbatical to revise this book, a patient related this dream: "My father was going away for a long trip. I was with a group of people. My father left us a thirty-foot boat, but rather than giving it to me to steer, he gave it to one of my friends and I was angry about this." This is not the place to discuss this dream fully. Suffice it to say that the patient's father had deserted the family when the patient was young, and left him to be tyrannized thereafter by an older brother. The patient said that this was the first time he had thought of his father in years. The events of the group—the therapist's leaving, his place being taken by a new therapist, the patient's attraction to the co-therapist (a woman), his resentment toward another dominating patient in the group—all acted in concert to awaken long slumbering memories.

Thus, the family haunts the group. Group events, member sibling rivalry, therapist-parents, and regressive group fantasies all pitch the patient back to his or her early life in the family. The patient re-enacts early family scripts in the group and, if therapy is successful, is able to experiment with new behavior and to break free from the family role into which he or she has long been locked.

While I believe these are important phenomena in the therapeutic process, it is altogether a different question to ask whether the group should focus explicitly upon these phenomena. I think not. I think that this process is part of the internal, often silent, homework of the group patient. Major shifts in our perspective on the past occur because of the vitality of the work in the present; change does not occur through a direct summons and inquiry of the spirits of the past. There are, as I shall discuss in chapter 6, many overriding reasons for the group to maintain an ahistoric focus. To focus unduly on people who are not present, on parents and siblings, on oedipal strivings, on sibling rivalries, or on incorporative or patricidal desires is to deny the reality of the group and the other members as a living experience in the here-and-now.

EXISTENTIAL FACTORS

The category of existential factors was almost an afterthought. My colleagues and I first constructed the Q-sort instrument with eleven major factors. It appeared neat and precise but incomplete. Something was missing. Important sentiments expressed by both patients and therapists had not been represented, and hence we added a factor consisting of these five items:

1. Recognizing that life is at times unfair and unjust
2. Recognizing that ultimately there is no escape from some of life's pain and from death
3. Recognizing that no matter how close I get to other people, I must still face life alone
4. Facing the basic issues of my life and death, and thus living my life more honestly and being less caught up in trivialities
5. Learning that I must take ultimate responsibility for the way I live my life no matter how much guidance and support I get from others

Several issues are represented in this cluster: responsibility, basic isolation, contingency, the recognition of our mortality and the ensuing consequences for the conduct of our life, the capriciousness of existence. What to label this category? We finally settled, with much hesitation, on "existential factors." I did not care for the word *existential*— it had become embedded in its own mystique; it meant something to everyone yet nothing precise to anyone.

Despite the unceremonious origin of this category, it is clear that the "existential" items strike responsive chords in patients, and many cite some of the five statements as having been crucially important to them. In fact, the entire category of existential factors is ranked highly by patients, ahead of such greatly valued modes of change as universality, altruism, recapitulation of the primary family experience, guidance, identification, and instillation of hope. One of the items—"Learning that I must take ultimate responsibility for the way I live my life no matter how much guidance and support I get from others" (60)—was highly ranked by the patients, and its mean score ranked it fifth of the entire sixty items.

The same findings are reported by other researchers. Every single project that includes an existential category reports that the patients rank the category at least among the upper 50 percent. In some projects, for example, with therapy groups in prison, in day hospitals and in psychiatric hospitals, the existential category is ranked among the top three factors.[30] It is important to listen to our data; obviously the existential factors in therapy deserve far more consideration than they generally receive.

It is more than happenstance that the existential factors category was included almost as afterthought and yet proved to be so important to patients. Existential factors play an important but generally unrecognized role in psychotherapy. There is no discrete school of existential psychotherapy, no formal training institute, no single accepted body of existential theory and techniques; nonetheless a considerable proportion of American therapists consider themselves to be existentially oriented. During the past decade I have addressed approximately twenty-five thousand therapists in lectures or workshops on group therapy and have asked the audience about their primary therapy orientation: Freudian analytic? Interpersonal? Behavioral? Gestalt? T.A.? Existential? Without exception, between 30 percent and 60 percent of the audience identified themselves as existential in orientation.

Even therapists who nominally adhere to other orientations are surprised when they look deeply at their techniques and at their basic view of the human situation and find that they are existentially oriented. Most therapists who consider themselves psychoanalytically oriented inwardly eschew or at best ignore much of the fundamental analytic theory. Keep in mind that classical psychoanalytic theory is based explicitly on a highly materialistic view of human nature. It is not possible to understand Freud fully without considering his allegiance to the Helmholtz school, an ideological school that dominated Western European medical and basic research in the latter part of the nineteenth century. The basic Helmholtzian doctrine was simply stated:

No other forces than the common physical-chemical ones are active within the organism; that, in those cases which cannot at the time be explained by these forces one has either to find the specific way or form of their action by means of the physical-mathematical method, or to assume new forces equal in dignity to the chemical-physical forces inherent in matter, reducible to the force of attraction and repulsion.[31]

Freud never swerved from his adherence to this postulate and to its implications about human nature; many of his more cumbersome, more relentless formulations (for example, the dual instinct theory, the theory of libidinal energy conservation and transformation) were the result of his unceasing attempts to fit human behavior to Helmholtzian rules. This doctrine posits that man is precisely the sum of his parts; it is deterministic, antivitalistic, and materialistic (in that it attempts to explain the higher by the lower). *The Helmholtzian manifesto constitutes a negative definition of the existential approach.* If you feel restricted by its definition of yourself, if you feel that there's something missing, that the doctrine has no place for some of the central features that make us human—that is, purpose, responsibility, sentience, will, values, courage, spirit—then to that degree you are an existentialist.

I must be careful not to slip off the surface of these pages and glide into another book. This is not the place to discuss, in depth, the existential frame of reference in therapy. I refer interested readers to my book *Existential Psychotherapy.*[32]

For now, it is sufficient to note that modern existential therapy represents an application of two merged philosophical traditions. The first is substantive—*Lebens-philosophie* (the philosophy of life, or philosophical anthropology); and the second is methodological—phenomenology —a more recent tradition, fathered by Edmund Husserl, which argues that the proper realm of the study of the human being is consciousness itself. In this latter tradition, understanding takes place from within, by bracketing the natural world and attending instead to the inner experience which is the author of that world.

The existential therapeutic approach—with its emphasis on awareness of death, freedom, isolation, and life purpose—has until recently been far more acceptable to the European therapeutic community than to the American one. The European philosophic tradition, the geographic and ethnic confinement, the greater familiarity with limits, war, death, and uncertain existence, all favored the spread of the existential influence. The American zeitgeist of expansiveness, optimism, limitless horizons, and pragmatism embraced instead the scientific positivism proffered by a mechanistic Freudian metaphysics or a hyperrational, empirical behaviorism (strange bedfellows!). During the past two decades, there has been a major development in American psychotherapy: the emergence of what has come to be known as the "third force" in American psychology (third after Freudian psychoanalysis and Watsonian behaviorism). This force has often been labeled "humanistic" or "existential" psychology, and its influence upon modern therapeutic practice has been enormous. Note, however, that there has been an Americanization as well as an importation of the European existential tradition. The syntax is European, but the accent is unmistakably New World. The European focus is on the tragic dimensions of existence, on limits, on facing and taking into oneself the anxiety of uncertainty and non-being. The humanistic psychologists, on the other hand, speak less of limits and contingency than of human potentiality, less of acceptance than of awareness, less of anxiety than of peak experiences and oceanic oneness, less of life meaning than of self-realization, less of apartness and basic isolation than of I-Thou and encounter.

Of course, when a basic doctrine has a number of postulates, and the accent of each is systematically altered in a specific direction, there is significant risk of mutation of the original doctrine. To some extent this has occurred, and some humanistic psychologists have lost touch with their existential roots and espouse a monolithic goal of "self-actualization" with an associated set of quick actualizing techniques. This is a most unfortunate development; it is most important to keep in mind that the existential approach in therapy is not a set of technical procedures but basically an attitude toward the human being.

Existential therapy is a dynamic approach based on concerns that are rooted in existence. By "dynamic" approach, I mean a therapy that posits that the deep structures of personality encompass forces that are in conflict with one another, and that (and this is very important) these forces exist at different levels of awareness: indeed, some exist outside of conscious awareness. The existential definition of the content of the internal struggle differs greatly from the other dynamic systems. A Freudian approach, for example, addresses the struggle between the individual's fundamental drives (primarily sexual and aggressive) and an environment that frustrates satisfaction of those drives.

The existential approach posits that the human being's paramount struggle is with the givens, the ultimate concerns, of existence: death, isolation, freedom, and meaninglessness. Anxiety issues from basic conflicts in each of these realms: we wish to continue to be and yet are

95

aware of inevitable death; we crave ground and structure and yet must confront groundlessness; each of us desires contact, protection, to be part of a larger whole yet experiences the unbridgeable gap between self and others; we are meaning-seeking creatures thrown into a world that has no meaning.

The items in the Q-sort that struck meaningful chords in patients reflected some of these painful truths about existence. Patients realized that there were limits to the guidance and support they could receive from others, and that the ultimate responsibility for the conduct of their lives was theirs alone. They learned also that though one could be close to others, there was nonetheless a point beyond which one could not be accompanied: there is a basic aloneness to existence that must be faced and cannot be avoided. Many patients learned to face their limitations and their mortality with greater candor and courage. Coming to terms with one's own death in a deeply authentic fashion permits one to cast the troublesome concerns of everyday life in a different perspective. It permits one to trivialize life's trivia.

• The course of therapy of Gail, a patient who at the end of treatment selected the existential Q-sort items as having been instrumental in her improvement, illustrates many of these points. A twenty-five-year-old perennial student, Gail complained of depression, loneliness, purposelessness, and severe gastric distress for which no organic cause could be found. In her initial session she lamented repeatedly, "I don't know what's going on!" I could not discover what precisely she meant and, since this complaint was embedded in a lengthy litany of self-accusations, I soon forgot it. However, in the group, too, she did not understand what happened to her: she could not understand why others were so uninterested in her, why she developed a conversion paralysis, why she entered sexually masochistic relationships, why she so idealized the therapist.

In the group Gail was boring, dull, and absolutely predictable. Before every utterance she scanned the sea of faces about her looking for clues as to what others wanted and expected. She was willing to be almost anything so as to avoid offending others and possibly driving them away from her. (Of course, it resulted in her driving others away, not from anger but from boredom.) Gail was in chronic retreat from life, and the group tried endless approaches to halt the retreat, to find Gail within the cocoon of compliance she had spun about herself.

However, no progress occurred until the group stopped encouraging Gail, stopped attempting to force her to socialize, to study, to write papers, to pay bills, to buy clothes, to groom herself, but instead urged her to consider the blessings of failure. What was there in failure that was so seductive and so rewarding? Quite a bit, it turned out! Failing kept her young, kept her protected, kept her from deciding. Idealizing the therapist served the same purpose. Help was "out there." He knew the answers; her job in therapy was to enfeeble herself to the point where the therapist could not in all good conscience withhold his royal touch.

A critical event occurred when she had a biopsy performed on an enlarged lymph node. She feared cancer and came to the group that day still awaiting the results of the biopsy (which ultimately demonstrated that she had no malignant tumor). She had never been so near to her own death before, and we helped Gail plunge into the terrifying loneliness she experienced. There are two kinds of loneliness—the existential, primordial loneliness that Gail confronted then, and a social loneliness, an inability to "be with." The second, the social loneliness, is commonly and easily worked with in a group therapeutic setting. Basic loneliness is more rarely faced: groups often confuse the two and try to take away one's basic loneliness. But it cannot be taken away; it cannot be resolved; it can only be known.

Rather quickly, then, Gail changed. She reintegrated far-strewn bits of herself. She began to make decisions and to take over the helm of her life. She commented, "I think I know what's going on" (I had long forgotten her initial complaint). More than anything else, she had been trying to avoid the specter of loneliness. I think she tried to elude it by staying young, by avoiding choice and decision, by perpetuating the myth that there would always be someone who would choose for her, would accompany her, would always be there for her. Choice and freedom invariably imply loneliness, and as Fromm pointed out long ago, freedom holds more terror for us than tyranny does.

Recall the Q-sort item in table 4.1 that many patients found important: "Learning that I must take ultimate responsibility for the way I live my life no matter how much guidance and support I get from others" (60). In a sense, this is a double-edged factor in group therapy. Group members learn a great deal about how to relate better, how to develop greater intimacy with others, how to give to and ask for help from others. At the same time, they discover the limits of intimacy, they learn what they *cannot* obtain from others. It is a harsh lesson and leads both to despair and to strength. One cannot stare at the sun very long, and Gail on many occasions looked away and avoided her dread. Always she came back to it, however, and by the end of therapy had made major shifts within herself.

Therapy groups often tend to water down the tragedy of life. Their natural currency is interpersonal theory; and if care is not taken, they will make the error of translating existential concerns into interpersonal ones, which are more easily grasped in the group. For example, as Gail's case illustrates, existential loneliness may be erroneously translated into social loneliness. Another incorrect translation occurs when we mistake feelings of powerlessness arising from awareness of our basic contingency for a powerlessness based on a sense of social inferiority. The group misses the point completely if it attempts to deal with the first, the fundamental feeling of powerlessness, by attempting to increase the individual's sense of social adequacy.

An important concept in existential therapy is that the human being may relate to the ultimate concerns of existence in one of two possible modes. On the one hand, one may suppress or ignore one's "situation" in life and live in what Martin Heidegger termed a state of *"forgetfulness of being."*[33] In this "everyday" mode one lives in the world of things, in everyday diversions; one is absorbed in "chatter," tranquilized, lost in the "they"; one is concerned only about the *way* things are. Or, on the other hand, one may exist in a state of *mindfulness of being,* a state in which one marvels not at the *way* things are but *that* they are. In this state one is aware of being; one lives "authentically"; one embraces one's possibility and limits; one is aware of one's responsibility for one's life. (I prefer Sartre's definition of responsibility: to be "responsible" is to be the "uncontested author of. . . .")[34]

Being aware of one's self-creation in the authentic state of mindfulness of being provides one with the power to change. Thus the therapist must pay special attention to the factors that transport a person from the "everyday" to the "authentic" mode of existing. One cannot effect such a shift merely by bearing down, by gritting one's teeth. But there are certain jolting "urgent experiences" (often referred to as "boundary experiences" in the philosophical literature) that effectively transport one into the "mindfulness of being" state.[35]

An extreme experience—such as Gail's encounter with a possibly malignant lymph node—is a good example of a boundary experience," an event that brought her sharply back to reality and placed her concerns in their proper perspective. Extreme experience, however, occurs only rarely during the course of a therapy group. Some group leaders attempt to generate extreme experience by using a form of existential shock therapy. With a variety of techniques, they try to bring patients to the edge of the abyss of existence. I have seen leaders begin personal growth groups, for example, by asking each patient to compose an epitaph for their tombstones. "Destination labs" may begin with each member drawing his or her lifeline and marking upon it his or her present position: how far is one from birth, how close to death? But our capacity for denial is enormous, and it is the rare group that perseveres, that does not slip back into less threatening concerns. Natural events in the course of a group—illness, death of others, and termination and loss—may jolt the group back, but always temporarily.

Some time ago I began a group composed of patients who lived continuously in the midst of extreme experience.[36] All the members had a terminal illness, generally metastatic carcinoma; and all were entirely aware of the nature and implications of their illness. I learned a great deal from that group—especially about the fundamental but concealed issues of life that are so frequently neglected in traditional psychotherapy.

For one thing, the members were deeply supportive to one another, and it was extraordinarily helpful for them to be helpful to one another. Offering help so as to receive it in reciprocal fashion was only one, and not the most important, aspect of the benefits to be gained. Being useful to someone else drew them out of morbid self-absorption and provided them with a sense of purpose and meaning. Almost every terminally ill person I have spoken to has expressed deep fear of a helpless immobility —not only of being a burden to others and being unable to care for oneself but of being useless and without value to others. Living, then, becomes reduced to survival, and the individual searches within, ever more deeply, for meaning. The group offered these patients the opportunity to find meaning outside of themselves. By activity, by extending help to another person, and by caring for others they found the sense of purpose that so often eludes the passive introspective gaze.

The support they offered one another took many forms. They provided transportation to meetings, they maintained telephone vigils when a member was in deep despair, they shared their methods of coping and of gaining strength. One patient, for example, taught the group meditation procedures; and the group members ended every meeting thereafter in darkness, meditating over a lighted candle to ease their minds of pain and dread. In other ways the group provided the members power to transcend themselves, to extend themselves into others. They welcomed student observers and community interest. They were eager to teach and to share their experiences.

They began the group with a common bond of enmity toward the medical profession. Much time was devoted to disentangling the threads of this anger. Some of the anger was displaced and irrational—

anger at fate, envious anger at the living, anger at doctors for not being all-knowing, all-powerful, and all-protecting. Some of the anger was entirely justified—anger at the doctors' lack of sensitivity, at their impersonality, their lack of time, their unwillingness to keep the patient fully informed and to include them in all important management decisions. We attempted to understand the irrational anger and place it where it belonged—on the basic uncertainty and the contingency of our existence. We faced the justifiable anger and attempted to cope with it by helping the members become effective in influencing the attitudes of the medical profession. The members invited oncologists and medical students to observe the group, and participated in medical school classes and conferences.

All of these approaches, these avenues to self-transcendence, can, if well traveled, increase one's sense of meaning and purpose as well as one's ability to bear what cannot be changed. Nietzsche, long ago, wrote: He who has a "why" to live can bear with almost any "how."[37]

It was clear to me (and demonstrated by empirical research) that the members of this group who plunged most deeply into themselves, who confronted their fate most openly and resolutely, passed into a mode of existence that was richer than that prior to their illness.[38] Their life perspective was radically altered; the trivial, inconsequential diversions of life were seen for what they were. Their neurotic phobias diminished. They appreciated more fully the elemental features of living: the changing seasons, the last spring, falling leaves, the loving of others. Rather than resignation, powerlessness, and restriction, some patients have experienced a great sense of liberation and autonomy. Most of the group members carry their own time bombs; they keep themselves alive by taking some form of medication, generally a steroid, and thus make a decision daily whether to live or to die. No one takes one's life with absolute seriousness without coming to terms with the power to end it.

We are all familiar with the centrality of the quality of the therapeutic relationship in the process of change. In group therapy a sound, trusting relationship between therapist and patients and among the patients themselves is a necessary mediating condition: it enhances trust, risk taking, self-disclosure, feedback, constructive conflict, working through problems centering around intimacy, and so on. But in addition to these mediating functions, the basic, intimate encounter has an intrinsic value, a value in and for itself.

What can you as therapist do in the face of the inevitable? I think that the answer lies in the verb *to be*. You do by *being*, by being there with the patient. "Presence" is the hidden agent of help in all forms of therapy. Patients looking back on their therapy rarely remember a single interpretation you made, but they always remember your presence, that you were there with them. It asks a great deal of the therapist to join this group, yet it is hypocrisy not to join. The group configuration is not "you," the therapist, and "they," the dying; but it is *we* who are dying, we who are banding together in the face of our common condition. The group well demonstrates the double meaning of the word *apartness:* we are separate, lonely, *apart from* but also *a part of.* One of my members put it elegantly when she described herself as a lonely ship in the dark. Even though no physical mooring could be made, it was nonetheless enormously comforting to see the lights of other ships sailing the same water.

Comparative Value of the Therapeutic Factors: The Therapist's View

Many group therapists have published their opinions about the therapeutic factors. This literature underscores the range of factors but says little about their comparative value.

R. Corsini and B. Rosenberg, in a widely cited report,[39] abstracted the therapeutic factors from 300 pre-1955 group therapy articles; 175 factors were clustered into nine major categories, which show considerable overlap with the factors I have described. Their categories, and my analogous categories in parentheses, are:

1. Acceptance (group cohesiveness),
2. Universalization (universality),
3. Reality testing (includes elements of recapitulation of the primary family, and of interpersonal learning),
4. Altruism,
5. Transference (includes elements of interpersonal learning, group cohesiveness, and imitative behavior),
6. Spectator therapy (imitative behavior),
7. Interaction (includes elements of interpersonal learning and cohesiveness),
8. Intellectualization (includes elements of imparting of information),
9. Ventilation (catharsis).

W. Fawcett Hill, in 1957, interviewed nineteen group therapists and offered these therapeutic factors: catharsis, feelings of belongingness, spectator therapy, insight, peer agency (that is, universality), and socialization.[40] The considerable overlap among these sets of therapeutic factors increases confidence in the exhaustiveness of the factors posited in this book.[41]

One pertinent issue that must be raised here is the question of whether the therapeutic factors (and relevant leader behavior) deemed important by the therapists actually occur in the group. Does a therapist's belief system correlate with his or her actual behavior? Some interesting studies highlight this issue.

Fiedler's study, described in chapter 3, indicates that experts, regardless of their school of conviction, closely resemble one another in the nature of their relationship with patients.[42] R. W. Heine, who studied the patients of therapists from different schools (psychoanalytic, Adlerian, nondirective), found that successfully treated patients attributed their improvement to similar factors, regardless of the particular discipline of the therapist.[43] Truax and Carkhuff's work, discussed in chapter 3, brings further evidence to support the conclusion that effective therapists operate similarly in that they establish a warm, accepting, understanding relationship with their patients.[44] H. Strupp, R. Fox, and K. Lessler, in a comprehensive study of 166 patients in individual therapy, reached a similar conclusion: successful patients underscored the fact that their therapists were attentive, warm, respectful, and, above all, "human."[45]

In their research on encounter groups, Lieberman, Yalom, and Miles (see chapter 14) studied leaders from ten different ideological schools.[46] These investigators closely observed the actual behavior of the leaders and learned that their ideological school (what they believed and what they said they did) bore little relation to their actual behavior. For example, two transactional analysis leaders resembled each other no more closely than they resembled any of the other sixteen leaders in the study. The researchers devised a new classification of leader style based on actual behavior and found that these clusters of leader style correlated with outcome; there were patterns of leader behavior (for example, extensive provision of support and cognitive structuring) that were unrelated to ideological schools and were highly conducive to successful outcome.

These studies suggest, then, that successful therapists closely resemble one another in several areas highly relevant to successful outcome and that the proclaimed differences between schools may be more apparent than real.

Other studies approach this topic from another perspective and compare the views of patients and therapists about effective therapeutic factors. J. Schaffer and S. Dreyer, studying one hundred acute inpatient group members and their thirty behaviorally oriented therapists report significant disagreements about the important therapeutic factors: the therapists underestimated the importance of altruism, advice, self-understanding, and universality and overestimated catharsis, modeling, and behavior experimentation.[47]

S. Bloch and J. Reibstein compared the therapeutic factors (using a "critical incident" method, see page 72) selected by thirty-three outpatients and twelve therapists, and noted broad agreement but that therapists valued instillation of hope and vicarious learning less than the patients did and interpersonal learning and cohesiveness slightly more than the latter did.[48]

H. Feifel and J. Eells studied seventy-three patients and their twenty-eight psychoanalytically oriented therapists and found that, although the patients attributed their successful therapy to relationship factors, their therapists gave precedence to technical skills and techniques.[49] G. Blaine and C. McArthur did a detailed retrospective study of the psychoanalytically oriented treatment of two patients.[50] The patients and their therapists were interviewed and queried about the factors regarded as therapeutic turning points: significant insights, derepression, and so on. There were startling differences between the patients' and the therapists' points of view. Major differences occurred in the weighting of unconscious factors which were made conscious and the correlation between childhood experiences and present symptoms: the therapist placed great importance on these factors, whereas the patients "denied that this sort of thing had occurred in therapy." The patients valued the personal elements of the relationship, the encounter with a new, accepting type of authority figure, and their changed self-image and perception of other people. A turning point in the treatment of one of the patients starkly illustrates the differences. In the midst of treatment, the patient had an acute anxiety attack and demanded and was granted an emergency interview with the therapist. Both therapist and patient regarded the incident as critical: the therapist, because he thought that during the emergency session there had been a derepression of memories of early incestuous sex play and a subsequent freeing up and working through of oedipal material; the patient, on the other hand, considered the content of the emergency session unimportant and instead valued the meeting because of the relationship implications —the fact that the therapist would see him in the middle of the night conveyed a caring and concern that was of the utmost importance.

A similar discrepancy between the patient's and the therapist's view of therapy is to be found in *Every Day Gets a Little Closer* (1974), which I co-authored with a patient (Ginny Elkin).[51] Throughout the treatment she and I wrote independent, impressionistic summaries of each meeting and handed them in, sealed, to my secretary. Every few months we read each other's summaries and discovered that we valued very different aspects of the therapeutic process. All my elegant interpretations? She never even heard them! What she remembered and treasured were the soft, subtle, personal exchanges which, to her, conveyed my interest and caring for her.

These studies, then, demonstrate that although effective therapists of different disciplines may disagree cognitively about the therapeutic processes, they resemble one another operationally. Furthermore, therapists and their patients may have different views about the responsible therapeutic factors. It is important to note the common conceptual thread running through the patients' views about therapy. They consistently emphasize the importance of the relationship and the personal, human qualities of their therapists.

THERAPEUTIC FACTORS: MODIFYING FORCES

It is not possible to construct an absolute hierarchy of therapeutic factors. There are many modifying forces: therapeutic factors are influenced by the type of group therapy, by the stage of therapy, by extragroup forces, and by individual differences.

Therapeutic Factors in Different Group Therapies

Different types of group therapy favor the operation of different clusters of curative factors. Consider, for example, the therapy group on an acute inpatient ward. Table 4.4 depicts the results of the nine studies investigating the therapeutic factors chosen by members of inpatient therapy groups. Note, first of all, that these patients did not select the same constellation of three factors (interpersonal learning, catharsis, and self-understanding) as did members of outpatient groups. (There is one exception: the patients in the Leszcz, Yalom, and Norden 1985c study; these higher-functioning patients meet in a high-functioning "level" group [see chapter 15] which is led in a fashion closely resembling interactional outpatient groups.)

Note also that inpatients select a wide range of therapeutic factors reflecting, I believe, both the heterogeneous composition of inpatient therapy groups and the "cafeteria" theory of improvement in group therapy. Patients who differ greatly from one another in ego strength, motivation, goals, and type and severity of psychopathology meet in

TABLE 4.4

Most Valued Therapeutic Factors in Inpatient Groups

STUDY	POPULATION	MOST-VALUED THERAPEUTIC FACTORS
Maxmen and Hannover, 1973[a]	Short-term psychiatric ward N = 100	Hope Cohesiveness Altruism Universality
Steinfeld and Mabli, 1974[b]	Correctional institution for narcotic addicts N = 50	Insight Existential factors Catharsis Interpersonal input
Butler and Fuhriman, 1980[c]	Day hospital long term treatment N = 28	Cohesiveness
Macaskill, 1982[d]	Long term inpatient Ward-borderline patients N = 9	Self-understanding Altruism Hope Catharsis Existential factors
Leszcz, Yalom, and Norden, 1985a[e]	Short-term team group, low-functioning patients N = 20	Responsibility Catharsis Hope
Leszcz, Yalom, and Norden, 1985b[f]	Short-term team group, higher functioning patients N = 31	Catharsis Responsibility Universality Vicarious learning
Leszcz, Yalom, and Norden, 1985c[g]	Short-term higher functioning group N = 31	Interpersonal learning Catharsis Self-understanding
Marcovitz and Smith, 1983[h]	Short-term psychiatric ward N = 30	Catharsis Cohesiveness Altruism Interpersonal learning (output) Self-understanding
Schaffer and Dreyer, 1982[i]	Short-term psychiatric ward N = 100	Responsibility Self-understanding Catharsis Advice

a. J. Maxmen and N. H. Hannover, "Group Therapy as Viewed by Hospitalized Patients," *Archives of General Psychiatry* 28 (March 1973): 404–8.
b. G. Steinfeld and J. Mabli, "Perceived Curative Factors in Group Therapy by Residents of a Therapeutic Community," *Criminal Justice and Behavior* 1 (3 [September 1974]):278–88.
c. T. Butler and A. Fuhriman, "Patient Perspective on the Curative Process: A Comparison of Day Treatment and Outpatient Psychotherapy Groups," *Small Group Behavior* 11 (4 [November 1980]):371–88.
d. N. Macaskill, "Therapeutic Factors in Group Therapy with Borderline Patients," *International Journal of Group Psychotherapy* 32(1) [January 1982]): 61–73.
e. M. Leszcz, I. Yalom, and M. Norden, "The Value of Inpatient Group Psychotherapy and Therapeutic Process: Patients' Perceptions," *International Journal of Group Psychotherapy,* in press, 1985.
f. Ibid.
g. Ibid.
h. R. Marcovitz and J. Smith, "Patient's Perceptions of Curative Factors in Short-term Group Psychotherapy," *International Journal of Group Psychotherapy* 33 (1983): 21–37.
i. J. B. Schaffer and S. F. Dreyer, "Staff and Inpatient Perceptions of Change Mechanisms in Group Psychotherapy," *American Journal of Psychiatry* 139 (1 [January 1982]): 127–28.

the same inpatient group and, accordingly, select and value different aspects of the group procedure. Many more inpatients than outpatients select the therapeutic factors of hope and assumption of responsibility (existential factors). Instillation of hope looms large in inpatient groups because so many patients enter the hospital in a state of utter demoralization. Until a patient acquires hope and the motivation to engage in treatment, no progress will be made. Often the most effective antidote to demoralization is the presence of other patients who have recently been in similar straits and discovered a way out of despair. Existential factors (defined on the research instruments generally as "assumption of ultimate responsibility for my own life") are of particular importance to inpatients because often hospitalization means that a patient has "hit bottom." (On one inpatient Q-sort study, the responsibility item (60) was ranked first of the sixty items.[52]) Hospitalized patients are confronted with the limits of other people; external resources have been exhausted; family, friends, therapists have failed; and, in the final analysis, they can rely only on themselves.

Other types of group offer members help from different therapeutic factors. For example, Alcoholics Anonymous and Recovery, Inc., primarily encourage the operation of instillation of hope, imparting information, universality, altruism, and some aspects of group cohesiveness. Discharge planning groups in psychiatric hospitals may use much "imparting of information" and "development of socializing techniques." Lieberman and Borman, in a study of self-help groups (women's consciousness raising, bereaved parents, widows, heart-surgery patients, and mothers) report that the most commonly chosen factor is universality, followed by guidance, altruism, and cohesiveness.[53]

When therapists form a new therapy group in some specialized setting or for some specialized patient population, the first step, as I stress in chapter 15, is to determine the appropriate goals and the appropriate therapeutic factors for that particular group. All else, all matters of therapeutic technique, follow from that framework. Thus, it is vitally important to keep in mind the persuasive research evidence that different types of group therapy make use of different therapeutic factors. Earlier, I presented evidence that patients and therapists often value different therapeutic factors. When this discrepancy is too great, when therapists emphasize therapeutic factors that are not compatible with the needs and capacities of the group members, then obviously the therapeutic enterprise will be derailed: patients will become bewildered and resistant; therapists, discouraged and exasperated.

Therapeutic Factors and Stages of Therapy

Intensive interactional group therapy exerts its chief therapeutic power through interpersonal learning (encompassing catharsis, self-understanding, and interpersonal input and output) and group cohesiveness; nevertheless, the other therapeutic factors play an indispensable role in the intensive therapy process. To appreciate the interdependence of the therapeutic factors, we must consider the therapeutic process in its longitudinal dimension.

Many patients expressed difficulty about rank-ordering therapeutic factors because they found various factors helpful at different stages of therapy. Factors of considerable importance early in therapy may be far less salient late in the course of treatment. In the early stages of development, the group is concerned chiefly with survival, with establishing boundaries and maintaining membership; in this phase, factors such as the instillation of hope, guidance, and universality seem especially important. A universality phase early in the group is inevitable, as members search out similarities and compare symptoms and problem constellations. The first dozen meetings of a group present a high-risk period for potential dropouts, and it is often necessary to awaken hope in the patients in order to keep them attending through this critical phase. Factors such as altruism and group cohesiveness operate throughout therapy; but their nature changes with the stage of the group. Early in therapy, altruism takes the form of offering suggestions or helping one another to talk with appropriate questions and attention. Later, it may take the form of a more profound caring and "being with." Group cohesiveness operates as a therapeutic factor at first by means of group support, acceptance, and the facilitation of attendance, and later by means of the interrelation of group esteem and self-esteem and through its role in interpersonal learning. It is only after the development of group cohesiveness that patients may engage deeply and constructively in the self-disclosure, confrontation, and conflict essential to the process of interpersonal learning. Butler and Fuhriman studied ninety-one patients from twenty-three outpatient groups and demonstrated that the therapeutic factors of cohesiveness, self-understanding and interpersonal output were more valued by patients the longer they participated in the group.[54]

Patients' needs and goals change during the course of therapy. In chapter 2, I described a common sequence in which patients first seek symptomatic relief and then, during the first months in therapy, formulate new goals—often interpersonal ones: they wish to be able to relate more deeply to others, to be able to love, to be honest with others. As patients' needs and goals shift during therapy, so, too, must the necessary therapeutic processes. Modern enlightened psychotherapy is often termed dynamic psychotherapy because it appreciates the dynamics, the motivational aspects of behavior, many of which are not in awareness. Dynamic therapy may be thought of also as changing, nonstatic, evolving psychotherapy: patients change, the group goes through a predictable developmental sequence; and so, too, the therapeutic factors shift in primacy and influence during the course of therapy.

Therapeutic Factors Outside the Group

Although major behavioral and attitudinal shifts would seem to require a degree of interpersonal learning, by no means is this invariably visible in the group. Occasionally patients make major changes without making what would appear to be the appropriate investment in the therapeutic process. This brings up an important principle in therapy: the therapist or the group does not have to do the entire job. Personality reconstruction as a therapeutic goal is as unrealistic as it is presumptuous. Our patients have many adaptive coping strengths which may have served them well in the past; and not infrequently, a boost from some event in therapy may be sufficient to help a patient to begin coping in an adaptive manner. I have previously used the term *adaptive spiral* to refer to the process in which one change in a patient begets changes in his or her interpersonal environment that beget further personal change. The adaptive spiral is the reverse of the vicious circle, in which so many patients find themselves ensnared—a sequence of events in which dysphoria has interpersonal manifestations that weaken or disrupt interpersonal bonds and consequently create further dysphoria.

Documentation of these points comes when we ask patients about other therapeutic influences or events in their lives which occurred concurrently with their therapy course. In one sample of twenty patients, eighteen described a variety of extragroup therapeutic factors. Most commonly cited was a new or an improved interpersonal relationship with one or more of a variety of figures (member of the opposite sex, parent, spouse, teacher, foster family, or a new set of friends).[55] Two patients claimed to have benefited by going through with a divorce that had long been pending. Many others cited success at work or school, which raised their self-esteem as they established a reservoir of real accomplishments; others became involved in some new social venture (YMCA groups or political committee work).

It is possible, of course, that these were fortuitous, independent factors which deserve, along with group therapy, credit for the successful outcome. On closer examination, however, it is apparent that usually the external factor was an auxiliary to therapy. The group mobilized the members to take advantage of environmental resources that, in fact, had long been available. After all, spouses, relatives, potential friends, social organizations, and academic or job opportunities were always "out there," available, waiting for the patient to seize them. The group may have given the patient only the necessary slight boost to allow him or her to exploit these previously untapped resources. Frequently the group members and the therapist are unaware of the importance of these factors and view the patient's improvement with skepticism or puzzlement.

A study of encounter group members who had very successful outcomes yielded corroborative results.[56] More often than not, the members did not credit the group for their change. Instead, they described the beneficial effects of new relationships they had made, new social circles they had created, new recreational clubs they had joined, greater work satisfaction they had found. However, closer inquiry indicated that the relationships, social circles, recreational clubs, and work satisfaction had not suddenly come into being *de novo*. They had always been available in the life space of the individual, but the group experience mobilized him or her to take advantage of these resources and exploit them for satisfaction and personal growth.

I have considered, at several places in this text, how the skills that group members acquire prepare them ably for new social situations in the future. Not only are extrinsic skills acquired but intrinsic capacities are released; psychotherapy removes neurotic obstructions which have stunted the development of the patient's own resources. At the risk of belaboring an obvious point, I recall a patient beginning therapy who described a weekend of skiing. What could have been an extraordinarily pleasant experience for him (fine, sunny weather, good snow conditions, agreeable companions) turned into a nightmarish one. He was obsessed by the thought that he would fall on the slopes, lose his skis, and that, by the time he had readjusted them, his friends would have decided not to wait for him at the lifts. He had a fear of abandonment which so pervaded all his experience that he could take no pleasure in any solitary activity. Therapy was quite successful in alleviating this fear, and once this obstruction was removed the patient blossomed and found gratification in diverse experiences. The view of therapy as "obstruction removal" lightens the burden of therapists and enables them to retain respect for the rich, never fully knowable capacities of their patients.

Individual Differences and Therapeutic Factors

Note that the rank-ordering of the therapeutic factors in tables 4.1, 4.2, 4.3, and 4.4 represents a mean or average value. Each study reports considerable individual variation in the rankings, and some researchers have attempted to determine the reasons behind these variations. Although factors such as sex, age, or education make little difference, there is evidence that level of functioning is significantly related to the ranking of therapeutic factors.

Higher-functioning outpatients value interpersonal learning (the cluster of interpersonal input and output, catharsis, and self-understanding) more than do the lower-functioning patients in the same group.[57] Leszcz, Yalom, and Norden report that in their inpatient groups all patients valued "awareness of responsibility" and catharsis. However, the lower-functioning patients also valued the "instillation of hope," whereas the higher-functioning patients in the same groups valued universality, vicarious learning, and interpersonal learning.[58] The Lieberman, Yalom, and Miles encounter group study indicates that high learners, in contrast to low learners, value vicarious learning: high learners are able to learn from the work of others as well as from their own.[59] Lastly, Freedman and Hurley, in a T-group of college students, demonstrated that an individual's perception of which therapeutic factors are helpful is linked to his or her level of self-acceptance and acceptance of others.[60] High self/other acceptors tended to value deeper insight into their interpersonal relations and into their family structure; low self/other acceptors placed more value on items that offered more safety and required less venturing: advice and guidance from other members and the group leaders, and universality.

Not everyone needs the same things or responds in the same way to group therapy; there are many therapeutic pathways through the group therapy experience. Consider, for example, catharsis: many restricted individuals benefit by experiencing and expressing strong affect; others, with contrasting problems of impulse control and great emotional liability, may, on the contrary, profit from acquiring an intellectual structuring and from reining in emotional expression. Narcissistic individuals need to learn to share and to give, whereas passive, self-effacing individuals need to learn to identify and express their needs. Some patients may need to develop satisfactory, even rudimentary social skills; others may need to work with more subtle issues—for example, a male patient who needs to stop sexualizing all women and devaluing or competing with all men.

In summary, it is clear that the comparative potency of the therapeutic factors is a complex question. Different factors are valued by different types of therapy group, by the same group at different developmental stages, and by different patients within the same group depending upon individual needs and strengths. Overall, however, the preponderance of research evidence indicates that the power of the long-term interactional outpatient group issues from its interpersonal properties. Interpersonal interaction and exploration (encompassing catharsis and self-understanding) and group cohesiveness are the *sine qua non* of effective long-term group therapy, and the effective group therapist must direct his or her efforts toward maximal development of these therapeutic resources. The next chapters will consider the role and the techniques of the group therapist from the viewpoint of these therapeutic factors.

5

THE THERAPIST:

BASIC TASKS

Now that I have considered *how* people change in group therapy, it is time to turn to the therapist's role in the therapeutic process. In this chapter I shall consider the basic tasks of the therapist and the techniques by which they may be accomplished.

The four previous chapters contend that therapy is a complex process consisting of elemental factors which interlace in an intricate fashion. The group therapist's job is to create the machinery of therapy, to set it into motion, and to keep it operating with maximum effectiveness. Sometimes I think of the therapy group as an enormous dynamo: often the therapist is deep in the interior, working, experiencing, interacting (and being personally influenced by the energy field); at other times the therapist dons mechanic's clothes and tinkers with the exterior, lubricating, tightening nuts and bolts, replacing parts.

Before turning to specific tasks and techniques, I wish to emphasize something to which I will return again and again in the following pages. Underlying all considerations of technique there must be a consistent, positive relationship between therapist and patient. The basic posture of the therapist to a patient must be one of concern, acceptance, genuineness, empathy. Nothing, no technical consideration, takes precedence over this attitude. There will be times when the therapist challenges the patient, shows anger and frustration, suggests that if the patient is not going to work he or she should consider leaving the group. But these efforts (which in the right circumstances may have therapeutic clout) are never effective unless they are experienced against a horizon of an accepting, concerned therapist-patient relationship.

I have chosen to discuss the techniques of the therapist in respect to three fundamental tasks: (1) creation and maintenance of the group, (2) culture building, and (3) activation and illumination of the here-and-now. I shall postpone the bulk of the discussion of the first task, creation and maintenance, until after the essential background material of chapters 8, 9, and 10. In this chapter, I shall focus primarily on culture building and, in chapter 6, on here-and-now activation and illumination.

Creation and Maintenance of the Group

The leader is, of course, solely responsible for creating and convening the group. Your offer of professional help serves as the group's initial *raison d'être*, and you naturally set the time and place for meetings. A considerable part of the maintenance task is performed before the first meeting; and, as I shall elaborate in later chapters, the leader's expertise in the selection and the preparation of members will greatly influence the group's fate.

Once the group begins, the therapist attends to gatekeeping, especially the prevention of member attrition. Occasionally a patient will have an unsuccessful group experience resulting in premature termination of therapy, and this may play some useful function in his or her overall therapy career; for example, failure in or rejection by a group may so unsettle the patient as to ideally prime him or her for another therapist. Generally, however, a patient who drops out early in the course of the group should be considered a therapeutic failure. Not only does the patient fail to receive benefit, but the progress of the remainder of the group is adversely affected. Stability of membership seems to be a *sine qua non* of successful therapy. If dropouts do occur, the therapist must—except in the case of a closed group (see chapter 10)—add new members.

Initially, the patients are strangers to one another and know only the therapist, who serves as a transitional object. You are the group's primary unifying force; the members relate to one another at first through their common relationship with you.

The therapist must recognize and deter any forces that threaten group cohesiveness. Continued tardiness, absences, subgrouping, disruptive extra-group socialization, and scapegoating all threaten the integrity of the group and command the intervention of the therapist. I shall discuss each of these issues fully in later chapters. For now, it is necessary only to emphasize the therapist's responsibility to superindividual needs. Your first task is to help create a physical entity—a group. There will be times when you must delay dealing with pressing needs of an individual patient and when, in fact, it will be necessary to sacrifice a patient (removing a member from the group) for the good of the other members.

• A clinical vignette illustrates some of these points:

I introduced two new women members into an outpatient group. This particular group had had some difficulty in keeping women members; there was a stable core of four male members, but two women members had dropped out in the previous few weeks. This meeting began a bit inauspiciously for one of the women who, lighting a cigarette, triggered a spasmatic bout of coughing in one of the men. Between gasps, he informed her that he was allergic to smoke and that the group had a no-smoking rule.

At this point another member, Mike, arrived in the group a couple of minutes late and, without even a glance at the two new women, announced, "I need some time today from the group. I was really shook up by the meeting last week. I went home from the group very disturbed by your comments about my being a time hog. I didn't like those insinuations from any of you [that is, the members] nor from you either [addressing me]. Later that evening I had an enormous fight with my wife who took exception to my reading a medical journal [Mike was a physician] at the dinner table, and we haven't been speaking since."

Now this particular opening is a good beginning for most group meetings. It had many things going for it: The patient stated that he wanted some time. (The more members who come to the group wanting time and wanting to work, the more energized will a meeting be.) Also, he wanted to work on issues that had been raised in the previous week's meeting. (As a general rule, and one I shall discuss later in this book, the more that group members work on themes continuously from meeting to meeting, the more powerful does the group become.) Furthermore, he began the meeting by attacking the therapist: this group had been treating me much too gently; and Mike's attack, though uncomfortable, was, I felt certain, going to produce important group work.

Thus I had many different options in the meeting, but there was one task to which I had to award greatest priority: the task of maintaining the physical integrity of the group. I had introduced two female members into a group that had had some difficulty retaining women. How had the group responded to these members? They had been very much excluded by the group. Mike had not even acknowledged their presence and had launched into his opening gambit—a gambit that, though personally important, systematically excluded the new women by its reference to the previous meeting.

It was important, then, for me to find a way to address this task and, if possible, also to address the issues Mike had raised. In chapter 2, I offered the basic principle that therapy should strive to turn all issues into here-and-now issues. It would have been folly to deal explicitly with Mike's fight with his wife. The data that Mike would have given about his wife would have been biased. He could "yes, but" the group to death. Fortunately, however, there was a way to address both issues at once. Mike's treatment of the two women in the group bore many similarities to his treatment of his wife at the dinner table. He had ignored and been as insensitive to their particular needs as to his wife's. As a matter of fact, this insensitivity was the precise issue for which the group had taken him to task in the previous meeting.

Therefore, after approximately a half-hour of the meeting, I pried Mike's attention away from his wife and last week's session by saying, "Mike, I wonder what hunches you have about how our two new members are feeling in the group today?" This inquiry led Mike into the general issue of empathy and his inability or unwillingness in many situations to enter the experiential world of the other. Fortunately, this tactic not only turned the other group members' attention to the way they all had ignored the two new women, but also helped Mike further his work on his core problem—his narcissism and his failure to recognize and appreciate the needs and wishes of others. Even were it not possible to address some of Mike's central issues, however, I still would have opted to attend to the integration of the new members. Physical survival of the group must take precedence over other tasks.

Culture Building

Once the group is a physical reality, the therapist's energies are occupied in shaping the group into a therapeutic social system. You endeavor to establish a code of behavioral rules, or norms, that will guide the interaction of the group. The desirable norms for a therapeutic group follow logically from the discussion of the therapeutic factors.

Consider for a moment the therapeutic factors outlined in the first four chapters. Who provides support, universality, advice, interpersonal feedback, testing, learning, opportunities for altruism, and hope? Obviously, the other members of the group! Thus, to a large extent, *it is the group that is the agent of change.*

Here lies a crucial difference in the basic roles of the individual therapist and the group therapist. In the individual format, the therapist functions as the solely designated direct agent of change; the group therapist, however, functions far more indirectly. Thus, if it is the group members who, in their interaction, set into motion the many therapeutic factors, then it is the group therapist's task to create a group culture maximally conducive to effective group interaction.

The game of chess provides a useful analogy. Expert players do not, in the beginning of the game, strive for checkmate or outright capture of a piece, but instead aim at obtaining strategic squares on the board and thereby increase the power of each of their pieces. In so doing, players are indirectly moving toward the ultimate goal since, as the game proceeds, this superior strategic position will favor an effective attack and ultimate material gain. So, too, the group therapist methodically builds a culture that will ultimately exert great therapeutic strength.

A jazz pianist, a member of one of my groups, once commented on the role of the leader by reflecting that very early in his musical career he deeply admired the great instrumental virtuosos. It was only much later that he grew to understand that the truly great jazz musicians were those who knew how to augment the sound of others, how to be quiet, how to enhance the functioning of the entire combo.

It is obvious that the therapy group has norms that radically depart from the rules, or etiquette, of typical social intercourse. Unlike almost any other kind of group, the members must feel free to comment on the immediate feelings they experience toward the group, the other members, and the therapist. Honesty and spontaneity of expression must be encouraged in the group. If the group is to develop into a true social microcosm, members must interact freely. In schematic form, the pathways of interaction should appear like the first, rather than the second, diagram, in which communications are primarily to or through the therapist.

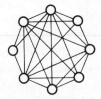 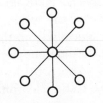

Other desirable norms include active involvement in the group, non-judgmental acceptance of others, extensive self-disclosure, desire for self-understanding, dissatisfaction with present modes of behavior, and eagerness for change. Norms may be a prescription for as well as a proscription against certain types of behavior. They have an important evaluative element in that members feel a particular mode of behavior *ought* or *ought not* to be performed. Norms may be implicit as well as explicit. In fact, the members of a group do not generally consciously formulate the norms of the group. Thus, to learn the norms of a group, the researcher is ill advised to ask the members for a list of these unwritten rules. A far better approach is to present the members with a list of behaviors and ask them to indicate which are appropriate and which inappropriate in the group.

Norms invariably evolve in every type of group—social, professional, and therapeutic. But by no means is it inevitable that a therapeutic group will evolve norms that facilitate the therapeutic process. System-atic observation of therapy groups readily reveals that many are encumbered with crippling norms. A group may, for example, so value hostile catharsis that positive sentiments are eschewed; a group may have a "take turns" format in which the members sequentially describe their problems to the group; or a group may have norms that do not permit members to question or challenge the therapist. Shortly I will discuss specific norms which hamper or facilitate therapy, but first I shall con-sider how norms come into being.

THE CONSTRUCTION OF NORMS

Norms of a group are constructed both from expectations of the members for their group and from the explicit and implicit directions of the leader and more influential members. If the members' expecta-tions are not firm, then the leader has even more opportunity to design a group culture which, in his or her view, will be optimally therapeutic. Obviously, the leader is the initial seat of influence in the group and is looked to by the members for direction.

G. Psathas and R. Hardert, conducting a careful analysis of the leader's interventions in a personal growth group, demonstrated that the leader's statements to the group play a powerful, though usually implicit, role in determining the norms established in the group.[1] D. Shapiro and L. Birk observed that "whenever the leader made a com-ment following closely after a particular member's actions this person became a center of attention in the group and often assumed a major role in future meetings."[2] Furthermore, the relative infrequency of the leader's comments augmented the strength of his or her interventions.

By discussing the leader as norm shaper, I am not proposing a new or contrived role for the therapist. Wittingly or unwittingly, the leader always shapes the norms of the group and must be aware of this function. The leader cannot *not* influence norms; virtually all of his or her early group behavior is influential. Moreover, what one does not do is often as important as what one does do; the late Don Jackson frequently said that "one cannot not communicate." Once I observed a group led by a British group analyst in which a member who had been absent the six previous meetings entered the meeting a few minutes late. The therapist in no way acknowledged the arrival of the patient and, after the session, explained to the student observers that he chose not to influence the group since he preferred that they make their own rules about welcoming tardy or prodigal members. It appeared clear to me, however, that his nonwelcome was an influential act and very much of a norm-setting message. His group had evolved, no doubt, as a result of many similar previous actions into a noncaring, insecure one, whose members sought methods of currying the leader's favor.

Norms are created relatively early in the life of a group and, once established, are difficult to change. Consider, for example, the small group in an industrial setting which forms norms regulating individual member output, or a delinquent gang which establishes codes of behavior, or a psychiatric ward which forms norms of expected staff and patient role behavior. To change entrenched standards is notoriously difficult and requires considerable time and often large turnover in group membership.

An interesting laboratory experiment by R. Jacobs and D. Campbell illustrates the tenacity and durability of norms.[3] Group members in a darkened room were asked to estimate how much a point of light (which was, in fact, stationary) moved (the "autokinetic response"[4]). A numerical group norm from which the individual members departed only minimally was rapidly established. The experimenters then replaced members, until there were several complete turnovers of membership. However, the group norm, which had been established by individuals long since departed from the group, remained fixed.

To summarize: every group evolves a set of unwritten rules or norms which determine the behavioral procedure of the group; the ideal therapy group has norms that permit the therapeutic factors to operate with maximum effectiveness; norms are shaped both by the expectations of the group members and by the behavior of the therapist; the therapist is enormously influential in norm setting—it is a function that he or she cannot avoid; norms constructed early in the group have considerable perseverance. The therapist is, thus, well advised to go about this important function in an informed, deliberate manner.

HOW DOES THE LEADER SHAPE NORMS?

There are two basic roles the therapist may assume in a group: technical expert and model-setting participant. In each of these roles the therapist helps to shape the norms of the group.

The Technical Expert

When assuming the role of technical expert, a therapist deliberately slips into the traditional garb of expert and employs a variety of techniques to move the group in a direction considered desirable. You explicitly attempt to shape norms during your early preparation of patients for group therapy. In this procedure, described fully in chapter 10, you carefully instruct patients about the rules of the group. You attempt to reinforce the instruction in two ways: by backing it with the weight of your authority and your experience, and by presenting the rationale behind your suggested mode of procedure in order to enlist the support of the patient's reason.

At the beginning of a group, therapists have at their disposal a wide choice of techniques to shape the group culture. These range from explicit instructions and suggestions to subtle reinforcing techniques. For example, as I described earlier, the leader must attempt to create an interactional network in which the members freely interact rather than directing all their comments to or through the therapist. To this end, you may implicitly instruct members in their pre-group interviews or in the first group sessions; you may, repeatedly during the meetings, ask for all members' reactions to another member or toward a group issue; you may wonder why conversation is invariably directed toward yourself; you may refuse to answer questions or may even close your eyes when you are addressed; you may ask the group to engage in exercises that teach patients to interact—for example, you may ask each member of the group, in turn, to give his or her first impressions of every other member; or you may, in a much less obtrusive manner, shape behavior by rewarding members who address one another—you may nod or smile at them, address them warmly, or shift your posture into a more receptive position. Exactly the same approaches may be applied to the myriad of other norms the therapist wishes to inculcate:

self-disclosure, open expression of emotions, promptness, self-exploration, and so on.

Therapists vary considerably in style. Although many do much of their norm shaping by explicit methods, all therapists, to a degree often greater than they suppose, perform their tasks through the subtle technique of social reinforcement. Human behavior is continuously influenced by a series of environmental events (reinforcers) which may have a positive or negative valence and which exert their influence on a conscious or a subliminal level.

Advertising science and political propaganda techniques are but two examples of a systematic harnessing of reinforcing agents. Psychotherapy, no less, relies on the use of subtle, often nondeliberate social reinforcers. Although no self-respecting therapist likes to consider himself or herself a social reinforcing agent, nevertheless the therapist continuously exerts influence in this manner, unconsciously or deliberately. You may positively reinforce behavior by numerous verbal and nonverbal acts, including nodding, smiling, leaning forward, an interested "Mmm," or a direct inquiry for more information. On the other hand, you may decline to reinforce behavior that you do not deem salubrious by not commenting, not nodding, ignoring the behavior, turning your attention to another patient, looking skeptical, raising your eyebrows, and so on. Any obvious verbal directive from therapists is an especially effective reinforcer because of the paucity of their interventions.

Every form of psychotherapy is a learning process, relying in part on operant conditioning. I agree with Shapiro, who states that "therapy without manipulation is a mirage which disappears on close scrutiny."[5] Judd Marmor, speaking from the vantage point of psychoanalysis, says, "What goes on in the psychotherapeutic 'working through' process is a kind of conditioned learning in which the therapist's overt and covert responses act as 'reward-punishment' cues which reinforce more mature patterns of behavior and inhibit less mature patterns."[6]

Considerable research documents the efficacy of operant techniques in the shaping of group behavior. Using these techniques deliberately, one can reduce silences[7] or increase personal and group comments, expressions of hostility to the leader, or intermember acceptance.[8] Though there is evidence that they owe much of their effectiveness to these learning principles, psychotherapists often eschew this evidence because of their unfounded fear that such a mechanistic view will undermine the essential human component of the therapy experience. The facts are compelling, however, and an understanding of their own behavior does not strip therapists of their spontaneity. The therapist who recognizes that he or she does exert great influence through social reinforcement, and who has formulated a central organizing principle of therapy, will be more effective and consistent in making therapeutic interventions. The experienced therapist does not become less spontaneous but acts on these principles reflexly as they become internalized determinants of his or her behavior.

The Model-Setting Participant

You as leader shape norms not only through explicit or implicit social engineering but through the example you set in your personal group behavior. The therapy group culture represents a radical departure from the social rules to which the patient is accustomed. The patient is asked to discard familiar social conventions, to try out new behavior, and to take many risks. How can you demonstrate to the patient that new behavior will not have the anticipated adverse consequences? One method, which has considerable research backing, is modeling: the patient is encouraged to alter his or her behavior by observing you engaging freely and without adverse effects in the behavior under question. A. Bandura has demonstrated in many well-controlled research endeavors that individuals may be influenced to engage in more adaptive behavior (for example, the overcoming of specific phobias[9]) or less adaptive behavior (for example, unrestrained aggressivity[10]) through observing and assuming the therapist's or the therapist-surrogate's behavior.

The leader may, by offering a model of nonjudgmental acceptance and appreciation of others' strengths as well as their problem areas, help to shape a group that is health-oriented. If, on the other hand, you conceptualize your role as that of a detective of psychopathology, the group members will follow suit. For example, one group patient had actively worked on the problems of other members for months but steadfastly had declined to disclose herself. Finally in one meeting she began to discuss her problems and "confessed" that one year previously she had had a two-month stay in a state psychiatric hospital. The therapist responded reflexively, "Why haven't you told us this before?" This comment, perceived as punitive by the patient, served only to reinforce her fear and discourage further self-disclosure. Obviously, there are questions and comments that will close people down and others that will help them to open up. The therapist, for example, might have commented that this woman now seemed to trust the group sufficiently to talk about herself, or might have commented on how difficult it must have been for her previously in the group, wanting to share this disclosure and yet being afraid to do so.

You set a model of interpersonal honesty and spontaneity; however, you must keep in mind the current needs of the members and demonstrate behavior that is congruent with those needs. I do not mean, however, that you should freely express all feelings. Total disinhibition is no more salubrious in therapy groups than in other forms of human encounter and, if faithfully enacted, may lead to ugly, wanton, destructive interaction. The therapist must model responsibility and appropriate restraint as well as honesty. The concept of the totally analyzed therapist who experiences no destructive feelings and fantasies toward patients is, in my experience, illusory. But the judicious use of your own feelings is an invaluable part of your armamentarium as leader. Consider the following therapeutically effective intervention:

• In the first session of a group of business executives meeting for a five-day human relations laboratory, a twenty-five-year-old, aggressive, swaggering member who had obviously been drinking heavily that day proceeded to dominate the meeting and make a fool of himself. He boasted of his accomplishments, belittled the group, monopolized the meeting, interrupted, outshouted, and insulted every other member. All attempts to deal with the situation failed: for example, feedback about how angry or hurt he had made others feel or interpretations about the meaning and cause of his behavior. Then my co-leader commented sincerely, "You know what I like about you? Your fear and lack of confidence. You're scared here, just like me. We're all scared about what will happen to us this week." That statement permitted the patient to discard his facade and, eventually, to become a valuable group member. Furthermore, the leader, by modeling an empathic nonjudgmental style, helped to establish a gentle, accepting group culture.

Interacting as a group member requires, among other things, that you accept and admit your personal fallibility. Therapists who need to appear infallible offer a perplexing and impeding example for their patients, and may be so reluctant to admit error that they may be withholding or devious in their relationship with the group.

• For example, in one group, the therapist, who needed to appear omniscient, was to be out of town for the next meeting. He suggested to the group members that they meet without him and tape record the meeting, and he promised to listen to the tape before the next session. He forgot to listen to the tape but, because of his need not to be wrong, was unable to admit this to the group. Consequently, the subsequent meeting, in which the therapist bluffed by avoiding mention of the previous leaderless session, turned out to be diffuse, confusing, and discouraging.

• Another example involved a neophyte therapist with similar needs. A patient attacked him by accusing him of making long-winded, confusing statements. Since this was the first confrontation of the therapist in this young group, the members were tense and perched on the edge of their chairs. The therapist responded by wondering whether he didn't remind the patient of someone from the past. The attacking patient clutched at the suggestion and volunteered his father as a candidate; the crisis passed, and the group members settled back in their chairs. However, it so happened that previously this therapist had himself been a member of a group (of psychiatric residents), and his colleagues had repeatedly focused on his tendency to make longwinded confusing comments. In fact, then, what had transpired was that the patient had seen the therapist quite correctly but was persuaded to relinquish his perceptions. If one of the goals of therapy is to help patients to test reality and to clarify their interpersonal relationships, then this transaction was antitherapeutic. (This illustrates, too, a point made earlier in regard to re-enactment of the primary family as a therapeutic factor: undue emphasis on the past may serve to deny the immediate reality of the group.)

Another consequence of the need to be perfect occurs when therapists become overly cautious. Fearing error, one weighs one's words so carefully, interacting so deliberately and with such poor timing, that one sacrifices spontaneity and may mold a group that is stilted and lifeless. Often a therapist who maintains an omnipotent, distant role is also saying, in effect, "Do what you will; you can't hurt or touch me." This pose may have the unwanted effect of aggravating a sense of impotence in patients, and thus is obviously counterproductive since one of the important norms of an effective therapy group is that the members take very seriously what each says to the other.

• In one group, Les, a young male patient, had made little movement for months despite vigorous efforts by the leader. In virtually every meeting the leader attempted to bring Les into the discussion, but to no avail. Instead, Les became more defiant and withholding, and the therapist became more active and angry. Finally Joan, another patient, commented to the therapist that he was a stubborn father treating Les like a stubborn son and was bound and determined to *make* Les change. Les, she added, was relishing the role of the rebellious son who was determined to defeat his father. This rang true for the therapist; it clicked with his internal experience, and he acknowledged this to the group and thanked Joan for her comments. The therapist's behavior in this example was extremely important for the group. In effect, he said, "I value you [the patients], this group, and this mode of learning." Furthermore, he reinforced norms of self-exploration, the interpretative mode, honesty, and confrontation with the therapist. The transaction was helpful to the therapist (unfortunate are the therapists who cannot learn more about themselves in their therapeutic work) and to Les, who fully explored his delight in defiantly frustrating the therapist.

Occasionally, less modeling is required of the therapist because of the presence of some "ideal" group patients who fulfill this function. In fact, there have been studies in which selected model-setting patients were deliberately introduced into a group. A. Schwartz and H. Hawkins introduced a pair of experienced group patients to serve as models in each of two inpatient schizophrenic groups.[11] It was known from their past group behavior that one pair of patients habitually made affect-laden statements whereas the other pair made impersonal, unemotional statements. The discussions of the groups were recorded and analyzed. The results attest to a significant amount of imitative behavior: the group with the models who expressed affect showed an increment in the amount of affect expressed, whereas the other group increasingly made unemotional, impersonal statements.

A. Goldstein et al. report an exploratory study in which they introduced a trained confederate (not a patient but a psychology graduate student) into two outpatient groups.[12] The "plants" pretended to be patients but met regularly in group discussions with the therapists and supervisors. Their role and behavior were planned to facilitate, by their personal example, self-disclosure, free expression of affect, confrontation with the therapists, silencing of monopolists, clique busting, and so on. The two groups were studied (through patient-administered cohesiveness questionnaires and sociometrics) for twenty sessions. The results indicated that the "plants," though not the most popular members, were regarded by the other patients as facilitating therapy; moreover, the authors concluded (though there were no control groups) that the "plants" served to increase group cohesiveness. Although a trained "plant" would contribute a form of deceit incompatible with the process of long-term group therapy, the use of such individuals has intriguing implications. It is entirely feasible, for example, to "seed" new therapy groups with an "ideal" group therapy patient from another group, who then continues therapy in two groups. Or, a patient who has recently satisfactorily completed group therapy might serve as a model-setting auxiliary therapist during the formative period of a new group.

Despite these provocative possibilities, it is you, the therapist, who, willingly or unwillingly, will continue to serve as the chief model-setting figure for the group patients. Consequently, it is of the utmost importance that you have sufficient self-confidence to fulfill this function. The less comfortable you feel, the more likely you are to encounter difficulties in this aspect of your role and to veer to one extreme or the other in your personal engagement in the group: either you will fall back into a comfortable, concealed professional role, or you will escape from the anxiety and responsibility inherent in the leader's role, by abdication and becoming simply "one of the gang." Either extreme has unfortunate consequences for the development of group norms. If you are an overly concealed professional leader, you create norms of caution and guardedness. If you are "one of the gang," you are unable to use the wide range of methods at your disposal for the shaping of norms; furthermore, you create a confused group which is unlikely to work fruitfully on important transference issues.

The issue of the transparency of the therapist has implications far beyond the task of norm setting. When you the therapist disclose yourself in the group, not only do you model behavior but you perform an act that has considerable significance in many other ways for the therapeutic process. Many patients develop conflicted and often distorted feelings toward the therapist; the transparency of the therapist plays a crucial role in the working through of transference. I shall discuss the ramifications of therapist transparency in great detail in chapter 7. It is time now to discuss the specific types of norms to incubate in the group.

EXAMPLES OF THERAPEUTIC GROUP NORMS

The Self-Monitoring Group

It is important that the group begin to assume responsibility for its own functioning. If this norm fails to develop, group passivity ensures the members are dependent upon the leader to supply movement and direction, and the leader feels increasingly fatigued and irritated by the burden of making everything work. Something has gone awry in the early development of such a group. When I lead groups like this, I often experience the members of the group as moviegoers. They visit the group each week to see what's playing; if it happens to interest them, they become engaged in the meeting. If not, "Too bad, Irv. Hope there'll be a better show next week!" My task in the group is to help members understand that they *are* the movie: if they do not perform, the screen is blank; there is no performance.

From the beginning of its life, I attempt to transfer the responsibility of the group to the members. Keep in mind that, in the beginning of a group, you as therapist are the only one who has a good definition of what constitutes a good "work" meeting. Your task, then, is to share that definition with the members. If the group has a particularly good meeting, I like to label it so. For example, I might comment at the end, "It's time to stop. It's too bad, I hate to bring a meeting like this to an end." In future meetings, I often make a point of referring back to that meeting. In a young group, a very hard-working meeting is often followed by a meeting in which the members step back a bit from the intensive interaction. I might comment after a half-hour, "I wonder how everyone feels about the meeting today? How would you compare it with last week's meeting? What did we do differently last week?"

Or you might help members develop a definition of a good meeting by asking them to examine and evaluate parts of a single meeting. For example, in the very early meetings of a group, I may interrupt and remark, "I see that an hour has gone by and I'd like to ask, How has the group gone today? Are you satisfied with it? What's been the most involving part of the meeting so far today? The least involving part?" The general point is that I endeavor to shift the evaluative function from myself to the patients. I say to them, in effect, "You have the ability (and responsibility) to determine when this group is working effectively and when it is wasting its time."

If a member laments, for example, that "the only involving part of this meeting was the first ten minutes—after that we just rapped for forty-five minutes," my reflex response is, "Then why did you let it go on? How could you have stopped it?" Or, "All of you seemed to have known this. What stopped you from acting? Why is it always my job to do what you are all able to do?" You begin to learn that there is generally very good consensus about productive and unproductive group work. (And productive work is almost invariably related to the presence or the absence of the here-and-now focus, which I shall discuss in the next chapter.)

Self-Disclosure

Group therapists may disagree about many aspects of the group therapeutic procedure, but there is great consensus about one issue: self-disclosure is absolutely essential in the group therapeutic process. Patients will not benefit from group therapy unless they self-disclose and do so fully. I prefer to lead a group with norms that say, in effect, that self-disclosure must occur but at each member's own pace. I prefer that members not experience the group as a forced confessional where deep revelations are wrung from members one by one.

During pre-group individual meetings, I make these points explicit to patients so that they enter the therapy group fully informed that, if they are to benefit from therapy, sooner or later they must share very intimate parts of themselves with the other group members.

Keep in mind that it is the subjective aspect of self-disclosure that is truly important. There may be times when therapists or group observers will mistakenly conclude that the group is not truly disclosing or that the disclosure is superficial or trivial in nature. Often there is an enormous discrepancy between subjective and objective self-disclosure—a discrepancy that, incidentally, confounds research that measures self-disclosure on some standardized scale. Many group therapy patients have had few important intimate confidants, and what appears to be minor self-disclosure may be the very first time a member has shared this material with anyone.

What about the "big secret"? A patient may come to therapy with an important "secret" which involves some central aspect of his or her life —for example, compulsive shoplifting, alcoholism, homosexuality, transvestism, incest. They may wish to join a therapy group but at the same time express a strong disinclination to share their secret with a large group of people. In my individual pre-group meetings I make it clear to a patient that sooner or later he or she will have to share the secret with the other group members. I emphasize that one may do this at one's own pace, that one may choose to wait until one feels great trust in the group, but that, ultimately, the sharing must come if therapy is to proceed. A group member who decides not to share a big secret merely re-creates in the group the same duplicitous modes of relating to others that exist outside the group. To keep the secret hidden, one must guard every possible avenue that might lead to it. Vigilance and guardedness are increased, spontaneity is decreased, and the individual bearing the secret spins an ever-expanding web of inhibition around himself or herself.

Sometimes it is adaptive to delay the telling of the secret. I think of two patients in my groups who did so. One patient had been a transvestite since the age of twelve and cross-dressed frequently but secretly.

Another patient entered the group with cancer. He stated that he had done a lot of work learning to cope with his cancer. He knew his prognosis: he would live for approximately two or three more years. He sought group therapy in order to live his remaining life more fully. He especially wanted to relate more intimately with the important people in his life. This seemed like a legitimate goal for group therapy, and I introduced him into a regular outpatient therapy group. (I have fully described this patient's course of treatment elsewhere.)[13]

Both of these patients chose not to disclose their secrets for many sessions. By that time I was getting edgy and impatient. I gave them knowing glances or subtle invitations. Eventually each became fully integrated into the group, developed a deep trust in the other members, and, after about a dozen meetings, chose to reveal himself very fully. In retrospect, their decision to delay was a very wise one. The group members knew each of these two patients as people, as John and Charles, who were faced with major life problems, not as a transvestite or as a cancer patient. John and Charles were justifiably concerned that, if they revealed themselves too early, they would be stereotyped, and that the stereotype would block other members from knowing them fully.

What happens when someone reveals the big secret? An important distinction must be made between "vertical" and "horizontal" self-disclosure. I believe that when an individual reveals the big secret, the therapist must help him or her disclose *even more* about the secret but in a "horizontal" rather than a "vertical" mode. By *vertical disclosure* I refer to greater in-depth disclosure about the secret itself. For example, when John disclosed his transvestism to the group, the members' natural inclination was to explore the secret "vertically." They asked about details of his cross-dressing: "How old were you when you started?" "Whose underclothes did you begin to wear?" "What sexual fantasies do you have when you cross-dress?" "How do you publicly pass as a woman with that mustache?"

But John had already disclosed a great deal vertically about his secret, and it was more important for him to reveal *horizontally:* that is, disclosure about the interactional aspects of disclosure, or *meta-disclosure.* For example, when John revealed his transvestism, I asked such questions as: "John, you've been coming to the group for approximately twelve meetings and not been able to share this with us. I wonder what it's been like for you to come each week and remain silent about your secret?" "How uncomfortable have you been about the prospect of sharing this with us?" "It's not felt safe for you to share this in the past. Today you chose to do so. What's happened in the group or in your feelings toward the group today that's allowed you to do this?" "What were your fears about revealing to us in the past? What did you think would happen? Who did you feel would respond in which ways?"

John responded that he feared he would be ridiculed or laughed at or thought weird. In keeping with the here-and-now inquiry, I guided him deeper into the interpersonal process by inquiring, "Who in the group would ridicule you? Who would think you were weird?" And then, after John selected certain members, I invited him to check out those assumptions with them.

Self-disclosure is always an interpersonal act. What is important is not that one discloses oneself but that one discloses something important in the context of a relationship to others. The act of self-disclosure takes on real importance because of its implications for the nature of ongoing relationships; even more important than the actual unburdening of oneself is the fact that disclosure results in a deeper, richer, and more complex relationship with others.

If undue pressure is placed on a member to disclose, I will, depending on the problems of the particular patient and his or her stage of therapy, respond in one of several ways. For example, I may relieve the pressure by commenting: "There are obviously some things that John doesn't yet feel like sharing. The group seems eager, even impatient to bring John aboard, while John doesn't yet feel safe or comfortable enough." (The word *yet* is important since it conveys the appropriate expectational set.) At other times I may shift the emphasis of the group from "wringing" the disclosure out of the patient to exploring the obstacles to disclosure. What does he or she fear? What are the anticipated dreaded consequences? From whom in the group does the patient anticipate disapprobation?

The patient should never be punished for self-disclosure. One of the most destructive events that can occur in a group is for members to use personal, sensitive material, which has been disclosed in the group, against one another in times of conflict. The therapist should intervene vigorously at this point; not only is it "dirty fighting," but it undermines important group norms. This "vigorous intervention" can take many forms. In one way or another, the therapist must call attention to the violation of trust. Often I will simply "stop action," interrupt the conflict, and point out that something very important has just happened in the group. I ask the offended member for his or her feelings about the incident, ask others for theirs, wonder whether others have had similar experiences, point out how this will make it difficult for others to reveal themselves, and so on. Any other work in the group is temporarily postponed; the important point is that the incident be underscored to reinforce the norm that self-disclosure is not only important but safe. Only after the norm has been established does the therapist turn to other aspects of the incident. The therapist may, for example, help the offending party examine his or her behavior—its impact on others, its occurrence in other life situations, its unconscious meaning.

Procedural Norms

The optimal procedural format in the group is unstructured, unrehearsed, and freely interacting. But such a format never evolves naturally: much active culture shaping is required on the part of the therapist. There are many trends the therapist must counter. The natural tendency of a new group is to devote an entire meeting to each of the members in rotation. Members may take turns; often the first person to speak or the one who presents the most pressing life crisis that week obtains the group floor for the meeting. Some groups have enormous difficulty changing the focus from one member to another, because a norm has somehow evolved whereby a change of topic is considered bad form, rude, or rejecting. Members may lapse into silence: they feel they dare not interrupt and ask for time for themselves; yet they refuse to keep the other member supplied with questions because they hope, silently, that he or she will soon stop talking.

These patterns hamper the development of a potent group and ultimately result in group frustration and discouragement. I prefer to deal with these antitherapeutic norms by calling attention to them and indicating that, since the group has constructed them, it has the power to change them. For example, I might say, "I've been noticing that over the past four weeks, the entire meeting has been devoted to only one person, often the first one who speaks that day, and also that others seem unwilling to interrupt and are, I believe, sitting silently on many important feelings. I wonder how this practice ever got started and whether or not we want to change it." A comment of this nature may be liberating to the group; the therapist has not only given voice to something that everyone knows to be true, but has also raised the possibility of other procedural options.

The Importance of the Group to Its Members

The more important the members consider the group, the more effective it becomes. I believe that the ideal therapeutic posture is when patients consider their therapy group meeting to be the most important event in their lives each week. The therapist is well advised to reinforce this belief in any available manner. If I am forced to miss a meeting, I inform the members well in advance and convey to them my concern about my absence. I arrive punctually for meetings. If I have been thinking about the group between sessions, I may share some of these thoughts with the members. I reinforce members when they give testimony of the group's usefulness to them or when they indicate they have been thinking about other members during the week.

The more continuity between meetings, the better. A well-functioning group continues to work through issues from one meeting to the next. (This is more easily done if the group meets more than once a week.) The therapist does well to encourage continuity; more than anyone else the therapist is the group "time binder," connecting events and fitting experiences into the temporal matrix of the group. "That sounds very much like what John was working on two weeks ago," or, "Ruthellen, I've noticed that ever since you and Jill had that run-in three weeks ago, you have become more depressed and withdrawn. What are your feelings now toward Jill?" I rarely start a group meeting, but when I do, it is invariably in the service of providing continuity between meetings. Thus, I might begin a meeting: "The last meeting was very heavy! I wonder what types of feelings you took home from the group and what those feelings are now?"

In chapter 14, I describe the group summary, a technique that serves to increase the sense of continuity between meetings. I write a detailed summary of the group meeting each week (an editorialized narrative description of content and process) and mail it to the members between sessions. One of the many important functions of the summary is that it offers the patient another weekly contact with the group and increases the likelihood that the themes of a particular meeting will be continued in the following one.

The group increases in importance when members come to recognize it as a rich reservoir of information and support. When members express curiosity about themselves, I, one way or another, convey the belief that any information members might desire about themselves is present in the group room, provided they learn how to tap it. Thus, when Ken wonders whether he is too dominant and threatening to others, my reflex is to reply, in effect, "Ken, there are many people who know you very well in this room. Why not ask them?"

Events that strengthen bonds between members enhance the potency of the group. It augurs well when group members go out together after a meeting for coffee, hold long discussions in the parking lot, or phone one another during the week in times of crisis. (Such extragroup contact is not without possible complication, however. This topic is complex, and I shall discuss it in detail in chapter 11.)

Members as Agents of Help

The group functions best if its members appreciate the valuable help they can provide one another. If the group continues to regard the therapist as the sole source of aid, then the group fails to achieve an optimal level of autonomy and self-respect. To reinforce this norm, the therapist may call attention to incidents demonstrating the mutual helpfulness of members. The therapist may also teach members more effective methods of assisting one another. For example, after a patient has been working with the group on some issue for a long portion of a meeting, the therapist may comment, "Reid, could you think back over the last forty-five minutes? Which comments have been the most helpful to you and which the least?" Or, "Victor, I can see you've been wanting to talk about that for a long time in the group and until today you've been unable to. Somehow Eve helped you to open up. What did she do? And what did Ben do today that seemed to close you down rather than open you up?" And so on.

Behavior undermining the norm of mutual helpfulness should not be permitted to go unnoticed. If, for example, one member challenges another concerning his treatment of a third member, stating, "Fred, what right do you have to talk to Peter about that? You're a hell of a lot worse off than he is in that regard," I might intervene by commenting, "Phil, I think you've got some negative feelings about Fred today coming from another source. Maybe we should get into them. I can't, however, agree with you when you say that because Fred is similar to Peter, he can't be helpful. In fact, quite the contrary has been true here in the group. People who *are* similar may have some special insight and thus be particularly helpful to the others."

Support

As I emphasized in my discussion of cohesiveness, it is essential that the members of a therapy group perceive it as a safe, supportive environment. Ultimately, in the long course of therapy, many uncomfortable issues must be broached and explored. Many patients have problems with rage or are arrogant or condescending or insensitive or just plain cantankerous. The therapy group cannot offer help without these particular traits emerging during the members' interactions. Ultimately, conflict must occur in the therapy group and, as I shall discuss in chapter 12, it is essential for the work of therapy. At the same time, however, too much conflict early in the course of a group can cripple its development. Before members feel free enough to express disagreement, they must feel safe enough and must value the group highly enough to be willing to tolerate uncomfortable meetings.

Thus the therapist must build a group with norms that permit conflict only after firm foundations of safety and support have been established; it is often necessary to intervene in order to prevent the proliferation of too much conflict too early in the group.

• A clinical illustration: In a new therapy group, there were two particularly hostile, critical members; and, by the third meeting, there was considerable open carping, sarcasm, and conflict. The fourth meeting was opened by Estelle (one of these two members) emphasizing how unhelpful the group had been to her thus far. Estelle had a way of turning every positive comment made to her into a negative, combative one. She complained, for example, that she could not express herself well and that there were many things she wanted to say but was so inarticulate she couldn't get them across. When another member of the group disagreed and stated that she found Estelle to be extremely articulate, Estelle turned that remark into unpleasantness by challenging the other patient for doubting her judgment about herself. Later in the group she complimented another of the women members by stating, "Ethel, you're the only one here who's ever asked me an intelligent question." Obviously Ethel was made quite uncomfortable at receiving this hexed compliment.

At this point I felt it was imperative to challenge the norms of hostility and criticism that had developed in the group, and intervened forcefully. I asked Estelle: "How do you think your statement to Ethel makes others in the group feel?" Estelle hemmed and hawed but finally offered that they might possibly feel insulted. I suggested that she check that out with the other members of the group. She did so and learned that her assumption was correct. Not only did every member of the group feel insulted, but Ethel, the recipient of Estelle's intended compliment, also felt irritated and put off by the statement. I then inquired, "Estelle, it looks as though you're correct, that you did insult the group, and that you knew that this was likely to occur. I wonder what's the payoff for you? What do you get out of it?"

Estelle suggested two possibilities. First she said, "I'd rather be rejected for insulting people than for being nice to them." That seemed a piece of twisted logic but nonetheless was comprehensible. Her second statement was: "At least this way I get to be the center of attention." "Like now"? I asked. She nodded. "How does it feel right now?" I wondered. Estelle said, "It feels good." "How about the rest of your life?" I wondered. She responded ingenuously, "It's lonely. In fact, this is it. This hour and a half is the people in my life." I ventured, "Then this group is a really important place for you?" Estelle nodded. I commented, "Estelle, you've always stated that one of the reasons you're critical of others in the group is that there's nothing more important than total honesty. If you want to be absolutely honest with us, however, I think you've got to tell us also how important we are to you and how much you like being here. That you never do, and I wonder if you can begin to investigate why it is so painful or dangerous for you to show others here how important they are to you."

By this time Estelle had become much more conciliatory, and I was able to obtain more leverage by enlisting her agreement that her hostility and insults did constitute a problem for her and that it would help her if we called her on it—that is, if we instantaneously labeled any insulting behavior on her part. It is always helpful to obtain this type of contract from a patient: in future meetings the therapist can confront members with some particular aspect of their behavior which they have asked to be called to their attention. Since they experience themselves as allies in this spotting and confrontative process, they are far less likely to feel defensive about the intervention.

SUMMARY

Many of these examples of therapist behavior may seem deliberate, pedantic, even pontifical. They are not the nonjudgmental, nondirective, mirroring, or clarifying comments typical of a therapist's behavior in other aspects of the therapeutic process. It is vital, however, that the therapist attend deliberately to the tasks of group creation and culture building. These tasks underlie and, to a great extent, precede much of the other work of the therapist.

It is time now to turn to the third basic task of the therapist: the activation and illumination of the here-and-now.

6

THE THERAPIST:
WORKING IN
THE HERE-AND-NOW

Introduction

The major difference between an outpatient therapy group which hopes to effect extensive and enduring behavioral and characterological change and such groups as A.A., Recovery, Inc., bulimia groups, groups of expectant mothers, weight-reduction groups, and cancer support groups is that the therapy group strongly emphasizes the importance of the here-and-now experience.

In chapter 2, I presented some of the theoretical underpinnings of the use of the here-and-now. Now it is time to focus on the clinical application of the here-and-now in group therapy. First, keep in mind that the here-and-now focus, to be effective, consists of two symbiotic tiers, neither of which has therapeutic power without the other.

The first tier is an "experiencing" one: the members live in the here-and-now; they develop strong feelings toward the other group members, the therapist, and the group. These here-and-now feelings become the major discourse of the group. The thrust is ahistoric: the immediate events in the meeting take precedence over events both in the current outside life and in the distant past of the members. This focus greatly facilitates the development and emergence of each member's social microcosm; it facilitates feedback, catharsis, meaningful self-disclosure, and acquisition of socializing techniques. The group becomes more vital, and *all* of the members (not only the one who is "working" that session) become intensely involved in the meeting.

But the here-and-now focus rapidly reaches the limits of its usefulness without the second tier, which is the illumination of process. If the powerful therapeutic factor of interpersonal learning is to be set into motion, the group must recognize, examine, and understand process. It must examine itself; it must study its own transactions; it must transcend pure experience and apply itself to the integration of that experience.

Thus, the effective use of the here-and-now is dualistic: the group lives in the here-and-now, and it also doubles back on itself; it performs a self-reflective loop and examines the here-and-now behavior that has just occurred.

here-and-now self-reflective loop

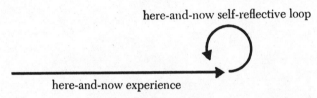

here-and-now experience

If the group is to be effective, both aspects of the here-and-now are essential. If only the first—the experiencing of the here-and-now—is present, then the group experience is intense, members feel deeply involved, and emotional expression is high. Members will finish the group agreeing, "Wow, that was a powerful experience!" Yet it will also prove to be an evanescent experience: members have no cognitive framework that permits them to retain the group experience, to generalize from it, and to apply what they have learned to "back home" situations. In fact, this is precisely the error made by many encounter group leaders of the 1960s and 1970s. If, on the other hand, only the second part of the here-and-now (the examination of process) is present, then the group loses its liveliness and meaningfulness; it degenerates into a sterile intellectual exercise. This error is made by overly rigid, formal, aloof therapists. Accordingly, the therapist has two discrete functions in the here-and-now: to steer the group into the here-and-now and to guide the self-reflective loop (or "process commentary"). Much of the here-and-now steering function can be shared by the group members; but, for reasons I shall examine later, process commentary remains to a large extent the task of the therapist.

INTRODUCTION

DEFINITION OF PROCESS

The term *process,* used liberally throughout this text, has a highly specialized meaning in other fields—law, anatomy, sociology, anthropology, psychoanalysis, and descriptive psychiatry. In interactional psychotherapy, *process* refers to the nature of the relationship between individuals who are interacting with one another.

Process may be contrasted with *content.* Imagine two individuals in a discussion. Now examine the content and the process of that discussion. The content consists of the explicit words spoken, the substantive issues, the arguments advanced. The process is an altogether different matter. When we ask about process, we ask, "What do these explicit words, the style of the participants, the nature of the discussion, tell *about the interpersonal relationship of the participants?"*

A therapist who is process oriented is concerned not primarily with the verbal content of a patient's utterance, but with the how and the why of that utterance, especially insofar as the how and the why illuminate aspects of the patient's relationship to other people. Thus, the therapist considers the metacommunicational* aspects of the message: Why, from the relationship aspect, is the patient making the statement at this time, to this person, in this manner? Consider, for example, this transaction: During a lecture a student raised his hand and asked, "What was the date of Freud's death?" The lecturer replied, "1938," only to have the student inquire, "But sir, wasn't it 1939?" The student asked a question whose answer he already knew. Obviously his motivation was not a quest for information. ("A question ain't a question if you know the answer.") We might infer that the process of the transaction was that the student wished to demonstrate his knowledge, or that he wished to humiliate or defeat the lecturer.

Frequently, in the group therapy setting, the understanding of process becomes more complex; we search for the process not only behind a simple statement but behind a sequence of statements made by a patient or by several patients. What does this sequence tell us about the relationship between one patient and the other group members, or between clusters or cliques of members, or between the members and

---

Metacommunication refers to the communication about a communication. Compare, for example: "Close the window!" "Wouldn't you like to close the window? You must be cold." "I'm cold, would you please close the window?" "Why is this window open?" Each of these statements contains a great deal more than a simple request or a command; each conveys a metacommunication: that is, a message about the nature of the relationship between the two interacting individuals.

the leader, or, finally, between the group as a whole and its primary task?

Some clinical vignettes may further clarify the concept:

• Early in the course of a group therapy meeting, Burt, a tenacious, intense, bulldog-faced graduate student, exclaimed to the group in general and to Rose (an unsophisticated, astrologically inclined cosmetologist and mother of four) in particular, "Parenthood is degrading!" This provocative statement elicited considerable response from the group, all of whom possessed parents, and many of whom were parents; and the ensuing donnybrook consumed the remainder of the group session.

Burt's statement can be viewed strictly in terms of *content*. In fact, this is precisely what occurred in the group; the members engaged Burt in a debate of the virtues versus the dehumanizing aspects of parenthood—a discussion that was affect-laden but intellectualized and brought none of the members closer to their goals in therapy. Subsequently, the group felt discouraged about the meeting and angry with themselves and with Burt for having dissipated a meeting.

On the other hand, the therapist might have considered the *process* of Burt's statement from any one of a number of perspectives:

1. Why did Burt attack Rose? What was the interpersonal process between them? In fact, the two had had a smoldering conflict for many weeks, and in the previous meeting Rose had wondered why, if Burt was so brilliant, he was still, at the age of thirty-two, a student. Burt had viewed Rose as an inferior being who functioned primarily as a mammary gland; once, when she had been absent, he had referred to her as a brood mare.

2. Why was Burt so judgmental and intolerant of nonintellectuals? Must he always maintain his self-esteem by standing on the carcass of a vanquished or humiliated adversary?

3. Assuming that Burt was chiefly intent upon attacking Rose, why did he proceed so indirectly? Is this characteristic of Burt's expression of aggression? Or is it characteristic of Rose that no one dares, for some unclear reason, to attack her directly?

4. Why did Burt, through an obviously provocative and indefensible statement, set himself up for a universal attack by the group? Although the words were different, this was a familiar melody for the group and for Burt, who had on many previous occasions placed himself in this position. Was it possible that Burt was most comfortable when relating to others in this fashion? He once stated that he had always loved a fight; indeed, he used almost to lick his chops at the appearance of a row in the group. His early family environment was distinctively a fighting

environment. Was fighting, then, a form (perhaps the only available form) of involvement for Burt?

5. The process may be considered from the even broader perspective of the entire group. Other relevant events in the life of the group must be considered. For the past two months the session had been dominated by Kate, a deviant, disruptive, and partially deaf member who had, two weeks previously, dropped out of the group with the face-saving proviso that she would return when she obtained a hearing aid. Was it possible that the group needed a Kate, and that Burt was merely filling the required role of scapegoat? Through its continual climate of conflict, through its willingness to spend an entire session discussing in nonpersonal terms a single theme, was the group avoiding something —possibly an honest discussion of members' feelings concerning Kate's rejection by the group or their guilt or fear of a similar fate? Or were they perhaps avoiding the anticipated perils of self-disclosure and intimacy?

Was the group saying something to the therapist through Burt (and through Kate)? For example, Burt may have been bearing the brunt of an attack really aimed at the co-therapists but displaced from them. The therapists—bearded, aloof figures with a proclivity for rabbinical pronouncements—had never been attacked or confronted by the group (although the patients, in private, referred to them as "the Smith Brothers"). Surely there were strong, avoided feelings toward the therapists, which may have been further fanned by their failure to support Kate and by their complicity through inactivity in her departure from the group.

Which one of these many process observations is correct? Which one could the therapist have employed as an effective intervention? The answer is, of course, that any and all may be correct. They are not mutually exclusive; each views the transaction from a slightly different vantage point. By clarifying each of these in turn, the therapist could have focused the group on many different aspects of its life. Which one, then, should the therapist have chosen?

The therapist's choice should be based on one primary consideration —the needs of the group. Where was the group at that particular time? Had there been too much focus on Burt of late with the other members feeling bored, uninvolved, and excluded? In that case, the therapist might best have wondered aloud what the group was avoiding. The therapist might have reminded the group of previous sessions spent in similar discussions which left them dissatisfied, or have helped one of the members verbalize this point by inquiring about the members' inactivity or apparent uninvolvement in the discussion. If the group communications had been exceptionally indirect, the therapist might have commented on the indirectness of Burt's attacks or asked the group to help clarify, via feedback, what was happening between Burt and Rose. If, as in this group, an important group event was being strongly avoided (Kate's departure), then it should be pointed out. In short, the therapist must determine what he or she thinks the group needs most at a particular time and help it move in that direction.

• In another group, Saul sought therapy because of his deep sense of isolation. He was particularly interested in a group therapeutic experience because of his feeling that he had never been a part of a primary group. Even in his primary family he had felt himself an outsider. He had been a spectator all his life, pressing his nose against cold window-panes, gazing at warm, convivial groups within.

At Saul's fourth therapy meeting, another member, Barbara, began the meeting by announcing that she had just broken up with a man who had been very important to her. Barbara's major reason for being in therapy had been her inability to sustain a relationship with a man, and she was profoundly distressed in the meeting. Barbara had an extremely poignant way of describing her pain, and the group was swept along with her feelings. Everyone in the group was very moved; I noted silently that Saul, too, had tears in his eyes.

The group members (with the exception of Saul) did everything in their power to offer Barbara support. They passed Kleenex; they reminded her of all her assets; they reassured Barbara that she had made a wrong choice, that the man was not good enough for her, that she was lucky to be rid of that jerk.

Suddenly Saul interjected, "I don't like what's going on here in the group today, and I don't like the way it's being led" (a thinly veiled allusion to me, I thought). He went on to explain that the group members had no justification for their criticism of Barbara's ex-boyfriend. They didn't really know what he was like. They could see him only through Barbara's eyes, and probably she was presenting him in a distorted way. (Saul had a personal ax to grind on this matter, having gone through a divorce a couple of years previously. His wife had attended a women's support group, and he had been the "jerk" of that group.)

Saul's comments, of course, changed the entire tone of the meeting. The softness and support disappeared. The room felt cool; the warm bond among members was broken. Everyone was on edge. I felt justifiably reprimanded. Saul's position was technically correct: the group was probably wrong to condemn Barbara's ex-boyfriend.

So much for the content. Now examine the process of this interaction. First, note that Saul's comment had the effect of putting him outside the group. The rest of the group was caught up in a warm, supportive atmosphere from which he excluded himself. Recall his chief complaint —that he was never a member of a group, but always the outsider. The meeting provided an *in vivo* demonstration of how that came to pass. In his fourth group meeting Saul had, Kamikazi style, attacked and voluntarily ejected himself from a group he wished to join.

A second issue had to do not with what Saul said but with what he did not say. In the early part of the group, everyone, save Saul, had made warm supportive statements to Barbara. I had no doubt but that Saul felt supportive of her. The tears in his eyes indicated that. Why had he chosen to be silent? Why was he able to comment from his critical self and not from his warmer, more supportive self?

The examination of the process of this interaction led us to some very important issues for Saul. Obviously it was difficult for him to express the softer, affectionate part of himself. He feared being vulnerable, exposing his dependent cravings, and losing himself, his precious individuality, by becoming a member of a group. Behind the aggressive, ever-vigilant, hard-nosed defender of "honesty" (honesty of expression of negative but not positive sentiments) there is always the softer, submissive child thirsting for acceptance and love.

• In a T-group of clinical psychology interns, one of the members, Robert, commented that he genuinely missed the contributions of some of the members who had been generally very silent. He turned to two of these members and asked if there was anything he or others could do that would help them participate more. The two members and the rest of the group responded by launching a withering attack on Robert. He was reminded that his own contributions had not been substantial, that he was often silent for entire meetings himself, that he had never really expressed his emotions in the group, and so forth.

Viewed from the *content* level, this transaction is bewildering: Robert expressed concern for the silent members and, for his solicitude, was soundly buffeted. Viewed from the *process*—that is, relationship—level, however, it makes perfectly good sense: the group members were much involved in a struggle for dominance, and their inner response to Robert's statement was, "Who are you to issue an invitation to speak? Are you the host or leader here? If we allow you to comment on our silence and suggest solutions, then we acknowledge your dominion over us," and so on.

• In another group, Kevin, an overbearing business executive, opened the meeting by asking the other members—housewives, teachers, clerical workers, and shopkeepers—for help with a problem confronting him. The problem was that he had received orders to cut his staff immediately by 50 percent: he had to fire twenty out of his staff of forty.

The content of the problem was intriguing and the group spent forty-five minutes discussing such aspects as justice versus mercy: that is, whether one retains the most competent workers or workers with the largest families or those who would have the greatest difficulty in finding other jobs. Despite the fact that most of the members engaged animatedly in the discussion, which involved important problems in human relations, the therapist strongly felt that the session was unproductive: the members remained in "safe" territory, and the discussion could have appropriately occurred at a dinner party or any other social gathering; furthermore, as time passed, it became abundantly clear that Kevin had already spent considerable time thinking through all aspects of this problem, and no one was able to provide him with novel approaches or suggestions.

The continued focus on content was unrewarding and eventually frustrating for the group. What did this content reveal about the nature of Kevin's relationship to the other members? As the meeting progressed, Kevin, on two occasions, revealed the amount of his salary (which was more than twice that of any other member); in fact, the overall interpersonal effect of Kevin's presentation was to make others aware of his affluence and power. The process became even more clear when the therapist recalled the previous meetings in which Kevin had attempted, in vain, to establish a special kind of relationship with the therapist (he had sought some technical information on psychological testing for personnel). Furthermore, in the preceding meeting, Kevin had been soundly attacked by the group for his fundamentalist religious convictions which he used to criticize others' behavior but not his own propensity for extramarital affairs and compulsive lying. At that meeting he had also been termed "thick-skinned" because of his apparent insensitivity to others. One other important aspect of Kevin's group behavior was his dominance; almost invariably he was the most active, central figure in the group meetings.

With this information about process, a number of alternatives were available. The therapist might have focused on Kevin's bid for prestige, especially following his loss of face in the previous meeting. Phrased in a nonaccusatory manner, a clarification of this sequence might have helped Kevin become aware of his desperate need for the group members to respect and admire him. At the same time, the self-defeating aspects of his behavior could have been pointed out; despite his efforts to the contrary, the group had come to resent and, at times, even to scorn him. Perhaps, too, Kevin was attempting to disclaim the appellation of "thick-skinned" by sharing with the group in melodramatic fashion the personal agony he experienced in deciding how to cut his staff. The style of the intervention would have depended on Kevin's degree of defensiveness: if he had seemed particularly brittle or prickly, then the therapist might have underscored how hurt he must have been at the previous meeting. If Kevin had been more open, the therapist might have asked him directly what type of response he would have liked from the others. Other therapists might have preferred to interrupt the content discussion and ask the group what Kevin's question had to do with last week's session. Or the therapist might have chosen to call attention to an entirely different type of process by reflecting on the group's apparent willingness to permit Kevin to occupy center stage in the group week after week. By encouraging the members to discuss their response to his monopolization, the therapist could have helped the group initiate an exploration of their relationship to Kevin.

PROCESS FOCUS: THE POWER SOURCE OF THE GROUP

Process focus is not just one of many possible procedural orientations; on the contrary, it is indispensable and a common denominator to all effective interactional groups. One so often hears words to this effect: "No matter what else may be said about experiential groups (therapy groups, encounter groups, and so on), one cannot deny that they are potent—that they offer a compelling experience for participants." This process focus is the power cell of these groups; it is precisely because they encourage process exploration that they are potent experiences.

A process focus is the one truly unique feature of the experiential group; after all, there are many socially sanctioned activities in which one can express emotions, help others, give and receive advice, confess and discover similarities between oneself and others. But where is it permissible to comment, in depth, on here-and-now behavior, on the nature of the immediately current relationship between people? Possibly only in the parent-young child relationship, and even then the flow is unidirectional. The parent is permitted process comments: "Don't look away when I talk to you!" or, "Be quiet when someone else is speaking," or, "Stop saying 'I dunno.' " But process commentary among adults is taboo social behavior; it is considered rude or impertinent. Positive comments about another's immediate behavior often denote a seductive or flirtatious relationship. When an individual comments about another's manners, gestures, speech, physical appearance, we can be certain that the battle is bitter and the possibility of conciliation chancy.

Why should this be so? What are the sources of this taboo? M. Miles, in a thoughtful essay,[1] suggests the following reasons that process commentary is eschewed in social intercourse: socialization anxiety, social norms, fear of retaliation, and power maintenance.

Socialization Anxiety

Process commentary evokes early memories and anxieties associated with parental criticism of the child's behavior. Parents comment on the behavior of children; and although some of this process focus is positive, much more is critical and serves to control and alter the child's behavior. Adult process commentary often awakens old socialization-based anxiety and is experienced as critical and controlling.

Social Norms

If individuals felt free to comment at all times upon the behavior of others, social life would become intolerably self-conscious, complex, and conflicted. Underlying adult interaction is an implicit contract that a great deal of immediate behavior will be invisible to the parties involved. Each party acts in the safety of the knowledge that one's behavior is not being noticed (or controlled) by the others; this safety provides an autonomy and a freedom that would be impossible if each continuously dwelled on the fact that others observe one's behavior and are free to comment on it. The Freud-Jung correspondence provides an excellent illustration: toward the end of their relationship both men so carefully observed and analyzed every nuance of the other's behavior that the relationship became unbearable.[2] The reader, too, shares the mounting anxiety and longs for the liberating final dissolution. Thus, in a Darwinian sense, the process commentary taboo has originated and persists to permit survival of the interaction necessary for our social order.

Fears of Retaliation

We cannot monitor or stare at another person too closely. Unless the relationship is exceedingly intimate, such intrusiveness is almost always dangerous and anxiety provoking, and we can expect some retribution. Aside from intentional systems such as a therapy group, there is no forum for interacting individuals to test and to correct their observations of one another.

Power Maintenance

Process commentary undermines arbitrary authority structure. Industrial organizational-development consultants have long known that a social structure's open investigation of its own structure and process leads to power equalization—that is, a flattening of the hierarchical pyramid. Individuals high on the pyramid are not only more technically informed but also possess organizational information that permits them to influence and manipulate. They not only have skills that have allowed them to obtain a position of power but, once there, have such a central place in the flow of information that they are able to reinforce their position. The greater the authority structure of an institution, the more stringent are the precautions against open commentary about process (as in, for example, the military or the church). The individual who wishes to maintain a position of arbitrary authority is wise to inhibit the development of any rules permitting reciprocal process observation and commentary.

THE THERAPIST'S TASKS IN THE HERE-AND-NOW

In the first stage of the here-and-now focus—the activating phase—the therapist's task is to move the group into the here-and-now. By a variety of techniques, many of which I shall discuss shortly, you steer the group members away from discussion of outside material and focus their energy upon their relationship with one another. You expend more time and effort upon this task early than late in the course of the group. As the group progresses, the members share much of this task, and the here-and-now focus becomes an effortless and natural part of the group life flow. In fact, many of the norms described in the last chapter, which the therapist must establish in the group, foster a here-and-now focus. For example, the leader who sets norms of interpersonal confrontation, of emotional expressivity, of self-monitoring, of valuing the group as an important source of information, is, in effect, reinforcing the importance of the here-and-now. Gradually, members, too, come to value the here-and-now and will themselves focus on it and, by a variety of means, encourage their fellow members to do likewise.

It is altogether another matter with the second phase of the here-and-now orientation—process illumination. Forces prevent members from fully sharing that task with the therapist. One who comments on process sets oneself apart from the other members and is viewed with suspicion, as "not one of us." When a group member makes observations about what is happening in the group, the others often respond resentfully about the presumptuousness of elevating himself or herself above the others. If a woman member comments, for example, that nothing is happening today, or that the group is stuck, or that no one is self-revealing, or that there seem to be strong feelings toward the therapist, then she is courting danger; the response of the other members is predictable: they will challenge her to make something happen today, or to reveal herself, or to talk about *her* feelings to the therapist. Only the therapist is relatively exempt from that charge; only the therapist has the right to suggest that others "work," or that others reveal themselves without the therapist's having to engage personally in the act he or she suggests.

Throughout the life of the group, the members are involved in a struggle for favored positions in the hierarchy of dominance. At times the conflict around control and dominance is flagrant; at other times, quiescent. But it never vanishes. Some members strive nakedly for power, others subtly; others desire it but are fearful of assertion; others always assume an obsequious, submissive posture. Statements by members that suggest that they place themselves above or outside the group generally evoke responses that emerge from the dominance struggle rather than from consideration of the content of the statement. Therapists are not entirely immune to evoking this response; some patients are inordinately sensitive to being controlled or manipulated by the therapist. They find themselves in the paradoxical position of applying to the therapist for help and yet are unable to accept help because all statements by the therapist are viewed through spectacles of distrust. This is a function of the specific pathology of some patients (and it is, of course, good grist for the therapeutic mill); it is not a global, universal response of the entire group.

The therapist is an observer-participant in the group; the observer status affords the objectivity necessary to store information, to make observations about sequences or cyclical patterns of behavior, to connect events that have occurred over long periods of time. You are the group historian; only you are permitted to maintain a temporal perspective; and you remain immune from the charge that you remove yourself from the group or elevate yourself above the others. It is the therapist who keeps in mind the original goals of the patient and the relationship between these goals and the events that gradually unfold in the group.

• For example, two patients, Tim and Marjorie, had a sexual affair which eventually came to light in the group. The other members reacted in various ways but none so condemnatory nor so vehemently as Diana, a forty-five-year-old nouveau-moralist, who criticized them both for breaking group rules: Tim, for being "too intelligent to act like such a fool"; Marjorie for "her irresponsible disregard for her husband and child,'; and the "Lucifer therapist" (me) who just "sat there and let it happen." I eventually pointed out that, in her formidable moralistic broadside, some individuals had been obliterated, that the Marjorie and Tim with all their struggles and doubts and fears whom Diana had known for so long had suddenly been replaced by faceless one-dimensional stereotypes. Furthermore, I was the only one to recall the reasons for seeking therapy which Diana had expressed at the first group meeting: namely, that she needed help in dealing with her rage toward a nineteen-year-old, rebellious, sexually awakening daughter who was in the midst of a search for her identity and autonomy! From here it was but a short step for the group, and then for Diana herself, to enter the experiential world of her daughter and to understand with great clarity the nature of the struggle between mother and daughter.

There are many occasions when the process is obvious to all the members in the group but they cannot comment on it simply because the situation is too "hot": they are too much a part of the interaction to separate themselves from it. In fact, often, even at a distance, the therapist too feels the heat and is wary about naming the beast.

• One neophyte therapist, when leading a training group of hospital nurses, learned through collusive glances between members in the first meeting that there was considerable unspoken tension between the young progressive nurses and the older, conservative nursing supervisors in the group. The therapist felt that the issue, one reaching deep into taboo regions of the authority-ridden nursing profession, was too sensitive and potentially explosive to touch. His supervisor assured him that it was too important an issue to leave unexplored and that he should broach it, since it was highly unlikely that anyone else in the group could do what he dared not. In the next meeting, the therapist broached the issue in a manner that is almost invariably effective in minimizing defensiveness: he stated his own dilemma about the issue, and told the group that he sensed a hierarchical struggle between the junior nurses and the powerful senior nurses, but that he was hesitant to bring it up lest the younger nurses would either deny it or so attack

147

the supervisors that the latter would suffer injury or angrily scuttle the group. His comment was enormously helpful and plunged the group into an open and constructive exploration of a vital issue.

I do not mean that *only* the leader should make process comments. As I shall discuss later, other members are entirely capable of performing this function; in fact, sometimes their process observations are more readily accepted than those of the therapists. What is important is that they not perform this function to avoid the patient role or in any other way to distance themselves from or elevate themselves above the other members.

Thus far in this discussion I have, for pedagogical reasons, overstated two fundamental points which I must now qualify. Those points are: (1) the here-and-now approach is an ahistoric one, and (2) there is a sharp distinction between here-and-now experience and here-and-now process illumination.

Strictly speaking, an ahistoric approach is an impossibility: every process comment refers to an act already belonging to the past. (Sartre once said, "Introspection is retrospection.") Not only does process commentary involve behavior that has just transpired but it frequently refers to cycles of behavior or repetitive acts that have occurred in the group over weeks or months. Thus, the past of the group, events in which the group members have participated, are a part of the here-and-now and an integral part of the data on which process commentary is based.

Often it is helpful to ask patients to review their past experiences in the group. If a patient feels that she is exploited every time she trusts someone or reveals herself, I often inquire about the times she has experienced that feeling in this group. Another patient, depending upon the relevant issues, may be encouraged to discuss such experiences as the times he has felt most close to others, or most angry, or most accepted, or most ignored. Other patients may, with profit, discuss patterns of behavior that develop over time that they observe in others or in themselves.

My qualification of the ahistoric approach goes even farther. As I shall discuss later in a separate section, no group can maintain a total here-and-now approach. There will be frequent excursions into personal history and current life situations. In fact, this discourse is so inevitable that one becomes curious at its omission. What is important, however, is the accent: the crucial task is not to uncover, to piece together, and to understand the past, but to use the past for the help it offers in understanding (and changing) the individual's mode of relating to the others in the present.

The distinction between here-and-now experience and process commentary is not sharp: there is much overlap. For example, low-inference commentary ("feedback") is both experience and commentary. When one member remarks that another refuses to look at her or that she is furious at another for continually deprecating her, she is at the same time commenting on process and involving herself in the affective here-and-now experience of the group. Process commentary, like nascent oxygen, exists for only a short duration; it rapidly becomes incorporated into the experiential flow of the group and becomes part of the data from which future process comments will flow. For example, in a group meeting of mental health trainees, one member began the session with an account of some extreme feelings of depression and depersonalization. The group avoided pursuing this man's dysphoria and instead offered him much practical advice. The leader commented on the process—on the fact that the group veered away from asking the member about his depression and depersonalization. The leader's intervention seemed useful: the group members became more emotionally engaged, and several discussed their fear of self-revelation. Soon afterward, however, a couple of counterdependent members objected to the leader's intervention; they felt that the leader was dissatisfied with their performance in the group, that he was criticizing them, and, in his usual subtle manner, was manipulating the group to fit in with his preconceived notions of the proper conduct of a meeting. Other members took issue: they commented that some members seemed compelled to challenge every move of the therapist. Thus, the leader's process comments became part of the experiential ebb and flow of the group, and the members' criticism of the leader, at first process commentary, also became experience, and itself subject to process commentary.

SUMMARY

The effective use of the here-and-now focus requires two steps: experience in here-and-now and process illumination. The combination of these two steps imbues an experiential group with compelling potency.

The therapist has different tasks in each step: First, to plunge the group into the here-and-now experience; second, to help the group observe and understand the process of what occurred in the here-and-now experience: that is, the implications that the interaction contains about the nature of the members' relationships to one another.

The first step becomes part of the group norm structure, and the group members ultimately assist the therapist in this chore.

The second step is more difficult. There are powerful injunctions against process commentary in everyday social intercourse. The therapist must overcome resistance, and the task of process commentary, to a great extent, remains the responsibility of the therapist and consists, as I shall discuss shortly, of a wide and complex range of behavior—from labeling single behavioral acts, to juxtaposing several acts, to combining acts over time into a pattern of behavior, to pointing out the undesirable consequences of a patient's behavioral patterns, to more complex inferential explanations or interpretations about the meaning and motivation of such behavior.

TECHNIQUES OF HERE-AND-NOW ACTIVATION

In this section I wish to describe (but not prescribe) some techniques: each therapist must develop techniques consonant with his or her style. Indeed, therapists have a more important task than mastering a technique: they must fully comprehend the strategy and theoretical foundations upon which all effective technique must rest.

I suggest that you "think here-and-now." When you do so long enough, you automatically steer the group into the here-and-now. Sometimes I feel like a shepherd herding a flock into an ever-tightening circle; I head off errant, historical, or "outside" statements like strays and guide them back into the circle. Whenever an issue is raised in the group, I think, "How can I relate this to the group's primary task? How can I make it come to life in the here-and-now?" I am relentless in this effort, and I begin it in the very first meeting of the group.

Consider a typical first meeting of a group. After a short awkward pause, the members generally introduce themselves and proceed to tell something about why they have sought therapy and, often with help from the therapist, may discuss how they are feeling that very day. I often intervene at some convenient point well into the meeting and remark to the effect that, "We've done a great deal here today so far. Each of you has shared a great deal about yourself, your pain, your reasons for seeking help. But I have a hunch that something else is also going on, and that is that you're each sizing one another up, each arriving at some impressions of the other, each wondering how you'll fit in with the others. I wonder now if we could spend some time discussing what each of us has come up with thus far." Now this is no subtle, artful, shaping statement: it is a heavy-handed explicit directive. Yet I find that most groups respond favorably to such clear guide lines.

The therapist moves the focus from outside to inside, from the abstract to the specific, from the generic to the personal. If a patient describes a hostile confrontation with spouse or roommate, the therapist may inquire, "If you were to be angry like that with anyone in the group, with whom would it be?" or, "With whom in the group can you foresee getting into the same type of struggle?" If a patient comments that one of his problems is that he lies, or that she stereotypes people, or that he manipulates groups, the therapist may inquire, "What is the main lie you've told in the group thus far?" or, "Can you describe the way you've stereotyped some of us?" or, "To what extent have you manipulated the group thus far?" If a patient complains of mysterious flashes of anger or suicidal compulsions, the therapist underscores the importance of that patient's signaling to the group the very moment they occur during the session so that the group can track down and relate these experiences to events in the session.

If a member describes her problem as being too passive, too easily influenced by others, the therapist may move her directly into the issue by asking who in the group could influence her the most and who the least? If a member comments that the group is too polite and too tactful, the therapist may ask, "Who are the leaders of the peace-and-tact movement in the group?" If a member is terrified of revealing himself and fears humiliation, the therapist may ask him to identify those in the group he imagines might be most likely to ridicule him.

In each of these instances, the therapist can deepen interaction by encouraging responses from the others. "How do you feel about the stereotype?"; "Can you imagine yourself ridiculing him?"; "Does this resonate with feelings that you are indeed influential, angry, too tactful?"; and so on. Even simple techniques of asking patients to speak directly to one another, to use second-person rather than third-person pronouns, and to look at one another are very useful.

Easier said than done! These suggestions are not always heeded. To some patients they are threatening indeed, and the therapist must here, as always, employ good timing and attempt to experience what the patient is experiencing. Search for methods that lessen the threat. Begin by focusing on positive interaction: "Toward whom in the group do you feel most warm?" "Who in the group is most like you?" or, "Obviously, there are some strong vibes, both positive and negative, going on between you and John. I wonder what you most envy about him? And what parts of him do you find most difficult to accept?

The subjunctive tense provides safety and distance and often is miraculously facilitative. I use it frequently when I encounter initial resistance. If, for example, a patient says, "I don't have any response or feelings at all about Mary today. I'm just feeling too numb and withdrawn," I often say, "If you were not numb or withdrawn today, what might you feel about Mary?" The patient generally answers readily: the "once-removed" position affords a refuge and encourages the patient to answer honestly and directly. Similarly the therapist might inquire, "If you were to be angry at someone in the group, at whom would it be?" or, "If you were to go on a date with Albert [another group member], what kind of experience might it be?"

The therapist must often teach patients how to request and offer feedback. One important principle is to avoid global questions and observations. Questions such as, "Am I boring?" or "Do you like me?" are not usually productive. A patient learns a great deal more by asking, "What do I do that causes you to tune out?", "When are you most and least attentive to me?" or, "What parts of me [or aspects of my behavior] do you like least and most?" In the same vein, feedback such as, "You're O.K.," or "a nice guy," is far less useful than, "I like you when you're willing to be honest with your feelings, like in the last week's meeting when you said you were attracted to Mary but feared she would scorn you. I like you least when you're impersonal and start analyzing the meaning of every word said to you, like you did early in the meeting today."

Resistance occurs in many forms; often it appears in the cunning guise of total equality. Especially in the early course of the group, patients often respond to your here-and-now urgings by claiming that they feel exactly the same toward all of the group members: that is, they say that they feel equally warm toward all the members, or no anger toward any, or equally influenced or threatened by all. Do not be misled. Such claims are never true. Guided by your sense of timing, you push the inquiry farther. Sooner or later you must help members to differentiate one from the other. Eventually they will disclose that they do have slight differences of feeling toward some of the members. These slight differences are important and are often the vestibule to full interactional participation. I explore the slight differences (no one ever said they had to be enormous); sometimes I suggest that the patient hold up a magnifying glass to these differences and describe what he or she then sees and feels.

• Often resistance is deeply ingrained, and considerable ingenuity is required. For example, one patient, Bob, resisted participation on a here-and-now level for months. Keep in mind that resistance is not usually conscious obstinacy but more often stems from sources outside of awareness. Sometimes the here–and–now task is so unfamiliar and uncomfortable to the patient that it is not unlike learning a new language; one has to attend with maximal concentration in order not to slip back into one's habitual remoteness. Bob's typical mode of relating to the group was to describe some pressing current life problem. Often the problem assumed crisis proportions which placed powerful restraints on the group. First, the members felt compelled to deal immediately with the precise problem Bob presented; and second, they had to tread cautiously because he explicitly informed them that he needed all his resources to cope with the crisis and could not afford to be shaken up by interpersonal confrontation. "Right now," he might say, "don't push me, I'm just barely hanging on." Efforts to alter this pattern were unsuccessful, and the group members felt blocked and discouraged in dealing with Bob. They cringed when he brought in problems to the meeting.

One day he opened the group with a typical gambit: after weeks of searching he had obtained a new job but was convinced that he was going to fail and be dismissed. The group dutifully, but warily, investigated the situation. The investigation met with many of the familiar, treacherous obstacles that block the path of work on "outside" problems. There seemed to be no objective evidence that Bob was failing at work. He seemed, if anything, to be trying too hard, working eighty hours a week. The evidence, Bob insisted, simply could not be appreciated by anyone not there at work with him: the glances of his supervisor, the subtle innuendos, the air of dissatisfaction toward him, the general ambience in the office, the failure to live up to his (self-imposed and unrealistic) sales goals. Moreover, Bob was a highly unreliable observer; he always downgraded himself and minimized his accomplishments and strengths.

The therapist moved the entire transaction into the here-and-now by asking, "Bob, what grade do you think you deserve for your work in the group, and what do each of the others get?" Bob, not unexpectedly, awarded himself a "D minus" and staked his claim for at least eight more years in the group. He awarded all the other members substantially superior grades. The therapist replied by awarding Bob a "B" for his work in the group and then went on to point out the reasons: Bob's commitment to the group, perfect attendance, willingness to help others, great efforts to work despite anxiety and often disabling depression.

Bob laughed it off; he treated the incident as a gag or a therapeutic ploy. But the therapist held firm and insisted that he was entirely serious. Bob then insisted the therapist was wrong and pointed out his failings in the group (one of which was, ironically, the avoidance of the here-and-now); however, Bob's disagreement with the therapist was incompatible with his long-held, frequently voiced, total confidence in the therapist. (Bob had often invalidated the feedback of other members in the group by claiming that he trusted no one's judgment except the therapist's.)

The intervention was enormously useful and transferred the process of Bob's evaluation of himself from a secret chamber lined with the distorting mirrors of his self-perception to the open vital arena of the group. No longer was it necessary that the members accept Bob's perception of his boss's glares and subtle innuendoes. The "boss" (the therapist) was there in the group. The transaction, in its entirety, was available to the group.

I never cease to be awed by the rich, subterranean lode of data that exists in every group and in every meeting. Beneath each sentiment expressed there are layers of invisible, unvoiced ones. How to tap these riches? Sometimes after a long silence in a meeting, I express this very thought: "There is so much information that could be valuable to us all today if only we could excavate it. I wonder if we could, each of us, tell the group about some thoughts that occurred to us in this silence which we thought of saying but didn't." The exercise is more effective, incidentally, if you start it yourself or participate. For example, "I've been feeling on edge in the silence, wanting to break it, not wanting to waste time, but on the other hand feeling irritated that it always has to be me doing this work for the group." Or, "I've been feeling torn between wanting to get back to the struggle between you and me, Mike. I feel uncomfortable with this much tension and anger, but I don't know yet how to help understand and resolve it."

When I feel there has been a particularly great deal unsaid in a meeting, I have often used, with success, a technique such as this: "It's now six o'clock and we still have half an hour left, but I wonder if you each would imagine that it's already six-thirty and that you're on your way home. What disappointments would you have about the meeting today?"

Many of the observations the therapist makes may be highly inferential. Objective accuracy is not the issue; as long as you persistently direct the group from the nonrelevant, from the "then-and-there" to the "here-and-now," you are operationally correct. If a group spends time in an unproductive meeting discussing dull, boring parties, and the therapist wonders aloud if the members are indirectly referring to the present group session, there is no way of ascertaining with any certainty whether they in fact are. "Correctness" in this instance must be defined relativistically and pragmatically. By shifting the group's attention from "then-and-there" to "here-and-now" material, the therapist performs a service to the group—a service that, consistently reinforced, will ultimately result in a cohesive, interactional atmosphere maximally conducive to therapy. Following this model, the effectiveness of an intervention should be gauged by its success in focusing the group upon itself.

According to this principle, a group that dwells at length on the subject of poor health, and on a person's sense of guilt over remaining in bed during times of sickness, might be asked: "Is the group *really* wondering about my [the therapist's] recent absence?" Or, a group suddenly preoccupied with death and the losses each member has incurred might be asked whether they are also concerned with the group's impending four-week summer vacation. One psychotherapy group in a prison which was asked to meet in a different room to permit observation by visiting psychiatrists began its session with a lengthy discussion of the proliferation of police computers which can instantaneously produce massive amounts of information about any individual in the country. The therapist made the useful interpretation that the group was dealing with the issue of being observed; he wondered if the members were angry and disappointed with him and suspected that he, like the computer, had no regard for their feelings.

Obviously, these interventions would be pointless if the group had already thoroughly worked through all the implications of the therapist's recent absence, the impending four-week summer break, or the therapist's act of permitting observation. The technical procedure is not unlike the sifting process in any traditional psychotherapy. Presented with voluminous data in considerable disarray, the therapist selects, reinforces, and interprets those aspects he deems most helpful to the patient at that particular time. Not all dreams and not all parts of a dream are attended to by the therapist; however, a dream theme that elucidates a particular issue on which the patient is currently working is vigorously pursued.

Implicit here is the assumption that the therapist knows the most propitious direction for the group at a specific moment. As we have seen, this is not a precise matter; what is most important is that the therapist has formulated broad principles of ultimately helpful directions for the group and its members—this is precisely where a grasp of the therapeutic factors is essential.

Often, when activating the group, the therapist performs two simultaneous acts: steers the group into the here-and-now and, at the same time, interrupts the content flow in the group. Not infrequently, members feel resentful or rejected by the interruption, and the therapist must attend to these feelings for they, too, are part of the here-and-now. This consideration often makes it difficult for the therapist to intervene. Early in our socialization process we learn not to interrupt, not to change the subject abruptly. Furthermore, there are times in the group when everyone seems keenly interested in the topic under discussion; even though the therapist is certain that the group is not "working," it is not easy to buck the group current. Social psychological small group research strongly documents the compelling force of group pressure. To take a stand opposite to the perceived consensus of the group requires considerable courage and conviction.

My experience is that the therapist faced with this type of dilemma can increase the patient's receptivity by expressing both sets of feelings to the group. For example, "Mary, I feel very uncomfortable as you talk. I'm having a couple of strong feelings. One is that you're into something that is very important and painful for you, and the other feeling is that Ben [the new member] has been trying hard to get into the group for the last few meetings and the group seems unwelcoming. This didn't happen when other new members entered the group. Why do you think it's happening now?" Or, "Warren, I had two reactions as you started talking. The first is that I'm delighted you feel comfortable enough now in the group to participate, but the other feeling is that it's going to be hard for the group to respond to what you're saying because it's so very abstract and far removed from you personally. I'd be so much more interested in what it's been like inside for you the past

weeks in the group. Even though you've been silent
tuned in to many issues."

There are, of course, many more activating procedu
15, I will describe some basic modifications in the group
procedure which facilitate here-and-now interaction in sl
cialty groups. But my goal in this chapter is not to offer a   ...dum
of techniques. Quite the contrary. I describe techniques only to illuminate the underlying principle of here-and-now activation. These techniques, or "group gimmicks," are servants not masters. To use them
injudiciously, to fill voids, to jazz up the group, to acquiesce to the
members' demands that the leader lead, is seductive but not constructive for the group.

In an encounter group research project, the activating techniques
("structured exercises") of sixteen different leaders were studied and
correlated with outcome.[3] There were two important relevant findings:
(1) the more structured exercises the leader used, the *more competent* did members (at the end of the thirty-hour group) deem the leader
to be; and (2) the more structured exercises used by the leader, the *less
positive were the results* (measured at a six-month follow-up.) In other
words, members desire the leader to lead and equate a large number
of structured exercises with competence. Yet too many structured exercises are counterproductive.

Over all, leader activity correlates with outcome in a curvilinear
fashion (too much or too little activity led to unsuccessful outcome). Too
little leader activity results in a floundering group. Too much activation
by a leader results in a dependent group: the group members look to
the leader to supply too much.

Remember that sheer acceleration of interaction is not the purpose
of these techniques. The therapist who moves too quickly—using gimmicks to make interactions, emotional expression, and self-disclosure
too easy—misses the whole point. Resistance, fear, guardedness, distrust—in short, everything that impedes the development of satisfying
interpersonal relations—must be permitted expression. The goal is to
create not a slick-functioning, streamlined social organization, but instead one that functions well enough and engenders sufficient trust for
the unfolding of each member's social microcosm. Working through the
resistances to change is the key to the production of change. Thus, the
therapist wants to go not *around* obstacles but *through* them. (As we
shall see in chapter 16, this is one key difference between the therapy
and the encounter group.)

Techniques of Process Illumination

As soon as you have successfully steered patients into a here-and-now interactional pattern, you must concern yourself with turning this interaction to therapeutic advantage. This task is complex and consists of several stages. Patients must first recognize what they are doing with other people (ranging from simple acts to complex patterns unfolding over a long time); they must then appreciate the impact of this behavior upon others and how it influences others' opinion of them and consequently upon their own self-regard; they must decide whether they are satisfied with their habitual interpersonal style; and, lastly, be helped to exercise the will to change. Even when you have helped the patient transform intent into decision and decision into action, your task is not complete. You must help the patient to solidify the change and to generalize it from the group setting into his or her larger life environment.

Each of these stages may be facilitated by some specific cognitive input by the therapist, and I shall describe each step in turn. First, however, I must discuss several prior and basic considerations: How does the therapist recognize process? How can the therapist help the members to assume a process orientation? How can the therapist increase the receptivity of the patient to his or her process commentary?

RECOGNITION OF PROCESS

Obviously before you can help patients understand process, you yourself must learn to recognize it. The experienced therapist does this naturally and effortlessly, observing the group proceedings from a perspective that permits a continuous view of the process underlying the content of the group discussion. This difference in perspective is the major difference in role between the patient and the therapist in the group.

• Thus in a group meeting, a patient, Pete, discloses much heavy, deeply personal material. The group is moved by his account and devotes much time to listening, to helping him elaborate more fully, and to offering him support. You as the therapist share in these activities but you entertain other thoughts as well. For example, you may wonder why, of all the members, is it invariably Pete who reveals first and most. Why does Pete so often put himself in the role of the group patient whom all the members must nurse? Why must he always display himself as vulnerable? Why *today?* After the conflict in the group last meeting, one might have expected Pete to be angry; instead, he "shows his throat." Is he avoiding giving expression to his rage? And so forth.

•   At the end of a session in another group, Jay, a young, rather fragile patient, had, amidst considerable emotional upheaval, revealed for the first time his preference for homosexual relationships. At the next meeting the group urged him to continue. He attempted to do so but, nearly asphyxiated with emotion, blocked and hesitated. Just then, with indecent alacrity, Vicky filled the gap, saying, "Well, if no one else is going to talk, I have a problem." Vicky, an aggressive forty-year-old cab-driver, who sought therapy because of social loneliness and bitterness, proceeded to discuss in endless detail a complex situation involving an unwelcome visiting aunt. For the experienced, process-oriented therapist, the phrase "I have a problem" is a *double entendre.* Far more trenchantly than her words, Vicky's behavior says, "I have a problem," and her problem is manifest in her insensitivity to Jay, who, after months of silence, had finally mustered the courage to speak.

It is not easy to tell the beginning therapist how to recognize process; the acquisition of this perspective is one of the major tasks in the education of a therapist. And it is an interminable task: throughout your career, you increase your ability to penetrate deeply into the substratum of group discourse. This greater vision increases the keenness of a therapist's interest in the meeting. Generally, beginning students who observe meetings find them far less meaningful, complex, and interesting than does the experienced therapist.

Certain guidelines, though, may facilitate the neophyte therapist's recognition of process. Note the simple nonverbal sense data available: Who chooses to sit where? Which members sit together? Who chooses to sit close to the therapist? Who far away? Who sits near the door? Who comes to the meeting on time? Who is habitually late? Who looks at whom when speaking? Do some members, while speaking to another member, look at the therapist? If so, then they are relating not to one another but instead to the therapist through their speech to the others. Who looks at his watch, who slouches in her seat? Who yawns? Do the members pull their chairs away from the center at the same time as they are verbally professing great interest in the group? Are coats kept on? When in a single meeting or in the sequence of meetings are they removed? How quickly do the group members enter the room? How do they leave it? What about cigarettes? Who smokes and when? In what manner? (Milton Berger describes a beautiful, self-possessed woman who smoked not in moments of tension but only when the tension had subsided sufficiently to allow her to light and hold the cigarette with aplomb.)[4] A near-infinite variety of postural shifts may betoken discomfort; foot flexion, for example, is a particularly common sign of anxiety. A change in dress or grooming not uncommonly indicates change in a patient or in the atmosphere of the entire group. An unctuous, dependent man may express his first flicker of resentment toward the leader by wearing to a group session an open-necked sport shirt rather than his usual shirt and tie. Indeed, it is common knowledge that nonverbal behavior frequently expresses feelings of which a person is yet unaware; the therapist, through observing and teaching the group to observe nonverbal behavior, may hasten the process of self-exploration.

Sometimes the process is clarified by attending not only to what is said but to what is omitted: the female patient who offers suggestions, advice, or feedback to the male patients but never to the other women in the group; the group that never confronts or questions the therapist; the topics (for example, the taboo trio, sex, money, death) that are never broached; the patient who is never attacked; or the one who is never supported—all these omissions are part of the transactional process of the group.

• In one group, for example, a member stated that she felt others disliked her. When asked, "Who?," she selected John, one of the other members. John immediately bristled, "Why me? Tell me one thing I've said to you that makes you pick me." The first member stated, "That's just exactly the point. You've never said *anything* to me. Not a question, not a greeting. I just don't exist for you." John, much later, when completing therapy, cited this incident as a particularly powerful and illuminating instruction.

Physiologists commonly study the function of a hormone by removing the endocrine gland that manufactures it and observing the changes in the hormone-deficient organism. Similarly, in group therapy, we may learn a great deal about the role of a particular member by observing the here-and-now process of the group when he or she is absent. For example, if the absent member is aggressive and competitive, the group may feel liberated; and other patients, who had felt threatened or restricted in the missing member's presence, may suddenly blossom into activity. If, on the other hand, the group has depended on the missing member to carry the burden of self-disclosure or to coax other members into speaking, then it will feel helpless and threatened when he or she is absent. Often this absence elucidates interpersonal feelings that previously were entirely out of the group members' awareness, and the therapist may, with profit, encourage the group to discuss these feelings toward the absent member both at that time and later in his or her presence.

Similarly, a rich supply of data about feelings toward the therapist often emerges in the leaderless or alternate meeting. One leader led a T-group of mental health professionals composed of one woman and twelve men. The woman, though she habitually took the chair closest to the door, felt reasonably comfortable in the group until the therapist was out of town and a leaderless meeting was scheduled. At that meeting the group discussed sexual feelings and experiences far more blatantly than ever before, and the woman had terrifying fantasies of the group locking the door and descending upon her for a "gang bang." She realized how the therapist's presence had offered her safety against fears of unrestrained sexual behavior by the other members and against the emergence of her own sexual fantasies. (She realized, too, the meaning of her occupying the seat nearest the door!)

Search in every possible way to understand the relationship messages in any communication. Look for incongruence between verbal and nonverbal behavior. Be especially curious when there is something arrhythmic about a transaction: when, for example, the intensity of a response seems disproportionate to the stimulus statement; or when a response seems to be off target or to make no sense. At these times look for several possibilities: for example, parataxic distortion (the responder is experiencing the sender unrealistically), or metacommunications (the responder is responding, accurately, not to the manifest content but to another level of communication), or displacement (the responder is reacting not to the current transaction but to feelings stemming from previous transactions).

Common Group Tensions

Remember that certain tensions are always present, to some degree, in every therapy group. Consider, for example, such tensions as the struggle for dominance, the antagonism between mutually supportive feelings and sibling rivalrous ones, between greed and selfless efforts to help the other, between the desire to immerse oneself in the comforting waters of the group and the fear of losing one's precious individuality, between the wish to get better and the wish to stay in the group, between the wish to help others and the fear of being left behind. Sometimes these tensions are quiescent for months until some event wakens them and they erupt into forceful expression.

The therapist must not forget these tensions; they are always there, always fueling the hidden motors of group interaction. The knowledge of these tensions often facilitates the therapist's recognition of process. Consider, for example, one of the most powerful sources of tension: the struggle for dominance. Earlier in this chapter, I described an intervention where the therapist, in an effort to steer a patient into the here-and-now, gave him a grade for his work in the group. While the intervention was effective for that particular patient, it had repercussions on the rest of the group. In the next meeting two patients asked the therapist to clarify some remark he had made to them at a previous meeting. The remarks had been so supportive in nature and so straight-forwardly phrased that the therapist was puzzled at the request for clarification. Deeper investigation revealed that the two patients—and later others, too—were requesting grades from the therapist.

• In another experiential group of mental health professionals at several levels of training, the leader was deeply impressed at the group skills of Stewart, one of the youngest, most inexperienced members. The leader expressed his fantasy that Stewart was a plant, that he could not possibly be just beginning his training since he conducted himself like a veteran with ten years' group experience. The comment evoked a flood of tensions; it was not easily forgotten by the group and, for months to come, was periodically revived and angrily discussed. With his comment, the therapist planted the kiss of death on Stewart's brow since thereafter the group systematically challenged and "deskilled" him. The therapist who makes a positive comment or evaluation of one member is likely to evoke feelings of sibling rivalry. As in each of these two examples, a comment involving comparative evaluation will almost certainly fan the embers of sibling rivalry into full conflagration.

The struggle for dominance fluctuates in intensity throughout the group. It is much in evidence at the beginning of the group as members jockey for position in the pecking order. Once the hierarchy is established, the issue may become quiescent, with periodic flare-ups: for example, when some member, as part of his or her therapeutic work, begins to grow in assertiveness and to challenge the established order.

When new members enter the group, especially aggressive members who do not "know their place," who do not respectfully search out and honor the rules of the group, you may be certain that the struggle for dominance will rise to the surface.

• For example, in one group a veteran member, Betty, was much threatened by the entrance of a new, aggressive woman, Rena. A few meetings later, when Betty discussed some important material concerning her inability to assert herself, Rena attempted to help by commenting that she, too, used to be like that, and then she presented various methods she had used to overcome it. Rena reassured Betty that if she continued to talk about it openly in the group she, too, would gain considerable confidence. Betty's response was silent fury of such magnitude that several meetings passed before she could discuss and work through her feelings. To the uninformed observer, Betty's response would appear puzzling; but in the light of Betty's seniority in the group and Rena's vigorous challenge to that seniority, her response was entirely predictable. She responded not to Rena's manifest offer of help but instead to Rena's metamessage: "I'm more advanced than you, more mature, more knowledgeable about the process of psychotherapy, and more powerful in this group despite your longer presence here."

• In another group, Bea, an assertive, articulate woman, had for months been the most active and influential member. A new member, Bob, was introduced who was at least equally assertive and articulate. In his first meeting, he described his life situation with such candor and clarity that the other members were impressed and touched. Bea's response, however, was: "Where did you get your est training?" (Not, note, "Did you ever have est training?" or, "You sound like you've had some experience in examining yourself.") The wording of Bea's comment clearly revealed the struggle for dominance, as she said implicitly: "I've found you out. Don't think you can fool me with that jargon. You've got a long way to go to catch up with me!"

Primary Task and Secondary Gratification

The concepts of primary task and secondary gratification, and the dynamic tension between the two, provide the therapist with a useful guide to the recognition of process (and, as I shall discuss later, a guide as well to the factors underlying a patient's resistance to process commentary).

First some definitions. The *primary task* of the patient is, quite simply, to achieve his or her original goals: relief of suffering, better relationships with others, or to live more productively and fully.

The task may be much more complicated. Sometimes one's view of the primary task changes considerably as one progresses in therapy. Sometimes the patient and the therapist have widely different views of the primary task. I have, for example, known patients who verbalize a goal of relief from pain (for example, from anxiety, depression, or insomnia) but have a deeper and more problematic goal of a different nature: for example, one patient wished that through therapy she would become so well that she would "out-mental health" others, become even more superior to her adversaries; another patient wished to learn how to manipulate others even more effectively. These goals may be unconscious or, even if conscious, well hidden from others. Also these goals are not part of the initial "contract" the patient makes with the therapist, and yet they exert a pervasive influence in the therapeutic work. In fact, much therapy may have to occur before some patients can formulate an appropriate primary task.

The patient, then, is generally aware of what he or she wishes to achieve in the therapy experience. By methods that I have discussed, the therapist, in pre-group preparations of patients and in the first group meetings, makes each patient aware of what he or she must do in the group to accomplish their individual primary tasks. And yet once the group begins, very peculiar things begin to happen; patients seem deliberately to sabotage their works or their primary task. Some clinical vignettes illustrate this paradox:

• A young and handsome woman patient enjoyed the attention of all three of the men in the group. She withheld the information from the group that she was engaged to be married, even though her sadomasochistic relationship with her fiancé was an enormous problem for her. After she was married, she misrepresented her husband to the group by portraying him as a passive ne'er-do-well rather than an accomplished mathematician. She feared that if the men in the group realized what a formidable competitor her husband was, they would be frightened away. The sham continued for several months.

• Cal, a young man in another group, behaved analogously. He was much interested in seducing the women of the group and shaped his behavior in an effort to appear suave and charming. He concealed his feelings of awkwardness, his desperate wish to be "cool," his fear of women, and his envy of some of the men in the group. He could never discuss his compulsive masturbation and occasional voyeurism. When another male member discussed his disdain for the women in the group, Cal (pleased at the withdrawal of competition) praised him for his honesty. When another member discussed, with much anxiety, his homosexual fantasies, Cal deliberately withheld the solace he might have offered by sharing his own, similar fantasies. He never dared to discuss the issues for which he entered therapy; nothing took precedence over being "cool."

• Another patient devoted all her energies to achieving an image of mental agility and profundity. She, often in subtle ways, continually took issue with the therapist. She scorned any help the therapist attempted to offer her, and took great offense when he attempted to interpret her behavior. When the therapist reflected that she made him feel he had nothing of value to offer her, she experienced her finest hour and, beaming, said that perhaps *he* ought to join a therapy group to work on *his* problems.

• Another member enjoyed an enviable position in the group because of his mistress, a beautiful actress, whose picture he delighted in passing around in the group. She was his showpiece, a living proof of his natural superiority. When one day she suddenly and peremptorily left him, he was too mortified to face the group and dropped out of therapy.

These examples have one common feature: each patient gave priority not to the primary task but to some *secondary gratification* arising in the group: a relationship with another member; an image a patient wished to project; a group role in which a patient was the most sexually desirous, the most influential, the most wise, the most superior.

The pathology of each of these patient's obstructed his or her pursuit of the primary goal. And yet is this not as it should be? Have we not often stressed that patients re-create their interpersonal worlds in the social microcosm of the group? To be sure! But in the incidents described here, the portrayal of pathology, on a basic level, opposed the work of therapy. Patients diverted their energies from therapy to the pursuit of some gratification in the group. If this here-and-now behavior were available for study—if the patients could, as it were, be pulled out of the group matrix to observe in a more dispassionate manner their actions—then the entire sequence would become part of the therapeutic work. But in all these instances the gratification took precedence over the work to be done. Patients concealed information, misrepresented themselves, rejected the therapist's help, and refused to give help to one another.

This is a familiar phenomenon in individual therapy. Long ago, Freud spoke of the patient whose desire to remain in therapy outweighed his or her desire to be cured. The individual therapist satisfies a patient's wish to be succored, to be heard, to be cradled. Yet there is a vast, quantitative difference in this respect between individual and group therapy. The individual therapy format is far more insular; the group situation offers an enormous range of gratifications. To the extent that the group is a social microcosm, it contains the possibilities of satisfying virtually any social need in an individual's life. Moreover, the gratification offered is often compelling; our social needs to be dominant, to be admired, to be loved, to be revered are powerful indeed.

Is the tension that exists between primary task and secondary gratification nothing more than a slightly different way of referring to the familiar concept of resistance and especially of "acting out"? In the sense that the pursuit of secondary gratification obstructs the therapeutic work, it may generically be labeled "resistance." Yet there is a shade of difference I wish to emphasize. Resistance ordinarily refers to pain avoidance. Freud's original view was that the very same psychic energies that are responsible for the repression of a noxious experience act to guard the gateway to the abode of the repressed material and to fend off any inquiry threatening to disturb that material and to unleash the original dysphoria. The definition has broadened since then, but retains the general connotation of "protection." Obviously, resistance in this sense is much in evidence in group therapy, on both an individual and, as I shall discuss, a group level. What I wish to emphasize is the abundant availability of secondary gratification in the therapy group. Often the therapeutic work in a group is derailed not because patients are too defensively anxious to work but because they find themselves unwilling to relinquish gratification.

Often, when the therapist is bewildered by the course of events in the therapy group, the distinction between primary task and secondary gratification is most useful. If you ask yourself, "Is the patient working on his or her primary task?" You have a firm base of departure. And when the substitution of secondary gratification for primary task is well entrenched and resists intervention, you have no more powerful technique than to remind the patient of the primary task—the original reasons that he or she sought therapy.

The same principle applies to the entire group as well. It can be said that the group has a primary task which consists of the development and exploration of all aspects of the relationship of each member to each of the others, to the therapist, and to the group as an aggregate. The therapist and, later, the group members can easily enough sense when the group is working, when it is involved in its primary task, and when it is avoiding that task. You may be unclear about what your group is doing, but you do know that it is not involved in either developing or exploring relationships between members. If you have been successful in helping the group to identify its task, then you must conclude that it is actively evading the task either because of some dysphoria associated with the task itself or because of some secondary gratification that is sufficiently satisfying to supplant the therapy work.

The Therapist's Feelings

All of these guides to the therapist's recognition and understanding of process have their usefulness. But the most important clues you have are your own feelings in the meeting, feelings that you come to trust after living through many previous similar incidents in group therapy. The experienced therapist learns to trust his or her feelings; they are as useful to a therapist as a microscope to a microbiologist. If you feel impatient, frustrated, bored, confused, discouraged—any of the entire panoply of feelings available to a human being—you learn to consider this as valuable data and put it to work, if appropriate.

You do not have to understand your feelings or arrange and deliver a neat interpretive corsage. The simple expression of feelings is often sufficient to help a patient proceed farther.

• One therapist, for example, experienced a forty-five-year-old woman in an unreal, puzzling manner because of her rapidly fluctuating method of presenting herself. He finally commented, "Sharon, I have several feelings about you that I'd like to share. As you talk, I often experience you as a competent mature woman, but sometimes I see you as a very young, almost pre-sexual child trying to cuddle, trying to be pleasing to everyone. I don't think I can go any farther with this now, but I wonder what chords this strikes in you." The observation struck deep chords in the patient and helped her to explore her conflicted sexual identity and her separation anxiety.

It is often very helpful to the group if you share feelings of being shut out by a patient. Such a comment rarely evokes defensiveness because it always implies that you wish to get closer to the patient. Consider the following example from a multiple-impact therapy session (a psychotherapy teaching format[5] in which one patient meets with several therapists, with procedural rules similar to those of group therapy):

• In her fourth session, Adele, a severely ill narcotics addict with a marked inability to interact directly with others (a problem the group had been exploring), began with an involved, detailed account of a family argument. With its endless procession of names of cousins, great aunts, and neighbors, the story, whatever else it meant, had the effect of excluding the therapists from her world during the hour.

Finally, one therapist commented that he felt frustrated and very much shut out by her. Adele then took a note out of her purse and read something that she said she had written to the group of therapists. It was a long, rather chilling allegory involving her swimming aimlessly in circles, with children nearby trying to swim with weights on their feet which adults had placed there to help them develop power. She shouted for help to passers-by on the shore, and they encouraged her to swim harder and to rest in a boat which, however, was full of holes and drew water. She knew that, although it was good to rest, she could never learn to swim in a boat.

The allegory was poignant and intriguing; but the therapists, when they recalled the group's primary task, expressed once again their feelings of exclusion and frustration. The reading of the allegory had been an entirely autistic affair which effectively kept them at a great distance. Adele then remarked that she had to tell the group that she was drowning. A therapist said that he sensed her feeling of drowning in the very first session and wondered why she had to tell them in this beautiful but devious fashion. In an unusual burst of directness, she replied that she wished to pique their interest in her by showing how sensitive and clever she was. Other therapists pointed out that this was unnecessary and that they had, in fact, often thought and talked about Adele between sessions. They felt that though her strategy was in part successful (they *were* impressed by the allegory), it also resulted in annoying and distancing them; it was after she had unveiled both the allegory and her need to impress them that their interest in her was greatest. Although literary devotees may shudder at this dismissal of her allegory as interpersonal deviousness, it proved, nonetheless, good medicine for Adele who had seen Xanadu too often in her beclouded course through an unpeopled world.

To express feelings in the therapeutic process, the therapist must have a reasonable degree of confidence in their appropriateness. The more you respond unrealistically to the patient (on the basis of countertransference or possibly because of pressing personal emotional problems), the less helpful—in fact, the more antitherapeutic—will you be in presenting these feelings as if they were the patient's problem rather than your own. You need to use the delicate instrument of your own feelings, and to do so frequently and spontaneously. But it is of the utmost importance that this instrument be as reliable and accurate as possible. It is for this reason that I believe every therapist should obtain personal psychotherapy. (More about this in chapter 17.)

HELPING PATIENTS ASSUME A PROCESS ORIENTATION

It has long been known that observations, viewpoints, and insights arrived at through one's own efforts are valued more highly than those that are thrust upon one by another person. The mature leader resists the temptation to make brilliant virtuoso interpretations, but searches instead for methods that will permit patients to achieve self-knowledge through their own efforts. As S. Foulkes and E. Anthony put it, "There are times when the therapist must sit on his wisdom, must tolerate defective knowledge and wait for the group to arrive at solutions."[6]

The task, then, is to influence members to assume and to value the process perspective. Many of the norm-setting activities of the leader described in chapter 5 serve this end. For example, the therapist emphasizes process by periodically tugging the members out of the here-and-now and inviting them to consider more dispassionately the meaning of recent transactions. Though techniques vary depending on a therapist's style, the intention of these interventions is to switch on a self-reflective beacon. The therapist may, for example, interrupt the group at an appropriate interval to comment, in effect, "We are about halfway through our time for today and I wonder how everyone feels about the meeting thus far?"

By no means do you have to understand the process to ask for members' analyses. You may simply say, "I'm not sure what's happening in the meeting but I do see some unusual things. For example, Bill has been very silent, Jack's moved his chair back three feet, Mary's been shooting glances at me for the past several minutes. What ideas do you all have about what's going on today?"

A process review of a "highly charged" meeting is often necessary. It is important for the therapist to demonstrate that intense emotional expression provides material for significant learning. Sometimes you can divide such a meeting into two parts: the experiential and the analysis of that experience. At other times you may analyze at the following meeting; you can ask about the feelings that members took home with them after the previous meeting, or simply solicit further thoughts they have since had about what occurred there.

Obviously, you teach through modeling your own process orientation. There is nothing to lose and much to gain by your sharing whenever possible your perspective on the group. Sometimes you may do this in an effort to clarify the meeting: "Here are some of the things I've seen going on today. . . ." Sometimes you may wish to use a convenient device such as summarizing the meeting to a late arrival, whether co-therapist or member.

In chapter 14, I describe a technique that systematically shares the therapist's process observations with the patients. Following each meeting of an outpatient therapy group (which meets once weekly) I write a detailed summary of the meeting, including a full description of my spoken and unspoken process observations; I mail these summaries to the patients prior to the next meeting. In this approach the therapist, despite considerable personal and professional disclosure, does not seem to lose any effectiveness. Quite the contrary: in several ways the therapy work is facilitated. One particular effect is the increase in the patients' perceptivity to the process of the group.

HELPING PATIENTS ACCEPT PROCESS-ILLUMINATING COMMENTS

F. Scott Fitzgerald once wrote, "I was impelled to think. God, was it difficult! The moving about of great secret trunks." Throughout therapy, patients are asked to think, to shift internal arrangements, to examine the consequences of their behavior. It is hard work, and it is often unpleasant, frightening work. It is not enough simply to provide patients with information or explanations; you must also facilitate the assimilation of the new information. There are strategies to help patients in this work.

Be concerned with the framing of interpretive remarks. No comments, not even the most brilliant ones, can be of value if delivery is not accepted, if the patient rejects the package unopened and uninspected. The relationship, the style of delivery, and the timing are thus as essential as the content of the message.

Patients are always more receptive to observations that are framed in a supportive fashion. Rarely does a patient reject an observation that she distances or shuts out others, or that he is too unselfish and never asks for anything for himself, or that she is stingy with her feelings, or that he conceals so much of what he has to offer. All of the observations contain a supportive message: that is, the observer wishes to be closer, wishes to help, wishes to know one more intimately.

Beware of appellations that are categorizing or limiting: they are counterproductive; they threaten; they raise defenses. Patients reject global accusations—for example, dependency, narcissism, exploitation, arrogance. And with good reason, since a person is always more than any one or any combination of labels. It is far more acceptable (and far more true) to speak of traits or parts of an individual. For example, "I often can sense you very much wanting to be close to others, offering help as you did last week to Gina, but there are other times, like today, when I see you as aloof, almost scornful of the others. What do you know about this part of you?"

Often in the midst of intense group conflict, members hurl important truths at one another. Under these conditions, one cannot acknowledge the truth: it would be aiding the aggressor, committing treason against oneself. To make the conflict-spawned truths available for consumption, the therapist must appreciate and neutralize the defensiveness of the combatants. You may, for example, appeal to a higher power (the patient's desire for self-knowledge), or increase receptivity by limiting the scope of the accusation. For example, "Farrell, I see you now closed up, threatened, and fending off everything that Jamie is saying. You've been very adroit in pointing out the weaknesses of her arguments; but what happens is that you (and Jamie, too) end up getting nothing for yourself. I wonder if you could take a different tack for a while and ask yourself this" (and, later: "Jamie, I'd like to ask you to do the same"): "is there *anything* in what Jamie is saying that is true for you? What parts seem to strike an inner chord? Could you forget for a moment the things that are *not* true and stay with those that *are* true?"

These are certain repetitive patterns that, if clearly labeled, can be useful in the recognition and acceptance of process commentary. Eric Berne described, in extremely accessible and often humorous terms, several such repetitive patterns or "games."[7] These are often helpful for a start but, like any labeling techniques, become restrictive if depended upon so heavily that leaders attempt to fit all human interaction into a few procrustean beds.

Sometimes patients, in an unusually open moment, make a statement which may at some future time provide the therapist with great leverage. The thrifty therapist underscores these comments in the group and stores them for use at that time. For example, one patient who was both proud of and troubled by his ability to manipulate the group with his social charm, pleaded at one meeting, "Listen, when you see me smile like this I'm really hurting inside. Don't let me keep getting away with it." Another patient, who tyrannized the group with her tears, announced one day, "When I cry like this, I'm angry. I'm not going to fall apart, so stop comforting me, stop treating me like a child." These moments of truth can be of great value if recalled, in a constructive, supportive manner, at a time when the patient is closed and defensive.

Often it is useful to enlist the patient more actively in establishing contracts. For example, if a patient has worked hard in a session on some important trait, I might say something like: "Jane, you worked hard today and were very open to our feedback about the way you mother others and the way you use that mothering to avoid facing your own needs and pain. How did it feel? Did we push you too hard?" If the patient agrees that the work was helpful (as the patient almost always does), then you can nail down a future contract by stating, "Then is it all right for us to keep pressing you, to give you feedback whenever we note you doing this in future meetings?"

Process Commentary: A Theoretical Overview

It is not easy to discuss, in a systematic way, the actual practice of process illumination. How can one propose crisp, basic guidelines for a procedure of such complexity and range, such delicate timing, so many linguistic nuances? I am tempted to beg the question by claiming that herein lies the art of psychotherapy: it will come as you gain experience; you cannot, in a systematic way, come to it. To a degree, I believe this to be so; yet I also believe that it is possible to blaze crude trails, to provide the clinician with general principles that will accelerate education without limiting the scope of artistry.

The approach I shall take in this section closely parallels the approach I used in the beginning of this book to clarify the basic therapeutic factors in group therapy. At that time I asked the questions: How does group therapy help patients? In the group therapeutic process, what is "core" and what is "front"? This approach leads to the delineation of several basic therapeutic factors and does not, I believe, constrain the therapist in any way in the choice of methods to implement them.

In this section I shall proceed in a similar fashion. Here the issue is not, "How does group therapy help?," but "How does the act of process illumination lead to change?" The issue is complex and requires considerable attention, but the length of this discussion should not suggest that the interpretive function of the therapist take precedence over other tasks.

First, let me proceed to view in a dispassionate manner the entire range of interpretive comments. I shall ask of each the simplistic but basic question, "How does this interpretation, this process-illuminating comment, help a patient to change?" Such an approach, consistently followed, reveals a set of basic operational patterns.

I shall begin by studying a series of process comments that a therapist made to a male patient over several months of group therapy:

1. You are interrupting me.
2. Your voice is tight, and your fists are clenched.
3. Whenever you talk to me, you take issue with me.
4. When you do that, I feel threatened, and sometimes frightened.
5. I think you feel very competitive with me and are trying to devalue me.

6. I've noticed that you've done the same thing with all the men in the group. Even when they try to approach you helpfully, you strike out at them. Consequently, they see you as hostile and threatening.

7. In the three meetings when there were no women present in the group, you were more approachable.

8. I think you're so concerned about your sexual attractiveness to women that you view men only as competitors. You deprive yourself of the opportunity of ever getting close to a man.

9. Even though you always seem to spar with me, there seems to be another side to it. You often stay after the group to have a word with me; you frequently look at me in the group. And there's that dream you described three weeks ago about the two of us fighting and then falling to the ground in an embrace. I think you very much want to be close to me, but somehow you've got closeness and homosexuality entangled and you keep pushing me away.

10. You are lonely here and feel unwanted and uncared for. That rekindles so many of your bad feelings of unworthiness.

11. What's happened in the group now is that you've distanced yourself, estranged yourself from all the men here. Are you satisfied with that? (Remember that one of your major goals when you started the group was to find out why you've not had any close men friends and to do something about that.)

Note, first of all, that the comments form a progression from sense data commentary—observations of single acts—to a description of feelings evoked by an act, to observations about several acts over a period of time, to the juxtaposition of different acts, to speculations about the patient's intentions and motivations, to comments about the unfortunate repercussions of his behavior, to the inclusion of more inferential data (dreams, subtle gestures), to calling attention to the similarity between his behavioral patterns in the here-and-now and in his outside social world.

As the sequence progresses, the comments become more inferential. They begin with sense-data observations and gradually shift to complex generalizations based on sequences of behavior, interpersonal patterns, fantasy, and dream material. As the comments become more complex and more inferential, their author becomes more removed from the other person—in short, more a therapist process-commentator. Members often make some of the earlier statements to one another but, for reasons I have already presented, rarely make the ones at the end of the sequence.

There is, incidentally, an exceptionally sharp barrier between comments 4 and 5. The first four statements issue from the experience of the commentator. They are the commentator's observations and feelings; the patient can devalue or ignore them but cannot deny them, disagree with them, or take them away from the commentator. The fifth statement ("I think you feel very competitive with me and are trying to devalue me") is much more likely to evoke defensiveness and to close down constructive interactional flow. This genre of comment is intrusive; it is a guess about the other's intention and motivation and is often rejected unless an important trusting, supportive relationship has been previously established. If members in a young group make many type-5 comments to one another, they are not likely to develop a constructive therapeutic climate.

But how does this series (or any series of process comments) help the patient change? In making these process comments, the group therapist initiates change by escorting the patient through the following sequence:

1. *Here is what your behavior is like.* Through feedback and later through self-observation, members learn to see themselves as seen by others.
2. *Here is how your behavior makes others feel.* Members learn about the impact of their behavior on the feelings of other members.
3. *Here is how your behavior influences the opinions others have of you.* Members learn that, as a result of their behavior, others value them, dislike them, find them unpleasant, respect them, avoid them, and so on.
4. *Here is how your behavior influences your opinion of yourself.* Building on the information gathered in the first three steps, patients formulate self-evaluations; they make judgments about their self-worth and their lovability. (Recall Sullivan's aphorism that the self-concept is largely constructed from reflected self-appraisals.)

Once this sequence has been developed and is fully understood by the patient, once patients have a deep understanding that their behavior is not in their own best interests, that relationships to others and to themselves are a result of their own actions, then they have come to a crucial point in therapy: they have entered the antechamber of change. The therapist is now in a position to pose a question that initiates the real crunch of therapy. The question, presented in a number of ways by the therapist but rarely in direct form, is: "Are you satisfied with the world you have created? This is what you do to others, to others' opinion of you, and to your opinion of yourself—*are you satisfied with your actions?*"

When the inevitable negative answer arrives, the therapist embarks on a many-layered effort to transform a sense of personal dissatisfaction into a decision to change and then into the act of change. In one way or another, the therapist's interpretive remarks are designed to encourage the act of change. Only a few psychotherapy theoreticians (for example, Otto Rank, Rollo May, Silvano Arieti, Leslie Farber and Allen Wheelis, and Irvin Yalom[8]) include the concept of *will* in their formulations; yet it is, I believe, implicit in most interpretive systems. I discuss the role of will in psychotherapy in great detail elsewhere, and I refer interested readers to that publication.[9] For now, broad brushstrokes are sufficient.

The intrapsychic agency that initiates an act, that transforms intention and decision into action, is will. Will is the primary "responsible mover" within the individual. Although modern analytic metapsychology has chosen to emphasize the "irresponsible movers"[10] of our behavior (that is, unconscious motivations and drives), it is difficult to do without the idea of will in our understanding of change. We cannot bypass it under the assumption that it is too nebulous and too elusive, and, consequently, consign it to the black box of the mental apparatus, to which the therapist has no access.

Knowingly or unknowingly, every therapist assumes that each patient possesses the capacity to change through willful choice. The therapist, using a variety of strategies and tactics, attempts to escort the patient to a crossroads where he or she can choose, choose willfully in the best interests of his or her own integrity. The therapist's task is not to create will or to infuse it into the patient. That, of course, you cannot do. What you can do is to help remove encumbrances from the bound or stifled will of the patient.

The concept of will provides a useful construct for understanding the procedure of process illumination. The interpretive remarks of the therapist can all be viewed in terms of how they bear on the patient's will. The most common and simplistic therapeutic approach is exhortative: "Your behavior is, as you yourself now know, counter to your best interests. You are not satisfied. This is not what you want for yourself. Damn it, change!" The expectation that the patient will change is simply an extension of the moral philosophical belief that if one knows the good (that is, what is, in the deepest sense, in one's best interest), one will act accordingly. In the words of Aquinas: "Man, insofar as he acts willfully, acts according to some imagined good."[11] And, indeed, for some individuals this knowledge and this exhortation is sufficient to produce therapeutic change. To be sure, this often happens with individuals who change as a result of some short-term experiential group. However, patients with significant and well-entrenched psychopathology generally need much more than exhortation.

The therapist, through interpretative comments, proceeds to exercise one of several other options that help the patient to disencumber his or her will. Your goal is to guide the patient to a point where he or she accepts one, several, or all of the following basic premises:

1. "Only I can change the world I have created for myself."
2. "There is no danger in change."
3. "To attain what I really want, I must change."
4. "I can change, I am potent."

Each of these premises, if fully accepted by a patient, can be a powerful stimulant to willful action. Each exerts its influence in a different way. Though I shall discuss each in turn, I do not wish to imply a sequential pattern. Each, depending on the need of the patient and the style of the therapist, may be effective independently of the others.

"Only I can change the world I have created for myself."

Behind the simple group therapy sequence I have described (seeing one's own behavior and appreciating its impact on others and on oneself) there is a mighty overarching concept, one whose shadow touches every part of the therapeutic process. That concept is *responsibility;* and though it is rarely discussed explicitly, it is nonetheless woven into the fabric of most psychotherapeutic systems. *Responsibility* has many meanings—legal, religious, ethical. I shall use it in the sense that a person is "responsible for" by being "the basis of," the "cause," the "author" of something.

One of the most fascinating aspects of group therapy is that everyone is born again, born together in the group. Each member starts off on an equal footing. In the view of the others (and, if the therapist does a good job, in the view of oneself), each gradually scoops out and shapes a life space in the group. *Each member, in the deepest sense of the concept, is "responsible" for this space and for the sequence of events that will occur to him or her in the group.* The patient, having truly come to appreciate this responsibility, must then accept, too, that there is no hope for change unless he or she changes. Others cannot bring change; nor can change bring itself. One is responsible for one's past and present life in the group (as well as in the outside world) and similarly and totally responsible for one's future.

Thus, the therapist helps the patient to understand that the interpersonal world is arranged in a generally predictable and orderly fashion, that it is not that the patient *cannot* change but that he or she *will* not change, that the patient bears the responsibility for the creation of his or her world, and therefore, the responsibility for its transmutation.

"There is no danger in change."

These efforts may not be enough. The therapist may tug at the therapeutic cord and learn that the patient, even after being thus enlightened, still makes no significant therapeutic movement. In this case you attempt to apply additional therapeutic leverage. You help the patient face the paradox of continuing to act contrary to his or her basic interests. In a number of ways you pose the question, "How come? Why do you continue to defeat yourself?"

A common method of explaining "How come?" is to assume that there are obstacles to the patient's exercising willful choice—obstacles that prevent the patient from seriously considering altering his or her behavior. The presence of the obstacle is generally inferred; the therapist makes an "as if" assumption: "You behave *as if* you feel there were some considerable danger that would befall you if you were to change. You fear to act otherwise lest some calamity befall you." The therapist assists the patient to clarify the nature of the imagined danger, and then proceeds, in several ways, to detoxify, to disconfirm the reality of this danger.

The patient's reason may be enlisted as an ally; the process of identifying and naming the fantasied danger may, in itself, enable one to understand how far one's fears are removed from reality. Another approach is to encourage the patient, in carefully calibrated doses, to commit the dreaded act in the group. The fantasied calamity does not, of course, ensue, and the dread is gradually extinguished. For example, a patient may avoid any aggressive behavior because at a deep level he fears that he has a dammed-up reservoir of homicidal fury and must be constantly vigilant lest he unleash it and eventually face retribution from others. You help the patient express aggression in small doses in the group: his pique at being interrupted, his irritation at members who are habitually late, his anger at the therapist for charging him money, and so on. Gradually, the patient is helped to relate openly to the other members and to demythologize himself as an alien and homicidal being. Although the language and the view of human nature is different, this is precisely the same approach to change used in systematic desensitization—a major technique of behavior therapy.

"To attain what I really want, I must change."

Another explanatory approach used by many therapists to deal with a patient who persists in behaving counter to his or her best interests is to consider the payoffs of that patient's present behavior. Though the behavior of the patient sabotages many of his or her mature needs and goals, at the same time it satisfies another set of needs and goals. In other words, the patient has conflicting motivations that cannot be simultaneously satisfied. For example, a male patient may wish to be able to establish mature heterosexual relationships; but at another, often unconscious, level, he may wish to be nurtured, to be cradled endlessly, to assuage castration anxiety by a maternal identification or, to use an existential vocabulary, to be sheltered from the terrifying freedom of adulthood.

Obviously, the patient cannot satisfy both sets of wishes: he cannot establish an adult heterosexual relationship with a woman if he also says (and much more loudly), "Take care of me, protect me, nurse me, let me be a part of you."

The therapist attempts to clarify this paradox for the patient. "Your behavior makes sense if we assume that you wish to satisfy the deeper, more primitive, more infantile need." You try to help the patient to understand the nature of his conflicting desires, to choose between them, to relinquish those that cannot be fulfilled except at enormous cost to his integrity and autonomy. Once the patient realizes what he "really" wants (as an adult), and that his behavior is designed to fulfill opposing growth-retarding needs, he gradually concludes: "To attain what I really want, I must change."

"I can change, I am potent."

Perhaps the major therapeutic approach to the question, How come? ("How come you act in ways counter to your best interests?") is to offer explanation, to attribute meaning to the patient's behavior. The therapist says, in effect, "You behave in certain fashions *because* . . ." and the "because" clause generally involves motivational factors outside of the patient's awareness. It is true that the previous two options I have discussed also proffer explanation; but—and I shall clarify this shortly—the purpose of the explanation (the nature of the leverage exerted on will) is quite different in each of these approaches.

What type of explanation does the therapist offer the patient? And which explanations are correct, and which incorrect? Which "deep"? Which "superficial"? It is at this juncture that the great metapsychological controversies arise, since the nature of the therapist's explanation is a function of the ideological school to which he or she belongs. I think we can sidestep the ideological struggle by keeping a fixed gaze on the *function* of the interpretation, on the relationship between explanation and the final product—change. After all, our goal is change. Self-knowledge, derepression, analysis of transference, and self-actualization are all worthwhile enlightened pursuits, all probably related to change, preludes to change, companions and cousins to change; and yet they are not synonymous with change.

Explanation provides a system by which we can order the events in our lives into some coherent and predictable pattern. To name something, to place it into a logical (or paralogical) causal sequence, is to experience it as being under our control. No longer is our behavior or our internal experience frightening, inchoate, out of control; instead, we behave (or have a particular inner experience) *because*. . . . The "because" offers us mastery (or a *sense* of mastery which, phenomenologically, is tantamount to mastery). It offers us freedom and effectance. As we move from a position of being motivated by unknown forces to a position of identifying and controlling these forces, we move from a passive, reactive posture to an active, acting, changing posture.

If we accept this basic premise—that a major function of explanation in psychotherapy is to provide the patient with a sense of personal mastery—it follows that the value of an explanation should be measured by this criterion. To the extent that it offers a sense of potency, a causal explanation is valid, correct, or "true." Such a definition of *truth* is completely relativistic and pragmatic. It argues that no explanatory system has hegemony or exclusive rights; that no system is the correct, fundamental one or the "deeper" (and, therefore, better) one.

Therapists may offer the patient any of several interpretations to clarify the same issue; each may be made from a different frame of reference, and each may be "true." Freudian, interpersonal object relations, existential, transactional analytic, Jungian, Gestalt, transpersonal, cognitive, behavioral explanations—all of these may be true simultaneously. None, despite vehement claims to the contrary, have sole rights to the truth. After all, they are all based on imaginary, "as if" structures. They all say, "You are behaving (or feeling) *as if* such and such a thing were true." The superego, the id, the ego; the archetypes; the masculine protest; the internalized objects; the grandiose self and the omnipotent object; the parent, child, and adult ego state—*none of these really exists.* They are all fictions, all psychological constructs created for semantic convenience. They justify their existence only by virtue of their explanatory powers.

Do we therefore abandon our attempts to make precise, thoughtful interpretations? Not at all. Only, we recognize the purpose and function of the interpretation. Some may be superior to others, not because they are "deeper" but because they have more explanatory power, are more credible, provide more mastery, and are therefore more useful.

Obviously, interpretations must be tailored to the recipient; in general, they are more effective if they make sense, if they are logically consistent with sound supporting arguments, if they are bolstered by empirical observation, if they are consonant with a patient's frame of reference, if they "feel" right, if they somehow "click" with the internal experience of the patient, and if they can be generalized and applied to many analogous situations in the life of the patient. Higher-order interpretations generally offer a novel explanation to the patient for some large pattern of behavior (as opposed to a single trait or act). The novelty of the therapist's explanation stems from his or her unusual frame of reference, which permits an original synthesis of data; indeed, often the data is material that has been generally overlooked by the patient or is out of his or her awareness.

If pushed, to what extent am I willing to defend this relativistic thesis? When I present this position to students, they respond with such questions as: Does that mean that an astrological explanation is also valid in psychotherapy? These questions make me uneasy, but I have to respond affirmatively. If an astrological or shamanistic or magical explanation enhances a sense of mastery and leads to inner, personal change, then it is a valid explanation. There is much evidence from cross-cultural psychiatric research to support this position; the explanation must be consistent with the values and with the frame of reference of the human community in which the patient dwells. In most primitive cultures it is often *only* the magical or the religious explanation that is acceptable, and hence valid and effective.

An interpretation, even the most elegant one, has no benefit if the patient does not hear it. You should take pains to review some of your evidence with the patient and present the explanation clearly. (If you cannot, it is likely that the explanation is rickety or that you yourself do not understand it; the reason is not, as has been claimed, that the therapist is speaking directly to the patient's unconscious.)

Do not always expect the patient to accept an interpretation. Sometimes the patient hears the same interpretation many times until one day it seems to click. Why does it "click" that one day? Perhaps the patient may have come across some corroborating data from new events in the environment or from the surfacing in fantasy or dreams of some previously unconscious material. Sometimes a patient will accept from another member an interpretation that he or she would not accept from the therapist. (Patients are clearly capable of making interpretations as useful as those of the therapists; and members are receptive to these interpretations, *provided the other member has accepted* *the patient role and does not offer interpretations to acquire prestige, power, or a favored position with the leader.)**

The interpretation will not click until the patient's relationship to the therapist is just right. For example, a patient who feels threatened and competitive with the therapist is unlikely to be helped by any interpretation (except one that clarifies the transference). Even the most elegant, thoughtful interpretation will fail because the patient may feel defeated or humiliated by the proof of the therapist's perceptivity. An interpretation becomes maximally effective only when it is delivered in a context of acceptance and trust.

It is not possible to discuss in more detail the types of effective interpretations, as I should have to describe the vast number of explanatory schools. Three venerable concepts are, however, so deeply associated with interpretation that they deserve special treatment here. These concepts are the use of the past, mass group interpretations, and transference. I shall turn now to the past and to mass group interpretations. So many interpretative systems involve transference (indeed, traditional analytic theory decrees that *only* the transference interpretation can be effective) that I shall devote chapter 7 entirely to the issue of transference and transparency.

The Use of the Past

Too often, explanation is confused with "originology" (the study of origins). I have discussed already that an explanatory system may effectively postulate a "cause" of behavior from any of a large number of perspectives. Still, many therapists continue to believe that to find the "real," the "deepest" causes of behavior, it is necessary to refer to the past. This position was staunchly defended by Freud, a committed psychosocial archaeologist. To the very end of his life he relinquished neither his search for the primordial (that is, the earliest) explanation nor his tenacious insistence that successful therapy hinges on the excavation of the earliest layers of life's memories.

The powerful and unconscious factors that influence human behavior are by no means limited to the past. As I shall discuss, the future is also a significant determinant of behavior. In addition to past and future,

*Educators have long been aware that the most effective teacher is often a near peer, an individual who is close enough to the student to be accepted and who, by identifying with the student's mental processes, is hence able to present material in a timely, accessible fashion.

unconscious field forces in the immediate present incessantly influence our feelings and actions.

The past may affect our behavior through pathways fully described by traditional Freudian analytic theory and by learning theorists (strange bedfellows). However, the "not yet," the future, is a no less powerful determinant of behavior, and the concept of future determinism is fully defensible. We have at all times within us a sense of purpose, an idealized self, a series of goals for which we strive, a death toward which we veer. These factors, both conscious and unconscious, all arch into the future and profoundly influence our behavior. Certainly the knowledge of our isolation, our destiny, and our ultimate death deeply influences our conduct and our inner experience. Though we generally keep them out of awareness, the terrifying contingencies of our existence play upon us without end. We either strive to dismiss them by enveloping ourselves in life's many diversions, or we attempt to vanquish death by faith in an afterlife or by striving for symbolic immortality in the form of children, material monuments, and creative expression.

The Galilean concept of causality which stresses current field forces has considerable explanatory potency for human behavior. As we hurtle through space, not only is our behavioral trajectory influenced by the nature and direction of the original push, and the nature of the goal that beckons us, but it is also influenced by all the current field forces operating upon it. Thus, explanation ensues from the exploration of the concentric rings of conscious and unconscious current motivations which envelop our patients. To cite only one example, patients may have a need to attack, which covers a layer of dependency wishes that they do not express lest they be rejected. Note that we need not ask how they got to be so dependent. The past need not be a part of the explanation of the need to attack; in fact, the future (a person's anticipation of rejection) plays a more central role in the interpretation.

A clinical example of interpretation based on this current field-force model occurred in a group where two patients, Stephanie and Louise, expressed strong sexual feelings toward the male therapist of the group. (Both women, incidentally, had histories—indeed, chief complaints—of masochistic sexual gratification.) One meeting they discussed the explicit content of their sexual fantasies involving him. Stephanie fantasized her husband being killed; herself having a psychotic breakdown; the therapist hospitalizing her and personally nurturing her, rocking her, and caring for all her bodily needs. Louise had a different set of fantasies. She wondered if the therapist was well cared for at home. She imagined frequently that something happened to his wife and that she could care for him by cleaning his house and cooking his meals.

The shared "sexual" attraction (which, as the fantasies indicate, was not genital-sexual) had for Stephanie and Louise a very different "explanation." The therapist pointed out to Stephanie that she, throughout the course of the group, had suffered frequent physical illness or severe psychological relapses. He wondered whether, at a deep level, she felt as though she could get his love and that of the other members only by a form of self-immolation. However, it never worked. She never obtained the love she wanted; more often than not, she discouraged and frustrated others. Even more important was the fact that as long as she behaved in ways that caused her so much shame, she could not love herself. He emphasized that it was crucial for her to change the pattern since it defeated her in her therapy: she was afraid to get better since she felt that to do so would entail an inevitable loss of love and nurturance.

In his comments to Louise, the therapist juxtaposed several aspects of her behavior: her self-derogation, her refusal to assume her rights, her inability to get men interested in her. Her fantasy of taking care of the therapist explicated her motivations: if she could be self-sacrificing enough, if she could put the therapist deeply into her debt, then she should, in reciprocal fashion, receive the love she sought. However, Louise's search for love always failed. Her eternal ingratiation, her dread of self-assertion, her continued self-devaluation succeeded only in making her appear dull and spiritless to those whose regard she most desired. Louise, like Stephanie, whirled about in a vicious circle of her own creation: the more she failed to obtain love, the more frantically she repeated the same self-destructive pattern—the only course of behavior she knew or dared to enact.

These interpretations offered two explanations for a similar behavioral pattern: "sexual" infatuation for the therapist. Two different dynamic pathways to masochism were sketched. In each, the therapist assembled several aspects of their behavior in the group as well as fantasy material and suggested that, if certain assumptions were made (for example, that Stephanie acted as though she could obtain the therapist's love only by offering herself as severely damaged; that Louise acted as though she could obtain his love only by so serving him as to place him in her debt), then the rest of the behavior "made sense." Both interpretations were potent and had a significant impact upon future behavior. Yet neither broached the question, "How did you get to be that way? What happened in your earlier life to create such a pattern?"

Both dealt instead with currently existing concentric patterns: the desire for love, the conviction that it could be obtained only in certain ways, the sacrifice of autonomy, the resulting shame, the ensuing increased need for a sign of love, and so on.

One formidable problem with explanations based on the distant past is that they contain within them the seeds of therapeutic despair. A formidable paradox: if we are fully determined by the past, whence comes the ability to change? As is evident in such later works as *Analysis Terminable and Interminable,* Freud's uncompromising deterministic view of man led him to, but never through, this Gordian knot.

The past, moreover, no more determines the present and the future than it is determined by them. The "real" past exists for each of us only as we constitute it in the present against the horizon of the future. Jerome Frank reminds us that patients, even in prolonged therapy, recall only a minute fraction of their past experience and may selectively recall and synthesize the past so as to achieve consistency with their present view of themselves.[12] (Erving Goffman suggested the term *apologia* for this reconstruction of the past.[13]) In the same way that one (as a result of therapy) alters one's self-image, one may reconstitute the past. One may, for example, recall long-forgotten positive experiences with parents; one may humanize them and, rather than experiencing them solipsistically (as figures who existed by virtue of their service to oneself), one may begin to understand them as harried, well-intentioned individuals struggling with the same overwhelming facts of the human condition that one faces oneself. Once one reconstitutes the past, a new past can further influence one's self-appraisal; however, it is the *reconstitution,* not simply the *excavation,* of the past that is crucial.

If explanations are not to be sought from an "originological" perspective, and if the most potent focus of the group is the ahistoric here-and-now, does the past therefore play no role at all in the group therapeutic process? Not at all! The past is a frequent visitor to the group and an even more frequent visitor to the inner private world of each of the members during the course of therapy. Not infrequently, for example, the past plays an important role in the development of group cohesiveness by increasing intermember understanding and acceptance.

The past is often invaluable in conflict resolution. Consider, for example, two members locked in a seemingly irreconcilable struggle, each of whom finds many aspects of the other repugnant. Often a full understanding of the developmental route whereby each arrived at his or her particular viewpoint can rehumanize the struggle. A man with a regal air of hauteur and condescension may suddenly seem understandable, even winsome, when we learn of his immigrant parents and his desperate struggle to transcend the degradation of a slum childhood. Individuals are benefited through being fully known by others in the group and being fully accepted; knowing another's process of becoming is a rich and often indispensable adjunct to knowing the person.

An ahistoric "here-and-now" interactional focus is never fully attainable. Discussions of future anticipation, both feared and desired, and of past and current experiences are an inextricable part of human discourse. Often the *omission* of the past, or of one's current outside life, is important group material. It is worth noting that a certain patient often speaks of his father but never of his mother, or that he never mentions his children to the group and in fact has little integration of his role as husband or parent, or that he never tells the group of changes in his relationships to other people. Each of these omissions sheds light upon the current experiential world of the patient. What is important is the accent; the past is the servant and not the master. It is important in that it explicates the current reality of the patient who is in the process of unfolding in relation to the other group members. As C. Rycroft states:

It makes better sense to say that the analyst makes excursions into historical research in order to understand something which is interfering with his present communication with the patient (in the same way that a translator might turn to history to elucidate an obscure text) than to say that he makes contact with the patient in order to gain access to biographical data.[14]

To employ the past in this manner involves an anamnestic technique differing from that often employed in individual therapy. Rather than a systematic, careful historical survey, the therapist periodically attempts a sector analysis to explore the development of some particular interpersonal stance. Consequently, many other aspects of a patient's past remain undiscussed. It is not uncommon, for example, for group therapists to conclude a course of successful therapy with a patient and yet be unfamiliar with such significant aspects of the patient's early life as school history, physical illnesses, occupation of parents, or geographical moves.

The explicit mention of the past in the therapy group does not accurately reflect the consideration of the past which occurs within each patient during therapy. The intensive focus on the relationship between members does not, of course, have as its goal the formation of enduring relationships between them but is, instead, training, a dress rehearsal for the work that must be done with the truly important individuals in a patient's life. At the end of therapy, patients commonly report significant additudinal improvements in relationships that have rarely been explicitly discussed in the group; many of these involve family members with whom one has had a relationship stretching far back into the past. So the past, more often implicitly than explicitly, plays a role in the working-through process, and the therapist should be aware of this silent important homework. You should not use the group meeting for this function, though, because to do so would sacrifice the therapeutic potency of the here-and-now interactional focus.

Mass Group Process Commentary

A specific type of process explanation remains to be discussed. Some leaders choose to focus primarily or entirely on mass group phenomena. These leaders refer, in their statements, to "the group" or "we" or "all of us"; they attempt to clarify the relationship between the "group" as an entity and its primary task (the investigation of intermember—and I include the leader here—relationships), or between the "group" and one of its members, a subgroup, the leader, or some shared concern. For example, return for a moment to the "parenthood is degrading" incident described on pages 138–40. In that incident the therapist had many process commentary options, some of which were mass group explanations. He might, for example, have raised the issue of whether the "group" needed a scapegoat and whether, with Kate gone, Burt filled the role; or whether the "group" was actively avoiding an important issue—that is, their guilty pleasure and fears about Kate's departure.

Throughout this text I interweave comments related to mass group phenomena: for example, the tasks of the therapist in the construction of a social system, norm setting, the role of the deviant, scapegoating, emotional contagion, role suction, subgroup formation, group cohesiveness, group pressure, the regressive dependency fostered by group membership, the response of the group toward termination, toward the addition of new members, toward the absence of the leader, and so on. There is no question, then, of the importance of mass group phenomena. All group leaders would agree that there are forces inherent in a group that significantly influence behavior; individuals behave differently in a group than they do in dyads (a factor that, as I discussed in chapter 8, makes group selection difficult). There is wide agreement that an individual's behavior cannot be fully understood without an appreciation of his or her environmental press.

What leaders do not agree about, however, is the application of this knowledge in the group therapy process. Some leaders choose to focus heavily on mass group phenomena. In fact, some leaders—for example, the Tavistock school, which I shall discuss shortly, insist that every statement of the leader consist of (or contain) a mass group interpretation; whereas other leaders rarely comment on mass group phenomena.

RATIONALE OF MASS GROUP PROCESS COMMENTARY

I shall begin by clarifying my position. The therapist uses mass group phenomena continuously in the course of therapy: many of the major therapeutic factors, such as cohesiveness, relate to mass group properties. I assist a group to develop cohesiveness in a variety of ways, beginning with the selection and preparation of patients. I may, for example, reinforce self-disclosure, encourage members to bring in group dreams, clarify how the group goals are confluent with the individual member's goals, or encourage the expression of positive as well as negative inter-member affect. However, it does not follow that the leader need make mass group comments. I would maintain that only a small percentage of the therapist's interventions need be on that level. In fact, as I shall argue, a role in which the leader focuses exclusively on mass group phenomena is restrictive and severely limits the therapist's effectiveness.

There are, however, times when mass group process commentary is needed. When? Let me suggest a simplifying principle: *The purpose of a mass group interpretation is to remove some obstacle that has arisen to obstruct the progress of the entire group.* The two common types of obstacle are anxiety-laden issues and antitherapeutic group norms.

Anxiety-Laden Issues
Often some issue arises that is so threatening that the group, on either a conscious or an unconscious level, refuses to confront the problem and takes some evasive action. This evasion takes many forms, all of which are commonly referred to as "group flight." Here is a clinical example of flight from an anxiety-laden issue:

• Six members were present at the sixty-fifth group meeting; one member, John, was absent. For the first time and without previous mention, one of the members, Mary, brought her dog to the meeting. The group members, usually animated and active, were unusually subdued and nonproductive. Their speech was barely audible, and throughout the meeting they discussed safe topics on a level of impersonality appropriate to any large social gathering. Much of the content centered on study habits (three of the members were graduate students), on examinations, and on teachers (especially their failings and untrustworthiness). Moreover, the senior member of the group discussed former members who had long since departed from the group —the "good old days" phenomenon. The dog (a wretched, restless creature who spent most of the group session noisily licking his genitals) was never mentioned. Finally, the therapist, thinking he was speaking for the group, brought up the issue of Mary's bringing the dog to the meeting. Much to the therapist's surprise, Mary—a highly unpopular, narcissistic member—was unanimously defended; everyone denied that the dog was in any way distracting and left the therapist as a lonely protester.

The therapist considered the entire meeting as a flight meeting and accordingly made appropriate mass group interpretations which I will discuss. But first, what is the evidence that such a meeting is "flight"? And flight from what? We must consider the age of the group; in a young group meeting, let us say, for the third time, such a session may be a manifestation not of resistance but of the group members' uncertainty about their primary task and of their groping to establish procedural norms. However, this group had already met for fourteen months; furthermore, the previous meetings had been strikingly different in character.

We are persuasively convinced of the presence of flight when we examine the preceding group meeting. At this meeting, John, the member absent from the meeting under consideration, had been twenty minutes late and happened to walk down the corridor at the precise moment when the door of the adjoining observation room was opened. John heard the voices of the other group members and saw a room full of observers viewing the group; moreover, the observers at that moment happened to be laughing at some private joke. John, like all the group members, had been told that the group was being observed by students, nevertheless this shocking and irreverent confirmation stunned him. When John, in the last moments of the meeting, was finally able to discuss it with the other members, they were equally stunned. John, as we have seen, missed the next session.

This event was a catastrophe of major proportions for the group—for that matter, it would be for any group. It raised serious questions in the minds of the members about the therapeutic situation. Was the therapist to be trusted? Was he, like his colleagues in the observation room, inwardly laughing at them? Was anything he said genuine? Was the group, once perceived as a human situation, in fact a sterile, contrived, laboratory specimen being studied dispassionately by a therapist who probably felt closer allegiance to "them" (the others, the observers) than to the group? Despite—or, rather, because of—the magnitude of these painful group issues, the group declined to confront the matter. Instead, it engaged in flight behavior, which now begins to be understandable. Exposed to an outside threat, the group members banded tightly together for protection; they spoke softly about safe topics so as to avoid sharing anything with the outside menace (the observers and, through association, the therapist). The therapist was unsupported when he asked about the obviously distracting behavior of the dog; the "good old days" was a reference to and yearning for bygone times when the group was pure and verdant and the therapist could be trusted. The discussion of examinations and untrustworthy teachers was also a thinly veiled expression of attitudes toward the therapist.

The precise nature and timing of the intervention is largely a matter of individual style. Some therapists, myself included, tend to intervene when they sense the presence of group flight even though they do not clearly understand its source. I may, for example, comment that I feel puzzled or uneasy about the meeting and inquire whether "there is something the group is not talking about today," or whether "the group is avoiding something"; or I might ask about the "hidden agenda." I may increase the power of my inquiry by citing the evidence—for example, the whispering, the sudden shift toward neutral topics and a noninteractive mode of communication, my experience of being left out or of being deserted by the others in the dog issue. Furthermore, I might add that the group is strangely avoiding all discussion both of the previous meeting and of John's absence today.

In this clinical example, I would not be satisfied merely with getting the group back on the track to a discussion of more meaningful material. The issues being avoided were too crucial to the group's existence to be left submerged. This consideration was particularly relevant in this group whose members had insufficiently explored their relationship to me. Therefore, I repeatedly turned the group's attention back onto the main issue (the members' trust or confidence in me) and tried not to be misled by substitute behavior—for example, the group's offering for discussion another theme, perhaps even a somewhat charged one. My task was not simply to circumvent the resistance, to redirect the group to work areas, but to plunge the members into the source of the resistance—not *around,* but *through,* anxiety.

Another clue to the presence and strength of resistance is the group's response to your resistance-piercing commentary. If your comments, even when repeated, fall on deaf ears, if you feel ignored by the group, if you find it extraordinarily difficult to influence the group, then you recognize both the involvement of the "group," rather than of a few members, and the considerable underlying resistance.

Another common way in which the group flight manifests itself is through intellectualization. For example, after a meeting in which two members disclosed their homosexuality, a group launched into a discussion of prejudice which lasted for two sessions. Prejudicial feelings in the abstract about Jews, blacks, Asian-Americans, and gays were discussed. Avoided, however, were a swarm of deeply personal feelings aroused by the two homosexual patients. The members avoided their scorn, their fears of their own latent homosexual feelings, their anger toward the therapists for having chosen these two when, as one woman member stated later, "the group so badly needed men." The group may also avoid work by more literal flight—by absence or by tardiness. Whatever the form, however, the result is the same: in the language of the group dynamicist, locomotion toward the attainment of group goals is impeded, and the group is no longer engaged in its primary task.

Not uncommonly, the issue precipitating the resistance is discussed symbolically. Uneasiness about observers may be discussed metaphorically by group members who launch into a long conversation about other types of confidentiality violation: for example, public posting of grades for a school course, or family members opening one another's mail. Hidden anger provoked by the therapist's absence may prompt discussions of parental feelings or death or illness. Generally, the therapist may learn something of what is being resisted by pondering "Why is this particular [non-work] topic being discussed, and *why now?*"

Antitherapeutic Group Norms

Another type of group obstacle warranting a mass group interpretation occurs when antitherapeutic group norms are elaborated by the group. For example, a group may, as I discussed earlier, establish a "take turns" format in which an entire meeting is devoted, sequentially, to each member of the group. Such a format is undesirable since it discourages free interaction; furthermore, members are often forced into premature self-disclosure and, as their "turn" approaches, may experience extreme anxiety or even decide to terminate therapy. Or, a group may establish a pattern of devoting the entire session to the first issue raised in that session with strong invisible sanctions against changing the subject. Or, there may be a "Can you top this?" format in which the members engage in a spiraling orgy of self-disclosure, or a tightly knit, closed pattern that excludes outlying members and does not welcome new ones.

To be effective in such instances, the therapist's interpretations about the mass group phenomena should clearly describe the process, specifically citing the deleterious effects on the members or on the group at large and emphasizing that there may be alternatives to these normative patterns.

Frequently a group, during its development, bypasses certain important phases or never incorporates certain norms into its culture. For example, a group may develop without ever going through a period of examining its views about, or without ever confronting or attacking, the therapist. Or a group may develop without a whisper of intermember dissension, without status bids or struggles for control; it may meet for a year or more with no hint of real intimacy or closeness arising among the members. Such a collaborative avoidance is a result of the group members, both consciously and unconsciously, constructing norms dictating this avoidance. If you sense that the group is providing a one-sided or incomplete experience for the members, you may then comment on the missing aspect of group life in that particular group. (Such an intervention assumes, of course, that there are regularly recurring, predictable phases of small group development with which you are familiar—a topic I shall discuss in chapter 11.

THE CONCEPT OF THE "GROUP"

The general principle I have just described—that the purpose of a mass group interpretation is to remove some obstacle to the progress of the entire group—is deceptively simple; from both a theoretical and a practical standpoint, the matter is far more complex.

Gradually over the years, the myth of the "group" has been elaborated and has generated considerable confusion in the field. As psychoanalysts entered the field of group therapy, they brought with them time-honored concepts and techniques of their discipline.

They attempted to apply traditional psychoanalytic techniques, with some modifications, to group therapy; however, they considered the "group" as an autonomous organism and regarded the "group," and not the individual, as the patient. They formulated vague concepts like *group ego* and *group superego* and replaced free association by an individual patient with "group association."[15] As one group analyst put it: "The group tends to speak and react to a common theme as if it were a living entity, expressing itself in different ways through various mouths. All contributions are variations on this single theme, even though the groups are not consciously aware of that theme and do not know what they are really talking about."[16]

Now, obviously, the concept of the group as a system with characteristic properties is valuable; what has happened, however, is that many workers have tended to anthropomorphize the group. Just as we have instilled life into a stock market that "attempts to fight off a selling wave" or "desperately guards the 1200 Dow Jones level," so, too, have we conceptually breathed life into the group. It is not, I feel, fatuous to point out that the group is not a living entity; it is but an abstraction created for our semantic and conceptual convenience. When it becomes so metapsychologized that it promotes not clarity but obfuscation, then it no longer serves its original function.

As an example of the conceptual pitfalls involved, consider the process of diagnosing the state of the group. How do we know what is the dominant group culture, the common group tension, or the group mind? How many of the group members must be involved before we conclude it is the "group" speaking? Some group analysts—for example, W. Bion and H. Ezriel—make the dubious assumption that silence by a group member signifies collusion or agreement with the individuals "speaking for the group."[17] The result is a "group mind" or "group culture" interpretation made on the basis of a small percentage of the membership.

THE TIMING OF GROUP INTERVENTIONS

For pedagogical reasons, interpersonal phenomena and mass group phenomena have been discussed as though they were quite distinct; in practice, of course, the two often overlap, and the therapist is faced with the question of when to emphasize the interpersonal aspects of the transaction and when to emphasize the mass group aspects. This matter of clinical judgment cannot be neatly prescribed; as in any therapeutic endeavor, judgment develops from experience (particular supervised experience) and from intuition. As Melanie Klein stated, "It is a most precious quality in an analyst to be able at any moment to pick out the point of urgency."[18]

The point of urgency is far more elusive in group therapy than in individual treatment. As a general rule, however, an issue critical to the existence or functioning of the entire group always takes precedence over narrower interpersonal issues. As an illustration let me return to the group that engaged in whispering, discussion of neutral topics, and other forms of group flight during the meeting after a member had inadvertently discovered the indiscreet group observers (see page 188). In the meeting under consideration, Mary (who had been absent at the previous meeting) brought her dog. Under normal circumstances this act would clearly have become an important group issue: Mary had neither consulted with nor informed the therapist or other members of her plans to bring a dog to the group; she was, because of her great narcissism, an unpopular member, and her act was representative of her insensitivity to others. However, in the meeting under consideration, there was a far more urgent issue—one threatening the entire group; and the dog was discussed not from the aspect of facilitating Mary's interpersonal learning but as he was used by the group in its flight. Only later, after the obstacle to the group's progress had been worked through and removed, did the members return to a meaningful consideration of their feelings about Mary bringing the dog.

TOTAL GROUP INTERVENTIONS: OTHER VIEWS

In past decades, there was much debate around the issue of mass group commentary. Many group leaders took a very different position from mine. Rather than view mass group interventions as a mode of removing obstacles to the work of the group, they considered commentary on mass group process as the chief, or even the sole, procedural task of the therapist. Wilfred Bion, a British Kleinian analyst, was one of the key theorists and developed a mode of group therapy, commonly referred to as "Tavistock group therapy," which was used by many group therapists both in Britain and the United States during the 1960s and 1970s.[19] It was always my belief that, for reasons I shall mention shortly, this group approach was not only ineffective but often countertherapeutic.

Accordingly, in previous editions of this book, I devoted considerable space to a description and a critique of this approach to therapy. That debate seems to have ended. No longer (not even at the Tavistock Clinic) is the classical Tavistock method used as a therapy approach. (Some group dynamists find Tavistock techniques to be a useful mode of teaching group dynamics and often offer experimental workshops for students.) Therefore I shall abbreviate my descriptions of this approach and refer interested readers to primary sources.[20]

Wilfred Bion and the Tavistock Approach

Bion studied his groups through holistic spectacles. Searching for total group currents, he noted that at times the group appeared to be pursuing its primary task* in a rational, effective fashion. Bion called this group culture the "work group" culture. At other times he noted that the group no longer seemed to be pursuing its primary task but, instead, appeared to be dominated by certain massive emotional states which resulted in behavior incompatible with the primary task. He described three types of basic, recurring emotional state (a "constellation of discrete feelings that permeate all the group's interactions")[21]: (1) aggressiveness, hostility, and fear; (2) optimism and hopeful anticipation; (3) helplessness or awe.

From these primary observations, Bion postulated that in each of these emotional states the group was acting "as if" the members shared some common belief from which their affect stemmed.[22] For example, while in an optimistic or hopefully anticipatory state, the group acts "as if" its aim is to preserve itself by finding strength or a new leader from its peer membership. When it is in a helpless or awed state, it acts "as if" its aim is to obtain support, nurturance, strength from something outside the group—generally the designated leader. When it is in an aggressive or fearful state, it acts "as if" its aim is to avoid something by fighting or running away from it. Bion termed each of these three emotional states "basic assumption cultures" and thus spoke of three types of basic assumption group: basic assumption pairing, basic assumption dependency, and basic assumption flight-fight, respectively. Thus, at any given time a group may be described as either a work group, or as one of the three basic assumption groups, or in some transitional phase.

Bion's focus on the individual group member centered on that member's relationship to the group culture. The concept of *valency* was

---

*Bion considered the primary task of the therapy group to be an exploration of its own intragroup tensions.

developed to describe an individual's attraction to a particular group culture. This attraction, analogous to tropism in plants,[23] is a force that leads a member into being the chief spokesman or a participant or a major rebel in one of the basic assumption cultures.

One other important aspect of Bion's view of groups is that it is *leader-centered.* All three basic assumption states are oriented around the issue of leadership. Each type of group searches for a leader—one who will meet its needs: the basic assumption dependency group attempts in various ways to coax or coerce the professional leader to guide them; the flight-fight group searches for a member who will lead them in this direction; the pairing group optimistically pairs and waits, hopeful that a leader will "emerge from the offspring of the pair."[24]

Bion's goal in group therapy was to help patients achieve the ability to become effective members of work groups. Thus, his interpretations were always mass group ones; he repeatedly confronted the group with its basic assumption behavior, especially insofar as that behavior related to the therapist. By confronting the group repeatedly in this manner, Bion attempted to reinstate the work group culture. He hoped that patients, as they became aware of the nature and unrealizability of their demands, would gradually learn more realistic and adaptive methods of group functioning.

Bion described three specific types of conflict that complicate group function, and suggested that it is the task of the therapist and the work group to expose, clarify, and work through these conflicts: (1) a desire on the part of the individual for "a sense of vitality by total submergence in the group," which exists alongside a desire for "a sense of individual independence by total repudiation of the group"; (2) the conflict between the group and the patient whose desires are often at cross-purposes to the needs of the group; and (3) the conflict between the problem-oriented work group and the basic assumption group.

My objection to the Tavistock approach has always been based upon the limited role of the group leader. Bion prescribed a role that was entirely limited to interpretation—and impersonal mass group interpretation at that. The leader remained impersonal: he or she did not interact with the group members and did not engage in many of the other functions of the leader I have described in this book—such functions as modeling, norm setting, activating the here-and-now, and support. Outcome research in psychotherapy presents convincing evidence against a limited, distant, therapist role: a positive, accepting, warm patient-therapist relationship is essential to good therapeutic outcome.[25] An outcome study by D. Malan indicated that patients treated in Tavistock groups had extremely poor outcome, experienced their group therapy as a depriving and frustrating experience, and resented the impersonal, cold, aloof stance of their group therapist.[26] Other researchers have demonstrated that therapists who limit their observations to mass group comments are ineffectual; interventions made to the group as a whole are far less likely to instigate self or interpersonal interaction than are interventions made to an individual member or a dyad.[27]

Whitaker and Lieberman

D. S. Whitaker and M. Lieberman have described a very different approach to mass group process. They state their position in a series of propositions.[28]

Proposition 1: Successive individual behaviors are linked associatively and refer to a common underlying concern about the here-and-now situation.

The comments and activities of a group therapy session are not diverse; they all hang together in relationship to some underlying issue. Seemingly unrelated acts gain coherence if one assumes that there is some concern which is shared by the members of the group.

Proposition 2: The sequence of diverse events which occur in a group can be conceptualized as a common, covert conflict (the group focal conflict) which consists of an impulse or wish (the disturbing motive) opposed by an associated fear (the reactive motive). Both aspects of the group focal conflict refer to the current setting.

For example, the members of a group may share a common wish to be singled out by the therapist for special attention (the disturbing motive), and yet they fear that such a wish will result in disapproval from the therapist and from other patients (reactive motive). The interaction between the wish and the fear is the group focal conflict.

Proposition 3: When confronted with a group focal conflict, the patients direct efforts toward establishing a solution which will reduce anxiety by alleviating the reactive fears and, at the same time, satisfy to the maximum possible degree the disturbing impulse.

In the group just described the members may arrive at the solution of searching for similarities among themselves; it is as if each were saying, "We are all alike, no one is asking for special favors." This solution, though it temporarily relieves tension, is by no means productive of growth; instead, the disturbing wish (to be unique and be singled out by the therapist for special gratification) is merely suppressed in the service of comfort. Other solutions, however, may be more enabling of group and personal growth.

Proposition 4: Successful solutions have two properties. First, they are shared; the behavior of all members is consistent with or bound by the solution. Second, successful solutions reduce reactive fears; individuals experience greater anxiety prior to the establishment of a successful solution, less anxiety after the solution is established.

Proposition 5: Solutions may be restrictive or enabling in character. A restrictive solution is directed primarily to alleviating fears and does so at the expense of satisfying or expressing the disturbing motive. An enabling solution is directed toward alleviating fears and, at the same time, allows for some satisfaction or expression of the disturbing motive.

For example, the disturbing motive in one group was the wish to express angry destructive feelings toward the therapist. The reactive motive (fear) was that the therapist would punish or abandon the group members. The group solution (an enabling solution) was to band together to express anger toward the therapist. Following one meeting the members discussed the matter and found strength in an implicit agreement that each would express his or her anger toward the therapist.

Keep in mind that the specific group focal conflict is not within the conscious awareness of the group members who are most involved, and the solution is not deliberately planned but is a vector, a course of action which "clicks" with the unconscious wishes and fears of each member. Should the solution be clearly unsatisfactory to one of the members, a new group conflict is created which culminates in a modified group solution. In this instance, the reactive fear was alleviated by the mutual support of the group members, and the disturbing wish was therefore expressed. Such a solution will, over the long term, be enabling for the patients since only by gradual exposure and expression of their disturbing wishes can the necessary reality testing occur.

In their therapeutic approach, Whitaker and Lieberman are most concerned with the nature of the group solution. Therapeutic intervention is required when a group solution appears that is restrictive to the group and to the members. Furthermore, an interpretation that elucidates the total group configuration is only one of a number of mechanisms that may be employed to influence the group. These researchers suggest, for example, that the therapist may, with efficacy, deal with a restrictive solution by modeling for the patients a different form of behavior. Thus, the role of the therapist is flexible: the therapist may ask questions, report on his or her personal reactions, focus on an individual's idiosyncratic mode of operating within the group, or—as we have seen—focus on total group process.

Whitaker and Lieberman do not lose sight of the fact that their tripartite (disturbing motive, reactive motive, and solution) system is but an abstraction rather than an entity in the animistic sense. Its purpose is to clarify the meaning and origin of behavior patterns that are restrictive for the group. Thus, in their views about total group phenomena and in their application of this information to the therapy process, Whitaker and Lieberman's approach, despite a semantic difference, overlaps significantly with the approach I have discussed earlier in this chapter.

To summarize, the problem of the orientation of the mass group therapist is one more of omission than of commission. While I do not quarrel with the importance of mass group phenomena in the behavior and experience of the members, I strenuously disagree with a restriction of the therapist's role. Interpretation, as I have indicated, does play an important role in therapy, but it is only one of many ingredients in successful therapy. Mass group phenomena obviously occur in small groups and may impede the work of the group. At these times, you as the group therapist, require a conceptual framework that enables you to identify and clarify the phenomena. Bion, Lieberman and Whittaker, and other therapists such as Foulkes[29] and Ezriel,[30] whom I have not discussed, have supplied enabling frames of reference and vocabulary. By employing an appropriate mass group explanation, you experience a personal sense of conceptual mastery; your personal confusion and anxiety diminish and, at this point, the process of resolution begins. You identify the process in appropriate language to the members and then proceed to pursue the group work, whether it be to explore the inner meaning of each member's involvement in the mass group process or to continue the interactional exploration that the mass group process has blocked.

7

THE THERAPIST:
TRANSFERENCE
AND TRANSPARENCY

Having discussed the mechanisms of therapeutic change in group therapy, the tasks of the therapist, and the techniques by which the therapist accomplishes these tasks, I shall in this chapter turn from what the therapist must *do* in the group to how the therapist must *be*. Do you, as therapist, play a role? To what degree are you free to be yourself? How "honest" can you be? How much transparency can you permit yourself?

Any discussion of therapist "freedom" does well to begin with transference, which can be either an effective therapeutic tool or a set of shackles which encumbers your every movement. In his first and extraordinarily prescient essay on psychotherapy (the final chapter of *Studies on Hysteria* [1895]), Freud noted several possible impediments to the formation of a good working relationship between patient and therapist.[1] Most of these could be resolved easily, but one stemmed from deeper sources and resisted efforts to banish it from the therapeutic work. Freud labeled this impediment "transference," since it consisted of attitudes toward the therapist that he believed had been "transferred" from earlier attitudes toward important figures in the patient's life. These feelings toward the therapist were "false connections," new editions of old impulses.

Only a few years passed before Freud realized that transference was far more than an impediment to therapy; if used properly, it could be the therapist's most effective tool.[2] What better way to help the patient recapture the past than to allow him or her to re-experience and re-enact ancient feelings toward parents through the current relationship to the therapist? Furthermore, the conflicted relationship with the therapist, the transference neurosis, was amenable to reality testing; the therapist could treat it and, in so doing, could simultaneously treat the infantile conflict. Considerable evolution in psychoanalytic technique has occurred over the last half-century, but, until recently, certain basic principles regarding the role of transference in psychoanalytic therapy have endured with relatively little change:

1. Analysis of transference is the major therapeutic task of the therapist.
2. Since the development (and, then, the resolution) of transference is crucial, it is important that you facilitate its development by concealing your real self so that the patient can encloak you in feelings and attitudes, much as one might dress a mannequin after one's own fancy (the rationale, of course, behind the traditional "blank screen" role of the analyst).
3. The most important type of interpretation the therapist can make is one which clarifies some aspect of transference (James Strachey referred to the transference interpretation as the "mutative interpretation."[3]).

In the past two decades, however, many analysts have perceptively shifted position as they have recognized the importance of other factors in the therapeutic process. For example, in 1973, a lead article in the *American Journal of Psychiatry* by a prominent analyst stated: "Psychoanalysts have begun, in general, to feel more free to enter into active communicative exchanges with patients instead of remaining bound to the incognito 'neutral mirror' model of relative silence and impassivity." He continued by pointing out that therapy is a learning process wherein patients acquire new models of thinking, feeling, and behavior:

Moreover, these new models are not always achieved cognitively and consciously; as often as not they are acquired subtly, as a result of overt or covert suggestion, unconscious identification with the therapist, corrective emotional experiences in the interaction with him, and a kind of operant conditioning via implicit or explicit expressions of his approval or disapproval. In this process, the nature and quality of the patient-therapist interaction, the real personalities of both patient and doctor, and the degree of faith, hope, trust, and motivation that the patient brings to the therapeutic situation are of paramount importance in enabling the new learning to take place successfully.[4]

Few would quarrel with the importance of the development, appreciation, and resolution of transference in individual dynamically oriented therapy.* At issue, however, is the priority of the transference work relative to other therapeutic factors in the therapeutic process. The problem is substantial since the tasks are not complementary but are, to an extent, mutually exclusive: the therapist cannot focus sheerly upon transference and at the same time hope to utilize the many other potential therapeutic factors.

These problems, troublesome to the individual therapist, constitute an issue of great urgency to the group therapist who—as we have seen in these many pages—having a variety of tasks to perform cannot afford to be limited to investigating transference.

The difference between therapists who consider the resolution of therapist-patient transference as the paramount therapeutic factor, and those who attach equal importance to the interpersonal learning ensuing from relationships between members and from the many other therapeutic factors is more than theoretical: in practice, marked differences of technique ensue. The following two vignettes from a group led by a formal British analyst who made only transference interpretations illustrate this point:

• At the twentieth meeting, the members discussed at great length the fact that they did not know one another's first names. They then dealt with the general problem of intimacy, discussing, for example, how difficult it was to meet and really know people today. How does one make a really close friend? Now, on two occasions during this discussion, a member had erred or forgotten the surname of another member. From this data the group leader made a transference interpretation: namely, that by forgetting the others' names, the members were each expressing a wish that all the other members would vanish so that each alone could have the therapist's sole attention.

• In another session two male members were absent, and four women members bitterly criticized the one male patient present, a homosexual, for his detachment and narcissism, which precluded any interest in the lives or problems of others. The therapist suggested that the women

---

*In the psychoanalytic literature, definitions of *transference* differ from one another in degree of freedom.[5] The more rigorous definition of *transference* is that it is a state of mind of a patient toward the therapist and is produced by displacement onto the therapist of feelings, ideas, and so on, that derive from previous figures in the patient's life. Other psychoanalysts extend *transference* to apply not only to the analyst-analysand relationship but to other interpersonal situations. In this discussion, as elsewhere in this text, I use the term liberally to refer to the irrational aspects of any relationship between two people. In its clinical manifestations the concept is synonymous with *parataxic distortion*. As I shall discuss, there are more sources of transference than the simple transfer or displacement of feeling from a prior to a current object.

were attacking the male patient because he did not desire them sexually. Moreover, he was an indirect target; the women really wanted to attack the therapist for his refusal to engage them sexually.

In each instance the therapist selectively attended to the data and, from the vantage point of his conception of the paramount therapeutic factor—that is, transference resolution—made an interpretation that was pragmatically correct since it focused the members' attention upon their relationship with the leader. However, in each instance the therapist-centered interpretation was incomplete and denied the important reality of intermember relationships; in fact, in the first vignette, the members, in addition to their wish for the therapist's sole attention, *were* considerably conflicted about intimacy and about their desires and fears of engaging with one another. In the second vignette, the homosexual patient *had* in fact been narcissistic and detached in his relationship to the women in the group, and it was exceedingly important for him to recognize and understand his behavior.

Any mandate that limits the group therapist's flexibility renders him or her less effective. I have seen some therapists hobbled by a conviction that they must at all times be totally "honest" and transparent, and others by the dictum that they must make interpretations only of transference or only of mass group phenomena or, even worse, only of mass-group–transference.

This chapter attempts to clarify the following issues related to transference:

1. Transference *does* occur in therapy groups; indeed, it is omnipresent and radically influences the nature of the group discourse.
2. Without an appreciation of transference and its manifestations, the therapist will often not be able to understand the process of the group.
3. The therapist who ignores transference considerations may seriously misunderstand some transactions and confuse rather than guide the group members; but if you see *only* the transference aspects of your relationships with members, you fail to relate authentically to them.
4. There are patients whose therapy hinges on the resolution of transference distortion; there are others whose improvement will depend upon interpersonal learning stemming from work not with the therapist but with another member around such issues as competition, exploitation, or sexual and intimacy conflicts; and there are many patients who choose alternate therapeutic pathways in the group and derive their primary benefit from other therapeutic factors.
5. Attitudes toward the therapist are not all transference based: many are reality based, and others are irrational but flow from other sources of irrationality inherent in the dynamics of the group. (As Freud knew, not all group phenomena can be explained on the basis of individual psychology.)[6]

6. By maintaining flexibility, you may make good therapeutic use of these irrational attitudes toward you, without at the same time neglecting your many other functions in the group.

Transference in the Therapy Group

Every patient, to a greater or lesser degree, perceives the therapist incorrectly because of transference distortions. Few patients are entirely conflict-free in their attitudes toward such issues as parental authority, dependency, God, autonomy, and rebellion—all of which are often personified in the person of the therapist. These distortions are continually at play under the surface of the group discourse; indeed, hardly a meeting passes without some clear token of the powerful feelings embodied by the therapist. Witness the difference caused by the therapist's entrance: the group may be engaged in animated conversation only to lapse into complete silence when the therapist appears. (Someone once said that the group therapy meeting officially begins when suddenly nothing happens!) The therapist's arrival not only reminds the group of its task but also evokes early constellations of feelings in each member about the adult, the teacher, the evaluator. Without you the group can frolic; your presence is experienced as a stern reminder of the responsibilities of adulthood.

Seating patterns often reveal complex and powerful feelings toward the leader. Frequently, the members attempt to sit as far away from you as possible; a paranoid patient often takes the seat directly opposite you, perhaps in order to watch you more closely; a dependent patient generally sits close to you. If co-therapists sit close to each other with only one vacant chair between them, the members may be disinclined to occupy it. One member, after eighteen months of group therapy, still described a feeling of great oppression when seated between the therapists.

Over a couple of years, for research purposes, I asked group members to fill out a questionnaire following each meeting. One of their tasks was to rank-order every member for activity (according to the total number of words each spoke). There was excellent intermember reliability in their ratings of the other group members but exceedingly poor reliability in their ratings of the group therapist. In the same meetings some patients rated the therapist as the most active member, whereas others considered him the least active. The powerful and unrealistic feelings of the members toward the therapist prevented an accurate appraisal, even on this relatively objective dimension. Some techniques to demonstrate this phenomenon have been developed for group dynamic classroom teaching. In one simple procedure, each member is requested to estimate the amount of money the group leader has in his or her pocket. The estimates vary enormously but generally show a concordance with transference set.

One patient, when asked to discuss his feelings toward me, stated that he disliked me greatly because I was cold and aloof. He reacted immediately to his disclosure with intense discomfort. He imagined possible repercussions: I might be too upset by his attack to be of any more help to the group; I might retaliate by kicking him out of the group; I might humiliate him by mocking him for some of the homosexual fantasies he had shared with the group; or I might use my psychiatric wizardry to harm him in the future.

On another occasion a group noted that I was wearing a copper bracelet. When they learned it was for tennis elbow, their reaction was extreme. They felt angry that I should be superstitious or ascribe to any quack cures. (They had berated me for months for not being human enough!) Some mused that if I would spend more time with my patients and less time on the tennis court, all of us would be better off. One patient, who always idealized me, said that she had seen copper bracelets advertised in *Sunset Magazine,* but guessed that mine was more special—perhaps something I had bought in Switzerland!

Some members characteristically address all their remarks to the therapist, or may speak to other members only to glance furtively at the therapist at the end of their statement. It is as though they speak to others in an attempt to reach you, seeking your stamp of approval for all their thoughts and actions. They forget, as it were, their reasons for being in therapy: they continuously seek to gain conspiratorial eye contact with you; to be the last to leave the session; to be, in a multitude of ways, your favorite child. One middle-aged woman described to the group a dream in which the group therapy room was transformed into the therapist's living room, which was bare and unfurnished. Instead of the other members, the room was crowded with my family, which consisted of several sons. I introduced her to them, and she felt intense warmth and pleasure. Her association to the dream was that she was overjoyed at the thought there was a place for her in my home. Not only could she furnish and decorate my house (she was a professional interior decorator) but, since I had only sons (in her dream), there was room for a daughter.

In the last chapter I described the group's strong response to any indication that the leader favors any one member of the group. In a

T-group of psychiatry residents one member, Herb, was so shaken by a stormy meeting that, as the members were leaving the room, I suggested to him that he phone if he needed to talk about what had happened (there was a two-week Christmas break following the meeting). Herb did phone for a brief conversation, and I forgot, when the group reconvened three weeks later, to mention this to the other members. Weeks later, when the group was attacking me for my inaccessibility, Herb defended me by mentioning, in passing, the phone call. The response of the group was fierce: they felt betrayed; they mocked my remark that the invitation to Herb to call was only a natural, human gesture of no great moment, and that I had simply forgotten to mention it to the group. "Where is your unconscious?," they jeered. "Innocent" surface acts by the leader often have deep implications for the members, and huge underground neural cables may soon be crackling with affect.

Transference is so powerful and so ubiquitous that the dictum "the leader shall have no favorites" seems to be essential for the stability of every working group. Freud suggested that group cohesiveness, curiously, derives from the universal wish to be the favorite of the leader.[7] The prototypic human group, the sibling group, is dominated by intense feelings of rivalry. Every child wishes to be the favorite and resents his or her rivals for their claims to maternal love. The older child wishes to rob the younger of privileges or to eliminate the child altogether. And yet each realizes that the rival children are equally loved by their parents; therefore, one cannot destroy one's siblings without incurring parental wrath and thus destroying oneself. The only possible solution is to insist on equality: if one can not be the favorite, then there must be no favorite at all. Everyone is granted an equal investment in the leader, and out of this demand for equality is born what we have come to know as "group spirit." (Freud at this juncture is careful to remind us that the demand for equality applies only to the other members. They do not wish to be equal to the leader, but quite the contrary; they have a thirst for obedience—a "lust for submission," as Erich Fromm put it[8]—and wish to be ruled. I shall return to this shortly.)

Freud was very sensitive to the powerful and irrational manner in which group members view their leader, and made a major contribution by systematically analyzing this phenomenon and applying it to psychotherapy. Obviously, however, the psychology of member and leader has existed since the earliest human grouping, and Freud was not the first to note it. To cite only one example, Tolstoy in the nineteenth century was keenly aware of the subtle intricacies of the member-leader relationship in the two most important groups of his day: the church and the military. His insight into the overevaluation of the leader gives *War and Peace* much of its pathos and richness. Consider Rostov's regard for the Tsar:

He was entirely absorbed in the feeling of happiness at the Tsar's being near. His nearness alone made up to him by itself, he felt, for the loss of the whole day. He was happy, as a lover is happy when the moment of the longed-for meeting has come. Not daring to look around from the front line, by an ecstatic instance without looking around, he felt his approach. And he felt it not only from the sound of the tramping hoofs of the approaching cavalcade, he felt it because as the Tsar came nearer everything grew brighter, more joyful and significant, and more festive. Nearer and nearer moved this sun, as he seemed to Rostov, shedding around him rays of mild and majestic light, and now he felt himself enfolded in that radiance, he heard his voice—that voice caressing, calm, majestic, and yet so simple. . . . And Rostov got up and went out to wander about among the campfires, dreaming of what happiness it would be to die— not saving the Emperor's life—(of that he did not dare to dream), but simply to die before the Emperor's eyes. He really was in love with the Tsar and the glory of the Russian arms and the hope of coming victory. And he was not the only man who felt thus in those memorable days that preceded the battle of Austerlitz: nine-tenths of the men in the Russian army were at that moment in love, though less ecstatically, with their Tsar and the glory of the Russian arms.[9]

(Indeed, it would seem that submersion in the love of a leader is a prerequisite for war. How ironic that more killing has probably been done under the aegis of love than under the banner of hatred!)

Napoleon, that consummate leader of men, was, according to Tolstoy, not ignorant of "transference"; nor did he hesitate to utilize it in the service of victory. In *War and Peace,* Tolstoy had him deliver this dispatch to his troops on the eve of battle:

Soldiers! I will myself lead your battalions. I will keep out of fire, if you, with your habitual bravery, carry defeat and disorder into the ranks of the enemy. But if victory is for one moment doubtful, you will see your Emperor exposed to the enemy's hottest attack, for there can be no uncertainty of victory, especially on this day, when it is a question of the honor of the French infantry, on which rests the honor of our nation.[10]

As a result of transference, the therapy group may grant the leader superhuman powers. Your words are given more weight and imbued with more wisdom than they possess. Equally austute contributions made by other members are ignored or distorted. All progress in the group is attributed to you. Your errors, faux pas, and absences are seen as deliberate techniques which you employ to stimulate or provoke the

group for its own good. Groups, including groups of professional therapists, overestimate your presence and knowledge. They believe that
there are great calculated depths to each of your interventions, that you
predict and control all the events of the group. Even when you confess
puzzlement or ignorance, that, too, is regarded as part of your technique, deliberately intended to have a particular effect on the group.

Who shall be the leader's favorite child? For many group members
this longing serves as an internal horizon against which all other group
events are silhouetted. No matter how much each cares for the other
members of the group, no matter how much each is pleased to see
others work and receive help, there is a background of envy, of disappointment that one is not basking alone in the light of the leader. The
desire for sole possession of the leader and the ensuing envy and greed
lie deeply embedded in the substructure of every group. An old collo-
quialism for the genital organs is "privates." However, today many
therapy groups discuss genitality and sexuality with much ease, even
relish. The "privates" of a group are more likely to be the fee structure,
because often money and fees act as electrodes upon which condense
much of the feeling toward the leader. The fee structure is an especially
charged issue in many mental health clinics which charge members of
a group different fees dependent upon income. How much one pays is
often one of the group's most tightly clenched secrets, since differences
in payment by the members (and the silent insidious corollary, differences in rights, in the degree of ownership) threaten the very cement
of the group: equality for all members.

Members often expect the leader to sense their needs; often this
expectation is most clearly apparent to them when the group has an
alternate (leaderless) meeting (see chapter 14) in which they may feel
unprotected and uncared for; there is no one there who will know,
without their having to ask, what they are feeling and what they wish
from the group. One member wrote a list of major issues that troubled
him; he brought it to meeting after meeting, waiting for the therapist
to divine its existence and to ask him to read it. Obviously, the content
of the list meant little. If he had really wanted to work on the problems
enumerated there, he could have taken the initiative himself to present
the list to the group. No, what was important was the therapist's presence and nurturance. This member's transference was such that he had
incompletely differentiated himself from the therapist; their ego
boundaries were blurred; to know or feel something was, for him, tantamount to the therapist's knowing and feeling it. Patients carry the

therapist around with them: you are in them; you observe their actions from over their shoulder; you participate in imaginary conversations with them.

When several members of a group share this desire for an all-knowing, all-caring leader, then the meetings take on a characteristic flavor. The group seems helpless and dependent. The members deskill themselves and seem unable to help themselves or others. Deskilling is particularly dramatic in a group composed of professional therapists who suddenly seem unable to ask even the simplest questions of one another. For example, in one meeting a group may talk about loss. One member mentions, for the first time, the recent death of his mother. Then silence. There is sudden group aphasia. No one is even able to say, "Tell us more about it." They are all waiting—waiting for the touch of the therapist. No one wants to encourage anyone else to talk for fear of lessening his or her chance of obtaining the leader's ministrations.

Then, too, the opposite occurs. Members challenge the leader continuously. You are distrusted; your motivations are misunderstood; you are treated as though you were the enemy. Examples of such negative transference are very common. One patient, just beginning the group, expended considerable energy in an effort to dominate the other members. Whenever the therapist attempted to point this out, the patient regarded his intentions as malicious: the therapist was interfering with his growth; the therapist was threatened by him and was attempting to keep him subservient; or, finally, the therapist was deliberately blocking his progress lest he improve too quickly and thus diminish the therapist's income.

Another paranoid patient, who had a long history of broken leases and lawsuits brought against her by irate landlords, recapitulated her litigiousness in the group. She refused to pay her small clinic bill because she claimed that there was an error in the account. However, she could not find the time to come to talk to the clinic administrator. When the therapist, on a number of occasions, reminded her of the account, she compared him to a Jew slumlord or a greedy capitalist who would have liked her to damage her health permanently by slaving in a coal mine. Another patient habitually became physically ill with flu symptoms whenever she grew depressed. It was impossible for the therapist to work with her without her feeling that he was accusing her of malingering in much the same way that her parents had done. One therapist, on a couple of occasions, accepted a cigarette from a female member; another member responded strongly and accused him both of "mooching" and of exploiting the women in the group.

Many reasons exist for unrealistic attacks upon the therapist, but some stem from the same feelings of helpless dependency that result in the worshipful obedience I have described. Some patients ("counter-dependents") respond counterphobically to their dependency by incessantly defying the leader. Others validate their integrity or potency by attempting to triumph over the big adversary; a sense of exhilaration and power ensues from twisting the tail of the tiger and emerging unscathed.

The most common charge that members levy against the leader is of being too cold, too aloof, too inhuman. In part, this charge is based on reality. For reasons, both professional and personal, that I shall discuss shortly, many therapists do keep themselves hidden from the group. Also, their role of process commentator requires a certain distance from the group. But there is more to it. Although the members insist that they wish you to be more human, they have the simultaneous counterwish that you be more than human. Freud often made this observation and eventually, in *The Future of an Illusion,* based his explanation for religious belief on the human being's thirst for a superbeing.[11] It seemed to Freud that the group integrity depended upon the existence of some superordinate figure who, as I have discussed, fosters the illusion of loving each member equally. Solid group bonds become chains of sand if the leader is lost. If the general perishes in battle, it is imperative that the news be kept secret lest panic ensue. So, too, for the leader of the church. Freud was fascinated by a 1903 novel, *When It Was Dark,* in which Christ's divinity was questioned and ultimately disproved.[12] The work depicted the catastrophic effects on Western European civilization; previously stable social institutions deconstituted like parts of a model airplane whose glue has suddenly deteriorated.

And so there is great ambivalence about the members' directive to the leader to be more human. They claim that you tell them nothing of yourself, yet they rarely make explicit inquiry. They demand that you be more human yet excoriate you for wearing a copper bracelet, mooching a cigarette, or forgetting to tell the group that you have conversed with a member over the phone. They prefer not to believe you if you profess puzzlement or ignorance. The illness or infirmity of a therapist always arouses considerable discomfort among the members; somehow the therapist should be beyond biological limitation. The followers of a leader who abandons his or her role are in deep distress. When Shakespeare's Richard II laments his "hollow crown" and gives vent to his discouragement and need for friends, his court bids him to be silent.

A group of psychiatric residents I once led put the dilemma very clearly. They often discussed the "big people" out there in the world —their therapists, group leaders, supervisors, and the adult community of senior practicing psychiatrists. The closer these residents came to completion of their training, the more important and problematic did the "big people" become. I wondered, Was it possible that they, too, would soon become "big people"? Could it be that even I had my "big people"? There were two opposing sets of concerns about the "big people," and both were equally frightening: first, that the "big people" were real, that they possessed superior wisdom and knowledge and would dispense an honest but terrible justice to the young, presumptuous frauds who tried to join their ranks; or, secondly, that the "big people" themselves were frauds, that the members were all Dorothys facing Oz's wizard. The second possibility had more frightening implications than the first: it brought them face to face with their intrinsic loneliness and apartness. It was as if, for a brief time, life's illusions were stripped away, exposing the naked scaffolding of existence—a terrifying sight, one that we conceal from ourselves with the heaviest of curtains. The "big people" are one of our most effective curtains: as frightening as their judgment may be, it is far less terrible than that other alternative—that there are no "big people," and that one is finally and utterly alone.

The leader is thus seen unrealistically by members for many reasons: true transference or displacement of affect from some prior object is one source; conflicted attitudes toward authority—dependency, autonomy, rebellion, and so on—which become personified in the therapist, are another; and still another source is the tendency to imbue the therapist with superhuman features so as to use him or her as a shield against existential anxiety. One further source lies in the members' explicit or intuitive appreciation of the great power of the group therapist. Your presence and your impartiality are, as I have already discussed, essential for group survival and stability. You cannot be deposed; you have at your disposal enormous power; you can expel members, add new members, mobilize group pressure against anyone you wish.

In fact, the sources of intense, irrational feelings toward the therapist are so varied and so powerful that transference will occur, come what may. I do not believe that a therapist need be unduly concerned with the task of generating or facilitating the development of transference. You need not, for example, assume a pose of unflinching neutrality. Better that you spend your time attempting to turn the transference to therapeutic account. A clear illustration of transference occurred with a patient who often attacked me for aloofness, deviousness, and hiddenness. He accused me of manipulation—of pulling strings to guide each member's behavior, of not being clear and open, of never really coming out and telling the group exactly what I was trying to do in therapy. It is striking that this patient was a member of a group in which I had been writing very clear, very honest, very transparent group summaries and mailing them to the members before the next meeting (see chapter 14). Never has any therapist, I believe, made a more earnest attempt to demystify the therapeutic process. Yet earlier in the very meeting where he attacked me, he informed the group that he had not read the summaries and in fact had a large number of them unopened lying on his desk.

As long as a group therapist assumes the responsibility of leadership, transference will occur. I have never seen a group without a deep, complex underpinning of transference. The problem is, thus, not *evocation* but, on the contrary, *resolution* of transference. The therapist who is to make therapeutic use of transference must help patients to recognize, to understand, and to change their distorted attitudinal set toward the leader.

Two major approaches facilitate transference resolution in the therapy group: consensual validation and increased therapist transparency. The therapist may encourage a patient to validate his or her impressions of the therapist against those of the other members. If many or all of the group members concur in the patient's view of and feelings toward the therapist, you may conclude either that the reaction to you stems from global group forces related to your role in the group, or that the reaction is not unrealistic at all: the patients are perceiving you accurately. If, on the other hand, one member alone of all the group members possesses a particular view of you, then this member may be helped to examine the possibility that he or she sees the therapist, and perhaps other people, too, through an internal distorting prism.

Thus, one method of facilitating reality testing is to encourage patients to check out their perceptions with one another. The other major method calls for the use of the therapist's person; you allow the patient to confirm or disconfirm impressions of you by gradually revealing more of yourself. You press the patient to deal with you as a real person in the here-and-now. You respond to the patient, you share your feelings, you acknowledge or refute motives or feelings attributed to you, you look at your own blind spots, you demonstrate respect for the feedback the members offer you. In the face of the mounting data the patient has about you, it becomes increasingly difficult to maintain fictitious beliefs about you.

The group therapist undergoes a gradual metamorphosis during the life of the group. In the beginning you busy yourself with the many functions necessary in the creation of the group, with the development of a social system in which the many therapeutic factors may operate, and with the activation and illumination of the here-and-now. Gradually you begin to interact with each of the members; as the group progresses, you relate more personally to them, and the early stereotypes the patients cast onto you become more difficult to maintain. This process between you and each of the members is not qualitatively different from the interpersonal learning that ensues as a result of each member's relationship with other members. After all, you have no monopoly on authority, dominance, sagacity, or aloofness, and many of the members work out their conflicts in these areas not with the therapist (or not *only* with the therapist) but with other members who have these attributes.

This change in the degree of transparency of the therapist is by no means limited to group therapy; someone once said that when the analyst tells the analysand a joke, you can be sure the analysis is approaching its end. However, the pace, the degree, the nature of the therapist transparency and the relationship between this activity of the therapist and the therapist's other tasks in the group is problematic and deserves careful consideration. More than any other single characteristic, the nature and the degree of therapist self-disclosure differentiates the various schools of group therapy.

The Psychotherapist and Transparency

Major "lasting" psychotherapeutic innovations appear and vanish with bewildering rapidity; only a truly intrepid observer would attempt to differentiate evanescent from potentially important and durable trends in the diffuse, heterodox American psychotherapeutic scene. Nevertheless, it seems that there is evidence, in widely varying settings, of a shift in the therapist's basic self-presentation. Consider the following vignettes:

• Therapists leading therapy groups that are observed through a one-way mirror reverse the roles at the end of the meeting. The patients are permitted to observe while the therapist and the students discuss or "rehash" the meeting. Or, in inpatient groups, the observers enter the room twenty minutes before the end of the session to discuss their observations of the meeting. In the final ten minutes, the group members react to the observers' comments.[13]

• At a university training center, a tutorial teaching technique has been employed in which four psychiatric residents meet regularly with an experienced clinician who conducts an interview in front of a one-way mirror. The patient is often invited to observe the post-interview discussion.

• Similarly, I have for many years used as a teaching vehicle a multiple therapy format in which one patient is treated simultaneously by several therapists (usually four psychiatric residents and two experienced clinicians).[14] One of the important ground rules is that there is no post-session rehash; everything that is said must be said in the presence of the patient, including disagreements about diagnosis, the appropriate plan of therapy, as well as criticism of one therapist by another.

• A group therapist began a meeting by asking a patient who had been extremely distressed at the previous meeting how he was feeling today and whether the therapy session had been helpful to him. The co-therapist then said to him, "Tom, I think you're doing just what I was doing a couple of weeks ago—pressing the patients to tell me how effective my therapy is. We both seem on a constant lookout for reassurance. I think we are reflecting some of the general discouragement in the group. I wonder whether the members may be feeling pressure that they have to improve to keep up our spirits."

• In several groups at an outpatient clinic, as I mentioned earlier, the therapists write a detailed summary (see chapter 14) after each meeting and mail it to the patients before the next session. The summary contains many things, including not only a narrative account of the meeting, a running commentary on process, and each member's contribution to the session, but also contains much therapist disclosure: the therapist's ideas about what was happening to everyone in the group that meeting; a relevant exposition of the theory of group therapy; exactly what the therapist was attempting to do in the meeting; the therapist's feelings of puzzlement or ignorance about events in the group; the therapist's own personal feelings, including both those said and unsaid in the session. These summaries are virtually indistinguishable from summaries the therapists had previously written for their own private records.

Without discussing the merits or the disadvantages of the approaches demonstrated in these vignettes, it can be said for now that there is no evidence that these approaches corroded the therapeutic relationship or situation. On the psychiatric ward, in the tutorial, and in therapy groups, the patients, rather than lose faith in their all too human therapists, developed more faith in a process in which the therapists were willing to immerse themselves. The patients who observed their therapists in disagreement learned that, although "no one true way" exists, the therapists are nonetheless dedicated and committed to finding ways of helping their patients.

In each of these vignettes the therapists abandon their traditional role and share some of their many uncertainties with their patients. Gradually, the therapist is defrocked, the therapeutic process demystified. The past two decades have witnessed the demise of the concept of psychotherapy as an exclusive domain of psychiatry. Not long ago therapy was indeed a private closed-shop affair: psychologists were under surveillance lest they be tempted to practice "therapy" rather than "counseling"; social workers could do "casework" but not psychotherapy. The eggshell era of therapy, in which the patient was considered so fragile, and the mysteries of technique so deep, that only the individual with the ultimate diploma dared treat one, is gone forever.

Instead, the last two decades have witnessed the establishment of diverse programs, many sponsored by the National Institute of Mental Health, designed to train nonprofessionals to do psychotherapy. For example, M. J. Rioch, under the auspices of the Washington School of Psychiatry, established courses to train housewives in both individual and group therapy.[15] Psychiatric technicians are being trained by intensive NIMH-sponsored courses to be group therapists in psychiatric hospitals.[16] Well-integrated college students have been successfully used as psychotherapists for disturbed adolescents at both Stanford University and Berkeley.[17] Ex-addicts, with only brief training, have been widely used as therapists for groups of addicts. The number of professions that engage in psychotherapy has grown greatly. There are vast differences in parts of the country depending upon state licensure laws and third-party insurance policies. But, in many states, psychotherapy practitioners in clinics and private practice include psychiatric nurses, marriage and family counselors, pastoral counselors, body workers, occupational therapists, movement and dance and art therapists. The recent groundswell of groups designed to offer psychological help but meeting without the presence, authority, or often consultation of the mental health professional, is of great interest. To cite only a few of the scores of such groups: by the end of the decade of the 1970s, Alcoholics Anonymous had over 30,000 chapters, Compassionate Friends (for bereaved parents) had 126 chapters, Parents Anonymous had over 1,000 groups, and GROW had over 400 groups (in Australia).[18]

Nor is this re-evaluation of the therapist's role and authority solely a modern phenomenon. There were adumbrations of such experimentation among the earliest dynamic therapists. For example, Sandor Ferenczi, an early disciple of Freud, out of dissatisfaction with the therapeutic results of psychoanalysis, continually challenged the aloof, omniscient role of the classical psychoanalyst. During his last several years he openly acknowledged his fallibility to patients and, in response to a just criticism, felt free to say, "I think you may have touched upon an area in which I am not entirely free myself. Perhaps you can help me see what's wrong with me."[19] S. H. Foulkes stated thirty years ago that the mature group therapist was truly modest—one who could sincerely say to a group, "Here we are together facing reality and the basic problems of human existence. I am one of you, not more and not less."[20]

All of these approaches argue that therapy is a rational, explicable process. They espouse a humanistic attitude to therapy, in which the patient is considered a full collaborator in the therapeutic venture. No mystery need surround the therapist or the therapeutic procedure; aside from the ameliorative effects stemming from expectations of help from a magical being, there is little to be lost and perhaps much to be gained through the demystification of therapy. A therapy based on a true alliance between therapist and enlightened patient reflects a greater respect for the capacities of the patient and, with it, an increased reliance on self-awareness rather than on the easier but precarious comfort of self-deception.

Greater therapist transparency is, in part, a reaction to the old authoritarian medical healer who, for many centuries, has colluded with the distressed human being's wish for succor from a superior being. Healers have harnessed and indeed cultivated this need as a powerful agent of treatment. In countless ways they have encouraged and fostered a belief in their omniscience: Latin prescriptions, specialized language, secret institutes with lengthy and severe apprenticeships, imposing offices, and pyramids of diplomas—all have contributed to the image of the healer as a powerful, mysterious, and prescient figure.

In unlocking the shackles of this ancestral role, the therapist of today has at times sacrificed effectiveness at the altar of self-disclosure. However, the dangers of indiscriminate therapist transparency (which I shall consider shortly) should not deter us from exploring the judicious use of therapist self-disclosure.

THE EFFECT OF THERAPIST TRANSPARENCY
ON THE THERAPY GROUP

The primary sweeping objection to therapist transparency is, as I have discussed, based on the traditional analytic belief that the paramount therapeutic factor is the resolution of patient-therapist transference. From this point of view, it is necessary for the therapist to remain relatively anonymous or opaque in order to foster the development of unrealistic feelings toward him or her. It is my position, however, that other therapeutic factors are of equal or greater importance, and that the therapist who judiciously uses his or her own person increases the therapeutic power of the group by encouraging the development of these factors. You gain considerable role flexibility and maneuverability and may, without concerning yourself about role spoilage, directly attend to group maintenance, to the shaping of the group norms, and to here-and-now activation and process illumination. By decentralizing your position in the group, you hasten the development of group autonomy and cohesiveness.

One objection to self-disclosure, a groundless objection I believe, is the fear of escalation, the fear that once you as therapist reveal yourself, the group will insatiably demand even more. Recall that powerful forces in the group oppose this trend. The members are extraordinarily curious about you yet, at the same time, wish you to remain unknown and powerful. My own clinical work has at times been complicated by my occasionally leading human development laboratories (intensive T-groups). The "re-entry phenomenon" (discussed in chapter 14) often results in abrupt but transient shifts in my role as a leader; yet I find that my therapy groups are neither confused nor, later, more personally demanding of me. I became aware that groups do not escalate demands for therapist disclosure, when many years ago, I led a therapy group session immediately after returning from a week-long residential human relations laboratory.

• Four members, Don, Russel, Janice, and Martha, were present at the twenty-ninth meeting of the group. One member and the co-therapist were absent; one other member, Peter, had at the previous meeting dropped out of the group. The first theme that emerged was the group's response to Peter's terminating. The group discussed this gingerly from a great distance, and I commented that we had, it seemed to me, never honestly discussed our feelings about Peter when he was present, and that we were avoiding them now even after his departure. Among the responses was Martha's comment that she was glad he had left, that she had felt they couldn't reach him, and that she didn't feel it was worth her while to try. She then commented on his lack of education and noted her surprise that he had even been included in the group—an oblique swipe at the therapists.

I felt the group had not only avoided discussing Peter but had also declined to confront Martha's judgmentalism and incessant criticism of others. I thought I might help Martha and the group explore this issue by asking her to go around the group and describe those aspects of each person she found herself unable to accept. This task proved very difficult for her, and she generally avoided it by phrasing her objections in the past tense: that is, "I once disliked some trait in you but now it's different." When she had finished with each of the patients, I pointed out that she had left me out; indeed, she had never expressed her feelings toward me except through indirect attacks. She proceeded to compare me unfavorably with the co-therapist, stating that she found me too retiring and ineffectual; with dispatch she then attempted to undo the remarks by commenting that "still waters run deep" and recalling examples of my sensitivity to her.

The other members suddenly stated that they'd like to tackle the same task, and did; in the process they revealed many long-term group secrets, such as Don's effeminacy, Janice's slovenliness and desexualized grooming, and Russel's lack of empathy with the women in the group. Martha was compared to "a golf ball, tightly wound up with an enamel cover." I was attacked by Don for my deviousness and lack of interest in him. The group then asked me also to go around the group in the same manner as they had done. Being fresh from a seven-day T-group, and no admirer of the Duke of Playa Toro who led his army from the rear, I agreed. I told Martha that her quickness to judge and condemn others made me reluctant to show myself to her, lest I, too, be judged and found wanting. I agreed with the golf ball metaphor and added that her judgmentalism made it difficult for me to approach her, save as an expert technician. I told Don that I felt his gaze on me constantly; I knew he desperately wanted something from me, and that the intensity of his need and my inability to satisfy that need often made me very uncomfortable. I told Janice that I missed a spirit of opposition in her; she tended to accept and exalt everything that I said so uncritically that it became difficult at times to relate to her as an autonomous adult. The meeting continued at an intense involved level, and at its end the observers expressed grave concerns about my behavior. They felt that I had irrevocably relinquished my leadership role and become a group member; that the group would never be the same; and that, furthermore, I was placing my co-therapist, who would return the following week, in an untenable position.

In fact, none of these predictions materialized. In subsequent meetings the group plunged more deeply into work; several weeks were required to assimilate the material generated in that single meeting. In addition, the group members, following the model of the therapist, related to one another far more forthrightly than before and made no demands on the therapist for escalated self-disclosure.

There are many different types of therapist transparency depending upon the therapist's personal style and goals in the group at a particular time. Are you trying to facilitate transference resolution? Are you model setting in an effort to set therapeutic norms? Are you generally attempting to assist the interpersonal learning of the members by working upon their relationship with you? Are you attempting to support and demonstrate your acceptance of members by saying in effect: "I value and respect you and demonstrate this by giving of myself?"

• An incident of therapist disclosure that was enormously helpful to the group occurred in a meeting when all three women members discussed their strong sexual attraction to me, one of the group therapists. Much work was done on the transference aspects of the situation, on the women being attracted to a man who was obviously unattainable, older, in a "superior" position, and so on. I then pointed out that there was still another side of it. None of the women had expressed similar feelings toward the other therapist (also male); and, furthermore, other female patients who had been in the group previously had had the same feelings. I could not deny that it gave me pleasure to hear these sentiments expressed, and I asked them to help me look at my blind spots: that is, what I was doing unbeknownst to myself to encourage their positive response? My request opened up a long and fruitful discussion by the group members of important feelings about both therapists. There was much agreement that the two of us were very different: I was more vain, took much more care about my physical appearance and clothes, and had an exactitude and preciseness about my statements that created about me an attractive aura of suave perfection. The other therapist was sloppier in appearance and behavior: he spoke more often when he was unsure of what he was going to say; he took more risks, was willing to be wrong, and, in so doing, was more often helpful to the patients. The feedback sounded right to me; I had heard it before and so informed the group. I thought about their comments during the week and, at the following meeting, thanked the group and told them that they had been helpful to me.

General principles that prove useful to the therapist when receiving feedback, especially negative feedback, are:

1. Take it seriously: Listen to it, consider it, and respond to it. Respect the patients and let their feedback matter to you; if you don't, you merely increase their sense of impotence.
2. Obtain consensual validation: Find out how other members feel. Is the feedback primarily a transference reaction, or does it closely correspond to the reality about you? If it is reality, you must confirm it; otherwise, you impair rather than facilitate a patient's reality testing.
3. Check your internal experience: Does the feedback fit? Does it click with your internal experience?

With these principles as guidelines, the therapist makes such commands as: "You're right. There are times when I feel irritated with you but at no time do I feel I want to impede your growth, or see you work in a coal mine, or slow your therapy so as to earn more money from you. That simply isn't part of my experience of you." Or: "It's true that I dodge some of your questions. But often I find them unanswerable. You imbue me with too much wisdom. I feel uncomfortable by your deference to me. I always feel that you've put yourself down very low, and that you're always looking up at me." Or: "I've never heard you challenge me so directly before. Even though it's a bit scary for me, it's also very refreshing." Or: "I feel restrained, very unfree with you because you give me so much power over you. I feel I have to check every word I say because you give so much weight to all of my statements."

Note that these therapy disclosures are all part of the here-and-now of the group. Each discloses something of the inner world that the therapist experiences in the group. Most therapists prefer not to reveal aspects of their personal life to the group, though there are some who choose to do so in the service of providing a model for the patients. For example, M. Berger states, "It is at times very helpful for the therapist to share some past or current real-life problem and to afford a model for identification through his capacity to come through such a problem constructively."[21]

M. B. Allan studied the effects of therapist disclosure on a group over a seven-month period and noted many beneficial effects from therapist transparency.[22] First, therapist disclosure was more likely to occur when therapeutic communication among members was not taking place. Secondly, the effect of therapist disclosure was to shift the pattern of group interaction into a more constructive, sensitive direction. Finally, therapist self-disclosure resulted in an immediate increase of cohesiveness. Yet many therapists shrink from self-disclosure without being clear about their reasons for doing so. Too often, perhaps, they rationalize by cloaking their personal inclinations in professional garb. There is little doubt, I believe, that the personal qualities of a therapist influence both professional style and choice of ideological school.

• An incident that occurred at a group therapy seminar aptly illustrates some of these issues. An experienced, competent group therapist brought up the following dilemma: Several months after the completion of group therapy, a male patient named Oscar invited him to dine at his home. Oscar wanted the therapist to meet his new wife; he had spoken of her often during his stay in the group and married her shortly after termination. The therapist felt that Oscar had had a successful course of therapy: he had worked exceedingly well and resolved many important issues (including transference distortions); in fact, the therapist could not remember having had a patient with a more successful course of therapy. Moreover, he liked Oscar, would have enjoyed seeing him, and was curious to meet his wife.

Yet the therapist declined the invitation. He felt that it would be professionally improper and unwise but had much difficulty being more explicit. Several themes emerged in the workshop discussion. Would it not totally undermine the therapeutic relationship? Suppose the patient might need the therapist again? Should the therapist not rotate in a professional orbit around Oscar so as to be available for immediate recall? (Yet the therapist felt that Oscar had had a completely successful course of therapy, and there was no reason to suspect further treatment would be necessary.) Would it not, in some ill-defined way, retrospectively undo some of the therapeutic work? Would it not be unsettling for the patient to see the therapist in a different light? (Yet Oscar had worked on and resolved transference issues. This was no tenuous cure on the basis of suggestion, a "transference cure," or "crooked cure," as Freud put it.)[23] Was the therapist impeding the process of termination by continuing to see the patient? (Often this is the case. Yet Oscar had worked long and well on termination.) Is it not bad practice from the standpoint of the other members of the group? Does not favoritism split the group? (True enough, yet Oscar had terminated therapy many months before; and, since many other members had been ready to terminate shortly, the group ended and was now no longer in existence.) Does the therapist not have to protect his private time? Does it not immeasurably complicate life and therapy to mix social and professional roles? (Most certainly. Yet Oscar was no longer a patient. Moreover the therapist *wanted* to dine with him.)

It seemed that every "professional" reason for the therapist's behavior proved to be rationalization. The closest the therapist could come to the truth, he said, was that he was made very uncomfortable at the prospect of a patient seeing him eat or act ill at ease in social conversation—not skillfully engaging in the introductions, not adeptly taking his leave at the end of the evening. The truth is, of course, that the therapist wanted to protect not the patient but himself! To protect himself from the odious charge of being human—of eating, of faltering, in short of being less than godlike.

Many therapists decline to reveal themselves to the group because of their fears about where it will lead. What further information will the patients demand? I have often posed this question to successfully treated patients at the end of therapy. Most express a wish that the therapist had been more open, more personally engaged in the group. None would have wanted the therapist to have discussed more of his or her private life or personal problems with them. The therapist, I think, need not fear being stripped and asked to stand shivering and naked before the group. Furthermore, there is evidence that leaders are more transparent than they know. One team of researchers, for example, demonstrated that group members are very much aware of which members the leaders like most.[24]

The real fear lies elsewhere. One group patient (the same one who likened the therapist to a Jew slumlord) had this dream: "We [the group] were all sitting around a long table with you [the therapist] at the head. You had in your hand a slip of paper with something written on it. I tried to snatch it away from you but you were too far away." Months later as this patient was approaching the crisis and turning point of her therapy, she recalled the dream and added that she knew all along what I had written on the paper, but hadn't wanted to say it in front of the group. It was my answer to the question, "Do you love me?" I think this question enormously threatens therapists.

But there is an even worse question: the collective one, "How much do you love each of us?" or, "Whom do you love best?" These questions threaten the very frame of the psychotherapeutic contract. They challenge tenets that both parties have agreed to keep invisible. They are but a step away from a commentary upon the "purchase of a friendship" model: "If you really care for us, would you see us if we had no money?" They come perilously close to the ultimate, terrible secret of the psychotherapist, which is that the intense drama in the group room plays a very small compartmentalized role in his or her life. As in Tom Stoppard's play *Rosencrantz and Guildenstern Are Dead*, key figures in one drama rapidly become shadows in the wings as the therapist moves immediately onto the stage of another drama.

Only once have I been blasphemous enough to lay this bare before a group. A therapy group of psychiatric residents were dealing with my departure (for several months' sabbatical). My personal experience during that time was one of saying goodbye to a number of patients and to several groups, some of which were more emotionally involving for me than the resident group. Termination work was difficult, and the group members attributed much of the difficulty to the fact that I had been so involved in the group that I was finding it hard to say goodbye. I acknowledged my involvement in the group but presented to them the fact that they knew but refused to know: that is, I was vastly more important to them than they were to me. After all, I had many patients; they had one therapist. They were clearly aware of this imbalance in their psychotherapeutic work with their own patients and yet had never applied it to themselves. There was a gasp in the group as this truth, this denial of specialness, this inherent cruelty of psychotherapy, came home to them.

Is there, therefore, no place in therapy for concealment? Is the most helpful therapist the one who is most fully and most consistently self-disclosing? Let us turn our attention to the limitations of transparency.

PITFALLS OF THERAPIST TRANSPARENCY

Some time ago I observed a group led by two neophyte group therapists who were at that time much dedicated to the ideal of therapist transparency. They formed an outpatient group and conducted themselves in an unflinchingly honest fashion, expressing openly in the first meetings their uncertainty about group therapy, their self-doubts, and their personal anxiety. In so doing, however, they jettisoned the function of group maintenance; the majority of the members dropped out of the group within the first six sessions.

The time-extended "marathon groups" popular in the 1970s (see chapter 10), which met from twenty-four to forty-eight consecutive hours, placed paramount emphasis on self-disclosure. The sheer physical fatigue wore down defenses and abetted maximal disclosure by both members and therapist. Then, of course, there is the ultimate in self-disclosure: "group therapy in the nude." In the late 1960s and early 1970s, the mass media (for example *Time* magazine[25]) gave considerable coverage to nude marathons in Southern California.* Indeed, at an American Psychiatric Association convention, fifteen hundred psychiatrists tried to cram into an auditorium seating seven hundred in order to watch a movie of nude marathon therapy. Specialized methods have evolved in these groups which, short of proctoscopy, carried disclosure to its ultimate (for example, the group might "spread-eagle" a member to afford maximal genital disclosure).

Many untrained leaders undertake to lead groups with the monolithic credo "Be yourself" as a central organizing principle for all other technique and strategy. Yet what these therapists have achieved is not freedom but tyranny. The paradox is that freedom and spontaneity in extreme form can result in a leadership role as narrow and restrictive as the traditional blank-screen leader. Under the freedom banner of "anything goes if it's genuine" (at any time, to any degree), the leader sacrifices flexibility. Consider the issue of timing. The neophyte, fully honest therapists I have just mentioned overlooked the fact that leadership behavior that may be appropriate at one stage of therapy may be quite inappropriate at another. If patients need initial support and structure to remain in the group, then it is the therapist's task to provide it. There are situations when, as Maslow puts it, "The good leader must keep his feelings to himself, let them burn out his own guts, and not seek the relief of catharting them to followers who cannot at that time be helped by an uncertain leader."[26]

Research that investigates group members' attitudes toward therapist self-disclosure reports that members are sensitive to the timing and the content of disclosure.[27] Therapists' disclosures judged as harmful in early phases of the group are considered facilitative as a group matures. Furthermore, members who have had much group therapy experience are far more desirous of therapist self-disclosure than are inexperienced group members. Content analysis demonstrated that members prefer leaders who disclose positive strivings (for example, personal and professional goals) and normal emotions (loneliness, sadness, anger, worries and anxieties); members disapprove of a group leader's expressing negative feelings about any individual member or negative feelings (for example, boredom or frustration) about the group experience. Lastly,

---

*Many of the wilder innovations in therapy have sprung from Southern California. It brings to mind Saul Bellow's fanciful notion in *Seize the Day* of someone tilting a large flat map of the United States and observing that "everything that wasn't bolted or screwed down slid into Southern California."[28]

both members and experienced leaders agree that greater overall leader transparency is more appropriate in encounter than in therapy groups.

The leader who strives only to create a mystique of egalitarianism between member and leader may in the long run provide no leadership at all. It is a naïve misconception to view effective role behavior of the leader as unchanging; as the group develops and matures, different forms of leadership are required. Furthermore, the "honest" comment of the dedicated leader may be the pragmatically correct response, rather than an indiscriminate expression of what may be the therapist's distortions or misperceptions. After all, as M. Parloff states, "The honest therapist is one who attempts to provide that which the patient can assimilate, verify and utilize."[29] Ferenczi years ago underscored the necessity for proper timing. The analyst, he said, must not admit his flaws and uncertainty too early. First, the patient must feel sufficiently secure in his own abilities before being called upon to face defects in the one on whom he leans.[30]*

In a sense, what happened in the 1960s and 1970s was that leader transparency became so cherished and romanticized as to achieve an autonomy of its own; it was then considered an end rather than a means to an end. There were attempts to justify this transformation by workers such as S. Jourard, O. H. Mowrer, and F. Stoller, who presented self-disclosure as the keystone of an oversimplified approach to psychopathology and therapy.[31] Jourard states, for example, that "people become clients because they do not disclose themselves in some optimal degree to the people in their life."[32] The corollary is that psychotherapy should reverse this process, with the therapist leading the way by personal example.

Thus, it is argued that the therapist sets an invaluable model for patients by full self-disclosure. Yet who ever said that full disclosure was possible or desirable in the therapy group or in the outside world? On the contrary, personal and interpersonal concealment and deception seem to be an integral ingredient of any functioning social order.

---

*A rich example of this principle is found in the novel *Magister Ludi,* in which Hermann Hesse describes an event in the lives of two renowned healers.[33] Joseph, one of the healers, severely afflicted with feelings of worthlessness and self-doubt, sets off on a long journey to seek help from his rival, Dion. At an oasis Joseph describes his plight to a stranger, who turns out to be Dion; whereupon Joseph accepts Dion's invitation to go home with him in the role of patient and servant. In time, Joseph regains his former serenity and zest and becomes the friend and colleague of his master. Only after many years have passed, and Dion lies on his deathbed, does he reveal to Joseph that when the latter encountered him at the oasis, he, Dion, had reached a similar impasse in his life and was en route to request Joseph's assistance.

Eugene O'Neill illustrated this in dramatic form in *The Iceman Cometh.* [34] In that play a group of derelicts live, as they have for twenty years, in the back room of a bar. The group is exceedingly stable, with many well-entrenched group norms. Each man maintains himself by a set of illusions ("pipe dreams," O'Neill labels them). One of the most deeply entrenched group norms is that no member challenge another's pipe dreams. Then enters Hickey, the iceman, a traveling salesman, a totally enlightened therapist, a false prophet who believes he brings fulfillment and lasting peace to each man by forcing him to shed his self-deceptions and stare with unblinking honesty at the sun of his life. Hickey's surgery is deft. He forces Jimmy Tomorrow (whose pipe dream is to unhock his suit, sober up, and get a job "tomorrow") to act now. He gives him clothes and sends him, and then the other men, out of the bar to face today.

The effects on each man and upon the group are calamitous. One member commits suicide, others grow severely depressed, the "life goes out of the booze," members attack each others' illusions, the group bonds disintegrate, and the group veers toward dissolution. In a sudden, last-minute convulsive act, the group labels Hickey psychotic, banishes him, and gradually re-establishes its old norms and cohesion. These "pipe dreams"—or "vital lies," as Ibsen calls them in *The Wild Duck* [35]—are often essential to personal and social integrity. They should not be taken lightly or impulsively stripped away in the service of honesty.

Commenting on the social problems of the United States, Victor Frankl once suggested that the Statue of Liberty on the East Coast be balanced by a Statue of Responsibility on the West Coast. [36] In the therapy group, freedom becomes possible and constructive only when it is coupled with responsibility. None of us is free from impulses or feelings that, if expressed, could be destructive to another. I suggest that we encourage patients and therapists to speak freely, to shed all internal censors and filters save one—the filter of responsibility.

I do not mean that no unpleasant sentiments are to be expressed; indeed, growth cannot occur in the absence of conflict. I do mean, however, that responsibility, not total disclosure, is the superordinate principle. The therapist has a particular type of responsibility—responsibility to patients and to the task of therapy. Patients have a human responsibility toward one another; and, as therapy progresses, as solipsism diminishes, as empathy increases, they come to exercise that responsibility in interactions with one another.

Thus, your *raison d'être* as group therapist is not primarily to be honest or fully disclosing. In times of confusion about your behavior, you may profit from stepping back momentarily to reconsider your primary tasks in the group. Therapist self-disclosure is an aid to the group because it sets a model for the patients and permits some patients to reality-test their feelings toward you. Ask yourself, Where is the group now? Is it a concealed, overly cautious group which may profit from a leader who models personal self-disclosure? Or has it already established vigorous self-disclosure norms and is in need of other assistance? You must, as I have noted, consider whether your behavior will interfere with your group-maintenance function. You must know when to recede into the background. Unlike the individual therapist, the group therapist does not have to be the axle of therapy. In part, you are midwife to the group: you must set a therapeutic process in motion and take care not to interfere with that process by insisting on your centrality.

An overly restricted definition of the role of group therapist—whether based on transparency or, for that matter, on any other criterion—may cause the leader to lose sight of the individuality of each patient's needs. Despite your group orientation, you must retain some individual focus; not all patients need the same thing. Some, perhaps most, patients need to relax controls; they need to learn how to express their affect—anger, love, tenderness, hatred. Others, however, need the opposite: they need to gain impulse control because their life styles are already characterized by labile and immediately acted-upon affect.

One final consequence of more or less unlimited therapist transparency is that the cognitive aspects of therapy may be completely neglected. As I have noted previously, mere catharsis is not in itself a corrective experience. Cognitive learning or restructuring (much of which is provided by the therapist) seems necessary for the patient to be able to generalize group experiences to outside life; without this transfer or carryover, we have succeeded only in creating better, more gracious therapy group members. Without the acquisition of some knowledge about general patterns in interpersonal relationships, the patient may, in effect, have to discover the wheel anew in each subsequent interpersonal transaction.

8

THE SELECTION OF
PATIENTS

Good group therapy begins with good patient selection. Patients improperly assigned to a therapy group are unlikely to benefit from their therapy experience. Furthermore, an improperly composed group may die stillborn, never having developed into a viable treatment mode for any of its members.

In this chapter I shall consider the clinical and research evidence bearing upon selection: How can the therapist determine whether a given patient is a suitable candidate for group therapy? The chapter following considers group composition: once it has been decided that a patient is a suitable group therapy candidate, then into which specific group shall that patient go?

This chapter and the following one address the question of patient selection and group composition of a specific type of group therapy: the heterogeneous, long-term interactional outpatient group with the ambitious goals of symptomatic relief and character change. As I have stressed throughout, and shall discuss in detail in chapter 15, there are many group therapies, and selection criteria are always relative to the specific type under consideration. There is scarcely any patient who will not fit well into some group. A secretive, nonpsychologically minded anorexic-bulimic patient, for example, is a poor candidate for a long-term interactional group but may be ideal for a homogeneous, behaviorally oriented, eating-disorders group.

Much research has been done on the issue of selection of patients. One would expect that research methodology would have much to offer: after all, researchers need only investigate a panoply of patient characteristics before the patient enters the group, and correlate these characteristics with some appropriate dependent variable, such as therapy outcome, attendance, mode of interaction, or cohesiveness. Yet the matter turns out to be far more complex: the methodological problems are severe; a true measure of psychotherapy outcome is elusive; each individual and each group is exquisitely complex and refuses to simplify itself in order to be precisely measured. Thus, to date, empirical research has failed to deliver. G. Bond and M. Lieberman, who wrote one of the most competent reviews of the empirical research on selection, begin their report with this caveat: "Readers who bring to this chapter a hope for guidance for better patient selection are best advised to read no farther."[1]

In this chapter, therefore, I must rely heavily upon my own clinical experience and the clinical contributions of others. Whenever possible I will discuss the research literature either to draw upon the best available evidence or to delineate areas where further research seems possible and necessary.

The great majority of clinicians do not select patients for group therapy. Instead, they deselect. Given a pool of patients, they determine that certain ones cannot possibly work in a therapy group and should be excluded, and then proceed to accept all the other patients. It would be preferable if the selection process were more finely tuned, but it is far easier to specify exclusion than inclusion criteria (one feature is sufficient to exclude a patient, whereas a more complex profile must be delineated to justify inclusion). Accordingly, I shall begin by examining criteria for exclusion.

Criteria for Exclusion

There is considerable clinical consensus that patients are poor candidates for a heterogeneous outpatient intensive therapy group if they are: brain damaged,[2] paranoid,[3] hypochondriacal,[4] addicted to drugs or alcohol,[5] acutely psychotic,[6] or sociopathic.[7]

These patients seem destined to fail because of their inability to participate in the primary task of the group; they soon construct an interpersonal role that proves to be detrimental to themselves as well as to the group. Consider the sociopathic patient, an exceptionally poor risk for outpatient, interactional group therapy. Characteristically, these patients are destructive in the group. Although early in therapy they may become important and active members, they will eventually manifest their basic inability to relate, often with considerable dramatic and destructive impact.

• To cite a clinical example: Felix, a thirty-five-year-old, highly intelligent patient with a history of alcoholism, transiency, and impoverished interpersonal relationships, was added with two other new patients to an ongoing group, which had been reduced to three by the recent graduation of members. The group had shrunk so much that it seemed in danger of collapsing, and the therapists were anxious to re-establish its size; they realized Felix was not an ideal candidate, but they had few applicants and decided to take the risk. In addition, they were somewhat intrigued by his alleged determination to change his life style. (The classic sociopath is forever reaching a turning point in life.) Felix, by the third meeting, had become the social-emotional leader of the group—seemingly able to feel more acutely and suffer more deeply than the other members. He presented the group, as he had the therapists, with a largely fabricated account of his background and current life situation. By the fourth meeting, as the therapists learned later, he had seduced one of the female members and, by the fifth meeting, spearheaded a discussion of the group's dissatisfaction with the brevity of the meetings. He proposed that the group, with or without the permission of the therapist, meet more often, perhaps at one of the members' homes, without the therapist. By the sixth meeting he had vanished, without prior notification to the group. The therapists learned later that he had suddenly decided to take a two-thousand-mile bicycle trip, hoping to sell the trip journal to a magazine.

This rather extreme example demonstrates many of the reasons why inclusion of a sociopathic individual in a heterogeneous outpatient group is ill-advised: his social "front" is deceptive; he often consumes such an inordinate amount of group energy that his departure leaves the group bereft, puzzled, and discouraged; he rarely assimilates the group therapeutic norms and instead often exploits other members and the group as a whole for his immediate gratification. Again, I wish to emphasize that I do not mean that group therapy is contraindicated for these patients. In fact, a specialized form of group therapy with a more homogeneous population and a sagacious utilization of strong group and institutional pressure may well be the treatment of choice[8] as is true also for the other contraindications I have just listed. Specialized groups, for example, have been shown to be effective with mentally defective patients, chronic aftercare patients, and patients addicted to alcohol or other drugs.[9]

Most clinicians agree that patients in the midst of some acute situational crisis are not good candidates for group therapy, but are far better treated in crisis-intervention therapy in an individual, family, or social network format.[10] Deeply depressed suicidal patients are best not referred to group therapy: they are often too retarded to use the group; they do not receive the very specialized attention they require in a group setting (except at enormous expense of time and energy to the other members); furthermore, the threat of suicide is too taxing, too anxiety provoking for the other group members to manage.[11]

Stable attendance is so necessary for the development of a cohesive group that it is wise to exclude patients who may not attend regularly. I do not accept patients who, because of their work, must travel and miss even one out of every five or six meetings. Similarly, I am hesitant to accept patients whose transportation to the group depends upon others or who have a very long commute to the group (I use a rough rule of thumb of sixty to ninety minutes as the maximum commute.) Too often, especially early in the course of a group, a patient may feel neglected or dissatisfied with a meeting: another member may have received the bulk of the group time and attention, or the group may have been busy building its own infrastructure—work that may not offer obvious immediate gratification. Deep feelings of frustration may, if coupled with a long strenuous commute, result in sporadic attendance. Obviously, there are many exceptions: some therapists tell of patients who faithfully fly to meetings from remote regions month after month. However, as a general rule, the therapist does well to heed this factor. For a patient who lives at considerable distance and has equivalent groups closer to home, it is in everyone's interests to refer him or her to one of those groups.

These clinical criteria for exclusion are broad and crude. Some therapists have attempted to arrive at more refined criteria through systematic study of patients who have failed to derive benefit from group therapy. Let me examine the research on one category of unsuccessful patients—the group therapy dropouts.

GROUP THERAPY DROPOUTS

There is evidence that premature termination from group therapy is bad for the patient and bad for the group. In a study of thirty-five patients who dropped out of heterogeneous interaction outpatient groups, in twelve or fewer meetings, I found that only three reported themselves as improved;[12] moreover, even those three patients made only marginal symptomatic improvement. None of these thirty-five patients left therapy because they had satisfactorily concluded their work; each terminated dissatisfied with the therapy group experience. These premature terminators had, in addition, an adverse effect on the remaining members of the group, who were threatened and demoralized by the early dropouts. The proper development of a group requires membership stability; a rash of dropouts may delay the maturation of a group for months.

Early group termination is thus a failure for the patient and a detriment to the therapy of the remainder of the group. It is also a common phenomenon. Dropout rates reported in the literature are: 57 percent (three or fewer meetings—university outpatient clinic);[13] 51 percent (nine or fewer meetings—Veterans Administration outpatient clinic);[14] 50 percent (V.A. outpatient clinic—sixteen or fewer meetings)[15] 35 percent (twelve or fewer meetings—university outpatient clinic);[16] 30 percent (three or fewer meetings—clinic and private outpatient groups);[17] 25 percent (twenty or fewer meetings—inpatient and outpatient groups);[18] 35 percent (twelve months or less—long-term analytic group therapy).[19] 17 percent (outpatient clinic—twelve or fewer meetings).[20]

A study of early dropouts may help to establish sound exclusion criteria and, furthermore, may provide an important goal for the selection process. If, in the selection process, we learn to screen out members destined to drop out of therapy, that in itself would constitute a major achievement. Although the early terminators are not the only failures in group therapy, they are unequivocal failures. (We may, I think, dismiss as unlikely the possibility that they have gained something positive which will manifest itself later. A recent outcome study of encounter group participants noted that individuals who had a negative experience in the group did not, when studied six months later, "put it all together" and enjoy a delayed benefit from the group experience.[21] If they left the group shaken or discouraged, they were likely to remain that way.) Keep in mind that the study of group dropouts tells us nothing about the group continuers; group continuation is a necessary but not sufficient factor in successful therapy. However, this research strategy circumvents some taxing problems of methodology, especially the critical problem of defining and measuring success in psychotherapy.

REASONS FOR PREMATURE TERMINATION

Let me now consider some of the reasons for premature termination of therapy that are relevant to the selection process.

B. Kotkov compared twenty-eight continuers and twenty-eight dropouts (seven meetings or less) in a Veterans Administration outpatient clinic on the basis of data collected at the initial interview.[22] The dropouts significantly differed, in several respects, from those who continued. The former, at their initial interview, were either more "spontaneous-composed," more hostile, or were, on the other hand, more placid and needed prodding. They complained less frequently of tension and more often demonstrated somatization of conflicts rather than "emotional reactivity." They complained of headaches and severe insomnia and demonstrated motor restlessness. Often they appeared to be less motivated toward treatment and were less psychologically minded.

In other studies, also in Veterans Administration outpatient clinics, dropouts were studied with the Rorschach projective test. They had less capacity to withstand stress, less desire for empathy, and less ability to achieve emotional rapport.[23] However, the discriminating power of the Rorschach in the task was modest, scarcely better than the crudest interview screening. (To the best of my knowledge, no predictive Rorschach studies have been done.) The dropouts had a lower Wechsler verbal scale I.Q. and came from a lower socioeconomic class.* M. Grotjahn studied his outpatient analytic groups and noted that, over a six-year period, forty-three patients (35 percent) dropped out within the first twelve months of therapy.[24] He felt that, in retrospect, approximately 40 percent of the dropouts were predictable and fell into three categories: (1) patients with diagnoses of manifest or threatening psychotic breakdowns either depressive, paranoid, or, in one instance, catatonic in nature; (2) patients who used the group for crisis resolution and dropped out when the emergency had passed; (3) highly schizoid, sensitive, isolated individuals who needed more careful, intensive preparation for group therapy.

E. Nash and his co-workers studied thirty group therapy patients in a university outpatient clinic.[25] The seventeen dropouts (three or fewer meetings) differed significantly from the thirteen continuers in several respects. Dropouts were more socially ineffective than continuers, and the few continuers who were socially ineffective scored exceptionally high on discomfort; the continuers had a history of fluctuating illness (which implies that the dropouts more likely experienced their illness

---

*That dropouts (from any psychotherapeutic format) are disproportionately high amongst the lower socioeconomic class is a finding corroborated by many other studies.[26]

as progressive and urgent); the dropouts were high deniers and often terminated therapy as their denial crumbled in the face of confrontation by the group.

S. Rosenzweig and R. Folman studied thirteen dropouts from V.A. outpatient clinic groups and found that though a battery of psychological tests* did not distinguish between the continuers and the drop-outs, the therapists' pre-therapy judgments about their ability to empathize with the patient, their patients' ability to form a therapeutic relationship, and the therapists' overall liking of a patient were significantly predictive of premature termination (sixteen meetings or less).[27]

These studies then suggest that, on initial interview, patients destined to drop out of groups are likely to have the following characteristics: high denial; high somatization; lower motivation; lower psychological mindedness; more severe, psychotic pathology; less likable (at least by therapists); lower socioeconomic class, social effectiveness, and I.Q. It would seem, then, that one way to view these findings is that as the rich get richer, the poor get poorer. Those patients with the least skills and attributes to work in a group are most likely to fail!

I shall discuss one final study in greater detail since it has considerable relevance for the selection process.[28] I studied the first six months of life of nine therapy groups in a university outpatient clinic and investigated all patients who terminated in twelve or fewer meetings. A total of ninety-seven patients were involved in these groups (seventy-one original members and twenty-six later additions); of these, thirty-five were early dropouts. Considerable data were generated from interviews and questionnaire studies of the dropouts and their therapists, as well as from the records and observations of the group sessions and historical and demographic data from the case records.

An analysis of the data suggested nine major reasons for the patients' dropping out of therapy:

1. External factors
2. Group deviancy
3. Problems of intimacy
4. Fear of emotional contagion
5. Inability to share the doctor
6. Complications of concurrent individual and group therapy
7. Early provocateurs
8. Inadequate orientation to therapy
9. Complications arising from subgrouping

*Barron ego strength scale, Stroop color word test, and Wechsler-Bellevue.

Usually more than one factor is involved in the decision to terminate. Some factors are more closely related to external circumstances or to enduring character traits which the patient brings to the group, and thus are relevant to the selective process; whereas others are related to problems arising within the group and thus are more relevant to therapist technique (I discuss them in chapters 10 and 11). Most relevant to the establishment of selection criteria are the patients who dropped out because of external factors, group deviancy, and problems of intimacy.

External Factors

1. *Physical reasons for terminating therapy* (for example, irreconcilable scheduling conflicts, moving out of the geographic area) played a negligible role in decisions to terminate. When this reason was offered by the patient, closer study usually demonstrated the presence of group-related stress more pertinent to the patient's departure. Nevertheless, in the initial screening session, the therapist should always inquire about any such pending major life change. There is considerable evidence to suggest that dynamic group therapy is not a brief form of therapy and that patients should not be accepted into a group if there is a considerable likelihood of forced termination within the next several months. Such patients are better candidates for closed groups (for example, a group with fixed membership, meeting for a predetermined number of sessions. Such groups are very common, for example, in university mental health clinics where summer vacations make ongoing therapy impossible).

2. *External stress* was considered a factor in the premature dropout of several patients who were so disturbed by external events in their lives that it was difficult for them to expend the energy for involvement in the group. They could not explore their relationships with other group members while they were consumed with the threat of disruption of relationships with the most significant people in their lives. It seemed especially pointless and frustrating to these patients to hear other group members discuss their problems when their own problems seemed so compelling. Among the external stresses were: severe marital discord with impending divorce, impending career or academic failure, disruptive relationship with family members, bereavement, and severe physical disease.

The importance of external stress as a factor in premature group termination was difficult to gauge, since often it appeared secondary to internal forces. A patient's psychic turmoil may cause disruption of his or her life situation so that secondary external stress occurs; or a patient may focus on an external problem, magnifying it as a means of escaping anxiety originating from the group therapy. Several patients considered external stress as the chief reason for termination; but in each instance, careful study indicated that external stress seemed at best a contributory but not sufficient cause for the dropout. Undue focusing on external events often seemed to be one manifestation of a denial mechanism which was helping the patient to avoid something perceived as dangerous in the group. The patients use the external stress as a rationalization for termination in order to avoid the anticipated dangers of self-disclosure, aggression, intimacy, or facing unknown aspects of themselves.

In the selection process, therefore, an unwarranted focusing on external stress may be an unfavorable sign, whether it represents an extraordinary amount of stress or manifestation of denial. Another unfavorable referral is the patient who has been propelled into therapy by an external crisis and has well-delineated goals—for example, a person distressed by a recent major loss through death or rejection.

Group Deviancy

The study of patients who drop out of therapy because they are group deviants offers a rich supply of information relevant to the selection process. But, first, the term *deviant* must be carefully defined. Almost every group patient represents an extreme in at least one variable— that is, the youngest, the only unmarried member, the sickest, the only Asian-American, the only nonstudent, the angriest, or the quietest. However, many patients (33 percent of the dropouts) deviated significantly from the rest of the group in areas crucial to their group participation; and this deviancy and its consequent repercussions were considered to be the primary reason for their premature termination. The patients' roles varied from those who were silent nonparticipators to those who were loud, angry, group disruptors, but always they were isolates and were perceived by the therapists and by the other members as retarding group locomotion.

It was said of all these patients by the group, by the therapists, and sometimes by the patients themselves that they just "didn't fit in." This distinction is difficult to translate into objectively measurable factors. The most commonly described characteristics are: lack of psychological sophistication, lack of interpersonal sensitivity, and lack of personal psychological insight manifested in part by the common utilization of denial. The patients were often of lower socioeconomic status and educational level than the rest of the group. The therapists, when describing their group behavior, emphasized that these patients retarded the group. They functioned on a different level of communication from that of the rest of the group. They remained at the symptom-describing, advice-giving and seeking, or judgmental level and avoided discussion of immediate feelings and here-and-now interaction.

There was an important subcategory of several dropouts who were chronic schizophrenics and, after individual treatment, were making a borderline adjustment. They had "sealed over" and utilized much denial and suppression. Their peculiarity was obvious to the other group members by their bizarre dress, mannerisms, and verbal content.

Two other patients in the study who did not drop out differed from the other members of their group in style of life. One had a history of prostitution and had an illegitimate child; another had a history of drug addiction and dealing. However, these two patients did *not* differ from the others in ways that impeded group locomotion (psychological insight, interpersonal sensitivity, and effective communication) and never became group deviants.

Group Deviancy: Empirical Research

Considerable social-psychological data from research with laboratory groups helps us to understand the fate of the deviant in the therapy group. Group members who are unable to participate in the group task, and who impede group locomotion toward the completion of the task, are much less attracted to the group and are motivated to terminate membership.[29] Individuals whose contributions fail to match high group standards have a high rate of group dropout—a tendency particularly marked when the individuals have a lower level of self-esteem.[30] The task of therapy groups is to engage in meaningful communication with the other group members, to reveal oneself, to give valid feedback, and to examine the hidden and unconscious aspects of one's feelings, behavior, and motivation. Individuals who fail at this task are those who lack the requisite skills or motivation. They lack the required amount of psychological-mindedness, are less introspective, less inquisitive, and more likely to utilize self-deceptive defense mechanisms; or they are reluctant to accept the role of patient and the accompanying implication that some personal change is necessary. D. Lundgren and D. Miller have shown in research upon Bethel T-groups that the individuals who are most satisfied with themselves, and who are inclined to overestimate others' opinions of them, tend to profit less from the group experience.[31] The Lieberman, Yalom, and Miles encounter group study demonstrated that group members who did not highly value or desire personal change were likely to terminate prematurely.[32] The ability to face one's deficiencies, even to the point of undue self-criticism, and a degree of sensitivity to the feelings of others seem to be requisite skills for successful group membership. Similarly in group therapy, members who on post-group questionnaires cannot accurately perceive how others view them are more likely to remain, at best, peripheral members.[33]

What happens to individuals who are unable to engage in the basic group task and are perceived by the group and, at some level of awareness, by themselves as impeding the group? S. Schachter has demonstrated that, in a small group, communication toward a deviant is very great initially and then drops off sharply as the group rejects the deviant.[34] The rejection (on sociometric measures) was proportional to the extent to which the deviancy was relevant to the purpose of the group. Much research has demonstrated that one's position in the group communication network significantly influences ones satisfaction with the group.[35] J. M. Jackson has shown also that an individual's attraction to a group is directly proportional to the extent to which this individual is considered valuable by the other members of the group.[36] It also has been demonstrated that the ability of the group to influence an individual is dependent partly on the attractiveness of the group for that member and partly on the degree to which the member communicates with the others in the group.[37] It is also well known from the work of M. Sherif[38] and S. E. Asch[39] that an individual will often be made exceedingly uncomfortable by a deviant group role; and there is evidence that individuals in a deviant or isolate group role, who cannot or do not verbally express anxiety, may experience physiological anxiety correlates.[40] Lieberman, Miles, and I demonstrated that encounter group members who were deviants (members considered "out of the group" by the other members, or those individuals who grossly misperceived the group norms) had virtually no chance of benefiting from the group and an increased likelihood of suffering negative consequences.[41]

To summarize, there is experimental evidence that the group deviant derives less satisfaction from the group, experiences anxiety, is less valued by the group, is less likely to be influenced or benefited by the group, is more likely to be harmed by the group, and is far more likely than nondeviants to terminate membership.

These experimental findings coincide notably with the experience of deviants in the therapy groups studied. Of the eleven deviants, there was only one who did not terminate prematurely. This patient managed to continue in the group because of massive support he received in concurrent individual therapy. However, he not only remained an isolate in the group but, in the opinion of the therapists and other members, impeded the progress of the group. What happened in that group was remarkably similar to the phenomena described above by Schachter[42] in experimental groups: at first considerable group energy was expended on the deviant; then the group gave up and the deviant was, to a great extent, excluded from the communicational network; but the group could never entirely forget the deviant, who slowed the pace of the work. If there is something important going on in the group that cannot be talked about, there will always be a degree of generalized communicative inhibition. With a disenfranchised member, the group is never really free; in a sense, it cannot move much faster than its slowest member.

These findings bear heavily upon the selection process. The patients who will assume a deviant role in therapy groups are not difficult to identify in screen interviews. The denial, the de-emphasis of intrapsychic and interpersonal factors, the tendency to attribute dysphoria to somatic and external environmental factors are evident in a carefully conducted interview.

The sample of chronic, "sealed over" schizophrenic patients was particularly recognizable. These patients maintained a precarious adjustment and could not intimately involve themselves in a rapidly moving interactional group without seriously threatening this adjustment. The chronic schizophrenic patients were all introduced into the group for similar reasons: their individual therapists felt that they had probably reached a plateau in treatment and now needed to develop socializing skills; in some instances, a transfer to group therapy was utilized as a method of gradual termination so as to relieve the therapist of guilt feelings.

The error thus occurs not in the identification of these patients but in the assumption that, even if they will not "click" with the rest of the group, they will, nevertheless, still benefit from the overall group support and the opportunity to improve their socializing techniques. In our experience, this expectation is not realized. The referral is a poor one, with neither the patient nor the group profiting. Eventually the group will extrude the deviant. The members may smile at one another when the deviant speaks or behaves irrelevantly; they will mascot the deviant; they will ignore the deviant rather than invest the necessary time to understand his or her interventions. In short, an environment will be created that can only be inimical to the therapeutic process.

Rigid attitudes coupled with proselytizing desires may rapidly propel an individual into a deviant position. A very difficult patient to work with in groups is the individual who employs fundamentalist religious views in the service of denial. The defenses of this patient are often impervious to ordinarily potent group pressures because they are bolstered, in his or her self system, by the norms of another anchor group —the particular religious sect. To tell the patient that he or she is applying certain basic tenets with unrealistic literalness is often not effective, and a frontal assault on these defenses merely rigidifies them.

It is important that the therapist attempt to screen out patients who will become marked deviants *relative to the goals of the particular group for which one is being considered.* Patients become deviants because of their interpersonal behavior in the group sessions and not because of a deviant life style or past history. There is no type of past behavior too deviant for a group to accept once therapeutic group norms are established. I have seen individuals with life styles including prostitution, exhibitionism, incest, voyeurism, kleptomania, infanticide, and histories of various other heinous criminal offenses accepted by a middle-class "straight" group. Alcoholics, to cite an example, often do poorly in mixed intensive outpatient groups, not because of their drinking but because of their interpersonal behavior: not infrequently an alcoholic's serious drinking problem manifests oral character traits that in the group setting take the form of insatiable demands for support, confirmation, and reassurance. The alcoholic often is fixed upon receiving nurturant supplies from the therapist, whom he or she is unable to share with the other members. Frustration tolerance is low, and when the alcoholic's threshold is reached, he or she may respond in ways that are inaccessible to group influence, usually through some motoric expression—for example, by increased drinking, absenteeism, tardiness, and drunken arrivals at meetings. (A cautionary note: To the extent that a single appellation such as *alcoholic* fails to render a whole person, these remarks are generalizations, and many group therapists have successfully treated individuals with alcoholic problems.[43])

Problems of Intimacy

Several patients dropped out of group therapy because of conflicted feelings about intimacy.* They manifested their intimacy conflicts in

---

*The dropout categories are heavily overlapping. For example, the chronic schizophrenic "group deviants" were also, undoubtedly, heavily conflicted in the area of intimacy and would have encountered considerable difficulty in this area in the group, had not their deviant group role forced their dropout earlier. Conversely, many of the patients who dropped out because of problems of intimacy began to occupy a deviant role because of the behavioral manifestations of their problems in intimacy. Had the stress of the internal intimacy conflict not forced them to terminate, it is most likely that the inherent stresses of the deviant role would have created pressures leading to termination.

various ways: (1) schizoid withdrawal, (2) maladaptive self-disclosure (promiscuous self-disclosures or pervasive dread of self-disclosure), and (3) unrealistic demands for instant intimacy.

Several patients, who were diagnosed as having either schizoid personality disorder or avoidant personality disorder (because of their social withdrawal, interpersonal coldness, aloofness, introversion, and tendency toward autistic preoccupation) experienced considerable difficulty relating and communicating in the group. Each had begun the group with a resolution to express feelings and to correct previous maladaptive patterns of relating. They failed to accomplish this aim and experienced frustration and anxiety, which in turn further blocked their efforts to speak. Their therapists described their group role as "schizoid-isolate," "silent member," "nonentity," "peripheral," "nonrevealer," "doctor's helper." Most of these patients terminated treatment thoroughly discouraged about the possibility of ever obtaining help from group therapy. I have occasionally seen such patients benefit from therapeutic factors such as universality, identification, altruism, and development of socializing techniques, early in the course of a new group. After a few months, as the group matures and members begin to involve themselves deeply with one another, the schizoid patient is out of his or her level and reaches a point of diminishing returns in therapy. The group members, in time, often grow impatient with the patient's silence, and weary of drawing him or her out (of playing "twenty questions," as one group put it), and turn against the patient. If the patient chooses to leave the group before this point, or if the therapist is wise (or courageous) enough to remove the patient from the group (see chapter 11), then the patient will have profited from the group experience.

Another intimacy-conflicted patient, whose diagnosis lay closer to schizophrenia (schizotypal personality disorder—DSM–III) dropped out for different reasons—his fears of his own aggression against other group members. He originally applied for treatment because "of a feeling of wanting to explode . . . a fear of killing someone when I explode . . . which results in my staying far away from people." He participated intellectually in the first four meetings he attended, but was frightened by the other members' expression of emotion. In the fifth meeting one patient monopolized the entire meeting with a repetitive, tangential discourse. The patient became extremely angry with the monopolizer and with the rest of the group members for their complacency in allowing this to happen—and, with no warning, abruptly terminated therapy.

Other patients manifested their problems with intimacy in other ways: some experienced a constant, pervasive dread of self-disclosure which precluded participation in the group and ultimately resulted in their dropping out; others engaged in premature, promiscuous self-disclosure and abruptly terminated; whereas still others made such inordinate demands on their fellow group members for immediate, prefabricated intimacy that they created an inviable group role for themselves.

This entire category of patients with severe problems in the area of intimacy presents a particular challenge to the group therapist in the areas both of selection and of therapeutic management (to be considered in chapter 13). The irony is that these patients whose attrition rate is high are the very ones for whom a successful group experience could be particularly rewarding. R. Harrison and B. Lubin reported that, in a human relations laboratory (see chapter 16), individuals designated as "work-oriented" (as opposed to "person-oriented") learn more and change more as a result of their group experience even though they are significantly more uncomfortable in the group.[44] Harrison and Lubin do not use the label *schizoid*, but their description of "work-oriented" individuals suggests a strong overlap: "Constriction of emotionality . . . threatened by expression of feelings by others . . . hard for them to experience and express their own emotional reactions." Therefore, these patients, whose life histories are characterized by ungratifying interpersonal relationships, stand to profit much from successfully negotiating an intimate group experience; and yet if their past interpersonal history has been too deprived, the group will prove too threatening for them and they will drop out of therapy more demoralized than before.

Thus, this general category represents at the same time a specific indication and counterindication for group therapy. The problem, of course, is one of early identification and screening out of those who will be overwhelmed in the group. If only we could, with accuracy, quantify this critical cut-off point! The prediction of group behavior from pre-therapy screening sessions is a complex task which I will discuss in detail in the next chapter. However, it may be noted here that an individual who, in the screening procedure, is severely schizoid and isolated, with a pervasive dread of self-disclosure, is an unfavorable candidate for interactional group therapy. If these patients are dissatisfied with their interpersonal styles, express a strong motivation for change, and manifest curiosity about their inner lives, then they stand a better chance of benefiting from a therapy group, especially a young one. Mildly or moderately schizoid patients and patients with an avoidant personality disorder *(DSM-III)*, on the other hand, are excellent candidates for group therapy and rarely fail to benefit therefrom. Great caution should be exercised when the therapist is seeking a replacement member for an already established, fast-moving group. If you decide on a therapeutic trial, then you should adequately prepare the schizoid patient for the group (see chapter 10) and consider also the possibility of short-term individual therapy conducted concurrently with the early phases of group therapy.

The Fear of Emotional Contagion

Several patients who dropped out of group therapy reported that they had been extremely adversely affected by hearing the problems of the other group members. One patient stated that, during his three weeks in the group, he was very upset by the others' problems, dreamed about them every night, and relived their problems during the day. Other patients reported being upset by one particularly disturbed patient in each of their groups; they were all frightened by seeing aspects of the other patient in themselves, fearing that they, too, might become as mentally ill as the severely disturbed patient or that continued exposure to this patient would evoke a personal regression. Another patient in this category experienced a severe revulsion toward the other group members, stating, "I couldn't stand the people in the group. They were repulsive. I got upset seeing them trying to heap their problems on top of mine. I didn't want to hear their problems. I felt no sympathy for them and couldn't bear to look at them. They were all ugly, fat, and unattractive." She bolted the first group meeting thirty minutes early and never returned. She had a lifelong history of being upset by other people's illnesses and avoiding sick people; once when her mother fainted, she "stepped over her" to get away rather than trying to help. Others also, as Nash et al. reported in an earlier study, had a long-term proclivity to avoid sick people.[45] They reported a lack of curiosity about others and, if they had been present at an accident, were "the first to leave" or tended to "look the other way." Most of them reported being very upset at the sight of blood.

Such fear of contagion has many possible dynamics. Some patients with borderline personal disorder report such fears (it is a common phenomena in inpatient group therapy), and it is often regarded as a sign of permeable ego boundaries and an inability to differentiate oneself from significant others in one's environment. Fears of contagion are frequently often associated with an intolerable fear of being alone and an irrational sense that one does not exist unless one is being observed or attended to by another. Other patients with fear of contagion are individuals who rely heavily upon projection: they disown undesirable personal traits or motivations by projecting them onto another and then develop strong negative feelings toward the person who serves as a receptacle for their feelings.

A fear of emotional contagion, unless it is extremely marked and clearly manifest in the pre-therapy screening procedure, is not an extremely useful index for group inclusion or exclusion. Generally, it is difficult to predict this behavior from screening interviews; furthermore fear of emotional contagion is not in itself sufficient cause for failure. Therapists who are sensitive to the problem can deal with it effectively in the therapeutic process. Occasionally patients must gradually desensitize themselves; I have known patients who dropped out of several therapy groups but who persevered until they were finally able to remain in one. The therapist may help by clarifying for the patient the crippling effects of his or her attitudes toward others' failings. Logic thus dictates that these attitudes do not rule out group therapy. Quite the contrary, this form of pathology has crippling effects on the patient's interpersonal life; and if the discomfort can be contained, the group may well offer the ideal therapeutic format for such a patient.

Other Reasons

The other reasons for group therapy dropouts—inability to share the therapist, complications of concurrent individual and group therapy, early provocateurs, problems in orientation to therapy, and complications arising from subgrouping—were generally a result not so much of faulty selection but of faulty therapeutic technique and will be discussed in later chapters. None of these categories, though, belongs purely to the selection or therapy technique rubric. For example, some patients terminated out of an inability to share the therapist. They never relinquished the notion that progress in therapy was dependent solely upon the amount of goods (time, attention, and so on) they received from the group therapist. Although it may have been true that these patients tended to be excessively dependent and authority-oriented, it was also true that they had been incorrectly referred to and prepared for group therapy. They had all been in individual therapy, and the group was considered as a method of therapy weaning. Obviously, group therapy is not a modality to be used to facilitate the termination phase of individual therapy, and the therapist, in pre-therapy screening, should be alert to inappropriate patient referrals.

Criteria for Inclusion

The most important criterion for inclusion is the most obvious one— motivation. The patient must be highly motivated for therapy in general and for group therapy in particular. It will not do to start group therapy because one has been "sent"—whether by spouse, probation officer, individual therapist, or any individual or agency outside oneself. To permit a patient to enter the group with this reluctant motivational set is to curtail greatly his or her chances for success. Many erroneous prejudgments of the group may be corrected in the preparation procedure (see chapter 10), but if you discern in a person a deeply rooted unwillingness to accept responsibility for treatment or deeply entrenched unwillingness to enter the group, you should not accept him or her as a patient.

Most clinicians agree that an important criterion for inclusion is whether a patient has obvious problems in the interpersonal domain: loneliness; shyness and social withdrawal; inability to be intimate or to love; excessive competitiveness, aggressivity, abrasiveness, or argumentativeness; suspiciousness; problems with authority; narcissism, including an inability to share, to empathize, or to accept criticism and a continuous need for admiration; feelings of unlovability; fears of assertiveness; obsequiousness, and dependency. In addition, patients must be willing to take responsibility for these problems or, at the very least, acknowledge them and entertain a desire for change.

Some clinicians suggest that patients who are impulsive, who find it difficult to control the need to act immediately on their feelings, are far better handled in group than in individual therapy.[46] The individual therapist often finds it difficult to remain both participant and observer, whereas in the group these two roles are divided among the members: some members may, for example, rush to battle with the impulsive patient, while others egg them on ("Let's you and him fight"), while others may act as disinterested reliable witnesses whose testimony the impulsive patient is often far more willing to trust than the therapist's.

In cases where interpersonal problems are not paramount (or not obvious to the patient), group therapy may still be the treatment of choice. For example, patients who are extremely intellectualized may do better with the affective stimuli available in a group. Some patients fare poorly in individual therapy because of severe problems in the transference: they either so distort the therapeutic relationship or become so deeply involved with (or oppositional to) the therapist, that they need the reality testing offered by other group members to make therapy possible.

Many patients seek therapy without an explicit interpersonal complaint. These may cite the common problems that propel the contemporary patient into therapy: a sense of something missing in life, feelings of meaninglessness, diffuse anxiety, anhedonia, identity confusion, mild depression, self-derogation or self-destructive behavior, compulsive workaholism, fears of success. Each of these complaints has its interpersonal underpinnings, and each may be treated as successfully in group therapy as in individual therapy.

RESEARCH ON INCLUSION CRITERIA

Any systematic approach to defining criteria for inclusion must issue from the study of successful group therapy patients, who theoretically should offer valuable information for the selection process. Imagine a rigorously controlled study in which a large number of patients are systematically studied before entering group therapy and then followed and evaluated after it. These patients should have different rates of success; and by correlating their pre-therapy data with outcome, we should be able to determine those patient characteristics predictive of favorable outcome. Unfortunately difficulties are inherent in such a study: patients drop out of therapy; many obtain ancillary individual therapy; group therapists vary in competence and technique; and initial diagnostic technique is unreliable and often idiosyncratic.

A team of researchers (P. Houts, S. Zimerberg, K. Rand, and myself) attempted, in 1965, to study factors evident before group therapy that might predict successful outcome in group therapy.[47] Forty patients (in five outpatient therapy groups) were followed through one year of group therapy. Outcome was evaluated and correlated with many variables studied before the onset of therapy. The results indicated that many factors were *not* predictive of success in group therapy, including level of psychological sophistication, the therapists' prediction of outcome, previous self-disclosure, and demographic data. In fact, the only variables predictive of success were the patients' attraction to the group and the patients' general popularity in the group (both measured at the sixth and the twelfth meetings).[48] The finding that popularity correlated highly with successful outcome has some implications for selection, because the researchers found that high previous self-disclosure, activity in the group, and the ability to introspect were some of the prerequisites for group popularity.

The Lieberman, Yalom, and Miles encounter group study (see chapter 16) demonstrated that, on pre-group testing, those who were to profit most from the group were those who highly valued and desired personal change; who viewed themselves as deficient both in understanding their own feelings and in their sensitivity to the feelings of others; who had a high expectational set for the group, anticipating that it would provide relevant opportunities for communication and help them correct their deficiencies.[49]

J. Melnick and G. Rose, in a project involving forty-five encounter group members, determined at the onset of the group each member's risk-taking propensity and expectations regarding the quality of interpersonal behavior to be experienced in the group and then determined each member's actual behavior in the group (including self-disclosure, feedback given, risk taking, verbal activity, depth of involvement, attraction to the group).[50] They found that both high-risk propensity and more favorable expectations correlated with therapeutically favorable behavior in the group.

The finding that a positive expectational set is predictive of favorable outcome has substantial research support: the more a client expects therapy to be useful, the more useful will it be.[51] This finding has implications both for the selection process and for the preparation of patients for therapy. As I discuss in chapter 10, it is possible, through proper preparation, to create a favorable expectational set.

To the best of my knowledge, no other systematic outcome studies demonstrate a relationship between patient trait or behavior (as observed before therapy) and subsequent outcome in group therapy—a glaring defect and one that must be corrected before it is possible to establish a sound scientific base for selection of patients for group therapy.

THE PATIENT'S EFFECT ON OTHER GROUP MEMBERS

Other inclusion criteria become evident when we also consider the other members of a group into which the patient may be placed. Thus far, for pedagogical clarity, I have oversimplified the problem by attempting to identify only absolute criteria for inclusion or exclusion. Unlike individual therapy recruitment, where we need consider only the questions whether the patient will profit from therapy and whether he or she and a specific therapist can establish a working relationship, recruitment for group therapy cannot, in practice, ignore the remainder of the group members. It is conceivable, for example, that a dependent alcoholic, a compulsive talker, or a sociopath might derive some benefit from a group but also that such a patient's presence would render the group less effective for several other members. Conversely, there are patients who would do well in a variety of treatment modalities but are placed in a slowly moving group because of their catalytic qualities or because of some specific need of a particular group. For example, some groups at times seem to need an aggressive member, or a strong male, or a soft feminine member. While borderline patients often have a stormy course of therapy, they also often have a beneficial influence on the group therapy process. They are more aware of their unconscious, less dedicated to formal social inhibitory techniques, and may lead the group into a more candid and eventually intimate culture. Considerable caution must be exercised, however, in including a member whose ego strength is significantly less than that of the other members. If these patients have socially desirable behavioral traits and are valued by the other members because of their openness and deep perceptivity, they will generally do very well. If, however, their behavior alienates others, and if the group is so fast moving or threatening that, rather than lead, they retard the group, then they will be driven into a deviant role and their experience is likely to be counter-therapeutic.

THE THERAPIST'S FEELING TOWARD THE PATIENT

One final, and important, criterion for inclusion is the therapist's personal feeling toward the patient. Regardless of the source, the therapist who experiences a strong dislike for or disinterest in a patient should refer that patient elsewhere. This caveat is obviously relative, and you must establish for yourself the intensity of such feelings that would preclude effective therapy. It is my impression that the issue is somewhat less crucial for group therapists than for individual therapists: with the consensual validation available in the group from other patients and from the co-therapist, many therapists find that they are more often able to work through initial negative feelings toward patients in group therapy than in individual therapy. Whether you like or dislike a patient is also a function of experience and of your personal maturity. As therapists gain experience and self-knowledge, they usually develop greater generosity and greater tolerance and find themselves actively disliking fewer and fewer patients.

An Overview of the Selection Procedure

The material I have presented thus far about selection of patients has a disturbingly disjunctive nature. I can, I believe, introduce some order by applying to this material a central organizing principle—a simple punishment-reward system. Patients are likely to terminate membership in a therapy group, and are thereby poor candidates, when the punishments or disadvantages of group membership outweigh the rewards or the anticipated rewards. When speaking of punishments or disadvantages of group membership, I refer to the price the patient must pay for group membership: this includes an investment of time, money, and energy, as well as a variety of dysphorias arising from the group experience, including anxiety, frustration, discouragement, and rejection.

The patient should play an important role in the selection process. It is preferable that one deselect oneself before entering the group than undergo the discomfort of dropping out of the group. The patient can make a judicious decision, however, only if provided with sufficient information: for example, the nature of the group experience, the anticipated length of therapy, what is expected of him or her in the group. I shall say more about this in the discussion on preparation of the group patient in chapter 10.

The rewards of membership in a therapy group consist of the various satisfactions members obtain from the group. Let us consider those rewards, or determinants of group cohesiveness, that are relevant to the selection of patients for group therapy.[52]

Members are satisfied with their groups (attracted to their groups and likely to continue membership in them) if:

1. They view the group as meeting their personal needs—that is, their goals in therapy;
2. They derive satisfaction from their relationships with the other members;
3. They derive satisfaction from their participation in the group task; and
4. They derive satisfaction from group membership vis-à-vis the outside world.

Each of these factors, if absent or of negative value, may outweigh the positive value of the others and result in group termination.

DOES THE GROUP SATISFY PERSONAL NEEDS?

The explicit personal needs of group therapy members are at first expressed in their "chief complaint"—their purpose for seeking therapy. These personal needs are usually couched in terms of relief from suffering, less frequently in terms of self-understanding or personal growth. Several factors are important here: there must be significant personal need; the group must be viewed as an agent with the potential of meeting that need; and the group must be seen, in time, as making progress toward meeting that need.

The patient must, of course, have some discomfort in his or her life to provide the required motivation for change. The relationship between discomfort and suitability for group therapy is not linear but curvilinear. *Patients with too little discomfort* (coupled with only a modest amount of curiosity about groups or themselves) are usually unwilling to pay the price for group membership.

Patients with moderately high discomfort may, on the other hand, be willing to pay a high price provided they have faith or evidence that the group can and will help. This faith may derive from several sources, such as:

1. Endorsement of group therapy by the mass media, by friends who have had a successful group therapy experience, or by a previous individual therapist;
2. Explicit preparation by the group therapist (see chapter 10);
3. Belief in the omniscience of authority figures;
4. Observing or being told about improvement of other group members; and
5. Observing changes in oneself occurring early in group therapy.

Patients with exceedingly high discomfort stemming from either extraordinary environmental stress, internal conflicts, inadequate ego strength, or some combination of these may be so overwhelmed with anxiety and realistic management of the external stress that the group goals and activities seem utterly irrelevant. Initially, many groups are unable to meet highly pressing personal needs. Greatly disturbed patients may be unable to tolerate the frustration that occurs as the group gradually evolves into an effective therapeutic instrument. They may demand instant relief, which the group cannot supply; or they may develop anxiety-binding defenses which are so interpersonally maladaptive (for example, extreme projection or somatization) as to make the group socially nonviable for them.

Individuals variously described as "alexithymic,"[53] "nonpsychologically minded," "nonintrospective," "high deniers," "psychological illiterates," and "psychologically insensitive" may be unable to perceive the group as meeting their personal needs. In fact, they may perceive an incompatibility between their personal needs and the group goals. They reason: "How can exploring my relations with the group members help me with my bad nerves?" These individuals, too, may have few sources of group satisfaction available to them. Not only does the group not satisfy their personal needs, but they cannot satisfactorily engage in the group activities (which require the very abilities they lack—introspection, sensitivity, and so on); and they eventually are further burdened with the anxiety inherent in the role of group deviant. There is a need here for sensitive clinical judgment, since some highly motivated, more flexible individuals with these characteristics may be taught by the group to become working members of the group.

SATISFACTION FROM RELATIONSHIPS WITH OTHER MEMBERS

Group members derive satisfaction from their relationships with other group members, and often this source of attraction to the group may dwarf the others. The importance of relationships among members both as a source of cohesiveness and as a therapeutic factor was fully discussed in chapter 3, and I need pause here only to reflect that it is rare for a patient to continue membership in the prolonged absence of interpersonal satisfaction.

The development of interpersonal satisfaction may be a slow process. Psychotherapy patients are often contemptuous of themselves and are therefore likely to be initially contemptuous of their fellow patients. They have had, for the most part, few gratifying interpersonal relationships in the past and have little trust or expectation of gaining anything from close relationships with the other group members. Often the patients may use the therapist as a transitional object. By relating positively to the therapist at first, they may more easily grow closer with one another. M. B. Parloff has demonstrated that group patients who establish closer relationships with the group therapist are significantly more inclined to perceive other group members as socially attractive.[54]

SATISFACTION FROM PARTICIPATION IN GROUP ACTIVITIES

The satisfaction that patients derive from participation in the group task is largely inseparable from the satisfaction derived from relationships with the other group members. The group task (to achieve a group culture of intimacy, acceptance, introspection, understanding, and interpersonal honesty) is, in essence, interpersonal. However, research with a wide variety of groups has demonstrated that satisfactory participation in the group task, regardless of its nature, is an important source of satisfaction for the group members.[55] Patients who cannot introspect, reveal themselves, care for others, or manifest their feelings will derive little gratification from participation in group activities. Such patients include many of the types discussed earlier: for example, the schizoid personality, patients with other types of overriding intimacy problem, the deniers, the somatizers, and the mentally retarded. These patients are better treated in a homogeneous group that has a group task consonant with their abilities.

SATISFACTION FROM PRIDE IN GROUP MEMBERSHIP

Members of many groups derive satisfaction from membership because the outside world regards their group as highly valued or prestigious. Therapy groups obviously are at a disadvantage in this regard, and generally this source of attraction to the group is not readily available. Therapy group members will, however, usually develop some pride in their group: for example, they will defend it if it is attacked by new members. They may feel superior to outsiders (members of A.A. call them "earth creatures")—to people who are as troubled as they but lack the good sense to join a therapy group. If patients manifest extraordinary shame at membership and are reluctant to reveal their membership to intimate friends or even to spouses, then therapy group membership must appear to them dissonant with the values of other important anchor groups; it is not likely that such patients will become deeply attracted to the group. Occasionally, as J. D. Frank and E. J. Ends point out, outside groups (for example, family, military, or, more recently, industry) will exert pressure on the individual to join a therapy group.[56] Groups held together only by such coercion are tenuous; but the evolving group process may generate other sources of cohesiveness.

Summary

Selection for group therapy is, in practice, conducted by the process of deselection: group therapists exclude certain patients from consideration and accept all others. The study of failures in group therapy, especially those patients who drop out early in the course of the group, provides important exclusion criteria. Patients should not be placed in a group if they are likely to become deviant. Group deviants stand little chance of benefiting from the group experience and a fair chance of being harmed by therapy. A group deviant is one who is unable to participate in the group task. Thus, in a heterogeneous, interactional group, a deviant is one who cannot or will not examine one's self and one's relationship with others, especially with the other members of the group.

Patients are to be excluded if they are in the midst of a life crisis that can be more efficiently resolved by other therapy formats. Conflicts in the sphere of intimacy represent both indication and contraindication for group therapy: group therapy can offer considerable help in this domain; yet if the conflicts are too extreme, the patient will choose to leave (or be extruded) by the group. The therapist's task is to select those patients who are as close as possible to the border between need and impossibility.

If the markers for exclusion are not present, the vast majority of patients seeking therapy can be treated in group therapy.

9

THE COMPOSITION OF
THERAPY GROUPS

Imagine the following situation: a psychiatric outpatient clinic with ten group therapists ready to form groups and seventy patients who, on the basis of the selection criteria outlined thus far, are suitable group therapy candidates. Is there an ideal or superior way to compose those ten groups?

A second, more common clinical problem is closely related. Assume that one patient has been deemed a suitable group therapy candidate and that there are several therapy groups, each with one vacancy. Into which group should the patient go? Which group would offer the best fit for that particular patient? The solution to this problem is to be found in the solution to the first. If valid principles about the effective total composition of a group can be established, the corollaries of these principles may provide guidelines for replacing members who leave the group. We grope in the dark if we try to replace a missing unit without any knowledge of the organization of the total system.

In this chapter I shall examine research evidence and clinical observations bearing on group composition. Is it possible that the proper blend of individuals will form the ideal group? That the wrong blend remains an inharmonious aggregate, never coalescing into a working group?

First, we must be clear about the ingredients of our blend. Of the infinite number of human characteristics, which are germane to the task of composing a therapy group? The essence of the therapy group is interaction: each member must continually communicate and interact with the other members. Regardless of any other consideration, the actual behavior of the members of a group dictates the fate of that group. Therefore, if we are to deal intelligently with group composition, we must aim for a mix that will allow the members to interact in some desired manner. The entire procedure of group composition and selection of group patients is thus based on the important assumption that we can, with some degree of accuracy, predict the group behavior of an individual from pre-therapy screening. This assumption is the basis for my preceding pronouncements about group selection and the following ones about group composition.

The Prediction of Group Behavior

In the previous chapter I advise against the inclusion of certain patients in a group because their behavior has undesirable effects on themselves and the group. Generally, predictions limited to individuals with such extreme, fixed, maladaptive interpersonal behavior as the alcoholic, the sociopathic, and the floridly psychotic are reasonably accurate: the grosser the pathology, the greater the predictive accuracy. There is scarcely any room for error when considering a paranoid schizophrenic with an active, expanding, persecutory delusional system. We know how that patient will behave in the group: he or she will soon grow to distrust the group members, will become secretive, suspicious, perhaps openly accusatory, and then, as the delusional system generalizes, will ultimately regard the group members as inimical.

Ordinarily, however, in clinical practice the problem is far more subtle: most patients who apply for treatment have a wide repertoire of behavior, and their ultimate group behavior is far less predictable.

Several screening procedures have been employed to predict future behavior in group therapy. Let us examine the most common of these clinical and research procedures.

THE STANDARD DIAGNOSTIC INTERVIEW

The most common method of screening patients is the individual interview. Often it is the routine interview used at intake for all patients applying for treatment to a practitioner or a clinic. The interviewer, in addition to acquiring information about such issues as motivation for treatment, ego strength, environmental stresses, or past history, attempts to predict how the patient will behave in the group. These predictions are often highly remote inferences stemming from observations of a patient's behavior in the dyadic situation.

One of the traditional end products of the mental health interview is a diagnosis that, in capsule form, is meant to summarize the patient's condition and convey useful information to another practitioner. The standard psychiatric diagnosis based on standard classificatory systems (for example, *DSM-III* or *ICD-9*) has always been, as most group therapists will attest, of only limited value as an indicator of interpersonal behavior. Diagnostic nomenclature was never meant for this purpose; it stemmed from a disease-oriented medical discipline, and its basis has been primarily etiological and symptomatic.

The revised (1980) *Diagnostic and Statistical Manual of Mental Disorders (DSM-III)* is an improvement upon earlier psychiatric diagnostic systems: it provides more objective and mutually exclusive definitions for psychiatric diagnosis and pays far more attention to personality; it attempts to code personality upon a specific axis (Axis II) and recognizes that an individual may have personality pathology in more than one area apart from (or in addition to) other psychiatric disorders.

Nonetheless, the *DSM-III*, along with the most recent *International Classification of Disease (ICD-9)* and all other disease-based systems, has marked limitations for those practitioners who work primarily with patients with relatively minor disturbances. The descriptive categories are not discrete; they are based only on observable behavior and not on the inner life of the individual; and reliability rates, even for highly experienced clinicians, for personality disturbances are very unsatisfactory.[1]

The typical private practitioner finds that the great majority of patients have some characterologic disturbance classifiable only in some vague way in the official nomenclature. A few, but only a few, of the categories or subcategories are useful in predicting interpersonal behavior. A person labeled as having a severe schizoid personality disorder will most likely behave in a roughly predictable manner: he or she will probably remain detached, perhaps intellectualizing, will be unable to reach and share feelings with others, and will be perceived by others as cold, uncaring, and distant. However, two individuals with a borderline or a narcissistic personality disorder may manifest entirely different interpersonal styles in the therapy group.

Over all, the standard intake interview has been shown to have little value in predicting subsequent group behavior. For example, in a study of thirty outpatients referred to group therapy, W. Piper and M. Marrache[2] demonstrated that the intake interviewers' ratings of five important factors—(1) motivation for group therapy, (2) verbal skills, (3) chronicity of problems, (4) history of object relations, and (5) capacity for insight—were unrelated to how a patient actually functioned in the group (for example, verbal activity, work participation and responsivity to other members and to the leader, as measured by the Hill Interactional Matrix[3]).

That a diagnostic label fails to predict much about human behavior should neither surprise nor chagrin us. No label or phrase can adequately encompass an individual's essence or entire range of behavior. Any limiting categorization is not only errorful but offensive as well and stands in opposition to the basic human foundations of the therapeutic relationship. (Albert Camus once described hell as a place where one's identity was eternally fixed and displayed on personal signs: Adulterous Humanist, Christian Landowner, Jittery Philosopher, Charming Janus, and so on.[4] To Camus, hell is to have no way of explaining oneself, to be fixed, to be classified once and for all time.)

STANDARD PSYCHOLOGICAL TESTING

Several investigators have sought to use standard psychological diagnostic tests as predictors of group behavior. These have most prominently included the Rorschach, the MMPI, the TAT, the Sentence Completion, and Draw-a-Person tests.[5] All these tests failed to yield valid predictions, with the single trivial exception that individuals using considerable denial (as shown by the Rorschach and the TAT) more often made positive, agreeing statements in group therapy.

SPECIALIZED DIAGNOSTIC PROCEDURES

The failure of these standard diagnostic procedures to predict anything at all about group behavior suggests the necessity for new procedures focusing primarily on interpersonal behavior. Recent clinical observations and research have suggested several promising directions. I will discuss these under two headings:

1. A formulation of an interpersonal nosological system.
2. New diagnostic procedures that directly sample group-relevant behavior.

An Interpersonal Nosological System

The first known attempt to classify mental illness dates back to 1700 B.C.;[6] and the intervening years have seen a bewildering number of systems advanced, each unacceptable, each beset with its own internal inconsistency. The majority of systems have classified mental illness according either to symptoms or to presumed etiology. With the advent of the object-relations and the interpersonal systems of conceptualizing psychopathology, as well as the increase in the number of people seeking treatment for less severe problems in living, have come rudimentary attempts to classify individuals according to interpersonal styles of relating.

For example, Karen Horney viewed troubled individuals as moving exaggeratedly and maladaptively *toward, against,* or *away* from other people, and has described interpersonal profiles of these types and various subtypes.[7] In her system, individuals who chiefly move *toward* others invoke the "self-effacing solution" and conduct their interpersonal relationships with a currency of love. Those who move *against* others (the "expansive solutions") engage in an interpersonal search for mastery and are divided into three subgroups: the narcissistic, the perfectionist, and the arrogant vindictive. The third maneuver, moving *away from* people, is labeled "resignation," and individuals so designated handle interpersonal relationships by withdrawal, by "a search for freedom." Horney's formulations have been influential and valuable for many American clinicians. Unfortunately Horney's nosological types are, as she recognized, highly caricaturized and composite profiles; there has been, to my knowledge, no attempt to systematize and quantify this approach to diagnosis.

Much the same can be said for Erich Fromm's attempts to formulate nosological categories on the basis of the individual's basic interpersonal orientation (the marketing, the receptive, the hoarding, and the exploitative personalities).[8] These and other classificatory systems developed by interpersonally oriented clinicians may provide a philosophical background for the study of personality but have not been organized and systematized with the precision necessary for the development of a methodology for the scientific study of personality.

Although some brave researchers (for example, R. Plutchik,[9] H. Kellerman,[10] and T. Leary[11]) have developed comprehensive, quantifiable interpersonal models of personality, these have proven so complex and cumbersome that they have stimulated no research on the composition of therapy groups.

There have been several attempts to design new psychological tests to predict subsequent group behavior. Variants of the Thematic Apperception Test,[12] the Sentence Association Test,[13] the Sentence Completion Test,[14] personality trait inventories,[15] and a sixty-item, self-report Q-sort[16] have all been used for this purpose with only equivocal results.

A more common strategy has been to define and study a few discrete personality variables that are particularly salient to an individual's participation in groups. These include dogmatism,[17] preference for high or low structure,[18] social avoidance,[19] locus of control[20], social risk-taking propensity,[21] and interpersonal trust.[22]

J. Melnick and G. Rose, in a well-designed experiment involving five undergraduate student encounter groups, demonstrated that social risk-taking propensity (measured by a self-administered questionnaire[23]) was significantly predictive of therapeutically appropriate self-disclosure, risk-taking behavior, and high verbal activity in the group sessions.[24]

One of the most commonly used instruments to measure interpersonal behavior is the FIRO (Fundamental Interpersonal Relations Orientation) which was first described by W. Schutz in 1958.[25] He reviewed a large number of studies of interpersonal behavior from the child development field, social psychological research, and the clinical field and concluded that control, inclusion, and affection are the three basic interpersonal needs. On the basis of these three needs an interpersonal profile of an individual may be constructed. The profile attempts to describe the valence of the individual toward each of these needs. Does one very much wish to control others or to be controlled, or is one relatively unconflicted in this area? Does one wish to be included in social activities or excluded from them? Does one very much desire intimacy or desire to avoid it? The data is derived from a self-administered questionnaire, the FIRO-B (the B stands for "behavior"), which takes approximately fifteen to twenty minutes to complete.

Direct Sampling of Group Relevant Behavior

A. Goldstein, K. Heller, and L. Sechrest, in their scholarly consideration of this topic, suggest that the prediction of within-group behavior will be most accurate when based on direct behavioral measurement of the individual who is engaged in a task closely related to the group therapy situation.[26] In other words, the closer we can approximate the therapy group in observing the individual, the more accurately can we predict his or her behavior. Abundant research evidence supports this thesis. The behavior of an individual kept in the same interpersonal format will show a consistency over time even though the people with whom this individual must interact are rotated—as has been demonstrated with child-adult interaction, therapist-patient interaction and small group interaction.[27] For example, R. H. Moos and S. R. Clemes have demonstrated that a patient seen by several individual therapists in rotation not only will be consistent in behavior but will change the behavior of each of the therapists![28]

The implications of these findings are that, since we cannot accurately predict group behavior from behavior in an individual interview, we should consider obtaining data about behavior in a group setting. Indeed, there has been some practical application of this principle. For example, in screening applicants for positions that require group-related skills, a procedure for observing their behavior in related group situations has been used. Thus, a group interview test has been used to select officers for the Air Force, shipyard foremen, public health officers, as well as many types of public and business executives.[29]

This general principle can be refined further, however, since additional research demonstrates that behavior in one group is especially consistent with behavior in previous groups if the groups are similar in composition,[30] in group task,[31] in group norms,[32] in expected role behavior,[33] or in global group characteristics (such as, climate or cohesiveness).[34] In other words, although one's behavior is broadly consistent from one group to the next, nevertheless there is still a wide range of behavior at one's disposal. The individual's specific behavior in a new group is influenced by the task and the structural properties of the group and by the specific interpersonal styles of the other group members.

The further implication, then, is that we can obtain the most relevant data for prediction of subsequent group behavior by observing an individual behave in a group that is as similar as possible to the one for which he or she is being screened. The most literal application of this principle is to arrange for the applicant to meet with the therapy group under consideration and to observe his or her behavior in this setting. In fact, some clinicians invite prospective members to visit the group on a trial basis so that the group members may carry out their own selection.[35] Although there are several advantages to this procedure (which I shall discuss in chapter 11), it is often clinically inefficient: it tends to disrupt the group; the members are disinclined to reject a prospective member unless there is some glaring incompatibility; furthermore, the prospective member is "on trial," as it were, and may not behave naturally.

A promising development with implications for both research and clinical practice is the test, or waiting-list, group—a temporary group constituted from a clinic waiting list. The behavior of a prospective group therapy patient is observed in the test group; and on the basis of this data, he or she is then referred to a specific therapy or research group. In an exploratory study, A. Stone, M. Parloff, and J. Frank formed four groups of fifteen patients each from a group therapy waiting list, and these groups met once a week for four to eight weeks.[36] Observers noted that the waiting-list group behavior of the patients was predictive of their behavior in their subsequent long-term therapy group. These workers found, as did D. Abrahams and J. Enright,[37] who used a group diagnostic procedure for all patients applying for treatment, that the procedure is clinically benign; patients did not react adversely to the waiting-list group. D. Malamud and S. Machover organized large groups of approximately thirty patients from a clinic waiting list.[38] These groups were seen for fifteen sessions of highly structured work-shops designed to prepare them for therapy. This preparatory group proved very successful: not only were the patients tided over the wait-ing period, but many reported significant benefit from the experience.

Piper and Marrache, in an important, well-designed project, placed thirty patients on a group therapy waiting list into four one-hour train-ing sessions which were conducted according to a prepared protocol but also included opportunities for here-and-now interaction.[39] Meas-urements were made of each patient's participation by trained observ-er-raters and then correlated with each patient's behavior during the first sixteen sessions. These investigators demonstrated that pre-therapy group behavior is a powerful predictor of such important varia-bles as verbal participation and responsivity both to members and to patients.

This is the only group therapy project demonstrating the predictive power of pre-therapy group behavior, but there is so much corroborat-ing evidence from human relations group research[40] that we can accept with a reasonable degree of certainty the hypothesis that subsequent group behavior may be predicted from pre-therapy waiting or training groups. This strategy has a distinct practical limitation, however: Piper and Marrache stated that each four-hour training group required twenty-four hours of a trained rater's time.[41]

Another possible approach to initial screening may be through a simulated group test. A simulated group has been used in social psycho-logical research design to establish unity of environment. For example, a subject is given earphones and told to listen through them to a group discussion in an adjoining room, and then is asked for his or her reac-tions to the "group," which is actually a tape-recorded simulation of a group. Clinicians, to my knowledge, have not employed this technique. As a diagnostic tool, a feasible research design could employ, however, a movie or a videotape of a therapy group of patients (with proper permission, of course) or a simulated therapy group of actors following a script. At various points the film could be stopped and the patient questioned about his or her emotional response, or ideas about what seemed to be happening, or what he might say or do if he were in the group.

The Interpersonal Intake Interview

For practitioners or clinics with limited waiting lists and facilities, the concept of trial groups may be only an intriguing, perhaps fanciful, research idea. A less accurate but more practical method of obtaining similar data is an interpersonally oriented initial interview, instead of the traditional psychiatric diagnostic interview. The therapist should test the prospective group patient's ability to deal with the interpersonal reality of the interview. Is the patient able, for example, to comment upon the process of the interview or to understand or accept the therapist's process commentary? For example, is the patient obviously tense but denies being so when the therapist asks? Will the patient identify the most uncomfortable or pleasant parts of the interview? Or comment on how he or she wishes to be thought of by the therapist?

Detailed inquiry should be made into the patient's interpersonal and group relationships, relationships with early chums, closest prolonged friendships, and degree of intimacy with members of both sexes. Many of Harry Stack Sullivan's interview techniques are of great value in this task.[42] It is informative, for example, when inquiring about friendships to ask for the names of best friends and what has become of them. A detailed history of formal and informal groups is valuable, of childhood and adult cliques, of fraternities, of club memberships, of gangs, of teams, of elected offices, and informal roles and status positions. The predictive power of this type of interview is yet to be determined, but, to my mind, it seems far more relevant to subsequent group behavior than does an intrapsychically focused interview.

F. Powdermaker and J. Frank described an interpersonal relations interview that, along with a standard psychiatric interview and psychological testing, comprised their pre-therapy diagnostic work-up.[43] From this information, conjectures about patients' subsequent in-group behavior were made, many of which were correct. Examples of accurate predictions were: "will dominate the group by a flood of speech and advice"; "will have considerable difficulty in showing feelings but will have compulsion to please the doctor and other members"; will be "bland and socially skillful, tending to seek the doctor's attention while ignoring the other members"; "will have a wait-and-see attitude"; or "will have a sarcastic, superior 'show-me' attitude and be reluctant to discuss his problems."

Summary

In summary, the prediction of certain salient parameters of subsequent group behavior from a pre-therapy diagnostic procedure seems feasible. Of all the prediction methods, the traditional intake individual interview appears the least accurate and yet is the most commonly used. An individual's group behavior will vary depending on internal psychological needs, manner of expressing them, and the task, interpersonal composition, and norms of the social environment. A general principle, however, is that the more similar the intake procedure is to the actual group situation, the more accurate will be the prediction of a patient's behavior. The most promising single clinical method may be observation of a patient's behavior in an intake or a waiting-list group. If facilities do not permit this method, I recommend that group therapists modify their intake interview and focus on a patient's interpersonal functioning.

Principles of Group Composition

To return now to the central question: given the most ideal circumstances—a large number of patient applicants and a wealth of information by which we can predict behavior—how then to compose the therapy group?

Perhaps the reason for the scarcity of interest in the prediction of subsequent group behavior is that the amount of information about group composition is even more rudimentary. Why, indeed, bother refining tools to predict group behavior if we do not know how to use this information? Although most clinicians sense that the composition of a group profoundly influences its character, the actual mechanism of influence has eluded clarification. I have had the opportunity to study closely the conception, birth, and development of over one hundred therapy groups—my own and my students'—and have been struck repeatedly by the fact that some groups seem to "jell" immediately and some more slowly, whereas other groups founder painfully, spinning off members, and emerge as working groups only after several cycles of attrition and addition of members. It has been my impression that whether a group "jells" is only in part related to the competence or efforts of the therapist or to the number of "good" patients in the group; to a degree, the critical variable is some, as yet unclear, blending of the members.

A recent clinical experience vividly brought this principle home to me. I was scheduled to lead a T-group of mental health professionals, all at the same level of training and approximately the same age. At the first meeting, over twenty participants appeared—too many for one group. We decided that I should lead two groups, but could not arrive at a satisfactory method of dividing the participants. Finally, the participants agreed simply to move in random fashion around the room for five minutes and at the end of that time find themselves in one of the two ends of the room. (A few of the members chose one of the two groups to fit in with their schedules.) Each group met for an hour and a half, one group immediately following the other.

Although superficially it might appear that the groups had similar compositions, the subtle blending of personalities resulted in each having a radically different character. The difference was apparent in the first meeting and persisted throughout the life of the group.

One group assumed an extraordinarily dependent posture. In the first meeting I arrived on crutches with my leg in a cast because I had injured my knee. The group made no inquiry about my condition. The members did not by themselves arrange the chairs in a circle. (Remember that all were professional therapists, and most had led groups!) They asked my permission for such acts as opening the window and closing the door. Most of the group life was spent analyzing their fear of me, the distance between me and the members, my aloofness and coldness.

In the other group that same day, I had not entered halfway through the door before several members asked, "Hey, what happened to your leg?" The group moved immediately into hard work, and each of the members used his or her professional skills in a constructive manner. The chief feeling I had in this second group was that of being unnecessary to its work; and, during the group, it was only with considerable effort that I could focus the members' attention on their disregard of me.

So, without doubt, the composition of the two groups dramatically influenced the character of their subsequent work. If the groups had been ongoing rather than time-limited (sixteen session) T-groups, it is possible that the different environments might have made little eventual difference in the beneficial effect of the group on each of its members. In the short run, however, the members of the first group felt more tense, more deskilled, and more restricted and, because of the narrower range of experience of the group, learned less about themselves.

A similar example may be drawn from the Lieberman, Yalom, and Miles encounter group study.[44] Two groups, randomly composed, had an identical leader—a tape recording (the "Encountertape Program") which gave the group instructions about how to proceed at each meeting. Within a few meetings, two very different cultures emerged. One group was dependably obedient to the taped instructions and faithfully followed all the prescribed exercises. The other group developed a disrespectful tone to the "leader," soon referring to him as "George." It was common for members to mock the tape: for example, when the tape gave an instruction to the group, one member commented derisively, "That's a great idea, George." Not only was the culture different for these short-term groups but the outcome was as well. (At the end of the thirty-hour group experience [ten meetings], the irreverent group had an appreciably better outcome.)

Thus, we can be certain that composition affects the character and process of the group. Still, however, we are a long way from concluding that a given method X more effectively composes a group than does method Y. The problem rests, of course, in the assessment of effectiveness. Group therapy outcome studies are crude, and no rigorous study has investigated the relationship between group composition and the ultimate criterion—long-term therapy outcome. We must therefore rely on nonsystematic clinical observations and studies that, though relevant to composition, stem from nontherapy settings.

CLINICAL OBSERVATIONS

The impressions of individual clinicians regarding the effects of group composition must be evaluated with caution. The lack of a common language describing behavior, the problems of outcome evaluation, the theoretical biases of the therapist, and the limited number of groups that any one clinician may treat all limit the validity of clinical impressions in this area.

There appears to be a general clinical sentiment that heterogeneous groups have advantages over homogeneous groups for long-term intensive interactional group therapy.[45] Homogeneous groups, on the other hand, have many advantages if the therapist wishes to offer support or symptomatic relief over a brief period. They are often effective for individuals with monosymptomatic complaints or for the noncompliant patient. Homogeneous groups "jell" more quickly, become more cohesive, offer more immediate support to group members, are better attended, have less conflict, and provide more rapid relief of symptoms. They do not lend themselves to long-term psychotherapeutic work with ambitious goals of personality change. Clinicians widely believe that the homogeneous group, in contrast to the heterogeneous group, tends to remain at superficial levels and is an ineffective medium for the altering of character structure.

The issue becomes clouded when we ask, Homogeneous for what? Heterogeneous for what? For age? Sex? Symptom complex? Marital status? Education? Socioeconomic status? Verbal skills? Psychosexual development? Psychiatric diagnostic categories? Interpersonal needs? Which are the critical variables? Is a group composed of bulimic women homogeneous because of the shared symptom, or heterogeneous because of the wide range of personality traits of the members?

Whitaker and Lieberman help to clarify the issue by suggesting that the group therapist strive for maximum heterogeneity in the patients' conflict areas and patterns of coping, and at the same time strive for homogeneity of the patients' degree of vulnerability and capacity to tolerate anxiety.[46] For example, these investigators state that a homogeneous group of individuals, all with major conflicts about hostility that were dealt with through denial, could hardly offer therapeutic benefit to its members. However, a group with a wide range of vulnerability (loosely defined as ego strength) will, for different reasons, also be retarded: the most vulnerable patient will place limits on the group, which will become highly restrictive to the less vulnerable ones. In the same vein, Foulkes and Anthony suggest blending a "mixed bag of diagnosis and disturbances" to form a therapeutically effective group: "The greater the span between the polar types, the higher the therapeutic potential, if the group can stand it."[47]

Unfolding from these clinical observations is the rule that a degree of incompatibility must exist between the patient and the interpersonal culture of the group if change is to occur. This principle—that change is preceded by a state of dissonance or incongruity—is backed by considerable clinical and social psychological research and is a concept to which I will return. In the absence of adequate ego strength, however, group members cannot profit from the dissonance; therefore, for the long-term intensive therapy group, the rule is: *heterogeneity for conflict areas,* and *homogeneity for ego strength.*

Heterogeneity must not be maintained at the price of creating a group isolate. Consider the age variable: if there is one sixty-year-old member in a group of very young adults, that individual may choose or be forced to personify the older generation. Thus, this patient is stereo-typed (as are the younger patients), and the required interpersonal honesty and intimacy fail to materialize. A similar process may occur in an adult group with a lone late adolescent who assumes the unruly teenager role. Yet there are advantages to having a wide age spread in a group. Most of my outpatient groups have patients ranging in age from twenty-five to sixty: patients, through working out their relation-ships with other members, will come to understand their past, present, and future relationships with a wider range of significant people—parents, peers, and children.

One solution to the problem of maintaining heterogeneity without creating isolates may be to pair patients. One group therapist suggested the "Noah's Ark" principle of group composition, in which each mem-ber has a compeer.[48] Another therapist suggests a composition tech-nique of "group balance," in which the therapist attempts to balance the group for such factors as transference toward the therapist; counter-transference; passive aggressivity; ability to express affect, insight or introspective ability; homosexuality-heterosexuality; and ego strength.[49]

The concept of heterogeneity even with pairing or balance is not without limitations. For example, if the group has too extreme an age range, the life-stage problems of some members may be so alien to others as to seriously impair cohesiveness. Aged individuals concerned about their livelihood and disengagement from life are sometimes ir-reconcilably distant from late adolescents and young adults dealing urgently with identity crises.

Some therapists employ the concept of role heterogeneity in their approach to composition.[50] In adding a new member, the primary consideration is, What role is open in the group? In this view the thera-pist should strive to increase the group's "role repertoire, in order to obtain better complementation between roles." Theoretically, such an orientation seems desirable. Practically, however, it suffers from lack of clarity. An extraordinary range of therapy group roles has been sug-gested: task leader, social-emotional leader, provocateur, doctor's helper, help-rejecting complainer, self-righteous moralist, "star," the fight, flight, dependency, or pairing leader, group hysteric, technical executive leader, social secretary, group stud, group critic, group ro-mantic, "guardian of democracy," the "time keeper," "aggressive male," vigilante of honesty, the sociable role, the structural role, the divergent role, the cautionary role, the romantic, the scrutinizer, the innocent, the scapegoat, the intellectualizer, the child, the puritan, the reintegrater.[51]

Can we expand the list arbitrarily and indefinitely by listing behavior trait constellations, or are there fixed roles, constant from group to group, that members are forced to fill? Until we have some satisfactory frame of reference to deal with these questions, asking "What role is open in the group?" will contribute little toward an effective approach to group composition.

One final clinical observation. As a supervisor and researcher, I had an opportunity to study closely the entire thirty-month course of an outpatient group led by Dr. R. and Dr. M., two competent psychiatric residents. The group consisted of seven members, all in their twenties, six of whom could be classified as schizoid personalities. The one patient who was considerably different, a passive-aggressive phobic woman, was frightened by the interaction and dropped out of the group after five months. Another patient was called for military duty at the end of a year. Two new patients were brought in to replace the losses.

The most striking feature of this homogeneous schizoid group was its extraordinary dullness. Everything associated with the group—meetings, tape recordings, written summaries, supervisory sessions—seemed low-keyed and plodding. Often nothing seemed to be happening: there was no discernible movement individually among the patients or in the group as a whole. And yet the attendance was near perfect, and the group cohesiveness extraordinarily high.* Since all the group patients in the Stanford clinic over this period of time were subjects in outcome research,[52] thorough evaluations of clinical progress were available at the end both of one year and of thirty months. The patients in this group, both the original members and the replacements, did extraordinarily well and underwent substantial characterologic changes as well as complete symptomatic remission. In fact, few other groups I have studied have had comparably good results. My views about group composition were influenced by this group, and I have come to attach great importance to group stability, attendance, and cohesiveness.

Although in theory I agree with the concept of composing a group of individuals with varied interpersonal stresses and needs, I feel that in practice it may be a spurious issue. Given the limited predictive value

*Many outpatient groups in the Stanford outpatient clinic were involved in research involving the measurement of group cohesiveness.[53] The group led by Dr. R. and Dr. M. scored higher on cohesiveness (measured by self-administered questionnaires) than any other group.

of our traditional screening interview, it is probable that we delude ourselves if we think we can achieve the type of subtle balance and personality interlocking necessary to make a real difference in group functioning. For example, although six of the seven patients in Dr. R. and Dr. M.'s group were diagnosed as schizoid personalities, they differed far more than they resembled one another. This apparently homogeneous group, contrary to the clinical dictum, did not remain at a superficial level and affected significant personality changes in its members. Although the interaction seemed plodding to the therapists and researchers, it did not seem so to the patients. None of them had had past intimate relationships, and many of their disclosures, though objectively unremarkable, were subjectively exciting "first-time disclosures." Although I have studied many so-called homogeneous groups (such as ulcer patients, dermatological patients, obese women, parents of delinquent children) that have remained superficial, I felt that they did so not because of homogeneity but because of the set of the group leaders and the restricted culture they fashioned. The organization of a group of individuals around a common symptom or around their children's problems may convey powerful implicit messages which generate group norms of restriction, a search for similarities, submergence of individuality, and discouragement of self-disclosure and interpersonal honesty. Norms, as I elaborated in chapter 5, once set into motion, may become self-perpetuating and difficult to change.

SYSTEMATIC STUDIES OF GROUP COMPOSITION

Although no therapy group research on composition exists, there have been several attempts to study the relationship between composition and outcome in nontherapy experiential groups. I shall merely summarize the finding of these studies here; interested readers should refer to the articles cited for details of a particular study. First, let me present the general research procedure of these studies so that we may determine their relevance to group therapy.

The subjects are usually participants in a human relations laboratory: they are generally professionals from the fields of education, industry, or behavioral science, or college student volunteers; they may be broadly considered "normals," although no psychiatric screening is performed. Usually homogeneous or heterogeneous groups are formed on the basis of some cluster of personality variables which are obtained from psychological tests or from behavioral observations of the subjects in trial groups. The groups are short-term, meeting for six to fifteen sessions, generally over a short period (one to two weeks). Outcome of the groups and of the individuals is assessed by some observational method and/or by subject-administered questionnaires. The personality variables most often used are:

1. "Person-oriented" or "task-oriented" individuals. "Person-oriented" individuals value such characteristics as warmth, openness, sympathy, and genuineness; "task-oriented" individuals value competence, ability, responsibility, initiative, and energy. A similar, overlapping dichotomy used in other studies is the "low structure" versus the "high structure" individual:[54] "high structure" characteristics include a preference for clarity and order, with less interest in personal feelings, and a tendency to defer to authority figures; "low structure" characteristics include a readiness to recognize and examine positive and negative feelings and interpersonal relationships.
2. FIRO-B characteristics.
3. Group culture preference (Bionic basic assumption cultures of dependency, flight, pairing) obtained from a self-administered questionnaire.[55]
4. Miscellaneous measures including dogmatism, locus of control, dominance or love orientation.[56]

In general, the group composition experimental work is not of high quality, the highly sophisticated statistical technique and conclusive findings reported by several reviews notwithstanding.[57] With these reservations, let me consider the research findings:

1. Homogeneous groups of task-oriented, high-structure, impersonal individuals function as effective human relations groups that produce change in the members. Apparently these groups offer a combination of support and challenge. The members are supported by their perceived similarity and challenged by the task of the group, which demands that they interact more intensively and intimately than is their wont. The groups tend to be highly cohesive.[58]
2. Homogeneous groups of person-oriented, low-structure individuals do not function as effective human relations groups, although the groups are interactive and initially stimulating. Apparently these groups offer too little challenge to the members, who are comfortable with the group task and with the other members.[59]
3. Homogeneous groups of individuals with the same attitudes toward dominance produce less change than do groups that are heterogeneously composed for the same variable.[60]
4. Heterogeneous encounter groups (incompatible on FIRO affection scale) are more effective in producing greater self-actualization of members.[61]
5. There is lack of consensus about mixed half-and-half (person-oriented and task-oriented) groups. They have been generally found to be ineffective, incompatible, poorly cohesive groups, which do not move toward the goals

of exploration, sharing, and intimate interaction.[62] On the other hand, there is modest evidence from one study that they induce greater change in the members.[63]

6. Task groups that are homogeneous (FIRO-B compatibility) are more productive and more cohesive than heterogeneous groups.[64]

7. Task groups that are homogeneous for culture preference (flight or pairing)[65] are more efficient than mixed groups. There is a suggestion that the mixed groups suffer from the lack of a liaison person to bridge the two subgroups.

8. In general, the atmosphere of a group is predictable from its composition. Dogmatism, dominance, interpersonal compatibility, and interpersonal skills are particularly relevant dimensions.[66]

9. Heterogeneous groups whose members are in constant conflict are unable to operate effectively.[67]

Overview

It would be most gratifying at this point to integrate these clinical and experimental findings, to point out hitherto unseen lines of cleavage and coalescence, and to emerge with a crisp theory of group composition which not only has firm experimental foundations but also is immediately practical. Unfortunately the insubstantial data do not permit such a synthesis.

Let me consider, however, the most unequivocal findings. The composition of a group makes a difference and influences many aspects of group function. A group's composition can have certain predictable short-term characteristics: for example, high cohesion, high conflict, high flight, high dependency. Furthermore, we can, if we choose to use available procedures, predict to some degree the group behavior of the individual.

What we do *not* know, however, is the relationship between any of these group characteristics and the ultimate therapy outcome of the group members. Furthermore, we are unclear about the degree to which the group leader may alter these characteristics of the group, and we do not know how long an ongoing group will manifest them. The theoretical underpinning of the two general approaches to group composition may help clarify the issue. Underlying the heterogeneous approach to composition are two theoretical rationales which may be labeled the *social microcosm theory* and the *dissonance theory*. Underlying the homogeneous group composition approach is the *group cohesiveness theory*.

THE SOCIAL MICROCOSM THEORY

The social microcosm theory postulates that, since the group is regarded as a miniature social universe in which patients are urged to develop new methods of interpersonal interaction, the group should thus be heterogeneous in order to maximize learning opportunities. It should resemble the real social universe by being composed of individuals of different sexes, professions, ages, socioeconomic and educational levels; in other words, it should be a demographic heterodox.

THE DISSONANCE THEORY

The dissonance theory, as applied to group therapy, also suggests a heterogeneous compositional approach, but for a somewhat different reason. Learning or change is likely to occur when the individual, in a state of dissonance, acts to reduce that dissonance. Dissonance creates a state of psychological discomfort and propels the individual to attempt to achieve a more consonant state. Individuals who find themselves in a group in which membership has many desirable features (for example, hopes of alleviation of suffering, attraction to the leader and other members), but which, at the same time, makes tension-producing demands (for example, self-disclosure or interpersonal confrontation), will then experience a state of imbalance or, to use T. M. Newcomb's term, "asymmetry."[68]

Similarly, a state of discomfort occurs when, in a valued group, one finds that one's interpersonal needs are unfulfilled, or when one's customary style of interpersonal behavior produces discord. The individual in these circumstances will search for ways to reduce discomfort: for example, by leaving the group or, preferably, by beginning to experiment with new forms of behavior. To facilitate the development of adaptive discomfort, the heterogeneous argument suggests that the patient be exposed to other individuals in the group who will not fulfill his or her interpersonal needs (and thus reinforce this patient's neurotic position) but will be frustrating and challenging, making the patient aware of different conflict areas, and also demonstrating alternative interpersonal modes.

Therefore, it is argued, a group should include members with varying interpersonal styles and conflicts. If, however, frustration and challenge are too great, and the staying forces (the attraction to the group) too small, no real asymmetry or dissonance occurs; the individual does not change but, instead, physically or psychologically leaves the group. (Here the dissonance theory overlaps with the next model, the cohesiveness theory.) If, on the other hand, the challenge is too small, no learning occurs either; members will collude, and exploration will be inhibited. The dissonance theory thus argues for a broad personality heterodox.

THE COHESIVENESS THEORY

The cohesiveness theory, underlying the homogeneous approach to group composition, posits, quite simply, that attraction to the group is the intervening variable critical to outcome, and that the aim should be to assemble a cohesive, compatible group.

SUMMARY

How can we reconcile or decide among these approaches?

First, note that no group therapy research supports the dissonance model. There is great clinical consensus (my own included) that group therapy patients should be exposed to a variety of conflict areas, coping methods, and conflicting interpersonal styles, and that conflict in general is essential to the therapeutic process.[69] However, there is no evidence that deliberately composed heterogeneous groups facilitate therapy; and I have just cited modest evidence to the contrary.

On the other hand, a body of small group research supports the cohesiveness concept. Interpersonally compatible therapy groups will develop greater cohesiveness. Members of cohesive groups have better attendance, are more able to express and tolerate hostility; are more apt to attempt to influence others, and are in turn themselves more readily influenced; members with greater attraction to their group have better therapeutic outcome; patients who are less compatible with the other members tend to drop out of the therapy group as do any two members with marked mutual incompatibility; members with the greatest interpersonal compatibility become the most popular group members, and group popularity is highly correlated with successful outcome.

The fear that a homogeneous group will be unproductive, constricted, or conflict-free, or deal with a narrow range of interpersonal concerns, is unfounded for several reasons. First, there are few individuals whose pathology is indeed monolithic; few individuals who, despite their chief conflict area, do not also encounter conflicts in intimacy or authority, for example. Secondly, the group developmental process may demand that patients deal with certain conflict areas. For example, the laws of group development (see chapter 11) demand that the group ultimately deal with issues of control, authority, and the hierarchy of dominance. In a group with several control-conflicted individuals, this phase may appear early or very sharply. In a group lacking such individuals, other members who are less conflicted, or whose conflicts are less overt, in the area of dependency and authority may be forced nonetheless to deal with it as the group inevitably moves into this phase of development. If certain roles are not filled in the group, most leaders, consciously or unconsciously, alter their behavior to fill the void.[70]

Furthermore—and this is an important point—no therapy group with proper leadership can be too comfortable or fail to provide dissonance for its members because the members must invariably clash with the group task. To develop trust, to disclose oneself, to develop intimacy, to examine oneself, to confront others, are all discordant tasks to individuals who have significant problems in interpersonal relationships.

The nonproductive homogeneous group of person-oriented individuals reported in T-group research is not relevant to group therapy because of the exceedingly low probability that such a group of individuals would seek psychiatric aid. It is my impression that the homogeneous group of individuals, placed together because of a common symptom or problem that remains on a shallow, restricted level, is entirely an iatrogenic phenomenon—a self-fulfilling prophecy on the part of the therapist.

On the basis of our present state of knowledge, therefore, I propose that cohesiveness be the primary guideline in the composition of therapy groups. The hoped-for dissonance will unfold in the group, provided the therapist functions effectively in the pre-therapy orientation of patients and during the early group meetings. Group integrity should be a primary concern, and you must select patients with the lowest possible likelihood of premature termination. Patients with a high likelihood of being incompatible with the prevailing group culture, or of being markedly incompatible with at least one other member, should not be included in the group. Group cohesiveness, be it noted, is not synonymous with group comfort or ease. Quite the contrary: it is only in a cohesive group that conflict can be tolerated and transformed into productive work.

A Final Caveat

First, let me say that the idea of crafting an ideal group is seductive: it is a siren's wail which has lured many researchers and generated an enormous body of research, little of which, alas, has proved substantial, replicable, or clinically relevant. In fact, because of the current conditions under which group therapists work, the very topic of group composition is out of touch with the reality of everyday clinical practice. Virtually every contemporary group clinician in private practice and the great majority in public clinics are preoccupied with problems of group integrity and survival: group composition ranks low on their list of priorities. Clinicians have difficulty accumulating sufficient patients to form and to maintain groups. (And I have no doubt that this difficulty grows with each passing year—perhaps because there are in practice rapidly increasing numbers of psychotherapists from ever more professional disciplines.) The more therapists available, the more professional competition for patients, the harder is it to begin and maintain therapy groups. Therapists prefer to fill their individual hours and are reluctant to risk losing a patient through referral to a therapy group. If clinicians attempt to put some group candidates on "hold" while awaiting the perfect blend of group patients (assuming that we know the formula of the blend, which we do not), they could never form a group. Referrals accumulate so slowly that the first prospective members interviewed tire of waiting and find suitable therapy elsewhere.

Thus contemporary clinicians, myself included, generally form groups by accepting, within limits, the first suitable seven or eight candidates screened and deemed to be good group therapy candidates. Only the crudest principles of group composition are employed, such as having an equal number of men and women or a wide range of age or activity for example, if two males already selected for the group are particularly passive, it is desirable to create balance by adding more active men.

The therapist's paramount task is to create a group that coheres. Time and energy spent on delicately casting and balancing a group is not justified given our current state of knowledge; you do better to invest that time and energy in careful selection of patients for group therapy and in pre-therapy preparation (to be discussed in the next chapter). There is no question that composition radically affects the group's character, but, if the group holds together, and if you appreciate the therapeutic factors and are flexible in your role, you can make therapeutic use of any conditions (other than lack of motivation) that arise in the group.

10

CREATION OF THE GROUP: PLACE, TIME, SIZE, PREPARATION

Preliminary Considerations

Before a group is convened, there are certain decisions to be made about its circumstances. The therapist must secure an appropriate meeting place and establish policy about the life span of the group, admission of new members, frequency of meetings, duration of each session, and size of the group.

THE PHYSICAL SETTING

Group meetings may be held in any setting, provided that the room affords privacy and freedom from distraction. Some therapists prefer to have the members seated about a large circular table (a rectangular table is unwieldy since not all the members on the same side will be able to see each other). Most therapists prefer to have no central obstruction so as to be able to see the entire body of each member and, thus, to more readily observe nonverbal or postural responses.

If the group session is to be videotaped or observed through a viewing screen by students, the group members' permission must be obtained in advance and ample opportunity provided for discussion of the procedure. A group that is to be observed continuously appears to forget about the viewing screen after a few weeks, but often when working through authority issues with the leader, members periodically return to it with renewed interest throughout therapy. If there are only one or two student observers, they are best seated in the room, though out of the group circle—an arrangement that, in the long run, proves less distracting than the viewing screen and allows the students to sample more of the group affect, which inexplicably is often filtered out by the screen. Observers who are not to take part in the therapy session should be cautioned to remain silent and to resist any attempts of the group members to draw them in; once an observer has spoken, it is increasingly difficult to be silent thereafter.

OPEN AND CLOSED GROUPS

At its inception a group is designated by its leader as *open* or *closed:* a closed group, once begun, shuts its gates, accepts no new members, and meets usually for a predetermined number of sessions; an open group maintains a consistent size by replacing members as they leave the group. An open group, too, may have a predetermined life span; for example, groups in a university student health service may plan to meet only for the nine-month academic year. Usually open groups continue indefinitely, even though every couple of years there may be a complete turnover of group membership and even of leadership. I have known of therapy groups in psychiatric training centers which have endured for twenty years, being bequeathed every two to three years by a graduating therapist to an incoming student.

Though a closed group with total stability of membership has much to recommend it, the exigencies of outpatient practice diminish its feasibility. Invariably, members will drop out, move away, or face an unexpected scheduling incompatibility; new members must be added at these times lest the group perish from attrition. A closed group format may, however, be practical in a setting that assures considerable stability, such as a prison, a military base, a long-term psychiatric hospital, or occasionally an outpatient analytic group in which all members are concurrently in individual analysis with the group leader. Some therapists lead a closed group for six months, at which time members re-evaluate their "contracts" and decide whether to commit themselves to another six months. Ordinarily, the great majority of outpatient groups are conducted as open groups.

DURATION AND FREQUENCY OF MEETINGS

Until the mid-1960s, the length of a psychotherapy session seemed fixed: the fifty-minute individual hour and the eighty-to-ninety-minute group therapy session were part of the entrenched folk wisdom of the field. Most group therapists agree that, even in well-established groups, at least sixty minutes is required for the warm-up interval and for the unfolding and working through of the major themes of the session. There also is some consensus among therapists that, after about two hours, a point of diminishing returns is reached: the group becomes weary, repetitious, and inefficient. Furthermore, many therapists appear to function best in segments of eighty to ninety minutes; longer sessions often result in fatigue, which renders the therapist less effective in subsequent therapy sessions on the same day.

The frequency of meetings varies from one to five times a week. I prefer a twice-weekly schedule. It is generally difficult to assemble outpatients more frequently. A once-weekly schedule is the most common format in outpatient work; but in my experience, the group tends to suffer from the long interval between meetings. Often much that cannot be ignored has occurred in the lives of the members; and the group has a tendency to veer away from interaction into crisis resolution. When the group meets more than once a week, it increases in intensity, the members continue to work through issues raised the previous week, and the entire process takes on the character of a continuous meeting.

The considerable experimentation, during the 1960s and 1970s, with the time variable was so extreme in its reaction to conventional modes of therapy as to border on procedural anarchy. Therapists held groups for weekly four-, six-, or eight-hour sessions. Some therapists chose to meet less frequently but for longer periods—for example, a six-hour meeting every other week. Individual therapists often referred their patients to a weekend time-extended group. Some group therapists referred their entire group for a weekend with another therapist; or, more commonly, they themselves conducted a marathon meeting with their own group sometime during the course of therapy. Some psychiatric wards or correctional institutions instituted an intensive group therapy week, during which the patients met in small groups for eight hours a day for five consecutive days; another program offered sixteen hours of group therapy each weekend for sixteen weeks.

THE TIME-EXTENDED, OR MARATHON, GROUP

The "marathon" group, so christened by G. Bach,[1] was described in many popular American magazines, newspapers, and fictionalized accounts.[2] It met for a prolonged session, perhaps as much as twenty-four to forty-eight hours, with little or no time permitted for sleep. The participants were required to remain together for the entire designated time; meals were served in the therapy room; and sleep, if required, was snatched during short naps in the session or in short, scheduled sleep breaks. The emphasis of the group was on total self-disclosure, intensive interpersonal confrontation, and affective involvement and participation.

The time-extended therapy session had several roots. Undoubtedly, psychotherapy has been influenced by the sensitivity-training field and its frequent use of intensive residential workshops in which the participants live together and meet in groups for several hours daily over several days (see chapter 16). Another influence was the inpatient psychiatric community which some clinicians came to regard as a potential twenty-four-hour-a-day therapy group. Intensive family therapy techniques may also have helped set the stage; R. MacGregor, in 1962, for example, described a mode of multiple impact therapy in which a psychiatric team devoted its total attention to one family for two to three full days.[3]

Proponents of the time-extended group claimed that the procedure had several advantages:[4] the acceleration of group development, the intensification of the emotional experience, the condensation of a lengthy course of therapy into twenty-four hours. Leaders claimed that the social microcosm unfolded more quickly because patients ate, slept, cried, and lived together continuously in a setting where there was no place to hide. The fatigue resulting from lack of sleep was also thought to accelerate the patients' abandonment of social facades. (As one marathon group leader stated, "Tired people are truthful; they do not have the energy to play games." A ninety-minute session is not long enough to compel people to "take off their masks.")[5]

The results of marathon group therapy that were first reported in the mass media and in scientific journals were extraordinary and boggled the mind. "Eighty percent of the participants undergo significant change as the result of a single meeting."[6] "Thirty-six hours of therapy have proved comparable to several years of conventional ninety-minute weekly group therapy sessions."[7] "Ninety percent of 400 marathon group members considered the meeting as one of the most significant and meaningful experiences of their lives."[8] "Marathon group therapy represents a breakthrough in psychotherapeutic practice."[9] "The marathon group has become a singular agent of change which allows rapidity of learning and adaptation to new patterns of behavior not likely to occur under traditional arrangements,"[10] "If all adults had been in a marathon, there would be no more war; if all teenagers had been in a marathon, there would be no more juvenile delinquency,"[11] And so on.

Yet despite these claims, the marathon movement has come and gone. The therapists who still regularly or periodically hold time-extended group meetings represent a small minority of practitioners. Articles and scholarly papers devoted to time-extended groups peaked in the years 1968–71.[12] Seventeen doctoral dissertations were written on marathon groups in 1971–72, but none appeared ten years later, 1981–82. Nonetheless, it is important to write and read about the movement: not, as I say, because it is current clinical practice; not to pay homage to it; not as a chapter in the history of psychotherapy; but because, from the standpoint of how therapists make decisions about clinical practice, the phenomenon has implications for the future of the field. Psychotherapy in general and group therapy in particular have, over the past four decades, been taken by storm by a series of ideological and stylistic fads; and, as M. Parloff (in a discussion of group marathons) states, "No sooner does a new group therapy Tinker Bell appear on the scene than a number of practitioners will offer to sustain its weak and flickering light by life-supporting shouts of 'I believe! I believe!' "[13]

Many therapeutic fads come and go so quickly that little thought and even less research addresses the issues they raise. Not so for the time-extended meeting. Because the format lends itself to experimentation (it is far easier to do outcome research on a group that lasts, for example, half a day than on one that lasts for six months: there are fewer dropouts, fewer life crises, no opportunities for subjects to obtain ancillary therapy) and arose in the National Training Laboratories (see chapter 16)—an institution that has always coupled innovation and research—there is considerable research literature on the time-extended meeting.

The extravagant claims I just mentioned were based entirely on anecdotal reports of various participants or on questionnaires distributed shortly after the end of a meeting—an exceedingly untrustworthy approach to evaluation. In fact, any outcome study based entirely on interviews, testimonials, or patient self-administered questionnaires obtained at the end of the group is of questionable value. At no other time is the patient more loyal, more grateful, and less objective about a group than at termination; at this juncture there is a powerful tendency to recall and to express only positive, tender feelings. Experiencing and expressing negative feelings about the group at this point would be unlikely for at least two reasons: (1) there is strong group pressure at termination to participate in positive testimonials; few group participants, as S. E. Asch has shown,[14] can maintain their objectivity in the face of apparent group unanimity; and (2) members reject critical feelings toward the group at this time to avoid a state of cognitive dissonance. The individual has chosen to invest considerable emotion and time in the group and, furthermore, has often developed strong positive feelings toward other members. To question the value or activities of the group would be to thrust oneself into a state of dissonance.

The systematic outcome literature on time-extended groups involves groups composed primarily of college student volunteers: only a handful of studies of patient groups have been reported.[15] The overall conclusions strongly indicate that there is no proof for the efficacy of the time-extended format: a few studies showed positive results, generally testimonial, which evaporated quickly and had disappeared at long-term follow-up.

Does a time-extended meeting accelerate the maturation of a therapy group? My colleagues and I explored the effect of a six-hour, time-extended meeting on the development of cohesiveness (operationally defined as involvement of members with each other and with the group as a whole) and on the development of a here-and-now, interactive communicational mode.[16] We studied six newly formed groups in a psychiatric outpatient department for the first sixteen sessions. Three of these groups held a six-hour first session, while the other three held a six-hour eleventh session. Thus, during their first sixteen meetings, each group had one six-hour session and fifteen meetings of conventional length (ninety minutes). Tape recordings of the second, sixth, tenth, twelfth, and sixteenth meetings were analyzed to classify the verbal interaction.[17] Post-group questionnaires measuring members' involvement with the group and with each other were obtained at these same meetings.

The results show that the time-extended meeting did *not* favorably influence the communication patterns in meetings after the marathon session.[18] In fact, there was a trend in the opposite direction: that is, the groups, following the six-hour meetings, appeared to engage in *less* here-and-now interaction. The influence of the six-hour meeting on cohesiveness was quite interesting. In the three groups that held a six-hour *initial* meeting, there was a trend toward *decreased* cohesiveness in subsequent meetings. In the three groups that held a six-hour *eleventh* meeting, however, there was a significant *increase* in cohesiveness in subsequent meetings. Thus, timing is a consideration: it is entirely possible that, at a particular juncture in the course of a group, a time-extended session may help increase member involvement in the group.

During the 1960s and 1970s, many therapists referred individual therapy patients to weekend marathon groups; and in the 1980s, many send patients to marathon sessions of large-group awareness training (for example, est and Lifespring). Is it possible that an intensive affect-laden time-extended group may open up a patient who is stuck in therapy? My colleagues and I studied thirty-three such patients referred by individual therapists for a weekend encounter group. We assigned them to one of three groups: two affect-evoking gestalt marathons and a control group (a weekend of meditation, silence, and Tai Chi).[19] Six weeks later, the experimental subjects showed slight but significant improvement in their individual therapy as compared with the control subjects. However, by twelve weeks, all differences had disappeared, and there were no remaining measurable effects upon the process of individual therapy.

The marathon group phenomenon makes us mindful of the issue of "transfer of learning." There is no question that the time-extended group can evoke powerful affect and can encourage members to experiment with new behavior. But does a change in one's behavior in the group invariably betoken a change in one's outside life? Clinicians have long known that change in the therapy session is not tantamount to therapeutic success; that change must be carried over into important outside interpersonal relationships and endeavors. It is only natural that therapists should wish to accelerate the process of change; but, nonetheless, it seems the laborious process of transfer of learning demands a certain irreducible temporal segment of life.*

Consider for example, a male patient who, because of his early experience with an authoritarian, distant, and harsh father, tends to see all

---

*M. Lorr reviewed the pertinent clinical research on intensity and duration of treatment and concluded that "duration of treatment is a more influential parameter than the number of treatments . . . change would appear to require the passage of time. Insights are put into practice in daily living. New ways of reacting interpersonally must be tested again and again in natural settings before what has been learned becomes consolidated. Trial and error testing seems a prerequisite for the process of growth and change."[20]

other males, especially those in a position of authority, as having similar qualities. In the group he may have an entirely different emotional experience with a male therapist and perhaps one of the male members. What has he learned? Well, for one thing he has learned that not all men are frightening bastards; at least there are one or two who are not. Of what lasting value is this experience to the patient? Probably very little unless he can generalize the experience to future situations. As a result of the group, the individual learns that at least some men in authority positions can be trusted. But which ones? He must learn how to differentiate between people so as not to perceive all men in a predetermined manner. A new repertoire of perceptual skills is needed. Once he is able to make the necessary discriminations, he must learn how to go about forming relationships on an egalitarian, distortion-free basis. For the individual whose interpersonal relationships have been impoverished and maladaptive, these are formidable and lengthy tasks which often require the continual testing and reinforcement available in the long-term therapeutic relationship.

SIZE OF THE GROUP

My own experience and a consensus of the clinical literature suggest that the ideal size of an interactional therapy group is approximately seven or eight, with an acceptable range of five to ten members. The lower limit of the group is determined by the fact that a critical mass is required for an aggregation of individuals to become an interacting group. When a group is reduced to four or three members, it often ceases to operate as a group; member interaction diminishes, and therapists often find themselves engaged in individual therapy within the group. Many of the advantages of a group—the opportunity for broad consensual validation and to interact and analyze one's interaction with a large variety of individuals—are compromised as the group's size diminishes.

C. Fulkerson, D. Hawkins, and A. Alden studied five groups (out of a total of nineteen groups in their clinic) that met for six months or longer with four or fewer members.[21] These researchers noted that these groups had several striking characteristics: (1) limited member-to-member interaction (the group interaction occurred primarily between patients and therapists); (2) passivity (group direction, sharing of time, and the nature of problem solving were all determined by the therapist); (3) a negative group "image," (members regarded the group as a "loser's group"); (4) good attendance (because of a sense of obligation rather than of true alliance); (5) poor group development (inhibited, competitive, uninvolved groups). Obviously these are characteristics of unproductive, poorly functioning groups. Replacement of members is a high priority; if new members are unavailable, it is preferable to meld two small groups rather than to continue meeting with insufficient membership.

The upper limit is determined by sheer economic principles: as the group increases in size, less and less time is available for the working through of any individual's problems.

Since it is likely that one or, possibly, two patients will drop out of the group in the course of the initial meetings, it is advisable to start with a group slightly larger than a preferred size; thus, to obtain a group of seven or eight members, many therapists start a new group with eight or nine. Although most outpatient therapists set an upper limit of eight or nine on their groups, sensitivity-training groups generally include more members, usually twelve to sixteen. It is possible to conduct a face-to-face group with this number—each member may interact in a meaningful way with each of the other members; however, there will not be enough time to work through with any thoroughness the problem areas that are identified. Such large groups may offer a therapeutic experience to those members who choose to take advantage of the opportunity, but their size precludes intensive psychotherapeutic work with each member.

To some extent, the optimal group size is a function of the duration of the meeting: the longer the meeting, the larger the number of patients who can profitably engage in the group. Thus, many of the marathon therapy groups included up to sixteen members. Still larger groups ranging from twenty to eighty are conducted by Alcoholics Anonymous, Recovery, Inc., and therapeutic communities. However, these groups rely on different therapeutic factors; the A.A. and Recovery, Inc., groups use inspiration, guidance, and suppression; whereas the large therapeutic community relies on group pressure and interdependence to encourage reality testing, to combat regression, and to instill a sense of individual responsibility toward the social community.

Little research has been done to explore the relationship between size and group effectiveness. G. F. Castore investigated the relationship between the size of a group and the number of different member-to-member verbal relationships initiated (that is, the number of other members to whom each individual directed at least one remark—a measure of the spread of interpersonal interaction in the group) in fifty-five inpatient therapy groups ranging in size from five to twenty patients.[22] They noted a marked reduction in interactions between members when there were as many as nine members in the group, and there was a second marked reduction when seventeen or more members were present. The implication of the research is that, in inpatient settings, groups of five to eight offer a greater opportunity for total patient participation.

Several studies of nontherapy groups suggest that, from the perspective of the group member, five-member groups are the most harmonious problem-solving groups.[23] Other studies show that as the size of a group increases, there is a corresponding tendency for cliques and disruptive subgroups to form.[24] A comparison between twelve-member and five-member problem-solving groups indicates that the larger groups are more dissatisfied and show less consensus.[25] As a group increases in size, research demonstrates, too, that only the more forceful and aggressive members are able to express themselves, whereas the less forceful members are unable to express their ideas or abilities.[26]

Preparation for Group Therapy

There is great variation in clinical practice regarding individual sessions with patients prior to group therapy. Some therapists, after seeing a patient once or twice in selection interviews, do not meet with him or her individually again, whereas other therapists continue individual sessions until the patient starts in the group. It may require several weeks to assemble seven or eight patients for a group; and, to avoid losing the early candidates, the therapist must continue to meet with each of them periodically.

Some therapists prefer to see the patient several times in individual sessions primarily for the purpose of building rapport—rapport that may help keep them in the group during periods of discouragement and disenchantment early in the course of group therapy. It is my clinical impression that the more often patients are seen before entering the group, the less likely they are to terminate prematurely from the group. Often the first step in the development of bonds among members is their mutual identification with a common shared object—the therapist. Keep in mind that the purpose of the individual pre-group sessions is to build a therapeutic alliance. To use the sessions primarily for anamnestic purposes is not a good use of clinical time; I would agree with S. H. Foulkes that any truly relevant material will be forthcoming in the group setting.[27]

One other overriding task must be accomplished in the pre-group interview or interviews: that is, the preparation of the patient for group therapy. If I had to choose one single aspect of group therapy research and practice where recent exciting innovations have occurred, I would select this area. Strong clinical consensus and highly persuasive research evidence (which I shall discuss shortly) argue that preparation of the patient for the group is an absolutely essential task of the therapist.

Several goals must be accomplished in the preparatory procedure: to clarify misconceptions, unrealistic fears, and expectations; to anticipate and diminish group therapy problems; to provide patients with a cognitive structure that will enable them to participate effectively in the group.

MISCONCEPTIONS ABOUT GROUP THERAPY

Certain misconceptions and fears about group therapy occur with such regularity that their presence can reasonably be taken for granted: thus, if they go unmentioned by the patient, the therapist should point them out as potential problems. Despite recent sympathetic presentation by the mass media, the belief is still widespread that group therapy is second-rate: that is, it is cheap therapy, a sop for people who cannot afford individual therapy; or, it is diluted therapy because each patient has only twelve to fifteen minutes of the therapist's time each week; or, it exists only because the number of patients greatly exceeds the supply of therapists.

These misconceptions may produce a set of expectations so unfavorable to group therapy as to make successful outcome unlikely. There is substantial research evidence that a patient's initial expectations of and faith in therapy and in the therapist are positively and significantly related to his or her remaining in treatment and to an ultimately favorable outcome.[28]

In addition to evaluative misconceptions, patients are usually further encumbered with procedural misconceptions and unrealistic interpersonal fears. Many of these are evident in the following dream which a patient reported at her second pre-group individual session shortly before she was to attend her first group meeting:

- "I dreamed that each member of the group was required to bring cookies to the meeting. I went with my mother to buy the cookies that I was to take to the meeting. We had great difficulty deciding which cookies would be appropriate. In the meantime, I was aware that I was going to be very late to the meeting, and I was becoming more and more anxious about getting there on time. We finally decided on the cookies and proceeded to go to the group. I asked directions to the room where the group was to meet and was told that it was meeting in room 129A. I wandered up and down a long hall in which the rooms were not numbered consecutively and in which I couldn't find a room with a number A. I finally discovered that 129A was located behind another room and went into the group. When I had been looking for the room, I had encountered many people from my past, many people whom I had gone to school with and many people whom I had known for a number of years. The group was very large, and about forty or fifty people were milling around the room. The members of the group included members of my family—most specifically, two of my brothers. Each member of the group was required to stand in front of a large audience and say what they thought was their difficulty and why they were there and what their problems were. The whole dream was very anxiety provoking, and the business of being late and the business of having a large number of people was very distracting."

Although time did not permit intensive analysis of the dream, several themes were abundantly clear. The patient anticipated the first group meeting with considerable dread. Her concern about being late reflected a fear of being excluded or rejected by the group. Furthermore, since she was starting in an ongoing group—one that had already met for several weeks—she feared that she would be left behind, the others having progressed far past her position. (She could not find a room with an "A" marked on it.) She dreamed that the group would number forty or fifty. Concerns about the size of the group are common; patients fear that their unique individuality will be lost as they become one of the mass. Moreover, patients erroneously apply the model of the economic distribution of goods to the group therapeutic experience, assuming that the size of the crowd is inversely proportional to the goods received by each individual.

The dream image of each member confessing problems to the group audience reflects one of the most basic and pervasive fears held by individuals entering a therapy group: the anticipation of having to reveal oneself and to confess shameful transgressions and fantasies to an alien audience. Further inquiry reveals the expectation of a critical, scornful, ridiculing, or humiliating response from the other members. The experience is fantasied as an apocalyptic trial before a stern, uncompassionate tribunal. The dream also suggests that pre-group anticipation resulted in a recrudescence of anxiety linked to early group experiences in the patient's life, including those of school, family, and play groups. It is as if her entire social network—all the significant people and groups she had encountered in her life—would be present in this group. (In a metaphorical sense this is true: to the degree that she had been shaped by other groups and other individuals, to the degree that she internalized them, she would carry them into the group with her since they are part of her character structure; furthermore, she would, through paratoxic distortions, re-create in the therapy group her early significant relationships.)

It is clear from the reference to room 129 (an early schoolroom in her life) that the patient was associating her impending group experience with a time in her life when few things were more crucial than the acceptance and approval of a peer group. She expected the therapist to be like her early teachers—an aloof, unloving evaluator.

Closely related to the dread of forced confession is the concern about confidentiality. The patient anticipated that there would be no group boundaries, that every intimacy she disclosed would be known by every significant person in her life.

Other common concerns, not evident in this dream, include a fear of mental contagion, of being made sicker through association with other psychiatric patients. Often, but not exclusively, this is a preoccupation of schizophrenic or borderline patients. In part, this concern is a reflection of the self-contempt of patients who project onto others their feelings of worthlessness. Such dynamics underlie the common query, "How can the blind lead the blind?" Convinced that they themselves have nothing of value to offer, patients find inconceivable the notion that they might profit from others like themselves. Other patients fear their own hostility: that, if they ever unleash their rage, it will engulf themselves as well as others. The notion of a group where anger is freely expressed is terrifying as they think silently, "If others only knew what I really thought about them.

The unrealistic expectations that, unchecked, lead to a rejection or a blighting of group therapy can be allayed by adequate preparation of the candidate. Before outlining a preparation procedure, I shall consider some problems, commonly encountered early in the course of the group, that may be ameliorated by preparation before therapy begins.

COMMON GROUP PROBLEMS

One important source of perplexity and discouragement for patients early in therapy is perceived goal incompatibility; they may be unable to discern the congruence between group goals (such as group integrity, construction of an atmosphere of trust, and an interactional confrontive focus) and their individual goals (relief of suffering). What bearing, they wonder, does a discussion of their personal reactions to other members have on their symptoms of anxiety, depression, phobias, impotence, or insomnia?

A high turnover in the early stages of a group is, I have already shown, a major impediment to the development of an effective group. The therapist, from the very first contact with a patient, should discourage irregular attendance and premature termination. The issue is more pressing than in individual therapy, where absences and tardiness can be profitably investigated and worked through. In the initial stages of the group, irregular attendance results in a discouraged and disjunctive group; the group as a whole has so much pressing business to do that resistance expressed through physical absence is especially destructive.

Group therapy, unlike individual therapy, often does not offer immediate gratification. Patients may be frustrated by not getting enough "air time" in the first few meetings, or their anxiety may even be exacerbated by the anxiety intrinsic in the task of direct interpersonal interaction. The therapist should anticipate and address this frustration and anxiety in the preparatory procedure.

"Subgrouping and extragroup socializing," which has been referred to as the "Achilles heel of group therapy," may be encountered at any stage of the group. The problem is complex, and I shall consider it in detail in chapter 12. For the present, it is sufficient to point out that the therapist may begin to shape the group norms regarding subgrouping in the very first contact with the patients.

A SYSTEM OF PREPARATION

There are many approaches to preparing patients for group therapy. The simplest, and the one most easy to effect in the harried world of everyday clinical practice, is in the pre-group interviews to offer a patient, in a thorough, systematic way, the information necessary to facilitate optimal entrance into the group. I am careful to set aside sufficient time for this presentation. I attempt to see a patient at least twice; but even if I see a patient only once before he or she enters the group, I reserve at least half the hour to address each of the foregoing misconceptions, erroneous expectations, and initial problems of group therapy. Misconceptions and expectations should be explored in detail and corrected not by empty exclamation but by an accurate and complete discussion of each. I predict to a patient the early problems in therapy and present a conceptual framework and clear guidelines to effective group behavior. Although each patient's preparation must be individualized according to his or her presenting complaints, questions and concerns raised in the interview, and level of sophistication regarding the therapy process, I have found that a preparatory interview similar to the general outline that follows is of considerable value.

I present patients with a brief explanation of the interpersonal theory of psychiatry, beginning with the statement that although each person manifests his or her problems differently, all who seek help from psychotherapy have in common the basic difficulty of establishing and maintaining close and gratifying relationships with others. I remind patients of the many times in their lives that they have undoubtedly wished to clarify a relationship, to be really honest about their positive and negative feelings with someone and get reciprocally honest feedback. The general structure of society, however, does not often permit totally open communication; feelings are hurt; relationships are fractured; misunderstandings arise; and, eventually, communication ceases. I describe the therapy group as a social laboratory in which such honest interpersonal exploration vis-à-vis the other members is not only permitted but encouraged. For if people are conflicted in their methods of relating to others, then a social situation that encourages honest interpersonal exploration can provide a clear opportunity to learn many valuable things about themselves. I emphasize that working on their relationships directly with other group members will not be easy; in fact, it may be very stressful. But it is crucial because if one can completely understand and work out one's relationships with the other group members, there will be an enormous carryover to the outside world. One will then find pathways to more rewarding relationships with significant people in one's life now and with people one has yet to meet. I emphasize that the therapy group does not eventuate in a single ejaculation of "honest disclosure"; instead, it offers a new social contract which encourages both disclosure and a responsibility to continue communication despite pain and anxiety.

I advise patients that the way they can help themselves most of all is to be honest and direct with their feelings in the group at that moment—especially their feelings toward the other group members and the therapists. I emphasize this point many times and refer to it as the "core of group therapy." I say that patients may, as they develop trust in the group, reveal intimate aspects of themselves, but that the group is not a forced confessional and that people have different rates of developing trust and revealing themselves. I urge patients to consider the group as a forum for risk taking and when they trust the group sufficiently, to try new types of behavior in the group setting.

I predict certain stumbling blocks. I warn patients that they may feel puzzled and discouraged in the early meetings. It will, at times, not be apparent how working on group problems and intragroup relationships can be of value in solving the problems that brought a patient to therapy. This puzzlement, I stress, is to be expected in the typical therapy process; and I strongly urge patients to stay with the group and to ignore any inclination to give up therapy. It is almost impossible to predict the eventual effectiveness of the group during the first dozen meetings, and I ask patients to suspend judgment, to make a commitment of at least twelve meetings before even attempting to evaluate the ultimate usefulness of the group. I tell them that many patients find it painfully difficult to reveal themselves or to express directly positive or negative feelings, and I discuss the tendency to withdraw emotionally, to hide feelings, to let others express feelings for one, to form concealing alliances with others. The therapeutic goals of group therapy are ambitious because we desire to change behavior and attitudes many years in the making; treatment is therefore gradual and long; no important changes will occur for months, and at least a year of treatment will be required.

I predict that patients are likely to develop feelings of frustration or annoyance with the therapist, and that they will expect answers that the therapist cannot supply. Help will often be forthcoming from other patients, however difficult it may be for a patient to accept this fact.

Next I describe briefly the history and development of group therapy —how group therapy passed from a stage during the Second World War, when it was valued for its economic advantages (that is, it allowed psychotherapists to reach a large number of patients), to its present position in the field, where it clearly has something unique to offer and is often the treatment of choice. I cite results of psychotherapy outcome studies in which group therapy is shown to be as efficacious as any mode of individual therapy.[29] My remarks in this area are focused on raising expectations and instilling faith in group therapy and on dispelling the false notion that group therapy is "second-class therapy."

Confidentiality, I state, is as essential in group therapy as it is in any doctor-patient relationship: for members to speak freely, they must have confidence that their statements will remain within the group. In my group therapy experience, I can scarcely recall a single serious breach of confidence and can therefore reassure patients on this matter with conviction. Occasionally, members may inquire whether they can discuss aspects of the group therapy experience with a spouse or a confidant. The best policy for the therapist to follow is never to "ban" anything but instead to provide sufficient information to allow the patient to share in the construction of procedural guidelines. Often a decision is made that permits a patient to share his or her own experience with someone outside the group but to keep the other members' experiences, and certainly their names, in strictest confidence.

Contacts outside the group between members, in one form or another, will occur in every psychotherapy group, and you must approach the issue in your preparatory interview. Two particularly important points must be stressed:

1. The group provides an opportunity for learning about one's problems in social relationships; it is not an assembly for meeting and making social friends; and it is the experience of therapists that if used in this manner the group loses its therapeutic effectiveness. In other words, the therapy group teaches one *how to develop intimate, long-term relationships, but it does not provide these relationships.*
2. However, if by chance or design, members do meet outside the group, it is their responsibility to discuss the salient aspects of that meeting inside the group.

It is particularly useless for therapists to prohibit extragroup socializing; almost invariably during the therapy, group members will engage in some outside socializing and, in the face of the therapist's "Thou shall not," may be reluctant to disclose it in the group. As I shall elaborate in the next chapter, extragroup relationships are not harmful *per se* (in fact, they may be extremely important in the therapeutic process); what impedes therapy is the conspiracy of silence which often surrounds such meetings.

A "Thou shall not" approach merely draws patients into the issue of rule setting and rule breaking. It is far more effective to explain at length why subgrouping may interfere with therapy. I, therefore, explain that friendships among group members often prevent them from speaking openly to one another in the group. Members may develop a sense of loyalty to a dyadic relationship and may thus hesitate to "betray" the other by reporting their conversations back to the group. Yet this reluctance will conflict with the openness and candor so essential to the therapy process. The primary task of therapy group members is, I remind them, to learn as much as possible about the way each relates to each other person in the group. All events that block that process ultimately obstruct therapy.

This strategy of providing full information to the members about the effects of subgrouping provides the therapist with far greater leverage than the strategy of the *ex cathedra* "Thou shall not." If patients engage in secretive subgrouping, you do not have to resort to the ineffectual, misdirected "Why did you break my rules?" but, instead, can plunge into the heart of resistance by inquiring, "How come you're sabotaging your own therapy?"

In summary, this cognitive approach to group therapy preparation has several goals: to provide a rational explanation of the therapy process; to describe what types of behavior are expected of patients; to establish a contract about attendance; to raise expectations about the effects of the group; to predict (and thus to ameliorate) problems and dysphoria in early meetings. Underlying everything the therapist says is the process of demystification. You convey a message that you respect the patient's judgment and intelligence, that therapy is a collaborative venture, that you are an expert who operates on a rational basis and are willing to share your knowledge with the patient. One final point is that comprehensive preparation also enables the patient to make an informed decision about whether to enter a therapy group.

OTHER APPROACHES TO PREPARATION

Straightforward cognitive preparation presented a single time to a patient may not be sufficiently powerful. Patients are anxious during their pre-group interviews and often recall astonishingly little of the content of the therapist's message or grossly misunderstand many key points. Some patients, for example, who I asked to remain in the group for twelve sessions before evaluating it, understood me to say that the group's entire life span would be twelve sessions.

Consequently it is necessary to repeat and to emphasize deliberately many key points of the preparation both during the pre-group sessions and during the first few sessions of the group. For my outpatient groups that meet once a week, I prepare a weekly written summary which I mail out to all the group members following each session (see chapter 14). These summaries provide an excellent forum to repeat in writing essential parts of the preparation procedure. When a new patient joins an ongoing group, I provide additional preparation by requesting that he or she read the group summaries of the previous six meetings.

Many therapists have described other methods to increase the potency of the preparatory procedure. These include distribution of written material, observation of a movie or an audio- or a videotape of meetings, or an experiential teaching format.[30] Some therapists have used another group member to sponsor and to prepare a new member.[31]

These approaches, used singly or in combination, can be highly effective modes of preparation; much research evidence, to which I shall turn shortly, attests to the general effectiveness of these auxiliary techniques. One of the simplest devices is to prepare a written document for each patient to study before entering a group. E. Gauron and E. Rawlings, for example, have developed a fine written preparation which includes the following directions: focus on the here-and-now, assume personal responsibility, avoid blaming others, avoid giving suggestions and fostering dependency, learn to listen to others, become aware both of feelings and of thoughts, attempt to experiment with new behavior.[32] Gauron and Rawlings offer specific instructions about how to give and receive feedback: for example, be specific, give it as soon as possible, be direct, share the positive and the negative, tell how the other makes you feel, don't deal with why—just deal with what you see and feel, acknowledge the feedback, don't make excuses, seek clarification, think about it, beware of becoming defensive, ask for feedback, and so on. Finally, these authors offer a model for how one person can relate intimately with another.

Many researchers have asked an incoming member to listen to or view a film or a tape of a group meeting.[33] Generally (for reasons of professional confidentiality) this is a professionally marketed tape in the public domain or a tape of a simulated group meeting with staff members or professional actors playing the roles of members. The scripts may be deliberately designed to demonstrate the major points to be stressed in the preparatory phase.

An even more powerful mode of preparing patients is to provide them with personal training in desired group behavior.[34] Several experiential formats have been described. S. Budman and his colleagues, for example, hold a single meeting with eighteen to twenty waiting-list patients who are asked to perform a series of carefully selected structured exercises, some involving dyads, some triads, some the entire group.[35] W. Piper and his colleagues developed a protocol in which a prospective group of patients met with a leader (not the eventual group therapist) for a series of four, twice weekly, pre-therapy training groups in which the group engaged in a series of structured exercises designed to teach patients how to use the here-and-now, how to express feelings, and how to become more self-disclosing and aware of the impact one has and wishes to have upon others.[36]

RESEARCH EVIDENCE

In a controlled experiment, my co-workers and I tested the effectiveness of a brief cognitive preparatory session.[37] Of a sample of sixty patients awaiting group therapy, half were seen in a thirty-minute preparatory session, whereas the other half were seen for an equal period in a conventional interview dedicated primarily to history taking. Six therapy groups (three of prepared patients, three of unprepared patients) were organized and led by group therapists unaware that there had been an experimental manipulation. (The therapists believed only that all patients had been seen in a standard intake session.) A study of the first twelve meetings demonstrated that the prepared groups had more faith in therapy (which, in turn, positively influences outcome)[38] and engaged in significantly more group and interpersonal interaction than did the unprepared groups,[39] and that this difference was as marked in the twelfth meeting as in the second. The research design required that identical preparation be given to each patient; we may surmise that had the preparation been more thorough and more individualized for each patient, its effectiveness might have been further enhanced.

The basic design and results of this project—a pre-group preparation sample, which is then studied during its first several group therapy meetings and shown to have a superior course of therapy as compared with a sample that was either not prepared or prepared in a different mode—has been replicated many times. The types of clinical population have varied, and particular modes of preparation and process and outcome-dependent variables have grown more sophisticated. But the amount of corroborative evidence supporting the efficacy of pre-group preparation is impressive; few studies failed to find positive effects of preparation.[40]

J. B. Heitler demonstrated the efficacy of cognitive preparation with patients from a lower socioeconomic class entering a Veterans Administration group.[41] Trained observers rated the groups (which met daily) for two weeks and concluded that the prepared patients participated to a greater extent, were more proactive and engaged in more self-exploratory behavior. The group therapist rated the prepared patients as more involved, as closer to his ideal of model group therapy patients, and as more initiative in self-exploratory efforts.

Other researchers have demonstrated that prepared subjects express more emotion,[42] assume more personal responsibility in a group,[43] have a better attendance and a lower dropout rate,[44] disclose more of themselves,[45] show increased verbal, "work-oriented" participation,[46] are better liked by the other members,[47] report less anxiety,[48] are more motivated to change,[49] are more likely to attain their primary goals in therapy,[50] and have fewer erroneous conceptions about the group procedure.[51] One project reported that an experiential approach to preparation was superior to more passive preparation (viewing a TV tape of a group).[52] One clinician merged two small groups, each of which had been differently prepared for the merger, and reported that the pre-merger preparation of the two groups greatly influenced the members' subsequent attendance and commitment to work in the new merged group.

THE RATIONALE OF PREPARATION

Let us consider briefly the rationale for preparation. The first dozen meetings of a therapy group are precarious and at the same time vitally important: many members grow unnecessarily discouraged and terminate therapy; the group is in a highly fluid state and maximally responsive to the influence of the therapist, who, if sensitive, can take giant strides in influencing the group to elaborate therapeutic norms. The early meetings are a time of considerable patient anxiety, both intrinsic unavoidable anxiety and extrinsic unnecessary anxiety.

The intrinsic anxiety issues from the very nature of the group: an individual who has encountered lifelong disabling difficulties in interpersonal relationships will invariably be stressed by a therapy group that demands not only that one attempt to relate deeply to other members but that one discuss these relationships with great candor. In fact, as I noted in chapter 9, much group research indicates that anxiety seems to be an essential condition for the initiation of change.[53] In group therapy, anxiety arises not only from interpersonal conflict but from dissonance, which springs from one's desire to remain in the group while at the same time feeling highly threatened by the group task.

An imposing body of evidence, however, demonstrates that there are limits to the adaptive value of anxiety in therapy.[54] An optimal degree of anxiety enhances motivation and increases vigilance, but excessive anxiety will obstruct one's ability to cope with stress. R. W. White notes, in his masterful review of the evidence supporting the concept of an exploratory drive, that excessive anxiety and fear are the enemies of environmental exploration; they retard learning and decrease exploratory behavior in proportion to the intensity of the fear.[55] In group therapy, crippling amounts of anxiety may prevent the introspection, interpersonal exploration, and testing of new behavior essential to the process of change.

Much of the anxiety experienced by patients early in the group is not intrinsic to the group task but is unnecessary, extrinsic, and sometimes iatrogenic. This anxiety is a natural consequence of being in a group situation in which one's expected behavior, the group goals, and their relevance to one's personal goals are exceedingly unclear. Research with laboratory groups demonstrates that if the group's goals, the methods of goal attainment, and expected role behavior are ambiguous, the group will be less cohesive and less productive, and its members more defensive, anxious, frustrated, and likely to terminate membership.[56] Effective preparation for the group will reduce the extrinsic anxiety that stems from uncertainty. By clarifying the group goals, by explaining how group and personal goals are confluent, by presenting unambiguous guidelines for effective behavior, by providing the patient with an accurate formulation of the group process, the therapist reduces uncertainty and the accompanying extrinsic anxiety.

A systematic preparation for group therapy by no means implies a rigid structuring of the group experience. I do not propose a didactic, directive approach to group therapy but, on the contrary, suggest a technique that will enhance the formation of a freely interacting, autonomous group. By averting lengthy ritualistic behavior in the initial sessions and by diminishing initial anxiety stemming from ambiguity, the group is enabled to plunge quickly into group work. In my view, anxiety caused by deliberate ambiguity is not necessary to prevent the group from becoming too socially comfortable. Patients are invariably highly conflicted about their interpersonal relationships, and groups that have a high rate of interpersonal interaction will continually present challenging and anxiety-provoking interpersonal confrontations. Therapy groups that are too comfortable are groups that avoid the task of direct interpersonal engagement.

Although some group therapists eschew systematic preparation for the group, close scrutiny reveals that all group therapists attempt to clarify the therapeutic process and the behavior expected of patients; the difference between therapists or between therapeutic schools is largely one of timing and style of preparation. By subtle or even sub-liminal verbal and nonverbal reinforcement, even the most nondirec-tive therapist attempts to persuade a group to accept his or her values about what is or is not important in the group process.[57]

Some therapists staunchly oppose preparation of the patient and hold that ambiguity of both patient and therapist role expectation is desir-able in the early phases of therapy.[58] Their argument is that the devel-opment and eventual resolution of patient-therapist transference dis-tortions is a key therapeutic factor; and that the therapist should seek, in the early stages of therapy, to enhance the development of transfer-ence. Enigma, ambiguity, absence of cognitive anchoring, and frustra-tion of conscious and unconscious wishes all facilitate regressive reac-tion to the therapist and help create an atmosphere favorable to the development of transference. These therapists wish to encourage such regressive phenomena and the emergence of unconscious impulses so that they may be identified and worked through in therapy.[59]

As I emphasized in chapter 7, I do not deny the importance of trans-ference in the therapy group. The issue is one of priority and technique. Transference is a hardy organism; it takes root and flourishes whether or not we prepare the soil, and it will not be smothered by adequate preparation for therapy. Furthermore, as I have so often emphasized, transference resolution and interpersonal learning are not the only therapeutic pathways through the therapy group. An opportunity to facilitate the development of the other therapeutic factors should not be sacrificed to the dubious assumption that it would impede the germi-nation of transference.

One final practical observation about preparation is in order. Group therapists often find themselves pressed to find group members. A sudden loss of members may provoke therapists into hasty activity to rebuild the group, often resulting in the selection of unsuitable, inade-quately prepared members. The therapist then has to assume the posi-tion of selling the group to the prospective member—a "sales" position generally obvious to the patient. The therapist does better to continue the group with reduced membership, to select new members very carefully, and then to present the group in such a way as to maximize a patient's desire to join it. In fact, research[60] indicates that the more difficult it is to enter a group and the more one wants to join, the more will the individual subsequently value the group. This is the general principle underlying initiation rites to fraternities or arduous selection and admission criteria for many organizations: an applicant cannot but reason that a group so difficult to join must be very valuable indeed.

11

IN THE BEGINNING

The work of the group therapist begins long before the first group meeting: indeed, as I have already emphasized, successful group outcome depends largely on the therapist's effective performance of the pretherapy tasks. In previous chapters I have discussed the crucial importance of proper group selection, composition, setting, and preparation. In this chapter I will consider the birth and development of the group: first, the natural history of the therapy group and, then, problems of attendance, punctuality, membership turnover, and addition of new members—important issues in the life of the developing group.

Formative Stages of the Group

INTRODUCTION

Every group, with its unique cast of characters, all interacting complexly with one another, undergoes a highly individual development. All the members begin to manifest themselves interpersonally, each creating his or her own social microcosm; in time, if led by an effective therapist, each member will begin to analyze his or her interpersonal style and eventually will experiment with new behavior. In light of the richness of human interaction compounded further by the grouping of several individuals with maladaptive styles, it is obvious that the course of a group, over many months or years, will be complex and, to a great degree, unpredictable. Nevertheless, mass forces operate in all groups to influence their course of development and to provide a crude but nonetheless useful schema of developmental phases.

There are compelling reasons for you as the therapist to familiarize yourself with the developmental sequence of groups. If you are to perform your task of assisting the group to form therapeutic norms and to prevent the establishment of norms that hinder therapy, then you must have a clear conception of the natural, optimal development of a therapy group. If you are to diagnose group blockage and to intervene in such a way as to allow the group to proceed, you must have a sense of favorable and of flawed development. Furthermore, a knowledge of broad developmental sequence will provide you with a sense of mastery and direction in the group, and prevent you from feeling confused and anxious, which would only compound similar feelings in the patients.*

Our knowledge of group development stems from a few empirical research inquiries with laboratory task groups and many observational studies of encounter and therapy groups. Although the descriptive language varies, there is considerable consistency regarding the basic phases of early group development. Broadly, a group goes through an initial stage of orientation, characterized by a search for structure and goals, by much dependency on the leader, and by concern about the group boundaries. Next, a group encounters a stage of conflict, as it deals with issues of interpersonal dominance. Thereafter, the group becomes increasingly concerned with intermember harmony and affection, while intermember differences are often submerged in the service of group cohesiveness. Much later, the mature work group emerges, which is characterized by high cohesiveness, considerable interpersonal and intrapersonal investigation, and full commitment to the primary task of the group and of each of the members.

THE FIRST MEETING

The first group therapy session is invariably a success. Patients (and neophyte therapists) generally anticipate the initial meeting with a dread so extreme that it is always allayed by the actual event. Some therapists choose to begin the meeting with a brief introductory statement about the purpose and method of the group (especially if they have not thoroughly prepared the patients beforehand); others may simply mention one or two basic ground rules—for example, honesty and confidentiality. The therapist may suggest that the members intro-

---

*An analogy may be made with the practice of psychoanalysis. There are many reasons for the analyst to be thoroughly familiar with the developmental phases of the analytic process; perhaps one of the more important ones is that the knowledge forestalls such incapacitating feelings in the analyst as frustration, discouragement, rage, and bewilderment.

duce themselves, or may elect to remain silent. Invariably, some member will suggest that the members introduce themselves; and usually within minutes, in American groups, the use of first names is established. Then a very loud silence ensues, which, like most psychotherapy silences, seems eternal but in actuality lasts only a few seconds. Generally the silence is broken by the patient destined to dominate the early stages of the group, who will say, "I guess I'll get the ball rolling," or words to that effect. Usually the patient then recounts his or her reasons for seeking therapy, which often elicit similar descriptions from other patients. An alternative course of events occurs when a member (perhaps spurred by the therapist's remark about the tension of the group during the initial silence) comments on his or her social discomfort or fear of groups. This remark may stimulate similar comments from other patients about first-level interpersonal pathology.

As I stressed in chapter 5, the therapist willingly or unwillingly begins to shape the norms of the group at its very conception. Furthermore, this task can be more efficiently performed when the group is yet young. The first meeting is, therefore, no time for the therapist to be inactive; many techniques, some described in chapter 5, are available for effective early intervention.

THE INITIAL STAGE: ORIENTATION, HESITANT PARTICIPATION, SEARCH FOR MEANING, DEPENDENCY

Two tasks confront members of any newly formed group: first, they must determine a method of achieving their primary task—the purpose for which they joined the group; second, they must attend to their social relationships in the group so as to create a niche for themselves that will not only provide the comfort necessary to achieve their primary task but will also result in additional gratification from the sheer pleasure of group membership. In many groups, such as athletic teams, college classrooms, and work details, the primary task and the social task are well differentiated; in therapy groups, although this fact is not often appreciated at first by members, the tasks are confluent—a fact vastly complicating the group experience of socially ineffective individuals.

Several simultaneous concerns are present in the initial meetings. Members, especially if unprepared, search for the rationale of therapy; they may be confused about the relevance of the group's activities to their personal goals in therapy. The initial meetings are often peppered with questions reflecting this confusion; and even months later, mem-

bers wonder aloud, "How is this going to help? What does all this have
to do with my problems?"

At the same time, the members are sizing up one another and the
group. One searches for a viable role for oneself and wonders if one will
be liked and respected or ignored and rejected. Although patients ostensibly come to a therapy group for treatment, social forces impel
them to invest most of their energy in a search for approval, acceptance, respect, or domination. To some patients, acceptance and approval appear so unlikely that they defensively reject or depreciate the
group by silently derogating the other members and by reminding
themselves that the group is unreal and artificial, or that they are too
special to care about a group that requires sacrificing even one particle
of their prized individuality. Members wonder what membership entails. What are the admission requirements? How much must one reveal
or give of oneself? What type of commitment must one make? At a
conscious or near conscious level they seek the answers to questions
such as these and maintain a vigilant search for the types of behavior
that the group expects and approves.

If the early group is puzzled, testing, and hesitant, so too is it dependent. Overtly and covertly, members look to the leader for structure
and answers, as well as for approval and acceptance. Many comments
in the group are directed at or through the therapist; surreptitious
reward-seeking glances are cast at you, as members demonstrate behavior that in the past has gained approval from authority. Your early
comments are carefully examined for directives about desirable and
undesirable behavior. Patients appear to behave as if salvation emanates solely or primarily from you, if only they can discover what you
want them to do. There is considerable realistic evidence for this belief:
your professional identity as a healer, your host role in providing a room
for the group, and your preparation of patients and charging a fee for
your services all reinforce their expectations that you will take care of
them. Some therapists unwittingly compound this belief by behavior
that offers unfulfillable promise of succor.

However, the existence of initial dependency cannot be totally accounted for by the situation, by the therapist's behavior, or by a morbid
dependency state on the part of the patient. I discussed in chapter 7 the
many irrational sources of the members' powerful feelings toward the
group therapist. Among the strongest of these is the human need for an
omnipotent, omniscient, all-caring parent—a need that colludes with
one's infinite capacity for self-deception to create a yearning for and a
belief in a superbeing. In young groups the members' fantasies play in

concert to result in what Freud referred to as the group's "need to be governed by unrestricted force . . . its extreme passion for authority . . . its thirst for obedience."[1] (Yet, who is God's god? I have often thought that the inordinately high suicide rate among psychiatrists[2] is one tragic commentary on this dilemma. Psychotherapists who are deeply depressed and who know that they must be their own superbeing, their own ultimate rescuer, are more likely than many of their patients to plunge into final despair.)

The content and communicational style of the initial phase is relatively stereotyped and restricted. The social code is consistent with that of a cocktail party or similar transient social encounters. Problems are approached rationally; the irrational aspects of the patient who presents a problem are suppressed in the service of support, etiquette, and group tranquillity. E. Semrad suggests the phrase "goblet issues" to refer to early group communication.[3] The phrase refers to the device of picking up a cocktail goblet at a party and figuratively using it to peer at and size up the other guests. Thus, at first, groups may endlessly discuss topics of apparently little substantive interest to any of the participants; these "goblet issues," however, serve as vehicles for the first interpersonal exploratory forays. A woman member, for example, discovers who responds favorably to her, who sees things the way she does, whom to fear, whom to respect; gradually she begins to formulate a picture of the role she will play in the group. "Goblet issues" in social settings include such burning subjects as the weather, "Do you know what's-his-name?" and "Where are you from?" In therapy groups symptom description is a favorite early issue, along with previous therapy experience, medications, and the like.

The search for similarities is common in early groups. Patients are fascinated by the notion that they are not unique in their misery, and most groups invest considerable energy in demonstrating how the members are similar. This process often offers considerable relief to members (see the discussion of universality in chapter 1) and provides part of the foundation for group cohesiveness.

Giving and seeking advice is another characteristic of the early group: patients present the group with the problems of dealing with spouses, children, employers, and so on; the group then attempts to provide some practical solution. As discussed in chapter 1, this guidance is rarely of functional value but serves as a vehicle through which members can express mutual interest and caring.

Many of these concerns are so characteristic of the initial stage of therapy that their presence can be used to estimate the age of a group.

If a group, for example, displays considerable advice giving and seeking, a search for similarities, symptom description, the meaning of therapy, and "goblet issues," then it is invariably either a very young group or an older one with a serious maturational block.

THE SECOND STAGE: CONFLICT, DOMINANCE, REBELLION

If the first core concern of a group is with "in or out," then the next is with "top or bottom."[4] The group shifts from preoccupation with acceptance, approval, commitment to the group, definitions of accepted behavior, and the search for orientation, structure, and meaning, to a preoccupation with dominance, control, and power. The conflict characteristic of this phase is between members or between members and leader. Each member attempts to establish his or her preferred amount of initiative and power; and gradually a control hierarchy, a social pecking order, emerges.

Negative comments and intermember criticism are more frequent; members often appear to feel entitled to a one-way analysis and judgment of others. As in the first stage, advice is given but in the context of a different social code: social conventions are abandoned, and members feel free to make personal criticism about a complainer's behavior or attitudes. Judgments are made of past and present life experiences and styles. It is a time of "oughts" and "shoulds" in the group, a time when the "peer-court," as Bach termed it,[5] is in session. Members make suggestions or give advice, not as a manifestation of acceptance and understanding—sentiments yet to emerge in the group—but as part of the process of jockeying for position.

The struggle for control is part of the infrastructure of every group: it is always present, sometimes quiescent, sometimes smoldering, sometimes in full conflagration. If there are members with strong needs to dominate, control may be the major theme of the early meetings. The dormant struggle for control often becomes more overt when new members are added to the group, especially new members who do not "know their place" and, instead of making obeisance to the older members in accordance with their seniority, make strong early bids for dominance.

The emergence of hostility toward the therapist is inevitable in the life sequence of a group. Many observers have emphasized an early stage of ambivalence to the therapist coupled with resistance to self-examination and self-disclosure.[6]

304

Hostility toward the leader has its source in the unrealistic, indeed magical, attributes with which patients secretly imbue the therapist. Their expectations are so limitless that they are bound to be disappointed by the therapist, however competent: gradually as they recognize the therapist's limitations, disenthrallment commences. By no means is this a clearly conscious process: the members may intellectually advocate a democratic group which draws on its own resources, but nevertheless may, on a deeper level, crave dependency and attempt first to create and then to destroy an authority figure. Group therapists refuse to fill the traditional authority role: they do not lead in the ordinary manner; they do not provide answers and solutions; they urge the group to explore and to employ its own resources. The members' wish lingers, however; and it is usually only after several sessions that the group members come to realize that the therapist will frustrate their yearning for a "real" leader.

Yet another source of resentment toward the leader lies in the gradual recognition by each member that one will not become the leader's favorite child. During the pre-therapy session, each member comes to harbor the fantasy that the therapist is his or her very own therapist, intensely interested in the precise details of that patient's past, present, and fantasy world. In the early meetings of the group, however, each member begins to realize that the therapist is no more interested in him or her than in the others; seeds are sown for the emergence of rivalrous, hostile feelings toward the other members. Each member feels, in some unclear manner, betrayed by the therapist.

These unrealistic expectations of the leader and consequent disenchantment are by no means a function of childlike mentality or psychological naïveté. The same phenomenon occurs, for example, in groups of professional psychotherapists. In fact, there is no better way for the trainee to appreciate the group's proclivity both to elevate and to attack the leader than to experience the feelings as a group member.

Some workers[7] who have taken Freud's *Totem and Taboo*[8] extremely literally regard the group's pattern of relationship with the leader as a recapitulation of the primal horde patricide. Freud does indeed suggest at one point that modern group phenomena have their prehistoric analogues in the ancient, misty events of the primal horde:

Thus the group appears to us as a revival of the primal horde. Just as primitive man survives potentially in every individual, so the primal horde may arise once more out of any random collection; insofar as men are habitually under the sway of group formation, we recognize in it the survival of the primal horde.[9]

The primal horde, not unlike the chorus in Sophocles' *Oedipus Tyrannus,* is able to free itself from restrictive growth-inhibiting bonds and progress to a more satisfying existence only after the awesome leader has been removed.[10]

The patients are never unanimous in their attack upon the therapist; invariably, some champions of the therapist will emerge from the group. The lineup of attackers and defenders may serve as a valuable guide for the understanding of characterologic trends useful for future work in the group. Generally, the leaders of this phase, those members who are earliest and most vociferous in their attack, are heavily conflicted in the area of dependency and have dealt with intolerable dependency yearnings by reaction formation. These individuals, sometimes labeled "counterdependents,"[11] are inclined to reject prima facie all statements by the therapist and to entertain the fantasy of unseating and replacing the leader.

- For example, approximately three-fourths of the way through the first meeting of a group I asked for the members' reflections on the meeting: How had it gone for them? Disappointments? Surprises? One member, who was to control the direction of the group for the next several weeks, commented that it had gone precisely as he had expected; in fact, it had been almost disappointingly predictable. The strongest feeling, he added, that he had had thus far was anger toward me because I had asked one of the members a question that evoked a brief period of weeping. He had felt then, "They'll never break *me* down like that." His first impressions were very predictive of his behavior for some time to come. He remained on guard and strove to be self-possessed and in control at all times. He regarded me not as an ally but as an adversary and was sufficiently forceful to lead the group into a major emphasis on control issues for the first months. If therapy is to be successful, counterdependent members must at some point experience their flip side and recognize and work through deep dependency cravings.

Other members immediately side with the therapist; they must be helped to investigate their need to defend the therapist at all costs, regardless of the issue involved. Occasionally patients defend you because they have encountered a series of unreliable objects and misperceive you as extraordinarily frail; others need to preserve you because they fantasize an eventual alliance with you against other powerful members of the group. Beware lest you unknowingly transmit covert signals of personal distress to which the rescuers appropriately respond.

Many of these conflicted feelings crystallize around the issue of the leader's name. Are you to be referred to by professional title (Dr. Jones, or, even more impersonally, "the doctor") or by first name? Some patients will use the therapist's first name or even a diminutive of the name immediately, before inquiring about the therapist's preference. Others, even after the therapist has wholeheartedly agreed to proceeding on a first-name basis, still cannot bring themselves to mouth such irreverence and continue to bundle the therapist up in a professional title.

Although I have posited disenchantment and anger with the leader as an ubiquitous feature of small groups, by no means is the process constant across groups in form or degree. The therapist's behavior may potentiate or mitigate both the experience and the expression of rebellion. Thus one prominent sociologist, who has for many years led sensitivity-training groups of college students, reports that inevitably there is a powerful insurrection against the leader, culminating in the members removing him or her bodily from the group room.[12] I, on the other hand, led similar groups for more than a decade and never encountered a rebellion so extreme that members physically ejected me from the room. Such a difference can be due only to differences in leader styles and behavior. Invoking greater negative response are those therapists who are ambiguous or deliberately enigmatic, who are authoritative yet offer no structure or guidelines for patients, and who covertly make unfulfillable promises to the group early in therapy.[13]

This stage is often difficult and personally unpleasant for group therapists. The neophyte therapist should be reminded, however, that the therapist is essential to the survival of the group: the members cannot afford to liquidate you, and you will always be defended. For your own comfort, however, you must learn to discriminate between an attack on your person and an attack on your role in the group. The group's response to the leader is similar to transference distortion in individual therapy in that it is not directly related to the therapist's behavior, but its source in the group must be understood both from an individual psychodynamic and from a group dynamic viewpoint.

Therapists who are particularly threatened by a group attack protect themselves in a variety of ways. Once I was asked to act as a consultant for two therapy groups, each approximately twenty-five sessions old, which had developed similar problems: both groups seemed to have reached a plateau, no new ground appeared to have been broken for several weeks, and the patients seemed to have withdrawn interest in the groups. A study of current meetings and past protocols revealed that neither group had yet directly dealt with any negative feelings toward the therapists. However, the reasons for this inhibition were quite different in the two groups. In the first group, the two co-therapists (who were leading their first group) had clearly shown their throats, as it were, to the group and, through their obvious anxiety, uncertainty, and avoidance of hostility-laden issues, had pleaded frailty. In addition, they both desired to be loved by all the members and had been at all times so benevolent and so solicitous that an attack by the patients would have appeared unseemly and ungrateful.

The therapists of the second group had forestalled an attack in a different fashion: they remained aloof Olympian figures whose infrequent interventions were oracular in their ambiguity and ostensible profundity. At the end of each meeting, they summarized the predominant themes and each member's contributions. To attack these therapists would have been perilous as well as impious and futile.

Such leadership tends to inhibit a group; suppression of important ambivalent feelings about the therapist results in a counterproductive taboo which opposes the desired norm of interpersonal honesty and emotional expression. Furthermore, an important model-setting opportunity is lost; the therapist who withstands an attack without being either destroyed or destructively retaliatory, but instead responds by attempting to understand and work through the sources and effects of the attack, demonstrates to the group that aggression need not be lethal and that it can be expressed and understood in the group.

One of the consequences of suppression of therapist-directed anger for the two groups in question, and for most groups, is the emergence of displaced, off-target aggression. For example, one group persisted for several weeks in attacking "doctors." Previous unfortunate experiences with doctors, hospitals, and individual therapists were described in detail, often with considerable group consensus on the injustices and inhumanity of the medical profession. In one group, a member attacked the field of psychotherapy by bringing in an article by H. J. Eysenck that purported to prove that psychotherapy is ineffective. At other times, police, teachers, and other representatives of authority are awarded similar treatment.

Scapegoating of other members is another "off target" manifestation and may become so intense that unless you intervene to direct the attack onto yourself, the sacrificial patient may be driven from the group. Other groups covertly appoint a leader from their ranks to replace the therapist—always an unsatisfactory process which leaves the group and the patient-leader discouraged and confused. Sensitivity training groups usually resolve the issue by defining the leader's role as that of a specialized member with certain technical skills. It is hoped that the group will learn to evaluate the therapist's contributions for their intrinsic value rather than accept them because of the authority behind them. Therapy groups do not resolve the problem for many months or years; again and again the group returns to the issue as members at different rates, according to their degree of dependency conflict, gradually work through their attitudes toward the therapist. It is essential, if this work is to be done, that the group feel free to confront the therapist, who must not only permit, but encourage, such confrontation.

THE THIRD STAGE: DEVELOPMENT OF COHESIVENESS

The third widely recognized formative phase of a group is the development of group cohesiveness. Following the previous period of conflict, the group gradually develops into a cohesive unit. Many varied phrases with similar connotations have been used to describe this phase: in-group consciousness;[14] common goal and group spirit;[15] consensual group action, cooperation, and mutual support;[16] group integration and mutuality;[17] we-consciousness unity;[18] external rivalry;[19] support and freedom of communication[20] and establishment of intimacy and trust between peers.[21] During this phase there is an increase of morale, mutual trust, and self-disclosure. Some members reveal the "real" reason they have come for treatment; sexual secrets may be shared; long-buried past transgressions are publicly unearthed. Post-group coffee meetings may be arranged; attendance improves, and patients evince considerable concern about missing members.

The chief concern of the group is with intimacy and closeness. W. Schutz, who characterizes patients' concerns in the first phase as "in or out" and in the second as "top or bottom," characterizes the third phase as "near or far"; the primary anxieties have to do with not being liked or close enough to people or with being too intimate.[22]

Although there may be greater freedom of self-disclosure in this phase, there may also be communicational restrictions of another sort: often the group suppresses all expression of negative affect in the service of cohesion. Compared with the previous stage of group conflict, all is sweetness and light, and the group basks in the glow of its newly discovered unity. The members, in a sense, unite against the rest of the world, with much intermember support, much pride in the group, and much condemnation of the members' adversaries outside the group. Eventually, however, the glow will pale, and the group embrace will seem ritualistic unless the hostility in the group is permitted to emerge. Only when all affects can be expressed, and constructively worked through in a cohesive group, does the group become a mature work group—a state lasting for the remainder of the group's life, with periodic short-lived recrudesences of each of the earlier phases. To underscore this transition, some researchers have suggested a division of this stage into two: a stage of cohesiveness (group against external world) and a stage of advanced group work or true teamwork in which the tension is between "work," or progress, and regression to an earlier stage.[23]

OVERVIEW

Now that I have outlined the early stages of group development, let me consider a series of qualifying conditions lest the novice take too literally the proposed developmental sequence. The developmental phases are, after all, constructs: entities that group leaders construct for their semantic and conceptual convenience. There exists no proof that stages do or must exist. The evidence for developmental stages of therapy groups stems from nonsystematic clinical observational studies: virtually no controlled research exists to substantiate this developmental sequence. Group developmental research in experiential groups has been rudimentary and inconclusive. For example, W. Bennis and other researchers, in a study of six sensitivity groups, tested the hypothesis that the groups would move through two developmental phases: a primary concern with authority and then a primary concern with intimacy.[24] Of these six groups studied, only one showed such a sequence; the other five showed continuous dealing and redealing with the two problems. At the very best, research demonstrates only a slight preponderance of comments during some temporal period of a group which can be coded as belonging to the domain of, let us say, control rather than affection.[25] Thus, the boundaries between phases are not clearly demarcated nor does a group permanently graduate from one phase.

In describing group development, Schultz uses the apt metaphor of replacing a wheel: one tightens the bolts one after another just enough so that the wheel is in place; then the process is repeated, each bolt being tightened in turn, until the wheel is entirely secure.[26] In a similar way, phases of a group emerge, become dominant, and then recede, only to have the group return again later to deal with the same issues with greater thoroughness. Perhaps, given these considerations, it would be more accurate to speak of developmental tasks rather than of developmental phases or developmental sequence. D. Hamburg suggests the term "cyclotherapy" to refer to this process of returning to the same issues but each time from a different perspective and each time in greater depth.[27] Often a therapy group will spend considerable time discussing some issue, such as fees, student observers in the group, or the relationship between the co-therapists, and then, months later, return to the same topic from an entirely different perspective.

The determination of the natural history of a therapy group becomes even more complex in light of the tendency of leaders to anticipate a certain development phase and, unbeknownst to themselves, to firmly guide the group through the predicted stages.[28] M. Lieberman has demonstrated that the leader unknowingly fills a gap in the group. He systematically composed a T-group from which were excluded all individuals with a need for pairing behavior, and compared its development, during a three-week human relations laboratory, with a naturally composed control group.[29] He found that the leaders of the control group expressed the same degree of pairing behavior throughout the course of the group; however, the leader of the experimental group expressed five times more pairing in the third week than in the first. Apparently, this leader was attempting to fill the need for warmth that had developed in the experimental group. With no control over the highly influential behavior of the leader, the determination of the "natural" developmental sequence becomes very difficult indeed.

Impact of Patients on Group Development

The developmental sequence I have described perhaps accurately portrays the unfolding of events in a theoretical, unpeopled therapy group and is much like the major theme of an ultramodern symphony which is unintelligible to the untrained ear. In the group, obfuscation derives from the richness and unpredictability of human interaction, which complicates the course of treatment and yet contributes to its excitement and challenge.

Generally, the course of events in the early meetings is heavily influenced by the group member with the "loudest" interpersonal pathology. By "loudest" I refer not to severity of pathology but to pathology that is most immediately manifest in the group: for example, monopolistic proclivities, exhibitionism, promiscuous self-disclosure, easily expressed anger, judgmentalism, or unbridled inclination to exert control. Not infrequently these patients receive covert encouragement from the therapist and other group members. Therapists value these patients because they provide a focus of irritation in the group, stimulate the expression of affect, and enhance the interest and excitement of a meeting. The other patients initially often welcome the opportunity to hide behind the protagonist as they themselves hesitantly examine the terrain.

In a study of the therapy dropouts of nine outpatient groups, I found that in five groups a patient with a characteristic pattern of behavior fled the therapy group within the first dozen meetings.[30] These patients ("early provocateurs") differed from one another dynamically but assumed a similar role in the group; they stormed in, furiously activated the group, and then vanished. The therapists described their role in the group in such terms as "catalysts," "targets," "hostile interpreters," or "the only honest one." Some of these early provocateurs were active counterdependents and challenged the therapist early in the group. One, for example, who asked in the third meeting why the session had to end when the therapist decreed, attempted to rally interest in a leaderless meeting or, only half jokingly, in an investigation of the leader's personal problems. Other provocateurs prided themselves on their honesty and bluntness, mincing no words in giving the other members candid feedback; while others, heavily conflicted in intimacy, both seeking it and fearing it, engaged in considerable self-disclosure and exhorted the group to reciprocate. Although the early provocateurs usually claimed that they were impervious to the opinions and evaluations of others, in fact they cared very much and, in each instance, deeply regretted the nonviable role they had created for themselves in the group.[31]

The therapist must recognize this phenomenon early in the group and, through clarification and interpretation of their role, help prevent these patients from committing social suicide. Perhaps, even more importantly, you must recognize and discontinue your own covert encouragement of their behavior. It is not uncommon for the therapist to be stunned at the early provocateur's dropping out: you may so welcome the behavior of these patients that you fail to appreciate both their distress and your own dependence on them for keeping the group energized. It is useful as a therapist to take note of your reactions to the absence of the various members of the group. (If some patients are never absent, you may fantasize their absences and your reaction to it.) If you dread the absence of certain patients, if you feel there would be no life in the group that day, then it is likely that there is too much burden on those patients and so much secondary gratification that they will not be able to deal with their primary task in therapy.

Despite these shortcomings, the proposed developmental sequence has much to recommend it. Many group leaders have observed that a group first deals with its *raison d'être* and boundaries, then with dominance and submission, and later, as shared experience increases, with issues of intimacy and closeness. Some time ago at a two-week group workshop, I took part in an intergroup exercise in which the sixty participants were asked to form four groups in any manner they wished and then to study the ongoing relationships among groups. The sixty participants, in near panic, stampeded from the large room toward the four rooms designated for the four small groups. The panic, an inevitable part of this exercise,[32] probably stems from primitive fears of exclusion from a group. In the group in which I participated, the first words spoken after approximately sixteen members had entered the room were, "Close the door. Don't let anyone else in!" The first act of the group was to appoint an official doorkeeper. Once the group's boundaries were defined and its identity vis-à-vis the outside world established, the group turned its attention to regulating the distribution of power by speedily electing a chairman, before multiple bids for power could immobilize the group. Only much later did the group experience and discuss feelings of trust and intimacy.

Once therapists have an idea of the developmental sequence, they are more easily able to maintain objectivity and to appreciate the course of a group despite considerable yawing. They may note that the group never progresses past a certain stage or omits others. At times, therapists may demand something for which the group is not yet ready: mutual caring and concern develop late in the group; in the beginning, members are likely to view one another as interlopers or rivals for the healing touch of the therapist.

Membership Problems

The early developmental sequence of a therapy group is powerfully influenced by membership problems. Turnover in membership, tardiness, and absence are facts of life in the developing group and often threaten its stability and integrity. Considerable absenteeism may redirect the group's attention and energy from its developmental tasks to the problem of maintaining membership. It is the therapist's task to discourage irregular attendance and, when necessary, to replace dropouts by adding new members.

MEMBERSHIP TURNOVER

In the normal course of events, 10 percent to 35 percent of the members drop out of the group in the first twelve to twenty meetings; if two or more members drop out, new members are usually added, and often a similar percentage of these additions drop out in their first dozen or so meetings. Only after this does the group solidify and begin to engage in matters other than those concerning group stability. Generally, by the time patients have remained in the group for approximately twenty meetings, they have made the necessary long-term commitment. In two attendance studies of five outpatient groups, there was considerable turnover in membership over the first twelve meetings, a settling in between the twelfth and twentieth, and near-perfect attendance, with excellent punctuality and no dropouts, between the twentieth and forty-fifth meetings (the end of the study).[33]

Another corroborative study of ninety group therapy patients reports a dropout rate of 29 percent in the first twelve meetings and only one dropout for the remainder of the first year of treatment.[34] Only one study reports a significantly different pattern.[35] The researchers studied five groups led by psychiatric residents (their first group experience) who were trained in analytic group techniques focusing on dynamics involving the group as a whole. Fourteen percent of the members dropped out in the first six months, and 36 percent dropped out between six and twelve months. Many dropped out because of discomfort arising from the greater intimacy arising in the group. Some groups had a wave of dropouts; one dropout seemed to seed others.

ATTENDANCE AND PUNCTUALITY

Despite the therapist's initial encouragement of regular attendance and punctuality, difficulties usually arise in the early stages of a group. At times the therapist, buffeted by gusts of excuses—babysitting problems, vacations, transportation difficulties, work emergencies, out-of-town guests, and so on—becomes resigned to the impossibility of synchronizing the schedules of eight busy people. Resist that conclusion! Tardiness and irregular attendance usually signify resistance to therapy and should be regarded in the same way in which you regard these phenomena in individual therapy. When several members are often late or absent, search for the source of the group resistance; for some reason, cohesiveness is limited and the group is foundering. When a group has solidified into a hard-working cohesive group, many months may go by with perfect attendance and punctuality.

At other times, the resistance is individual rather than group based. I am continually amazed by the transformation in some patients who for long periods have been tardy because of absolutely unavoidable contingencies—for example, periodic business conferences, classroom rescheduling, babysitting emergencies. These patients, after recognizing and working through the resistance, may become the most punctual members for months on end. Thus, one periodically late member hesitated to involve himself in the group because of his shame about his impotence and homosexual fantasies. After he disclosed these concerns and worked through his feelings of shame, he found that the crucial business commitments responsible for his lateness (commitments that, he later revealed, consisted of perusing his afternoon mail) suddenly ceased to exist.

Whatever the basis for resistance, it is behavior that must, for several reasons, be modified before it can be understood and worked through. For one thing, irregular attendance is destructive to the group; it is, in a sense, contagious and begets group demoralization and further absences. Obviously, it is impossible to work on an issue in the absence of the relevant patients; there are few exercises more futile than addressing the wrong audience by deploring irregular attendance with the group members who are present—the regular, punctual patients.

Various methods of influencing attendance have been adopted by therapists. During pre-therapy interviews, many therapists stress the importance of regular attendance. Patients who appear likely to have scheduling or transportation problems are best referred for individual therapy, as are patients who must be out of town every four weeks or who, a few weeks after the group begins, plan an extended out-of-town vacation. Charging full fees for missed sessions is standard practice unless a patient has an extraordinary excuse for absence and explains it to the therapist well in advance. Many group therapists charge patients a set fee per month, which is not reduced for missed meetings regardless of the reason.

It is extremely important for the therapist to be utterly convinced of the importance of the therapy group and of regular attendance. The therapist who acts on this conviction will transmit it to the patients. Thus, arrive punctually, award the group high priority in your own schedule, and, if you must be absent, take your own absence seriously and inform the group weeks in advance.

A patient who has a poor attendance record (whatever the reason) is unlikely to benefit from the group. Stone and his colleagues state that, in their study of ninety-eight patients, attendance (early in the group) was linearly related to late (six to twelve months) dropout.[36] Thus, inconsistent attendance demands decisive intervention.

• For example, in a new group, one member, Dan, was consistently late or absent. Whenever the co-therapists discussed his attendance, it was clear that Dan had exceedingly valid excuses: his life and his business were in such crisis that unexpected circumstances repeatedly arose to make attendance impossible. The group as a whole had not jelled; despite the therapists' efforts, other members were often late or absent, and there was considerable flight during the sessions. At the twelfth meeting, the therapists decided that decisive action was necessary, and advised Dan to leave the group, explaining that Dan's schedule was such that the group could be of little value to him. They offered to help Dan arrange individual therapy which would provide greater scheduling flexibility. Although the therapists' motives were not punitive, and although they were thorough in their explanation, Dan was deeply offended and, in anger, walked out midway through the meeting. The other members, extremely threatened, supported Dan to the point of questioning the therapists' authority to ask a member to leave.

Despite this initial reaction of the group, it was soon clear that the therapists had made the proper intervention. One of the co-therapists phoned Dan and saw him individually for a few sessions and then referred him to a competent therapist for long-term therapy. Dan soon appreciated that the therapists were acting not punitively but in his best interests. Irregular attendance at a therapy group would not have been effective therapy for him. The group was immediately affected: attendance abruptly improved and remained near-perfect over the next several months. The members, once they had recovered from their fear of similar banishment, gradually disclosed their approval of the therapists' act and their great resentment toward Dan and, to a lesser extent, toward some of the other members for having treated the group in such a cavalier fashion.

Other therapists attempt to improve attendance by harnessing group pressure—for example, by refusing to hold a meeting until a predetermined number of members (usually three or four) are present. Even if not formalized in this manner, the pressure exerted by the other members is the most effective lever brought to bear on errant ones. The group is often frustrated and angered by the repetitions and false starts necessitated by irregular attendance; the therapist should encourage the members to express their reactions to late or absent members. Be mindful, though, that the therapist's concern about attendance is not always shared by the members: a young or immature group often welcomes the small meeting, regarding it as an opportunity for more individual attention from the leader.

Like any event in the group, absences or latenesses are forms of behavior that reflect an individual's characteristic patterns of relating to others. If Mary comes late, does she apologize? Does Joe enter in a thoughtless, exhibitionistic manner? Does Peg ask for a recap of the events of the meeting? Is her relation with the group such that the members provide her with a recap? If Stan is absent, does he phone in advance to let the group know? Does he offer complex overelaborate excuses as though convinced he will not be believed? Not infrequently a patient's psychopathology is responsible for poor attendance. For example, one patient who sought therapy because of a crippling fear of authority figures and a pervasive inability to assert himself in interpersonal situations was frequently late because he was unable to muster the courage to interrupt a conversation or a conference with a business associate.

Thus, this behavior is part of a patient's social microcosm and, if handled properly, may be harnessed in the service of self-understanding; but for both the group's and the individual's sake, it must be corrected before being analyzed. No interpretation can be heard by an absent patient. In fact, the therapist must time any comments to the returning patient with care. Often patients who have been absent or late return to the meeting with some defensive guilt and are not in an optimal state of receptiveness for observations about their behavior. It is as if they experience a recrudescence of archaic concerns about arriving late at home or at school and have an expectational set of being scolded or punished. The therapist often does well to attend first to group maintenance and norm-setting tasks and then, later, when the timing seems right and defensiveness diminished, attempt to help the patient explore the meaning of his or her behavior.

A patient who is to miss a meeting or arrive late should, if possible, phone the therapist in advance, so as to spare the group from wasting considerable time expressing curiosity or concern about the missing member. Often, in advanced groups, the fantasies of patients about why a member is absent provide valuable material for the therapeutic process; however, in early groups, such speculations tend to be superficial and unfruitful.

An important adage of interactional group therapy, which I emphasize many times throughout this book, is that any event in the group can serve as grist for the interpersonal mill. Even the absence of a member can generate important previously unexplored material.

- For example, a group composed of four women and three men met for its eighth meeting one day when two of the men were unable to attend. Albert, the remaining male, had previously been withdrawn and submissive in the group. In the meeting in which he was alone with the four women, a dramatic transformation occurred: Albert suddenly erupted into activity, talked about himself, questioned the other members, spoke loudly and forcefully, and, on a couple of occasions, challenged the therapist. His nonverbal behavior was saturated with quasi-courtship bids directed at the women members—for example, frequent adjustment of his necktie knot and preening of the hair at his temples. Later in the meeting, the group focused on Albert's change, and he realized and expressed his fear and envy of the two missing males, both of whom were aggressive and assertive. He had long experienced a pervasive sense of social and sexual impotence which had been reinforced by his feeling that he had never made a significant impact on any group of people and especially a group of women. In subsequent weeks Albert did much valuable work on these issues—issues that might not have become accessible for many months without the adventitious absence of the two other members.

My clinical preference is to encourage attendance in most of these ways but never, regardless of how small the group, to cancel a session. There is considerable therapeutic value in the patient's knowing that the group is always there, stable and reliable; its constancy will in time beget constancy of attendance. Furthermore, I have had many small group sessions, even with two members, that have proven to be critical for the patients attending. The technical problem with such meetings, especially of three or fewer members, is that, without interaction, the therapist may revert to focusing on intrapsychic processes in a manner characteristic of individual therapy and forgo group and interpersonal issues. It is far more therapeutically consistent and technically undemanding to focus in depth on group and interpersonal processes even in the smallest of sessions. Consider the following clinical example from a ten-month-old group:

- For various reasons—vacations, illnesses, and resistance—only two members (and the therapist) attended: Wanda, a thirty-eight-year-old depressed borderline patient, who on two previous occasions had required hospitalization; and Martin, a twenty-three-year-old schizoid, who was psychosexually immature and suffered from moderately severe ulcerative colitis.

Wanda spent much of the early part of the meeting describing the depth of her despair, which during the past week had reached such proportions that she had been preoccupied with suicide and, since the group therapist had been out of town, had visited the emergency room at the hospital. While there, she had surreptitiously read her medical chart and seen a consultation note written a year previously by the group therapist in which he had diagnosed her as "borderline." She said that she had been anticipating this diagnosis and now wished the therapist to hospitalize her. Martin then recalled a fragment of a dream he had had several weeks before but had not discussed: the therapist is sitting at a large desk interviewing him; he, Martin, stands up and looks at the paper on which the therapist is writing, and there he sees in huge letters one word covering the entire page: IMPOTENT. The therapist helped both Wanda and Martin to discuss their feelings of awe, helpless dependence, and resentment toward him, as well as their inclination to shift responsibility and project onto him their bad feelings about themselves.

Wanda proceeded to underscore her helplessness by describing her inability to cook for herself and her delinquency in paying her bills, which was so extreme that she now feared police action against her. The therapist and Martin both commented on her persistent reluctance to comment on her positive accomplishments—for example, her continued excellence as a teacher. The therapist wondered whether her presentation of herself as helpless was not designed to elicit responses of caring and concern from the other members and the therapist—responses that she felt would be forthcoming in no other way.

Martin then mentioned that he had gone to the medical library the previous day to read some of the therapist's professional articles. In response to the therapist's question about what he really wanted to find out, Martin answered that he guessed he really wanted to know how the therapist felt about him and proceeded to describe, for the first time, his longing for the therapist's sole attention and love.

Later the therapist expressed his dismay at Wanda's reading his note in her medical record. Since there is a realistic component to a patient's anxiety upon learning that her therapist has diagnosed her as "borderline," the therapist candidly discussed both his own discomfort at having to use diagnostic labels for hospital records and the confusion surrounding psychiatric nosological terminology; he recalled as best he could his reasons for using that particular label and its implications.

Wanda then commented upon the absent members and wondered whether she had driven them from the group (a common reaction to the absence of members). She dwelled on her unworthiness and, at the therapist's suggestion, made an inventory of her baleful characteristics, citing her slovenliness, selfishness, greed, envy, and hostile feelings toward all those in her social environment. Martin both supported Wanda and echoed her, identifying many of these feelings in himself. He discussed how difficult it was for him to reveal himself in the group (Martin had disclosed very little of himself previously in the group). Later he discussed his fear of getting drunk or losing control in other ways: for one thing, he might become indiscreet sexually. He then discussed, for the first time, his fear of sex, his impotence, his inability to maintain an erection, and his last-minute refusals to take advantage of sexual opportunities. Wanda empathized deeply with Martin and, although she had for some time regarded sex as abhorrent, expressed the strong feeling (which, be it noted, she did not intend to act upon) that she would like to help him by offering herself to him sexually. Martin then described his strong sexual attraction to Wanda, and later both he and Wanda discussed their sexual feelings toward the other members of the group. The therapist made the observation, one that proved subsequently to be of great therapeutic importance to Wanda, that her interest in Martin and her desire to offer herself to him sexually belied many of the items in her inventory: her selfishness, greed, and ubiquitous hostility to others.

Thus, although only two members were present at this meeting, they met as a group and not as two individual patients. The other members were discussed *in absentia,* and previously undisclosed interpersonal feelings between the two patients and toward the therapist were expressed and analyzed. It was a valuable session, deeply meaningful to both participants.

THE GROUP DROPOUT

There is no more threatening problem for the neophyte group therapist (and for many more experienced therapists as well) than the dropout from group therapy. Dropouts concerned me greatly when I first started to lead groups, and my first group therapy research was a study of all the patients who had dropped out of the therapy groups in a large psychiatric clinic.[37] Nor is it a minor problem; as I discussed earlier, the group therapy demographic research demonstrates that a substantial number of patients will leave a group prematurely regardless of what the therapist does. (In fact, some clinicians suggest that dropouts are not only inevitable but necessary in the sifting process involved in building a cohesive group.)*

Elsewhere in this book, I have discussed the reasons for premature termination. In general, they stem from problems caused by deviancy, subgrouping, conflicts in intimacy and disclosure, the role of the early provocateur, external stress, complications of concurrent individual and group therapy, inability to share the leader, inadequate preparation, and emotional contagion. Underlying all these reasons is the considerable stress early in the group; patients who have maladaptive interpersonal patterns are exposed to unaccustomed demands for candor and intimacy; they are often confused about procedure; they suspect that the group activities bear little relevance to their problem; and, finally, too little support occurs for them in the early meetings to sustain their hope.

Preventing Dropouts

Let me first discuss the prevention of dropouts and then turn to the management of the process when it is a *fait accompli*. One important way of decreasing the dropout rate is, in pre-therapy preparation, to anticipate major group concerns and problems. This anticipation makes clear to the patient that periods of discouragement are expected in the therapy process. Patients are less likely to lose confidence in a therapist who appears to have the foreknowledge that stems from experience.

Some groups contain experienced group members who assume some of this predictive function.

• For example, one group that graduated several members, but contained three old members, was reconstituted with five new members. In the first two meetings, the old members briefed the new ones and, among other information, told them that, by the sixth or seventh meeting, some patient would decide to drop out and then the group "would have to drop everything for a couple of meetings to persuade him to stay." The old members went on to predict which of the new members would be the first to decide to terminate. This form of prediction is a most effective manner of ensuring that it is not fulfilled.

---

*An escape hatch may be essential to the group process, so as to allow some patients to make their first tentative commitments to the group. The group must have some decompression mechanism: mistakes in the selection process are inevitable, unexpected events in the lives of the new members occur, unanticipated group incompatibilities develop. Some intensive week-long human relations laboratories or encounter groups that meet at a geographically isolated place lack a way of escape; and on several occasions, I have observed psychotic reactions stemming from a patient's being forced to continue in an incompatible group.

Even despite painstaking preparation, however, many patients will consider dropping out. When a patient informs a therapist that he or she wishes to leave the group, the traditional approach is to urge the patient to return to the group to discuss it with the other group members. Underlying this practice is the assumption that the group will help the patient work through resistance and thereby dissuade him or her from terminating. This approach, however, is rarely successful. In one study of thirty-five dropouts from nine therapy groups (with an original membership of ninety-seven patients), I found that every one of the dropouts was urged to return for another meeting; not once did the final session avert premature termination.[38] (Furthermore, there were no group continuers who threatened to drop out and were salvaged by this technique.)

Generally the therapist is well advised to see a potential dropout for a short series of individual interviews to discuss the sources of group stress. Occasionally an accurate, penetrating interpretation may keep a patient in therapy.

• For example, one schizoid, alienated patient announced in the eighth meeting that he felt he was getting nowhere in the group and had decided to terminate. In an individual session the patient told the group therapist something he had never been able to say in the group: namely, that he had many positive feelings toward a couple of the group members. Nevertheless, he insisted that the therapy was ineffective and that he desired a more accelerated and more relevant form of therapy. The therapist correctly interpreted the patient's intellectual criticism of the group therapy format as a rationalization: he was, in fact, fleeing from the closeness he had felt in the group. The therapist again explained the social microcosm phenomenon and clarified for the patient that in the group he was repeating his lifelong style of relating to others: he had always avoided or fled from intimacy and no doubt would always do so in the future unless he stopped running and allowed himself the opportunity to explore his interpersonal problems *in vivo*. The patient returned to the group and eventually made considerable gains in therapy.

An inexperienced therapist is particularly threatened by the patient who threatens to drop out. You begin to fear that, one by one, your patients will leave and that you will one day come to the group and find that you (and perhaps a co-therapist) are the only ones there. (And what, then, do you tell your group supervisor?)

If this fantasy truly takes hold, you cease to be therapeutic to your patients. The balance of power shifts. You feel blackmailed. You begin to be seductive, cajoling—anything to entice the patients back to future meetings. Once this happens you, of course, have entirely lost your therapeutic leverage.

After struggling in my own clinical work with the problem of group dropouts over many years, I have finally achieved some resolution of the issue. Through a shift in personal attitude, I no longer have group therapy dropouts. But I do have group therapy "throwouts"! I do not mean that I frequently throw patients out of a therapy group, but I am perfectly prepared to do so if a patient is not working in the group. I am entirely convinced that group therapy is a highly effective mode of psychotherapy, and if a patient is not going to be able to profit from it, then I want to get that patient out of the group into a more appropriate mode of therapy for him or her and bring someone else into the group who will be able to use what it has to offer.

This method of reducing dropouts is more than a specious form of bookkeeping (converting "dropouts" to "throwouts") analogous to the procedure used by some hospitals to inflate the survival rate of various surgical procedures (that is, by transferring terminal patients to affiliated institutions), but reflects a posture of the therapist which increases the commitment to work. Once you have achieved this particular mental set, you communicate it to patients in direct and indirect ways. You convey your confidence in the therapeutic modality and your expectation that the patient will use the group for effective work. You, not the patient, retain responsibility for entrances and departures from the group.

Removing a Patient from the Group

To take a patient out of a therapy group is an act of tremendous significance for both that patient and the group and must be approached thoughtfully. Once you have determined that a patient is not working effectively, it is necessary to attempt to remove all possible obstacles in the way of his or her productive engagement in the group. If you have done everything in your power yet been unable to alter the situation, there is every reason to expect one of these outcomes: (1) the patient will ultimately drop out of the group without benefit (or without further benefit); (2) the patient may be harmed by further group participation (because of negative interaction and/or the adverse consequences of the deviant role [see chapter 8]); or (3) the patient will substantially obstruct the group work for the remaining patients. It is folly to adopt a *laissez-faire* posture: the time has come to remove the patient from the group.

How? There is only one way to take a patient out of a therapy group —gracelessly! An impasse has been reached in therapy, and there is no skillful, subtle way to do what must be done. Often it is a task better handled in an individual meeting with that patient than in the group. In fact, the very reason that the patient is being asked to leave the group is that he or she cannot work nondefensively and productively in the group. Furthermore, the situation is so anxiety-provoking for the other members that generally the therapist can expect little constructive group discussion. Nor, in my experience, is it helpful to invite the patient back for one final meeting to work things through with the group: If the patient were able to work things through in an open, nondefensive manner, then there would have been no need to ask him or her to leave the group. My almost invariable experience is that such final working-through meetings are closed, nonproductive, and frustrating.

When you remove a patient from the group, you may, without exception, expect a powerful reaction from the rest of the group. The ejection of a group member stirs up deep archaic levels of anxiety associated with ejection or abandonment by the primal group. Even if there is unanimous agreement among the members that the patient should have been asked to leave the group—even if, for example, the patient had developed a manic reaction and was disrupting the entire group— the members still are anxious and threatened by your decision to remove the patient.

There are two possible interpretations the members may give to your act of removing the patient. One interpretation is rejection and abandonment: that is, that you do not like the patient, you resent him or her, you're angry and you want the patient out of the group and out of your sight. The other interpretation (the correct one, let us hope) is that you are a responsible mental-health professional acting in the best interests of the patient being asked to leave the group and of the remaining patients. Every patient's treatment regimen is different, and you made a responsible decision about the fact that this form of therapy was not suited for a particular patient. Furthermore, you acted in a professionally responsible manner by ensuring that the patient will receive another form of therapy more likely to be helpful.

The remaining group members generally embrace the first—the rejection—interpretation. Your ultimate task is to help them arrive at the second interpretation; you may facilitate the process by making clear the reasons for your actions and also sharing your decisions about future therapeutic plans: for example, that you are seeing the patient in individual therapy or making a responsible referral.

The Departing Group Member: Therapeutic Considerations

When a patient is asked to leave or chooses to leave a group, then it is up to you to make the experience as constructive as possible; such patients ordinarily are considerably demoralized and tend to view the group experience as "one more failure." Even if the patient denies this feeling, you should still assume that it is present, and, in a private discussion with the patient, advance alternative methods of viewing the experience. For example, you may present the notion of "readiness" or "group fit." Some patients are able to profit from group therapy only after a period of individual therapy; others, for reasons unclear to us, are never able to work effectively in therapy groups. It is also entirely possible that the patient may have a successful course of therapy in another group, and this possibility should be explored. In any case, the patient should be helped to understand that it is not he or she who has failed but that, due to several possible reasons, a form of therapy has proven unsuccessful.

You may use the final interview to review in detail the patient's experience in the group in a manner useful for the patient. Occasionally a therapist is uncertain about the usefulness or the advisability of confronting a patient who is terminating therapy. Should you, for example, confront a denying male patient who attributes his dropping out of the group to his hearing difficulties when, in fact, he had been an extreme deviant and was clearly rejected by the group? As a general principle, it is useful to view the patient from the perspective of his or her entire career in therapy. If the patient is very likely to re-enter therapy, a constructive confrontation will, in the long run, enable him or her to use any subsequent therapy more effectively. If, on the other hand, there is little likelihood that the patient will pursue a dynamically oriented therapy, there is little point in presenting a final interpretation that he or she will never be able to use or to extend. Test the denial. If it is deep, leave it be: there is little point in undermining defenses, even self-deceptive ones, if you cannot provide a satisfactory substitute.

THE ADDITION OF NEW MEMBERS

Whenever the group census falls undesirably low (generally five or less), the therapist should introduce new members. This may occur at any time during the course of the group, but often there are major junctures in the long-term outpatient group when new patients are added: during the first twelve to twenty meetings (to replace early dropouts) and after approximately twelve to eighteen months (to replace improved, graduating members).

Timing

The success of this operation depends, in part, upon proper timing: there are favorable and unfavorable times to introduce new members into a group. Generally a group that is in crisis, or is actively engaged in an internecine struggle, or has suddenly entered into a new phase of development does not favor the addition of new members; often it will reject the newcomers or else will evade confrontation with the pressing group issue and instead redirect its energy toward the incoming members. An example would be a group that is, for the first time, dealing with hostile feelings toward a controlling, monopolistic patient; or a group that has recently developed such cohesiveness and trust that a member has, for the first time, shared an extremely important secret with it. Some therapists postpone the addition of new members even when the census of the group is down to four or five if the group is working well. I prefer not to delay and promptly begin to screen prospective candidates. Small groups, even highly cohesive ones, will eventually grow even smaller through absence or termination and soon will lack the interaction necessary for effective work.

The most auspicious period for adding new members is during a phase of stagnation in the group. Many groups, especially older ones, sensing the need for new stimulation, actively encourage the therapist to add members.

Response of the Group

A *Punch* cartoon, cited by Foulkes,[39] portrays a harassed woman and her child trying to push their way into a crowded train compartment. The child looks up at his mother and says, "Don't worry, Mother, at the next stop it will be our turn to hate!" The parallel to new patients entering the group is trenchant. Hostility to the newcomer is evident even in the group that has beseeched the therapist to add new members.

I have observed many times that when new members are slated to enter a meeting, the old members arrive late; often they may remain for a few minutes talking together animatedly in the waiting room while the therapists and the new patients wait in the therapy room. A content analysis of the session in which a new member or members are introduced reveals several themes that are hardly consonant with benevolent hospitality. The group suddenly spends far more time than in previous meetings discussing "the good old days." Long-departed group members and events of bygone meetings are avidly recalled, as new members are guilelessly reminded, lest they have forgotten, of their novitiate status.

Similarly, members may express resemblances they perceive between the new member and some member no longer present in the group. I once observed a meeting in which two members were introduced; the group noted a similarity between one of them and Matthew, a patient who (the newcomer shortly learned) had committed suicide a year before; the other patient was compared with Minerva, a patient who had dropped out, discouraged and unimproved, after three months of therapy. These groups, be it noted, were unaware of the invidiousness of their greetings and consciously felt that they were extending a welcome to the newcomers.

A group may also express its ambivalence by discussing, in a newcomer's first meeting, threatening, confidence-shaking issues. For example, in its seventeenth session (one in which two new members entered), one group discussed for the first time the co-therapists' competence. The members noted that the therapists were listed in the hospital catalogue as resident-students and suspected they might be leading their first group. This issue—a salient and important one, which must be discussed—was nonetheless highly threatening to new members. It is of interest that the information was already known to several group members but had never until that meeting been broached in the group.

There are, of course, simultaneous feelings of welcome and support for new members which are particularly marked if the group has been searching for new members. The members may exercise great gentleness and patience in dealing with new members' initial fear or defensiveness. The group, in fact, may collude in many ways to increase its attractiveness for the newcomer. Often patients may gratuitously offer testimonials and describe the various ways in which they have improved. In one such group, a newcomer asked a disgruntled, resistive woman member about her progress; and, before she could reply, two other members, sensing that she would devaluate the group, interrupted and described their own progress. Although groups may unconsciously wish to discourage newcomers, they seem to prefer to do so by threatening the new member or by severe initiation rites; members are not willing to deter new members by so devaluating their group that the candidates choose not to join it.

Reasons for a Group's Response

There are several reasons for a group's ambivalent response to new members. Some members who highly prize the solidarity and cohesiveness of the group may consider any proposed change as a threat to the status quo. Others may envision new members as potential rivals for the therapist's and the group's attention and perceive their own fantasied role as favored child to be in jeopardy. Still other members, particularly those conflicted in the area of control and dominance, may regard the new member as a threat to their position in the hierarchy of power. In one group where a new female patient was being introduced, the two incumbent female members, desperately protecting their stake, employed many prestige-enhancing devices, including the recitation of poetry. When John Donne is quoted in a therapy group as part of the incoming ritual, it is hardly for an aesthetic end.

A common concern of a group is that, even though new members are needed, they will nonetheless slow up the group. The group fears that familiar material will have to be repeated for the newcomers, and that the group must recycle, as it were, and relive the stages of gradual social introduction and ritualistic etiquette. This expectation proves to be unrealistic: new patients introduced into an ongoing group generally move quickly into the prevailing level of group communication and bypass the early testing phases characteristic of members in a newly formed group. One additional but less frequent source of ambivalence issues from the threat posed by the newcomer to group patients who have improved and who fear to see in that person themselves as they were at the beginning of their own therapy. In order to avoid reexposure to painful, past periods of life, they will frequently shun new patients who appear as reincarnations of their earlier selves.

Therapeutic Guidelines

Patients entering an ongoing group require not only the standard preparation to group therapy I discussed in chapter 10, but also preparation to help them deal with the unique stresses accompanying entry into an established group. Entry into any established culture—be it new living situation, work, school, hospital, and so on—produces anxiety and, as extensive research indicates, demands orientation and support.[40]

I prefer to anticipate for patients their feelings of exclusion and bewilderment at entering an unusual culture and to reassure them that they will be allowed to enter and participate at their own rate. New patients entering established groups may be daunted by the sophistication, openness, interpersonal facility, and daring of more experienced members; they may also be frightened or fear contagion, since they are immediately confronted with patients revealing "sicker" sides of themselves than are revealed in the first meetings of a new group. These contingencies should therefore be discussed with the patient. It is generally helpful to describe to the incoming patient the major events of the past few meetings. If the group has been going through some particularly intense, tumultuous events, it is wise to brief the new patient even more thoroughly. If you use a written summary technique (see chapter 14), then you may ask the new patient to read the summary of the past few meetings.

I make an effort to engage the new patient in the first meeting or two. Often it is sufficient merely to inquire about his or her experience of the meeting—something to the effect of: "Bob, this has been your first session. What has the meeting felt like for you? Does it seem like it will be difficult to get into the group? What concerns are you aware of so far?" It's often useful to help the patient assume some control over his or her participation. For example, you might say, "Bob, I note that several questions were asked of you earlier. How did that feel? Too much pressure? Or did you welcome them?" Or, "Bob, I'm aware that you were silent today. The group was deeply engaged in business left over from meetings when you were not present. How did that feel? Relieved? Or would you have welcomed questions directed at you?"

Many therapists prefer to introduce two new members at a time. Such a practice may have advantages both for the group and for the new members. Introduction in pairs probably does not result in a statistically lower dropout rate[41] and occasionally, if one patient is integrated into the group much more easily than the other, may backfire and create even greater discomfort for a newcomer. Nevertheless, introduction in pairs has much to recommend it: the group conserves energy and time by assimilating two patients at once; the new patients may ally with each other and thereby feel less alien.

The number of new patients introduced into the group distinctly influences the pace of absorption. A group of six or seven can generally absorb a new member with scarcely a telltale ripple; the group continues work with only the briefest of pauses and rapidly pulls the new member along. On the other hand, a group of four confronted with three new members often comes to a screeching halt as all ongoing work ceases and the group devotes all its energy to the task of incorporating the new members. The old members will wonder how much they can trust the new ones. Dare they continue with the same degree of self-disclosure and risk taking? To what extent will their familiar, comfortable group be changed forever? The new members will be searching for guidelines to behavior. What is acceptable in this group? What is forbidden? If their reception by the established members is not gracious, they may seek the comfort inherent in an alliance of newcomers. The therapist who notes frequent "we" and "they," or "old members" and "new members" statements should heed these signs of schism; until incorporation is complete, little further therapeutic work can be done.

A similar situation often arises when the therapist attempts to amalgamate nuclei of two groups that have been reduced in number. This procedure is not easy. Too often a clash of cultures and cliques formed along lines of the previous groups may persist for a remarkably long time; and the therapist must actively prepare patients for the merger.

An interesting strategic variation on the process of adding new members consists of including the group in the selection decision. For example, the therapist may permit the entire group to interview prospective members and, after the candidate leaves, vote on his or her inclusion. While this may sound like a frightening ordeal for the new patient, it need not ·be. The therapist, in an initial individual screening session, may prepare the patient for the group interview, presenting it as a means of finding the proper "fit" between patient and group; furthermore, the procedure may be a two-way interview: the candidate may assess the group as well as be assessed by it. Of course, should the group decide not to accept the patient (and that occurs rarely), then the therapist assumes full responsibility for placing the patient in another group.

This procedure is cumbersome and time consuming and should be used only with a group that has matured into a seasoned work group. However, it offers several advantages to both patient and group. The patient, having had to overcome barriers to joining the group, comes to value it more highly. Is this not the principle behind fraternity initiations, freemasonry, novitiate study, and long, costly apprenticeships in such organizations as psychoanalytic societies? The group members, on the other hand, having had an active role in the decision-making process, will assume responsibility for their decision and invest considerable energy to help the new member become a part of the group. Is this not the principle behind all forms of the democratic group process?

The introduction of new patients may, if properly considered, enhance the therapeutic process of the old members who may respond to a newcomer in highly idiosyncratic styles. An important principle of group therapy, which I have discussed previously, is that every major stimulus presented to the group elicits a variety of responses by the group members. The investigation of the reasons behind these different responses is generally rewarding and clarifies aspects of character structure. To observe others' response to a situation in a manner markedly different from one's own is an arresting experience which can provide considerable insight into one's behavior. Such an opportunity is unavailable in individual therapy but constitutes one of the chief strengths of the group therapeutic format. An illustrative clinical example may clarify this point:

• A new member, Alice—a forty-year-old, attractive divorcée—was introduced at a group's eighteenth meeting. The three men in the group greeted her in strikingly different fashions.

Peter arrived fifteen minutes late and thereby missed the introduction. For the next hour he was active in the group, discussing issues left over from the previous meeting as well as events occurring in his life during the past week. He totally ignored Alice, avoiding even glancing at her—a formidable feat in a group of six people in close physical proximity. Later in the meeting, as others attempted to help Alice participate, he, still without introducing himself, fired questions at her like a harsh prosecuting attorney. A twenty-eight-year-old devout Catholic father of four, Peter had sought therapy because he, as he phrased it, loved women too much and had had a series of extramarital love affairs. In subsequent meetings, the group used the events of Alice's first meeting to help Peter investigate the nature of his "love" for women. Gradually he came to recognize how he used women, including his wife, as part objects, valuing them for their genitals only and remaining insensitive to their feelings and experiential world.

The two other men in the group, Brian and Arthur, on the other hand, were preoccupied with Alice during her first meeting. Arthur, a twenty-four-year-old homosexual who sought therapy in order to change his sexual orientation, reacted strongly to Alice and found that he could not look at her without experiencing the strongest sense of embarrassment. His discomfort and blushing were apparent to the other members, who helped him explore far more deeply than he had previously his relationship with the women in the group. Arthur had desexualized the other two women in the group by establishing in his fantasy a brother-sister relationship with them. Alice, who was sexually attractive, divorced and "available," and at the same time old enough to evoke in him affect-laden feelings about his mother, presented a special problem for Arthur, who had previously been settling into too comfortable a niche in the group.

Brian, on the other hand, transfixed Alice with his gaze and delivered an unwavering broad smile to her throughout the meeting. An extraordinarily dependent twenty-three-year-old, Brian had sought therapy for depression following the breakup of a love affair. Having lost his mother in infancy, he had been raised by a succession of governesses and had had only occasional contact with an aloof, powerful father of whom he was terrified. His romantic affairs, always with considerably older women, had invariably collapsed because of the insatiable demands he made on the relationship. The other women in the group in the past few meetings had similarly withdrawn from him and, with progressive candor, had confronted him with, as they termed it, his puppy-dog presentation of self. Brian thus welcomed Alice, hoping to find in her a new source of succor. In subsequent meetings Alice proved helpful to Brian as she revealed her feeling, during her first meeting, of extreme discomfort at his beseeching smile and her persistent feeling that he was asking for something important from her. She said that she did not know what it was, but she knew that it was more than she had to give.

Freud once compared psychotherapy to chess in that far more is known and written about the opening and the end games than about the middle game. Accordingly, the opening stages of therapy and termination may be discussed with some degree of precision, but the vast bulk of therapy cannot be systematically described. Thus, the following chapters deal in a general way with issues and problems of later stages of therapy and with some specialized therapist techniques.

12

THE ADVANCED GROUP

Once a group has survived its first few months, it is no longer possible to describe discrete stages of development. When a group achieves a degree of stability, the long working-through process begins, and the major therapeutic factors described in the earlier chapters operate with increasing force and effectiveness. Members gradually engage more deeply in the group and discover and share their problems in living. There is no limit to the richness and complexity of the group sessions.

No one, therefore, can offer specific procedural guidelines for each contingency. In general, the therapist must strive to encourage development and operation of the therapeutic factors. The application of the basic principles of the therapist's role and technique to specific group events and to each patient's therapy (as discussed in chapters 5, 6, and 7) constitutes the art of psychotherapy; and for this, there is no substitute for experience, supervision, and intuition.

Certain issues and problems occur, however, with sufficient regularity to warrant discussion. In this chapter, I consider subgrouping, self-disclosure, conflict, and termination of therapy; and in chapter 13, "The Problem Patient," I discuss certain recurrent behavioral configurations in patients that present a challenge to the therapist and to the group.

Subgrouping

Fractionalization—the splitting off of smaller units—occurs in every social organization. The process may be transient or enduring, helpful or harmful, for the parent organization. Therapy groups are no exception; subgroup formation is an inevitable and often disruptive event in the life of the group; and yet there, too, the process, if understood and harnessed properly, may further the therapeutic work.

333

A subgroup in the therapy group arises from the belief of two or more members that they can derive more gratification from a relationship with each other than from one with the entire group. Extragroup socializing is often the first stage of subgrouping. A clique of three or four members may begin to have telephone conversations, to have coffee or dinner, to visit each other's homes, or even to engage in business ventures with one another. Occasionally, two members will become sexually involved. A subgroup may occur, however, completely within the confines of the group therapy room, as members who perceive themselves to be similar form coalitions. There may be any number of common bonds: comparable educational level; similar values; similar age, marital status, or group status (for example, the "old-timer" original members). Social organizations, especially if larger than a therapy group, characteristically develop opposing factions—two or more conflicting subgroups; but such is not often the case in therapy groups, where one clique forms but the remaining group members, excluded from it, generally do not possess effective social skills and do not usually coalesce into a second subgroup.

The members of a subgroup may be identified by a general code of behavior: they agree with one another regardless of the issue and avoid confrontations among their own membership; they may exchange knowing glances when a member not in the clique speaks; they may arrive and depart from the meeting together.

THE EFFECTS OF SUBGROUPING

Subgrouping can have an extraordinarily disruptive effect on the course of the therapy group. In a study of thirty-five patients who prematurely dropped out from group therapy, I found that eleven (31 percent) dropped out largely because of problems arising from subgrouping.[1] Complications arise whether the patient is included in or excluded from a subgroup.

Inclusion

Those included in a twosome or a larger subgroup often find that group life is vastly more complicated and less rewarding. As a patient transfers allegiance from the group goals to the subgroup goals, loyalty becomes a major issue. Should one abide by the group procedural rules of free and honest discussions of feelings if, in so doing, one would be breaking a confidence established secretly with another member?

- For example, two group members, Christine and Jerry, often met

334

after the therapy session to have long, intense conversations. Jerry had remained withdrawn in the group and had sought out Christine because, as he informed her, he felt that she alone could understand him. After obtaining her promise of confidentiality, he soon was able to reveal to her his homosexual obsessions and occasional pedophilic involvements. Back in the group, Christine felt restrained by her promise and avoided open interaction with Jerry, who eventually dropped out unimproved. Ironically, Christine was an exceptionally sensitive member of the group who might have been particularly useful to Jerry by encouraging him to participate in the group had she not been restrained by the antitherapeutic subgroup norms (that is, her promise of confidentiality).

Another example of the conflict between group and subgroup norms is cited by H. Lindt and M. Sherman:

An older, paternal man had been giving two other patients a ride home and had invited them to see television at his house. The visitors witnessed an argument between the older patient and his wife, and at a subsequent group session told him that they felt he was mistreating his wife. The older patient, evidently feeling betrayed and considering the group his enemy rather than his friend, seemed to develop feelings of rejection and dropped out of treatment.[2]

Severe clinical problems occur when group members engage in sexual relations: they often hesitate to "besmirch" (as one patient phrased it) an intimate relationship by giving it a public airing. Freud, who never practiced clinical group therapy, wrote in 1921 a prescient essay on group psychology in which he underscored the incompatibility between a sexual love relationship and group cohesiveness.[3] Though we may disagree with the cornerstone of his argument (that inhibited sexual instincts contribute to the cohesive energy of the group), his conclusions are compelling: that is, no group tie—be it race, nationality, social class, or religious belief—can remain unthreatened by the overriding importance that two people in love can have for each other. Obviously, the ties of the therapy group are no exception. Members of a therapy group who become involved in a love-sexual relationship will almost inevitably come to award their dyadic relationship higher priority than their relationship to the group. They sacrifice their value for each other as helpmates in the group; they refuse to betray confidences; in their efforts to be charming to one another, they affect poses in the group; they perform for one another, blotting out the therapists, other members of the group, and, most importantly, their primary goals in therapy. Often the other group members are dimly aware that something important is occurring which is being actively avoided in the group discussion —a state of affairs that usually results in global group inhibition.

• Chance provided empirical evidence to substantiate these comments.[4] A research team happened to be studying closely a therapy group in which two members developed a clandestine sexual relationship. Since the study began months before the liaison occurred, good baseline data is available. Several observers (as well as the patients themselves in post-group questionnaires) rated each meeting along a seven-point scale for: amount of affect expressed, amount of self-disclosure, and general value of the session. In addition, the communication-flow system was recorded with the number and direction of each patient's statements charted on a who-to-whom matrix. During the observation period, two patients, Bruce and Geraldine, developed a sexual relationship that was kept secret from the therapist and the group for three weeks. During these three weeks, there was a steep downward gradient in the scoring of the quality of the meetings, with particularly diminished verbal activity, expression of affect, and self-disclosure. Moreover, scarcely a single verbal exchange between Geraldine and Bruce was recorded! This last finding is the quintessential reason that subgrouping impedes therapy. Keep in mind that the primary goal of group therapy is to facilitate each member's exploration of his or her interpersonal relationships. Here were two people who knew each other well, had the potential of being deeply helpful to one another, and yet scarcely exchanged a word in the group.

The couple resolved the problem by deciding that one of them would drop out of the group (not an uncommon form of resolution). Geraldine dropped out; and in the following meeting, Bruce discussed the entire incident with relief and with great candor. (The ratings by both patients and observers indicated this meeting to be valuable, with active interaction, strong affect expression, and much disclosure from others as well as Bruce.)

Exclusion
Exclusion from the subgroup also complicates group life. Anxiety associated with earlier exclusion experiences is evoked which, if not discharged by working through, may become disabling. Often it is exceptionally difficult for members to comment on their feelings of exclusion; they may be disinclined to intrude into a relationship or to risk incurring the wrath of the involved members by discussion of the subgroup in the session.

Nor are therapists immune to this problem. Recently one of my supervisees observed two of his group patients (both married) walking arm in arm along the street. The therapist found himself unable to comment on this event for several reasons: the therapist should not assume the position of spy or disapproving parent in the eyes of the group; the therapist is not free to bring up nongroup material; the involved members will, when they are psychologically ready, discuss the problem. However, these are rationalizations; there is no more important issue than the interrelationship of the group members. The therapist who is unwilling to bring in all material bearing on member relationships can hardly expect members to do so. If you feel yourself trapped in a dilemma—on the one hand, needing to bring in such observations and, on the other, unhappy about seeming like a spy— then often the best approach is to share your dilemma with the group —both your observations and your personal uneasiness and reluctance to discuss them.

THE CAUSES OF SUBGROUPING

Subgrouping is caused by both group and individual forces. Some groups (and some therapists) have a disproportionately high incidence of subgrouping; some individuals will invariably become involved in subgrouping in whatever group they are placed.

Subgrouping may be a manifestation of a considerable degree of undischarged hostility in the group, especially toward the leader. In their classic research on three different styles of leadership, R. White and R. Lippit noted that a group is more likely to develop disruptive in-group and out-group factions under an authoritarian, restrictive style of leadership.[5] The members, unable to express their anger and frustration directly to the leader, release these feelings obliquely by binding together and mobbing or scapegoating one or more of the other members.

I have in my discussion of primary task and secondary gratification (in chapter 6) already presented one of the major dynamics underlying subgrouping. Patients who violate group norms by secret liaisons are opting for need gratification rather than for pursuit of personal change —their primary reason for being in therapy. Need frustration occurs early in therapy: for example, patients with strong needs for intimacy, dependency, sexual conquests, or dominance may soon sense the impossibility of gratifying these needs in the group and often attempt to gratify them outside of the formal group. In one sense, these patients are "acting out" in that, outside the therapy setting, they engage in an organized, symbolically determined form of behavior which relieves inner tensions. Except in retrospect, it is exceptionally difficult to discriminate "acting out" from acting or participation in the therapy group. The course of the therapy group is a continual cycle of action and analysis of this action. The social microcosm concept depends on patients engaging in their habitual patterns of behavior, which are then examined by the patient and the group. "Acting out" as a form of resistance to therapy occurs only when one refuses to examine and to allow the group to examine one's behavior. Extragroup behavior that is *not* examined in the group becomes then a particularly potent form of resistance, whereas extragroup behavior that is subsequently brought back into the group and worked through may prove to be of considerable therapeutic import.

THERAPEUTIC CONSIDERATIONS

By no means, then, is subgrouping, with or without extragroup socializing, invariably disruptive. If the goals of the subgroup are consonant with the goals of the parent group, subgrouping may ultimately enhance group cohesiveness: for example, a coffee group or a bowling league may operate successfully within a larger social organization. In therapy groups, some of the most significant incidents in therapy occur as a result of some extragroup member contacts which are then fully worked through in therapy.

• For example, two women members who went to a dance together after a meeting discussed new observations and sets of feelings that had arisen in the social setting. One of the pair had been far more flirtatious, even openly seductive, than she had been in the group; furthermore, much of this was "blind spot" behavior—out of her awareness.

• Another group scheduled a beer party for one member who was terminating. Unfortunately, he had to leave town unexpectedly, and the party was canceled. The member acting as social secretary notified the others of the cancellation but by error neglected to contact one member, Jim. On the night of the party Jim waited, in vain, at the appointed place for two hours experiencing many familiar feelings of rejection, exclusion, and bitter loneliness. The discussion of these reactions and of Jim's lack of any annoyance or anger and his feeling that his being excluded was natural, expected, "the way it should be," led to much fruitful therapeutic work for him. When the party was finally held, considerable data was generated for the group. Members displayed different aspects of themselves. For example, the member who was least influential in the group, because of his emotional isolation and his inability or unwillingness to disclose himself, assumed a very different role because of his wit, store of good jokes, and easy social mannerisms. Another experienced and sophisticated group patient re-encountered his dread of social situations and inability to make small talk and took refuge behind the role of host, devoting his time busily to refilling empty glasses.

• In another group, a dramatic example of effective subgrouping occurred when the patients became concerned about one member who was in such despair that she considered suicide. Several group members maintained a week-long telephone vigil, which proved to be beneficial both to the patient and to the cohesiveness of the entire group.

• The vignette of the "man who liked Robin Hood," described in chapter 2, is another example of subgrouping which enhanced therapeutic work. The patient attempted to form an extragroup alliance with every member of the group and ultimately, as a result of his extragroup activity, arrived at important insights about his manipulative modes of relating to peers and about his adversarial stance toward authority figures.

Thus, the principle is clear: any contact outside a group may prove considerably useful provided that the goals of the parent group are not relinquished. If such meetings are viewed as part of the group rhythm of action and subsequent analysis of this action, much valuable information can be made available to the group. To achieve this end, the involved members must inform the group of all important extragroup events. If they do not, the disruptive effects on cohesiveness I have described will take place. *It is not the subgrouping per se that is destructive to the group, but the conspiracy of silence that generally surrounds it.*

In practice, groups that meet only once weekly often experience more of the disruptive effects of subgrouping than the beneficial ones. Much extragroup socializing never comes directly to the group's attention, and the behavior of the involved members is never made available for analysis in the group. For example, the extragroup relationship described earlier between Christine and Jerry, in which Jerry revealed in confidence his homosexual behavior, never was made known to the group. Christine disclosed the incident over a year later to a research psychiatrist who interviewed her in a psychotherapy outcome study.

The therapist should, then, encourage open discussion and analysis of all extragroup contacts and all in-group coalitions. As I said in the discussion on preparation, the therapist must emphasize that it is the patient's responsibility to bring extragroup contacts into the group. The therapist who surmises from glances between two members in the group, or from their appearance together outside the group, that a special relationship exists between them should not hesitate to present this feeling to the group. No criticism or accusation is implied, since the investigation and understanding of an affectionate relationship between two members may be as therapeutically rewarding as the exploration of a hostile impasse. The therapist must attempt to disconfirm the misconception that psychotherapy is reductionistic in its ethos, that all experience will be reduced to some fundamental (and base) motive. Furthermore, other members must be encouraged to discuss their reactions to the relationship, whether they be envy, jealousy, rejection, or vicarious satisfaction.

One practical caveat: patients engaged in some extragroup relationship that they are not prepared to discuss in the therapy group may request the therapist for an individual session and ask that the material discussed not be divulged to the rest of the group. If you give such a promise of confidentiality, you may soon find yourself in an untenable collusion from which extrication is difficult. I would suggest that the group therapist *never* offer a promise of confidentiality: instead, you should assure the patients that you will be guided by your professional judgment and act in their therapeutic behalf.

Therapy group members may establish sexual relationships with one another but not with great frequency. The therapy group is not prurient; patients have severe sexual conflicts, resulting in such problems as impotence, frigidity, social alienation, and sexual guilt. Probably far less sexual involvement occurs in a therapy group than in an equally long-lasting social or professional group.

The therapist cannot, by edict, prevent the formation of sexual relations or any other form of subgrouping. I agree with A. Wolf, who states:

men and women who become so engaged do so compulsively and generally drift into physical familiarity whether the physician forbids it or not. Then the therapist is faced with their sense of guilt, a tendency to hide aspects of the relationship and a secret defiance that complicates and obscures the significance of the act. Furthermore, patients who leap into bed with one another do so rather extensively with people outside the group. In the therapeutic setting, the repetition of the sexual act has the advantage of subjecting compulsive promiscuity to examination under the microscope.[6]

Consider the clinical example of the "Grand Dame" (described in chapter 2) of Valerie, Charles, and Louis. Recall that Valerie seduced

Charles and Louis as part of her struggle for power with the group therapist. The episode was, in one sense, disruptive for the group: Valerie's husband learned of the incident and threatened Charles and Louis, who, along with other members, grew so distrustful of her that dissolution of the group appeared imminent. The crisis was resolved by the group's expelling Valerie (who continued therapy in another group). Despite these catastrophic complications, some benefits occurred. The episode was thoroughly explored within the group, and the participants obtained considerable help with their sexual pathology. For example, Charles, who had a history of a Don Juan style of relationships with women, at first disclaimed all responsibility in the matter. He washed his hands of the incident by pointing out that Valerie had asked him to go to bed, and, as he phrased it, "I don't turn down a piece of candy when it's offered." Louis also tended to disclaim responsibility for his relationships with women, whom he customarily regarded as an object or "piece of ass." Both Charles and Louis were presented with powerful evidence of the implications of their act—the effects on Valerie's marriage and the effects on their own group—and so came to appreciate their personal responsibility for their acts. Valerie, for the first time, realized the sadistic nature of her sexuality; not only did she employ sex as a weapon against the therapist but, as I have already described, as a means of depreciating and humiliating Charles and Louis.

If subgrouping cannot be forbidden, neither should it be encouraged. I have found it most helpful to make my position on this problem explicit to patients in the preparatory or initial sessions. I tell them that extragroup activity often impedes therapy, and clearly describe the complications caused by subgrouping. I underscore that if extragroup meetings occur, fortuitously or by design, then it is the subgroupers' responsibility to the other members and to the group to keep the others fully informed. The therapist must help the patients understand that the group therapy experience is a dress rehearsal for life; it will teach the skills necessary to establish durable relationships but will not provide the relationships. If patients do not transfer their learning, they derive their social gratification exclusively from the therapy group, and therapy becomes interminable.

It is my experience that it is unwise to include two members in an outpatient group who already have a long-term special relationship: husband and wife, roommates, business associates, and so on. It is perfectly possible to focus group therapy on the improvement of a long-term relationship, but that entails a different kind of therapy group (for example, a marital couples' group, conjoint family therapy, multiple family therapy) than that described in this book.

In inpatient psychotherapy groups, the problem is even more complex, since the group members spend their entire day in close association with one another.

• For example, in a group in a psychiatric hospital for criminal offenders, a subgrouping problem had created great divisiveness. Two members, who were by far the most intelligent, articulate, and educated of the group, had formed a close friendship and spent much of every day together. The group sessions were characterized by an inordinate amount of tension and hostile bickering, much of it directed at these two men, who by this time had lost their separate identities and were primarily regarded, and regarded themselves, as a dyad. Much of the attacking was off target, and the therapeutic work of the group had become overshadowed by the attempt to destroy the dyad. As the situation progressed, the therapist, with good effect, helped the group explore several themes. First, the group had to consider that the two members could scarcely be punished for their subgrouping since everyone had an equal opportunity to form such a relationship. The issue of envy was thus introduced, and gradually the members discussed their own longing and inability to establish a friendship. Furthermore, they discussed their feelings of intellectual inferiority to the dyad, as well as their sense of exclusion and rejection by them. The two members had, however, augmented these responses by their actions; both had, for years, maintained their self-esteem by demonstrating their intellectual superiority whenever possible. When addressing other members, they deliberately used polysyllabic words and maintained a conspiratorial attitude which accentuated the others' feelings of inferiority and rejection. Both members profited from the group's description of the subtle rebuffs and taunts they had meted out and came to realize that others had suffered painful effects from their behavior.

CLINICAL EXAMPLE

I shall end this section with a lengthy clinical illustration. It is the longest clinical tale told in the book, and I include it because it illustrates in depth not only many of the issues involved in subgrouping but also other aspects of group therapy discussed in other chapters, including the differentiation between primary task and secondary gratification and the issue of assumption of responsibility in therapy.

The group of outpatients, led by me, met twice weekly. The patients were young, ranging in age from twenty-five to thirty-five years. At the time we join the group, two women had recently graduated, leaving only four male patients (and, of course, myself). Bill, the male lead in the drama that unfolded, was a tall, handsome thirty-two-year-old divorced dentist and had been in the group for approximately eight months without significant progress. He originally sought therapy because of chronic anxiety and episodic depressions. He was socially self-conscious to the degree that simple acts—for example, saying good night at a party—caused him much torment. If he could have been granted one wish by some benevolent therapeutic muse, it would have been "to be cool." He was dissatisfied with work, he had no male friends and followed a Don Juan pattern of relating to females. Though he had been living with one woman for a few months, he felt neither love nor commitment to her.

The group, waiting for new members, met for several sessions with only four men and established a virile, Saturday night, male-bonded subculture. Issues that had rarely surfaced while women were in the group occupied much of the center stage: the men discussed masturbatory practices and fantasies, fighting, feelings of cowardice, concerns about physique, feelings about the large breasts of a former group member, and their fantasies of a group gang-bang with the bearer of those large breasts.

Two women were then introduced into the group, and never has a well-established culture disintegrated so quickly. The Saturday night camaraderie was swept away by a flood of male dominance behavior. Bill boldly, brazenly competed not for one but for both of the women. The other men in the group reacted to the first meeting with the two women members in accordance with their dynamic patterns. One, a twenty-five-year-old graduate student, arrived at the meeting in short pants (lederhosen), the only time in eighteen months of therapy he thus bedecked himself, and during the meeting was quick to discuss, in detail, his homosexual proclivities. Another member made an appeal to the maternal instincts of the new patients by presenting himself as a fledgling with a broken wing. The remaining member removed himself from the race by remarking, after the first forty minutes, that he wasn't going to join the others in the foolish game of competing for the women's favors; besides, he had been observing the new members and concluded that they had nothing of value to offer him.

One of the women was Jan, an attractive twenty-eight-year-old divorceé with two children. She was a language teacher who sought therapy

343

for many reasons: depression, promiscuity, infanticidal obsessions, lone-liness. She complained that she could not say no to an attractive man. Men used her sexually: they would make a sexual call at her home for an hour or two in the evening but would not be willing to be seen with her in the daylight. There was an active willful part of it, too, as she boasted of having had sexual relations with most of the heads of the departments at the college where she taught. Because of poor judg-ment she was in deep financial trouble. She had written several bad checks and was beginning to flirt with the idea of prostitution: if men were exploiting her sexually, then why not charge them for her favors?

In the pre-group screening interviews and preparatory sessions, I realized that her great promiscuity made her a likely candidate for self-destructive sexual acting out in the group. Therefore, I took much greater pains than usual to emphasize that outside social involvement with other group members would not be in her or the group's best interests.

After the entrance of the two women, Bill's group behavior altered radically: he disclosed himself less; he preened; he crowed; he played a charming, seductive role; he became far more deliberate and self-conscious in his actions. In short, in pursuit of secondary sexual gratifica-tion, he appeared to lose all sense of why he was in a therapy group. Rather than welcome my comments to him, he resented them: he felt they made him look bad in front of the women. He rapidly jettisoned his relationship to the men in the group and thenceforth related to them dishonestly. For example, in the first meeting, when one of the male members told the women he felt they had nothing of value to offer him, Bill rushed in to praise him for his honesty though Bill's primary feeling at that point was one of exhilaration that the other had folded his tent and left him in sole possession of the field of women. At this stage, Bill resisted any intervention. I tried many times during these weeks to illuminate his behavior for him, but it was like trying to strike a match in the midst of a monsoon.

After approximately three months Jan made an overt sexual proposi-tion to Bill which I learned of in a curious way. Bill and Jan chanced to arrive early in the group room; and in their conversation, Jan invited Bill to her apartment to view some pornographic movies she had re-cently obtained. Observers viewing the group through a one-way mir-ror had also arrived early, overheard the proposition, and related it to me after the meeting. I felt uneasy about "big brotherism" but brought up the incident in the next meeting, only to have Jan and Bill deny that a sexual invitation had been made. The discussion ended with Jan angrily stomping out midway through the meeting. In succeeding weeks, after each meeting she and Bill met in the parking lot for long talks and embraces. Jan brought these incidents back into the meeting but, in so doing, incurred Bill's anger at her for betraying him. Eventually Bill made an overt proposition to Jan, who, on the basis of much work done in the group, decided it would be against her best interests. For the first time, she said no to an attractive, interested, attentive man and received much group support for her stance.

(I am reminded of an episode Victor Frankl once told me of a patient who had consulted him on the eve of his marriage. He had had a sexual invitation from a strikingly beautiful woman, his fianceé's best friend, and felt he could not pass it up. When would such an opportunity come his way again? It was, he insisted, a unique, once-in-a-lifetime opportunity! Dr. Frankl—quite elegantly, I think—pointed out that he did indeed have a unique opportunity and, indeed, it was one that would never come again. It was the opportunity to say no in the service of his responsibility to himself and his chosen mate!)

Bill, meanwhile, was finding life in the group increasingly complex; not only was he pursuing Jan but also Gina, who had entered the group with Jan. At the end of each meeting Bill struggled with such conundrums as how to walk out of the group alone with each woman at the same time. Jan and Gina were, at first, very close, almost huddling together for comfort when entering an all-male group. It was to Bill's advantage to separate them; and in a number of ways, he contrived to do so. Not only did Bill have a "divide and seduce" strategy, but he also found something intrinsically pleasurable in the process of splitting. He had had a long history of splitting and seducing roommates and, before that, of investing energy in order to interpose himself between his mother and sister.

Gina had passed through, with the help of much prior therapy, a period of promiscuity similar to Jan's. She was more desperate for help, more committed to therapy than Jan, and very committed to a relationship with her boyfriend. Consequently, she was not eager to consummate a sexual relationship with Bill; but as the group progressed, she developed a strong attraction to him and an even stronger determination that, if she could not have him, neither should Jan. One day in the group, Gina unexpectedly announced that she was getting married in three weeks and invited the group to the wedding. She described her husband-to-be as a rather passive, clinging, ne'er-do-well; it was only many months later that the group learned he was a gifted mathematician who was considering faculty offers from several leading universities. Thus, Gina, too, often pursued secondary gratification rather than her primary task. In her efforts to keep Bill interested in her and to compete with Jan, she misrepresented her relationship with another man, underplaying the seriousness of her involvement until her marriage forced her hand. Even then, she presented her husband in a fraudulently unfavorable light so as to nourish Bill's hopes that he still had an opportunity for a liaison with her. In so doing, Gina sacrificed the opportunity to work on her relationship with her fiancé—one of the urgent tasks for which she had sought therapy!

After several months in the group, Jan and Bill decided upon a sexual relationship and announced to the group their planned assignation two weeks later. The group members reacted strongly. The two women (another had entered the group by this time) were angry. Gina felt secretly hurt at Bill's rejection of her; in the group she expressed much anger at their threatening the integrity of the group. The new patient, who had a relationship with a man similar to Bill, identified with Bill's girlfriend. Some of the men participated vicariously; they perceived Jan as a sexual object and rooted for Bill to score. Another said (and as time went by in the group, this sentiment was heard more often) that he wished Bill would hurry up and screw her so that they could talk about something else in the group. He was an anxious, timid man who had had no heterosexual experience whatsoever; the sexual goings-on in the group were, as he phrased it, so much out of his league that he could not participate in any way.

Rob, another man in the group, silently wished that the heterosexual preoccupation of the group were different. He had been having increasing concern about homosexual obsessions; yet he delayed discussing them in the group for many weeks because of his sense that the group would be unreceptive to his needs and that he would lose the respect of the members who placed such extraordinary value on heterosexual prowess. Eventually, however, he did discuss these issues with some relief. (It is of importance to note that Bill, aside from advice and solicitude, offered Rob very little. Some ten months later, after Rob left the group and after the Bill-Jan pairing had been worked through, Bill disclosed his own homosexual concerns and fantasies. Had Bill, whom Rob admired very much, shared these at the appropriate time, they would have offered Rob considerable help. Bill would not at that time, however, disclose anything that might encumber his campaign to seduce Jan—another instance of secondary gratification that rendered the group less effective.)

After their sexual liaison began, the Jan-Bill relationship became even more inaccessible for group scrutiny and for therapeutic work. They began speaking of themselves as "we" and resisted all exhortations of mine or of other members to learn about themselves by analyzing their behavior. At first it was difficult to know what was operating between the two aside from powerful lust. I knew that Jan's sense of personal worth was outwardly based. To keep others interested in her she needed, she felt, to give gifts—especially sexual ones. Furthermore, there was a vindictive aspect: she had triumphed over important men previously (department chairmen and several employers) by sexual seduction. It seemed likely that Jan felt powerless in her dealings with the therapists; her chief interpersonal coinage—sex—afforded her no significant influence over them, but it did permit an indirect victory through the medium of Bill. I learned much later how she and Bill would gleefully romp in bed, relishing the thought that they had put something over on the therapists. Bill not only recapitulated in the group his sexualization of relationships, his repetitive efforts to prove his potency by yet another seduction, but found particularly compelling the opportunity for oedipal mastery—the taking of women away from the leader.

Thus, Bill and Jan, in a rich behavioral tapestry, displayed their dynamics and re-created their social environment in the microcosm of the group. Bill's narcissism and inauthentic mode of relating to women was clearly portrayed. He often made innuendos to the effect that his relationship to the girl with whom he lived was deteriorating, thus planting a seed of marital hope in Jan's imagination. Bill's innuendos colluded with Jan's enormous capacity for self-deception: she alone of any of the group members considered marriage a serious possibility. When the other members tried to help her hear Bill's primary message—that she was not important to him, that she was a sexual object and merely another conquest—she reacted defensively and angrily.

Gradually, the dissonance between Bill's private statements and the group's interpretations of his intentions created so much discomfort that Jan considered leaving the group. I reminded her that this was precisely what I had warned her about before she entered the group; if she dropped out of therapy, all that had happened in the group would come to naught. She had had many brief and unrewarding relationships in the past; the group offered her a unique opportunity: that is, the opportunity to stay with a relationship and, for once, play the drama through to its end. Jan decided to stay, perhaps as much to prove me wrong as for any other self-serving reason.

Jan and Bill's relationship was exclusive: neither related in any significant way to anyone else in the group, except that Bill attempted to keep erotic channels open to Gina ("to keep his account open at the bank," as he put it). Gina and Jan persisted in a state of unrelenting enmity so extreme that they both had homicidal fantasies toward the other. (When Gina married, she invited to the wedding everyone in the group save Jan. Only when a boycott was threatened by the others was a frosty invitation proffered her.) Bill's relationship to me had been very important to him before Jan's entry; during the first months of his liaison with her, he seemed to forget my presence. Gradually, however, his concern about me returned. One day, for example, he brought in a dream in which I escort all the members, save him, into an advanced postgraduate group, he himself being demoted to a more elementary, retarded group.

Jan and Bill's relationship consumed enormous amounts of group energy and time. Relatively few unrelated themes were worked on in the group, but all of the members worked on personal issues relating to the pairing—for example, sex, jealousy, envy, fears of competition, concerns about physical attractiveness. There was a sustained high level of emotion in the group. Attendance was excellent: over a thirty-meeting stretch there was not a single absence!

Gradually their relationship began to sour. Jan had always maintained that all she wanted from Bill was his sheer physical presence—one night a month with him was what she required. Now she was forced to realize that she wanted much more. She felt pressured in life: she had lost her job and was beset by financial concerns; she had given up her promiscuity but felt sexual pressures and now began to say to herself, "Where is Bill when I really need him?" She grew depressed, but, rather than work on the depression in the group, she minimized it. Once again secondary considerations were given priority over primary, therapeutic ones, for she was reluctant to give Gina and the other members the satisfaction of seeing her depressed: they had warned her months ago that a relationship with Bill would ultimately be self-destructive.

And where, indeed, was Bill? That question plunged us into the core issue of Bill's therapy—responsibility. As Jan grew more deeply depressed (a depression punctuated by accident proneness, such as an automobile accident and a kitchen accident in which she burned herself), the group confronted Bill with an awesome question: Had he known in advance the outcome of the adventure, would he have done anything different? Bill said that he would not have. "If I do not look after my own pleasure, who will?" he rejoined. The other members of the group and now Jan, too, attacked him for his self-indulgence and his lack of responsibility for others. Bill pondered over this confrontation, only to advance a series of rationalizations at the subsequent meeting. He was not irresponsible; he was high-spirited, impish, a life-loving Peer Gynt. Life contains little enough pleasure; why was he not entitled to take what he could? He insisted that the group members and therapists, guilefully dressed in the robes of responsibility, were, in fact, trying to rob him of his life force and freedom.

For many sessions, the group plunged into the issues of love, freedom, and responsibility. Jan, with increasing directness, confronted Bill. She jolted him in the group by asking exactly how much he cared for her. He squirmed and alluded both to his love for her and to his unwillingness to establish an enduring relationship with any woman. In fact, he found himself turned off any woman who wanted a long-term relationship. I was reminded of a comparable attitude toward love in the novel *The Fall*, where Camus expresses Bill's paradox with shattering clarity:

It is not true, after all, that I never loved. I conceived at least one great love in my life, of which I was always the object . . . sensuality alone dominated my love life. . . . In any case, my sensuality (to limit myself to it) was so real that even for a ten-minute adventure I'd have disowned father and mother, even were I to regret it bitterly. Indeed—*especially* for a ten-minute adventure and even more so if I were sure it was to have no sequel.[7]

The group therapist, if he was to help Bill, had to make certain that there was to be a sequel.

Bill did not want to be burdened with Jan's depression. He had women in various cities around the country who loved him (and whose love made him feel alive); yet for him these women did not have an independent existence. He preferred to think that his women came to life only when he appeared to them. Once again, Camus said it for him:

I could live happily only on condition that all the individuals on earth, or the greatest possible number, were turned toward me, eternally in suspense, devoid of independent life and ready to answer my call at any moment, doomed in short to sterility until the day I should deign to favor them. In short, for me to live happily it was essential for the creatures I chose not to live at all. They must receive their life, sporadically, only at my bidding.[8]

Jan pressed Bill relentlessly. She told him that there was another man who was seriously interested in her, and she pleaded with Bill to level with her, to be honest about his feelings to her, to set her free. By now Bill was quite certain that he no longer desired Jan. (In fact, as we were to learn later, he had been gradually increasing his commitment to the girl with whom he lived.) Yet he could not allow the words to pass his lips. A strange type of freedom, then, as Bill himself gradually grew to understand: the freedom to take but not the freedom to relinquish. (Camus wrote, "Believe me, for certain men at least, not taking what one doesn't desire is the hardest thing in the world!")[9] He insisted he be granted the freedom to choose his pleasures; yet, as he came to see, he had not the freedom to choose for himself. His choice almost invariably resulted in his thinking less well of himself; and the greater his self-hatred, the more compulsive, the less free, was his mindless pursuit of sexual conquests that afforded him only an evanescent balm.

Jan's pathology was equally patent. She ceded her freedom to Bill (a logical paradox); only he had the power to set her free. I confronted her with her pervasive refusal to accept her freedom: Why could she not say "no" to a man? How could men use her sexually unless she chose that they use her? It was evident, too, that she punished Bill in an inefficient, self-destructive manner: she attempted to induce guilt through accidents, depression, and through her lamentations that she had trusted a man who had then betrayed her and that she would now be ruined for life.

Bill and Jan circled these issues for months. From time to time they would re-enter their old relationship but always with slightly more sobriety and slightly less self-deception. During a period of nonwork, I sensed that the timing was correct, and confronted them in a forcible manner. Jan arrived late at the meeting complaining about the disarray of her financial affairs. She and Bill giggled as he commented that her irresponsibility about money made her all the more adorable. I stunned the group by observing that Jan and Bill were doing so little therapeutic work that I wondered if it made sense for them to continue in the group. Jan and Bill accused me of hypermoralism. Jan said that for weeks she only came to the group to see Bill and to talk to him after the group; if he left, she did not think she would continue. I reminded her that the group was not a dating bureau: surely there were far more important tasks for her to pursue. Bill, I continued, would play no role in the long scheme of her life and would shortly fade from her memory. Bill had no commitment to her, and if he were at all honest he would tell her so. Jan rejoined that Bill was the only one in the group who truly cared for her. I disagreed and said that Bill's caring for her was clearly not in her best interests.

Bill left the meeting furious at me (especially at my comment that he would soon fade from Jan's mind). For a day he fantasized marrying her to prove me wrong, but returned to the group to plunge into serious work. As his honesty with himself deepened, as he faced a central feeling of emptiness which a woman's love had always temporarily filled, he entered and worked his way through a painful depression. Jan was deeply despondent for two days following the meeting and then made significant decisions for herself about work, money, men, and therapy.

The group then entered a phase of productive work, which was further deepened when I introduced a much older woman patient who brought with her many neglected themes in the group: parents, death, marriage, physical deterioration. Jan and Bill fell out of love; they began to examine their relationships to others in the group, including the therapists; Bill stopped lying; first to Jan, then to Gina, then to the other members, and, finally to himself. Jan continued in the group for six more months, and Bill for another year.

The outcome for both Jan and Bill was—judged by any outcome criteria—stunning. In interviews nine months after their termination, both showed impressive changes. Jan was no longer depressed, self-destructive, or promiscuous. She was involved in the most lengthy, stable, and satisfying relationship with a man she had ever had. The infanticidal obsessions had disappeared (with, incidentally, scarcely a mention of them during her entire course of therapy). She had gone into a different and, for her, more rewarding professional career. Bill, once he understood that he had made his relationship with his girl-friend tenuous to allow him to seek what he really didn't want, allowed himself to feel more deeply and married shortly before leaving the group. His anxious depressions, his tortured self-consciousness, his pervasive sense of emptiness had all been replaced by their respective, vital counterparts.

I am not able in these few pages to sum up all that was important in the therapy of Jan and Bill. There was much more to it, including many important interactions with other members and with the co-therapist and me. The development and working through of their extragroup relationship was, I believe, not a complication but an indispensable part of their therapy. It is unlikely that Jan would have had the motivation to remain in therapy had Bill not been present in the group. It is unlikely that, without Jan's presence, Bill's central problems would have surfaced clearly and become accessible for therapy. The price paid by the group, however, was enormous. Vast amounts of group time and energy were consumed by Jan and Bill. Other members were neglected; many important issues, untouched. It is most unlikely that a new group, or a group that met less frequently than twice a week, could have afforded the price. It is also unlikely that Jan and Bill would have been willing to persevere in their therapeutic work and to remain in the group had they not already been committed to the group before their love affair began.

Conflict in the Therapy Group*

Conflict cannot be eliminated from human groups, whether they are dyads, small groups, macrogroups, or such megagroups as nations and blocs of nations. If conflict is denied or suppressed, invariably it will manifest itself in oblique, corrosive, and often ugly ways. Although our immediate association with conflict is negative—destruction, bitterness, war, violence—a moment of reflection brings to mind positive associations: conflict brings drama, excitement, change, and development to human life and societies. Therapy groups are no exception. Conflict is inevitable in the course of a group's development; its absence, in fact, suggests some impairment of the developmental sequence. Furthermore, conflict can be harnessed in the service of the group; the group members can, in a variety of ways, profit from conflict, provided its intensity does not exceed their tolerance, and provided that proper group norms have been established. In this section, I will consider conflict in the therapy group—its sources, its meaning, and its value in therapy.

There are many sources of hostility in the therapy group. There are antagonisms based on mutual contempt, a contempt that arises from the patient's own self-contempt. Indeed, often months pass before some patients really begin to hear and respect the opinions of other members; they have so little self-regard that it is at first inconceivable that others, similar to themselves, have something valuable to offer.

Transference or parataxic distortions often generate hostility in the therapy group. One may respond to others not on the basis of reality but on the basis of an image of the other distorted by ones own past relationships and one's current interpersonal needs and fears. One may see in others aspects of significant individuals in one's own life. Should the distortion be negatively charged, then a mutual antagonism may be easily initiated.

Mirroring is a form of parataxic distortion and a particularly common source of hostility in the therapy group.[10] Individuals may have suppressed, for years or their entire lives, some traits or desires of which

*This discussion draws much from essays by Jerome Frank[11] and Carl Rogers.[12]

they are much ashamed; when they encounter another person who embodies these very traits, they generally shun, or experience a strong but inexplicable antagonism toward him or her. The process may be close to consciousness and recognized easily with guidance by others, or it may be deeply buried and understood only after many months of investigation.

• For example: One patient, Vincent, a second-generation Italian-American who had grown up in the Boston slums and obtained a good education with great difficulty, had long since dissociated himself from his roots. Having invested his intellect with considerable pride, he spoke with great care in order to avoid betraying any nuance of his background. In fact, he abhorred the thought of his lowly past and feared that he would be found out—that others would see through his front to his core, which he regarded as ugly, dirty, and repugnant. In the group, Vincent experienced extreme antagonism for another member, also of Italian descent, who had, in his values and in his facial and hand gestures, retained his identification with his ethnic group. It was through his investigation of his antagonism toward the other that Vincent arrived at many important insights about himself.

J. Frank described a double mirror reaction:

In one group a prolonged feud developed between two Jews, one of whom flaunted his Jewishness while the other tried to conceal it. Each finally realized that he was combatting in the other an attitude he repressed in himself. The militant Jew finally understood that he was disturbed by the many disadvantages of being Jewish, and the man who hid his background confessed that he secretly nurtured a certain pride in it.[13]

• In a group of psychiatric residents, one member, Pat, agonized over whether to transfer to another more academically oriented residency. The group, led by one particular member, Clem was singularly unsympathetic to Pat's plight. They resented his taking group time, they rebuked him for his weakness and indecisiveness, they insisted that he "crap or get off the pot." When the therapist guided the group members into an exploration of the sources of their anger toward Pat, many dynamics became evident (several of which I shall discuss in chapter 17). One of the strongest sources was uncovered by Clem, who discussed his own paralyzing indecisiveness. He had, a year previously, dealt with the same decision that Pat faced and, unable to make an active decision, had resolved the dilemma by passively deciding not to decide and by suppressing the entire problem. Pat's behavior reawakened the whole agonizing problem for Clem, who resented the other man not only for disturbing his uneasy slumber but also for struggling with the issue more honestly and more courageously than he had.

Projective identification, an unconscious process involved in mirroring, consists of projecting some of one's own (but disowned) attributes onto another, toward whom one subsequently feels an uncanny attraction—repulsion. A stark literary example of projective identification occurs in Dostoevsky's nightmarish tale *The Double,* in which the protagonist encounters a man who is his double physically and yet the personification of all the dimly perceived, hated aspects of himself.[14] The tale depicts with astonishing vividness the uncanny attraction and the horror and hatred that develop between the protagonist and his double.

L. Horwitz emphasizes both the intrapsychic and the interpersonal aspects of projective identification.[15] The contents of one's disowned self are not only put *onto* another, as in simple projection, but *into* another so that the behavior of the other actually changes. The projector relates to the recipient or the vessel on the basis of the disowned, projected characteristics—for example, with disgust, horror, or pity— and, in so doing, alters the other's behavior. Projective identification resembles "two distorting mirrors facing each other and producing increased distortions as the reflected images bounce back and forth."[16]

Rivalry may be yet another source of conflict. Patients may compete with one another in the group for the largest share of the therapist's attention or for some particular role: the most powerful, respected, sensitive, disturbed, or needy person in the group.

• In the fiftieth meeting of one group, a new member, Ginny, was added. In many aspects she was similar to Douglas, one of the original members: they were both artists, mystical in their approach to life, often steeped in fantasy, and both too familiar with their unconscious. It was not an affinity, however, but an antagonism that developed between the two. Ginny immediately established the role she invariably assumed with others: she behaved in a spiritlike, irrational, and disorganized fashion in the group. Douglas, who saw his role as the sickest and most disorganized member being usurped, reacted to her with less tolerance and understanding than to any of the "squarer" members of the group. Only after active interpretation of the role conflict and Douglas's assumption of a new role ("most improved member") was an entente between the two members achieved.

Occasionally, antagonisms may also develop on the basis of differences in outlook based on different life experiences. Members of different generations may dispute drugs, the work ethic, the sexual code, or

354

religious beliefs. Liberals and conservatives may develop considerable heat over political issues.

As the group progresses, the members may grow increasingly impatient and angry at patients who have not adopted the group's norms of behavior. If a woman, for example, continues to hide behind a facade, the group may coax her, attempt to persuade her, and finally angrily demand that she be honest with herself and the others in the group.

Certain patients, because of their character structure, will invariably be involved in conflict and will engender conflict in any group to which they belong. Consider a man with a paranoid personality disorder whose assumptive world is that there is danger in the environment. He is eternally suspicious and vigilant. He examines all experience with an extraordinary bias as he searches for clues and signs of danger. He is tight, ready for an emergency. He does not play or permit himself abandonment and looks suspiciously upon such behavior in others. Obviously, these traits will not endear the paranoid patient to the other group members: sooner or later, anger will erupt all around him; and the more severe and rigid the character structure, the more extreme will be the conflict.

In chapter 11, I discuss another source of hostility in the group: the growing disenchantment and disappointment with the therapist for frustrating patients' unrealistic expectations. If the group is unable to confront the therapist directly, it may create a scapegoat—a highly unsatisfactory solution for both victim and group. In fact, scapegoating is a method by which the group can discharge anger arising from any source and is a common phenomenon in any therapy group. The choice of a scapegoat is not, of course, arbitrary. Some people embrace a scapegoat role in a variety of social situations.[17]

Regardless of its source, the discord, once begun, follows a predictable sequence. The antagonists develop the belief that they are right and the others are wrong, that they are good and the others bad. Moreover, although it is not recognized at the time, these beliefs are characteristically held with equal conviction and certitude by each of the two opposing parties. Where such a situation of opposing beliefs exists, we have all the ingredients for a deep and continuing tension.

Generally a breakdown in communication ensues. The two parties cease to listen to each other with any understanding. Often, in a social situation, the two opponents completely rupture their relationship at this point, and the correction of misunderstandings is thus permanently prevented.

Not only do the opponents stop listening, but they also may unwittingly distort their perceptions of one another. Perceptions are filtered through a screen of stereotype. The opponent's words and behavior are shaped to fit a preconceived view. Contrary evidence is ignored or distorted; conciliatory gestures may be perceived as deceitful tricks. (The analogy to international relations is all too obvious.)

Distrust is the basis for this sequence: opponents view their own actions as honorable and reasonable and the behavior of others as scheming and evil. If this sequence, so common in human events, were permitted to unfold in therapy groups, the group members would have little opportunity for change or learning. A group climate and group norms that preclude such a sequence must be established early in the life of the group.

Cohesiveness is the prime prerequisite for the successful management of conflict. Members must develop a feeling of mutual trust and respect and must come to value the group as an important means of meeting their personal needs. The patients must understand that communication must be maintained if the group is to survive; all parties must continue to deal directly with one another, no matter how angry they become. Furthermore, everyone is to be taken seriously; when a group treats one patient as a mascot whose opinions and anger are lightly regarded, the hope of effective treatment for that patient has all but officially been abandoned. Moreover, group cohesiveness will have been seriously compromised, since the next most peripheral member will have reason to fear similar treatment. The cohesive group in which everyone is taken seriously soon elaborates norms that obligate members to go beyond name calling. Each member must pursue and explore derogatory labels; one must be willing to search more deeply within oneself to understand one's antagonism and to make explicit those aspects of others that anger one. Norms must be established that make it clear that group members are there to understand themselves, not to defeat or ridicule others.

A member who realizes that others accept and are trying to understand him or her finds it less necessary to hold rigidly to beliefs, and may be willing to explore previously denied aspects of self. Gradually one may develop motivational insight and recognize that not all of one's motives are as one has proclaimed, and that some of one's attitudes and behavior is not so fully justified as one has been maintaining to one's opponent and to the world. When this step has been achieved, a breakthrough may occur in which the individual's perception of the situation changes, and he or she realizes that the problem can be viewed in more than one way.

Empathy is an important element in conflict resolution and facilitates humanization of the struggle. Often understanding the past plays an important role in the development of empathy: once an individual appreciates the aspects of an opponent's earlier life that have resulted in the latter's current stance, the position of this other not only makes sense but may even appear right for him or her. *Tout comprendre, c'est tout pardonner.*

Conflict resolution is often impossible in the presence of off-target or oblique hostility.

• For example: In one group, a woman patient began a session by requesting and obtaining the therapist's permission to read a letter she was writing in conjunction with a court hearing on her impending divorce, which involved considerable property settlement and custodianship of children. The letter reading consumed considerable time and was eventually interrupted by the therapist and then the other members, who disputed the contents of the letter. The sniping by the group and defensive counterattacks by the protagonist continued until the group atmosphere was crackling with irritability. The group made no constructive headway until the therapist explored with the patients the process of the meeting. The therapist was annoyed with himself for having permitted the letter to be read and with the patient for having put him in that position. The group members were angry at the therapist for having given permission and at the patient both for consuming so much time and for relating to them in the frustrating impersonal manner of letter reading. Once the anger had been directed away from the oblique target of the letter's contents onto the appropriate targets of the therapist and the letter reader, steps toward conflict resolution could begin.

Permanent conflict abolition, let me note, is not the final goal of the therapy group; conflict will continually recur in the group despite successful resolution of past conflicts and despite the presence of considerable mutual respect and warmth. However, neither is unrestrained expression of rage a goal of the therapy group.

Although some relish conflict, the vast majority of patients (and therapists) are highly uncomfortable when expressing or receiving anger. The therapist's task is to harness conflict and use it in the service of growth. One important principle is to find the right level: too much or too little conflict is counterproductive. Thus, you need to titrate conflict carefully, especially on the upper end. It is unnecessary to evoke conflict deliberately: if the group members are interacting with one another openly and honestly, conflict will invariably emerge. But conflict easily gets out of hand, and the therapist must often intervene actively to keep it within constructive bounds.[18]

Keep in mind that the therapeutic use of conflict, like all other behavior in the here-and-now, is a two-step process: experience (affect expression) and the understanding of that experience. You may control conflict by switching the group from the first to the second stage. Often a simple direct appeal is effective: for example, "We've been expressing some heavy feelings here today as well as last week. To prevent us from overload, perhaps it might be valuable to stop what we're doing and try together to understand what's been happening and where all these powerful feelings come from."

Receiving negative feedback is painful and yet, if accurate and sensitively delivered, helpful. The therapist can make it more palatable by making the benefits of feedback clear to the recipient and enlisting that patient as an ally in the process. Often you can facilitate that sequence by obtaining verbal contracts from patients early in therapy and referring back to the contract when the patient obtains feedback. For example, if a woman patient comments that her fiancé (as well as other men in the past) has accused her of trying to tear him down, and that she wishes to work on that problem in the group, you may nail down a contract by a statement such as: "Carolyn, it sounds like it would be helpful to you if we could identify similar trends in your relationships to others in the group. How would you feel if, from now on, we point this out to you as soon as we see this happen?" Once this contract has been agreed upon, store it in your mind and, when the occasion arises (that is, the patient receives honest feedback), remind the patient that, despite the discomfort, the feedback is precisely the information that may be most useful in helping her relationship with her fiancé.

Almost invariably two group members who feel considerable mutual antagonism have the potential to be of great value to each other. Each obviously cares about how the other regards him or her. Generally there is much envy and much mutual projection and thus the opportunity to uncover hidden parts of oneself. In their anger each will tell the other important (though unpalatable) truths about that other. The self-esteem of the antagonists may be increased by the conflict; when people become angry at one another, this in itself may be taken as an indication that they are important to one another and take one another seriously. Synanon refers to an angry relationship as "hard love." Individuals who truly care nothing for one another ignore each other. At other times, patients learn that, although others may respond negatively to some trait, mannerism, or attitude, they themselves are valued.

For patients who have been unable to express anger, the group may serve as a testing ground for taking risks and learning that such behavior is neither dangerous nor necessarily destructive. In chapter 2, I described incidents cited by patients as turning points in their therapy; a majority of these critical incidents involved the expression, for the first time, of strong negative affect. It is also important for patients to learn that they can withstand attacks and pressure from others. Overly aggressive patients may learn some of the interpersonal consequences of blind self-assertion. Through feedback, they appreciate their impact on other individuals and gradually come to terms with the self-defeating pattern of their behavior. For many, angry confrontations may provide valuable learning opportunities, since therapy group members learn to remain in mutually useful contact despite their anger.

Patients may be helped to express anger more directly and more fairly. Even in all-out conflict, there are tacit rules of war which, if violated, make satisfactory resolution all but impossible. For example, in therapy groups combatants will occasionally take information disclosed by the other in a previous spirit of trust and use it later to scorn or humiliate the other. Or, they may refuse to examine the conflict because they claim to have so little regard for the other that they do not wish to waste any further time. These postures require vigorous intervention by the therapist. One of the most common indirect and self-defeating modes of fighting is the one used by Jan in the clinical illustration of subgrouping I described earlier in this chapter. This strategy calls for the patient, in one form or another, to injure himself or herself in the hope of inducing guilt in the other—the "see what you've done to me" strategy. Usually, much therapeutic work is required to change this pattern; it is generally deeply engrained, with roots stretching back to earliest childhood. (Remember the common childhood fantasy of one's imagined funeral and anguished parents and other tormentors beating their breasts in endless guilt.)

In the process of disagreeing, each patient may learn more about the reasons for his or her position and may, in fact, discover new and more valid reasons. One may also understand that, despite the source of one's anger, one expresses oneself in self-defeating, maladaptive ways. Some patients may learn from feedback that they habitually display scorn, irritation, or disapproval. Human sensitivity to facial gestures and nuances of expression far exceeds proprioceptive sensitivity[19]; only through feedback do we learn that we communicate something that is not intended or, for that matter, even consciously experienced.

Patients who do not experience anger are common and always challenging in therapy. They learn that others in their situation would feel angry; they learn to read their own body language ("My fists are clenched so I *must be* angry"); they learn to magnify rather than suppress the first flickerings of anger; they learn that it is safe, permissible, and in their best interests to feel and express anger.

Strong shared affect may enhance the importance of the relationship. In chapter 3, I described how group cohesiveness is increased when members of a group go through intense emotional experiences together, regardless of the nature of the emotion. "In this manner," as Frank says, "members of a successful therapy group are like members of a closely knit family who may battle each other, yet derive much support from their family allegiance."[20] A dyadic relationship, too, that has weathered much stress is likely to be especially rewarding. An experience in which two individuals in group therapy experience an intense mutual hatred and then, through some of the mechanisms I have described, resolve the hatred and arrive at mutual understanding and respect is always of great therapeutic value.

Self-Disclosure

Self-disclosure—both feared and valued by participants—plays an integral part in all group therapies. Without exception, group therapists believe that it is important for patients to reveal personal material in the group—material that they could not otherwise learn and that the individual patient would rarely disclose to others. The self-disclosure may involve past or current events in one's life, fantasy or dream material, hopes or aspirations for the future, and current feelings toward other individuals. In group therapy, the latter category (feelings toward other members) often assumes major importance.

RISK

Every self-disclosure involves some risk on the part of the discloser. The risk of disclosure depends, in part, upon the nature of what is disclosed. If one discloses material that has been previously undisclosed, highly personal, and emotionally charged, then obviously the risk is greater. There is always a particularly great risk with first-time disclosures: that is, the first time one has shared certain information with anyone else.

The risk also depends upon the individual(s) to whom one discloses. If one knows that the receiver shares similar concerns and is sensitive and will react as one intends, then the risk decreases. If the receiver is well known, a person with whom one has had frequent similar transactions, and is vulnerable through having previously disclosed personal information, then the risk becomes less.[21]

SEQUENCE OF SELF-DISCLOSURE

In conventional social relationships, in which one participant has an inclination for self-disclosure, a predictable sequence usually occurs. The discloser begins by making disclosures. The receiver who is involved in a lasting relationship with the discloser (and not merely a casual acquaintance at a cocktail party) is likely to feel charged with certain responsibilities or obligations to the discloser. This person generally responds to the disclosure by some appropriate comment, depending on the nature of the disclosure, and then reciprocates with some disclosure of his or her own. The receiver now, as well as the original discloser, is vulnerable, and the relationship usually deepens, with the participants continuing to make slightly more open and intimate disclosures in turn until some optimal level of their relationship is reached.

ADAPTIVE FUNCTIONS OF SELF-DISCLOSURE

Self-disclosure is a prerequisite for the formation of meaningful interpersonal relationships in a dyad or in a group. As disclosures proceed in group, the entire membership gradually increases its involvement, responsibility, and obligation to one another. If the timing is right, nothing will commit an individual to a group more than to receive or to reveal some intimate secret material. There is nothing more exhilarating than for a member to disclose for the first time material that has been burdensome for years and to be understood and fully accepted. Interpersonalists such as Sullivan and Rogers have maintained that self-acceptance must be preceded by acceptance by others; it follows, then, that to accept oneself, one must gradually permit others to know one as one really is.

Research evidence validates the importance of self-disclosure in group therapy. In chapter 3, I described the relationship between self-disclosure and popularity in the group. Popularity (determined from sociometrics) correlates positively with therapy outcome;[22] patients who disclose extensively in the early meetings often are very popular in their groups.[23] People reveal more to individuals they like; and, conversely, those who reveal themselves are more likely to be liked by others.[24] But the relationship between liking and self-disclosure is not linear. One who discloses too profusely arouses anxiety in others rather than affection.[25]

Several research inquiries have demonstrated that high disclosure (either naturally occurring or experimentally induced) increases group cohesiveness.[26]

Peres demonstrated that successfully treated patients in group therapy made almost twice as many self-disclosing personal statements during the course of therapy as did unsuccessfully treated patients.[27] C. Truax and R. Carkhuff also found that patients' success in group therapy correlated with their transparency during the course of the group.[28] Lieberman, Yalom, and Miles found that, in encounter groups, individuals who had negative outcomes revealed less of themselves than did the other participants.[29]

The concept of carryover is vital here: not only are patients rewarded by the other group members for self-disclosure; but the behavior, thus reinforced, is integrated into an individual's relationships outside the group, where it is similarly rewarded. Often the first step in revealing to a spouse or a potential close friend is the "first time" disclosure in the therapy group.

S. Bloch considers self-disclosure so central to the therapeutic process that he lists it as one of the therapeutic factors.[30] He studied thirty-three outpatient group members who were asked to describe the most important event for them in a group. The events were then coded by trained raters into therapeutic factors. "Self-disclosure" was the second most common (after "self-understanding") "important event." I, too, highly value self-disclosure but have chosen not to consider it one of the primary therapeutic factors because I believe it is a part process which is valued by patients because of its role in catharsis and its position in the matrix of interpersonal learning. Patients consider an act of self-disclosure as important not only, or not primarily, because of the sheer act of disclosing but because of the simultaneous expression of emotion and because of the interpersonal response to their disclosure. To reveal oneself *and then* to be accepted and supported is deeply confirming. Patients often entertain some calamitous fantasy about self-disclosure: to disclose and to have that fantasy disconfirmed is highly therapeutic.

MALADAPTIVE SELF-DISCLOSURE

Self-disclosure is related to optimal psychological and social adjustment in a curvilinear fashion: too much or too little self-disclosure signifies maladaptive interpersonal behavior.

Too little self-disclosure usually results in severely limited opportunity for reality testing. Those who fail to disclose themselves in a relationship generally forfeit the opportunity to obtain valid feedback. Furthermore, they prevent the relationship from developing further; without reciprocation, the other party will either desist from further self-disclosure or else rupture the relationship entirely.

Those who do not disclose themselves in the group have little chance of genuine acceptance by the other members and therefore little chance of experiencing a rise in self-esteem. L. Vosen has demonstrated this very point experimentally. In his study, "a self-perceived lack of self-disclosure resulted in reduced self-esteem."[31] Should it occur that one is accepted on the basis of a (false) image one projects, no enduring boost in self-esteem occurs; moreover, one is even less likely at this point to engage in valid self-disclosure because of the added risk of losing the acceptance gained through one's false presentation of self.[32]

Some individuals dread self-disclosure, not primarily because of shame or fear of nonacceptance but because they are heavily conflicted in the area of control: to them self-disclosure is dangerous because it makes them vulnerable to the control of others. When others in the group have made themselves exceedingly vulnerable through self-disclosure, then and only then is such a person willing to reciprocate.

Self-disclosure blockages will impede individual members as well as entire groups. One who has an important secret that one dares not reveal to the group may find participation on any but a superficial level very difficult because one must conceal not only the secret but all possible avenues to it. In chapter 5, I discussed in detail how, in the early stages of therapy, the therapist might best approach the patient with a top secret. To summarize, it is advisable for the therapist to counsel the patient that the latter must, in order to benefit from therapy, share the secret with the group. The pace and timing are up to the patient, but the therapist may offer to make the act easier in any way the patient wishes.

These are times when the therapist, unwittingly, discourages self-disclosure. The most terrifying secret I have known a patient to possess occurred in a newly formed group led by a neophyte therapist. The patient had, one year previously, murdered her two-year-old child and then failed in a suicide attempt. (The court ruled her insane and released her on the provision that she be in therapy.) After fourteen weeks of therapy, not only had the patient told nothing of herself but by her militant promulgation of denial and suppressive strategies (such as astrological tables and ancient mystical sects) had impeded the entire group. Despite his supervisor's counsel, the group therapist could find no method to help the patient (or the group) move into therapy. The supervisor then observed some group sessions and noted that the patient provided the therapist with many opportunities to help her discuss the secret. A productive supervisory session was devoted to the therapist's countertransference. His feelings about his own two-year-old child, his horror (despite himself) at the patient's act, colluded with her guilt to silence her in the group. In the following meeting, the gentlest question by the therapist was sufficient to free the patient's tongue and to change the entire character of the group.

In some groups, self-disclosure is discouraged by a general climate of judgmentalism. Members are reluctant to disclose "shameful" aspects of themselves lest others lose respect for them. In groups of mental health professionals, this issue is even more pressing. Since our chief professional instrument is our own person, at risk is professional as well as personal loss of respect.

• In one group, for example, a psychiatric resident discussed her homosexuality, while another discussed his lack of confidence as a physician and his panic whenever he was placed in a life or death situation. Bob, another member, reported that their fears of revealing this material were well founded since he did lose respect for them and doubted whether he would, in the future, refer patients to them. The group continued, with the other members condemning Bob for his judgmentalism and suggesting that they would be reluctant to refer patients to him. An infinite regress of judgmentalism can easily ensue, and it is incumbent on the therapist at these times, to make a vigorous process intervention.

You must differentiate, too, between a healthy need for privacy and neurotic compulsive secrecy. Some people, who seldom find their way into groups, are private in an adaptive way: they share intimacies with only a few intimate friends and shudder at the thought of self-disclosure in a group. Moreover, they enjoy private self-contemplative activities. This is a far different thing from privacy based on fear, shame, or crippling social inhibitions. In fact, as Abraham Maslow suggests, the resolution of neurotic privacy may be an essential first step toward the establishment of a healthy desire for privacy.[33] Many patients who are nondisclosers have, at the same time, a fear of being alone and involve themselves in many unrewarding dependent relationships; they so fear loneliness that they can no longer experience the pleasures of privacy. Their sense of self is so stunted that the world takes on a reality only as it is perceived through the experience of another. Thus, they cannot enjoy a movie alone or a play or a sporting event: they await the newspaper review or the reactions of others to experience the realness of an event. They may be so sensitized to rejection or abandonment that the experience of being alone fills them with dread. Others are so painfully self-conscious that they torture themselves while alone by dwelling on how they appear to others: Do others think them friendless, lonely, pitiable, and so on?

Too much self-disclosure can be as maladaptive as too little. Indiscriminate self-disclosure is not a goal of mental health nor a pathway to it. Some patients make the grievous error of reasoning that if self-disclosure is desirable, then total and continuous self-disclosure must be a very good thing indeed. But, as Erving Goffman noted, urban life would become unbearably sticky if every contact between two people entailed sharing personal concerns and secrets.[34] Obviously, the relationship that exists between discloser and receiver should be the major factor in determining the pattern of self-disclosure. Several research investigations have demonstrated this truth experimentally: individuals disclose different types and amounts of material, depending on whether the receiver is a mother, father, best male friend, female friend, work associate, or spouse.[35]

However, some maladaptive disclosers disregard and thus jeopardize their relationship to the receiver. The individual who in self-disclosure fails to discriminate between intimate friends and distant acquaintances perplexes associates. We have all, I am certain, experienced confusion or betrayal upon learning that supposedly intimate material confided to us has been shared with many others. Furthermore, a great deal of self-disclosure may frighten off an unprepared recipient. In a rhythmic, flowing relationship, one party leads the other in self-disclosures, but never by too great a gap.

In group therapy, members who reveal early and promiscuously will often drop out early in the course of therapy. Patients should be encouraged to take risks in the group; such behavior change results in positive feedback and reinforcement and encourages further risk taking. But if they reveal too much too early, they may exceed their tolerance: they feel so much shame that any interpersonal rewards are offset; furthermore, they may threaten others willing to support them but not yet prepared to reciprocate.[36] The high discloser is then placed in a position of such great vulnerability in the group that he or she often chooses to flee.

All of these observations suggest that self-disclosure is a complex, social act which is situation- and role-bound. One does not self-disclose in solitude: time, place, and person must always be considered. Appropriate self-disclosure in a therapy group, for example, may be disastrously inappropriate in other situations. (This failure to demarcate boundaries—and the ensuing grief therefrom—happens to many individuals who have an exhilarating short-term experience in an encounter group [see chapter 16]).

Appropriate self-disclosure for one stage of a therapy group may be inappropriate for another stage. These points are particularly evident in the case of self-disclosure of one's feelings toward other members ("feedback"). It is my belief that the therapist should help the members be guided as much by responsibility to others as by freedom of expression. I have seen vicious, destructive events occur in groups under the aegis of honesty and self-revelation: "You told us that we should be honest about expressing our feelings, didn't you?" But, in fact, we always selectively reveal our feelings. There are always layers of reactions that we rarely share—feelings about unchangeable attributes, physical characteristics, deformity, professional or intellectual mediocrity, social class, lack of charm, and so on. For some individuals, disclosure of overt hostile feelings is "easy—honest." What about the underlying meta-hostile feelings—feelings of fear, envy, guilt, sadistic pleasure in vindictive triumph? For many individuals, high-risk disclosure consists not of negative but of positive feelings—feelings of admiration, concern, empathy, physical attraction, love.

The patient who has just disclosed a great deal faces a moment of vulnerability and requires support from the members and/or the therapist. Regardless of the circumstances, no patient should be attacked for important self-disclosure.

• A clinical vignette is illustrative. Five members were present at a meeting of a year-old group. (Two members were out of town, and one was ill.) Joe, the protagonist of this episode, began the meeting with a long rambling statement about feeling uncomfortable in a smaller group. He had a style of talking difficult to characterize except to say that, when he talked, people didn't want to listen and longed for him to stop. No one had really dealt honestly with these vague, unpleasant feelings about Joe until this meeting when Betsy interrupted him and stated, "Joe, I wish you'd stop talking. I can't bear to listen to you. I don't know who you're talking to—perhaps to the ceiling, perhaps to the floor, but I know that you're not talking to me. I care about everyone else in this group. I think about them. They mean a lot to me. I hate to say this to you but, for some reason, Joe, you don't matter to me."

Joe was stunned by this and attempted to get some information about the reason behind Betsy's feelings and was given some feedback about his failure to reveal himself and to relate personally to any of the members of the group. Joe then took it upon himself to go around the group and describe his personal feelings toward each of the members of the group.

I thought that Joe revealed more than he had previously but still remained in fairly safe territory. I asked, "Joe, if you were to think about revealing yourself on a ten-point scale with "one" representing cocktail party stuff and "ten" representing the most you could ever imagine revealing about yourself to another person, how would you rank what you did in the group over the last ten minutes?" Joe thought about it for a moment and said he guessed he would give himself "three" or "four." I asked, "Joe, what would happen if you were to move it up a rung or two?"

Joe deliberated for a moment and then said, "If I were to move it up a couple of rungs, I would tell the group that I was an alcoholic."

This was a staggering bit of self-disclosure. Joe had been in the group for a year, and neither I, my co-therapist, nor the group members had known of this. Furthermore, it was vital information. For weeks, for example, Joe had bemoaned the fact that his wife was pregnant and had decided to have an abortion rather than to bear his child. The group was baffled and ultimately highly critical of his wife for such behavior. The fact that Joe was an alcoholic was a crucial missing link and cast the marital relationship in a new light.

My initial response was one of anger. I recalled all those futile hours Joe had led the group on a wild-goose chase. I was tempted to exclaim, "Damn it, why haven't you told us that before?" But that is just the time to bite your tongue. The important thing is not that Joe did not give us this information earlier but that he *did* tell us today; and, rather than being punished for his previous concealment, he should be reinforced for having made a breakthrough and been willing to take an enormous risk in the group. The proper technique consisted of supporting Joe and facilitating further "horizontal" disclosure (see pages 128–30).

In chapter 7, I discussed some of the role-bound properties of group leader self-disclosure. One important function of leader self-disclosure is to encourage member self-disclosure. But leader transparency must always be placed in the context of what is useful to the functioning of a particular group at a particular time. The general who, after having made an important tactical decision, goes around wringing his hands and verbally expressing his uncertainty is certain to undercut the morale of his entire command.[37] Similarly, the therapy group leader should not disclose feelings that would undermine the effectiveness of the group, such as impatience with the group, a desire to get home to dinner, a preoccupation with a patient or a group seen earlier in the day, his or her list of favorites in the group, or a host of other deeply personal concerns.

Termination

TERMINATION OF THE PATIENT

Termination is more than the end of therapy; it is an integral part of the process of therapy and, if properly understood and managed, may be an important force in the instigation of change. Throughout, I have emphasized that group therapy is a highly individual process. Each patient will enter, participate in, use, and experience the group in a uniquely personal manner. The end of therapy is no less individual. Only general assumptions about the length and overall goals of therapy may be made. Most patients require approximately twelve to twenty-four months to undergo substantial and durable change, although it is possible to resolve crises and achieve symptomatic relief in far briefer periods. The goals of therapy have never been stated more succinctly than in Freud's "to be able to love and to work." Some people would add a third, "to play"; and others would hope, too, that one would be able to love oneself, to allow others to love one, to be more flexible, and to search for and trust one's own values. Some patients may achieve a great deal in a few months, whereas others require years of group therapy. Some patients have far more ambitious goals than others do; it would not be an exaggeration to state that some patients, satisfied with their therapy, terminate in approximately the same state in which others may begin therapy. Some patients may have highly specific goals in therapy and, because much of their psychopathology is ego-syntonic, choose to limit the amount of change they are willing to undertake. Others may be hampered by important external circumstances in their lives. All therapists have had the experience of helping a patient improve to a point at which further change would make him or her worse.

For example, a patient might, with further change, outgrow, as it were, his or her spouse; continued therapy would result in the rupture of an irreplaceable relationship unless concomitant changes occur in that spouse. If that contingency is not available, the therapist may be well advised to settle for the positive changes that have occurred, even though the personal potential for greater growth is clear.

Termination of professional treatment is but a stage in the individual's career of growth. Patients continue to change, and one important effect of successful therapy is to enable patients to use constructively the resources in their personal environment. I have seen many successful patients in long-term follow-up interviews who have not only continued to change after termination but who, after they have left the group, recall an observation or interpretation made by another member or the therapist that only then, months later, became meaningful to them. Not only growth but setbacks occur following termination: many successfully treated patients will, from time to time, encounter severe stress and need temporary help. In addition, all patients experience anxiety and depression following departure from a group; a period of mourning is an inevitable part of the termination process.

The timing of termination is as inexact and as individual as the criteria for termination. Some therapists find that termination from group therapy is less problematic than termination from long-term individual therapy, in which patients often become so dependent on the therapeutic situation that they are loath to part with it. Group therapy patients are usually more aware that therapy is not a way of life but a process with beginning, middle, and end. In the therapy group, there are many living reminders of the therapeutic sequence. Patients see new members enter therapy and improved members terminate; they observe the therapist beginning the process over and over again to help the beginners over difficult phases of therapy. Thus, they realize the bittersweet fact that though the therapist is a person with whom they have had a real and meaningful relationship, he or she is also a professional whose attention must shift to others and who will not remain as a permanent and bottomless source of gratification for them.

Not infrequently a group places subtle pressure on a member not to terminate; not only will the remaining members miss that member but they will miss his or her contributions. There is no doubt that patients who have worked in a therapy group for many months or years acquire interpersonal and group skills that make them particularly valuable to the other members. (I think that this may be one important *qualitative* difference between group therapy and individual therapy outcome: group therapy members often become expert process diagnosti-cians and facilitators. Perhaps this proposition could be demonstrated by testing patients with videotaped group segments and obtaining their observations about the underlying process.)

• For example, one graduating patient pointed out in his final meet-ing that, in four of the last five sessions, it was Albert who started the meeting but that rapidly the group switched over to Dave, who was more entertaining and engaging. Following that, he noted that Albert, aside from occasional sniping, slumped into silence for the rest of the meeting. He also remarked that two other members never com-municated directly to each other; instead, they always used a third-party mediator. Another patient in her last meeting remarked that she had noted the first signs of the breakdown of a long-term collusion between two patients in which they had, in effect, agreed never to say anything challenging or unpleasant to the other. In the same meeting, she chided the members of the group who were asking for clarification about the group ground rules about subgrouping: "Answer it for your-selves. It's your therapy. You know what you want to get out of the group. What would it mean to you? Will it get in your way or not?" All of these comments are highly sophisticated—worthy of any ex-perienced group therapist.

Therapists may so highly value these members' contributions as to share at times in the latter's reluctance to allow a patient to terminate; there is, of course, no justification for such a posture and therapists should explore this openly as soon as they become aware of it. I have, incidentally, noted that a sort of 'role suction' operates at such times: once the senior member leaves, another moves into a position where he or she is able similarly to exercise skills acquired in the group.

Some socially isolated patients may postpone termination because they use the therapy group as a social group rather than as a means for developing the skills to create a social life for themselves in their home environment. The therapist must in this instance focus on transfer of learning and encourage risk taking outside the group. Others may pro-long unduly their stay in the group by hoping for some guarantee that they are indeed safe from future difficulties; they may suggest that they remain in the group for a few more months until they start a new job, or get married, or graduate from college. If the improvement base seems secure, however, these delays are generally unnecessary: one can never be certain, one is always at risk.

Not infrequently patients experience a brief recrudescence of their original symptomatology shortly before termination. Rather than pro-long their stay in the group, the therapist should help the patients understand this event for what it is—protest against termination.

• One patient, three meetings before termination, re-experienced much of the depression and meaninglessness that had brought him into therapy. The symptoms rapidly disappeared with the therapist's interpretation that he was searching for reasons not to leave the group. That evening the patient had a dream which he brought into the next meeting: "You [the therapist] offered me a place in another group in which I would receive training as a therapist. I felt that I had duped you into thinking I was better." The dream represents an ingenious strategem to defeat termination and offers two alternatives: the first is that the patient goes into another of the therapist's groups in which he receives training as a therapist; the second is that he has duped the therapist and has not really improved (and thus should continue in the group). Either way the dream is taken, the patient does not have to terminate.

Some patients improve gradually and consistently during their stay in the group. Others go about things arrhythmically and improve in bursts. I have known many patients who, though committed to the group and hard-working, make no apparent progress whatsoever for six, twelve, even eighteen months and then suddenly, in a short period of time, seem to transform themselves. (What do we tell our students? That change is often slow, that they should not look for immediate gratification from their patients. Instead, if they build solid, deep therapeutic foundations, change is sure to follow. So often we think of this as a sop—a platitude designed to bolster neophyte therapists' morale— that we forget it is true.)

The same staccato pattern of improvement is often true for the group as a whole. Sometimes groups struggle and labor for months on end with no visible change in any member and then suddenly enter a phase in which everyone seems to get well together. S. Rutan uses the apt metaphor of building a bridge during a battle.[38] The group labors mightily to construct the bridge and may suffer losses; but once the bridge is in place, it escorts many individuals to a better place.

There are certain patients for whom even a consideration of termination is problematic. These patients are particularly sensitized to abandonment: their self-regard is so low that they consider their illness to be their only currency in their traffic with the therapist and the group. If they were to improve, the therapist would leave them; therefore, they must minimize or conceal progress. Of course, it is not until much later that they discover the key to the absurd paradox: once they truly improve, they will no longer need the therapist!

One useful sign suggesting readiness for termination is that the group becomes less important to the patient. One terminating member commented that Mondays and Thursdays (the days of the group meetings) were now like any other day of the week. When she began in the group, she lived for Mondays and Thursdays, with the rest of the days inconsequential wadding between meetings.

I have made a practice of recording the first individual interview with a patient. Not infrequently these tapes are useful in arriving at the termination decision. By listening, many months later, to their initial session, patients can obtain a clearer perspective of what they have accomplished and what remains to be done.

Therapists who use alternate sessions (see chapter 14) report that when a patient's behavior in the leaderless meeting is identical to that patient's behavior in the presence of a therapist, the optimal time for termination may be at hand.

The group members are an invaluable resource in helping one another decide about termination, and a unilateral decision made by a patient without consulting the other members is often premature. Generally a well-timed termination decision will be discussed for a few weeks in the group, during which time the patient works through any feelings about leaving the group. Not infrequently patients make an abrupt decision to terminate membership in the group immediately. I have often found that such patients find it difficult to express gratitude and positive feeling; hence they attempt to abbreviate the separation process as much as possible. These patients must be helped to understand and correct their jarring, unsatisfying method of ending relationships. To ignore this phase is to neglect an important area of human relations. Termination is, after all, a part of almost every relationship, and throughout one's life one must, on many occasions, say goodbye to important people.

Many terminating patients attempt to lessen the shock of departure by creating bridges to the group which they can use in the future. They seek assurances that they may return, collect telephone numbers of the other members, or arrange social meetings so as to keep themselves informed of important events of the group. These efforts are only to be expected, and yet the therapist must not collude in such a way as to deny termination. On the contrary, you must help the members to explore it to its fullest extent. The patient is truly leaving; he or she cannot really return; the group will be irreversibly altered; replacements will enter the group; the present cannot be frozen; time flows on cruelly and inexorably. These facts are evident to the remaining members as well—there is no better stimulus than a departing member to encourage the group to deal with issues about the rush of time, loss, separation, death, aging, and the contingencies of existence. Termination is thus more than an extraneous event in the group; it is the microcosmic representation of some of life's most crucial and painful issues.

The group may need some sessions to work on their loss and to deal with many of these termination issues. After a member leaves the group, it is generally wise not to introduce new patients into the group without a hiatus of one or more meetings. A member's departure is often an appropriate time for others to take inventory of their own progress in therapy. Members who entered the group together with the terminating patient may feel some pressure to move more quickly. Other reactions are a function of conflict areas. Some members may misperceive the member's leaving as a forced departure and may feel a need to reaffirm a secure place in the group—by regressive means if necessary. Other more competitive members may rush toward termination prematurely.

We therapists must also look to our own feelings during the termination process because occasionally we unaccountably and unnecessarily delay a patient's termination. Some perfectionist therapists may unrealistically expect too much change in their patients and refuse to accept anything less than total recovery; moreover, they lack faith in a patient's ability to continue growth following the termination of formal therapy. Other patients bring out Pygmalion pride in us: we find it difficult to part with someone who is, in part, our own creation; saying goodbye to some patients is saying goodbye to a part of ourselves. Furthermore, it is a permanent goodbye; if we have done our job properly, the patient no longer needs us and breaks all contact. Nor, of course, are we exempt from feelings of loss and bereavement. There are many members to whom we have grown close. We will miss them as they miss us. To us as well as to the patient, termination is a jolting reminder of the built-in cruelty of the psychotherapeutic process.

TERMINATION OF THE GROUP

Groups terminate for various reasons. Some therapists set a time limit at the beginning of a group. Often external circumstances dictate the end of a group: for example, groups in a university mental health clinic usually run for eight to nine months and disband at the beginning of the summer vacation. Other groups end when the therapist leaves the area, although this is not inevitable since the co-therapist, if present, may continue the group, or the group may be transferred to another therapist (who may, incidentally, aid in the transition by attending the original therapist's last few meetings). Occasionally a therapist may decide to end a group because the great majority of patients all are ready to terminate at approximately the same time.

Often a group avoids the difficult and unpleasant work of termination by ignoring or denying the members' concerns, and it is the therapist who must keep the task in focus for them. The end of a group is a real loss: patients gradually come to realize that it can never be reconvened, that even if they continue a relationship with one member or a fragment of the group, nevertheless the entire group will be gone forever.

The therapist must often repeatedly call the members' attention to the impending termination. If avoidance is extreme—manifested, for example, by increased absence—the therapist must confront the group with this behavior. Usually, with a mature group, the best approach is direct: the members can be reminded that it is their group, and they must decide how they want to end it. Irregularly attending members must be helped to understand their behavior. Do they feel their absence makes no difference to the others, or do they so dread expressing positive feelings toward the group, or perhaps negative feelings to the therapist for ending it, that they avoid confrontation? Pain over the loss of the group is, in part, dealt with by a sharing of past experiences: exciting and meaningful past group events are remembered; patients remind one another of "the way you were then"; personal testimonials are invariably heard in the final meetings. It is important that the therapist not bury the group too early; otherwise it is in for several ineffective "lame duck" sessions. You must find a way to hold the issue of termination before the group and yet help it keep working until the very last minute.

Throughout, we facilitate the group work by disclosing our own feelings about separation. Therapists, as well as patients, will miss the group. For us, too, it has been a place of anguish, conflict, fear, and also of great beauty: some of life's truest and most poignant moments occur in the small and yet limitless microcosm of the therapy group.

13

PROBLEM PATIENTS

I have yet to encounter the unproblematic patient, the patient whose course of therapy resembles a newly christened ship gliding smoothly down the slip into the water. Each patient *must* be a problem: the success of therapy depends on each individual's encountering and mastering basic life problems in the here-and-now of the group. Each problem is complex and unique: the intent of this book is not to provide a compendium of problems but to describe the strategy and set of techniques that will enable a therapist to adapt to any problem arising in the group. Some common recurring behavioral constellations, however, prove taxing to the therapist and merit particular attention. I shall discuss, in this chapter, nine such problems: the monopolist, the schizoid patient, the silent patient, the boring patient, the help-rejecting complainer, the self-righteous moralist, the psychotic patient, the narcissistic patient, and the borderline patient.

The Monopolist

The *bête noire* of many group therapists is the habitual monopolist, a person who seems compelled to chatter on incessantly. These patients are anxious if they are silent; if others get the floor, the monopolists reinsert themselves with a variety of techniques: by rushing in indecently to fill the briefest silence, by responding to every statement in the group, by continually noting similarities between the problems of the speaker and the monopolist's own, with the recurring refrain, "I'm like that, too." The monopolist may persist in describing, in endless detail, conversations with others (often taking several parts in the conversation) or in presenting accounts of newspaper or magazine stories that may be only slightly relevant to the group issue. Some monopolists hold the floor by assuming the role of interrogator, and still others capture the members' attention by enticing them with bizarre or sexually piquant material. I have known some patients who monopolized by puzzling the others: they described rare, "out of the blue" *déjà vu* or depersonalization episodes, often omitting to mention important clarifying details, such as severe precipitating stress. Grand hysterics may monopolize the group by means of the crisis method: they regularly present the group with major life upheavals, which always seem to demand urgent and lengthy attention. Other members are cowed into silence, their problems seeming trivial in comparison. ("It's not easy to interrupt *Gone With the Wind*," as one of my patients put it.)

EFFECTS ON GROUPS

Although a group may in the initial meeting welcome and perhaps encourage the monopolist, the mood soon turns to one of frustration and anger. Other group members are often disinclined to silence a member for fear that they will thus incur an obligation to fill the silence. They anticipate the obvious rejoinder of, "All right, I'll be quiet. *You* talk." And, of course, it is not possible to talk easily in a tense, guarded climate. Members who are not particularly assertive may not deal directly with the monopolist for some time; instead, they may smolder quietly or make indirect hostile forays. Generally, oblique attacks on the monopolist will only aggravate the problem and fuel a vicious circle. The monopolist's compulsive speech is an attempt to deal with anxiety; as the patient senses the growing group tension and resentment, her* anxiety rises, and the tendency to speak compulsively correspondingly increases. Some monopolists are consciously aware, at these times, of assembling a smokescreen of words in order to divert the group from making a direct attack.

Eventually this source of unresolved tension will have a detrimental effect on cohesiveness—an effect manifested by such signs of group disruption as indirect, off-target fighting, absenteeism, dropouts, and subgrouping. When the group does confront the monopolist, it is often in an explosive, brutal style; the spokesman for the group usually receives unanimous support—even, in my experience, a round of ap-

---

*Although I have so far in this book avoided the generic masculine pronoun, the stylistic nature of this chapter requires a specific pronoun for each type of patient. Hence, I have used masculine and feminine pronouns according to the predominance, in my experience, of a particular disorder among one or the other sex. In each category, of course, are found patients of both sexes.

plause. The monopolist may then sulk, be completely silent for a meeting or two ("See what they do without me"), or leave the group. In any event, little that is therapeutic has been accomplished.

THERAPEUTIC CONSIDERATIONS

The overall task of the therapist is to interrupt the behavioral pattern of the monopolist in a therapeutically effective fashion. Despite the strongest provocation and temptation to shout the patient down or to silence her by edict, such an assault has little value except as a temporary catharsis for the therapist. The patient is not helped: no learning has accrued; the anxiety underlying the monopolist's compulsive speech persists and will erupt again in further monopolistic volleys or, if no outlet is available, will force the patient to drop out of the group. Neither is the group helped; regardless of the circumstances, the others are threatened by the therapist's silencing, in a heavy-handed manner, one of the members. Therapy is perceived as potentially dangerous, and a crystal of caution and fear is implanted in the mind of each member lest a similar fate befall her.

Nevertheless, the monopolistic behavior must be checked, and generally it is the therapist's task to do so. While often, with good reason, the therapist does well to wait for the group to handle a group problem, the monopolistic patient is one problem that the group, and especially a young group, often cannot handle. The monopolistic patient seems to pose a threat to the procedural underpinnings of a group: group patients are encouraged to speak in a group, yet this patient who speaks a great deal must be silenced. The therapist must address this issue, prevent the elaboration of therapy-obstructing norms, and, in addition, intervene to prevent the monopolistic patient from committing social suicide. A two-pronged approach is most effective: consider both the monopolizing patient and the group that has allowed itself to be monopolized.

From the standpoint of the group, bear in mind the principle that, by definition, no monopolistic patient may exist in a vacuum; that patient always abides in a dynamic equilibrium with a group that permits or encourages such behavior. You may thus inquire why the group permits or encourages one member to carry the burden of the entire meeting. Such an inquiry may startle the members, who have only perceived themselves as passive victims of the monopolist. After the initial protestations are worked through, the group members may then, with profit, examine their exploitation of the monopolist; for example, they may have been relieved by not having to participate verbally in the group. They may have permitted the patient to do all the self-disclosure, or to make a fool of himself, or to act as a lightning rod for the group members' anger, while they themselves assumed little responsibility for the therapeutic goals of the group. Once the members disclose and discuss their reasons for inactivity, their personal commitment to the therapeutic process is augmented. They may, for example, discuss their fears of assertiveness, or of harming the monopolist, or of a retaliatory attack by some specific member or by the therapist; they may wish to avoid seeking the group's attention lest their greed be exposed; they may secretly revel in the monopolist's plight and enjoy being a member of the victimized and disapproving majority. A disclosure of any of these issues by a hitherto uninvolved patient signifies progress and greater engagement in therapy.

The group approach to this problem must be complemented by work with the monopolistic patient. The basic principle is a simple one: you do not want to silence the monopolist; *you do not want to hear less from the patient; instead, you want to hear more.* The seeming contradiction is resolved when we consider that the monopolist uses compulsive speech for self-concealment. The issues the monopolist presents to the group do not reflect deeply felt personal concerns but are selected for other reasons—to entertain, to gain attention, to justify her position, to present grievances, and so on. Thus, the monopolist sacrifices the opportunity for therapy to the insatiable need for attention and control. Although each therapist will fashion interventions according to personal style, the essential message to the monopolist must be that, through such compulsive speech, she holds the group at arm's length and prevents others from relating meaningfully to her. Thus you do not reject but instead issue an invitation to engage more fully in the group. If you harbor only the singular goal of silencing the patient, then you have, in effect, abandoned the therapeutic goal and might as well remove the patient from the group.

In addition to grossly deviant behavior, the social sensory system of the monopolist has a major impairment. She seems peculiarly unaware both of her interpersonal impact and of the response of others to her; moreover, she lacks the capacity or inclination to empathize with others in her social setting. Data from an exploratory research endeavor support this conclusion.[1] Patients and student observers were asked to fill out questionnaires at the end of each group meeting. One of the areas explored was activity; the participants were asked to rank the group members, including themselves, for the total number of words uttered during a meeting. There was excellent reliability in the activity ratings among patients and observers, with two exceptions: (1) the ratings of the therapist's activity by the patients showed large discrepancies (a function of transference; see chapter 7); and (2) monopolistic patients placed themselves far lower on the activity rankings than did the other members, who were often unanimous in ranking a monopolist as the most active member in the meeting.

The therapist must, then, help the monopolist be self-observant by encouraging the group to provide her with continual feedback; without the leader's encouragement, the group may, as I mentioned, provide the feedback only in a disjunctive, explosive manner, which only makes the monopolist defensive. Such a sequence has little therapeutic value and merely recapitulates a drama and a role which the patient has performed far too often.

• For example, in the initial interview one male monopolist complained about his relationship with his wife, who, he claimed, often abruptly resorted to such "sledgehammer tactics" as publicly humiliating him or accusing him of infidelity in front of his children. The sledgehammer approach accomplished nothing durable for this patient; once his bruises had healed, he and his wife began the cycle anew. Within the first few meetings of the group, a similar sequence unfolded: because of his monopolistic behavior, judgmentalism, and inability to hear the members' response to him, the group pounded harder and harder until finally, when he was forced to listen, the message was cruel and destructive.

Often the therapist must help to increase a patient's receptivity to feedback. You may have to be forceful and directive, saying, for example, "Charlotte, I think it would be best now for you to stop speaking because I sense there are some important feelings about you in the group which I think would be very helpful for you to know." You should also help the group disclose their responses to Charlotte rather than their interpretations of her motives. Far more useful and acceptable is a statement such as "When you speak in this fashion I feel . . ." rather than, "You are behaving in this fashion because. . . ." The patient may often perceive motivational interpretations as accusatory but can hardly reject the validity of others' subjective responses to her.

Too often we confuse or interchange the concepts of interpersonal manifestation, response, and cause. The cause of monopolistic behavior may vary considerably from patient to patient: some individuals speak in order to control others; many so fear that they will be influenced or penetrated by others that they compulsively defend each of their statements; others so overvalue their own ideas and observations that they cannot delay and all thoughts must be immediately expressed. Generally the cause of the monopolist's behavior is not well understood until much later in therapy, and interpretation of the cause offers little help in the early management of disruptive behavior patterns. It is far more effective to concentrate on the patient's manifestation of self in the group and on the other members' response to her behavior. Gently but repeatedly, patients must be confronted with the paradox that, however much they may wish to be accepted and respected by others, they persist in behavior that generates only irritation, rejection, and frustration.

A clinical illustration of many of these issues occurred in a therapy group in a psychiatric hospital in which sexual offenders were incarcerated:

- Walt, who had been in the group for seven weeks, launched into a familiar lengthy tribute to the remarkable improvement he had undergone. He described in exquisite detail how his chief problem had been that he had not understood the damaging effects his behavior had on others, and how now, having achieved such understanding, he was ready to leave the hospital. The therapist observed that some of the members were restless, one softly pounded his fist into his palm, while others slumped back in a posture of indifference and resignation. He stopped the monopolist by asking the group members how many times they had heard Walt relate this account. The group members agreed that they had heard it at every meeting; in fact, they had heard Walt speak this way in the first meeting he attended; furthermore, they had never heard him talk about anything else and knew him only as a "story." The members discussed their irritation with Walt, their reluctance to attack him for fear of seriously injuring him, of losing control of themselves, or of painful retaliation. Some spoke of their hopelessness about ever reaching Walt, and of the fact that he related to them only as matchstick figures without flesh or depth. Still others spoke of their terror of speaking and revealing themselves in the group; therefore, they welcomed Walt's monopolization. A few members expressed their total lack of interest or faith in therapy and therefore failed to intercept Walt because of apathy.

Thus the process was overdetermined: a host of interlocking factors resulted in a dynamic equilibrium called monopolization. By halting the runaway process, uncovering and working through the underlying factors, the therapist obtained maximum therapeutic benefit from a potentially crippling group phenomenon. Each member moved closer to group involvement. Walt was no longer permitted or encouraged to participate in a fashion that could not possibly be helpful to him or the group.

It is essential to enlist the patient as an ally in the therapeutic work. The monopolist must have some reasons for wishing to change monopolistic patterns, especially since she has not entered therapy with this complaint. For example, the monopolist may be helped to consider the sequence of events in the group. When she entered the group, what kind of response was she hoping to get from the group members? What has actually transpired? How does she explain the discrepancy? Is she satisfied with the group's response to her?

The therapist must help the monopolist generalize beyond the group. The monopolist may devalue the importance of learning about the group's reaction to her, or suggest that the group consists of disturbed people. She may protest, "This is the first time something like this has ever happened to me." If the therapist is sufficiently in control to have prevented scapegoating, then this statement is always untrue: the patient *is* in a very familiar place—vis-à-vis others. What is different in the group is the presence of norms that permit the others to comment openly on her behavior.

The therapist increases therapeutic leverage by encouraging the patient to examine and discuss interpersonal difficulties (the fact of feeling lonely, of having no close friends, of not ever being listened to by others, of being shunned without reason, and so on). Once these are made explicit, the therapist can, more convincingly, demonstrate to the patient the importance and relevance of examining her in-group behavior. Good timing is necessary; there is no point in attempting to do this work with a closed defensive patient in the midst of a firestorm. Repeated, gentle, properly timed interventions are required.

The Schizoid Patient

The schizoid condition, the malady of our times, perhaps accounts for more patients entering psychotherapy than does any other psychopathological configuration. These patients are emotionally blocked, isolated, distant individuals who often seek group therapy out of a vague sense that something is missing: they cannot feel, cannot love, cannot play, cannot cry. They are spectators of themselves, they do not inhabit their own bodies, they do not experience their own experience.

Sartre in *The Age of Reason* vividly describes the experiential world of such a person:

He closed the paper and began to read the special correspondent's dispatch on the front page. Fifty dead and three hundred wounded had already been counted, but that was not the total, there were certainly corpses under the debris. . . . There were thousands of men in France who had not been able to read their paper that morning without feeling a clot of anger rise in their throat, thousands of men who had clenched their fists and muttered: "Swine!" Mathieu clenched his fists and muttered: "Swine!" and felt himself still more guilty. If at least he had been able to discover in himself a trifling emotion that was veritably if modestly alive, conscious of its limits. But no: he was empty, he was confronted by a vast anger, a desperate anger, he saw it and could almost have touched it. But it was inert—if it were to live and find expression and suffer, he must lend it his own body. It was other people's anger. "Swine!" He clenched his fists, he strode along, but nothing came, the anger remained external to himself. . . . Something was on the threshold of existence, a timorous dawn of anger. At last! But it dwindled and collapsed, he was left in solitude, walking with the measured and decorous gait of a man in a funeral procession in Paris. . . . He wiped his forehead with his handkerchief and he thought: "One can't force one's deeper feelings." Yonder was a terrible and tragic state of affairs that ought to arouse one's deepest emotions. . . . "It's no use, the moment will not come. . . ."[2]

The schizoid patient is often in a similar predicament in the therapy group. In virtually every group meeting, the patient, unless he selectively inattends to the proceedings, has confirmatory evidence that the nature and intensity of his emotional experience differs considerably from that of the other members. The patient may be puzzled at this discrepancy and may conclude that the other members are melodramatic, excessively labile, phony, overly concerned with trivia, or simply of a different temperament. Eventually, however, schizoid patients begin to wonder about themselves; like Sartre's Mathieu, they grow to suspect that somewhere inside themselves is a vast reservoir of feeling that they cannot reach.

In one way or another, by what he says or does not say, the schizoid patient conveys this emotional isolation to the other members. In chapter 2, I described a male patient who could not understand the members' concern about the therapist's leaving the group or a member's obsessive fears about her boyfriend being killed. He saw people as interchangeable. He had his need for an M.D.R. (minimum daily requirement) of affection (without, it seemed, proper concern about the source of affection). He would be "bugged" by the departure of the therapist because it would slow up his therapy. He would be annoyed with himself for not having made better use of the therapist. But he did not share in the feeling expressed by the others: grief at the loss of the person who is the therapist. In defense of himself, he maintained, "There's not much sense to my having any strong feelings about the therapist's leaving since there is nothing I can do about it." Another patient, chided by the group because of his lack of empathy toward two highly distressed members, responded, "So, they're hurting. There are millions of people hurting all over the world at this instant. If I let myself feel badly for everyone who was hurting, I'd find it a full-time occupation." In other words, feelings are awarded priority according to the dictates of rationality; they must be justified pragmatically—if they serve no purpose, why have them?

The group is often keenly aware of a discrepancy between a patient's words, experience, and emotional response. One patient, who had been criticized for withholding information from the group about his relationship with a girlfriend, frostily asked, "Would you like to bring your camera and climb into bed with us?" When questioned, however, he denied feeling any anger and could not account for the tone of sarcasm. At other times, the group reads the schizoid patient's emotions from postural or behavioral cues. Indeed, the patient may relate to himself in a similar way and join in the investigation, commenting, for example, "My heart is beating fast, so I must be frightened."

The response of the other members is characteristic and proceeds from curiosity and puzzlement through disbelief, solicitude, irritation, and frustration. They will repeatedly ask the patient, "What do you *feel* about . . . ?" and only much later come to realize that they were demanding that he quickly learn to speak a foreign language. Soon members become increasingly active in helping to resolve what has at first appeared to be a minor affliction. They begin to tell the patient what he *should* feel and what *they* would feel were they in his situation. Eventually, frustration sets in. The group tries even harder, almost always with no noticeable results. Soon a sledgehammer approach may be used as members try to force an affective response by increasing the intensity of the stimulus. Meetings may become very predictable and very discouraging. Sometimes the group mascots the patient, who thus becomes the source of much amusement to the group. (Henri Bergson felt that a central aspect of the comic situation was man as machine.[3] There seems to be something intrinsically comic in the spectacle of a human being acting in a routine, mechanical manner, as in much Chaplinesque humor or Laurel and Hardy slapstick. I think it is this factor that leads the group to find humor in an apparently unfunny situation.)

The therapist must avoid joining in the quest for a "breakthrough." I have never seen a schizoid patient significantly change by virtue of a dramatic incident; change is a prosaic process of grinding labor, repetitive small steps, and almost imperceptible progress. It is tempting and often useful to employ some activating, nonverbal, or gestalt techniques to hasten a patient's movement. These approaches may hasten the patient's recognition and expression of nascent or repressed feelings; but keep in mind that if you do excessive, one-to-one directive work, the group may become less potent, less autonomous, more dependent and leader-centered. (I shall discuss these issues at length in chapter 14).

In chapter 6, I described several here-and-now activating techniques which are useful in work with the schizoid patient. Encourage the patient to differentiate between members; despite his protestations, the patient does not feel precisely the same way toward everyone in the group. Help the patient to move into feelings he passes off as inconsequential. When the patient admits, "Well, I may feel slightly irritated or slightly hurt . . . ," suggest that he stay with these feelings; no one ever said that it was necessary to discuss only big feelings. "Hold up a magnifying glass to the hurt; describe exactly what it is like." Try to cut off the patient's customary methods of avoidance: "Somehow, you've gotten away from something that seemed important. Can we go back to where we were five minutes ago? When you were talking to Julie, I thought you looked near tears. Something was going on inside." Encourage the patient to observe his body. Often the patient may not experience affect but will be aware of the affective autonomic equivalents—tightness in the stomach, sweating, throat constriction, flushing, and so on. Gradually the group may help the patient to translate those feelings into their psychological meaning; the members may, for example, note the timing of the patient's reactions and their appearance in conjunction with some event in the group.

You as therapist should also beware of assessing events solely according to your own experiential world. As I have shown previously, patients may experience the same event in totally different manners: a seemingly trivial event to you or to one patient may be an exceedingly important experience to another patient. A slight show of irritation by a restricted schizoid patient may be for him a major breakthrough; it may be the first time in adulthood that the patient has expressed anger and may further enable him to test out new behavior both in and out of the group.

In the group, the schizoid is both a high-risk and a high-reward patient. The patient who can manage to persevere, to continue in the group and not be discouraged by the inability to change his relationship style quickly, is almost certain to profit considerably from the group therapy experience.

The Silent Patient

The converse of the monopolist, the silent member, is a less disruptive but often equally challenging problem for the therapist. Is the silent member always a problem in the group? Perhaps the patient profits silently. A story, probably apocryphal, that has circulated among group therapists for years tells of a patient who attended a group for a year without uttering a word. At the end of the fiftieth meeting, he announced to the group that he would not return; his problems had been resolved, he was due to get married the following day, and he wished to express his gratitude to the group for the help they had given him.

Some reticent patients may profit from vicariously engaging in treatment through identifying with active patients with similar problems; it is possible that changes in behavior and in risk taking can gradually occur in such a patient's relationships outside the group while he remains silent and seemingly unchanged in the group. The encounter group research project of Lieberman, Yalom, and Miles indicated that some of the participants who changed the most seemed to have a particular ability to maximize their learning opportunities in a short-term group (thirty total hours) by engaging vicariously in the group experience of other members.[4] There was evidence, though, that, in general, the *more active and influential a member was in the group matrix, the more likely he was to benefit.* Lundgren and Miller have demonstrated in T-groups that—regardless of what the participants said —the more words they spoke, the greater the positive change in their picture of themselves.[5] R. Coyne and R. Silver demonstrated that, in an experiential group, vicarious experience, as contrasted with direct participation on a combination of vicarious and direct experience, was ineffective in producing either change or an attraction to the group process.[6]

There is much clinical consensus that, in long-term therapy, the silent patient does not profit from the group. The greater the verbal participation, the greater the sense of involvement, and the more the patient is valued by others and ultimately by himself. I would suggest, then, that we not be lulled by the legendary story of the silent patient who got well. A silent patient is a problem patient and rarely benefits significantly from the group.

Patients may be silent for many reasons. Some may experience a pervasive dread of self-disclosure: every utterance, they feel, may commit them to progressively more disclosure. Others may feel so conflicted about aggression that they cannot undertake the self-assertion inherent in speaking. Others who demand nothing short of perfection in themselves never speak for fear of falling short when they open their mouths; whereas other patients keep their distance from the group or manage to control it by maintaining a lofty superior silence. Some patients are especially threatened by a particular member in the group and habitually speak only in the absence of that member. Others participate only in smaller meetings or in alternate (leaderless) meetings. Some are afraid of displaying weakness and remain silent lest they shatter, plead, or cry. Others may lapse into a periodic silent sulk in an effort to punish others or to force the group to attend to them.

The important point, though, is that silence is never silent; it is behavior and, like all other behavior in the group, has meaning both in the framework of the here-and-now and as a representative sample of the patient's typical way of relating to his interpersonal world. The therapeutic task, therefore, is not only to change the behavior (that is essential if the patient is to remain in the group) but to help the patient gain self-knowledge from his behavior.

Proper management depends in part on the dynamics of the silence, which the therapist ascertains from the pre-group individual interviews and from the patient's nonverbal cues, as well as from the few verbal contributions. A middle course must be steered between placing undue pressure on the patient and, on the other hand, allowing him to slide into an extreme isolate role. The therapist may still maintain an attitude of allowing each patient to modulate his or her own degree of participation and yet periodically including the silent patient by commenting on nonverbal behavior: that is, when, by gesture or demeanor, the patient is evincing interest, tension, sadness, boredom, or amusement. Often the therapist may hasten the member's participation by encouraging the other members to reflect on their perceptions of him and then asking the silent member to validate these perceptions. Even if repeated prodding, cajoling, or inviting is necessary, it is still possible to avoid making the patient a passive object by repeated process checks. "Is this a meeting when you want to be prodded? How did it feel when Mike put you on the spot? Did he go too far? Can you let us know when we make you uncomfortable? What's the ideal question we could ask you today to help you come into the group?" In these and other ways, the therapist can enlist the patient as active collaborator in the campaign against his silence. If, resisting all these efforts, a patient's participation remains very limited even after three months of meetings, my experience has been that the prognosis is poor. The group will become increasingly frustrated and puzzled at vainly coaxing, encouraging, or challenging a silent, blocked patient to participate. In the face of group discouragement and disapproval, the patient's position in the group becomes even more nonviable and the likelihood of participation ever more remote. Concurrent individual sessions may be useful in helping the patient at this time; if this fails, the therapist should seriously consider withdrawing the patient from the group.

The Boring Patient

Rarely does anyone seek therapy because of being boring. Yet, in thinly disguised garb, the complaint is not uncommon. Patients complain that they never have anything to say to others; that they are left standing alone at parties; that no member of the opposite sex will go out with them more than once; that others use them only for sex; that they are inhibited, shy, socially awkward, empty, or bland. Like silence, monopolization, or selfishness, boredom is to be taken seriously. It is an extremely important problem for the patient, whether he explicitly identifies it as such or not.

In the social microcosm of the therapy group, boring patients recreate these problems and bore the members of the group—and the therapist. The therapist dreads a small meeting in which only two or three boring members are present; if they were to leave the group, they would simply glide away leaving nary a ripple in the pond.

Boredom is a highly individual experience. Not everyone is bored by the same situation, and it is not easy to make generalizations. In general, though, the boring patient in the therapy group is one who is massively inhibited, who lacks spontaneity, never takes risks. The boring patient's utterances are always "safe" (and, alas, always predictable). He is obsequious and carefully avoids any sign of aggressivity; he is often masochistic (rushing into self-flagellation before anyone else can pummel him); he says what he believes the social press requires: that is, before speaking, he scans the faces of the other members to determine what they expect him to say and squelches any contrary sentiment coming from within.

The particular social style of the individual varies considerably: one may be silent; another stilted and hyperrational; another timid and self-effacing; still another dependent, demanding, or pleading.

The group members often escalate their efforts to encourage spontaneity in the boring patient. They ask the patient to share fantasies about members, to scream, to curse—anything to pry something unpredictable from the patient.

• One of my patients, Nora, drove the group to despair by her constant clichés and self-deprecatory remarks. After many months in the group, her outside life began to change for the better, but each report of success was accompanied by the inevitable self-derogatory neutralizer. She was accepted by an honorary professional society ("That is good," she said, "because it is one club that can't kick me out"), she received her graduate degree ("but I should have finished earlier"), she had gotten all A's ("but I'm a child for bragging about it"), she looked better physically ("shows you what a good sunlamp can do"), she had been asked out by several new men in her life ("sheer luck"), she obtained a good job ("it fell into my lap"), she had had her first vaginal orgasm ("give the credit to marijuana").

The group tried to tune her in to her self-effacement; one engineer suggested bringing an electric buzzer to the group to ring each time Nora knocked herself. One member, trying to shake her into a more spontaneous state, commented on her bra, which he felt could be improved. (This was Ed, discussed in chapter 2, who generally related only to the sexual parts of women.) He said he would bring her a present, a new bra, next session. Sure enough, the following session he arrived with a present, a huge box, which Nora said she would prefer to open at home. So there it sat, looming in the group and, of course, inhibiting any other topic. Nora was asked at least to guess what it contained, and she ventured, "A pair of falsies."

She was finally prevailed upon to open the gift and did so laboriously and with enormous embarrassment. The box contained nothing but styrofoam stuffing. Ed explained that this was his idea for Nora's new bra: that she should wear no bra at all. Nora promptly apologized to Ed (for guessing he had given her falsies) and thanked him for the trouble he had taken. The incident launched much work for both members. (I shall not here discuss the sequel for Ed.) The group held up for Nora the fact that Ed had humiliated and embarrassed her, and yet she responded by apologizing to him. She had politely thanked someone who had just given her a gift of precisely nothing! The incident created the first robust spark of self-observation in Nora. She began the next meeting with: "I've just set the world ingratiation record. Last night I received an obscene phone call and I apologized to the man!" (She said, "I'm sorry you must have the wrong number.")

The underlying dynamics of the boring patient vary enormously from individual to individual. Many have a core dependent position and so dread rejection and abandonment that they eschew any aggressive remark that might initiate retaliation. They mistakenly confuse healthy self-assertion with aggression and by refusing to grow and to present themselves as full, differentiated individuals with their own desires, interests, and opinions, they bring to pass (by boring others) the very rejection and abandonment they had hoped to forestall.

If you, as the therapist, are bored with a patient, that boredom is important data. You must counter your boredom with curiosity. Ask yourself: "What makes the patient so boring? When am I most and least bored? How can I find the person—the real, the lively, spontaneous, creative, person—within this boring shell?" No urgent "breakthrough" technique is indicated. Since the boring patient is tolerated by the group much better than the abrasive, narcissistic, or monopolistic patient, you have much time. In fact, the group members, in coming to know the boring patient more deeply, accept that patient more and find him less boring than do people in the outside social world.

Lastly, keep in mind that the task is not one of inspiriting boring patients, of injecting color, spontaneity, or richness *into* them, but is instead to inquire why they have squelched all their creative, vital, childlike parts and to encourage them to allow these qualities, which reside in all of us, to find expression.

The Help-Rejecting Complainer

The help-rejecting complainer, a variant of the monopolist, was first identified and christened by J. D. Frank in 1952;[7] since then, the behavior pattern has been recognized by many group clinicians, and the eponym appears frequently in psychiatric literature.[8] In this section, I shall discuss the rare, fully developed, help-rejecting complainer; however, this pattern of behavior is not a distinct, all-or-nothing clinical syndrome. Patients may arrive at this style of interaction through various psychodynamic pathways and may persistently manifest this behavior in an extreme degree with no external provocation; others may demonstrate only a trace of this pattern; whereas still others may become help-rejecting complainers only at times of particular stress.

DESCRIPTION

The help-rejecting complainer (hereafter HRC) has a distinctive behavioral pattern in the group, implicitly or explicitly requesting help from the group by presenting problems or complaints, and then rejecting any help offered. The HRC continually brings environmental or somatic problems to the group and often describes them in a manner that causes them to appear insurmountable; in fact, the HRC seems to take pride in the insolubility of her problems. Often the HRC focuses wholly on the therapist in a tireless campaign to elicit medication or advice. Clearly this behavior indicates a need not for approval or respect but for help. The HRC seems oblivious to the group's reaction to her and is apparently willing to appear ludicrous so long as she is allowed to persist in the search for help. She bases her relationship to the other members along the singular dimension of establishing that she is more needy of aid than they. The HRC rarely shows competitiveness in any area except when another member makes a bid for the therapist's or group's attention by presenting a problem; at this juncture the HRC often attempts to belittle others' complaints by comparing them unfavorably with her own. One such patient stated explicitly, "It seems like such a waste to me listening to you when my problems involve life and death and yours seem so superficial." The HRC seems entirely self-centered: she speaks only of herself and her problems. In fact, however, her problems are not clearly formulated to the group or to herself; they are obscured by her propensity to exaggerate them and to blame others, often authority figures on whom she depends in some fashion.

When the group and the therapist do respond to the HRC's plea, the entire bewildering configuration takes form, as the patient rejects the help offered. The rejection is unmistakable, though it may assume many varied and subtle forms; sometimes the advice is rejected overtly, sometimes indirectly; sometimes while accepted verbally, it is never acted upon or, if acted upon, inevitably fails to improve the plight of the patient.

EFFECTS ON THE GROUP

The effects on the group are obvious: the other members become bored and irritated, then frustrated and confused. The HRC appears to them as a greedy whirlpool, sucking down the group's energy. Worse yet, no deceleration of the HRC's demands is evident. Faith in the group process suffers, as members experience a sense of impotence and, further, as they despair of making their own needs appreciated by the group. Cohesiveness is undermined as absenteeism occurs or as patients subgroup in an effort to exclude the HRC.

DYNAMICS

The behavioral pattern of the HRC appears to be an attempt to resolve highly conflicted feelings about dependency. On the one hand, the patient feels helpless, insignificant, and totally dependent on others, especially on the therapist, for a sense of personal worth. Any notice and attention from the therapist temporarily enhance the HRC's self-esteem. On the other hand, the HRC's dependent position is vastly confounded by a pervasive distrust and enmity toward authority figures. A vicious circle results, one that has been spinning for much of the patient's life: consumed with need, the HRC turns for help to a figure whom she anticipates as unwilling (or unable) to help; the anticipation of refusal so colors her style of requesting help that the prophecy is fulfilled, and further evidence is accumulated for the HRC's belief in the malevolence of the potential caregiver.

M. Berger and M. Rosenbaum, who report several cases, particularly emphasize the HRC's latent motivation to frustrate and defeat the group and the therapist.[9] Their series of HRCs were subject to severe deprivation early in life: parents were either absent or seriously disturbed. Often marked depressive trends were evident as well as a pervasive need to deprive others of pleasure as the HRCs themselves had been deprived. Should an HRC undergo positive change, it will often be withheld from the group until several months after the fact.

GUIDELINES FOR MANAGEMENT

A severe HRC is an exceedingly difficult clinical challenge, and many such patients have won a Pyrrhic victory over therapist and group by failing in therapy. It would thus be presumptuous and misleading to attempt to prescribe a careful therapeutic plan; however, certain generalizations may be posited. Surely it is a blunder for the therapist to confuse the help requested for the help required. The HRC solicits advice not for its potential value but in order to spurn it; ultimately, the therapist's advice, guidance, and medication will be rejected, forgotten, or, if used, will prove ineffective or, if effective, will be kept secret. It is also a blunder for the therapist to express any frustration and resentment to the patient. Retaliation merely completes the vicious circle; the HRC's anticipation of ill treatment and abandonment is once again realized, and she finds justification for her own anger. Once again the HRC is able to affirm that no one can ever really understand her.

What course, then, is available to the therapist? One clinician suggests, perhaps in desperation, that the therapist interrupt the vicious circle by indicating that he or she "not only understands but shares the patient's feelings of hopelessness about his situation, thus refusing to perpetuate his part in a futile relationship."[10] Two brave co-therapists who led a group composed only of help-rejecting complainers warn the therapist against investing in a sympathetic, nurturing relationship with the patient.[11] They suggest that you sidestep any expression of optimism, encouragement, or advice and adopt, instead, a pose of irony in which you the therapist agree with the content of the patient's pessimism while maintaining a detached affect.

In general, however, the therapist should attempt to mobilize the major therapeutic factors in the service of the patient. Once a cohesive group has been formed and the patient—through universality, identification, and catharsis—has come to value membership in the group, then the therapist can encourage interpersonal learning by continually focusing on feedback and process in much the same manner as I have described in discussing the monopolistic patient. Once the HRC cares about her interpersonal impact on the other members, then she should be helped to recognize her characteristic pattern of relationships. One therapist, having once identified the process, called the group's attention to it by humming the tune "Nobody Knows the Trouble I've Seen" when the HRC engaged in typical behavior.[12] Eric Berne, who considers the HRC pattern to be the most common of all social and psychotherapy group games, has christened it "Why don't you—yes but."[13] The use of such easily accessible descriptive labels often makes the process more transparent and acceptable to the group members. But the therapist must be careful when using a bantering approach: it is easy to cross the line that separates playful caring from mockery.

The Self-Righteous Moralist

The self-righteous moralist (SRM), first described by D. Rosenthal, J. Frank, and E. Nash, evinces a pattern of behavior evident in the early group meetings.[14] The most outstanding characteristic of the self-righteous moralist is the need to be right and to demonstrate that the other person is wrong, particularly when some moral issue is involved. The SRM's interpersonal motives differ from those of the patients with the other behavioral patterns I have discussed. The monopolist wants to control others for sundry reasons. The help-rejecting complainer wants to solicit help and then to defeat the benefactor. The self-righteous moralist, on the other hand, is relatively unconcerned about being liked or respected; above all, he wishes to be right, to be respected for moral integrity, and to be successful in imposing his values on other people.

In the first meeting, the SRM usually appears calm and self-assured, demonstrating superiority through poise. He is often silent at first until he is clear about the group or some member's position. The SRM then usually becomes the key figure in the discussion because of the intensity of his convictions and his propensity to belabor his viewpoint indefatigably. Characteristically, the SRM refuses to concede any points, to admit any error, or to make any modification of his original formulation.[15] When others discuss problems, he participates in a manner that will enhance his status. The SRM may point out that he has survived greater environmental stress, that he has continued to succeed despite manifold handicaps, and that his solutions may serve as models for others. Although the group may empathize with the SRM when first presenting these problems, the empathy is soon transformed into irritation when the members realize that his primary interest is in attaining a position of moral superiority rather than in sharing experiences. If another member attempts to assume a position of superiority in the group, the self-righteous moralist feels challenged and engages the interloper by attempting to prove him wrong. The therapist, too, is challenged, though often only obliquely; the patient may express doubts about therapy and refer to the opinions of other experts in the field or cite reputable authorities in other fields. When particularly threatened, the SRM may challenge and attack the therapist's moral values.

The self-righteous moralist mobilizes so much resentment that, unless the therapist intervenes, the former is soon forced out of the group. Not only must the patient be protected, but the group must be helped to deal with the patient's provocative behavior. One of the key concepts in the dynamics and treatment of the SRM is shame: the patient has done the "right thing" in life, has struggled and suffered, but has received little success or recognition. In an attempt to deal with shame, the individual seeks recognition for nobility of character rather than for achievements. If the group can be helped to sense the shame underlying the angry, self-righteous polemics of the patient, their response to him will be constructive. The therapist, once attuned to the patient's deep sense of failure and shame, will respond accordingly rather than be drawn into the same catastrophic interpersonal sequence that the patient usually creates in relating to the world.

Often, however, before the therapist fully recognizes the pattern, the entire malignant sequence has unfolded and become irreversible: the group has responded to the self-righteous moralist at first with patience, then with irritation, at times with studied indifference, and finally with fury. By devaluing the group and by convincing himself that the group's opinion is of little import, the patient often defends himself and rationalizes the fact that he has not attained the respect he desires.

Many of these issues are illustrated in this clinical vignette:

• Max, a twenty-nine-year-old man who sought therapy because of intense sexual urges toward adolescent girls, immediately slid into the self-righteous moralist pattern in the group. He established his moral superiority by an ingenious maneuver: he underscored his ability to lead a good Christian life despite the handicap of ego-alien sexual impulses. His behavior in the group conformed closely to the pattern I have described, and he especially berated the group and the therapists for their personal disregard of Christian ethics. The group's response to him, even their pointing out that his contempt and scorn for them was not only infuriating but highly un-Christian, apparently went unheeded. The feelings of the members toward him degenerated to name calling, and three members expressed deep, ungovernable feelings of hatred toward Max.

He expressed little concern for the opinions of pagans and, by the twentieth meeting, when the situation became unbearable, dropped out of the group. To the casual observer, his experience in the group was not only unhelpful but catastrophic. However, he immediately began therapy in a married couples' group and proved to be far more receptive when he received the same feedback from his wife and from other couples. Follow-up interviews confirmed that he had learned a great deal in the group but had reflexly locked himself into a relationship with the group which precluded experimentation with new behavior. His behavior, however, in the initial meetings of the second group was considerably different from his behavior in the first.

This vignette illustrates a point I have made elsewhere in the text: therapy does not terminate with termination from the group. Successful patients may continue to grow and to integrate new experiences for the rest of their lives. Unsuccessful patients who, because of "role lock," found their position in the group not to be viable, and who were thus unable to change (or to admit change), are sometimes able to profit from their experience nonetheless and to use their subsequent therapy more effectively.

The Psychotic Patient

The therapy group is severely challenged when a member develops a psychosis during treatment. The fate of the psychotic patient, the response of the other members, and the effective options available to the therapist all depend, in part, upon when the psychosis occurs in the history of the group. In general, in an older and mature group where the psychotic patient has occupied a central, valued role, the group members are more likely to be tolerant and effective in the crisis.

THE EARLY PHASES OF A GROUP

In chapter 8 on the selection of patients, I emphasized that, in the initial screening, the grossly psychotic patient should be excluded from outpatient, interactional group therapy. If, by accident or design, such a severely ill patient is included in the group, both the group and the patient almost invariably suffer. The group is impeded in its progress in a manner I shall illustrate shortly; the patient soon slides into a deviant role in the group and eventually terminates treatment, often much the worse for the experience.

At times, despite cautious screening, a patient, because of unanticipated stress from life circumstances or from the group, becomes psychotic in the early stages of therapy, creating substantial problems for the newly formed group. In this book I have repeatedly stressed that the early stages of the group are a time of great flux and great importance. The young group is easily influenced, and norms that are established early are often exceedingly durable. An intense sequence of events unfolds as, in a few weeks, an aggregate of frightened, distrustful strangers evolves into an intimate, mutually helpful group. Any event that, in the early part of a group, consumes an inordinate amount of time, and diverts energy from the tasks of the developmental sequence, is potentially destructive to the group. Some of the relevant problems are illustrated by this clinical example:

• Sandy, a thirty-seven-year-old housewife who had once, several years before, been hospitalized and treated with electroconvulsive therapy for depression, sought group therapy at the insistence of her individual therapist, who thought that an understanding of her inter-personal relationships would help her to improve her relationship with her husband. In the early meetings of the group, she was an active member who tended to reveal far more intimate details of her past history than did the other members. Occasionally Sandy expressed anger toward another member and then engaged in excessively profuse apologies coupled with self-deprecatory remarks. By the sixth meeting, her behavior became still more inappropriate. For example, she discoursed at great length on her son's urinary problems and described, with intricate detail, the surgery that had been performed to relieve urethral stricture. At the following meeting, she noted that the family cat had also developed a blockage of the urinary tract; she then pressed the other members of the group to describe their pets.

In the eighth meeting, Sandy decompensated completely. She behaved in a bizarre, irrational manner, insulting members of the group, openly flirting with the male members to the point of stroking their bodies, and finally lapsed into punning, clang associations, and inappropriate laughter and tears. One of the therapists then escorted her from the room, phoned her husband, and arranged for immediate psychiatric hospitalization. Sandy remained in the hospital in a manic, psychotic state for a month and then gradually recovered.

The members during the meeting were obviously extremely uncomfortable, their feelings ranging from bafflement and fright to annoyance. After Sandy left, they expressed feelings of guilt for, in some unknown manner, having triggered her behavior. Others spoke of their fear, and one recalled another person who had acted in a similar fashion but had also brandished a gun.

During the subsequent meeting, the members discussed many feelings related to the incident. One member expressed his conviction that no one could be trusted; even though he had known Sandy for seven weeks, her behavior proved to be totally unpredictable. Others expressed their relief that they were, in comparison, psychologically healthy; others, in response to their fears of similarly losing control, employed considerable denial and veered away from discussing these problems. Some expressed a fear of Sandy's returning and making a shambles of the group. Others expressed their diminished faith in group therapy; one member asked for hypnosis, and another brought to the meeting an article from a scientific journal claiming that psychotherapy was ineffective. A loss of faith in the therapists was expressed in the dream of one member, in which the therapist was in the hospital and was rescued by the patient.

In the next few meetings, all these themes went underground; the meetings became listless, shallow, and intellectualized. Attendance dwindled, and the group seemed resigned to its own impotence. At the fourteenth meeting, the therapists announced that Sandy was improved and would return the following week. A vigorous, heated discussion ensued. The members feared that:

1. They would upset her, that an intense meeting would make her ill again, and that therefore the group would be forced to move slowly and superficially.
2. Sandy would be unpredictable; at any point she might lose control and display dangerous, frightening behavior.
3. Sandy would, because of her lack of control, be untrustworthy; nothing in the group would remain confidential.

At the same time, the members expressed considerable anxiety and guilt for wishing to exclude Sandy from the group, and soon tension and a heavy silence prevailed. The extreme reaction of the group persuaded the therapist to delay for a few weeks the reintroduction of Sandy (who was, incidentally, in concurrent individual therapy).

When she re-entered the group, she was treated as a fragile object, and the entire group interaction was guarded and defensive. By the twentieth meeting, five of the seven members had dropped out of the group, leaving only Sandy and one other member.

The therapists reconstituted the group by adding five new members. It is of interest that, despite the fact that only two of the old members and the therapists continued in the reconstituted group, the old group culture persisted: Sandy was treated so delicately and so obliquely by the new members that the group moved slowly, floundering in its own politeness and social conventionality. Only when the therapists openly confronted this issue and discussed in the group their own fears of upsetting Sandy and thrusting her into another psychosis were the members able to deal with their feelings and fears about her. At that point, the group moved ahead more quickly. Sandy remained in the new group for a year and made decided improvements in her ability to relate with others and in her self-concept.

LATER IN THE COURSE OF A GROUP

An entirely different situation may arise when a patient who, for many months, has been an involved, active group member decompensates into a psychosis. Other members are then primarily concerned for the patient rather than for themselves or for the group. Since they have previously known and understood the now-psychotic patient as a person, they often react with great concern and interest; the patient is less likely to be viewed as a strange and frightening object to be avoided. The popular stereotype of the insane person includes a strong element of differentness; the patient's appearance and behavior seem totally dissimilar to anything in an observer's own inner experience.*

Although perceiving similarity may enhance the other members' ability to continue relating to a distressed patient, it also creates a personal upheaval in some members, who begin to fear that they, too, can lose control and slide into a similar abyss. It is most important for the therapist to anticipate this reaction so as to enable the others to work through their dread.

When faced with a psychotic patient in a group, many psychiatrists reflexly revert to their early medical model and symbolically "dismiss" the group by intervening forcefully in a one-to-one fashion. In effect, they say to the group, "This is too serious a problem for you to handle." Such a maneuver, however, is often antitherapeutic: the patient is frightened, and the group emasculated.

It has been my experience that a mature group is perfectly able to deal with the psychiatric emergency and, although there may be false starts, to consider every contingency and take every action that the therapist might have considered. Consider the following clinical example:

- In the forty-fifth meeting Rhona, a forty-three-year-old divorcée, arrived a few minutes late in a disheveled, obviously disturbed state. Over the previous few weeks she had gradually been sliding into a depression, but clearly the process had suddenly accelerated. She was tearful, despondent, and suicidal and evidenced psychomotor retardation. During the early part of the meeting, she wept continuously and expressed feelings of great loneliness, hopelessness, and inability to love, hate, or, for that matter, have any deeply felt emotion; she described her feeling of great detachment from everyone, including the group, and, when prompted, discussed her suicidal ruminations.

The group members responded to Rhona with great empathy and concern. They inquired about events during the past week and helped

---

*R. Moos and I demonstrated, for example, that medical students assigned for the first time to a psychiatric ward regarded the psychotic patients as extremely dangerous, frightening, unpredictable, and dissimilar to themselves.[16] At the end of their five weeks' assignment, these attitudes underwent considerable change: the students grew less isolated and frightened of their patients, as they learned that "psychotics" were but confused, deeply anguished human beings, more like themselves than they had previously thought.

her discuss two important occurrences that seemed related to the depressive crisis: (1) she had for months saved money and planned a summer trip to Europe; her seventeen-year-old son had, during the past week, decided to decline a summer camp job which had been offered him and refused to search for other jobs—a turn of events that, in Rhona's eyes, jeopardized her trip; (2) she had, after months of hesitation, decided to attend a dance for divorced middle-aged people which proved to be a disaster: no one had approached her to dance, and she had left for home consumed with feelings of total worthlessness.

The group helped her to explore her relationship with her son: she, for the first time, expressed rage at him for his lack of concern for her. With the group's assistance, she attempted to define the limits of her responsibility toward him. It was difficult for Rhona to discuss the dance because of the amount of shame and humiliation she felt. Two other women in the group, one single and one divorced, empathized deeply with her and shared their experiences and reactions to the scarcity of suitable males. Rhona was also reminded by the group of the many times she had, during sessions, interpreted every minor slight as a total rejection and condemnation of herself. Finally, after much attention, care, and warmth had been offered her, one of the members pointed out to Rhona that the experience of the dance was being disconfirmed right in the group: several people who knew her well were deeply concerned and involved with her. Rhona rejected this idea by claiming that the group, unlike the dance, was an artificial, unreal situation in which people followed artificial, unnatural rules of conduct. The members quickly pointed out that quite the contrary was true: the dance— the contrived congregation of strangers, the attractions based on split-second, skin-deep impressions—was the artificial situation and the group was the real one; it was there that she was truly and completely known.

Rhona, consumed with the conviction of her own worthlessness, then berated herself for her inability to feel reciprocal warmth and involvement with the group members. One of the members quickly intercepted this maneuver by pointing out that it was a familiar and repetitive pattern of hers: that she experienced some feelings toward the other members which were evidenced by her facial expression and body posture, but then her "shoulds" took over and tortured her by insisting that she "should" feel more, "should" feel more warmth and more love than anyone else. The net effect was that the real feeling she did have was rapidly extinguished by the winds of her impossible self-demands.

In essence, what then transpired was Rhona's gradual recognition of the discrepancy between her public and private esteem (described in chapter 3). At the end of the meeting, Rhona responded by bursting into tears and crying for several minutes. The group was reluctant to leave but did so when the members had all convinced themselves that suicide was no longer a serious consideration. Throughout the next week, the members maintained an informal vigil, each phoning Rhona at least once.

Rather early in the session the therapist realized the important dynamics operating in Rhona's depression and, had he chosen, might have made the appropriate interpretations to allow the patient and the group to arrive much more quickly at a cognitive understanding of the problem—but to do so would have detracted considerably from the meaningfulness and value of the meeting to both the protagonist and the other members. For one thing, the group would have been deprived of an opportunity to experience its own potency; every success adds to the group's cohesiveness and enhances the self-regard of each of the members. It is difficult for some therapists to refrain from interpretation, and yet it is essential to learn to sit on your wisdom. There are times when it is foolish to be wise and wise to be silent.

At times, as in this clinical episode, the group chooses and performs the appropriate action; at other times, the group may decide that the therapist must act. But there is a vast difference between a group's hasty decision stemming from infantile dependence and unrealistic appraisal of the therapist's powers and, on the other hand, a decision based on the members' thorough investigation of the situation and mature appraisal of the therapist's expertise.

These points lead me to an important principle of group dynamics, one substantiated by considerable research. A group that reaches an autonomous decision based on a thorough exploration of the pertinent problems will employ all of its resources in support of its decision; a group that has a decision thrust upon it is likely to resist that decision and be even less effective in making valid decisions in the future.*

A widely cited study by L. Coch and J. French is relevant here.[17] The authors studied a pajama-producing factory in which periodic changes in jobs and routine were necessitated by advances in technology. For many years these changes were resisted by the employees; with each change, there was an increase in absenteeism, turnover,

---

*Hardly an ultramodern principle! Thomas Jefferson once stated that "that government is the strongest of which every man feels a part."[18]

aggression toward the management, as well as decreased efficiency and output. An experiment was designed to test various methods of over-coming the employees' resistance to change. The critical variable stud-ied was the degree of participation of the group members (the em-ployees) in planning the change. The employees were divided into three groups, and three variations were tested: (1) the first variation involved no participation by the employees in planning the changes, though an explanation was given to them; (2) the second variation involved participation through elected representation of the workers in designing the changes to be made in the job; (3) the third variation consisted of total participation by all the members of the group in designing the changes. The results showed conclusively that, on all measures studied (aggression toward management, absenteeism, effi-ciency, number of employees resigning from the job), the success of the change was directly proportional to the degree of participation of the group members.

The implications for group therapy are apparent: members of a ther-apy group who personally participate in planning a course of action will be more committed to the enactment of the plan. They will, for exam-ple, invest themselves more fully in the care of a psychotic member if they recognize that it is their problem and not the therapist's alone.

At times, as in the previous clinical example, the entire experience is beneficial to the development of group cohesiveness; sharing intense emotional experiences usually strengthens ties among members. The danger to the group occurs when the psychotic patient consumes a massive amount of energy for a prolonged period. Then other members may drop out, and the group may deal with the disturbed patient in a cautious, concealed manner or attempt to ignore him; all of these meth-ods never fail to aggravate the problem. In such critical situations, one important option always available to the therapist is to see the disturbed patient in individual sessions for the duration of the crisis (this option will be dealt with more fully in the discussion of concurrent individual therapy). However, here too the group should thoroughly explore the implications and share in the decision.

One of the worst calamities that can befall a therapy group is the presence of a manic member. A patient in the midst of a severe hypo-manic thrust is perhaps the single most disruptive problem for a group. (In contrast, a full-blown manic episode presents little problem since the solution is clear: hospitalization.)

- For over a year, one of my therapy groups attempted to deal with a patient with a bipolar affective disorder. Most of the time the patient was an extraordinarily valuable member; she was fully committed to the group, insightful, sensitive, and provocative. When she became depressed, the group was deeply concerned for her, feared suicide, and devoted many hours to bolstering her self-concept and dissuading her from resignation or suicide. When she grew manic, she dominated the group: she could not refrain from responding to every comment made in the meeting; she interrupted other members continuously; and she also stirred up great concern on the part of the other members, who grew alarmed at the many unwise and impulsive economic and personal life decisions she made. Gradually the depressive and manic episodes grew more severe, and the lucid interval between episodes, shorter. Eventually hospitalization was required, and she left the group with no benefit from her experience.

The patient with a major bipolar affective disorder is best managed pharmacologically and is probably impervious to psychologically based treatment. It is obviously unwise, then, to allow the group to invest much energy and time in treatment that has such little likelihood of success. However, considerable support can be offered to medicated patients in homogeneous specialty groups.[19]

The Narcissistic Patient

A healthy love of oneself is essential to the development of self-respect and self-confidence; excessive narcissism takes the form of loving oneself to the exclusion of others, of losing sight of the fact that others are sentient beings, that others, too, are constituting egos, each constructing and experiencing a unique world. In short, narcissists are solipsists who experience the world and other individuals as existing solely for them.

Narcissistic problems range in severity from patients who have slight narcissistic traits and appear vain, selfish, or conceited to those with such hypertrophied narcissistic trends that the whole personality is organized around exaggerated self-love. Before discussing the severely impaired narcissistic patient, I shall address the general problems evoked by narcissistic behavior in the group.

GENERAL PROBLEMS

The narcissistic patient generally has a stormier but more productive course in group than in individual therapy. In fact, the individual format provides so much gratification that the core problem emerges much more slowly: the patient's every word is listened to; every feeling, fantasy, and dream examined; everything is given to and little demanded from her. In the group, however, the patient is expected to share time, to understand, to empathize with and to help other patients, to form relationships, to be concerned with the feelings of others, to receive feedback that may be critical. Often narcissistic patients feel alive when onstage: they judge the group's usefulness to them on the basis of how many minutes of the group's and the therapist's time they have obtained at a meeting. They guard their specialness fiercely and often object when anyone points out similarities between themselves and other members; for the same reason, they also object to being included with the other members in mass group interpretations.

• One patient, Vicky, frequently criticized the group format by commenting on her preference for the one-to-one format. She often supported her position by citing psychoanalytic literature critical of the group therapy approach. She felt bitter at sharing time in the group. For example, one day three-fourths of the way through a meeting, the therapist remarked that he perceived Vicky and John to be under much pressure. They both admitted that they needed and wanted help from the group; after a moment's awkwardness, John gave way, saying he thought his problem could wait till the next session. Vicky consumed the rest of the meeting and, at the following session, continued where she left off. When it appeared that she had every intention of using the entire meeting, one of the members commented that John had been "left hanging" last session. But there was no easy transition since, as the therapist pointed out, only Vicky could release the group and she gave no sign of doing so graciously (Vicky had lapsed into a sulking silence). Nonetheless, the group turned to John, who was in the midst of a major life crisis. John presented his situation, but no good work was done. At the very end of the meeting, Vicky began weeping silently; and the group members, thinking that she wept for John, turned to her. On the contrary, however, she wept, she said, for all the time, which she could have used, that was wasted on John. What Vicky could not appreciate for at least a year in the group was that this type of incident did not support her request for individual therapy—quite the contrary; the fact that such difficulties arose in the group was precisely the reason that the group format was especially indicated for her.

The fact that other members identify with, object to, and block the narcissistic patient's bids for attention frustrates the patient but, at the same time, constitutes a major advantage of the group therapeutic mode for such patients. Furthermore, the group is catalyzed as well: other members profit from having to take assertive stands against the narcissistic patient's bids for attention; and particularly non-assertive members may use aspects of the narcissistic patient's behavior as excellent modeling.

• Another narcissistic patient, Ruth, who sought therapy for her inability to maintain deep relationships, participated in the group in a highly stylized fashion: she insisted on filling the members in every week on the minute details of her life and especially on her relationships to men—her most pressing problem. Many of these details were extraneous, but she was insistent (much like the "watch me" phase of early childhood); aside from "watching her," there seemed no way the group could relate to Ruth without her feeling deeply rejected. She insisted that friendship consisted of sharing intimate details of one's life; yet we learned through a follow-up interview with a member who terminated the group that Ruth frequently called her for social evenings but she could no longer bear to be with Ruth because of her propensity to use friends in the same way one might use an analyst— as an ever-patient, ever-solicitous, ever-listening ear.

Some narcissistic patients who have a deep sense of specialness feel that not only do they deserve maximum group attention but that it should be forthcoming without their expending any effort. They expect the group to care for them, to reach out for them despite the fact that they reach out for no one; they expect gifts, surprises, compliments though they give none; they expect concern though they show none themselves; they expect to be able to express anger and scorn but to remain immune from retaliation; they expect to be loved and admired for simply being there. I have seen this posture especially pronounced in beautiful women who had been beautiful children and who had been praised all their lives simply by virtue of their appearance and their presence.

The lack of awareness of or empathy for others is obvious in the group. After several meetings, members begin to note that although the patient does personal work in the group, she never questions, supports, or assists others. The narcissistic patient may describe her life experiences with great enthusiasm but is a poor listener and grows bored or drowsy when others speak.

• One member felt no hesitation at asking openly for a transfer from the group. After eight months, he had overcome much of his problem with shyness, had learned what the other members thought about him, and now felt that he was reaching a point of diminishing return in the group: for the most part, he had gotten what he could from the other members. This same member gave virtually nothing to the group, not even information about himself; the group often remarked on his parsimoniousness; he did not speak to them, they said, but sent verbal telegrams wasting as few words as possible. The group members honed in on this trait, causing the patient to look deeply at his narcissistic assumptive world. When the group confronted him with the fact that there is only one relationship in life where one individual receives without reciprocating to the other—the mother and the young infant— he was deeply moved and, by way of assent, noted that customarily he would send letters of a few sparse lines to his mother and receive in return several generous pages with sentences overflowing into the margins. This trait carried over to his academic work as well, since he could never write a luxuriant colorful essay; instead, he turned in terse outlines and was bewildered at his instructor's lack of appreciation for his efforts.

In the last chapter, I described, in the long account of Bill and Jan's relationship, many of Bill's narcissistic modes of relating to other people. Much of his failure or inability to view the world from the position of the other was summed up in a statement he made to the "other woman" in the group, Gina, after sixteen months together. He once wistfully said that he regretted that "nothing ever really happened" between them. Gina sharply corrected him: "You mean nothing sexual, but a great deal has happened for me. You tried to seduce me. For once I refused. I didn't fall in love with you, and I didn't go to bed with you. I didn't betray myself or my husband. I learned to know you and to care for you very deeply with all your faults and with all your assets. Is that nothing happening?" Several months after the end of therapy, I asked Bill in a follow-up interview to recall some of the most significant events or turning points in therapy. He described a session late in therapy when the group watched a videotape of the previous session. Bill was stunned to learn that he had completely forgotten most of the session, remembering only those few points in which he was centrally involved. His egocentricity was powerfully brought home to him and affirmed what the group had been trying to tell him for months.

NARCISSISTIC PERSONALITY DISORDER

Thus far I have described problems that arise in a group as a result of narcissistic behavior, and discussed patients with a relatively stable personality structure who manifest narcissistic traits—conceit, selfishness, vanity. But many patients have a more profound personality disturbance, which we refer to as "narcissistic personality disorder." The 1980 American Psychiatric Association *Diagnostic and Statistical Manual of Mental Disorders (DSM–III)* provides descriptive criteria, which include a grandiose sense of self-importance; a preoccupation with fantasies of unlimited success; a requirement for constant attention and admiration; an extreme sensitivity to criticism, indifference, or defeat, which often results in rage, inferiority, shame, or feelings of emptiness; and the presence of at least two of the following disturbances in interpersonal relationships—entitlement, interpersonal exploitativeness, alternation between overidealization and devaluation, and lack of empathy.[20] Otto Kernberg adds that these individuals have a shallow emotional life, derive little enjoyment from life other than tributes received from others, and tend to depreciate those from whom they expect few narcissistic supplies.[21]

The *DSM–III* description of this disorder is an improvement on previous classificatory systems. It officially recognizes the vast numbers of patients who are highly vulnerable, who are neither neurotic nor psychotic but somewhere in between. Yet the category still lacks precision, often serves as a catch-all for personality that clinicians cannot otherwise diagnose, and will, in all likelihood, undergo further transformation in future classificatory systems.[22]

Although, in the psychoanalytic community today, there is considerable debate about the psychodynamics and the developmental origins of the narcissistic personality disturbance,[23] this debate is tangential to group therapy practice. What is important for the group therapist is, as I have stressed throughout this book, not the question—elusive and unanswerable—how one got to be the way one is but rather the nature of the current forces, both conscious and unconscious, that influence the way the narcissistic patient relates to other people.

The major task for the group therapist is not precise analytic diagnosis. Whether the diagnosis be severe narcissistic or borderline personality disorder, the primary issue, which I will address in the next section, is the same: the management of the highly vulnerable patient in the therapy group.

The Borderline Patient[24]

For decades, psychotherapists have known about a large cluster of patients who are unusually difficult to treat and who fall between the major diagnostic criteria of severity of impairment: more disorganized than neurotic patients but more integrated than psychotic patients. Their outward veneer of integration is thin and conceals a chaotic primitive personality structure. Under stress, these borderline patients are highly unstable: they act out through drug and alcohol abuse and many other self-destructive modes; they develop psychoses that resemble schizophrenic psychosis yet are circumscribed, short-lived, and episodic.

In recent years, a great deal more clarity about borderline patients has emerged, thanks especially to the work of Otto Kernberg,[25] who emphasized the overriding instability of the borderline patient—instability of mood, thought, and interpersonal activity; and in 1980, for the first time, the standard classificatory system included a category for these patients. *DSM–III* states that five of these eight criteria must be present to make the diagnosis of borderline personality disorder:

1. Self-destructive impulsivity or unpredictability (for example, substance abuse, shoplifting, overeating, self-mutilation);
2. Unstable and intense interpersonal relationships (for example, idealization, devaluation, manipulation, marked shifts of attitude);
3. Inappropriate intense anger or lack of control of anger;
4. Identity disturbance manifested by uncertainty about such issues as self-image, gender identity, values, career choice, loyalties;
5. Instability of mood (marked shifts from normal mood to depression, irritability or anxiety usually lasting a few hours and only rarely more than a few days;
6. Intolerance of being alone;
7. Physically self-damaging acts (suicidal gestures, recurrent accidents, or physical fights);
8. Chronic feelings of emptiness or boredom.[26]

Not only has there been a recent explosion of interest in the diagnosis, the psychodynamics, and the individual therapy of the borderline patient, but much group therapy literature has also focused upon the vulnerable patient—the individual with a borderline or narcissistic personality disturbance. Group therapists have developed an interest in these patients for two major reasons. First, because borderline patients are difficult to diagnose in a single screening session, many clinicians unintentionally introduce borderline patients into therapy groups consisting of patients functioning at a higher level of integration. Once in the group, the patient poses a severe challenge to the group therapist: the primitive affects and the highly distorted perceptual tendencies of the borderline patient vastly influence the course of group therapy. Second, many therapists have arrived at the conclusion that group therapy (generally with conjunctive individual therapy) is the treatment of choice for the borderline patient.[27] Furthermore, research evidence indicates that borderline patients highly value their group therapy experience—often more than their individual therapy experience.[28]

Keep in mind that many therapists suggest group therapy for borderline patients not because these patients work well or easily in therapy groups but because they are so extraordinarily difficult to treat in individual therapy. Many individual therapists have reported that the borderline patient cannot easily tolerate the intensity and the intimacy of the one-to-one treatment setting. Crippling transference problems—both transference and countertransference—invariably emerge in therapy. Therapists often find it difficult to deal with the demands and the primitive anger of the borderline patient, particularly since the patient so often acts them out (for example, through absence, lateness, drug abuse, or self-mutilation). Massive regression often occurs, and many patients are so threatened by the emergence of painful, primitive affects that they flee therapeutic engagement.

One of the major advantages that a therapy group may have for the treatment of a borderline patient is the powerful reality testing provided by the ongoing stream of feedback and observations from the other group members. Thus, the regression of a patient is far less pronounced; the patient may distort, act out, or express primitive, chaotic needs and fears, but the continuous reminders of reality in the therapy group keep these feelings muted.

• A clinical illustration: Val, a high-level borderline patient was insulting, unempathic, and highly sensitive to even the mildest criticism. In one meeting, she lamented at length that she never received support or compliments from anyone in the group and least of all from the therapists. In fact, she could remember only three positive comments to her in the seventy group meetings she had attended. One member responded immediately and straightforwardly: "Oh, come on, Val, get off it. Last week both of the therapists supported you a whole lot. In fact, you get more stroking in this group than anyone else." Every other member of the group agreed and offered several examples of positive comments that had been given to Val over the last few meetings.

Later in the same meeting, Val responded to two incidents in a highly maladaptive fashion. Two members were locked together in a painful battle over control. Both were shaken and extremely threatened by the degree of anger expressed, both their own and their antagonist's. Many of the other group members offered observations and support. Val's response was that she didn't know what all the commotion was about and that the two were jerks for getting themselves so upset about nothing at all.

Later, in the same meeting, Farrell, a member who had been very concealed and silent, was pressed to reveal more about herself. With considerable resolve, she disclosed, for the first time, intimate details about a relationship she had recently entered into with a man. She disclosed her fear that the relationship would collapse because she desperately wanted children and, once again, had started a relationship with a man who had made it clear that he wanted no children. Many members of the group responded empathically and supportively to her disclosure. Val was silent and, when called upon, stated that she could see Farrell was having a hard time talking about this, but couldn't understand why. It didn't seem like a "big deal" revelation.

The group's response to Val in both of these incidents was immediate and direct. The two people whom she had accused of acting like jerks let her know that they felt put down by her remarks. One commented, "If people talk about some problem that you don't have, then you dismiss it as being unimportant or jerky. Look, I don't have the problems that you have about not getting enough compliments from the therapists or other members of the group. It simply is not an issue for me. How would you feel if I called you a jerk every time you complained about that?" Farrell, the person Val had responded to with "It's no big deal," commented, "Thanks a lot. That really hurts, Val, and makes me want to have nothing to do with you from now on. I'd like to put as much distance as possible between the two of us."

This meeting illustrates several features of group work with a borderline patient. Val was inordinately adversarial and had developed an intense and disabling negative transference in several previous attempts in individual therapy. In this session, she expressed distorted perceptions of the therapists (that they had given her only three compliments in seventy sessions when, in fact, they had been strongly supportive of her). In individual therapy, Val's distortion might have led to a major impasse because her transferential distortions were so marked that she did not trust the therapists to provide an accurate view of reality. The therapy group neatly avoided that impasse: the therapists did not have to serve as champions of reality because several group members assumed that role.

In general, the potential for intense and crippling transference distortions is reduced in the therapy group situation. First, as in this session, other members correct distorted views of the therapist (borderline patients often oscillate between devaluation and idealization of the therapist). Furthermore, the transference opportunity is diluted in the group therapy setting: either the patient may develop less intense feelings toward several individuals in the group or may temporarily rest, withdraw, or disengage in the therapy group setting in a way that is often not possible in the one-to-one format.

Val, like many borderline patients, was inordinately sensitive to criticism. (M. Pines compares the borderline with the hemophiliac patient who bleeds at the slightest injury and lacks the resources to staunch the flow of blood.)[29] The group members were aware that Val was highly vulnerable and tolerated criticism poorly. Yet they did not hesitate to confront her directly and consistently. Although Val was wounded in this meeting, as in so many others, she also heard the larger message that the group members took her seriously and respected her ability to take responsibility for her actions and to change her behavior. I believe that it is crucially important that a group assume this stance toward the vulnerable patient. Once a group begins to ignore, patronize, or mascot a borderline patient, then therapy fails. The group no longer provides reality testing, and the patient assumes the noxious deviant role.

The work ethic of psychotherapy is often more readily apparent in a group. Individual therapy with borderline patients may be marked by the absence of a therapeutic alliance. The patient may be unable or unwilling to use therapy for personal change and, instead, demands gratification or revenge from the therapeutic relationship. The observation of others working in the group and pursuing concrete goals and manifesting changes often supplies an important corrective to the sole exclusive focus on extracting supplies from the therapist.

Borderline patients also profit from the therapeutic factor of *identification*. The group provides the patient with an opportunity to obtain greater distance from the therapist; and from that vantage point, the patient is able to observe and to internalize aspects of the therapist's behavior.[30] For example, patients may note how the therapist listens and supports and then may incorporate the same behavior into their own relationships with other group members or other individuals in their lives.

The borderline patient's core problems lie in the sphere of intimacy, and the therapeutic factor of cohesiveness is often of decisive import. If the patient is able to accept the reality testing offered by the group, and if his or her behavior is not so disruptive as to create a deviant or scapegoat role, then the group may become a postive "holding environment"—an enormously important, supportive refuge from the stresses the patient experiences in everyday life.[31] Once the borderline patient develops trust in the group, she may serve as a major stabilizing influence. Separation anxiety is so great, and the patient is so anxious to preserve the continued presence of important figures in her environment, that she helps to keep the group together: the borderline patient may be the most faithful attender and chide other members for being absent or tardy. The borderline patient's sense of belongingness is augmented by the fact that often she is a great asset to the therapy group. The patient's great access to unconscious needs, fantasies, and fears may loosen up a group and facilitate the therapeutic work—especially the therapy of schizoid, inhibited, constricted individuals.

Keep in mind that the course of group therapy for the borderline patient is never easy. The other group members, the therapist, and the patient are taxed by the work. The duration of therapy is long: there is considerable clinical consensus that borderline patients require many years of therapy, and generally the borderline patient will stay in a group longer than any of the other members. The borderline patient's vulnerability and tendency to distort are so extreme that generally adjunctive individual therapy is required. Many therapists suggest that the most common reason for treatment failure of borderline patients in therapy groups is the omission of adjunctive individual therapy.[32]

Despite the heroic diagnostic efforts of *DSM–III*, the borderline personality disorder does not represent a homogeneous diagnostic category. One borderline patient may be markedly dissimilar from another. The frequently hospitalized chaotic patient is grossly different (and has a very different course of therapy) from the less severely disabled individual with an "unanchored self."[33] Thus, the decision about whether to include a borderline patient in a group depends upon the characteristics of the particular individual being screened rather than upon the broad diagnostic category. The therapist has to assess not only a patient's ability to tolerate the intensity of the therapy group but also the group's ability to tolerate the demands of that particular patient. Most heterogeneous outpatient groups can, at best, tolerate only one or possibly two borderline patients. The major considerations influencing the selection process are the same as those described in chapter 8. It is particularly important to assess the possibility of the patient's becoming a deviant in the group. Rigidity of behavioral patterns, especially those that antagonize other people, should be carefully scrutinized. Patients who are grandiose, contemptuous, and disdainful are unlikely to have a bright future in a group.[34] It is necessary for a patient to have the capacity to tolerate minimal amounts of frustration or criticism without serious acting out. A patient with an erratic work record, a history of transitory relationships, or a history of quickly moving on to a new situation, when slightly frustrated in an old one, is likely to respond in the same way in the therapy group.

14

THE TECHNIQUE
OF THE THERAPIST:
SPECIALIZED FORMATS
AND PROCEDURAL AIDS

The standard group therapy format in which one therapist meets with six to eight patients is often complicated by other factors: the patient may be in concurrent individual therapy; there may be a co-therapist in the group; occasionally the group may meet without the therapist—in fact, many self-help groups operate completely without a therapist being present. I shall discuss these contingencies in this chapter and describe, in addition, some specialized techniques and approaches that, though not essential, may at times facilitate the course of therapy.

Concurrent Individual and Group Therapy

While many different combinations of group and individual therapy may be practiced, no systematic data permit firm conclusions about the effectiveness of any of them. Guidelines must thus be formulated from clinical judgment and from deductive reasoning based on the posited therapeutic factors. My own clinical experience leads me to conclude that concurrent individual therapy is neither necessary nor helpful except in certain instances. If members are selected with a moderate degree of care, a therapy group meeting once or, preferably, twice a week is ample therapy and should benefit the great majority of patients.

If concurrent group and individual therapy are conducted, the optimal combinations in order of my personal preference are: (1) all or some members in concurrent individual therapy with other therapists—"conjoint therapy";[1] (2) all group members in concurrent individual therapy with the group therapists—"combined therapy";[2] (3) some members in concurrent individual therapy with group therapist.

The realities of clinical practice are such that the ideal format for a patient is not always ideal or even feasible for a therapist. Psychotherapists in solo private practice generally must form their groups from the ranks of their individual patients, some or most of whom continue in individual therapy. Large, busy clinics, however, are more likely to offer group therapy without concurrent individual therapy. (In fact, budgetary concerns have prompted some state mental health agencies to decree such a therapy format.)

Some patients may go through a severe life crisis that requires considerable individual temporary support in addition to group therapy. Occasionally individual therapy is required in order to enable a patient to use the group: a patient may be so fragile or blocked by anxiety or fearful of aggression as to be unable to participate effectively in the group therapeutic process. Active intervention may be necessary to escort a patient into a therapeutic position in the group and prevent him or her from becoming locked into a cramped role and, as some studies suggest,[3] from having an unrewarding or injurious group therapy experience. Not infrequently individual therapy is required to prevent a patient from dropping out of the group.

- For example, Ginny,* a young borderline patient participating in her first group, was considerably threatened by the first few meetings. She had felt increasingly alienated because her bizarre fantasy and dream world seemed so far from the experience of the other members. In the fourth meeting, she attacked one of the members and was, in turn, attacked. For several nights thereafter, she had terrifying nightmares: for example, (1) her mouth turning to blood (which appeared related to her fear of being verbally aggressive because of her world-destructive fantasies); (2) walking along the beach and being engulfed by a huge wave (related to her fear of losing her boundaries and identity in the group); and (3) being picked up and then held down by several

---

*This is Ginny Elkin (pseudonym), with whom I wrote *Every Day Gets a Little Closer* (Basic Books, 1975).

men while the therapist performed an operation on her brain—his hands being, however, guided by the men holding her down (obviously related to her fears of therapy and of the therapist's being overpowered by the members).

Her hold on reality grew more tenuous, and it seemed unlikely that she could continue in the group without added support. Concurrent individual therapy with another therapist was arranged; it enabled her to remain in the group and to derive much support therefrom.

• Another clinical example: Mr. A was referred to a group by an analyst who had treated him for six years and was now terminating analysis.[4] Despite considerable improvement, Mr. A still had not mastered the symptom for which he had originally sought treatment—fear of women. He found it difficult even to dictate to his secretary. In one of his first meetings, his difficulty became evident: he was made extremely uncomfortable by a woman in the group who complimented him. He stared at the floor for the rest of the session and, after the session, called his analyst to state that he wanted to drop out of the group and re-enter analysis. His analyst discussed the situation with the group therapist and agreed to resume individual treatment on the condition that Mr. A return to the group as well. For the next few months, they had an individual hour after each group session. The individual therapist and the group therapist had frequent consultations, and the group therapist was able to modulate the noxious stimuli in the group sufficiently to allow Mr. A to continue in therapy. Within a few months, he was able to reach out emotionally to women for the first time and gradually grew more at ease with women in the real world.

There are times when it is helpful to supplement ongoing individual therapy with group therapy.[5] For example, some patients in individual therapy are arid and unable to produce the material necessary for productive work. Often the rich affective interpersonal interaction of the group is marvelously evocative and generates ample data for both individual and group work. Other patients may improve in behavior in the individual therapy hour yet be unable to transfer the learning to outside life. The group setting may serve as a valuable way station permitting patients to experiment with new behavior in a protected low-risk environment. New material may be generated with the disconfirmation of a patient's fantasies of the calamitous consequences that might follow new behavior, and gradually the patient becomes able to transfer to outside life what he or she has learned. Sometimes in individual therapy severe unreconcilable problems in the transference and countertransference arise; the therapy group, as I discussed in the section on borderline patients in the previous chapter, may be particularly helpful in diluting transference and facilitating reality testing.

Concurrent individual therapy can complicate life in the therapy group in several ways. When there is a marked difference in the basic approach of the individual therapist and group therapist, the two therapies may work at cross-purposes. If, for example, the individual approach is oriented toward understanding genetic causality and delves deeply into past experiences while the group focuses primarily on here-and-now material, the patient is likely to become confused and to judge one approach on the basis of the other. Generally, patients beginning group therapy are discouraged and frustrated by the initial group meetings, which offer less support than their individual therapy hours, where their narcissistic needs are gratified by the therapist's exclusive attention and by the exploration of the minute details of their past and present life, dreams, and fantasies. Sometimes such patients, when attacked or stressed by the group, may defend themselves by unfavorably comparing their group to their individual experience; such an attack on the group invariably results in further attacks on the individual and further deterioration of the situation. Later in therapy, patients often reverse their comparative evaluations of the two modes.

Another complication of concurrent therapy arises when patients use individual therapy to drain off affect from the group. The patient may interact like a sponge in the group, taking in feedback and reacting to it in the safer domain of the individual therapy hour. One common form of resistance inherent in this pattern is the altruistic rationalization: "I will allow the others to have the group time since I have my own hour." When this pattern is pronounced, the group therapist, in collaboration with the individual therapist, may insist that either the group or the individual therapy be terminated. I have known several patients whose involvement in the group dramatically accelerated when their concurrent individual therapy was stopped.

If two conditions are met, the individual and the group therapeutic approaches may complement each other. First, the individual and the group therapist must be in frequent communication with each other, and the patient must be made aware that the individual and the group therapist will share all information. Second, the individual therapy must complement the group approach by being itself here-and-now oriented and by devoting time to explore, in depth, a patient's feelings toward the group members and toward incidents and themes of current meetings. Such an exploration can serve as rehearsal for further involvement in the life of the group. The patient is often able to examine an uncomfortable, turbulent relationship in the individual setting long before being able to confront the issue in the group. The individual therapist also can with great profit focus on transfer of learning, on helping the patient apply what he or she has learned in the group to new situations —for example, to the patient's relationship with the individual therapist as well as to important figures in outside life. It is obvious, too, that each therapist must avoid undermining the other therapy format. An effort by the individual therapist to explore the group experience in the individual therapy hour is viewed by the patient as a vote of confidence in the group.

Some potential complications of concurrent therapy can be avoided if the group therapist serves also as the individual therapist. For one thing, the therapist has control over the type of individual therapy conducted. Furthermore, a group in which all members are in concurrent individual therapy with the group leader is generally stable, with few dropouts. This format, however, has its own inherent complications. Some therapists become confused about confidentiality: it becomes increasingly difficult to remember who said what in which setting. Can the therapist repeat in the group intimate material that was revealed in an individual session? Or couch a remark in vague language identifiable only by the one patient? As a general rule, it is ill advised to make any contract of confidentiality regarding the individual sessions; the therapist should retain the privilege of bringing up any individual material in the group, according to his or her professional judgment. If important material from individual therapy (regardless of whether the patient be in conjoint or combined therapy) is kept secret from the group, therapy is often sabotaged, and the patient's conviction reinforced that he or she is unspeakably unacceptable.[6] Some therapists feel so strongly about this point that they obtain in writing the patient's permission for the group and the individual therapist to share information.

I shall discuss co-therapists in the next section. For now, I wish to point out that the complexities are compounded if two therapists lead a group, and some patients see one therapist individually, some another, and some neither. If special exclusive relationships exist, and if group material is removed from the purview of the group, then the group is rendered less potent and effective.

At times factionalism and sibling rivalry are pronounced in a group whose members see the leader in concurrent individual therapy; intermember resentment may be particularly extreme if some of the mem-

concurrent therapy because they cannot afford the fee.

it may be necessary for the therapist to see a group mem-
in crisis for a few individual sessions: for example, patients
severely troubled by a loss (such as death, separation, or di-
or by some other major environmental stress (such as academic
or, failure). Sometimes individual sessions are indicated for a patient
on the verge of dropping out of the group. The individual attention a
patient receives in these instances rarely arouses resentment from
other members, particularly if they have shared in the decision that
extra help is needed at this time.

Combined group and individual therapy may present special problems for neophyte group therapists. Some find it difficult to see the same
patient in two formats since they customarily assume a different role in
the two types of therapy: in group, a therapist tends to be informal,
open, and actively engaged with patients; in individual therapy, the
therapist, unfortunately, tends to remain impersonal and distant. Often
therapists in training prefer that patients have a "pure" treatment
experience—that is, that patients be solely in group therapy without
any concurrent individual therapy with themselves or other therapists
—in order to discover for themselves what to expect from each type of
therapy.

Co-Therapists

Some group therapists choose to meet alone with a group, but the great
majority prefer to work with a co-therapist.[7] No research has been
conducted to determine the relative efficacy of the two methods, and
clinicians differ in their opinions.[8] My clinical experience has taught me
that the co-therapy approach may have special advantages but potential hazards as well.

First, consider the advantages. Co-therapists complement and support one another. Together their cognitive and observational range is
greater: their two points of view generate more hunches and more
strategies. When one therapist, for example, is intensively involved
with one member, the co-therapist may be far more aware of the remaining members' responses to the interchange.

Together, co-therapists broaden the possible range of tranferential
reactions. Moreover, the nature and degree of the transference-based
distortions become more evident because patients will differ among

themselves in their reactions to each of the co-therapists and to the co-therapists' relationship.

Most co-therapy teams deliberately or, more often, unwittingly split roles: one therapist assumes a provocative role—much like a Socratic gadfly—while the other is supportive and serves as a harmonizer in the group.[9] When the co-therapists are male and female, the roles are usually (but not invariably) assumed accordingly. There is much agreement among clinicians that a male-female co-therapist team may have unique advantages: the image of the group as the primary family may be more strongly evoked; among the group members, many fantasies and misconceptions about the relationship between the two therapists arise and may, with profit, be explored.[10] Many patients may benefit from the model setting of a male-female pair working together with mutual respect and without the destructive competition, mutual derogation, exploitation, or pervasive sexuality that they too often associate with male-female pairings.

From my observations of over eighty therapy groups led by neophyte therapists, I consider the co-therapy format to have special advantages for the beginning therapist. For one thing, the presence of a co-therapist lessens initial anxiety and permits the therapist greater equanimity and objectivity in his or her efforts to understand the meeting. In the post-meeting rehash, the co-therapists can provide valuable feedback about each other's behavior. Until therapists obtain sufficient experience to be reasonably clear of their own self-presentation in the group, this co-therapist feedback is vital in enabling therapists to differentiate what is real and what is transference distortion in patients' perceptions. The presence of a co-therapist often increases the usefulness of the supervisory session (see chapter 17). Often, much professional and personal growth is generated by the co-therapists (often with the supervisor's aid) working through their relationship with one another.

It is especially difficult for beginning therapists to maintain objectivity in the face of massive group pressure. For example, the members of one group unanimously prescribed for one young male member that he take advantage of several available casual sexual opportunities in an effort to work through his sexual timidity. In actuality, the advice was destructive for the patient, who was, with great difficulty, working on his relationship to his new wife. Unable to oppose the group current, however, the therapist found himself agreeing with the group's advice to the patient—advice that would have been unthinkable were he seeing the patient in individual therapy. Group decisions are often intemperate (a phenomenon known to social psychologists as the "risky shift"), and the presence of a co-leader may be a necessary stabilizer for the inexperienced therapist.

One of the more unpleasant and difficult chores for the neophyte therapist is to weather a group attack upon oneself and to help the group make constructive use of it. When you are under the gun, you may be too threatened either to clarify the attack or to encourage further attack without appearing defensive or condescending. There is nothing more squelching than an individual, under fire, saying, "It's really great that you're attacking me. Keep it going!" A co-therapist may prove invaluable here: he or she may help the members continue to express their anger at the other therapist and ultimately to examine the source and meaning of that anger.

A father-son co-therapy team has been described with interesting results.[11] The therapists concluded that the presence of a parent and a son working together harmoniously was a living demonstration to the patients of the successful resolution of parent-child conflicts. Patients at first distorted and misperceived the relationship in several ways: they interpreted benign remarks by the father as criticism or attacks on the son; they refused to believe that the son made independent interpretations in the group; they felt that he had to "clear" them first with his father. By working through such issues, the members were helped to understand their own relationship with parents and parental imagos.

Whether co-therapists should openly express disagreement during a group session is an issue of some controversy. I have generally found co-therapist disagreement unhelpful to the group in the first few meetings; at that point, the group is too unstable and not yet cohesive enough to tolerate such divisiveness in leadership. Later, however, therapist disagreement may contribute greatly to therapy. In one study, I asked twenty patients who had concluded long-term group therapy about the effects of therapist disagreement on the course of the group and on their own therapy.[12] The patients were unanimous in their judgment that it was beneficial. It was a model-setting experience for some patients: they observed individuals whom they respected disagree openly and resolve their differences with dignity and tact. Other patients found it most useful in working through some of their feelings about authority figures: they witnessed the therapists make mistakes, differ with their colleagues, and experience discomfort, without permanently harming themselves. In short, the therapists are experienced as humans who, despite their imperfections, are genuinely attempting to help the patients. Such a humanization process is inimical to irrational stereotyping, and patients learn to differentiate others according to their individual attributes rather than their roles.

Some patients were made uncomfortable by co-therapists' disagreement and likened it to witnessing parental conflict; nonetheless, it strengthened the honesty and the potency of the group. I have observed many stagnant groups spring into life when the two therapists differentiated themselves as individuals.

The disadvantages of the co-therapy format flow from problems in the co-therapy relationship. It is important that the co-leaders feel comfortable and open with one another. They must learn to exploit one another's strengths: one may be more able to nurture and support; the other, more able to confront and to tolerate anger. If the co-leaders are competitive, and each pursues his or her own star interpretations rather than supports a line of inquiry the other has begun, then the group will be distracted and unsettled.

It is important that therapists speak the same professional language. A survey of forty-two co-therapy teams revealed that the most common source of co-therapy dissatisfaction was differing theoretical orientation.[13] Some training programs have utilized an apprenticeship format in which a neophyte therapist participates as a junior therapist in a group led by a senior clinician. This status differential results in tension and lack of clarity about the leadership role if the relationship between the therapists is not made explicit. If two therapists of markedly different levels of experience do co-lead a group, it is important that each be mature, comfortable with each other, and comfortable in their roles as co-workers and as teacher and apprentice. The senior leader teaches by modeling and by encouraging a co-leader to participate in every way possible. The student strives to avoid destructive competition as well as obsequious nonassertiveness.

It follows, then, that the choice of co-leader is an important step and not to be taken lightly. I have seen many classes of psychiatric residents choose co-leaders and have had the opportunity to follow the progress of these groups. I am convinced that the ultimate success or failure of a group depends to a large part upon the correctness of that choice. If the co-leaders are uncomfortable with each other or are closed, competitive, or in wide disagreement about style and strategy (and if these differences are not resolvable in supervision), there is little likelihood that their group can develop into an effective work group. Consultants or supervisors called in to assist with a group that is not progressing satisfactorily can often offer the greatest service by directing their attention to the relationship between co-therapists. (I shall discuss this fully in chapter 17.)

Co-therapist choice should not be made blindly: do not agree to co-lead a group with someone you do not know well. Do not make the choice on an inability to say no to an invitation: it is far too important and too binding a relationship.* If the therapists are themselves in an experiential group, they have an ideal opportunity to see one another's group behavior, and I suggest to my students that they delay decisions about co-therapists until after such a group. You do well to select a co-leader toward whom you feel close but who is dissimilar to yourself: such complementarity enriches the experience of the group. There are, as I discussed, advantages in a male-female team, but you do far better to lead a group with someone compatible of the same sex than with a colleague of the opposite sex with whom you do not work well. Husbands and wives frequently co-lead a marital couples group (generally of short term and focused on improvement of dyadic relationships); co-leadership, however, of a long-term singles group requires an unusually mature and stable marital relationship. I advise therapists who are involved with each other in a newly formed intense relationship, romantic or otherwise, not to lead a group together; it is advisable to wait until the relationship has developed stability and permanence. Two former lovers, now estranged, do not a good co-therapy team make.

Splitting is a phenomenon that often occurs in groups led by co-therapists. Some patients respond to their feelings of impotence and helplessness in the presence of adults by attempting to split the therapists, in much the same way as they may have, in their primary family, attempted to split their parents. They may attempt in a variety of ways to undermine the therapists' interrelationship and to intrude between them. Some patients are quite perceptive about tensions in the co-therapists' relationship and will, in a destructive fashion, play upon these tensions. For example, if a senior therapist feels threatened by a younger co-therapist, a member might be marvelously influenced by anything the younger therapist said and untouched by the contributions of the older, regardless of the content of their offerings. Such a

---

*In Evelyn Waugh's *Brideshead Revisited*, the protagonist, on departing for his first year of college, is counseled by his father that if he were not circumspect, he would have to devote a considerable part of his second year at college to getting rid of undesirable friends he had made during his first year.[14]

process should be noted and interpreted; it is an indication of highly conflicted attitudes toward authority images.

Some groups become split into two factions, with each co-therapist having a "team" of patients with whom he or she has a special relationship. Sometimes this split has its genesis in the relationship that the therapist and those patients established before the onset of the group, in prior individual therapy or in consultation. (For this reason, it is advisable that both therapists interview a patient, preferably simultaneously, in the pre-group screening. I have noted patients who have continued to feel a special bond throughout their entire group therapy course with the member of the co-therapy team who first interviewed them.) Other patients align themselves with one therapist because of his or her personal characteristics, or because they feel a particular therapist is more intelligent, more senior, more sexually attractive than the other therapist or more ethnically or personally similar to them. Whatever the reasons for the subgrouping, the process should be noted and openly discussed.

One essential ingredient of a good co-therapy team is discussion time. Co-therapists must set aside time to talk together. At the very least, they need a few minutes before a meeting (to talk about the last session and to examine possible agendas for that day's meeting) and fifteen to twenty minutes at the end to debrief and to share their reflections about each other's behavior. If the group is supervised, it is imperative that both therapists attend the supervisory session.

The Leaderless Group

Leaderless groups have been used in group psychotherapy in two major forms: (1) the occasional or regularly scheduled leaderless meeting that serves as an adjunct to traditional therapist-led therapy groups; and (2) the self-directed group—a group that meets for its entire lifespan without a designated leader.

THE LEADERLESS MEETING

In 1949 Alexander Wolf, a pioneer in the development of group therapy, first suggested the use of regularly scheduled "alternate" meetings without a therapist.[15] His groups, which met three times weekly, were asked to meet an additional two or three times without him at one of the members' homes. Since then, other therapists have reported the use of alternate meetings in a variety of temporal arrangements: some suggest two therapist-led meetings and one alternate meeting weekly; whereas others, myself included, prefer only an occasional leaderless meeting. Although some therapists have spoken out vociferously against the leaderless meeting, describing the chaotic acting out and disruption that may ensue,[16] the general clinical consensus is that such fears are unfounded. Over the last decade, there has been a decrease of interest in leaderless meetings.[17] Few articles on the subject have appeared, and I have learned from informal surveys that few contemporary clinicians use regularly scheduled leaderless meetings in their practice.

Even though we cannot be certain about the efficacy of the alternate meeting in the overall course of therapy, there is little doubt that the events and reactions surrounding it have important implications for the understanding of the dynamics of the member-leader relationship. Members generally do not initially welcome the suggestion of the leaderless meeting: it evokes many unrealistic fears and consequences of the therapist's absence. In one study, I asked a series of patients who had been in group therapy for at least eight months, "What would have happened in the group if the group therapists were absent?"[18] (This is another way of asking what function the group therapists perform in the group.) The replies were varied. Although a few patients stated that they would have welcomed leaderless meetings, most of the others expressed, in order of frequency, these general concerns:

1. *The group would stray from the primary task.* A cocktail hour atmosphere would occur, problems would be avoided, long silences would transpire, the discussions would become increasingly irrelevant. "We would end up in left field without the doctor to keep us on the track!" "I could never express my antagonisms without the therapist's encouragement." "We need him there to keep things stirred up." "Who else would bring in the silent members?" "Who would make the rules? We'd spend the entire meeting simply trying to make rules."

2. *The group would lose control of its emotions.* Anger would be unrestrained, and there would be no one available either to rescue the damaged members or to help the aggressive ones maintain control.

3. *The group would be unable to integrate its experiences and to make constructive use of them.* "The therapist is the one who keeps track of loose ends and makes connections for us." "She helps clear the air by pointing out where the group is at a certain time." The therapist was viewed by the members as the "time binder"—the group historian who sees patterns of behavior longitudinally and points out that what a mem-

ber did today, last week, and last month fits into a coherent pattern. The members were saying in effect that, however great the action and involvement without the therapist, they would be unable to make use of it.

Many of the members' concerns are clearly unrealistic and reflect an infantile, dependent posture. It is for this very reason that a leaderless meeting may play an important role in the therapy process. The members are helped to experience themselves as autonomous, responsible, and resourceful adults who, though they may profit from the therapist's expertise, are nevertheless able to control their emotions, to pursue the primary task of the group, and to integrate their experience. In a sense, the rationale is identical to that underlying the therapeutic community. M. Jones,[19] D. Daniels,[20] and many other clinicians have pointed out that not only does the traditional authority-bound mental hospital fail to counteract feelings of helplessness and inadequacy on the part of hospitalized patients but its authoritarian total-care structure reinforces these very features. Thus, it is reasoned, a new patient-directed intentional social system, which encourages patients' personal growth and decision-making capacity, must be constructed.

If the leaderless meeting is to be a constructive experience, it is important that the patients' unrealistic predictions about their own helplessness are not realized. Proper timing is important: before suggesting that alternate meetings be considered, the therapist must be certain that the therapy group has developed cohesiveness and established productive norms.

The leaderless meeting not only fosters a sense of autonomy and responsibility but has several other advantages. Issues arise in the alternate meetings which yield important insights about each patient's relation to the therapist(s). Some patients feel liberated and are far more active and uninhibited in the absence of the therapist; others are, for the first time, able to express critical feelings toward him or her; still others display their contempt for their peers (and thus their self-contempt) by refusing to participate on the grounds that all benefit emanates solely from the therapist.*

Although many therapists fear that intense sexual acting out will occur in leaderless meetings, experience has shown this fear to be

---

*The alternate meeting becomes divisive if some members do not attend. A patient's steadfast refusal to come to leaderless meetings is a significant matter and deserves much attention in the group. If this matter cannot be resolved, and if the therapist is firmly committed to the group's holding alternate meetings, he or she should consider transferring the patient to another group; the patient has a poor chance for improvement in a group to which he or she is only partially committed.

unfounded. However, it is common for groups to assume a more playful (often sexually tinged) character in the absence of the leader. The transformation is often startlingly abrupt; no sooner does the teacher leave the room than the class erupts into unrestrained, mirthful play. One group planned a party on a nearby nude beach; another discussed a nude swimming party; another (a group of alcoholics) talked about a marijuana party; another burlesqued the mannerisms, beard, and careful carelessness of the therapist's grooming and clothing.

In assessing the possible hazards of leaderless meetings, keep in mind the distinction between acting and acting out. *Acting out* is, by definition, a resistance to therapy; it is action concealed from the group's analytic eye; patients discharge through action those impulses that should be discussed and examined in therapy. *Acting* is far different. As Lieberman states, "For acting read trying out, reality testing, practice, and the distinction becomes clear."[21] All change must be preceded by action; and all action in therapy meetings that is available for the group's analytic scrutiny may be useful in the process of change. "Rightly understood and accepted, all experiences are good and the bitter ones best of all."[22]

The way in which a group chooses to communicate to the therapist the events of the alternate meeting is often of great interest. Do the members attempt to conceal or distort information, or do they compulsively brief the therapist on all details? Sometimes the ability of a group to withhold information from the therapist is in itself an encouraging sign of group maturation, although therapists are usually uncomfortable at being excluded. In the group, as in the family, not only must one strive for autonomy but the leader must be willing to allow one to do so. Often the leaderless session and subsequent events allow the therapist to experience and understand his or her own desires for control and feelings of being threatened as patients become less dependent.

SELF-DIRECTED GROUPS

The alternate session has two primary goals: to increase the group's and the members' sense of personal responsibility and autonomy and to hasten the emergence of several important themes for subsequent working through with the therapist's help. The self-directed group operates on another principle: the primary healing forces are inherent in the group and may be evoked and harnessed without the presence of a formal leader. In part, the self-directed group has sprung into being

426

as a result of the shortage of professional manpower; in part, it is a reflection of a humanistic trend that decries the need for an authority structure perceived as restrictive and growth-inhibiting.

Although no formal inventory of self-directed groups exists, there is no doubt that it is a movement of considerable magnitude. Approximately 250 national organizations sponsor self-help groups; and perhaps 10 million Americans have been members of such groups.[23] Alcoholics Anonymous, for example, has an enormous membership with chapters meeting in virtually every major city of the world. Other well-known groups include TOPS and Weight Watchers, Grow Groups, Schizophrenics Anonymous, Neurotic Anonymous, Recovery, Inc. (mental illness), Mended Hearts (heart surgery patients), Compassionate Friends (bereaved parents), NAIM and THEOS (widows), and women's consciousness-raising groups.

Self-directed groups are a heterogeneous lot; few are, in actuality, leaderless but rely instead on leaders drawn from the ranks of former members—for example, Alcoholics Anonymous and Recovery, Inc. Some may remain nominally leaderless, such as a self-led group of mental health professionals or a women's consciousness-raising group, but yet be guided by a natural leader who has emerged from the ranks.

Outcome evaluation of these groups is still in its infancy. In well-designed studies, Lieberman has demonstrated that self-help groups of widows (Theos) and of heart surgery patients (Mended Hearts) produce significant improvement in members on many mental health indices of depression, well-being, self-esteem, and life satisfaction.[24]

One of the more interesting action-research ventures into the self-directed group field was conducted by B. Berzon and her associates, who developed a series of audio tapes which provide guidance to self-directed personal growth groups.[25] These tapes were designed to help the group members accomplish certain goals: to encourage participation, to focus attention on the here-and-now, and to encourage helping behavior.

In Berzon's work leaders are eliminated and their functions built in artificially, using ingenious techniques. For example, in a ten-session program, three basic stages were proposed: (1) group building (first four sessions); (2) intensification of feelings (fifth through ninth sessions); and (3) separation (last session).[26] A task was designated and an exercise assigned, via an audio tape, for each session according to the principles of group development. Following each exercise, the group members spent the remainder of the time discussing their reactions to it.

Berzon has reported on several evaluative studies of versions of this program. These studies indicate that members of self-directed therapy groups become more interpersonally sensitive, self-accepting, and self-reliant than do no-treatment controls. One study compared seventy-five subjects in self-directed groups to forty-four comparable subjects who had no group experience.[27] Self-concept (measured by a semantic differential rating scale) was significantly higher, at the end of the ten meetings, in the group members than in the controls after a comparable period of time.[28] No change occurred on the other measure, "personal efficacy" (a five-item forced-choice instrument).[29] A study comparing a professionally led, self-directed group (an eighteen-session programmed protocol) and a control sample demonstrated that both professionally directed and self-directed groups showed positive change on self-concept and on global adjustment ratings, but that the changes in the professionally directed groups were more marked and durable.[30]

Lieberman, Yalom, and Miles studied the outcome of a ten-session leaderless, programmed encounter group of normal college students.[31] In the entire project, seventeen groups were studied, fifteen led by leaders of varying ideological schools (see chapter 16) and two groups led by the "Encounter Tape Program." Of the twenty-two members who began these two leaderless groups, one dropped out, one had a negative outcome, thirteen (60 percent) were unchanged, five (22.5 percent) had a positive outcome, and two (9 percent) a very positive outcome. Although these are, at best, modest results and unacceptable outcomes for most group therapists, the two groups nevertheless compared favorably to many leader-led groups in the project. (Their six months' follow-up placed the two groups third and eighth most effective of the seventeen groups.) Keep in mind, however, that these were short-term (thirty hours total) groups of nonpatients; the extrapolation of these results to therapy group outcome is difficult.

My impression of the two groups from my observation of the meetings and interviews with the members was that they were safe, supportive, low-key groups. The type of learning available was highly selective in that little opportunity existed for investigation of attitudes toward either conflict or authority. For example, in one meeting, a woman member grew very angry at another member and, weeping, ran out of the meeting. Next week she returned, but the tape provided another agenda for that meeting, and the incident was permanently buried. There was no leader present to bring the group back to the issue; no one took the responsibility of ensuring that the group not only resolved the conflict but also learned from it.

Dreams

The number and types of dreams that patients bring to therapy is largely a function of the therapist's behavior. Your response to the first dreams presented by patients will influence the choice of dreams subsequently presented. The intensive, detailed, personalized investigation of dreams practiced in analytically oriented individual therapy is hardly feasible in group therapy. For groups meeting once or twice weekly, such a practice demands that a disproportionate amount of time be spent on one patient; the process is, furthermore, minimally useful to the remaining members who become mere bystanders.

What useful role, then, can dreams play in group therapy? In individual analysis or analytically oriented treatment, therapists are usually presented with many dreams and dream fragments. They never strive for complete analysis of all dreams (Freud always held that a total dream analysis should be a research, not a therapeutic, endeavor) but, instead, elect to work on dreams or aspects of dreams that seem pertinent to the current phase of therapy. Therapists may ignore some dreams and may ask for extensive associations to others.

Generally, individual therapists will use dreams to explore the current theme in therapy: for example, if a male patient who is currently working on concerns about his sexual identity brings in a dream with male-female doubles as well as a heavily disguised patricidal theme, the therapist will generally select the former theme for work and ignore or postpone the second theme for later work. Moreover, the process is self-reinforcing. It is well known that patients who are deeply involved in therapy dream or remember dreams compliantly: that is, they produce dreams that corroborate the current thrust of therapy and reinforce the theoretical framework of the therapist ("tag along" dreams, Freud termed them).

Substitute "group work" for "individual work," and the group therapist may use dreams in precisely the same fashion. The investigation of certain dreams accelerates group therapeutic work. Most valuable are group dreams—dreams that involve the group as an entity—or dreams that reflect the dreamer's feelings toward one or more members of the group. Either of these types may elucidate not only the dreamer's but other members' concerns which until then have not become fully conscious. Some dreams may introduce, in disguised form, material that is conscious but that members have, for various reasons, been reluctant to discuss in the group. In either case, the dream may be used in the service of a primary task of the group: to explore the here-and-now interpersonal relationships of the group members.

Some illustrative examples of members' dreams in group therapy may clarify these points:

- In the sixth meeting of a group, a woman patient related a dream fragment: "We [the group] are in a strange large room. We are expected to undress. Everyone else takes off their clothes. I am afraid and run out of the room."

In discussing her dream, the patient, who had until then been an almost completely silent member, spoke of her great fears of self-disclosure and her feeling that once she began to participate in the group in any manner she would be humiliated by being forced to disrobe completely. As the group encouraged her to explore her fear more deeply, she spoke of her particular dread of one of the co-therapists and one of the dominant members of the group; she dreaded, especially, their disapprobation of her current extramarital sexual activities. The dream thus enabled her both to enter the group and to forewarn the group about her great sensitivity and vulnerability to criticism.

- At the twentieth meeting, a woman patient related this dream: "I am walking with my younger sister. As we walk she grows smaller and smaller. Finally I have to carry her. We arrive at the group room where the members are sitting around drinking tea. I have to show the group my sister. By this time she is so small she is in a package. I unwrap the package but all that is left of her is a tiny bronze head."

The investigation of this dream clarified several previously unconscious concerns of the patient. The dreamer had been extraordinarily lonely and had immediately become deeply involved in the group; in fact, it represented her only important social world. At the same time, however, she feared her intense dependence on the group; it had become too important to her. She modified herself rapidly to meet group expectations and, in so doing, lost sight of her own needs and identity. The rapidly shrinking sister symbolized herself becoming more infantile, more undifferentiated, and finally inanimate as she immolated herself in a frantic quest for the group's approval. Some of the manifest content of the dream becomes clearer through a consideration of the content of the meeting preceding the dream: the group had spent considerable time discussing her body—she was moderately obese; and finally another woman member had offered her a diet she had recently seen in a magazine. Thus her concerns about losing her personal identity took the dream form of shrinking in size.

- Shortly afterward in the same group, a male patient brought in

430

this dream fragment: "I bring my sister in to meet the group. She is beautiful and I want to show her off to the members."

This patient had had many dreams involving family members, all of whom had died at Auschwitz, but he had never before had a dream involving the group. His Don Juan style of life had for many years served to bolster his self-esteem by enabling him to possess beautiful women whom other men would desire. The dream helped to uncover these dynamics as they operated in the microcosm of the group. He dreamed of eliciting respect and admiration from the members by showing off his possession, his beautiful (but dead) sister; behind this desire was the conviction that he had little intrinsic personal substance for which other members would value him.

• The following dream illustrates how the therapist may shift the material and selectively focus on those aspects which further the group work: "My husband locks me out of our grocery store. I am very concerned about the perishables spoiling. He gets a job in another store, where he is busy cleaning out the garbage. He is smiling and enjoying this, though it is clear he is being a fool. There is a young, attractive clerk there who winks at me, and we go out dancing together."

This patient was the middle-aged woman who was introduced into a younger group in which two members, Jan and Bill (see chapter 13), were involved in a sexual relationship. From the standpoint of her personal dynamics, the dream was highly meaningful. Her husband, distant and work-oriented, locked her out of his life; she had a strong feeling of her life slipping by unused (perishables spoiling). She had referred to her own sexual fantasies as "garbage"; she felt considerable anger toward her husband to which she could not give vent (in the dream she made an absurd figure of him). Yet the therapist chose to refrain from sampling these tempting dream morsels and, instead, focused on the group-relevant themes. She had many concerns about being excluded from the group; she felt older, less attractive, and very isolated from the other members. Accordingly, the therapist focused on the theme of being "locked out" and on her desire for more attention from the men in the group (one of whom resembled the clerk who takes her dancing at the end of the dream).

• The following is an example of a dream that clarifies a previously undisclosed fact of a patient's interpersonal behavior: A female patient dreamed: "I go to a dance recital given by Fern [one of the members]. Jim is there. I go over to him at intermission and ask him where he is sitting. He stammers and hesitates so that I grow uncomfortable and run away."

Jim, a homosexual, responded to this dream by commenting on its prescience: if he were to see any members of the group at a social event, he would be so ashamed of their meeting any of his gay friends that he would go to any lengths to avoid encountering the group members. The other member's dream thus enabled Jim to plunge into the crucial issue of his shame and his need to conceal himself continually from the straight world.

The following three dreams illustrate how conscious but avoided material may, through dreams, be brought into the group for examination.

• "There are two rooms side by side with a mirror in my house. I feel there is a burglar in the next room. I think I can pull the curtain back and see a person in a black mask stealing my possessions."

This dream was brought in at the twentieth meeting of a therapy group which was observed through a one-way mirror by the therapist's students. Aside from a few comments in the first meeting, the group members had never voiced and explored their feelings about the observers. A discussion of the dream led the group into a valuable discussion of the therapist's relationship to the group and to his students. Were the observers "stealing" something from the group? Was the therapist's primary allegiance toward his students, and were the group members merely a means of presenting a good show or demonstration for them?

It was session time. The session took place in a big blue bathroom like the therapist's. We all sat down around the bathtub, in a circle, with our feet in the water. We all had our shoes on, so the water in the bathtub became very dirty. The faucet was opened to clean up the water. Someone suggested that we should take our shoes off. Some agreed with this, but others did not. I was ashamed because my feet are ugly, so I had to agree with those who wanted to keep their shoes on. To solve the problem, someone brought some wooden mats to put under our feet, but there were too few mats and we began to argue and quarrel. At this moment, I woke up full of anguish.[32]

The group listened to this dream and reported that, following the previous meeting, four of the seven members had gone to a bar and formed two heterosexual couples. To them the bathtub represented the group, in which they deposited their dirty feelings. Later in the session, one of the members mentioned that he could never profit from the sessions because whenever he talked, someone always interrupted him. The group then began to argue about how various members usurped the others' time, and several illustrative episodes from recent meetings were recalled. The dream image of the members fighting for the few wooden mats of the therapist brought to light long-smoldering feelings of rivalry and competition for the therapist's attention.

• A patient in another group presented a similar dream fragment: "The whole group is sitting around the bathtub washing their feet. The dirt slowly goes down the drain."

This was the group that, two sessions previously, had expelled Valerie (see chapter 2) because she had, by breaking the rule of confidentiality, become exceedingly disruptive to the group. The meeting immediately prior to the dream was a breast-beating session in which all members, including the therapists, had felt extraordinarily guilty at expelling her. The dream, by its stark and cruel symbolism—"washing the dirt out of the group"—reminded the members not to become overwhelmed by guilt: there had been a very valid reason for their drastic action.

FANTASY

Waking dreams or fantasies may play an important role in the therapeutic process. A great wealth of material exists just below consciousness and, if made available to the therapy process, greatly enriches the work. Some therapists regularly ask for recall of fantasy material. They encourage members to discuss the fantasies they have had about the group or the members during the interval since the previous meeting. They may, for example, ask members to share the fantasies about the group they have had on the way to the meeting that day. Other therapists may guide fantasy formation during the meeting. For example, if two members are deeply involved, the therapist may clarify their relationship by asking not for their feelings toward each other (often these are not clearly known) but for a fantasy of doing something with each other. One twenty-eight-year-old woman was told by a male member that he would simply like to walk alone with her in the woods with his head on her shoulder. Since one of her primary problems centered on her inability to attract men to her, it proved of great benefit to her to discover how she had been manifesting herself maternally rather than sexually to the other member.

The Use of Video Tapes

Modern scientific technology, which has largely contributed to the dehumanization of present-day society and, consequently, to the necessity for group therapy, has at the same time created an instrument—

433

the video-tape recorder—that has considerable potential benefit for the teaching, practice, and understanding of group therapy.

Video-tape recording has proven its value in the teaching of all forms of psychotherapy. Students and supervisors are permitted to view a session with a minimum of distortion. Important nonverbal aspects of behavior of both students and patients, which may be completely missed in the traditional supervisory format, become available for study. The student-therapist has a rich opportunity to observe his or her own presentation of self and body language. Confusing aspects of the meeting may be viewed several times until some order appears. Valuable teaching sessions which clearly illustrate basic principles of therapy may be stored and a teaching video-tape library created. These features suggest that video tapes are a significant advance over older methods of observation such as audio tapes, closed-circuit television, or one-way mirrors.

The potential benefit for the group therapy patient is self-evident. Do we not wish patients to obtain an accurate view of their behavior? Do we not search for methods to encourage self-observation and to make the self-reflective aspect of the here-and-now as salient as the experiencing aspect?

Though these potential benefits seem formidable, the proper role and application of this new technique in ongoing therapy is far from settled. Some therapists make the video-tape recording a central feature and, in a sense, structure the group around it; others, myself included, find the technique of value and periodically make use of it as an auxiliary aid in the therapeutic process; others, frustrated by the mechanical difficulties and disappointed in the technique's failure to live up to expectations (often unrealistic ones), have abandoned video recording entirely. There was an initial wave of great enthusiasm, and a host of articles on the use of television in psychotherapy appeared in professional journals in the late 1960s and early 1970s. With the exception of one well-edited text, however,[33] little literature about video tape and group therapy has appeared in the past decade.

Many clinicians stress the importance of immediate playback and arrange for a patient to view the tape as soon as possible after the experience. This procedure necessitates great instrumental flexibility: camera, tape deck, and monitor must be in the group room, and the tape rewound on the spot for viewing and commentary by members and therapists. Obviously, certain segments must be selected for this type of viewing ("focused feedback"[34]); selection may be made by the group or by the therapist. Some therapists use an auxiliary therapist whose chief task is to operate the camera and associated gadgetry and to select suitable portions for playback. Other therapists prefer the less complicated method of video taping an entire meeting and devoting the following session to playback and reactions to it. Some therapists schedule an extra playback meeting in which most of the previous tape is observed; others tape the first half of the meeting and observe the tape during the second half. Still other therapists use a "serial-viewing" technique: they video tape every session and retain short representative segments of each which, later in therapy, they play back to the group.[35]

Patient response depends upon the timing of the procedure. M. Berger notes that the patient's response to the first playback session differs from his or her response to later sessions.[36] In the first playback, patients attend primarily to their own image and are relatively less involved with the process of the group. Later, they may be more attentive to their styles of responding and relating to others. For this reason, it is far more efficient, later in therapy, to select certain important segments for viewing rather than to view, indiscriminately, an entire session.

Often a patient's long-cherished self-image is radically challenged by a first video-tape playback. It is not unusual to recall and to accept previous feedback one has gotten from other members; often, with dramatic impact, one understands that the group has been honest and, if anything, overprotective in previous confrontations. The group is no longer experienced as a critical or destructive tribunal, and the patient may become more amenable to future interpretations. Although feedback about one's behavior from others is important, it is not as convincing as information one discovers for oneself: video tape provides feedback that is not mediated through a second person. Often profound self-confrontations occur: one cannot hide from oneself, and patients may subsequently abandon defensive and incongruent facades. Many initial playback reactions are concerned with physical attractiveness and mannerisms; whereas in subsequent playback sessions, patients note their interactions with others, their withdrawal, self-preoccupation, hostility, or aloofness. They are far more able to be self-observant and objective than when actually involved in the group interaction.

I have on occasion found video recording to be enormously useful in crisis situations. For example, one alcoholic patient arrived at the group intoxicated and proceeded to be monopolistic, insulting, and crude. An intoxicated patient rarely profits from such a meeting since this mental state renders one incapable of retention and integration. However, the meeting was video taped, and a subsequent viewing of the meeting was enormously helpful to the patient: he had been told but really never knew how destructive alcohol was to himself and to others.

• On another occasion in an alcoholic group, a patient arrived intoxicated and in deep despair. He lost consciousness and lay stretched out on the sofa while the group, encircling him, discussed various courses of action. Some time later, the patient viewed the tape with profound effect. He had often been told, but without impact, that he was self-destructive, that he was killing himself with alcohol. The sight of himself on video tape, laid out as if on a bier, brought his suicidal life pattern and his death home to him with undeniable force. Berger describes a similar episode.[37] A periodically manic patient, who had never accepted that her behavior was unusual, had an opportunity to view herself in a particularly high, disorganized state. In each of these instances, the videotape provided a powerful self-observatory experience —a necessary first step in the therapeutic process.

Many therapists are reluctant to inflict a television camera on a group; they feel that it will inhibit the group's spontaneity, and that the group members will resent, though not necessarily overtly, the intrusion. In my opinion, the situation is not dissimilar to the introduction of the audio tape recorder into psychotherapy in the 1950s. The person who often experiences the most discomfort is the therapist. If you regard the camera as an intrusion and alter your behavior accordingly, obviously the technique will obstruct therapy. Many therapists who have become accustomed to video tapes report that, after the initial adjustment, the process of the meeting is not altered, other therapists dispute that point and claim that the sound and sight of the machinery, the presence of a cameraman, the interruptions to the group, and the unnatural seating pattern (if only one camera is used, the group members must, for everyone to be seen, sit in a horseshoe pattern) are always an interference in the group. Patients who are to view the playback are usually receptive to the suggestion of video taping. Often, however, they are concerned about confidentiality and need reassurance on this issue. If the tape is to be viewed by anyone other than the group members (for example, students, researchers, or supervisors), the therapist must be explicit about the purpose of the viewing and the identity of the viewers and must obtain written permission from all the members.

Written Summaries

For the past ten years, I have regularly employed an ancillary technique in my outpatient group therapy. At the end of each session, I dictate a detailed summary of the group session.[38] The summary is an editorialized narrative which describes the flow of the session, each member's contribution to the meeting, my contributions (not only what I said but what I wished I had but did not say, or what I did say and regret), and any hunches or questions that occur to me after the session. This dictation is then transcribed and mailed to the members the following day. Dictation of the summaries (two to three single-spaced pages) requires approximately twenty to thirty minutes of a therapist's time and is best done immediately at the end of the session. If there are co-therapists, I recommend that they alternate the task from week to week. To date, my students and colleagues and I have written and mailed thousands of group summaries to group members. It is my strong belief that the procedure greatly facilitates therapy.

My first experience with the written summary was in individual therapy. A young woman, Ginny, had attended a therapy group for six months but had to terminate because she moved out of town and could not arrange transportation to get to the group on time. Moreover, her inordinate shyness and inhibition had made it difficult for her to participate in the group. Ginny was inhibited in her work as well: she was a gifted writer but crippled by severe writer's block. I agreed to treat her in individual therapy but with one unusual proviso: that after each therapy hour, she write an impressionistic, free-wheeling summary of the underground of the session—what she was really thinking and feeling but had not verbally expressed. My hope was that the assignment would help to penetrate the writing block and would encourage greater spontaneity. I agreed to write an equally candid summary. Ginny had a pronounced idealized transference, and my hope was that a written summary conveying my honest feelings—pleasure, discouragement, puzzlement, fatigue—would permit her to relate more genuinely to me.

Over a year and a half, Ginny and I wrote weekly summaries. We handed them, sealed, to my secretary, and every few months we read each other's summary. The experiment turned out to be highly success-

437

ful: Ginny did well in therapy, and the summaries contributed greatly to that success.*

I developed sufficient courage from the venture (and courage is needed: it is difficult at first for a therapist to be so self-revealing) to think about adapting the technique to a therapy group. The opportunity arose shortly in two groups of alcoholic patients.[39] My co-therapists and I had attempted to lead these groups in an interactional mode. The groups had gone well in that the members were interacting openly and productively. However, here-and-now interaction always entails anxiety, and alcoholic patients are notoriously poor anxiety binders. By the eighth meeting, patients who had been dry for months were drinking again (or threatening to drink again if they ever had another meeting like last week's!). We hastily sought methods of modulating anxiety: increased structure, a suggested (written) agenda for each meeting, video playback, and written summaries distributed after each meeting. The patients considered the written summary to be the most efficacious method, and soon it replaced the others. Subsequently I have, over the past twelve years, used the written summary technique in all my once-weekly outpatient groups.

I believe that the summaries are most valuable if they are honest and straightforward about the process of therapy. They are virtually identical to summaries I make for my own files (which provide most of the clinical material for this book), and are based on the assumption that the patient is a full collaborator in the therapeutic process, that psychotherapy is strengthened not weakened by demystification.

The summary serves several functions: it provides understanding of the events of the session, labels good (or resistive) sessions, notes and rewards patient gains, predicts (and thus prevents) undesirable developments, brings in silent members, increases cohesiveness (by underscoring similarities and caring in the group, and so on), provides interpretations (either repetition of interpretations made in the group or new interpretations occurring to the therapist later), and provides hope

---

*I learned a great deal about psychotherapy from this experiment. For one thing, it brought home to me the *Rashomon* nature of the therapeutic venture. The patient and I had extraordinarily different perspectives of the hours we shared. All my marvelous, elegant interpretations? She never even heard them! Instead, Ginny heard, and valued, very different parts of the therapy hour—the deeply human exchanges; the fleeting supportive, accepting glances; the brief moments of real intimacy. The exchange of summaries provided interesting instruction about psychotherapy, and I used the summaries in my teaching. Years later, the patient and I decided to write a prologue and an afterword and publish the summaries as a book: *Everyday Gets a Little Closer: A Twice-Told Therapy* (Basic Books, 1975).

to the patients (helping them realize that the group is an orderly process and that the therapists have some coherent sense of the group's long-term development). In fact, the summary may be used to augment every one of the group leader's tasks in a group. In the following discussion of the functions of the summary, I shall cite excerpts from summaries and end this section with an entire summary.

REVIVIFICATION AND CONTINUITY

The summary becomes another group contact during the week; the meeting is revivified for the members and the group is more likely to assume continuity. Earlier, in chapter 5, I stated that groups assume more power if the work is continuous, if themes begun one week are not dropped but are explored, ever more deeply, in succeeding meetings. The summary augments this process. Not infrequently patients begin a meeting by referring to the previous summary—either a theme they wish to explore or a statement with which they disagree.

UNDERSTANDING PROCESS

The summary helps patients re-experience and understand important events of a meeting. In chapter 6, I described the here-and-now as consisting of two phases: experience and the understanding of that experience. The summary facilitates the second stage—the understanding and the integration of the affective experience. Often group sessions may be so threatening or unsettling that members move into a defensive, survival position. Only later (often with the help of the summary) can they review significant events and convert them into constructive learning experiences. The therapist's interpretations (especially complex ones) delivered in the midst of a melee tend to fall on deaf ears. Interpretations repeated in the summary are often effective because the patient is able to consider them at length, far from the intensity of engagement.

SHAPING GROUP NORMS

The summaries may be used to reinforce norms both implicitly and explicitly. For example, the following excerpt reinforced the here-and-now norm:

Phil's relationship with his boss is very important and difficult for him at this time, and as such is certainly material for the group. However, the members do not know the boss, what he is like, what he is thinking and feeling—and thus are limited in offering help. However, they are beginning to know one another and can be more certain of their own reactions to one another in the group. They can give more accurate feedback about feelings that occur between them rather than trying to guess what the boss may be thinking.

Or consider the following excerpt which encourages the patients to make process commentary and to approach the therapist in an egalitarian manner: (In the excerpt, Irv is the therapist.)

Jed did something very different in the group today, which was to make an observation about the bind that Irv was in. He noted, quite correctly, that Irv was in a bind of not wishing to change the topic from Dinah because of Irv's reluctance to stir up any of Dinah's bad feelings about being rejected or abandoned in the group, but on the other hand Irv wanted very much to find out what was happening to Pete, who was obviously hurting today.

THERAPEUTIC LEVERAGE

The therapist may, in the summary, keep the patient's attention on his or her primary task, reminding the patient of his or her original purpose in coming to therapy. For example:

Mary Lou felt hurt at Jim's calling her an observer of life and fell silent for the next forty-five minutes. Later she said she felt clamped up and thought about leaving the group. It is important that Mary Lou keep in mind that her main reason for being in therapy was that she felt estranged from others and unable to create closer, sustained relationships, especially with men. In that context, it is important for her to recognize and understand her impulse to clamp up and withdraw as a response to feedback.

Or the therapist may take care to repeat statements by patients that will offer leverage in the future. For example:

Emily began weeping at this point, but when Ed tried to console her she snapped, "Stop being so kind. I don't cry because I'm miserable, I cry when I'm pissed off. When you console me or let me off the hook because of my tears, you always stop me from looking at my anger."

NEW THOUGHTS

Often the therapist understands an event after the fact. On other occasions, the timing is not right for a clarifying remark during a session (too much cognition might squelch the emotional experience); or there has simply been no time available in the meeting; or a patient has been so defensive that he or she would reject any efforts at clarification. The summaries provide the therapist with a second chance to convey important thoughts. In this excerpt, the therapists communicate a message that emerged in their post-meeting discussion. The summary describes and attempts to counteract undesirable developments in the session: the shaping of countertherapeutic norms and scapegoating. (Rick and Carla are new members in the group.)

Ethel and Al were particularly vehement today in pointing out several times that Bea had been confrontative and insensitive to Ted and, as Al put it, was very very hard on people. Is it possible that what was going on in the group today might be viewed from another perspective: the perspective of what types of message the group was giving to the new members about how they would like them to be in the group? Is it possible that the group was suggesting to Rick and Carla that they take pains not to be critical and that open criticism is something that simply is not done here in this group? It may also be true that, to some degree, Bea became the fall guy for this transaction: that is, is it possible that, at some unconscious level, the group concluded that she was tough enough to take this and they could get a message to the new members through Bea, through a criticism of her behavior?

TRANSMISSION OF THE THERAPIST'S TEMPORAL PERSPECTIVE

Far more than any member of the group, the therapist maintains a long-range temporal perspective and is cognizant of changes occurring over months, both in the group and in each of the members. There are many times when the sharing of these observations offers hope, support, and meaning for the members. For example:

Seymour spoke quite openly in the group today about how hurt he was by Jack and Burt switching the topic off him. We [the co-therapists] were struck by the ease with which he was able to discuss these feelings. We can clearly remember his hurt, passive, silence in similar situations in the past, and are impressed with how markedly he has changed his ability to express his feelings openly.

Or again:

Jackie described the despair she has been experiencing. In some ways it sounded almost identical to the kinds of despair Jackie described in the group when she first entered—having to do with loneliness, with the feeling that there was no one in the world who cared about her, with the feeling that she always had to ask people to be with her and to do things with her, that no one ever sought her out. However, there was an important difference in her state now and her condition at that time. The major difference was that several months ago Jackie presented these things as though that's the way the world *was*—that there really *was* no one in the world for her. This time she has much more of a realistic view of it. She realizes that this is the way she is thinking right now. She feels badly and angry because she experiences the fact that there is so much more work to do. She is upset at the fact that she allows others to define her, to tell her whether she is worthwhile or not, rather than having a stable sense of self-worth inside of her.

The summaries provide temporal perspective in yet another way. Since the patients almost invariably save and file the reports, they thus have a comprehensive account of their progression through the group, an account to which they may, with great profit, refer in the future.

Therapist Self-Disclosure

The therapist, in the service of the patients' therapy, may use the summary as a vehicle to disclose a great deal of personal here-and-now feelings (of puzzlement, of discouragement, of irritation, of pleasure) and of his views about the theory and meaning underlying his behavior in the group. Consider these illustrative excerpts (Irv and Louise are the therapists):

Irv and Louise both felt considerable strain in the meeting. We felt caught between our feelings of wanting to continue more with Dinah, but also being very much aware of Al's obvious hurting in the meeting. Therefore, even at the risk of Dinah's feeling that we were deserting her, we felt strongly about bringing in Al before the end of the meeting.

We felt very much in a bind with Seymour. He was silent during the meeting. We felt very much that we wanted to bring him into the group and help him talk, especially since we knew that the reason he had dropped out of his previous group was because of his feeling that people were uninterested in what he had to say. On the other hand, today we decided to resist the desire to bring him in because we knew that by continually bringing Seymour into the group, we are infantalizing him, and it will be much better if, sooner or later, he is able to do it by himself.

Irv had a definite feeling of dissatisfaction with his own behavior in the meeting today. He felt he dominated things too much, that he was too active, too directive. No doubt this is due in large part to his feeling of guilt at having missed the previous two meetings and wanting to make up for it today by giving as much as possible.

Louise wondered whether the fact that Sarah was leaving the group was only due to her new work schedule or whether she was leaving the group because in fact she was considerably improved. It is striking that Louise said this only a few seconds before Irv was going to say it. The therapists are always looking for reassurances that their patients feel better.

FILLING GAPS

An obvious and important function of the summary is to fill in gaps for patients who miss meetings because of illness or vacation. The summaries keep them abreast of events and enable them to move more quickly back into the group.

NEW PATIENTS

As I described in chapter 11, the entrance of a new patient may be facilitated by providing summaries of the previous few meetings. I routinely ask new members to read such summaries before attending the first meeting.

GENERAL IMPRESSIONS

I believe that the written summary facilitates therapy. Patients have been unanimous in their positive evaluation: most read and consider the summaries very seriously; many reread them several times; almost all file them for future use. The patient's therapeutic perspective and commitment is deepened; the patient-therapist relationship is strengthened; and no serious transference complications occur.

I have noted no adverse consequences. Many therapists have asked about confidentiality, but I have encountered no problems in this area: patients are asked to regard the summary with the same degree of confidentiality as any event in the group. As an extra precaution, I use only first names and avoid explicit identification of any particularly delicate issue (for example, an extramarital affair).

Like any event in the group, the summaries generate differential responses: for example, those patients with severe dependency yearnings will cherish every word; those with a severe counterdependent posture will challenge every word or, in one instance, be unable to spare the time to read them at all; obsessive patients obsess over the precise meaning of the words; and paranoid patients search for hidden meanings. Thus, although the summaries provide a clarifying force, they do not thwart the formation of the distortions necessary to therapy.

A SUMMARY OF A GROUP'S TWENTIETH MEETING*

Terri was absent because of illness. Bea opened the meeting by raising an important question for her left over from last week. During her interchange with Edith she thought that she saw Paul give Ethel a knowing glance. Paul assured Bea that that was, indeed, not the case. He had looked at Ethel but it was for a different reason entirely—it had been because of his deep concern about Ethel's depression last week hoping to find a way to involve Ethel more in the group. The matter was dropped there, but it seemed a particularly useful way for Bea to have used the group. It is not an uncommon experience for individuals to feel that others exchange glances when they are talking and it seemed as though Bea had a certain sense of being excluded or perhaps of Paul dismissing her or possibly Paul being uninterested in what she and Edith were up to.

The next issue which emerged consumed a considerable portion of the meeting and, in some ways, was tedious for many of the members but, at the same time, was an exceptionally valuable piece of work. Paul took the floor and began talking about certain types of insight he had had during the last week or two. He took a very long time to describe what he had been feeling and did so in a highly intelligent but intellectualized and vague fashion. People in the group, at this point, were either straining to stay with Paul and understand what he was coming to or, as in the case of Bill and Ted, had begun to tune Paul out. Eventually what transpired was that Paul communicated to the group that he had some real doubts about whether or not he, indeed, really wanted to go back to law school, and was wrestling with those doubts.

During Paul's entire presentation he seemed, at some level, aware that he was being unclear and that he was communicating what he had to say in a highly oblique fashion. He asked, on several occasions, whether the group was following him and whether he was clear. At the end of his presentation, he puzzled individuals in the group by commenting that he felt very good about what had happened in the group and felt that he was in exactly the place he wanted to be in. Ethel questioned this. She, like others in the group, felt a little puzzled about what on earth it was that Paul had gotten from the whole sequence. But apparently what had happened was that Paul had been able to convey to the group the struggle he was having about this decision and, at the same time, covertly to make it clear to the group that he did not want any active

---

*The summary is unedited aside from slight stylistic improvement and change of names. It is approximately 20 percent longer, better written, and more lucid than most summaries. I dictated this summary on a portable cassette recorder in approximately twenty to twenty-five minutes (driving home from a meeting). Several weeks are required to learn to dictate meetings comfortably and quickly. It is best to dictate immediately after a session. I use this dictating plan: I first think of the two to four major issues of the meeting and the transitions between issues. Then I describe each member's contribution to the discussion of each issue. Do not be perfectionistic: one cannot recall or remember everything. My secretary types my summary the following day and mails it out. I do not proofread it; patients overlook errors and omissions.

This is a representative sample out of a file of hundreds of summaries. Should any of my readers wish to visit and peruse other summaries, please contact me at the Department of Psychiatry, Stanford University School of Medicine, Stanford, CA 94305.

help with the content of the decision. When we wondered why Paul couldn't come out and say what it took him a very long time to say in just a sentence or two—that is, "I'm struggling with the decision to enter law school and I'm not certain if I want to go"—he said he would have felt extremely frightened had he said that. It seemed, as we analyzed it, that what he was frightened of was that somehow the group, as his family had done, would take the decision away from him—would rob him of his autonomy, would enter into and make the decision for him in some fashion.

Then we suggested another approach for Paul. Would it have been possible for him to have started the meeting by being explicit about the whole process: that is, "I'm struggling with an important decision. I don't know if I really want to go to law school. I want you all to know this and be able to share this with you, but I don't want anyone in the group to help me actually make the decision." Paul reflected upon this and commented that that sounded very possible—something, indeed, he could have done. We'll need to look for future situations when Paul does become intellectualized and somewhat vague for ways to help him communicate the thought succinctly and directly—to get what he wants to get from it and, at the same time, not puzzle or discourage listeners.

At the very end of this, the group seemed to have some difficulty letting Paul go, and more questions were asked of him. Al, in particular, asked Paul several questions about the content of his decision, until Edith finally commented that she'd like to change the topic, and it was clear that Paul was more than glad to do so. We did not discuss in the group today Al's questioning of Paul, which is not dissimilar from some other meetings in the past where Al became intensely interested in the content of the enterprise. One speculation we have (which will undoubtedly be rejected outright) is that Al may be filling the time of the group as a way to keep the group away from asking him some questions about the pain in his life.

There was a very brief interchange between Edith and Bea. After their confrontation last week, Edith said that Bea had come up to her after the meeting and made it clear to her that Edith should not be upset about what was, at least in part, Bea's problem. Edith felt grateful at that and let Bea know that. At the same time, however, Bea could comment to Edith that when Edith first started to talk to her in the meeting today she felt this pang of fear again.

We did not pursue that any further, but we wonder if that's not an important event: that is, that it might be important not only to Bea but to Edith as well to know that Bea has this fear of her—a fear that Paul commented he also shared at times. The reason this might be important is that Edith stated that she wants to do some work on the attitude of attack that she often assumes. She has been alerted to that by comments from the man whom she is dating. Is it possible that the aspect of Bea's fear that may be important to Edith is that Bea has been attacked by Edith on several occasions in the past and that Bea remembers these and is (understandably) cautious. Edith, on the other hand, has a sense that, because she has forgotten or dismissed the previous attack, Bea should therefore, of course, do so also—and that's where the discrepancy begins to come in. Indeed, in the previous meeting, Edith seemed rather astonished that Bea would still continue to feel that pain and that fear. This may be an important theme that should be examined in future meetings.

Irv attempted to bring Ted into the meeting because everyone has been aware that Ted has been withdrawn and silent in the meeting and his participation has been much missed. Ted talked, once again, about feeling that the group was unsafe and feeling fearful of talking because he was attacked for almost anything he said. We then talked about the fact that, as Bea pointed out, when he talked about issues that were personal and close to himself—like his loneliness or his difficulties making friends—then, indeed, there was no attack at all.

The group began to try to help differentiate that there are things that Ted may do that evoke attack, but there are plenty of other ways he could interact in the group that would, indeed, not culminate in any type of attack. For example? Well, Irv pointed out that Ted might make positive comments about people or focus on some of the things he liked about people in the group, and it was suggested that he do this. Edith asked him for some positive feedback, and for a few moments Ted was blocked and then finally commented that Edith "had a pleasant personality . . . usually."

The phrasing of this sentence soon resulted in some antagonistic exchanges, and soon Ted was back in a very familiar unsafe situation in the group. Bea and others pointed out that he had phrased that compliment in such a way as to undo it and make it seem less like a compliment and almost more like something negative. Al and others pointed out how the adding of the word "usually" made it seem ironical rather than a genuine compliment. Ted defended himself by saying that he had to be honest and had to be accurate. He also pointed out that, if he were simply to say that Edith was intelligent or sensitive, she would immediately conclude that he meant that she was the most intelligent person in the room. Edith pointed out that, indeed, that was not the case, and she was pleased to hear him give that kind of compliment. Ted might have been in a little less of a bind, as Bill pointed out, had he made a more limited type of compliment: that is, rather than talk about something as global as personality, make it somewhat more narrow. For example, Ted might have commented on some aspect of Edith that he liked, even her dress or her hair or some particular mannerism.

When we questioned Ted about how he had gotten back into this situation in the group and whether he bore any responsibility for it, Ted was very quick to point out that, indeed, he had and that he did share a good part of the burden of responsibility for the position of being attacked that he was in. We attempted to point out to Ted that feeling the group as unsafe is an extremely important issue for him to work on because this is very much the way that he experiences the world outside, and the more that he can explore ways to live in the group so that it appears less dangerous, the more he will be able to generalize to his life outside.

In the last few minutes of the group, the focus turned to Bill. Edith and others commented that they had been missing his participation. Bill stated he'd been aware of his inactivity and been disappointed that he'd shared so little of himself. His silence has been somewhat different from Ted's silence in that he does not experience the group as unsafe but instead has a sense of letting things pass by. If he has some questions or opinions, he's perfectly willing to let them

446

go by without expressing them. This posture of letting the life in the group go by may be extremely important for Bill because it reflects how he lives in the world at large—where he does let much of life go by and often experiences himself more as an observer than as a participant. Changing that posture in the group would be the first step to changing that posture in life.

Ethel was rather quiet in the group today, but the comments that she did make earlier in the meeting reflected that she, at least visibly, appears less depressed and distressed than she was during the previous meeting.

This summary illustrates several of the functions I described earlier. It clarifies process. A good deal of the meeting was consumed by Paul's obsessive, confusing monologue (which was rendered more confusing yet by his comment that he had gotten a very great deal from his recitation). The summary explained the process of that transaction. It also reinforced norms (by, for example, supporting Bea for checking out glances passing between two members). It increased therapeutic leverage by linking in-group behavior with out-group problems (Edith's relationship with her boyfriend and Bill's observer posture in life). It added some afterthoughts (the comment to Al about filling time with questions about content to keep the group from questioning him). It attempted to identify behavioral and dynamic patterns (Edith's narcissistic sense of entitlement—that is, that she should be able to attack when she was angry and that the others should forget about it when she felt better).

Structured Exercises

I shall use the term *structured exercise* to denote any of the many activities in which a group follows some specific set of orders. An exercise is generally prescribed by the leader, but occasionally by some experienced member. The precise rationale of the procedures vary; but in general, structured exercises are thought to be accelerating devices: they attempt to speed up the group with "warm-up" procedures which bypass the hesitant, uneasy first steps of the group; they speed up interaction by assigning to interacting individuals tasks that circumvent ritualized, introductory social behavior; and they speed up individual work by techniques designed to help members move quickly to "get in touch with" suppressed emotions, with unknown parts of themselves, and with their physical body.

The structured exercise may require only a few minutes, or it may consume an entire meeting; it may be predominantly verbal or nonverbal (almost all nonverbal procedures, however, include a verbal component; generally, the exercise generates data that is subsequently discussed). The exercise may involve the entire group as a group (the group may be asked, for example, to build something or to plan an outing), or one member vis-à-vis the group (one member stands, eyes closed, in the center and falls, allowing the group to support, and then to cradle and rock, him or her), or the entire group as individuals (each member may be asked "go around" and to give his or her initial impressions of everyone else in the group), or the entire group as dyads (the "blind walk"—the group is broken into dyads and each pair takes a walk with one member blindfolded, led by the other), or a single, particular dyad (two members locked in a struggle may be asked to take turns pushing the other to the ground and then lifting the other up again), or one particular member (a member working in the "hot seat" may be asked to have an internal dialogue giving voice to inner conflicting roles or forces).

Structured exercises were first described in group work in the T-groups of the 1950s and became even more common and variegated with the evolution of the encounter group (see chapter 16). In the 1960s and 1970s, gestalt therapy provided an additional source of structured procedures. Though these exercises have an important place in group therapy, they have been used to excess by many leaders and by many training programs. Some group leader training programs rely heavily on texts of structured exercises and train technique-oriented leaders who conduct groups clutching a grabbag of gimmicks into which they reach whenever the proceedings flag. Large segments of the general public have come to identify group therapy with structured exercises through large group awareness courses (for example, est, lifespring). These courses, which I discuss elsewhere,[40] consist entirely of a two-to-four-day potpourri of structured exercises and didactic and inspirational instruction.

This current injudicious use of structured exercises is a miscarriage of the intent of the approaches that spawned these techniques. The T-group field formulated exercises that were designed to demonstrate principles of group dynamics (both between and within groups). They also fashioned accelerating aids; since the typical T-group met for a sharply limited period of time, the trainers sought methods to speed the group past the initial reserve and the traditional social ritualized behavior. Their aim was for members to experience as much as possible of the developmental sequence of the small group.

Gestalt therapy, another major source of structured exercises, is a therapy approach based on existential roots. Transcripts of Fritz Perls's sessions with patients as well as his theoretical essays demonstrate that Perls was basically concerned with problems of existence, of self-aware-ness, of responsibility, of contingency, of wholeness both within one individual and within the individual's social and physical universe.[41] Although Perls's approach was novel, his conception of the human being's basic dilemma is one he shares with a long skein of philosophers of life stretching back to the beginning of recorded thought. Paradoxi-cally, gestalt therapy has come to be considered by some clinicians as a speedy, gimmick-oriented therapy; whereas, in fact, it is a based on the deepest of truths. Unlike the brief therapies, it attempts to pene-trate denial systems and to bring patients to a new perspective on their position in the world. It basically decries a technical, packaged ap-proach; and yet some gestalt therapy trainees do not progress past technique, do not grasp the theoretical assumptions upon which all technique must rest.

How has it come about that the substance has been so often mistaken for the essence of the gestalt approach? The cornerstone for the error was unwittingly laid by the founder of gestalt therapy, Fritz Perls, whose creative, technical virtuosity acted in such consort with his flair for showmanship as to lead many people to mistake the medium for the message. Perls had to do battle with the hyperintellectualized emphasis of the early analytic movement and often overreacted and overstated his opposition to theory. "Lose your mind and come to your senses," Perls proclaimed. Consequently, he did not write a great deal and taught by illustration, trusting that his students would discover their own truths through experience rather than through the intellectual process. Yet, in his few expository essays, it is clear that Perls read and thought deeply and extensively; much of his work rests on the basic assumptions of such thinking men as Husserl, Heidegger, and Sartre.[42] The many half-day or whole-day workshops offered by some gestaltists, which consist of the same tired string of audience exercises ("Finish the sentence, 'I am aware . . . ' "; "Think of an incomplete decision in your life, give a voice to the opposing forces, and let those voices have a dialogue"), only perpetuate the erroneous view that gestalt therapy is a series of structured exercises.

What do we know about the effects of these procedures upon the process and outcome of the group? Lieberman, Yalom, and Miles's encounter group project (see chapter 16 for details) closely studied the impact of the structured exercise and came to the following conclu-sions.[43] Leaders who used many exercises were popular with their groups. Immediately at the end of a group, the members regarded

449

them as more competent, more effective, and more perceptive than leaders who used these techniques sparingly. Yet the members of groups with the most exercises had significantly *lower* outcome than did the members of groups with the fewest exercises. (The groups with the most exercises had fewer high changers, fewer total positive changers, and more negative changers. Moreover, the high changers of the exercise groups with most exercises were *less* likely to maintain change over time.) In short, the moral of this study is that if you want your group members to think you're competent and that you know what you're doing, then use an abundance of structured interventions; in doing so, in "leading," in providing explicit directions, in assuming total executive function, you fulfill their fantasies of what a leader should do. However, the outcome for your group members will not be improved; in fact, too much reliance upon these techniques renders a group less effective.

The research looked at other differences between groups with more and fewer exercises. There were no differences in the amount of self-disclosure nor were there differences in emotional climate between these groups. There were differences in the themes emphasized: the groups with more exercises focused on the expression of positive and negative feelings; those with fewer exercises had a greater range of thematic concerns: the setting of goals; the selection of procedural methods; closeness versus distance; trust versus mistrust; genuineness versus phoniness; affection; and isolation. It would seem, then, that many common themes groups must deal with are simply not considered in groups with many exercises; the leader's active approach settles these issues for the group. The exercises appear to plunge the members quickly into a great degree of expressivity, but the group pays a price for its speed; it circumvents many group developmental tasks and does not develop a sense of autonomy and potency.

It is not easy for group clinicians to evaluate their own use of structured techniques. In the encounter group project, almost all leaders used some structured exercises. Some of the more effective leaders attributed their success in large measure to these techniques. To take one example, many leaders used the "hot seat" technique (a format in which one member occupies the "hot seat," and the leader, in particular, and the other members focus on that member exclusively and exhaustively for long periods of time). However, the approach was as highly valued by the most ineffective leaders as by the effective ones. Obviously, other aspects of leader behavior accounted for the effective leaders' success; but if they erroneously credit their effectiveness to the structured exercise, then it is given a value it does not deserve (and is unfortunately passed on to students as the central feature of the process of change).

The Lieberman, Yalom, Miles encounter group project also demonstrated the central importance of psychosocial forces in the change process: change was heavily influenced by an individual's role in the group (centrality, level of influence, value congruence, activity) and by characteristics of the group (cohesiveness, climate of intensivity and harmoniousness, norm structure). In other words, the data failed to support the importance of the leader's centrality and of his or her direct therapeutic interaction with each member.

Though these findings issue from short-term encounter groups, they have much relevance for the therapy group. First, consider the concept of *acceleration*. In that they bypass early, "slow" stages of group interaction, in that they plunge members quickly into an expression of positive and negative feelings, structured exercises do indeed "accelerate" interaction.

But do they accelerate the process of therapy? I think that, in general, they do not. In short-term T-groups, it is often legitimate to employ techniques to bypass certain difficult stages, to help the group flit on when it is mired in an impasse. In long-term therapy groups, the "bypass" is less germane; the leader more often wishes to guide the group *through* anxiety, *through* the impasse or difficult stages, rather than *around* them. Resistance is not an impediment to therapy but is the stuff of therapy. The early psychoanalysts conceived of the analytic procedure in two stages: the analysis of resistance and then the "true" analysis (which consists of strip-mining the infantile unconscious roots of behavior). Later they realized that the analysis of resistance, if pursued thoroughly, is sufficient unto itself. Interactional group therapy, as I have indicated throughout, functions similarly: there is more to be gained by experiencing and exploring great timidity or suspiciousness or any of a vast number of dynamics underlying a member's initial guardedness than by providing the member with a vehicle that plunges him or her willy-nilly into deep disclosure or expressivity. Acceleration that results in material being untimely wrenched from individuals may be counterproductive if the proper context of the material has not been constructed. To illustrate this point, consider the following intervention from a gestalt therapy group:

One medical student in a group punctuated almost every remark (made in a very intense voice) with a flick of his head to the right. I had another student stand behind him and hold his head fairly tightly. After a minute or two, the head movement disappeared and the man began to flick his right wrist slightly at the end of each comment. Another student held his wrist. Soon a fairly noticeable shrug of the right shoulder appeared to replace that. At this point, I had him then exaggerate the shrug extensively, turning it into an entire body movement; within a minute or two, he was able to put this gesture into the words "who cares?" This was the miniaturized organismic counterpoint to his overtly expressed close interest in what I was saying.[44]

It would appear that the leader accelerated the surfacing of feelings of indifference or cynicism, and the emergence of these feelings is cited as validation of the technique. I would argue, though, that if this patient were in a therapy group in which proper norms were established— norms of trust, risk taking, free interpersonal exploration—then, without question, these attitudes would emerge in many ways without some dazzling midwife's trick. Furthermore, as time progressed, as the patient deepened interaction with each of the members and as each became more important to him or her, the "who cares?" would become even more meaningful. Because the patient works in a group for weeks or months before these feelings fully surface, we cannot conclude that these weeks or months are time wasted. On the contrary; they may represent essential time, time spent in building the social and interpersonal context which makes their subsequent emergence and working through "therapeutic."

I urge caution in the use of multiple structured exercises in therapy groups for yet another reason. The leader who prescribes structured tasks for a group runs the risk of establishing norms that impede the group from developing into a potent therapeutic force. Members of a highly structured, leader-centered group begin to feel that help (all help) emanates from the leader; they await their turn to work with the leader; they deskill themselves; they cease to avail themselves of the help and resources available in the group. They divest themselves of responsibility.

This is a curious development since Perls was acutely aware of the necessity for individuals to assume responsibility for themselves and their therapy. Much of Perls's modus operandi was, in fact, explicitly directed toward that end. Yet beneath the technique, beneath the imperative to assume responsibility, Perls created a bewildering paradox: on the one hand, he exhorted one to be, to do, to act for oneself; while, on the other hand, his leadership style implied: "I will take charge. I will lead you. Depend on me to provide energy and ingenious techniques." In a group, the paradox is even more striking as the members await their turn to work and are deprived of the opportunity to be autonomous as a group and to be helpful to one another. In short, the group is infantalized and, rather than a therapy group, becomes a congregation of individuals, each of whom does individual therapy in the presence of the other supplicants.

This outcome poses no problem to the gestalt therapist, who has never intended to use the group as a therapeutic agent; Perls always did individual therapy in a group: members came up one by one to occupy the "hot seat" and to work with him. Why, then, bother with a group at all? Perls employed the group as an omnipresent Greek chorus: when individuals work in the presence of others, they work with greater seriousness and with greater commitment. And so the group is used as a presence, as a symbolic equivalent of the watchful eyes of one's entire human community. At times, too, observing members do significant silent, internal work which is instigated by some aspect of the work of another. Occasional group interactions are encouraged, which the gestalt therapist may use to collect data about the individual. Sometimes other members may make useful observations or comments, but often the leader specifically asks them not to interfere in the "work." This formal, gestalt therapy concept of "individual therapy in a group" accounts for my not considering gestalt therapy at length in this text.* Though I agree with many of the goals and underlying assumptions of the gestalt school, I feel that Perls's group therapy technique is ill founded and makes inefficient use of a group's therapeutic potential. Many contemporary gestalt therapists have arrived at a similar conclusion, and recent gestalt therapy texts have described a group approach that is less leader-centered and

---

*It is for the same reason that I have not fully discussed transactional analytic group therapy, which also uses an individual-therapy-in-a-group model. T.A., as compared with gestalt therapy, is a less novel, less original movement in psychotherapy. In fact, its basic concerns, view of human beings, goals, and therapeutic approach are conventional; without exception, each of T.A.'s major concepts are to be found in the traditional psychological literature stretching back over the last forty years. What is most novel and most useful about the T.A. methodology is its vocabulary: arresting, lucid terminology for such concepts as interpersonal transactions ("games"), conflicting inner constellations of motives and drives ("parent, child, and adult ego states"), goals and therapy commitment ("contract"), genetic determinants of ego restrictions ("archaic decisions"); guiding fictions, life-style ("scripts"), parental expectations, superego (parental injunctions), and the like. To the extent that this vocabulary has made it possible for mental health workers (and especially those with little professional background) to obtain a more rapid and more incisive grasp of intrapersonal and interpersonal transactions, T.A. has made a significant contribution to the field. However, to the extent that it has restricted understanding by, for example, stuffing all the complexities of human behavior into a limited number of games, ego states, and scripts and to the extent that it has overemphasized the member-leader helping relationship to the neglect of the many other therapeutic factors in group therapy, the T.A. approach has not been productive.

more aware of the importance of member-to-member trans-action.[45]

In voicing these objections to the use of structured exercises, I have overstated the case. Surely there is a middle ground—a middle ground between, on the one hand, allowing the group to flounder profitlessly in some unproductive sequence and, on the other hand, to assume a frenetically active, structured leadership role. The Lieberman, Yalom, and Miles encounter group study reached that very conclusion.[46] It demonstrated that the degree to which leaders assumed an "executive," managerial function was related to outcome in a curvilinear fashion: that is, too much and too little were negatively correlated with good outcome; too much executive function created the types of problem I have discussed in the preceding section (leader-centered, dependent groups); too little (a laissez-faire approach) resulted in plodding, unenergetic, high attrition groups.

Indeed, many of the techniques I described in chapter 5 that the leader employs in norm setting, in here-and-now activation, and in process-illumination functions, have a prescriptive quality. ("Toward whom in the group do you feel closest?" "Can you look at Mary as you talk to her?" "If you were going to be graded for your work in the group, what grade would you receive?" And so on.) Every experienced group leader employs some structured exercises. For example, if a group is tense and experiences a silence of a minute or two (a minute's silence feels very long in a group), I often ask for a quick go-around in which each member says, quickly, what he or she has been feeling or has thought of saying, but did not, in that silence. The exercise usually generates much valuable data.

The important issue is one of degree, accent, and purpose. If structured interventions are suggested to help mold an autonomously functioning group, or to steer the group into the here-and-now, or to explicate process, they may be of value. If used, they should be properly timed; nothing is as disconcerting as the right idea in the wrong place at the wrong time. It is a mistake to use exercises as emotional space filler—that is, as something interesting to do when the group seems at loose ends.

Nor should a structured exercise be used to generate affect in the group. A properly led therapy group should not need energizing from without; if there seems insufficient energy in the group, if meetings seem listless, if time and time again the therapist feels it necessary to inject voltage into the group, there is most likely a significant developmental problem which the increased use of accelerating devices only

454

compounds. It is necessary, instead, to explore the obstructions, the norm structure, the members' passive posture toward the leader, the relationship of each member to his or her primary task, and so forth. My experience is that if the therapist prepares patients adequately and actively shapes expressive, interactional, self-disclosing norms in the manner described in chapter 5, there will be no paucity of activity and energy in the group.

Structured exercises often play a more important role in brief, specialized therapy groups than in the long-term general outpatient group. In the next chapter, I shall describe the way that structured exercises may be used in the acute inpatient therapy group.

15

THE SPECIALIZED
THERAPY GROUP

Introduction

Group therapy methods have proven to be so useful in so many different clinical settings that no longer is it correct to speak of "group
therapy." Instead, we must refer to "the group therapies." And, as one
can learn from even a cursory survey of professional journals, the number and scope of the group therapies is mind boggling. There are groups
for suicidal patients, for the aged, for the children of Alzheimer's patients, alcoholics, children of alcoholics, mothers of drug addicts, families of the mentally ill, fathers of delinquent daughters, children of
Holocaust survivors, renal dialysis patients, patients with multiple scle-
rosis, leukemia, asthma, sickle cell anemia, cancer, deafness, agora-
phobia, mental retardation, transexualism, bulimia, amputees, paraple-
gics, dying patients, asthmatics, non-orgasmic women, borderline
patients, college dropouts, patients who have had a myorcardial infarct
or a stroke, adopting parents, blind diabetic patients, patients in crisis,
day hospital patients, bereaved patients, post-divorced, and many,
many others.[1]

   Obviously no single text can, with any degree of depth, address each
of these specialized groups. Even were that possible, it would not constitute an intelligent approach to learning. No sensible student of
zoology, to take one example, undertakes the study of vertebrate
anatomical structure by memorizing the anatomy of each subspecies
separately; instead, the student first studies basic principles of form,
structure, and function and then proceeds to study the anatomy of a

prototypic primal specimen—for example, a representative amphibian. With this foundation in place, the student is in an ideal position to undertake the anatomical study of any species: it is necessary only to determine the particular environment and adaptational necessities of the species and to modify accordingly the primal anatomical patterns.

The extension of this analogy to group therapy is obvious. It is necessary that the student first master fundamental group therapy theory and then obtain a deep understanding of the primal prototypic therapy group.

But which group therapy represents the most archaic common ancestor? There has been such a luxuriant growth of group therapies that it requires great perspicacity to find, amidst the thicket, the primal trunk of group therapy. But if there is a primal or ancestral group therapy, it is the long-term outpatient group therapy described in this book: it was the first group therapy; it remains the most deeply studied, since patients are sufficiently motivated, cooperative, and stable to have allowed systematic research; furthermore, it has stimulated, over the last forty years, an imposing body of professional literature containing the observations and conclusions of thoughtful clinicians.

Once familiar with the primal therapy group, the student is ready for the next step—the adaptation of basic group therapy principles to any specialized clinical situation. That step is the goal of this chapter, and I have chosen to proceed via a clinical illustration: I shall discuss in detail how one may modify standard group therapy technique in order to lead effective groups on the acute psychiatric inpatient ward.

I have chosen the acute inpatient therapy group as my example for two reasons. First, it offers an opportunity to demonstrate many principles of strategic and technical adaptation. The clinical challenge is severe: as I shall discuss, the acute inpatient setting is so inhospitable for group therapy that radical modifications of technique are required. Second, this particular example may have intrinsic value to many readers since the inpatient group is the most common specialized group: therapy groups are led on virtually every acute psychiatric ward in the country.

Modification of Traditional Group Therapy for Specialized Clinical Situations: Basic Steps

When planning a specialized therapy group, I suggest the following three steps:

ASSESSMENT OF THE CLINICAL SITUATION

It is important to examine carefully all the clinical facts of life which will bear upon the therapy group. Take care to differentiate the intrinsic limiting factors from the extrinsic, traditional factors. The intrinsic factors (for example, mandatory attendance for patients on legal probation, or duration of group treatment in a ward group of hospitalized patients with cancer) are built into the clinical situation and cannot be changed. These factors correspond to the environmental press in our zoology analogy, and the group leader must adapt to them. The extrinsic factors (those factors that have become tradition or "policy") are arbitrary and within the power of the therapist to change.

FORMULATION OF GOALS

When you have a clear view of the clinical facts of life, your next step is to construct a reasonable set of clinical goals. You may not like the clinical situation, you may feel hampered by the many intrinsic restraints which prevent you from leading the "ideal" group, but do not wear yourself out by protesting an immutable situation. ("Better to light a candle than to curse the darkness.") With proper modification of goals and technique you will always be able to offer some form of help.

I cannot overemphasize the importance of setting clear and appropriate goals: it may be the most important step you make in your therapy. Nothing will so inevitably ensure failure as the presence of inappropriate goals. The goals of the long-term outpatient group I describe in this book are ambitious: to offer symptomatic relief and also to change character structure. If you attempt to apply these same goals to, let us say, an aftercare group of chronic schizophrenic patients, then you will rapidly become a therapeutic nihilist and stamp yourself and group therapy as hopelessly ineffective.

It is imperative to shape a set of goals that is appropriate to the clinical situation and achievable in the available time frame. The goals must be clear not only to the therapists but to patients as well. In my discussion of group preparation in chapter 10, I emphasized the importance of enlisting the patient as a full collaborator in treatment. You facilitate collaboration by making the goals and the group procedure explicit and by linking the two: that is, by clarifying how the procedure of the therapy group will help the patient attain those goals.

In time-limited, specialized groups, the goals must be limited, achievable, and tailored to the capacity and potential of the group members.

MODIFICATION OF TECHNIQUE

It is important that the group be a success experience: patients enter therapy feeling defeated and demoralized; the last thing they need is another failure.

MODIFICATION OF TECHNIQUE

When you are clear about the clinical conditions and have formulated appropriate, realizable goals, you must next consider the implication these conditions and these goals have for your therapeutic technique. In this phase, it is important to consider the therapeutic factors and to determine which factors will play the greatest role in the achievement of the goals. It is a phase of disciplined experimentation in which you alter technique, style, and, if necessary, the basic form of the group to adapt to the clinical situation and to the new goals of therapy.

In summary, to develop a specialized therapy group I recommend the following steps:
1. Assessment of the clinical setting: determine the immutable clinical restraints.
2. Formulation of goals: develop goals that are appropriate and achievable within the existing clinical restraints.
3. Modification of traditional technique. Retain the basic principles and therapeutic factors of group therapy but alter techniques to adapt to the clinical situation and to achieve the specified goals.

These steps are clear but too aseptic to be of immediate clinical usefulness. I shall now proceed to illustrate the entire sequence by describing, in detail, the development of a therapy group for the acute psychiatric inpatient ward.

The Acute Inpatient Therapy Group[2]

CLINICAL SETTING

The outpatient group that I describe throughout this book is freestanding: all important negotiations occur between the group therapist(s) and the seven or eight group members. Not so for the inpatient group! When you lead an inpatient group, the first clinical fact of life you must face is that your group is never an independent, free-standing entity: it always has a complex relationship to the larger group—the inpatient ward—in which it is ensconced.

The therapy group's effectiveness and often its very existence is heavily dependent upon administrative backing. If the ward medical director and the clinical nursing coordinator are not persuaded that the group therapy approach is effective, they are unlikely to support the group program: they will not accord prestige to the therapy groups; they will not assign staff members to group leader positions on a regular schedule, or provide supervision or even schedule group sessions at a convenient, consistent time. Therapy groups on such wards are rendered ineffective: the group leaders are demoralized and untrained; meetings are scheduled irregularly and are often disrupted by patients being called out for individual therapy or for a variety of other hospital appointments.

This state of affairs is *not* an intrinsic, immutable problem. Rather it is an extrinsic, attitudinal problem and stems from a number of sources. First, it is closely related to the professional education of the ward administrators. Many psychiatric training programs and nursing schools do not offer comprehensive curriculums in group therapy (and virtually no programs offer sound instruction in inpatient group psychotherapy). The professional literature too, has ignored the needs of the inpatient group therapist.[3] It is completely understandable that ward directors will not invest ward resources and energy in a treatment program about which they have little knowledge or faith. But I believe that these attitudes will change: it is difficult to ignore the rapidly accumulating body of research that demonstrates the effectiveness of inpatient group therapy.[4]

Often the debate about the role of group therapy on the inpatient unit has nothing to do with the effectiveness of group therapy but is, in reality, a debate about another issue entirely—the issue of professional territoriality. For many years, the inpatient therapy group has been organized and led by the psychiatric nursing profession. But what happens if the ward has a medical director who does not believe that psychiatric nurses (or occupational therapists, activity therapists, or recreational therapists) should do psychotherapy? In this instance, the group therapy program is scuttled, not because it is ineffective, but to safeguard professional territory.

These extrinsic factors are not immutable and the group therapist must struggle to change them. One method is to survey the research literature supporting the efficacy of a group program and to present the evidence to appropriate administrative bodies. I am optimistic about the prospects of staff attitudinal changes; the medical profession is gradually relinquishing its antediluvian insistence on psychotherapy hegemony. Professional interdisciplinary struggles, if present, need to be resolved in policy committees or staff meetings; the small therapy group must not be used as a battleground on which professional self-interests are contested.

In addition to these extrinsic, programmatic problems, the acute inpatient ward poses several major *intrinsic* problems for the group therapist. There are two particularly staggering problems that must be faced by every inpatient group therapist: the rapid turnover of the inpatient ward and the heterogeneity of psychopathology.

Every contemporary acute psychiatric ward is characterized by rapid patient turnover. The length of psychiatric hospitalization has inexorably shortened over the past two decades; and, on most wards, the average length of hospitalization ranges from one to three weeks. This means, of course, that the composition of the small therapy group will be highly unstable. I led a daily group on an inpatient unit for five years and rarely had the identical group for two consecutive meetings and almost never for three. This appears to be an immutable situation. The group therapist has little influence on ward admission and discharge policy. In fact, more and more commonly, discharge decisions are based on fiscal rather than on clinical concerns. Nor is there any reason to suspect that this situation will change in the future; the "revolving door" inpatient unit is here to stay and, if anything, the door will whirl even faster in the future.

Another important clinical fact of life on the inpatient unit is the great heterogeneity of psychopathology. The typical contemporary psychiatric inpatient unit (often one in a general community hospital) admits patients with a wide spectrum of pathology: acute schizophrenic psychosis, decompensated borderline or neurotic conditions, substance abuse, major affective disorders, eating disorders, post-traumatic stress disorders, or situational reactions.

Not only is there a wide diagnostic spread, but there are also broad differences in attitudes toward, and capacity for, psychotherapy: many patients may be unmotivated; they may be psychologically unsophisticated; they may not want to be in the hospital; they do not agree that they need help; they often are not paying for therapy; they may have neither introspective propensity nor inner-directed curiosity about themselves.

The presence of these two factors alone (the brief duration of treatment and the range of psychopathology) makes it evident that a radical modification of technique is required for the inpatient therapy group. These two intrinsic clinical conditions violate some of the necessary conditions of group therapy I describe earlier in this text. In chapter 3, I stressed the crucial importance of stability of membership. Gradually, over weeks and months, the sense of cohesiveness—a major therapeutic factor—develops, and patients often derive enormous benefit from the experience of being a valued member of an ongoing stable group. How then to lead a whirligig group in which new members come and go virtually every session? Similarly, in the chapter on composition, I stressed the importance of composing a group carefully and of paying special attention to avoiding deviants and to selecting members with roughly the same amount of ego strength. How then to lead a group in which one has almost no control over the membership—a group in which there may be floridly psychotic individuals sitting side by side with better functioning, integrated members?*

There are several other intrinsic clinical factors which are less dramatically confounding than the rapid patient turnover and the range of psychopathology but nonetheless still exert significant influence on the functioning of an inpatient psychotherapy group.

All of the patients in the group are generally profoundly disturbed; their immediate goal is alleviation of distress rather than self-exploration or personal growth. Once the acute crisis disappears, the patient is discharged. The therapist's time is very limited. Generally there is no time to see a patient in pre-group interviews to establish a relationship and to prepare him or her for the group. There is little time to integrate new members into the group, to work on termination (someone terminates the group almost every meeting), to work through issues that arise in the group, or to focus on transfer of learning.

The group boundaries are often blurred. Patients may be in other groups on the ward with some or many of the same members. Extra-

---

*Elsewhere I discuss some options the group therapist has for facing these two factors.[5] First, the leader can reduce the group turnover and instability by insuring that, whatever other types of groups offered, the ward holds daily group meetings of a "talking" group. There are two approaches to composition: the "team" approach and the "level" approach. In the team approach, the patients are assigned, usually according to order of admission, to one of two or three teams, depending upon the size of the ward. All the patients on one team meet in a small therapy group. Thus, the team small group is maximally heterogeneous with the entire range of psychopathology of the ward represented in the group. In the level approach, the patient is assigned to a more homogeneous group according to his or her level of functioning: severely ill psychotic patients are assigned to one group and "higher level" patients to another. Research indicates that patients value both small groups but tend to value their participation in the level group somewhat more highly.[6] Each of the two groups serve a different function. The team group contributes heavily to the harmony of the ward and opens channels of communication between the psychotic and the less severely disturbed patients. The level groups have the advantage of working at the proper level for each of the members: the groups can be tailored for the capacity of the members. My recommendation is that the psychiatric ward offer a daily team group and a daily level group for each patient.

group socializing is, of course, the rule rather than the exception: patients spend their entire day together. The boundaries of confidentiality are similarly blurred. There can be no true confidentiality in the small inpatient group: patients often share important small group events with other patients on the ward, and staff members freely share information with one another during rounds, nursing report, and staff meetings. Thus, the small inpatient group boundary of confidentiality is an elastic one which encompasses the entire ward and is not confined to any one group within that ward.

The role of the group leader is more complex since he or she may be involved with patients throughout the day in other roles. There is limited therapist stability as well as patient stability; group leaders are frequently psychiatric nurses who—because of the necessity of weekend, evening, and night coverage—are on a rotating schedule and often cannot be present at the group for several consecutive meetings.

Therapist autonomy is limited in other ways as well: for example, therapists have, as I shall discuss shortly, only limited control over group composition. They often have no choice about co-therapists, who are usually assigned on the basis of the rotation schedule.

Therapy is much more concentrated. Each patient has several therapists at the same time. The group leader rarely has time, for example, to discuss the therapy of his or her group patients with a patient's individual therapist. Lastly, the pace of the acute inpatient ward is so harried that there is little opportunity for supervision or even for post-meeting discussion between therapists.

FORMULATION OF GOALS

These then are the clinical facts of life of the inpatient therapy group. Once you have grasped them and differentiated intrinsic from extrinsic factors, it is time to ask this question: Given the many confounding intrinsic factors that influence (and hobble) the course of the inpatient group, what *can* the group accomplish? What are reasonable goals of therapy—goals that are attainable by the inpatient clinical population in the available time?

I may start by noting that the goals of the acute inpatient group are *not* identical to those of acute inpatient hospitalization. The goal of the group is *not* to resolve a psychotic depression, *not* to decrease psychotic panic, *not* to slow down a manic patient, *not* to diminish hallucinations or delusions. Groups can do none of these things. That's the job of other aspects of the ward treatment program—primarily of the psychopharmacological regimen. To set these goals for a therapy group is not only unrealistic but sentences the group to failure.

So much for what the inpatient group *cannot* do. What *can* it offer? I shall describe six achievable goals: engaging the patient in the therapeutic process; talking helps; problem spotting; decreasing isolation; being helpful to others; alleviation of hospital-related anxiety.

1. *Engaging the Patient in the Therapeutic Process.*

The contemporary pattern of acute psychiatric hospitalization—brief but repeated admissions to psychiatric wards in general hospitals—has proven to be more effective than longer hospitalization if (and only if) hospitalization is followed with adequate aftercare treatment.[7] Furthermore, there is persuasive evidence to suggest that group therapy aftercare is a particularly efficacious mode of aftercare treatment, more so than individual aftercare therapy in many studies.[8]

A primary goal of inpatient group therapy emerges from these findings: *to engage the patient in a process that he or she perceives as constructive and supportive and will wish to continue after discharge from the hospital.* Keep in mind that, for many patients, the inpatient psychotherapy experience is their first introduction to therapy. If their group therapy experience is sufficiently positive and supportive to encourage them to attend an aftercare group, then—all other factors aside —the inpatient therapy group will have served a very important function.

2. *Talking Helps.*

The inpatient therapy group helps patients learn that talking about their problems is helpful. They learn that there is relief to be gained in sharing pain and in being heard, understood, and accepted by others. From listening to others, one also learns that others suffer from the same type of disabling distress as oneself—that one is not unique in one's suffering. In other words, the inpatient group introduces patients to the therapeutic factors of cohesiveness and universality.

3. *Problem Spotting.*

The duration of therapy in the inpatient therapy group is far too brief to allow patients to work through problems. But the group can efficiently help patients spot problems that they may, with profit, work on in ongoing individual therapy, both during their hospital stay and in their post-hospital therapy. The therapy group teaches patients, in effect, that "here is where your work needs to be done"; and, by providing a focus for therapy, the groups increase the efficiency of other therapies. It is important that the problems that groups identify be problems with some therapeutic handle—a problem that the patient perceives as circumscribed and malleable (not some generalized problem—for example, depression or suicidal inclinations—that the patient was very aware of having and offers no handhold for therapy). The group is most adept at helping a patient identify problems in his or her mode of relating to other individuals. I mentioned earlier that group therapy is not an effective format to reduce anxiety or to ameliorate psychotic thinking or profound depression, but it is the therapy setting *non pareil* for individuals to learn about maladaptive, interpersonal behavior.

- For example, Emily was an extremely isolated young woman. She complained that she was always in the position of calling others for a social engagement. No one ever reciprocated. She never received invitations; she had no close girlfriends who sought her out. Her dates with men always turned into one-night stands: she attempted to please them by going to bed with them, but they never called for a second date. People seemed to forget her as soon as they met her. During the three group meetings she attended, the group gave her consistent feedback about the fact that she was always pleasant and always wore a gracious smile and always seemed to say what she thought would be pleasing to others. However, in this process, people soon lost track of who Emily was. What were her own opinions? What were her own desires and feelings? Her need to be eternally pleasing had a serious negative consequence: that is, people found her boring and predictable. A dramatic example occurred in her second meeting when I forgot her name and apologized to her. Her response was, "That's all right, I don't mind." I noted that the fact that she didn't mind was probably one of the reasons I had forgotten her name. In other words, had she been the type of person who would have minded or made her needs more overt, then most likely I would not have forgotten her name. In her three group meetings, Emily identified a major problem that had far-reaching consequences for her social relationships outside—that is, her tendency to submerge herself in a desperate but self-defeating attempt to capture the affection of others.

4. Decreasing Isolation.
The inpatient group can help to break down the isolation that exists between members. The group is a laboratory exercise intended to sharpen communication skills: the better the communication, the less

the isolation. It helps individuals share with one another and permits them to obtain feedback about how others perceive them. Through feedback individuals discover their blind spots: that, to take one example, though one may wish to express concern or interest, others often interpret one's gestures and comments as indicating impatience or disapproval.

Decreasing isolation between group members has two distinct payoffs. First, improved communicational skills will help patients in their relationship to others outside the hospital. Virtually every patient who is admitted in crisis to an inpatient ward suffers from a breakdown or an absence of important supportive relationships with others. If the patient is able to transfer communicational skills from the group to his or her outside life, then the group will have fulfilled a very important goal.

A second payoff in decreasing isolation is evident in a patient's behavior on the ward. The less the patient's isolation, the more is that patient able to use the therapy resources available on the ward. As communication improves, patients are able to make good use of their relationships with other patients. There is much research that indicates that a particularly valuable aspect of inpatient hospitalization is the help that patients get from their relationships with other patients.[9]

5. *Being Helpful to Others.*

This goal, the therapeutic factor of altruism, is closely related to the previous one. If patients are helped by other patients, then they are also helped by the knowledge that they themselves have been useful to others. Patients generally enter psychiatric hospitals in a state of profound demoralization. They feel that not only have they no way of helping themselves but that they have nothing to offer others. The experience of being valuable to other ward members is enormously confirming to one's sense of self-worth.

6. *Alleviation of Hospital-Related Anxiety.*

Much anxiety emanates from the process of psychiatric hospitalization. Many patients experience great shame; others are concerned about stigmatization and the effects of hospitalization on their jobs and friendships. Many patients are distressed by events on the ward: bizarre behavior of other patients, staff tension, acutely disturbed patients who monopolize large amounts of staff time.

Many of these secondary sources of tension compound the patient's primary dysphoria and must be addressed in therapy. The small therapy groups (as well as the therapeutic community group) provide a forum where patients can air these issues and often achieve reassurance simply from learning that these concerns are shared by other members as well.

MODIFICATION OF TECHNIQUE

Now that we have appraised the clinical setting of the inpatient group and formulated a realistic set of goals, we are ready to consider the implications of these steps for group therapy strategy and technique.

The Time Frame of the Therapist

In the outpatient therapy group I have described in this text, the time frame of the therapist is many weeks or months. Therapists must be patient, must build cohesiveness over many sessions, must work through issues repetitively from meeting to meeting (they recognize that psychotherapy is often "cyclotherapy" because they must return again and again to the same issues in the therapeutic work). The inpatient group therapist faces an entirely different situation: the group composition changes almost every day; members have a very brief duration of therapy—indeed, many members attend the group for only a single session.

It is clear that the inpatient group therapist must adopt a radically shortened time frame; and *I believe that the inpatient group therapist must consider the life of the group to be only a single session.* Perhaps there will be continuity from one meeting to the next; perhaps you may have culture bearers who will be present in several consecutive meetings, but do not count on it. The most constructive attitude to assume is that your group will last for only a single session, and that you must strive to offer something useful for as many patients as possible during that session.

Efficiency and Activity

The single-session time frame demands efficiency. You have no time to allow issues to build, to let things develop in the group and slowly work them through. You have no time to waste; you must work quickly and efficiently; you have only a single opportunity to engage a patient, and you must not squander it.

Efficiency demands activity on the part of the therapist. There is no place in inpatient group psychotherapy for the passive, reflective group therapist. A far higher level of activity is demanded in inpatient than in outpatient groups; you must activate the group and call on, actively support, and interact personally with members. The increased level of activity demanded requires a major shift in technique for the person who has been trained in long-term group therapy. However, in my opinion, it is an absolutely essential modification of technique.

Support

Keep in mind that one of the major goals of the inpatient therapy group is to engage patients in a therapeutic process they will wish to continue after leaving the hospital. Thus, it is imperative that the therapist create in the group an atmosphere that members experience as supportive, positive, and constructive. Members must feel safe; they must learn to trust the group and to experience it as a place where they will be understood and accepted. The inpatient therapy group is not the place for confrontation, for criticism, for the expression and examination of anger. There will often be patients in the group who are conning or manipulative and who may need powerful confrontation, but it is far better to let them pass unchallenged than to run the risk of making the group feel unsafe to the vast majority of patients.

In the long-term outpatient group, therapists provide support both *directly* and *indirectly: direct support,* by personal engagement, by empathic listening, by understanding, by accepting glances, nods and gestures; *indirect support,* by building a cohesive group which then becomes a powerful agent of support.

Inpatient group psychotherapists must learn to offer support more quickly and directly. Support is not something that therapists "of course" provide. In fact, many training programs in psychotherapy unwittingly extinguish a therapist's natural propensity to support patients. Therapists are trained to become sniffers of pathology—experts in the detection of weaknesses. They are often so sensitized to transferential and countertransferential issues that they hold themselves back from engaging in basically human, supportive behavior with their patients.

Support may be offered in a myriad of ways. The most direct, and the one most often overlooked by well-trained professional therapists, is to acknowledge openly the patients' efforts, intentions, strengths, positive contributions, and risks. If, to take an obvious example, one member states that he finds a woman in the group very attractive, it is important that this patient be supported for the risk he has taken. You may wonder whether he has previously been able to express his admiration of another so openly, and note, if appropriate, that this is reflective of real progress for him in the group. Or, if you may make a point of openly noting when another member, revealing delicate and important material, encourages other members to take similar risks. Do not assume that the patient automatically realizes that his or her disclosure has helped others take risks.

Try to emphasize the positive rather than the negative aspects of a defense. Consider, for example, the patient who persists in playing assistant therapist. Do not confront the person by challenging this refusal to be a patient and to work on personal issues, but offer instead positive comments about how helpful the patient has been to others and then gently remark on his or her selflessness and reluctance to ask for something personal from the group. It is the rare patient who resists the therapist's suggestion that he or she needs to learn to be more selfish and to ask for more from others.

The therapist also supports by helping patients obtain support from the group. Some patients, for example, obtain very little support from the group because they characteristically present themselves in a highly objectionable fashion. A self-centered patient who incessantly ruminates about a somatic condition will rapidly exhaust the patience of any group. When you identify such behavior, it is important to intervene quickly before animosity and rejection occur. A number of tactics are available: you may directly instruct the patient about other modes of behaving in the group. You may, for example, assign the patient the task of introducing new members into the group, or of giving feedback to other members, or of attempting to guess and express what each person's evaluation of the group is that day. Elsewhere I described a patient who talked incessantly about her many surgical procedures.[10] It became clear from listening to this woman's description of her life situation that she felt she had given everything to her children and had received nothing in return. She also described a deep sense of unworthiness and of being inferior to the other members of the group. I suggested that when she talked about her surgical procedures she was really saying: "I have some needs, too, but I have trouble asking for them. My preoccupation with my surgery is a way of asking: 'pay some attention to me.'" Eventually the patient agreed with my formulation and also to my request that, whenever she talked about her surgery, I had her permission to translate that into the real message, "Pay more attention to me." This patient's explicit request for help was effective, and the members responded to her positively—as they never did when she recited her irritating litany of somatic complaints.

Another approach to support is to focus upon making the group safe. Often that means that you must take care to avoid conflict in the group. In the long-term outpatient group, some degree of conflict and tension is necessary to the therapeutic work. It is an entirely different matter in the inpatient group, where patients are so vulnerable that tolerance for conflict and additional anxiety is limited.

Therefore, anticipate and avoid conflict whenever possible. If patients are irritable or want to learn more about how they can be assertive or disagree with others, then it is best to channel that work onto yourself: you are, let us hope, in a far better position to handle criticism than any of the group members. If two patients are locked in conflict, it is best to intervene quickly and to search for positive aspects of the conflict. For example, keep in mind that sparks often fly between two individuals because of mirroring: one sees aspects of oneself (especially negative aspects) in another whom one dislikes because of what one dislikes in oneself. Thus, you can deflect conflict by asking individuals to discuss the various ways in which they resemble their adversary.

There are many other conflict-avoiding strategies. Keep in mind, for example, that envy is often an integral part of interpersonal conflict. It is often constructive to ask adversaries to talk about those aspects of one another that they admire or envy. Role switching is sometimes a useful technique: ask adversaries to switch roles and to present the other's point of view. Often it is helpful to remind the group that opponents generally prove to be very helpful to one another, whereas those who are indifferent rarely help one another grow. Sometimes an adversarial position is a method of showing caring.

One reason some members experience the group as unsafe is that they fear things will go too far, that the group may coerce them to lose control—to say, think, or feel things that will result in interpersonal catastrophe. You can help these patients feel safe in the group by allowing them to exercise control over their participation. Check in with patients repeatedly with such questions as: "Do you feel we're pushing you too hard?" Or, "Is this too uncomfortable for you? Do you think you've revealed too much of yourself today?" Or, "Have I been too intrusive by asking you such direct questions today?"

When you lead groups of severely disturbed regressed patients, you must provide even more support and in an even more direct fashion. Examine the behavior of the severely regressed patients and find in it some positive aspect. Support the mute patient for staying the whole session; compliment the patient who leaves early for even having stayed twenty minutes; support the patient who arrives late for having shown up at the meeting; support inactive patients for having paid attention throughout the meeting. If statements are unintelligible or bizarre, nonetheless label them as attempts to communicate. If patients try to give advice, even inappropriate advice, reward them for their intentions to help.

Focus of the Inpatient Group: The Here-and-Now

Throughout this text, I have repeatedly emphasized the importance of here-and-now interaction in the group therapeutic process. I have stressed that work in the here-and-now is the heart of the group therapeutic process—the power cell that energizes the therapy group. Yet, whenever I have visited inpatient wards throughout the country, I have found that inpatient groups rarely focus on here-and-now interaction. Such avoidance of the here-and-now is, in my opinion, precisely the reason that so many inpatient groups are ineffective.

If the inpatient group does not focus on the here-and-now, what other options are there? Most inpatient groups adopt a "then-and-there" focus in which members, following the therapist's cues, take turns presenting their "back home" problems (the problems that brought them into the hospital), and the other members attempt to address these problems with exhortation and advice. This approach to inpatient group therapy is always a mistake; it is the *least* effective way to lead a therapy group and almost invariably sentences the group to failure. The problems that have brought a patient into the hospital are complex and overwhelming. They have generally foiled the best efforts of skilled mental health professionals, and they will, without question, stump the therapy group members. For one thing, the patient is always an unreliable reporter: the information he or she presents to the group will invariably be biased; and, because it is not possible to summarize all important background information in the short time available in a group meeting, it will be limited as well.

Not only is the group destined to fail to solve or to cast new light on the patient's "back home" problem, but there are many other disadvantages to this format. For one thing, it results in highly inequitable time sharing. If much or all of a meeting is devoted to one patient, many of the remaining patients will feel cheated or bored. Unlike outpatient group members, they cannot even bank on the idea that they have "credit" in the group—that is, that the group owes them time and attention. The duration of hospitalization is so short that either patients are discharged before their turn comes, or the group composition changes so rapidly that patients are left clutching worthless I.O.U.'s.

471

Some inpatient groups focus on ward problems—that is, ward tensions, staff-patient conflict, housekeeping disputes, and so on. Generally this is an unsatisfactory mode of using the small group: the average inpatient ward has approximately twenty patients; and, in any small group meeting, only half the members and one or two staff members will be present. Invariably the group members or the staff members discussed are in the *other* group. A much better arena for dealing with ward problems is the therapeutic community meeting in which all patients and the staff are present.

Other inpatient groups focus on common themes—for example, suicidal ideation, hallucinations, or drug side effects. Such meetings may be of value to some, but rarely to all, members. Furthermore, the information dispensed may easily be provided to patients via other formats. It is not the most powerful way of using the inherent strength of the small group modality.

The clinical circumstances of the inpatient group do not make the here-and-now focus any less important or less advisable. In fact, the here-and-now focus is as effective in inpatient as in outpatient therapy. However, the clinical conditions of inpatient work (especially the brief duration of treatment and the severity of illness) demand modifications in technique. As I mentioned earlier, there can be no time for working through interpersonal issues. Instead, you must help patients spot interpersonal problems, reinforce interpersonal strengths, and encourage them to attend aftercare therapy where they can pursue and work through the interpersonal issues identified in the group.

The most important point to be made about the use of the here-and-now in inpatient groups is already implicit in the foregoing discussion of support. I cannot emphasize too heavily that *the here-and-now is not synonymous with conflict, confrontation, or critical feedback.* I am certain that it is because of this erroneous assumption that so few inpatient group therapists capitalize on the value of here-and-now interaction.

Conflict is only one, and by no means the most important, facet of here-and-now interaction. The here-and-now focus helps patients learn many invaluable interpersonal skills: to communicate more clearly, to get closer to others, to express positive feelings, to become aware of personal mannerisms that push other people away, to listen, to offer support, to reveal oneself, to form friendships.

The inpatient group therapist must pay special attention to the issue of the relevancy of the here-and-now. The members of an inpatient group are in crisis; they are preoccupied with their life problems and immobilized with dysphoria or confusion. Unlike many outpatient group members who are interested in self-exploration, in personal growth, and in improving their abilities to cope with future crisis, inpatients are closed, in a survival mode, and unlikely to apprehend the relevancy for their problems of the here-and-now focus.

Therefore, you must provide explicit instruction about the relevancy of the here-and-now. I begin each meeting with a brief orientation to the new patients in which I emphasize that, though patients may enter the hospital for different reasons, everyone can benefit from examining how he or she relates to other people. Everyone can be helped by learning how to get more out of relationships with others. I stress that I focus on relationships in group therapy because that is what group therapy does best. The group provides an unusual opportunity for people to learn about relationships: in the group, there are other members and two mental health experts who are willing to provide feedback about how they see each person in the group relating to others. I also acknowledge that members have important and painful problems, other than interpersonal ones, but that these problems need to be addressed in other therapeutic modalities: in individual therapy, in social service interviews, in couple or marital therapy.

Structure

Just as there is no place in acute inpatient group work for the inactive therapist, there is no place for the nondirective group therapist. The great majority of patients on an inpatient ward are confused, frightened, and disorganized; they crave and require some external structure and stability. Consider the experience of patients newly admitted to the psychiatric unit: they are surrounded by other troubled, irrationally behaving patients; their mental acuity may be obtunded by medication; they are introduced to many staff members who, because they are on a complex rotating schedule, may not appear to have consistent patterns of attendance; they are exposed, sometimes for the first time, to a wide array of therapies and therapists.

Often the first step to acquiring internal structure is exposure to a clearly perceived externally imposed structure. Anxiety is relieved when one is provided with clear, firm expectations for behavior in a new situation.

In debriefing interviews with newly discharged patients, the overwhelming majority expressed a preference for group leaders who provided an active structure for the group.[11] They appreciated a therapist who started the group meeting and who provided crystal-clear direction for the procedure of the group. They preferred leaders who actively invited members to participate, who focused the group's attention on work, who assured equal distribution of time, who reminded the group of its basic group task and direction. Empirical research also demonstrates that both members and therapist consider structured group meetings as more therapeutic than unstructured ones.[12]

Modes of Structure

Group leaders can provide structure for the group in many ways: through setting clear spatial and temporal boundaries; through a lucid, confident personal style; through orienting and preparing patients for group therapy; through a consistent and coherent group procedure.

Spatial and Temporal Boundaries

An ideal physical arrangement for a therapy group consists of a circle of members meeting in an appropriately sized room with a closed door. The physical plan of many wards, however, makes these basic requirements difficult. Some units, for example, have only one group room and yet must schedule two groups to meet at the same time. In this case one group may have to meet in a very large, busy general activity room or in an open hallway without clear spatial demarcation. I believe that the lack of clear spatial boundaries vitiates intimacy and cohesiveness and compromises the work of the group; it is far preferable to find some closed space even if it means meeting off the ward. Some group rooms have long couches or benches which seat three or four members. To use these seats legislates against interaction: four members sitting in a row will be unable to see one another and will generally address the therapist rather than each other.

Structure is also provided by temporal stability. The ideal meeting begins with all members present and punctual, and meets with no interruptions whatsoever until its conclusion. It is difficult to approximate these conditions in an inpatient setting for several reasons: disorganized patients arrive late because they forget the time and place of the meeting; heavily medicated patients fall asleep during a session and interrupt the group flow; members are called out for some medical or therapy appointment; members with limited attention span may request to leave early; agitated or panicked patients may bolt from the group at any time.

Therapists must intervene in every way possible to provide maximum stability. They may urge the administration to declare the group time inviolable so that patients may not be called out of the group for any reason whatsoever. They may request the staff members to remind disorganized patients about the group meeting and escort them into the room. The group therapists may model promptness through their own personal example.

There are several approaches to the problem of "bolters." First, patients are made more anxious if they perceive that they will not be permitted to leave the room. Therefore it is best simply to express the hope that they can stay the whole meeting; and, if they cannot, suggest that they return the next day when they feel more settled. If a patient attempts to leave the room in mid-session, you cannot, of course, physically block him or her, but there are still available options. You may reframe the situation in a way that provides a rationale for the patient's putting up with the discomfort of staying: for example, in the case of a patient who has stated that he or she often flees from uncomfortable situations and is resolved to change that pattern, you might remind him or her of that resolution. You may comment: "Eleanor, it's clear that you're feeling very uncomfortable now, and I know you want to leave the room, but I remember your saying just the other day that you've always isolated yourself when you felt bad and that you want to try to find ways to reach out to others. I wonder if this might not be a good time to work on that by simply trying extra hard to stay in the meeting today?" You may decrease anxiety by suggesting that she simply be an observer for the rest of the session, or you may suggest that she change her seat to a place that feels more comfortable to her—for example, next to you.

Groups led for higher-level patients may be made more stable by a policy that prohibits latecomers from entering the group session. This policy, of course, is only effective with an optional group. It may present problems for therapists who feel uncomfortable at being strict gatekeepers; it runs against the grain of traditional clinical training to refuse admission to patients who want therapy. Of course, this policy creates resentment in patients who arrive at a meeting only a few minutes late, but it also conveys to them that you value the group time and work and that you want to get the maximum amount of uninterrupted work each session. Debriefing interviews with patients at discharge invariably reveal that patients resent interruptions and approve of all the therapist's efforts to ensure stability. Latecomers who are denied entrance to the group may sulk briefly but generally will be punctual the following day.

Therapist Style

The therapist also greatly contributes to the sense of structure through personal style. Confused or frightened patients are reassured by a therapist who is firm, explicit, and decisive yet who, at the same time, shares with patients the reasons for his or her actions. Many long-term outpatient group therapists allow events to run their course and then encourage the examination and integration of the event. Inpatient groups, however, are marked by repeated major disruptive events. Members are often too stressed and vulnerable to deal effectively with such events and are reassured if therapists act decisively and firmly. If, for example, a manic patient veers out of control and monopolizes the group's time, it is best that you intervene and prevent the patient from obstructing the group work in that session. Nothing is to be gained by allowing the patient to continue on course; it profits neither the patient nor the group. You may, for example, tell the patient that it is time to be quiet and to work on listening to others; or, if the patient is unable to exercise any control, you may escort him or her from the room. Generally, it is excellent model setting for therapists to talk about their ambivalent feelings in such a situation: for example, they may share both their conviction that they have made the proper move for the welfare of the entire group and their great discomfort at assuming an authoritarian pose.

At other times the group may engage in long discussions which the inpatient therapist realizes are not effective and do not constitute effective work. Again, the outpatient therapist has options available, including waiting out and then analyzing the resistance. However, in inpatient groups it is far more efficient to be direct—to, for example, interrupt the group with some explicit message such as, "I have a sense that this topic is of much interest to several of the people in the room, but I also feel it's not the best way to use the group time since it's a discussion that you could easily have outside the group. Groups are much more helpful if we help people learn more about how they relate and communicate with others, and I think it would be better if we could get back to . . ." (and at this point you can supply some clear alternative to the group).

Group Session Protocol

One of the most potent ways of providing structure is to build into each session a consistent, explicit sequence. This is a particularly radical departure from traditional outpatient group therapy technique; it is however, a necessary procedure in specialized groups and makes for

476

the most efficient use of a limited number of sessions. In the inpatient group, a structured protocol for each session has the advantage not only of efficiency but also of ameliorating anxiety and confusion in severely ill patients. Although group sessions, depending upon the task and compositon of the group, will have different sequences, natural lines of cleavage appear in the great majority of inpatient group therapy sessions.

1. *The first few minutes.* This is the time for the therapist to provide explicit structure for the group. If there are new members in the group in a session (and there generally are in the acute inpatient group), then this is the time for the therapist to prepare these new patients for therapy. (I shall shortly describe a model group in which I give a verbatim example of a preparatory statement.)

2. *Definition of the task.* The therapist, in this phase, attempts to determine the most profitable direction for the group to take in a particular session. Do not make the error of plunging in great depth into the first issue discussed, for, in so doing, you may miss other potentially productive agendas. You may determine the task in a number of ways: you may, for example, simply listen to get a feel of the urgent issues present that day; or you may (and I will give a description of this technique shortly) provide some structured exercise which will permit you to ascertain the most valuable direction for the group to take that day.[13]

3. *"Filling" the task.* Once you have a broad view of the potentially fertile issues for a session, you attempt to address these issues and, in the process, involve as many patients as possible in the group session.

4. *The final few minutes.* The last few minutes is the summing-up period. You indicate that the work phase is over, and you devote the remaining time to review and analysis of the meeting. This is the "self-reflective loop" of the here-and-now (see page 136) in which you attempt to clarify the group interaction that occurred in the session. You may also wish to do some final "mopping up": you may inquire about any jagged edges or ruffled feelings that members may take out of the session; or you may ask the members, both the active and the silent ones, about their experience and evaluation of the meeting?

Disadvantages of Structure

Several times in this text, I have remonstrated against excessive structure. For example, in discussing norm setting, I urged that the therapist strive to make the group as autonomous as possible, that an effective group is a group that takes maximum responsibility for its own functioning. Does not an excessively active therapist who structures the group tightly create a dependent group? Surely if the leader does everything for the patients, they will do too little for themselves.

Empirical research demonstrates the shortcomings of excessive structure. On pages 449–50 I described findings from an encounter group project which demonstrated that leaders who provide excessive structure may be positively evaluated by their members but their groups, nonetheless, will have less positive outcomes.[14]

A second finding from the same study is instructive: leader behavior that is structuring in nature (total verbal activity and amount of managerial behavior) is related in *curvilinear* fashion to positive outcome (both at the end of the group and at the six month follow-up.) In other words, the rule of the golden mean prevails: too much or too little leader structuring is detrimental to growth.

Thus, we face a dilemma. In many brief, specialized groups, we must provide structure; but if we provide too much, our group members will not learn to use their own resources. This is a major problem for the inpatient group therapist who must, for all the reasons I have described, structure the group and yet, at the same time, avoid infantalizing its members.

There is a way out of this dilemma—a way so important it constitutes a fundamental principle of therapy technique in the specialized group. The leader must *structure the group in a fashion that encourages each member's autonomous functioning.* If this principle seems paradoxical, wait! The following model of an inpatient group will clarify it.

THE HIGHER-LEVEL GROUP: A WORKING MODEL

I shall describe, in some detail, a format for the higher-level functioning inpatient group. Keep in mind that my intention in this section as throughout this chapter is not to prescribe a particular blueprint but to illustrate an approach to the modification of group therapy technique. My hope is that this model illustrates the strategy of modification and will assist you to construct an effective model for your own specialized clinical situation.

I suggest that an optional group be held for upper-level patients* for approximately seventy-five minutes five times a week. I have experimented with a variety of models over several years; the model I de-

---

*Upper-level patients are the talking, oriented patients. Elsewhere I have described an analogous model for the regressed, psychotic patient.[15]

scribe below is the most effective one that I have found, and I have used it for several hundred inpatient group therapy sessions.

The basic protocol of the meeting:

1. Orientation and preparation · · · 3 to 5 minutes
2. Agenda go-round (each member offers a personal agenda for the meeting) · · · 20 to 30 minutes
3. Agenda "filling" · · · 20 to 35 minutes
4. Review · · · 10 to 20 minutes

Orientation and Preparation

The preparation of patients for the therapy group is no less important in inpatient than in outpatient group therapy. The time frame, of course, is radically different. Instead of spending twenty to thirty minutes preparing a patient for group therapy during an individual session, the inpatient group therapist must accomplish such preparation in the first few minutes of the inpatient group session. If a new patient is present in the group that meeting (as is usually the case), then I suggest that the leader give a simple and brief introductory statement which includes: a description of housekeeping details (time, length of meeting, rules about punctuality), a clear exposition of the purpose of the group, and an outline of the basic procedure of the group describing the sequence of the meeting. The following is a typical preparatory statement (directed to the new patient(s) in a group on a particular day):

"John, I'm Irv Yalom and this is the afternoon therapy group which meets daily for one hour and fifteen minutes beginning at two o'clock. My co-therapist is ——, and she will be here four of the five meetings for the next four weeks. On the fifth day, another therapist will take her place.

"The purpose of this group is to help members learn more about the way they communicate and relate to others. People come into the hospital with many different kinds of important problems, but one thing that most individuals have in common here is some unhappiness about the way that some of their important relationships are going.

"There are, of course, many other urgent problems that people have, but those are best worked on in some of your other forms of therapy. What groups do best of all is to help people understand more about their relationships with others. One of the ways that we can best work is to focus on the relationships that exist between people in this room. The better your communication becomes with each of the people here, the better will your communication become with people in your outside life.

"It's important to know that observers are present almost every day to watch the group through this one-way mirror. [I point toward the mirror and also toward the microphone, in an attempt to orient the patient as clearly as possible to the spatial surroundings.] The observers will be professional mental health workers, often medical students, or other members of the ward staff.

"We begin our meetings by going around the group and checking with each person and asking each to say something about the kinds of problems they're having in their lives that they'd like to try to work on in the group. It is very hard to come up with an agenda during your first meetings. But don't sweat it. We will help you with it. That's our job. After the go-round we then try to work on as many of these problems as possible. In the last fifteen minutes of the group, the observers will come into the room and share their observations with us. After that, in the last few minutes, we check in with everyone here about how they size up the meeting and about the leftover feelings that should be looked at before the group ends."

The Agenda Go-Round

The second phase of the group is the definition of the task. The overriding task of the group (from which the various goals of the group emanate) is to help each member explore and improve his or her interpersonal relationships. An efficient method of task definition is a structured exercise which asks each patient to formulate a brief, personal agenda for the meeting. The agenda must be realistic and "do-able" in the group that day; it must focus on interpersonal issues and, if possible, on issues that in some way relate to one or more members of the group meeting.

To formulate an appropriate agenda is a complex task; patients need considerable assistance, especially in their first couple of meetings, from the therapist. Each patient is, in effect, asked to make a statement that involves three steps: (1) acknowledge that one wishes to change (2) in some interpersonal domain (3) which has some here-and-now manifestation.

Patients have relatively little difficulty with the first two aspects of the agenda but require considerable help from the therapist in the third—framing the agenda in the here-and-now. The third part is, however, less complex than it seems, and the therapist may move any agenda into the here-and-now by mastering only a few basic guidelines. Consider the following common agenda: "I want to learn to communicate better to others." The patient has already accomplished the first two steps of the agenda: that is, (1) he or she has expressed a desire for change (2) in an interpersonal area. All that remains is to move the agenda into the here-and-now—a step that the therapist can easily facilitate with a comment such as: "Please look around the room. With whom in the group do you communicate well? With whom would you like to improve your communication?"

Another common agenda is the statement, "I'd like to learn to get closer to people." The therapist's procedure is the same: to thrust it into the here-and-now by asking, "With whom in the group do you feel close? With whom in the group would you like to feel closer?" Another common agenda is: "I want to be able to express my needs and get them met. I keep my needs and pain hidden inside and keep trying to please everybody." Shift that into the here-and-now by asking: "Would you be willing to try to let us know today what you need? What kind of pain do you have? What would you like from us?"

Nota bene, the agenda is generally *not* the reason the patient is in the hospital. But, often unbeknownst to the patient, the agenda may be an underlying or contributory reason. The patient may have been hospitalized because of substance abuse, depression, or a self-destructive attempt. However, underlying such behaviors or events there are almost invariably important tensions or disruptions in interpersonal relationships.

Note also that the therapist strives for agendas that are gentle, positive, and nonconfrontational. In the examples I cited of agendas dealing with communication or closeness, I accented strength and achievement by inquiring first about the positive end of the scale.

Many patients offer an agenda that directly addresses anger: for example, "I want to be able to express my rage. The doctors say I turn my anger inward and that causes me to be depressed." This agenda must be handled with care. You do *not* want patients to express anger at one another, and you must reshape that agenda into a more constructive form. I have found it helpful to approach the patient in the following manner: "I believe that anger is often a serious problem because people let it build up to high levels and then are unable to express it. The release of so much anger would feel like a volcano exploding. It's frightening both to you and to others. It's much more useful in the group to work with "young anger," with anger before it turns into red anger. Thus, I'd like to suggest to you that today you focus on young anger—for example, impatience, frustration, or very minor feelings of annoyance. Would you be willing to express in the group any minor flickerings of impatience or annoyance when they first occur—for example, irritation, at the way I lead the group today?"

The agenda exercise has many advantages. For one thing, it is a solution to the paradox that structure is necessary but, at the same time, growth inhibiting. *The agenda exercise provides structure for the group, but it simultaneously encourages autonomous behavior on the part of the patient.* Patients are required to take responsibility for the therapy and to say, in effect: "Here is what I want to change about myself. Here's what I choose to work on in the group today." Thus, the agenda encourages patients to assume a more active role in their own therapy and to make better use of the group. They learn that straightforward, explicit agendas involving another member of the group will guarantee that they do productive work in the session: for example, "I tried to approach Mary earlier today to talk to her, and I have the feeling that she rejected me, wanted nothing to do with me, and I'd like to find out why."

Some patients have great difficulty stating their needs directly and explicitly. In fact, many enter the hospital because of self-destructive attempts which are indirect methods of signifying that they need help. The agenda task teaches them to state their needs clearly and directly and to ask explicitly for help from others. In fact, for many patients, the agenda exercise, rather than any subsequent work in the group meeting, is itself the therapy. If these patients can be taught to ask for help verbally rather than through some nonverbal, self-destructive mode then the hospitalization will have been very useful.

The agenda exercise also provides a "wide-angle" view of the group work that may be done that day; the group leader is quickly able to make an appraisal of what each patient is willing to do and of which patients' goals may interdigitate with other patients' goals in the group.

The agenda exercise is valuable but cannot immediately be installed in a group. Often a therapy group needs several meetings to catch on to the task and to recognize its usefulness. The agenda go-round is not an exercise that the group members can accomplish on their own: the therapist must be extremely facilitative, persistent, inventive, and often directive to make the exercise work. If a member is extremely resistant, sometimes a suitable agenda is for individuals to examine why it is so hard to formulate an agenda. Sometimes it is useful to ask other members to suggest a suitable agenda for a given patient. For example, a nineteen-year-old male offered an unworkable agenda: "My dad treats me like a kid." He could not comprehend the agenda concept in his first meeting, and I asked for suggestions from the other members. There were several excellent ones: "I want to examine why I'm so scared in here," and, "I want to be less silent in the group"; ultimately one perfect agenda was suggested: "I want to learn what I do that makes my dad treat me like a kid. Do I act like a kid in this group?"

Agenda Filling

Once the agenda go-round has been completed, the next phase of the group begins. In many ways, this segment of the group resembles any interactionally based group therapy meeting in which members explore and attempt to change maladaptive interpersonal behavior. But there is one major difference: therapists have at their disposal agendas for each member of the group which allow them to focus the work in a more "customized" and efficient manner. The time span of the inpatient group is only a single session, and the therapist must be efficient and provide the greatest good for the greatest number of patients.

If the group is large—let us say twelve members—and if there are new members in the group who require a good bit of time to formulate an agenda, then there may be only thirty minutes of the group in which to fill the twelve agendas. Obviously, work cannot be done on each agenda in the session, and it is important that patients be aware of this possibility. You may explicitly inform patients that the agenda go-round does not constitute a promise that each agenda will be focused upon in the group. You may also convey this possibility through conditional language in the agenda-formation phase: for example, "If time permits, what would you like to work on today?"

Nonetheless, the efficient and active therapist should be able to work on the majority of agendas in each session. The single most valuable guideline I can offer is try to fit agendas together so that you work on several at once. If, for example, John's agenda is that he is very isolated and would like some feedback from the members about why it's hard to approach him, then you can fill several agendas simultaneously by calling for feedback for John from members with agendas such as: I want to learn to express my feelings," "I want to learn how to communicate better to others," or, "I want to learn how to state my opinions clearly."

Similarly, if there's a patient in the group who is weeping and highly distressed, why should you, the therapist, comfort that patient when you have, sitting in the group, patients with the agenda of: "I want to learn to express my feelings," or, "I want to learn how to be closer to other people." By calling on these members, you lace several agendas together.

Generally, during the agenda go-round, the therapist collects several "letters of credit"—commitments from patients about certain work they want to do during the meeting. If, for example, one patient states it is important to learn to take risks in the group, it is wise to store this and, at some appropriate time, call on the patient to take a risk by, for example, giving feedback or evaluating the meeting. If a patient expresses the wish to open up and share his or her pain with others, it is facilitative to elicit some discrete contract from the patient, even if for two or three minutes of sharing, and then make sure the patient gets the time in the group. It is possible, with such contracts, to increase responsibility assumption by asking the patient to nominate one or two members to call on him or her if the patient has not fulfilled the contract by a certain time in the session.

The Review

The final phase of the group meeting signals a formal end to the body of the meeting and consists of review and evaluation of the meeting. I lead an inpatient group on a teaching unit and generally have two to four students observing the session through a one-way mirror. I prefer to divide the final phase of the group into two equal segments: (1) a discussion of the meeting by the therapist(s) and observer(s); and (2) the group members' response to this discussion.

In the first segment, therapists and observers form a small circle in the room and conduct an open analysis of a meeting just as though there were no patients in the room listening and watching. (If there are no observers in the meeting that day, the co-therapists hold a discussion between themselves or may invite the patients to contribute in a discussion in which everyone attempts to review and analyze the meeting.) In this discussion, leaders and observers review the meeting and focus upon the group leadership and upon the experience of each of the members. The leaders question what they missed, what else they might have done in the group, whether they left out certain members. The discussants make some comment about each member: the type of agenda formulated, the work done on that agenda, guesses about a patient's satisfaction with the group.

Although this group "wrap-up" format is unorthodox, it is, in my experience, effective. For one thing, it makes constructive use of observers. In the traditional teaching format, student-observers stay invisible and meet with the therapist in a post-group discussion to which the patients, of course, do not have access. Patients generally resent this observation format and sometimes develop paranoid feelings about being watched. To bring the observers into the group transforms the observers from a negative to a positive force in the group. In fact, patients often express disappointment when no observers are present.

This format requires therapist transparency and is an excellent opportunity to do invaluable modeling. Co-therapists may discuss their dilemmas or concerns or puzzlement. They may ask the observers for feedback about their behavior. Did, for example, the observers think they were too intrusive, or did they put too much pressure on a particular patient? What did the observers think about the relationship between the two leaders?

In the final segment of the review phase, the discussion is thrown open to the patients. Generally this is a time of great animation, since the therapist-observer discussion generates considerable data. There are two directions that the final few minutes can take. First, the patients may respond to the therapist-observer discussion: for example, they may comment on the openness, or lack thereof, of the therapists and observers. They may have reactions to hearing the therapist express doubt or fallibility. They may agree with or challenge the observations that have been made about their experience in the group.

The other direction this phase can take is for the patients to process and evaluate their own meeting. The therapist may guide a discussion in which he or she makes such inquiries as: "How did you feel about the meeting today? Did you get what you wanted out of it? What were your major disappointments with this session? If we had another half hour to go, how would you use the time?" The final few minutes are also a time for the therapist to make contact with the silent members and inquire about their experience: "Were there times when you wanted to speak in the group? What stopped you? Had you wanted to be called on, or were you grateful not to have participated? *If* you had said something, what would it have been?" (This last question is often miraculously facilitative.)

In a research project that specifically inquired into patients' reactions to this format, there was strong consensus among the patients that the final phase of the group was an integral central part of the group session.[16] When patients were asked what percentage of the value of the group stemmed from this final segment, they placed on it a value that far exceeded the actual time involved. Some patients, for example, ascribed to the final twenty minutes of the meeting a value of as high as 75 percent of the total group value.

16

GROUP THERAPY
AND THE
ENCOUNTER GROUP

Fads and fashions change in the fields of psychotherapy and personal growth. And it is difficult to overestimate the rapidity of that change. My previous edition of this book contained a heady forty-two–page chapter on encounter groups studded with extravagant predictions, my own and others, about the soaring, perdurable destiny of the entire encounter group movement.

Today, a decade later, as I poke around in the ashes of that movement, I consider deleting this chapter entirely. The encounter group movement has vaporized: growth centers and free universities have closed; university bulletin boards and underground newspapers post no encounter group offerings. Ten years ago, university dormitories churned with debates about whether to permit growth institutes to conduct marathon groups for the students in the dormitory common room. Today debates of equal intensity still rage—but about vastly different issues: for example, whether to allow the large cadre of born-again Christian students to conduct public Bible readings in those same common rooms.

Over the past three years, I have asked several thousand mental health professionals who have attended group therapy workshops whether they have been a member or a leader of an encounter group over the past couple of years. Only a handful, perhaps 1 percent, have responded affirmatively, and some beginning students have asked, "What *is* an encounter group?"

Yet I have decided against deletion. There are several reasons the well-educated group therapist should be familiar with the history, the mechanics, and the ethos of the encounter group. First, though the encounter group movement has been disassembled, the sophisticated technology of the encounter group persists and is employed by currently fashionable groups, both secular (communication workshops, social skills training groups, psychoeducational groups)[1] and religious.

Traditional religious institutions as well as new religious sects have made much use of encounter technology. New religions, such as the Jesus movement, the Divine Light Mission, and the Unification Church, offer many encounter-like small group meetings.[2] Over the last decade, there has developed a massive marriage encounter program sponsored primarily by Catholic and Jewish religious leaders (but also by other Christian denominations). Religious congregations are offered a wide variety of growth experiences: retreats for married couples, teenagers, engaged couples, families, the divorced and the bereaved, and people desiring a self-exploratory experience. These growth experiences use a behavioral technology similar to the encounter group technology.* In addition, several Christian denominations have been involved in another movement (the "Cursillo") using a group format. There is no national registry of these contemporary religious growth experiences; but while no accurate figures are available, it is clear that vast quantities of people have attended, and their number is steadily increasing.

Perhaps the most rapidly expanding group movement is the self-help group.[3] It has been estimated that in 1980 over 10 million Americans attended one of the vast number of self-help groups (for example, A.A., Recovery, Inc., Theos [widows], Compassionate Friends [bereaved parents], Mended Hearts [coronary surgery patients], Overeaters Anonymous); many of these groups also employ techniques developed in the encounter group movement.

---

*I do not mean to imply that the founders of this movement consciously and explicitly applied encounter group techniques. Indeed, the movement was begun by a Spanish priest, Father Carlo, who most likely knew nothing of the American encounter group. Even the name seems coincidental. The original Spanish term was *encuentro*, meaning "rediscovery" or to "meet again." Nonetheless, the evolution of the technique in the United States was influenced by a zeitgeist that, without doubt, was shaped by the encounter group movement. In fact, the movement has separated into two factions as a result of an American priest's (Father Gallagher) emphasis on the experience and sharing of feelings. Nor do I mean that traditional churches lead encounter groups; in fact, few of the programs use a small group (six to twenty persons) format. Nonetheless, the type of structured exercise, the emphasis upon personal exploration, identification and expression of feelings, and the development of genuine intimacy are highly reminiscent of encounter group technology.

The large group awareness programs—for example, est and Life-spring—have made much use of encounter group technology. These programs use a time-extended format which consists largely of inspirational lectures and a series of encounter group structured exercises arranged and presented in a high-tech, slickly packaged format. The large group consisting of two hundred to three hundred people is occasionally broken down into smaller groups or dyads for structured exercises. (I have described and discussed this format in detail elsewhere.[4]) Large numbers of people are involved. By 1984, over 650,000 people had had the basic est or Lifespring training. In addition to the large group format, Lifespring offers advanced training consisting of fifty hours of small group (twenty to thirty-five persons) meetings which differ little from the highly energized, interactional, cohesive encounter group of the 1960s and 1970s. Approximately 12,000 people have attended these Lifespring encounter groups, and the numbers, as of 1985, are still increasing. During 1983 alone, 1,200 people attended these advanced Lifespring training groups.

The attendance of all these group phenomena combined—secular workshops, religious growth experiences, self-help groups, large group experiences such as est and Lifespring—dwarfs the attendance enjoyed, in their heyday, by the free universities, Esalen, and other growth centers.

So, although the movement is over and an encounter group *qua* encounter group is hard to find, more people than ever before are having an encounter group experience.

Although we clinicians do not often lead these various new groups, we must remain informed. Many of our clients may, before or during therapy, engage in one of them. Furthermore, many people view, not without justification, these groups as an alternative mental health system.

Other reasons justify discussing encounter groups in this text. In the following chapter, I stress the importance, in the training of the group therapist, of some personal group experience. Some training programs may offer a traditional therapy group for trainees, but most sponsor some variant of an encounter group. (For the moment, I refer to all personal growth experiential groups as "encounter groups," but shortly I will define terms more precisely.) Thus, many group therapists enter the field through the portals of the encounter group.

Keep in mind, too, that the contemporary therapy group, as I have described it in this text, has been greatly influenced by the encounter group. No historical account of the development and evolution of group

488

therapy is complete without including a description of the cross-fertilization occurring between the therapy and the encounter traditions.

Lastly, and this may seem surprising to some readers, the encounter group, or at least the tradition from which it emerged, has been responsible for developing the best, the most sophisticated small group research technology. In comparison, group therapy research has been crude and unimaginative; much of the empirical research I have cited throughout this text has had its roots in the encounter group tradition.

So much for the justification of discussing encounter groups. Let me proceed to a definition and to a historical survey.

What Is an Encounter Group?

Encounter group is a rough, inexact generic term that encompasses a great variety of forms. Consider some of its many aliases: human relations groups, training groups, T-groups, sensitivity groups, personal growth groups, marathon groups, human potential groups, sensory awareness groups, basic encounter groups, truth labs, experiential groups, confrontation groups, and so on.

Although the nominal plumage is dazzling in its diversity, all these groups have several common denominators. The groups range in size from eight to twenty members—large enough to encourage face-to-face interaction, yet small enough to permit all members to interact. The groups are generally time-limited, often compressed into hours or days. They focus to a large extent on the here-and-now; they transcend etiquette and encourage the doffing of traditional social facades. Finally, these groups value interpersonal honesty, exploration, confrontation, heightened emotional expressiveness, and self-disclosure. The goals of a group are often vague. Occasionally they stress merely the provision of an experience—joy, a state of being "turned on," entertainment; but more often they implicitly or explicitly strive for some change—in behavior, in attitudes, in values, in life style, in degree of self-actualization; or in one's relation to others, to nature, to one's physical being; or in one's way of being in the world. The participants are not generally labeled "patients"; the experience is considered not therapy but "growth."

ANTECEDENTS AND EVOLUTION OF THE ENCOUNTER GROUP[5]

The term *encounter group* for an experiential group was coined by Carl Rogers in the mid-1960s. The most common term before then was *T-group* ("T" for "training in human relations").* The first T-group, the ancestral experiential group, was held in 1946. The State of Connecticut had passed a Fair Employment Practices Act and asked Kurt Lewin, a prominent social psychologist, to train leaders who could deal effectively with tensions among groups and thus help to change the racial attitudes of the public. Kurt Lewin organized a workshop that consisted of small groups of ten members each. These groups were led in the traditional manner of the day; they were basically discussion groups and analyzed "back home" problems presented by the group members.

Kurt Lewin always believed in "no research without action; no action without research." Consequently he assigned research observers to record and code the behavioral interactions of each of the small groups. During evening meetings, the group leaders and the research observers met and pooled their observations of leader, member, and group behavior. Soon some participants learned of these evening meetings and asked permission to attend. Reluctantly the staff agreed; they feared revealing their own inadequacies and were uncertain about the effects upon the members of hearing their behavior discussed openly.

Finally the members were permitted to attend and observe the evening meetings on a trial basis. Observers who have written about this experience report that the effect on both participants and staff was "electric."[6] There was something galvanizing about witnessing an in-depth discussion of one's own behavior. Soon the format of the evening meetings was widened to permit the participants to respond to the observations, and shortly thereafter all parties were involved in the analysis and interpretation of their interaction. Before many evenings had passed, all the participants were attending the evening meetings, which were often continued for as long as three hours. There was widespread agreement that the meetings offered the participants a new and rich understanding of their own behavior.

The staff immediately realized that they had, somewhat serendipitously, discovered a powerful technique of human relations education —experiential learning. Group members learn most effectively by studying the very interactional network in which they themselves are enmeshed. They profit enormously by being confronted, in an objective

*In this chapter, I shall use the terms *T-group* and *encounter group* loosely and interchangeably. As I shall discuss, the field is so sprawling that no single term is entirely satisfactory. Even here I shall retain a nuance of difference: *T-group*, when I want to accent the traditional human relations flavor; *encounter group*, to accent the unconventional personal growth aspect.

manner, with on-the-spot observations of their own behavior and its effects on others; they may learn about their interpersonal styles, the responses of others to them, and about group behavior in general.

From this beginning, research has been woven into the fabric of the T-group. I refer not only to formal research but to a research attitude on the part of the leader, who collaborates with the group members in a research inquiry designed to enable each participant to experience, understand, and change his or her behavior. This feature, together with the concept of the T-group as a technique of education, is essential, as I shall shortly show, in the differentiation of the T-group from the therapy group. It was a principle, however, that was gradually abandoned in the later metamorphosis of T-group to encounter group.

This laboratory was so successful that similar laboratories were held in successive years. The small discussion groups were called "basic skill training groups" (shortened in 1949 to "T-group"). By 1950, the sponsoring organization, the National Training Laboratory (N.T.L.), was established within the National Educational Association as a permanent year-round organization. In its heyday, the N.T.L. had a network of several hundred trained leaders and, during the 1960s, held human relations laboratories for thousands of participants.

The T-group was only one aspect of these human relations laboratories. Large group exercises were instituted. Intergroup relationships were studied. The laboratories emphasized theory and the application of in-group learning to "back home" situations.

At first the leaders maintained that the T-group was an educational venture in human relationships and not a psychotherapeutic one. Gradually, however, during the 1950s and 1960s, the training staff shifted from a sociological and educational emphasis to a clinical one. Rogerian and Freudian clinicians became involved with the human relations laboratory, and the language gradually grew less sociological and sociopsychological and more clinical.

Gradually, the T-group moved in the direction of ever greater emphasis on interpersonal interaction. Discussion of outside material ("there-and-then"), including "back home" current problems or past personal history, was discouraged, whereas here-and-now material was highly prized. The T-group made major technical innovations which were destined to exert much influence on both the encounter group and the psychotherapy group. These included feedback, unfreezing, observant participation, and cognitive aids.

491

Feedback

Feedback, a term borrowed from electrical engineering, was first applied to the behavioral sciences by Lewin (it is no accident that he was teaching at M.I.T. at the time).[7] The early trainers considered that an important flaw in society was that too little opportunity exists for individuals to obtain accurate feedback from their "back home" associates: bosses, fellow employees, husbands, wives, teachers, students, and so on. Feedback became an essential ingredient of all T-groups; without it the here-and-now focus had little meaning or vitality. Feedback seemed most effective in the group when it stemmed from here-and-now observations, when it followed the generating event as closely as possible, and when the recipient checked it out with other group members to establish its validity and reduce perceptual distortion.

Unfreezing

Unfreezing, also adopted from Lewinian change theory, refers to the process of disconfirming an individual's former belief system. Motivation for change must be generated before change can occur. One must be helped to re-examine many cherished assumptions about oneself and one's relations to others. The familiar must be made strange;[8] thus, many common props, social conventions, status symbols, and ordinary procedural rules were eliminated from the T-group, and one's values and beliefs about oneself were challenged. This was a most uncomfortable state to be in, a state tolerable only under certain conditions: one must experience the group as a safe refuge within which it is possible to entertain new beliefs and experiment with new behavior without fear of reprisal.

Observant Participation

Most trainers considered observant participation as the optimal method of involvement for all group participants. Members must both participate emotionally in the group and observe themselves and the group objectively. Often this is a difficult task to master and members chafe at the trainer's attempts to subject the group to objective analysis. Yet the dual task is essential to learning; alone, either action or intellectual scrutiny yields little learning. Camus once wrote, "My greatest wish: to remain lucid in ecstasy."[9] So, too, the T-group (and the therapy group) is most effective when its members can couple cognitive appraisal with emotional experience.

Cognitive Aids

Cognitive guides around which T-group participants could organize their experience were often presented in brief "lecturettes" by a T-group leader or another staff member. Today there is a resurgence of the use of cognitive aids in communication workshops and in specialized, homogenous therapy groups. One example used in early T-group work (and which is still useful in the contemporary therapy group) is the Johari window,* a four-celled personality paradigm which clarifies the function of feedback and self-disclosure.

	Known to Self	Unknown to Self
Known to Others	A	B
Unknown to Others	C	D

Cell A, "Known to self and Known to others," is the public area of the self; cell B, "Unknown to self and Known to others," is the blind area; cell C, "Known to self and Unknown to others," is the secret area; cell D, "Unknown to self and Unknown to others," is the unconscious self. The goals of the T-group, the trainer suggests, are to increase the size of cell A by decreasing cell B (blind spots) through feedback and cell C (secret area) through self-disclosure. In traditional T-groups, cell D (the unconscious) was considered "out of bounds."

The use of such cognitive aids, lectures, reading assignments, and theory sessions demonstrates that the basic allegiance of the T-group was to the classroom rather than to the consulting room. The participants were considered students; the task of the T-group was to facilitate learning for its members. Different trainers emphasized different types of learning: some focused primarily on group dynamics and helped the members to understand group development, group pressures, the leadership role, and common group tensions and obstacles; others emphasized personal learning and focused on the interpersonal style and communication of the members. These two emphases became more polarized until a formal distinction was made in laboratory planning between group process groups (which were more concerned with group properties, group functioning, and, on a larger scale, with organization development) and personal development groups. I shall pursue the evolution of the T-group most concerned

*Named after Joe Luft and Harry Ingram, who first developed the window.[10]

with personal development, since this form of T-group most closely resembles the therapy group and has spawned the many varieties of encounter groups.

From T-Group to Encounter Group

GROUP THERAPY FOR NORMALS

In the 1950s, the N.T.L. established several regional branches, and each of the various sectors gradually developed its own T-group emphasis. It was the West Coast, and particularly Southern California, that pursued the "personal development" model most vigorously. A 1962 article by Southern California trainers, which presented a model of a T-group as "group therapy for normals," clearly signaled the change in emphasis from group dynamics to individual dynamics, from stress on the development of interpersonal skills to a greater concern with personal growth.[11] The experiential group was still considered an instrument of education—not of therapy. However, a broader, more humanistically based definition of education was proposed: education is not, they argued, the process of acquiring interpersonal and leadership skills, not the understanding of organizational and group functioning; education is nothing less than full self-discovery, the development of one's full potential.

THE STRESSES OF NORMALITY

These group leaders worked with normal healthy members of society, indeed with individuals who by most objective standards had achieved considerable success. Yet they learned that though these members had much external success, their inner experience was one of tension, insecurity, and value conflict.

The highly competitive American culture, many behavioral scientists noted, encourages facade building. One who is considered successful by one's peers too often strives at all costs to protect one's public image. Doubts about personal adequacy are swallowed and one must maintain constant vigilance lest any uncertainty or discomfort slip through. This process is isolating and crippling since it curtails communication not only with others but with oneself. Gradually, in order to eliminate a perpetual state of self-recrimination, the successful individual comes to believe in the reality of his or her facade and attempts, through uncon-

494

scious means, to ward off internal and external attacks on that self-image. Thus, a state of equilibrium is reached but at great price: considerable energy is invested in maintaining intrapersonal and interpersonal separation, energy that might otherwise be used in the service of self-actualization. Creativity and self-knowledge are sacrificed as one turns one's gaze outward in a never-ending search for peer validation. Interpersonal relationships are shallow and unrewarding; one squelches spontaneity so that one's studied facade remains unruffled; one avoids self-disclosure, and refrains from confronting others to avoid reciprocal confrontation.

THE T-GROUP AS A SOCIAL OASIS

The T-group was promulgated as a respite from the insidious stresses of our culture. It offered an oasis where many of the restrictive norms I have described were unnecessary—in fact, were not permitted. The T-group did not reward individuals for material success, hierarchical position, a manner of unruffled aplomb, efficiency, or expertise in some specialized area. Instead, the T-group encouraged different values: interpersonal honesty and disclosure of self-doubts and perceived weaknesses.

Gradually individuals discovered that their pretense of self-satisfaction was not only unnecessary but an encumbrance. For years they had operated on the assumption of having to pay dearly if they let slip their facade—a cost envisioned as humiliation, rejection, and loss of social or professional status. The T-group experience challenged these assumptions and enables these people to experiment with openness and to differentiate its real costs from its pseudo costs. Obviously there are real risks in the disclosure of all one's thoughts and feelings: "The realities of living, of sensible interpersonal strategy and tactics, clearly dictate the advisability of keeping some things as part of our private selves."[12] But many of the pseudo costs are exposed. Letting one's facade slip does not result in rejection; in fact, members find themselves more completely accepted on the basis of a fully disclosed self rather than on that of a false projected image. Moreover, their deep sense of isolation is assuaged, as each becomes aware of the universality of secret doubts and fears. These processes are self-reinforcing since the experience of universality encourages each to be even more self-revealing. Members who have previously regarded interpersonal relationships as automated or threatening are able to sample the inherent richness and depth of human intimacy.

495

As the goal of the group shifted from education, in a traditional sense, to personal change, the name of the group shifted from "T-group" (training in human relations) or "sensitivity training group" (training in interpersonal sensitivity), to one more consonant with the basic thrust of the group. Several labels were advanced: "personal growth," "human potential," "human development," or "basic encounter" groups. "Encounter group," which stresses the basic authentic encounter between members (and between leader and members and between the disparate parts of each member), had the most staying power and became the most popular name for the "let it all hang out" experiential group prevalent in the 1960s and 1970s.

The "third force" in psychology (third after Freudian analysis and Watsonian-Skinnerian behaviorism), which emphasized a holistic, humanistic concept of the person, provided impetus and form to the encounter group from yet another direction. Psychologists such as A. Maslow, G. Allport, E. Fromm, R. May, F. Perls, C. Rogers, and J. Bugenthal (and the philosphers behind them—Sartre, Tillich, Jaspers, Heidegger, and Husserl) rebelled strongly against the mechanistic model of behaviorism, the determinism and reductionism of analytic theory. "Where," they asked, "is the person? Where is consciousness, will, decision, responsibility, and a recognition and concern for the basic and tragic dimensions of existence?"

All of these influences resulted in groups with a much broader, and vaguer, goal—nothing less than "total enhancement of the individual."[13] Time in the group was set aside for reflective silence, for listening to music or poetry. Members were encouraged to give voice to their deepest concerns—to re-examine these basic life values and the discrepancies between them and their life styles, to encounter their many false selves; to explore the long-buried parts of themselves (the softer, feminine parts in the case of men, for example).

Collision with the field of psychotherapy was inevitable. T-groups claimed that they offered therapy for normals, yet also that "normality" was a sham, that everyone was a patient: the disease, a dehumanized runaway technocracy; the remedy, a return to grappling with basic problems of the human condition; and the vehicle of remedy, the experiential group. The medical model could no longer be applied to mental illness. The differentiation between mental illness and health grew as vague as the distinction between treatment and education. Encounter group leaders claimed both that patienthood is ubiquitous and that "one need not be sick to get better."

496

The Effectiveness of the Encounter Group

In its early days the T-group was heavily researched. The social psychologists and sociologists associated with the National Training Laboratories generated an enormous amount of rigorous research into its process and outcome. Many of these studies still stand as paradigms of imaginative, sophisticated research.

The most extensive (and expensive) controlled research inquiry into the effectiveness or groups that purport to change behavior and personality, was conducted by Lieberman, Yalom, and Miles in 1973. Since I believe this research has much relevance to group therapy (I have drawn from this study often in this book), I shall describe the design and method before reporting the results. The project is complex, and I can only touch upon major features relevant to our present discussion; I refer interested, research-minded readers to *Encounter Groups: First Facts,* the monograph fully describing the project.[14]

We offered an experiential group as an accredited one-quarter course at Stanford University. Two hundred and ten participants (all undergraduate students, aged eighteen to twenty-two) signed up for the course and were then randomly distributed (aside from sex, race, and previous encounter group experience) to one of eighteen groups, each of which met for a total of thirty hours over a twelve-week period. Sixty-nine subjects, who were similar to the participants but who did not have a group experience, were used as a control population and completed all the outcome research instruments.

THE LEADERS

Since a major aim of the study was to investigate the effect of leader technique upon outcome, we sought to diversify leader style by employing leaders from several ideological schools. We selected experienced and expert leaders from ten such schools:

1. Traditional NTL (T-groups),
2. Encounter groups (personal growth group),
3. Gestalt groups,
4. Sensory awareness groups (Esalen group),
5. Transactional analytic groups,
6. Psychodrama groups,
7. Synanon,

8. Psychoanalytically oriented experiential groups,
9. Marathon groups,
10. Encounter-tapes groups.

There were a total of eighteen groups. Of the 210 subjects who started in the eighteen groups, 40 dropped out before attending half the meetings, and 170 finished the thirty-hour group experience.

WHAT DID WE MEASURE?

We were most interested in an intensive examination of outcome and the relationship between outcome, leader technique, and group process variables. To evaluate outcome, an extensive psychological battery of instruments was administered to each subject three times: before beginning the group, immediately after completing it, and six months after completion.

These self-administered instruments attempted to measure any possible changes encounter groups might effect—for example, self-esteem, self-ideal discrepancy, interpersonal attitudes and behavior life values, defense mechanisms, emotional expressivity, values, friendship patterns, and major life decisions. Much third-party outcome assessment was collected—evaluations by leaders, by other group members, and by a network of each subject's personal acquaintances. The assessment outcome was strikingly similar to that of a psychotherapy project but with one important difference: since the subjects were not patients but ostensibly healthy individuals seeking growth, no assessment of "target symptoms" or "chief complaints" was made.

Leader style was studied by teams of trained raters, who observed all meetings and coded all behavior of the leader, by tape recordings and written transcripts of the meetings in which all leader statements were recorded and analyzed, and by questionnaires filled out by participants.

Process data were collected by the observers and from questionnaires filled out by participants at the end of each meeting.

RESULTS: WHAT DID WE FIND?

First, the participants' testimony was very high. At the termination of the group, the 170 subjects who completed the groups considered them pleasant (65 percent), constructive (78 percent), a good learning experience (61 percent), and a "turned-on experience" (50 percent).

Over 90 percent felt that encounter groups should be a regular part of the elective college curriculum. Six months later, the enthusiasm had waned, but the overall evaluation was still positive. To put it another way, at the end of the group for every one participant who viewed the experience negatively, 4.7 participants perceived it as productive; six months later, the ratio was still positive but had dropped to 2.3 to 1.

So much for testimony. What of the overall, more objective battery of assessment measures? Each participant's outcome (judged from all assessment measures) was rated and placed in one of six categories: high learner, moderate changer, unchanged, negative changer, casualty (significant, enduring, psychological decompensation which was due to being in the group), and dropout. The results for all 206[15] experimental subjects and for the sixty-nine control subjects may be summarized in table 16.1. ("Short post" is at termination of group and "long post" is at six-month follow-up.)

Table 16.1 indicates that approximately one-third of the participants at the termination of the group and at the six months follow-up had undergone moderate or considerable positive change. The control population, who were studied with the same instruments, showed much less change, either negative or positive. The encounter group, thus, clearly influenced change, but for both better and worse. Maintenance of change was high: of those who changed positively, 75 percent maintained their change for at least six months.

Put in a critical fashion, one might say that table 16.1 indicates that, of all subjects who began a thirty-hour encounter group led by an acknowledged expert, approximately two-thirds found it an unrewarding experience (either dropout, casualty, negative change, or unchanged).

Viewing the results more generously, one might put it this way. "This is a college course. One does not expect that students who drop out will profit. Let us, therefore, eliminate the dropouts from the data. If that is done (see table 16.2), then it appears that 39 percent of all students taking a one-quarter college course underwent some significant positive personal change which persisted for at least six months—not a bad batting average for a twelve-week, thirty-hour course!"

However, even if we consider the goblet one-third full rather than two-thirds empty, it is difficult to escape the conclusion that, in this project, encounter groups did not appear to be a highly potent agent of change. Furthermore, a significant risk factor was involved: 16 (8 percent) of the 210 subjects suffered psychological injury which produced sequelae still present six months after the end of the group.

SOURCE: *Encounter Groups: First Facts*, by Morton A. Lieberman, Irvin D. Yalom, and Matthew B. Miles. New York: Basic Books, Inc., 1973.

TABLE 16.1

Index of Change for All Participants Who Began Study

	CASUALTIES	NEGATIVE CHANGER	DROPOUTS	UNCHANGED	MODERATE CHANGER	HIGH LEARNER	TOTAL
Short Post							
Participants	16 (08%)	17 (08%)	27 (13%)	78 (38%)	40 (20%)	28 (14%)	206
Controls		16 (23%)		41 (60%)	9 (13%)	3 (04%)	69
Long Post							
Participants	16 (10%)	13 (08%)	27 (17%)	52 (33%)	37 (23%)	15 (09%)	160
Controls		7 (15%)		32 (68%)	5 (11%)	3 (06%)	47

TABLE 16.2

Index of Change for Those Who Completed Group
(N = 179 Short Post, 133 Long Post)

	CASUALTIES	NEGATIVE CHANGER	UNCHANGED	MODERATE CHANGER	HIGH LEARNER
Short Post	09%	10%	44%	22%	16%
Long Post	12%	10%	39%	28%	11%

SOURCE: *Encounter Groups: First Facts*, by Morton A. Lieberman, Irvin D. Yalom, and Matthew B. Miles. New York: Basic Books, Inc., 1973.

Still, much caution must be exercised in the interpretation of the results. It would do violence to the data to conclude that encounter groups *per se* are ineffective or even dangerous. First, it is difficult to gauge the degree to which we can generalize these findings to populations other than an undergraduate college student sample. But, even more important, we must take note that these are all massed results: the data are handled as though all subjects were in one encounter group. There was no standard encounter group experience; there were eighteen different groups, each with a distinct culture, each offering a different experience, and each with very different outcomes. *In some groups, almost every member underwent some positive change with no one suffering injury; in other groups, not a single member benefited, and one was fortunate to remain unchanged.*

The next obvious question—and one very relevant to psychotherapy —is: Which type of leader had the best, and which the worst, results? The T-group leader, the gestalt, the T.A., the psychodrama leader, and so on? However, we soon learned that the question posed in this form was not meaningful. The behavior of the leaders when carefully rated by observers varied greatly and did not conform to our pre-group expectations. *The ideological school to which a leader belonged told us little about the actual behavior of that leader.* We found that the behavior of the leader of one school—for example, transactional analysis— resembled the behavior of the other T.A. leader no more closely than that of any of the other seventeen leaders. In other words, the behavior of a leader is not predictable from one's membership in a particular ideological school. Yet the effectiveness of a group was, in large part, a function of its leader's behavior.

To answer the question, Which is the more effective leadership style?, we need, then, a more accurate, empirically derived leader taxonomy. A factor analysis of a large number of leader behavior variables (rated by observers) resulted in four basic leadership functions:

1. Emotional stimulation (challenging, confronting, activity; intrusive modeling by personal risk-taking and high self-disclosure).
2. Caring (offering support, affection, praise, protection, warmth, acceptance, genuineness, concern).
3. Meaning attribution (explaining, clarifying, interpreting, providing a cognitive framework for change; translating feelings and experiences into ideas).
4. Executive function (setting limits, rules, norms, goals; managing time; pacing, stopping, interceding, suggesting procedures).

These four leadership functions had a clear and striking relationship to outcome. Caring and meaning attribution had a linear relationship to positive outcome: *the higher the caring and the higher the meaning attribution, the higher the positive outcome.*

The other two functions, emotional stimulation and executive function, had a curvilinear relationship to outcome—the rule of the golden mean: *too much or too little of this leader behavior resulted in lower positive outcome.* For example, too little leader emotional stimulation resulted in an unenergetic, devitalized group; too much stimulation (especially with insufficient meaning attribution) resulted in a highly emotionally charged climate with the leader pressing for more emotional interaction than the members could integrate. Too little executive function—a *laissez-faire style*—resulted in a bewildered, floundering group; too much executive function resulted in a highly structured, authoritarian arrhythmic group, which failed to develop a sense of member autonomy or a freely flowing interactional sequence.

The most successful leader, then, was one moderate in amount of stimulation and in expression of executive function and high in caring and meaning attribution. Both caring and meaning attribution seemed necessary: neither alone was sufficient to ensure success.

These findings from encounter groups strongly corroborate the functions of the group therapist as discussed in chapter 5. Both emotional stimulation and cognitive structuring are essential. The Rogerian factors of empathy, genuineness, and unconditional positive regard thus seem incomplete; we must add the cognitive function of the leader. The research does not tell us what kind of meaning attribution is essential. Several ideological explanatory vocabularies seemed useful. What seems important is the *process* of explanation which, in several ways, enabled a participant to integrate his or her experience to generalize from it, and to transport it into other life situations.*

The Relationship between the Encounter Group and the Therapy Group

Having traced the development of the encounter group to the point of collision with the psychotherapy group, I shall now turn to the evolu-

---

*The importance of meaning attribution received powerful support from another source. When members were asked to report (at the end of each session) the most significant event of a meeting and the reason for its significance, we found that those members who gained from the experience were far more likely to report incidents involving cognitive integration. (Even so revered an activity as self-disclosure bore little relationship to change unless it was accompanied by intellectual insight.) The pervasiveness and strength of this finding was impressive as well as unexpected (occurring in encounter groups with a fundamental anti-intellectual ethos).

tion of the therapy group in order to clarify the interchange between the two disciplines.

THE EVOLUTION OF GROUP THERAPY

The history of group therapy has been too thoroughly described in other texts to warrant repetition here.[16] A rapid sweep will reveal the basic trends. Joseph Hershey Pratt, a Boston internist, is generally acknowledged to be the father of contemporary group therapy. Pratt undertook, in 1905, the treatment of many patients with far-advanced tuberculosis. Recognizing the relationship between psychological health and the physical course of tuberculosis, Pratt undertook to treat the person rather than the disease. He designed a treatment regimen that included home visits, diary keeping by patients, and weekly meetings of a tuberculosis class of approximately twenty-five patients. At these classes, the diaries were inspected, weight gains were recorded publicly on a blackboard, and testimonials were given by successful patients. A degree of cohesiveness and mutual support developed which appeared helpful in combating the depression and insolation so common to tubercular patients.

During the 1920s and 1930s, several psychiatrists experimented with group methods. A. Adler employed group methods in Europe because of his awareness of the social nature of human problems and because of a desire to provide psychotherapeutic help to the working classes.[17] E. W. Lazell, in 1921, met with groups of schizophrenic patients in St. Elizabeth's Hospital in Washington, D.C., and delivered lectures on schizophrenia.[18] L. C. Marsh, a few years later, used groups for a wide range of clinical problems, including psychosis, psychoneurosis, psychophysiological disorders, and stammering.[19] He employed a variety of techniques, including such didactic methods as lectures and homework assignments as well as exercises designed to promote considerable interaction; for example, members were asked to "treat" one another; or all were asked to discuss such topics as one's earliest memory, ingredients of one's inferiority complex, night dreams, and daydreams. L. Wender used analytic group methods with hospitalized nonpsychotic patients in the 1930s,[20] while T. Burrows[21] and D. Schilder[22] applied these techniques to the treatment of psychoneurotic outpatients. S. Slavson, who worked with groups of disturbed children and young adolescents, exerted considerable influence in the field through his teaching and writing at a time when group therapy was not yet considered by most workers to be an effective therapeutic approach.[23] J. Moreno, who first used the term *group therapy*, employed group methods before 1920 but has been primarily identified with psychodrama, which he introduced into America in 1925.[24]

These tentative beginnings in the use of group therapy were vastly accelerated by the Second World War, when the many military psychiatric patients and the few trained psychiatric workers made individual therapy impractical and required more economic modes of treatment.

During the 1950s, the main thrust of group therapy was in a different direction: toward the application of group therapy in different clinical settings and for different types of clinical problems. Theoreticians—Freudian, Sullivanian, Horneyan, Rogerian—explored the application of their conceptual framework to group therapy theory and practice.

The T-group and the therapy group thus arose from different disciplines; and for many years, the two disciplines, each generating its own store of theory and technique, continued as two parallel streams of knowledge, even though some leaders straddled both fields and, in different settings, led both T-groups and therapy groups. The T-group maintained a deep commitment to research and continued to identify with the fields of social psychology, education, organizational science, and industrial management.

THERAPY GROUP AND ENCOUNTER GROUP: FIRST INTERCHANGES

The evolution of the T-group into the modern encounter group resulted in an entirely different concourse between the two fields. To speak of group therapy for normals and at the same time to suggest that, because of the stresses inherent in our culture, patienthood is ubiquitous can only lead to deep questioning about differences between the goals of encounter and therapy groups.

Considerable encounter group-therapy group traffic began to occur in the 1960s. Many mental health professionals participated in some form of encounter group during their training and subsequently led encounter groups and/or applied encounter techniques to their psychotherapeutic endeavors. Encounter group leaders, on the other hand, felt strongly that their group participants had had a therapeutic experience and that there was in reality no difference between personal growth and psychotherapy (between "mind expansion" and "head shrinking"). Furthermore, it became evident that there was much overlap between the population seeking psychotherapy and that seeking encounter experiences. Thus, many encounter group leaders concluded they were practicing psychotherapy—indeed, a more rapid and effective type of psychotherapy—and advertised their services accordingly.

The response of the traditional mental health field to this perceived encroachment was one of great concern. Psychotherapists were alarmed at the recklessness of the new groups and at possible risks to participants. They were equally concerned about ethical issues: the lack of clinical training of the encounter group leaders; the advertising that suggested that months, even years of therapy could be condensed into a single, intensive weekend; the lack of responsibility of many of the leaders. Polarization increased and soon in many communities, the mental health professionals launched campaigns urging their local governments to pass legislation to regulate encounter group practice and to hold leaders legally responsible for untoward effects.

In part, the vigorous response of the mental health profession was an irrational reaction to what it perceived as an invasion of territory. In part, however, the response was appropriate to certain excesses in some factions of the encounter field. These excesses issued from a crash-program mentality, successful in such ventures as space exploration and industrialization, but resulting in a *reductio ad absurdum* in human relations ventures. If something is good, more is better. If self-disclosure is good in groups, then total, immediate, indiscriminate disclosure in the nude must be better. If involvement is good, then prolonged, continuous, marathon involvement must be better. If expression of feeling is good, then hitting, touching, feeling, kissing, and fornicating must be better. If a group experience is good, then it is good for everyone—in all stages of the life cycle, in all life situations. These excesses were often offensive to the public taste and could, as research has indicated, be dangerous to some participants.

Before excessive polarization occurred, there was, during the 1960s and 1970s, constructive interchange between the group therapy and the sensitivity training fields. Clinical researchers learned a great deal from the T-group research methodology; T-groups were commonly used in the training of group therapists[25] and in the treatment program of chronically hospitalized patients;[26] some clinicians referred their individual therapy patients to a T-group for "opening-up" (just as, in the 1980s, some clinicians refer their patients to est or Lifespring[27]); and finally, some T-group techniques were adopted by clinicians, resulting in a gradual shift in the practice of group therapy. For example, the increased emphasis on the here-and-now, the concept of feedback, greater leader transparency, the use of group structured exercises (both verbal and nonverbal), and the time-extended meeting, have, in part, been the legacy of the T-group to group therapy.

THERAPY GROUP AND ENCOUNTER GROUP: SHARED PROPERTIES AND CONCERNS

Starting from their widely different points of origin, the encounter group and the therapy group converged to the point where many observers wondered whether there were any intrinsic differences between them.

Development of the Individual's Positive Potential

The traditions from which each type of group work have derived have undergone considerable evolution, which has resulted in a major shift in group goals, theory, and technology. Human relations education, as I have indicated, changed its emphasis from the acquisition of specific theory and interpersonal skills to the encounter group goals of total enhancement of the individual.

The field of psychotherapy underwent a gradual evolution from a model of personality development based on the transmutations of the individual's libidinal and aggressive energies to the current emphasis on ego psychology. Many theorists have posited the existence of an additional positively valenced drive which must perforce be allowed to unfold rather than be inhibited or sublimated; thus, Hendrick's "instinct to master,"[28] Berlyne's "exploratory drive,"[29] Horney's "self-realization,"[30] White's "effectance motivation,"[31] Hartmann's "neutralized energy,"[32] Angyal's "self-determination,"[33] and Goldstein, Rogers, and Maslow's "self-actualization."[34] Thus, the development of the individual entails more than the inhibition or sublimation of potentially destructive instinctual forces. One must, in addition, fulfill one's creative potential; and the efforts of the therapist are best directed toward this goal. Horney states that the task of the therapist should be to help remove obstructions; given favorable circumstances, one will realize one's own potential, "just as an acorn will develop into an oak."[35] Similarly, Rogers refers to the therapist as a facilitator.

A closely related trend in psychotherapy, beginning with Fromm, Reichmann, Erikson, and Lindemann, has been the strategy of building on the patient's strengths. Psychotherapists have come to appreciate, for example, that individuals may encounter great discomfort at certain junctures in the life cycle, not because of poor ego strength but because there have been inadequate opportunities for the learning relevant to that life stage to occur; psychotherapy may be directed toward the facilitation of this learning. This shift in therapy orientation has brought the group therapist and the T-group leader closer together. The T-group leader has always espoused the goal of acquisition of competence and believed that the reinforcement of strengths is no less vital than the correction of deficiencies.

Outcome Goals

Hoped-for changes occurring in the individual as a result of T-group experience closely parallel (despite differences in language) the changes that group therapists wish to see in their patients. For example, one T-group outcome study investigated the following fifteen variables: sending communication, receiving communication, relational facility, risk taking, increased interdependence, functional flexibility, self-control, awareness of behavior, sensitivity to group process, sensitivity to others, acceptance of others, tolerance of new information, confidence, comfort, and insight into self.[36] The Lieberman, Yalom, and Miles outcome criteria for their encounter group project also closely resembled psychotherapy outcome criteria, with the single obvious exception of target symptoms ("chief complaints").[37]

Group Composition

Encounter group and therapy group composition grew more similar over the years. Psychotherapists no longer worked only with individuals with major mental health problems; they began treating ever more fairly well-integrated individuals with minor problems in living. Conversely, many patients came to regard the encounter groups, especially the weekend marathon variety, as crash psychotherapy programs. Lieberman and Gardner studied participants of several growth centers and reported that 81 percent had had psychotherapy in the past or were currently in the therapy.[38] Moreover, using the criteria of amount of stress, symptomatology, and reasons for seeking help, they found that 70 percent closely resembled new patients applying for help at psychiatric outpatient clinics.

THERAPY GROUP AND ENCOUNTER GROUP: SIMILAR LEARNING ENVIRONMENTS

The Lieberman, Yalom, Miles encounter group project suggested that not only do encounter groups and therapy groups resemble each other in form but that similar rules of learning and change apply to both approaches. When the outcome (on both group and individual level) was correlated with the course of events during the life of a group, several conclusions emerged that have obvious relevance to the process of change in therapy group. For example, the study concluded that if encounter groups are to be effective vehicles of personal change, several basic encounter group maxims need to be reformulated in the following ways:

1. "Feelings not thought" should be altered to "feelings, only with thought."
2. "Let it all hang out" is best revised to "let more of it hang out than usual, if it feels right in the group, and if you can give some thought to what it means." In this study, self-disclosure, emotional expressiveness (of either positive or negative feelings), was not in itself sufficient for change.
3. "Getting out the anger is essential" to "getting out the anger may be okay, but keeping it out there steadily is not." Excessive expression of anger was counterproductive: it was not associated with a high level of learning, and it generally increased risk.
4. "There is no group, only persons" to "group processes make a difference in learning, whether or not the leader pays attention to them." Learning was strongly influenced by such group properties as cohesiveness, climate, norms, and the group role occupied by a particular member.
5. "High yield requires high risk" to "the risk in encounter groups is considerable and unrelated to positive gain." The high-risk groups, those that produced many casualties, did not at the same time produce high learners. The productive groups were safe ones. The high-yield–high-risk group is, according to our study, a myth.
6. "You may not know what you've learned now, but when you put it all together . . ." to "bloom now, don't count on later." It is often thought that individuals may be shaken up ("unfrozen") during a group experience but that later, after the group is over, they integrate their experience in it and come out stronger than ever. In our projects, individuals who had a negative outcome at the termination of the group *never* moved to the positive side of the ledger when studied six months later.

THERAPY GROUPS AND ENCOUNTER GROUPS: DIFFERENCES

Because there are similarities between encounter and therapy groups, we must not make the mistake of equating the two. There are, I believe, fundamental differences.

Setting
The encounter group differs from the therapy group in size, duration, and physical setting. Generally, it consists of ten to sixteen members

who may be total strangers or who may be associates at work. Sometimes the encounter group meets as part of a larger residential human relations laboratory lasting one to two weeks. The group, in this setting, usually meets in two- to three-hour sessions once or twice a day. The members usually spend the entire day with one another, and the encounter group atmosphere spills over into other activities. Often encounter groups meet, like therapy groups, in shorter sessions spaced over a longer period. Almost always, however, the encounter group's life spans a shorter time.

Unlike the therapy group, the encounter group's ethos is one of informality and pleasure. The physical surroundings are often like a resort, and more consideration is given to the pursuit of fun.

The Role of Leader

Generally there is a far greater gap between leader and members in a therapy group than in an encounter group—a result of both the leader's behavior and the characteristics of the members. Although encounter group members may overvalue their leader, generally they see him or her more realistically than do psychiatric patients. Encounter group members, partially because of their greater self-esteem and also because of their greater opportunity to socialize between meetings with the leader, perceive the leader as similar to themselves, except insofar as the leader has superior skill and knowledge in a specialized area. The leader earns prestige as a result of his or her contributions. Eventually, the leader begins to participate in a manner similar to the other members and in time assumes full membership in the group, although his or her technical expertise continues to be employed and appreciated.

Part of the encounter group leader's task is to transmit not only knowledge but also skills; the leader expects the group members to learn methods of diagnosing and resolving interpersonal problems. Often the leader explicitly behaves as a teacher—for example, by explicating some point of theory or by introducing some group exercise, verbal or nonverbal, as an experiment for the group to study. It is not unusual for encounter group members to seek further human relations education and subsequently to become leaders themselves. (Occasionally this practice has had unfortunate repercussions since some members with much zeal but without the necessary background have considered one or two experiences as a group member sufficient training for them to undertake a new career as a group leader.)

Group therapists are viewed far more unrealistically by their group members (see chapter 7). In part, the therapist's deliberately enigmatic and mystifying behavior generates this distortion. The therapist has entirely different rules of conduct from the other members in the group; is rarely transparent or self-disclosing, and too often reveals only a professional front. It is a rare therapist who socializes or even drinks coffee with group members. In part, however, the distortion resides within the patients and springs from their hope for an omniscient figure who will intercede in their behalf. They do not view the therapist merely as an individual similar to themselves aside from specialized professional skills; for better or for worse, they attribute to the therapist the archetypal abilities and powers of the healer.

Although, as the group proceeds, the therapist's role may change to be more like a member's, it is never that of a full group member: the therapist almost never presents personal problems in living to the group; the therapist's statements and actions continue to be perceived as powerful and sagacious regardless of their content. Furthermore, the therapist is not concerned with teaching his or her skills to the group members; rarely does a therapy group member use the group experience to start out on a career as a group therapist.

Beyond the Common Social Malady

Most of the fundamental differences between encounter groups and therapy groups derive from difference in composition. Although much overlapping may occur, the encounter group is generally composed of well-functioning individuals who seek greater competence and growth; whereas the therapy group has a population of individuals who often cannot cope with minor everyday stress without discomfort; they seek relief from anxiety, depression, or a sterile and ungratifying intrapersonal and interpersonal existence. Earlier in this chapter, I referred to the tensions inherent in our competitive culture, that to a greater or lesser degree affect all of us. However—and this point is often overlooked by clinically untrained encounter group leaders (as well as by large group awareness trainers)—psychiatric patients have, in addition, a set of far more pressing concerns. The common social malady is woven into the fabric of their personality but is not synonymous with their psychopathology: they have an additional, and deeper, basis for alienation and dysphoria.

Orientation to Learning

One of the basic tasks of the encounter group—the acquisition of interpersonal competence—requires a degree of interpersonal skill that most psychiatric patients do not possess. Encounter group leaders ordinarily make certain assumptions about their group members: they must be able to send and receive communications about their own and other members' behavior with a minimum of distortion; they must, if they are to convey accurate information and be receptive to feedback, have a relatively high degree of self-awareness and self-acceptance. Furthermore, participants must desire interpersonal change. They must be well intentioned and constructive in their relationships with the other members and must believe in a fundamental constructive attitude on the part of the others if a cohesive, mutually trusting group is to form. The members must be willing, after receiving feedback, to question previously cherished beliefs about themselves ("unfreezing"), to experiment with new attitudes and behavior, and to transfer their learning to their "back home" life.

These intrapersonal and interpersonal prerequisites, which most encounter group leaders take for granted in their group members, are the very attributes sorely deficient in the typical psychiatric patient, who generally has lower self-esteem and self-awareness. The stated group goals of increased interpersonal competence are often perceived as incompatible with their personal goals of relief from suffering, Their initial response to others is often based on distrust rather than trust, and, most important of all, their ability to question their belief system and to risk new forms of behavior is severely impaired. In fact, the inability to learn from new experience is central to the basic problem of the neurotic. To illustrate with a classic example, consider Anna Freud's study of Patrick, who during the London blitz in 1943 was separated from his parents and developed an obsessive-compulsive neurosis. In the evacuation center, he stood alone in a corner and chanted continuously, "Mother will come and put on my overcoat and my leggings, she will zip my zipper, she will put on my pixie hat," and so on.[39] Consequently, Patrick, unlike the other children, could not avail himself of the learning opportunities in the center. He remained isolated from the other adults and children and formed no other relationships that could have relieved his fear and permitted him to continue to grow and to develop social skills. The frozen compulsive behavior did provide some solace for Patrick by preventing panic but so tied up his energy that he could not appraise the situation and take new, adaptive action.

Not only does the neurotic defense preclude testing and resolution of the core conflict, but it characteristically generalizes to include an ever-widening sphere of the individual's life space. Generalization may occur directly or indirectly. It may operate directly, as in traumatic or war neuroses in which the feared situation takes an increasingly broader definition. For example, a phobia once confined to a specific form of moving vehicle may generalize to apply to all forms of transportation. Indirectly, individuals suffer since, as with little Patrick, the inhibition prevents them from exploring their physical and interpersonal environment and developing their potential. A vicious circle arises since maladaptive interpersonal techniques beget further stress and may preclude the formation of gratifying relationships.

The important point is that individuals with neurotic defenses are frozen into a closed position; they are not open for learning, and they are generally searching not for growth but for safety. C. Argyris puts it nicely in differentiating a "survival orientation" from a "competence orientation."[40] The more competence-oriented, the more receptive and flexible an individual is. One becomes an "open system" and, in the interpersonal area, is able to use one's experience to develop greater interpersonal competence. On the other hand, the survival-oriented individual is more concerned with self-protection. Through the use of defense mechanisms, one withdraws from, distorts, or attacks the environment.

Individuals are neither all open or all closed; they may be closed in specific areas and open in others. Nor, as I have stated, are all therapy group members more closed than all encounter group members. Consider for a moment the vast scope and diversity of the group therapies: it is possible, for example, that the affluent members of an analytic group in Manhattan may be as integrated and congruent as the members of an average encounter group. The label "patient" is often purely arbitrary and a consequence of a request for help, not of a need for help. Generally, however, the therapy group is composed of individuals who are oriented toward survival rather than competence and who therefore cannot readily take advantage of the interpersonal learning opportunities of the group. Therapy group members cannot easily follow the simple encounter group mandate to be open, honest, and trusting when they are experiencing profound feelings of suspicion, fear, distrust, anger, and self-hatred. A great deal of work must be done to overcome these maladaptive interpersonal stances so that patients can begin to participate constructively in the group. Jerome Frank came close to the heart of the matter when he said that "therapy groups are as much or more concerned with helping patients to unlearn old patterns as they are with helping them to learn new ones."[41]

DIFFERENCES: EARLY AND LATE

The therapy group, then, differs from the encounter group early and late. It differs early by beginning more painfully and laboriously. Encounter group members may begin a group with trepidation; they face an unknown situation in which they will be asked to expose themselves and to take risks. Nevertheless, they are generally backed up by relatively high self-esteem and a reservoir of professional and interpersonal success. Psychiatric patients, on the other hand, begin a therapy group with dread and suspicion. Self-disclosure is infinitely more threatening in the face of a belief in one's basic worthlessness and badness. The pace is slower; the group must deal with one vexing interpersonal problem after another. The encounter group, after all, does not often have to face the problem of an angry paranoid patient, or a suicidal depressive one, or a denying patient who attributes all difficulties in living to a spouse, or the unstable borderline patient, or the easily discouraged members who constantly threaten to leave the group. The therapist, unlike the encounter group leader, must constantly modulate the amount of confrontation, self-disclosure, and tension the group can tolerate.

The therapy group differs later by having a different termination point for each member. Unlike the encounter group, which invariably ends as a unit and generally at a predetermined time, the therapy group (or at least the open therapy group) continues for each member until his or her goals have been reached. In fact, as Frank points out, one reason that the therapy group is so threatening is that its task, "broad personal modification," has scarcely any limit; and, furthermore, there is no restriction about what can—and, perhaps, must—be discussed.[42] Often in an encounter group, it is enough for the members to recognize and surmount a problem area; not so in the therapy group, in which problem areas must be explored in depth for each of the members involved.

For example, in a twelve-session encounter group of mental health professionals which I once led, the members (who were also my students) experienced great difficulty in their relationship to me. They felt frightened and inhibited by me, vied for my attention, addressed a preponderance of their comments to me, overvalued the wisdom of my remarks, and harbored unrealistic expectations of me. I responded to this issue by helping the group members recognize their behavior, their distortions, and unrealistic expectations. I then helped them appreciate the effects of their unrealistic and dependent attitudes toward me on the course of the group and called their attention to the implications of this phenomenon on their future role as group therapists. Next, we discussed some of the members' feelings toward the more dependent members of the group: for example, how it felt to have someone ostensibly talk to you but at the same time gaze fixedly at the leader. Once these tasks were accomplished, I felt that it was important that the group move past this block and proceed to focus on other facets of the group experience, for it was abundantly clear that the group could spend all of its remaining sessions attempting to resolve fully its struggle with the issue of leadership and authority. I helped to turn the group's attention to other current but untouched group issues—for example, the members' feelings about three silent and seemingly uninvolved members, the hierarchy of dominance in the group, and the general issue of intermember competition and competence, always a specter looming large in encounter groups of mental health workers.

In a therapy group, I would approach the same issue in a different fashion with different objectives in mind. I would encourage the patients especially conflicted in this area to discuss in depth their feelings and fantasies toward me. Rather than consider ways in which to help the group move on, I would help plunge them into the issue so that each member might understand his or her overt behavior toward me, as well as avoided behavior and the fantasied calamitous effects of such behavior. Although I would, by a degree of transparency, assist the members in their reality testing, I would attempt to modulate the timing of this behavior so as to allow the formation and full exploration of their feelings toward me. (See chapter 7 for a detailed discussion of this issue.) The goal of clarifying other facets of group dynamics is, of course, irrelevant for the therapy group; the only reason for changing the focus of the group is that the current issue is no longer the most fertile one for the therapeutic work: either the group has pursued the areas as far as possible at a particular time, or some other more immediate issue has arisen in the group.

To summarize, the basic intrinsic difference between the encounter group and the therapy group arises from differences in their composition (and thereby their goals). As a general rule, psychiatric patients have different goals, more deeply disrupted intrapersonal and interpersonal relations, and a different (closed, survival-based) orientation to learning. These factors result in process and procedural differences both in the early stages and in the late working-through stages of the group.

17

TRAINING THE
GROUP THERAPIST

Group therapy is a curious plant in the garden of psychotherapy. It is hardy: the best available research has established that group therapy is effective, as robust as individual therapy.[1] Yet it needs constant tending; its perennial fate is to be periodically choked by the same old weeds: group therapy is "second rate"; "use it if no individual therapy is available or affordable"; group therapy is "superficial" or "dangerous."

Patients and many mental health professionals continue to underrate and to fear group therapy. Perhaps because it cannot cleanse itself of the anti-intellectual taint of the encounter group movement, or because of the formidable intrinsic methodological obstacles to rigorous, truly meaningful research,[2] it remains a fact that group therapy enjoys low academic prestige. Rarely does one earn university tenure on the basis of a career devoted to small group research. The same situation prevails in clinics and hospital administration hierarchies: rarely does the individual who is most invested in group therapy enjoy a position of professional authority.

Attempts to alter this situation have always worked—but for the briefest of times. An initial wave of renewed enthusiasm is followed by neglect, and soon all the old weeds crowd in once again. The moment demands a whole new generation of well-trained gardeners, and it behooves us to pay careful attention to the education of student group therapists.

In this chapter, I shall present my views about group therapy training, not only in specific recommendations for a training curriculum but also in the form of general considerations concerning an underlying philosophy of training. The approach to therapy described in this book is based both upon clinical experience and an appraisal of the best available research evidence. Similarly, in the educational process, a clinical and a research orientation are closely interrelated: the acquisition of a research or inquiring attitude to one's own work and to the work of others is necessary in the development of the mature therapist.

Many training programs for mental health professionals are based on the individual therapy model and either do not provide group therapy training or offer it as an elective part of the program. In fact, it is not unusual for students to be given excellent intensive individual therapy supervision and then, early in their program, to be asked to lead therapy groups with no specialized guidance whatsoever. The program directors apparently expect that students will be able, somehow, to translate their individual therapy training into group therapy skills.

Fortunately, increasing numbers of educators have recognized the folly of this approach, and mental health training programs are becoming ever more appreciative of the need for well-organized group training programs. Slowly, much too slowly, we have come to recognize that one-to-one psychotherapy cannot possibly suffice to meet the pressing mental health needs of the country. It is abundantly clear that, as time passes, we will rely on group approaches ever more heavily; and I believe that any psychotherapy training program that fails to acknowledge this, and does not expect students to become as fully proficient in group as in individual therapy, is failing to meet its responsibilities to the field.

Even though psychiatry in the 1980s continues its course of remedicalization, the percentage of programs offering a group therapy training program has increased. E. Pinney, in a 1983 survey of 194 residency programs, reports that 91 percent offer at least one year of group therapy training.[3] (Earlier surveys: 1950—48 percent,[4] 1961—72 percent,[5] 1978—78 percent.[6]) Similar surveys are not available for other professional disciplines, but my personal impression is that virtually all psychology, social work and marriage and family counseling programs offer group therapy training. (Two-thirds of the psychiatric residency programs train professionals from other disciplines in group therapy.)[7]

Every program has its own unique needs and resources. While I cannot hope to offer a blueprint for a universal training program, I shall, in the following section, discuss the four major components that I consider essential to a comprehensive training program. I believe that student group therapists profit from (1) observing experienced group therapists at work; (2) close clinical supervision of their maiden groups;

(3) a personal group experience; and (4) personal psychotherapeutic work.

Observation of Experienced Clinicians

Student therapists derive enormous benefit from watching an experienced group therapist at work. At first, clinicians often feel considerable dis-ease at the thought of being observed; but once they have taken the plunge, the process becomes not only comfortable but rewarding for all parties—students, therapists, and group members.

The format of observation depends, of course, on the physical facilities. I prefer using a one-way mirror, but if students' schedules do not permit them to be present at the group, the meeting may be videotaped and replayed in a seminar with the therapist. This procedure requires a greater time investment for the therapist and some increased discomfort for the members because of the presence of the television camera. If there are only one or two observers, they may sit in the group room without unduly distracting the members; but I suggest that they remain silent and outside the group circle. Regardless of the format employed, the group members should be fully informed about the presence of observers and the purpose of observation. I remind the patients that observation is necessary for training. I was trained in that fashion, and their willingness to permit observers will ultimately be beneficial to the unknown patients whom the student observers will treat in the future.

The total length of time students observe a group is, unfortunately, generally determined by service and training rotations. If there is sufficient program flexibility, I would suggest that observation continue at least four months, which generally provides a sufficient period of time for changes to occur in group development, in interactional patterns, and in perceivable intrapersonal growth. A format that I have used to my satisfaction is to have my students observe a group that meets twice weekly. If their schedules preclude their attendance at more than one meeting a week, I dictate a detailed summary of each meeting and distribute it to the students before the next meeting. In this way, they are able to follow a twice-weekly group, which has a greater likelihood of showing noticeable progression.

A post-meeting discussion is an absolute training necessity, and there is no better time for a group leader to meet with student observers than immediately following the meeting. I prefer to meet for approximately thirty to forty-five minutes, and I spend the time in a variety of ways: to obtain the students' observations, to answer questions about underlying reasons for my interventions, and to use the clinical material as a springboard for discussion of fundamental principles of group therapy. Other instructors prefer to delay the discussion and assign the students the task of writing a description of the meeting which focuses primarily on process (that is, the interpersonal relationships between the members of the group). The students exchange their summaries and meet later in the week for an analysis of the meeting.[8] Though some introductory didactic sessions are necessary, I find that much of the material presented in this book can be best discussed with students around appropriate clinical material that arises over several months of an observed group.[9]

The relationship between observers and group therapist is important; there will be times when an inordinate amount of carping ("Why didn't you . . . ?") creates discomfort for the therapist and impairs his or her efficiency. Indeed, I have on occasion conducted post-group discussions that focused more upon the process of the observer group than upon the therapy group. Not infrequently observers complain of boredom, and therapists feel some strain to increase the group's entertainment quotient. My experience is that, in general, boredom is inversely related to experience; as students gain in experience and sophistication, they appreciate, to a much greater extent, the many subtle layers underlying every transaction.

Group members respond differently to being observed by students. Like any group event, the different responses are grist for the therapeutic mill. If all members face the same situation (that is, observation), why do some respond with anger, others with suspicion and still others with pleasure, even exhilaration? The answer, of course, is that each member has a different inner world and the differing responses constitute a *via regia* to the examination of each inner world.

Nonetheless, for the majority of patients, traditional observation constitutes an intrusion. The most a leader can expect from patients is a grudging acceptance and, ultimately, a blocking of awareness of the presence of observers. There are methods, however, of incorporating observers into the therapeutic process in such a way as to turn the observation process to therapeutic advantage. I prefer to inform the group that the observers' perspectives are valuable to me as the leader. If appropriate, I inform the group of some comments made by the observers after the previous meeting, and I also let the group know that

I often incorporate some of the observers' comments into the written summary (see page 437).

Still another, more daring, strategy is to invite the group members to be present at the observers' post-meeting discussion. In chapter 15, I discussed a model of an inpatient group that regularly included a ten-minute observers' discussion that the group members observed.[10] I have used a similar format for outpatient groups: I invite members and observers to switch rooms at the end of a meeting so that the patients observe through the one-way mirror the observers' and co-therapists' post-group discussion. My only proviso is that the entire group elect to attend: if some members attend and some do not, the process may be divisive and retard the development of cohesiveness. A significant time commitment is required: forty-five minutes of post-group discussion plus a ninety-minute session make for a long afternoon or evening.

This format has interesting implications for teaching. Its advantages are several: it teaches a student how to be constructively transparent; it conveys a sense of respect for a patient as a full ally in the therapeutic process; and it demystifies therapy: it is a statement that therapy is a potent, rational, collaborative process requiring no part of Dostoevsky's Grand Inquisitor's triumvirate—magic, mystery, and authority.

If patients do observe the post-group discussion, then there must be supplemental teaching seminars prior or subsequent to the observation period. The post-meeting discussions that the patients observe differs from the typical post-group rehash. The discussion becomes part of the therapy itself; observers and therapists make statements to patients through one another. There is less time devoted to formal instruction of basic theory or strategic principles. The students tend to be inhibited in their questions and comments, and there is less free-ranging discussion of transference and countertransference.

Supervision

A supervised clinical experience is a *sine qua non* in the education of the group therapist. This book posits a general approach to therapy, delineates broad principles of technique, and, especially when discussing the opening and closing stages of therapy, suggests specific tactics. But the laborious working-through process that comprises the bulk of therapy cannot be thoroughly depicted in a text; an infinite number of situations arise, each of which may require a rich, imaginative approach. It is precisely at these points that a supervisor makes a valuable and unique contribution to a student therapist's education.

The neophyte therapist's first group is a highly threatening experience; without an experienced clinician as guide, the student, however eager to remain open to learning, instead grasps for the safety of a highly structured clinical approach. My colleagues and I once studied twelve nonprofessionals who led groups in a psychiatric hospital.[11] Half of the leaders received ongoing supervision as well as an intensive training course in group leadership; the others received neither. Naïve observers rated the therapists at the beginning of their groups and six months later. The results indicated that not only did the trained therapists improve *but the untrained therapists, at the end of six months, were less skilled than at the beginning.* Sheer experience, apparently, is not enough; without ongoing supervision and evaluation, original errors may be reinforced by simple repetition. For this reason, every training course must include a supervisory experience. The American Group Psychotherapy Association recommends a minimum of 180 hours of supervision in the training of group therapists.

In many ways, group therapy supervision is more taxing than individual therapy supervision. For one thing, mastering the cast of characters is in itself a formidable task. Furthermore, there is such an abundance of data that both student and supervisor must often be highly selective in their focus. A few practical recommendations. One supervisory hour per one group therapy session is, in my experience, the optimal ratio. At the very least, the supervisor must observe one or two sessions at the beginning of supervision: it permits the supervisor to fix names with faces and also to savor the affective climate of the group. Many supervisors prefer to observe meetings periodically throughout the year. Video tapes may serve this purpose also; audio tapes, too, though far less satisfactorily. It is wise to hold the supervisory session soon after the group session, preferably the following day.

One excellent format, if schedules permit, is to observe the last thirty minutes of each meeting and hold the supervisory session immediately thereafter. If much time elapses between the group meeting and the supervisory session, the events of the former fade, and students are well advised to make post-group notes to prod their memories. Therapists develop their own style of note taking. My preference is to record the major themes of each session—generally, from one to three. For example: (1) John's distress at losing his job, and the group's efforts to offer support; (2) Sharon's anger at the men in the group; (3) Annabelle's feeling inferior and unaccepted by the group).

Once this basic skeleton is in place, I fill in the other vital data: the transition between themes; each member's contribution to each of the themes; the therapist's interventions and feelings about the meeting as a whole and toward each of the members. Other supervisors suggest that students pay special attention to "choice points"—a series of critical points in the meeting where action is required of the therapist.[12] Still other supervisors make use of patient feedback obtained from questionnaires distributed at the end of a group session.[13]

A ninety-minute group session provides a wealth of material. If trainees present a narrative of the meeting, discuss each patient's verbal and nonverbal contribution as well as their own participation, and explore in depth their countertransference and realistically based feelings toward each of the members and toward their co-therapist, there should be more than enough important material to occupy the supervisory hour. If not, if the trainee runs quickly out of material and if the supervisor has to search for ways to be useful, something is going seriously wrong in the supervisory process. The supervisor would do well at these times to attend to the relationship between himself or herself and the trainee(s). Are the students guarded? Distrustful? Fearful of exposing themselves to their supervisor? Cautious lest the supervisor censure them or control them by placing pressure on them to operate in the group in a manner that feels alien to them?

The supervisory session is no less a microcosm than is the therapy group, and the supervisor should be able to obtain much information about the therapist's behavior in a therapy group by attending to his or her behavior in supervision. If students lead groups as co-therapy teams (and for reasons stated in chapter 14, I recommend that format for neophyte therapists), a process focus in the supervisory hour is particularly rich. Are the co-therapists open and trusting with one another and with their supervisor? Who reports the events of the meeting? Who defers to whom? Does the supervisor feel bewildered by two very different views of the group? Is there much competition for the supervisor's attention? Is there a sense of heightened tension in the supervisory session? The relationship between co-therapists is of crucial importance for the therapy group and, not infrequently, the supervisor may be maximally effective by focusing attention on this relationship.

For example, I recently supervised two residents whose personal relationship was strained. In the supervisory session, each vied for my attention; there was a dysrhythmic quality to the hour since neither pursued the other's lead but instead brought up different material, or the same material from an entirely different aspect. Supervision was a microcosm of the group, since in the therapy sessions they competed intensely with each other to make star interpretations and to enlist patients on their respective "teams." They never complemented each other's work by pursuing the theme that one had brought up; instead, each remained silent, waiting for an opportunity to introduce a different line of inquiry. The group paid the price for the therapists' poor working relationship: no good work was done, absenteeism was high, and demoralization evident. Supervision in this instance focused almost entirely on the co-therapy relationship and took on many of the characteristics of dyadic therapy. For example, one of the leaders brought in this transparent dream: "I organize a group of patients but have a bad feeling of having selected poorly. Jack and I are trying to lead the group, but the patients are too out of it to do anything but make a lot of noise with one another. Finally in frustration, I leap into the center and shout an interpretation at Jack which he can't hear and I wake up feeling very frustrated."

Our supervision focused on these therapists' competition and on their wish to impress me. One had just transferred from another residency and felt strongly pressed to prove her competence. The other felt that he had made a great mistake in blindly accepting a co-therapist, and felt trapped in the relationship. We considered dissolving the co-therapy team but decided that such a move would be countertherapeutic: what chance do we have of persuading patients to work on their relationships if we therapists refuse to do the same? If co-therapists can successfully work on their relationship, there is a double payoff: therapy is served (the group works better with an improved interleader relationship), and training is served (trainees learn first-hand some of the basic principles of conflict resolution).

In the ongoing work of supervision, it is important for the supervisor to focus on the student therapist's behavior in the group. Are the student's verbal and nonverbal interventions congruent with his or her feelings, and do they help to establish the types of group norm the supervisor considers useful to the group? At the same time, the supervisor must avoid making the student so self-conscious that spontaneity is stunted. Groups are not so fragile that a single statement markedly influences their direction; it is the therapist's overall gestalt that counts. Every supervisor will at times tell a supervisee what he or she would have said at some juncture of the group. This is a useful and perhaps essential part of the modeling process; however, many student therapists are inclined to ape the supervisor's comments at a not entirely appropriate spot in the following group meeting. The next supervisory session generally begins with "I did what you said, but. . . ." Thus, when, on occasion, I tell a student what I would have said, I preface my comments with a specific caveat: "Don't say this at the next meeting. . . ."

Many teachers have, with profit, expanded the supervisory hour into a continuous case seminar for several student therapists. The group leaders take turns presenting their group to the entire class. Since it takes time to assimilate data about all the members of a group, I prefer that one group be presented for four to six weeks before moving on to another. In this format, three to four groups can be followed throughout the year.

A Group Experience for Trainees

A personal group experience has become widely accepted as an integral part of a training program; for example, the accreditation committee of the American Group Psychotherapy Association has recommended a minimum requirement of sixty hours of participation in a group. Such an experience may offer many types of learning not elsewhere available. You are able to learn at an emotional level what you may previously have known only intellectually. You experience the power of the group, its power to wound or heal. You learn how important it is to be accepted by the group; what self-disclosure really entails; how difficult it is to reveal your secret world, your fantasies, feelings of vulnerability, hostility, and tenderness. You learn to appreciate your own strengths as well as weaknesses. You learn about your own preferred role in the group; and, perhaps most striking of all, you learn about the role of the leader by becoming aware of your own dependency and your unrealistic appraisal of the leader's power and knowledge.

Recent surveys indicate that 60 percent to 70 percent of group therapy training programs offer some type of personal group experience.[14] Some programs offer a simulated group in which one or two trainees are appointed co-therapists and the other trainees role-play the group patients. The most common model (which I shall discuss in detail shortly) is a T-group or "support group" composed of other trainees. This group may be short-term, lasting approximately a dozen sessions, or it may consist of an intensive weekend marathon; but the most common model, and the one I prefer, is a T-group that continues throughout the entire year.

I have led groups of psychology interns and psychiatric residents for over twenty years and, without exception, have found them to be a highly valuable teaching technique. Indeed, many students, when reviewing their training programs, have rated the T-group as the single most valuable experience in their curriculum. A group experience with one's peers has a great deal to recommend it: not only do the members reap the benefits of a group experience; but, if the group is led properly, it will so facilitate relationships and communication within the trainee class as to enrich the entire training experience. Students always learn a great deal from their peers, and any efforts that potentiate that process increase the value of the program.

Are there disadvantages as well as advantages to a group experience? One often hears storm warnings about the possible destructive effects of staff or trainee experiential groups. These warnings are, I believe, based on irrational premises: for example, that enormous amounts of destructive hostility would ensue once a group unlocks suppressive floodgates, or that a group would constitute an enormous invasion of privacy as forced confessionals are wrung one by one from each of the hapless trainees. We know now that responsibly led groups facilitate communication and constructive working relationships.

SHOULD GROUPS IN A TRAINING PROGRAM BE VOLUNTARY?

An experiential group is always more effective if the participants engage voluntarily and view it not only as a training exercise but as an opportunity for personal growth. Indeed, I prefer that trainees begin such a group with an explicit formulation of what they want to obtain from the experience personally as well as professionally. To this end, it is important that the group be introduced and described to the trainees in such a way that they consider it to be consonant with their personal and professional goals. I prefer to frame the group within the students' training career by asking them to project themselves into the field of the future. It is, after all, highly probable that mental health practitioners will spend an increasingly greater amount of their time in groups —as leaders of therapy groups and as members and leaders of treatment teams. To be effective in this role, the clinician of the future will simply have to know his or her way around groups. The clinician will have to learn how groups work, and to know, in the deepest possible sense, how he or she works in groups.

Once an experiential group is introduced as a regular part of a training program, and once the faculty develops confidence in the group as a valuable training adjunct, there is little difficulty in "selling" it to incoming trainees. Still, programs differ on whether to make the programs optional or mandatory. A 1980 survey indicates that, in the first year of training, approximately 50 percent of programs offer an optional group and 50 percent a mandatory one.[15]

My experience is that, if a group is presented properly, the trainees not only look forward to it with much anticipation but experience strong disappointment if for some reason the opportunity for a group experience is withheld from them. If a student steadfastly refuses to enter the training group or any other type of experiential group, it is my opinion that some investigation of such resistance is warranted. Occasionally such a refusal stems from misconceptions about groups in general, or is a reflection of some respected senior faculty member's negative bias toward groups; but, if not, if the refusal is based on a pervasive dread or distrust of group situations, and if the student does not have the flexibility to work on this resistance in individual therapy, in a supportive group, or in a bona-fide therapy group, I believe it may well be unwise for that student to pursue the career of psychotherapist.

WHO SHOULD LEAD AN EXPERIENTIAL GROUP FOR STUDENT PSYCHOTHERAPISTS?

A caveat to directors of training programs: Select the leader with great care. For one thing, the group experience is an extraordinarily influential event in the students' training career; the leader will often serve as an important role model for the trainees and should, therefore, have the highest possible professional standards with extensive clinical and group experience. The overriding criteria is, of course, the personal qualities and the skill of the leader: the professional degree (whether the leader be, for example, psychiatric social worker, psychiatrist, clinical psychologist, or marriage and family counselor) is a secondary consideration.

I believe also that a trainee's first group experience should not be in a highly specialized format (for example, T.A. or gestalt). For one thing, as I discussed in chapter 14, many such specialized approaches focus more on one-to-one work within a group and fail to provide the trainee with a basic foundation of interactional and group dynamics upon which he or she may then build to accommodate any of the specialized approaches. Furthermore, since the experiential group is an important and delicate enterprise, it may be unwise to burden it with unnecessary additional ideological freight. I have seen trainees fail to profit from an experiential group not because of a failure to accept the group approach but because of their rejection (or their supervisor's or role model's rejection) of the specialized approach.

Another reason that the leader should be selected with great care is that it is extremely difficult to lead groups of mental health professionals who will continue to work together throughout their training. The pace is slow; intellectualization is common; and self-disclosure and risk-taking are minimal. The chief instrument in psychotherapy is the therapist's own person. Realizing this truth, the neophyte therapist feels doubly vulnerable in self-disclosure: at stake are both personal and professional competence.

SHOULD THE LEADER BE A STAFF OR A FACULTY MEMBER OF A TRAINING PROGRAM?

A leader who wears two hats (group leader and program administrator) compounds the problem even further for the group members who feel restricted by the presence of someone who may in the future play an evaluative role in their careers. Mere reassurance to the group that the leader will maintain strictest confidentiality or neutrality is insufficient to deal with this very real concern of the members.

I have on many occasions been placed in this double role and have approached the problem in various ways but with only limited success. One approach is to confront the problem energetically with the group. I affirm the reality that I do have a dual role, and that, though I shall attempt in every way to be merely a group leader and shall remove myself from any administrative evaluative duties, I may not be able to free myself from all unconscious vestiges of the second role. I thus address myself in an uncompromising fashion to the problem facing the group. But, as the group proceeds, I also address myself to the fact that each member must deal with the "two hat" problem. Yet each may respond to it in a very different fashion: some may so distrust me that they choose to remain hidden in silence; some curry my favor; some trust me completely and participate with full abandon in the group; others persistently challenge me. All of these stances toward a leader reflect basic attitudes toward authority and are good grist for the mill, provided there is even a modicum of willingness to work. An additional approach that I as a dual-hatted leader often take is to be unusually self-disclosing—in effect to give the members more on me than I have on them. In so doing, I model openness and demonstrate both the universality of human problems and how unlikely it is that I shall adopt a judgmental stance toward them.

526

My experience has been that, even using the best techniques, the leader who is also an administrator is laboring under a severe handicap, and his or her group is likely to be restricted and guarded. The group becomes a far more effective vehicle for personal growth and for training if led by a leader outside the institution who will play no role in student evaluation. It facilitates the work of a group if, at its onset, the leader, in whatever administrative position, makes explicit his or her unwillingness, under any circumstances, ever to contribute letters of reference—either favorable or unfavorable—for the members.

IS THE TRAINING GROUP A THERAPY GROUP?

No other issue is so often used in the service of group resistance as the question whether the group is a therapy group. It is wise for the leader to present a clear position at the onset of the group. I begin by asking that the members make certain commitments to the group. Each member should be aware of the requirements for membership; that is, a willingness to invest oneself emotionally in the group, to disclose feelings about oneself and the other members, and to explore areas in which one would like to make personal changes.

There is a useful distinction to be made between a therapy group and a therapeutic group. A training group, though it is not a therapy group, is therapeutic in that it offers the opportunity to do therapeutic work. Some members take advantage of that opportunity and have an excellent therapeutic experience. By no means, though, is each member expected to do extensive therapeutic work.

The basic contract of the group, in fact, its *raison d'être*, is training, not therapy. To a great extent these goals overlap: A leader can offer no better group therapy model than that of an effective therapeutic group. Furthermore, every intensive group experience contains within it great therapeutic potential: members cannot engage in effective interaction, cannot fully assume the role of a group member, without therapeutic spinoff. Yet that is different from a therapy group that assembles for the purpose of accomplishing extensive therapeutic change for each member. In a therapy group, the intensive group experience, the expression and integration of affect, the recognition of here-and-now process, are all essential but secondary considerations to the primary goal of individual therapeutic change. In a training group of mental health professionals, the reverse is true.

COMMON GROUP THEMES

A training group of mental health professionals confronts all the common themes that emerge in experiential groups but, because of its unusual composition, also has unique characteristics. In no other type of group does the issue of competition and competence play such a pervasive role. The group members often experience one another as competitors—competitors for jobs in the future, competitors for professional standing; or, even more commonly, they view one another as a professional standard against which to measure themselves. Their professional competence is a function of their personal integration; consequently they fear that revelation of perceived weaknesses or flaws will result in negative professional judgment from their peers. And, in fact, it is true that some group members secretly make judgments about whether they would refer a patient to another member who is rigid, or insensitive, or gay, or who feels panic when faced with an emergency, or who is more depressed, drug dependent, insomniac or anxious than his or her patients.

Try as they will, it is difficult for group members to escape competition issues. They may, for example, participate together in other more academically oriented conferences where differences in intellectual ability are clearly evident; one member may have to be chosen as chief resident; one may choose to transfer to another, more "high powered," program; some members, because of superior performance, may be offered staff or faculty positions at the parent training institute.

Groups respond to this tension in several ways, the most common of which is a tacit or an explicit pact of equality: the group denies any intermember differences and often bands together against the evaluatory menace of the hostile outside world. There is often much shared resentment against tyrannical judging administrators or against certifying boards which evaluate candidates. In one training group, for example, one member was so severely disabled because of a severe depression that he missed several months of his training. The group unanimously condemned the administration for refusing to grant him training credit for this period; none of the members dared consider the obvious justification for the administration's action.

The group solution of equality has the effect of leveling or deskilling members. Even though all of the members may have had experience as group leaders or individual therapists, they do not feel able to exercise these skills in a group. Instead, the training group, even more than most patient groups, often becomes dependent upon the leader to make even the simplest, most natural inquiries.

Some other common themes of the training group include many shared concerns issuing from the members' professional experience: their confusion over the limits of their responsibility; their discouragement over their failures; or, should it occur, their anguish over the suicide of one of their patients. One very important concern is that trainees often feel drained by their patients, experiencing their own strong craving for nurturance yet despairing of finding either an opportunity to express it or a person to gratify it. As the end of training approaches, as the trainees prepare to cut their last comforting ties to institutionalized studenthood, the group often spends considerable time dealing with the emotions aroused by this final and true transition to adulthood. Feelings about being "grown up," being looked up to, being one of the "big people," and being on one's own surface again and again.

LEADER TECHNIQUE

The leader of a training group of mental health professionals has a demanding task: he or she not only provides a role model by shaping and conducting an effective group but must also make certain modifications in technique to deal with the specific educational needs of the group members.

The basic approach, however, does not deviate from the guidelines I have outlined earlier in this book. For example, the leader is well advised to retain an interactional here-and-now focus. It is an error, in my opinion, to allow the group to move into a supervisory format where members describe problems they encounter in their therapeutic work with patients: such discussion should be the province of the supervisory hour. Whenever a group is engaged in discourse that can be held equally well in another formal setting, I believe that it is failing to use its unique properties and full potential. Instead, members can discuss these work-related problems in more profitable group-relevant ways: for example, they might discuss how it would feel to be the patient of a particular member. The group is also an excellent place for two members who happen to work together in therapy groups, or in marital or family therapy, to work on their relationship.

There are many ways for a leader to use the members' professional experience in the service of the group work. For example, I have often made statements to the training group in the following vein: "The group has been very slow moving today. When I inquired, you told me that you felt 'lazy' or that it was too soon after lunch to work. If you were the leader of a group and heard this, what would you make of it? What would you do?" Or, "Not only are John and Stewart refusing to work on their differences but others are lining up behind them. What are the options available to me as a leader today?" And so on. In a training group, I am inclined, much more than in a therapy group, to explicate group process. In therapy groups, if there is no therapeutic advantage in clarifying group process, I see no reason to do so. In training groups, there is always the superordinate goal of education.

Often process commentary combined with a view from the leader's seat is particularly useful. For example: "Let me tell you what I felt today as a group leader. A half-hour ago I felt uncomfortable with the massive encouragement and support everyone was giving Tom. This has happened before and, though it was reassuring, I haven't felt it was really helpful to Tom. I was tempted to intervene by inquiring about Tom's tendency to pull this behavior from the group; but I chose not to, partly because I've gotten so much flak lately for being so nonsupportive. So I remained silent. I think I made the right choice since it seems to me that the meeting developed into a very productive one with some of you getting deeply into your feelings of needing care and support. How do the rest of you see what's happened today?"

Because of the superordinate goal of education, the training group leader has considerable freedom. To a much greater extent than the group therapist, the training group leader may conclude that anything that happens in the group is okay as long as the members are able to learn from it. Thus, the leader may feel completely comfortable if the members want to experiment with the format by, for example, focusing each meeting on a single member or using structured exercises, provided that after a period of time the members evaluate the effects of these procedures upon the work of the group. The leader of a training group also has a splendid opportunity to model a research or "inquiring" attitude toward his or her own clinical work by consistently using the group as a source of data about the process and progress of the group. One may, for example, ask a troubled member how useful he or she found a meeting, or which parts of the session and which lines of inquiry seemed helpful, and which seemed unproductive or even restrictive.

PERSONAL PSYCHOTHERAPY

A training group rarely suffices to provide all the personal therapy a student therapist requires. Though we cannot set firm guidelines for so individual a process, few would dispute that some extensive self-exploratory venture is necessary for the maturation of the group therapist. In fact, a recent survey of psychologist psychotherapists indicated that 83 percent had had personal psychotherapy (mean number of hours = 297) and rated their therapy as highly important in their training.[16]

The therapist's self-knowledge plays a role in every aspect of therapy. An inability to perceive countertransference responses, to recognize personal distortions and blind spots, to use one's own feelings and fantasies in one's work limits the effectiveness of any therapist. If you lack insight into your own motivations, for example, you may avoid conflict in the group because of your proclivity to mute your feelings; or you may unduly encourage confrontation in a search for aliveness in yourself. You may be overeager to prove yourself or to make consistently brilliant interpretations and thereby emasculate the group. You may fear intimacy and prevent open expression of feelings by premature interpretations. You may do the opposite—overemphasize feelings, make too few connections, and so overstimulate patients that they are left in agitated turmoil. You may so need acceptance that you are unable to challenge the group and, like the members, may be swept along by the prevailing group current; you may be so devastated by an attack on yourself and so unclear about your presentation of self as to be unable to distinguish the realistic from the transference aspects of the attack. A supervisor-observer, a co-therapist, or a video-recording playback may help to provide feedback for the student group therapist, who may thus discover many of these blind spots; however, some type of personal psychotherapy is usually necessary for fuller understanding and correction.

Several training programs—for example, the British Group Analytic Institute and the Ontario Group Psychotherapy Association—require candidates to participate as bona-fide patients in an outpatient therapy group led by a senior clinician and composed of nonprofessionals seeking personal therapy.[17] Advocates of such a program point out the many advantages to being a real member of a therapy group. There is less sibling rivalry than in a group of one's peers, less need to perform, less defensiveness, less concern about being judged. The anticipated pitfalls are surmountable. If a trainee attempts to play assistant therapist or in some other way avoids genuine therapeutic engagement, a competent group leader will be able to provide the proper direction.

I believe that experience as a full member of a bona-fide therapy group is invaluable and would encourage any trainee to seek such therapy. Unfortunately the right group is hard to find. The advocates of personal group therapy as a part of training hail from large metropolitan areas (London, New York, Toronto, Geneva). But in smaller urban areas, the availability of personal group therapy is limited: there are simply not enough groups that meet the proper criteria—that is, a group of high-functioning outpatients led by a senior clinician with an eclectic dynamic approach. In fact, I believe that ever fewer high-functioning outpatient groups will be led in the future because of the increasing competition in private practice. New psychotherapy professions (for example, marriage and family counselors, pastoral counselors, body workers of many ideological persuasions, psychiatric nurses) are swelling the numbers of therapists offering therapy for the higher-functioning patient. Economics dictates the form of clinical practice. In an economy of scarcity, the number of private practice groups dwindles; therapists generally fill their individual therapy hours before referring a patient to group therapy. The vast majority of existing outpatient therapy groups are offered by clinics. These groups usually contain some or many members with major psychological impairment and do not constitute a good fit for a group therapy trainee.

There is one other method of obtaining both group therapy training and personal psychotherapy. For several years, I have led a therapy group for practicing psychotherapists. It is a straightforward therapy group, not a training group; the ticket of admission is the need and the wish for personal therapy, and members are charged standard therapy group fees. Naturally in the course of their therapy the members—most, but not all, of whom are also group therapists—learn a great deal about the group therapy process.

Since every community has some experienced group therapists, this format makes group therapy available to large numbers of mental health professionals. The composition of the group is generally more compatible for the student group therapist in that there is great homogeneity of ego strength. The group is a "stranger" group; members are all professionals but do not work together. Thus, the group avoids many of the competitive problems that occur in groups of students in the same training program. Members are highly motivated, psychologically minded, and generally verbally active. The highly experienced group therapist will find that such groups are not difficult to lead. Occasionally members may test, judge, or compete with the leader, but the great majority of the members are there for "no nonsense" work and apply their own knowledge of psychotherapy to help the group become maximally effective.

SUMMARY

The training experiences I have thus far described—observation of an experienced clinician, group therapy supervision, experiential group participation, and personal therapy—constitute, in my view, the minimum essential components of a program to train group therapists. (I assume that a trainee has previously had, or is simultaneously being trained in, general clinical areas: for example, interviewing, psychopathology, personality theory, and other forms of psychotherapy.) The sequence of the group therapy training experiences may depend on the structural characteristics of a particular training institute. I prefer that observation, personal therapy, and the experiential group begin very early in the training program, to be followed in a few months by the formation of a group and ongoing supervision. I feel it is wise for trainees to have a clinical experience in which they deal with basic group and interactional dynamics in an open-ended group of nonpsychotic, highly motivated patients before they begin to work with goal-limited groups of highly specialized patient populations or with one of the new specialized therapy approaches.

Training is, of course, a life-long process. It is important that clinicians maintain contact with colleagues, either informally or through professional organizations, such as the American Group Psychotherapy Association.[18] For growth to continue, continual new input is required. Many formats for continued education exist, including reading, working with different co-therapists, teaching, participation in professional workshops, and informal discussions with colleagues.

Beyond Technique

The group therapy training program has the task of teaching students not only how to do but also how to learn. What clinical educators must not convey is a rigid certainty in either our techniques or in our underlying assumptions about therapeutic change: the field is far too primitive for disciples of unwavering faith. To this end, I believe it is most important that we teach and model a basic research orientation to continuing education in the field. By research orientation, I refer not to a steel-spectacled Chi square efficiency but instead to an open, self-critical, inquiring attitude toward clinical and research evidence and conclusions—a posture toward experience which is consistent with a sensitive and humanistic clinical approach.

We need to help students evaluate their own work in a critical fashion and maintain sufficient flexibility (both technically and attitudinally) so that they can be responsive to their own observations. The mature therapist is an evolving therapist, a therapist who regards each patient, each group, indeed his or her whole career as a learning experience.

It is equally important to train students to evaluate systematic group therapy research and, if appropriate, to adapt the research conclusions to their clinical work. The inclusion of readings and seminars in clinical research methodology is thus highly desirable. Although only a few clinicians will ever have the time, funding, and institutional backing to engage in large-scale research, many clinicians can engage in intensive single-patient or single-group research, and all clinicians must evaluate clinical research. If the group therapy field is to develop in a coherent fashion, it must respond to responsible, well-executed, relevant, and credible research; otherwise, group therapy will continue its capricious, helter-skelter course, and research will become even more of a futile, effete exercise.

To illustrate, let me consider how the student may be introduced to a major research problem: outcome assessment. Seminars may be devoted to a consideration of the voluminous literature on the problems of outcome research. (The several excellent recent reviews may serve to anchor these discussions.)[19] In addition to seminars, each student may engage in a research practicum by interviewing patients who, for one reason or another, have recently terminated group therapy. In fact, few training hours are more profitably spent. It is a valuable exercise for the student to attempt to evaluate the degree of change, the nature of change, the mechanisms whereby the group experience has effected that change, and the contributing role of other factors in a patient's environment. The exercise becomes richer yet if students have available a tape of the initial interview to which they and each patient can listen.

Once having engaged even to a limited extent in an assessment of change, the student becomes more sensitive and more critical toward research involving outcome. (And it is outcome that remains the single greatest problem in group therapy research.) The problem, as the student grows to understand, is that conventional research approaches continue to perpetuate the error of extensive design, of failing to individualize outcome assessment. Clinicians fail to heed or even to believe research in which outcome is measured by before-after changes on standardized instruments—and with good reason, for abundant clinical and research evidence indicates that change means something different to each patient. Some patients need to experience less anxiety or hostility; for other patients, improvement would be accompanied by greater anxiety or hostility.[20] Even self-esteem changes need to be individualized. It has been demonstrated that a high self-esteem score on traditional self-administered questionnaires can reflect *either* a genuinely healthy regard of self *or* a defensive posture in which the individual maintains a high self-esteem at the expense of self-awareness.[21] These latter individuals would, as a result of successful treatment, have *lower* (but more accurate) self-esteem as measured by questionnaires.

In short, it is important for clinician as well as researcher to recognize the severe limitations of the traditional standardized (nomothetic) approach to outcome. I can think of no alternative except a laborious individualized (ideographic) approach to outcome. A number of clinical researchers have demonstrated the feasibility of an individualized outcome scale for each patient.[22] D. Malan has proposed an outcome strategy in which each patient is interviewed before therapy and a judgment is made by experienced clinicians about what types of changes would occur if that patient were to improve in therapy.[23] At the conclusion of therapy, the patient is re-examined, and each of the predictions is examined.

Not only must the general strategy of outcome assessment be altered, but the criteria for outcome must also be reformulated. It may be an error to use, in group therapy research, criteria originally designed for individual therapy outcome. I suspect that, although group and individual therapies may be equivalent in overall effectiveness, each modality may affect different variables and have a different type of outcome. For example, group therapy graduates may become more interpersonally skilled, more inclined to be affiliative in times of stress, more capable of sustaining meaningful relationships, or more empathic, whereas individual therapy patients may be more self-sufficient, introspective, and attuned to inner processes.

For years, group therapists have considered therapy as a multidimensional laboratory for living, and it is time to acknowledge this factor in outcome research. As a result of therapy, some patients alter their hierarchy of life values and grow to place more importance on humanistic or aesthetic goals; other patients may make major decisions which will influence the course of their lives; others may be more interpersonally sensitive and more able to communicate their feelings; still others may become less petty and more elevated in their life concerns; others may have a greater sense of commitment to other people or projects; others may experience greater energy; others may come to terms in a meaningful manner with their own mortality; while still others may find themselves more adventuresome, more receptive to new concepts and experiences.

A research orientation demands that, throughout your career as a therapist, you remain flexible and responsive to new evidence and that you live with a degree of uncertainty—no small request. Uncertainty that stems from the absence of a definitive treatment system begets anxiety. Working with deeply troubled, anxious individuals also begets anxiety. Many practitioners seek solace by embracing the Loreleis of orthodox belief systems. They commit themselves to one of the many ideological schools of conviction that not only offer a comprehensive system of explanation but also screen out discrepant facts and discount new evidence. This commitment usually entails a lengthy apprenticeship and initiation. Once within the system, a student finds it difficult to get out: first, one has usually undergone such a lengthy apprenticeship that denouncement of the school is equivalent to denouncing a part of oneself; secondly, it is extremely difficult to abandon a position of certainty for one of uncertainty. Clearly, however, such a position of certainty is antithetical to growth and is particularly stunting to the development of the student therapist.

There are certain potential dangers in the abrogation of certainty. Anxious and uncertain therapists may be less effective. Deep uncertainty may engender therapeutic nihilism, and the student may refuse to master any organized technique of therapy. The teacher, by personal example, must offer an alternative model: that he or she believes, in accordance with the best evidence available, that a particular approach is effective, but expects to alter that approach as new information becomes available. Furthermore, the teacher makes clear to the student the pride he or she derives from being part of a field that attempts to progress and is honest enough to know its own limitations.

The practitioner who lacks a research orientation with which to evaluate new developments is in a difficult position. How is one, for example, to react to the myriad recent innovations in the field? Unfortunately, the adaption of a new method is generally a function of the vigor, the persuasiveness, or the charisma of its proponent, and some new therapeutic approaches have been extraordinarily successful in rapidly obtaining both visibility and adherents. Many therapists without a consistent and critical approach to evidence have found themselves unreasonably unreceptive to all new approaches or, on the contrary, swept along with some current fad and then, dissatisfied with its limitations, have gone on to yet another.

The critical problem facing group psychotherapy, then, is one of balance. A traditional, conservative sector is less receptive to change than is optimal; an innovative, challenging sector is less receptive to stability than is optimal. The field is swayed by fashion, whereas it should be influenced by evidence. Psychotherapy is a science as well as an art and there is no place in science for uncritical orthodoxy or for innovation solely for its own sake. Orthodoxy offers safety for adherents but leads to stagnation; the field becomes insensitive to the zeitgeist and is left behind as the public goes elsewhere. Innovation provides zest and a readily apparent creative outlet for proponents but, if unevaluated, results in a kaleidoscopic field without substance—a field "which rides off madly in all directions."[24]

NOTES

Chapter 1. The Therapeutic Factors in Group Therapy

1. M. A. Lieberman, I. Yalom, and M. Miles, *Encounter Groups: First Facts* (New York: Basic Books, 1973).

2. H. Feifel and J. Eells, "Patients and Therapists Assess the Same Psychotherapy," *Journal of Consulting and Clinical Psychology* 27(1963):310–18.

3. J. Schaffer and S. Dreyer, "Staff and Inpatient Perceptions of Change Mechanisms in Group Therapy," *American Journal of Psychiatry* 139(1982):127–28.

J. Flora-Tastado, "Patient and Therapist Agreement on Curative Factors in Psychotherapy," *Dissertation Abstracts International* 42(1981):371–B.

S. Bloch and J. Reibstein, "Perceptions by Patients and Therapists of Therapeutic Factors in Group Therapy," *British Journal of Psychiatry* 137(1980):274–78.

R. Cabral and A. Paton, "Evaluation of Group Therapy: Correlations Between Clients' and Observers' Assessments," *British Journal of Psychiatry* 126(1975):475–77.

4. T. Butler and A. Fuhriman, "Level of Functioning and Length of Time in Treatment Variables Influencing Patients' Therapeutic Experience in Group Psychotherapy," *International Journal of Group Psychotherapy* 33(4[October 1983]):489–504.*

5. J. Maxmen, "Group Therapy as Viewed by Hospitalized Patients," *Archives of General Psychiatry* 28(March 1973):404–8.

T. Butler and A. Fuhriman, "Patient Perspective on the Curative Process. A Comparison of Day Treatment and Outpatient Psychotherapy Groups," *Small Group Behavior* 11(4[November 1980]):371–88.

T. Butler and A. Fuhriman, "Curative Factors in Group Therapy A Review of the Recent Literature," *Small Group Behavior* 14(2[May 1983]):131–42.

M. Leszcz, I. Yalom, and M. Norden, "The Value of Inpatient Group Psychotherapy," *International Journal of Group Psychotherapy*, in press (1985).

E. Rynearson and S. Melson, "Short-term Group Psychotherapy for Patients with Functional complaint," submitted for publication, *Post Graduate Medicine* 76(1984):141–50.

6. B. Corder, L. Whiteside, and T. Haizlip, "A Study of Curative Factors in Group Psychotherapy with Adolescents," *International Journal of Group Psychotherapy* 31(3[July 1981]):345–54.

N. Macaskill, "Therapeutic Factors in Group Therapy with Borderline Patients," *International Journal of Group Psychotherapy* 32(1[January 1982]):61–73.

7. M.A. Lieberman and L. Borman, *Self-Help Groups for Coping with Crisis* (San Francisco: Jossey-Bass, 1979).

M. A. Lieberman, "Comparative Analyses of Change Mechanisms in Group" in R. Dies, K. R. Mackensie, eds., *Advances in Group Therapy* (New York: International Universities press, 1983).

8. F. Taylor, *The Analysis of Therapeutic Groups* (London: Oxford University Press, 1961).

*The numbers in brackets refer to the original complete citation of a reference in each chapter.

B. Berzon and R. Farson, "The Therapeutic Event in Group Psychotherapy: A Study of Subjective Reports by Group Members," *Journal of Individual Psychology* 19(1963): 204–12.

9. A. P. Goldstein, *Therapist-Patient Expectancies in Psychotherapy* (New York: Pergamon Press, 1962).

S. Bloch, et al., "Patients' Expectations of Therapeutic Improvement and Their Outcomes," *American Journal of Psychiatry* 133(1976):1457–59.

10. Goldstein, *Therapist-Patient Expectancies* [9], *in Psychotherapy* pp. 35–53.

E. Uhlenhuth and D. Duncan, "Some Determinants of Change in Psychoneurotic Patients," *Archives of General Psychiatry* 18(1968):532–40.

11. M. A. Lieberman and L. Bohrman, *Self-Help Groups for Coping in Crisis* (San Francisco: Jossey-Bass, 1979).

12. W. C. White and M. Boskind-White, "An Experiential-Behavioral Approach to the Treatment of Bulimarexia," *Psychotherapy: Theory, Research and Practice* 18(1981): 501–7.

J. Schneider and W. S. Agras, "A Cognitive Behavioral Group Treatment of Bulimia," *British Journal of Psychiatry* 146 (1985):66–69.

B. Kirkley, et al., "A Comparison of Two Group Treatments for Bulimia," *Journal of Consulting and Clinical Psychology,* in press.

13. M. Jones, "Group Treatment with Particular Reference to Group Projection Methods," *American Journal of Psychiatry* 101(1944):292–99.

14. J. W. Klapman, "The Case for Didactic Group Psychotherapy," *Diseases of the Nervous System* 11(1950):35–41.

15. L. C. Marsh, "Group Therapy and the Psychiatric Clinic," *Journal of Nervous and Mental Diseases* 82(1935):381–90.

16. H. Wechsler, "The Self-Help Organization in the Mental Health Field: Recovery, Inc.—A Case Study," *Journal of Nervous and Mental Diseases* 130(1960):297–314.

17. A. A. Low, *Mental Health Through Will Training* (Boston: Christopher Publishing House, 1950).

18. Lieberman and Borman, *Self-Help Groups* [11], pp. 194–234.

19. B. Yano, J. Shabert, and L. Alexander, "A Psychiatrist-Nutritionist Group Therapy Approach to the Management of Obesity," *International Journal of Group Psychotherapy* 29(1979):185–94.

20. D. K. Grenvold and G. J. Welch, "Structured Short Term Group Treatment of Postdivorce Adjustment," *International Journal of Group Psychotherapy* 29(1979):347–58.

21. E. Herman and S. Baptiste, "Pain Control: Mastery Through Group Experience," *Pain* 10(1981):79–86.

22. S. Price, A. Heinrich, and J. Golden, "Structured Group Treatment of Couples Experiencing Sexual Dysfunction," *Journal of Sex and Marital Therapy* 6(1981):247–57.

23. L. Gallese and E. Treuting, "Help for Rape Victims Through Group Therapy," *Journal of Psychosocial Nursing and Mental Health Services* 19(1981):20–21.

24. C. Appolone and P. Gibson, "Group Work with Young Adult Epilepsy Patients," *Social Work in Health Care* 6(1981):23–32.

25. T. Hackett, "Group Therapy in Cardiac Rehabilitation," *Cardiology* 62(1977):75–84.

R. H. Rahe, et al., "Group Therapy in the Outpatient Management of Post-Myocardial Infarction Patients," *Psychiatry in Medicine* 4(1973):77–78.

M. A. Ibrahim, et al., "Management after Myocardial Infarction: A Controlled Trial of the Effect of Group Psychotherapy," *International Journal of Psychiatric Medicine* 5(1974):253–68.

26. A. Lieber, W. Schlanger, and J. Levi, "Group Therapy with Hemodialysis Patients," *Dialysis and Transplantation* 7(May 1978):464–70.

27. D. I. Malamud and S. Machover, *Toward Self-Understanding: Group Techniques in Self-Confrontation* (Springfield, Ill.: Charles C Thomas, 1965).

28. I. D. Yalom, et al., "Preparation of Patients for Group Therapy: A Controlled Study," *Archives of General Psychiatry* 17(1967):416–27.

29. F. Fromm-Reichman, *Principles of Intensive Psychotherapy* (Chicago: University of Chicago Press, 1950).

30. J. Frank, "Emotional Reactions of American Soldiers to an Unfamiliar Disease," *American Journal of Psychiatry* 102(1946):631–40.

31. J. Frank, et al., "Behavioral Patterns in Early Meetings of Therapy Groups," *American Journal of Psychiatry* 108(1952):771–78.

C. Peters and H. Brunebaum, "It Could Be Worse: Effective Group Therapy with the Help-Rejecting Complainer," *International Journal of Group Psychotherapy* 27(1977): 471–80.

E. Berne, *Games People Play* (New York: Grove Press, 1964).

32. J. Flowers, "The Differential Outcome Effects of Simple Advice, Alternatives and Instructions in Group Psychotherapy," *International Journal of Group Psychotherapy* 29(1979):305–15.

33. J. Frank, *Persuasion and Healing, A Comparative Study of Psychotherapy*, (Baltimore: Johns Hopkins University Press, 1973).

34. V. Frankl, *The Will to Meaning* (Cleveland: World Publishing, 1969).

35. A. Bandura, E. B. Blanchard, and B. Ritter, "The Relative Efficacy of Desensitization and Modeling Approaches for Inducing Behavioral, Affective, and Attitudinal Changes," *J. Personality and Social Psychology* 13(1969):173–99.

A. Bandura, D. Ross, and S. Ross, "Vicarious Reinforcements and Imitative Learning," *Journal of Abnormal and Social Psychology* 67(1963):601–7.

36. J. L. Moreno, "Psychodramatic Shock Therapy," *Sociometry* 2(1939):1–30.

Chapter 2. Interpersonal Learning

1. J. Bowlby, *Attachment and Loss*, vol. III: *Loss: Sadness and Depression* (New York: Basic Books, 1980).

2. W. Goldschmidt, as quoted by D. A. Hamburg, "Emotions in Perspective of Human Evolution," in P. Knapp, ed., *Expressions of the Emotions of Man* (New York: International Universities Press, 1963), p. 308.

3. W. James, *The Principles of Psychology*, vol. I (New York: Henry Holt, 1890), p. 293.

4. J. Hartog, J. Audy, and Y. Cohen, eds., *The Anatomy of Loneliness* (New York: International Universities Press, 1980).

J. Lynch, *The Broken Heart: The Medical Consequences of Loneliness* (New York: Basic Books, 1977).

5. H. S. Sullivan, *The Interpersonal Theory of Psychiatry* (New York: W. W. Norton, 1953).

H. S. Sullivan, *Conceptions of Modern Psychiatry* (New York: W. W. Norton, 1940).

6. P. Mullahy, "Harry Stack Sullivan," in H. Kaplan, A. Freedman, and B. Sadock, eds., *Comprehensive Textbook of Psychiatry* (Baltimore: Williams & Wilkins, 1980).

P. Mullahy, *The Contributions of Harry Stack Sullivan*, (New York: Hermitage House, 1952).

7. Ibid., p. 22.

8. Ibid., p. 10.

9. H. S. Sullivan, "Psychiatry: Introduction to the Study of Interpersonal Relations," *Psychiatry* 1(1938):121–34.

10. Sullivan, *Conceptions* [5], p. 207.

11. Ibid., p. 237.

12. E. Kübler-Ross, *On Death and Dying* (New York: Macmillan, 1969).

13. F. Alexander and T. French, *Psychoanalytic Therapy: Principles and Applications* (New York: Ronald Press, 1946).

14. F. Alexander, "Unexplored Areas in Psychoanalytic Theory and Treatment," in G. Daniels, ed., *New Perspectives in Psychoanalysis Sandor Rado Lectures 1957–1963* (New York: Grune & Stratton, 1965), p. 75.

15. Ibid., pp. 79–80.

16. J. Frank and E. Ascher, "The Corrective Emotional Experience in Group Therapy," *American Journal of Psychiatry* 108(1951):126–31.

17. J. Breuer and S. Freud, *Studies on Hysteria* (London: Hogarth Press, 1955).

18. M. A. Lieberman, I. Yalom, and M. Miles, *Encounter Groups: First Facts* (New York: Basic Books, 1973).

19. Ibid.

20. K. Horney, *Neurosis and Human Growth,* (New York: W. W. Norton, 1950).

21. In order to ensure each patient's right to privacy, I have altered certain facts, such as name, occupation, and age. In addition, the interaction described in the text is not verbatim but has been reconstructed from detailed clinical notes taken after each therapeutic encounter.

22. B. Berzon, C. Pious, and R. Farson, "The Therapeutic Event in Group Psychotherapy: A Study of Subjective Reports by Group Members," *Journal of Individual Psychology* 19(1963):204–12.

G. Talland and D. Clark, "Evaluation of Topics in Therapy Group Discussion," *Journal of Clinical Psychology* 10(1954):131–37.

J. Frank, "Some Values of Conflict in Therapeutic Groups," *Group Psychotherapy* 8(1955):142–51.

J. D. Kaye, "Group Interaction and Interpersonal Learning, *Small Group Behavior* 4(1973):424–48.

A. German and J. Gustafson, "Patients' Perceptions of the Therapeutic Relationship and Group Therapy Outcome," *American Journal of Psychiatry* 133(1976):1290–94.

H. Frankiel, "Mutually Perceived Therapeutic Relationships in T-groups: The Co-trainer Puzzle", *Journal of Applied Behavioral Science* 7(1971):449–65.

D. Lundgren, "Developmental Trends in the Emergence of Interpersonal Issues in T-groups," *Small Group Behavior* 8(1977):179–200.

P. Smith, "Sources of Influence in the Sensitivity Group Laboratory," *Small Group Behavior* 7(1976):331–48.

D. Lundgren, "Authority and Group Formation," *Journal of Applied Behavioral Science* 15(1979):330–45.

R. Dies, "Clinical Implications of Research on Leadership in Short-Term Group Psychotherapy," in R. Dies and K. Mackenzie, eds., *Advances in Group Psychotherapy* (New York, International Universities Press: 1983), pp. 27–79.

J. Hodgson, "Cognitive versus Behavioral-Interpersonal Approaches to the Group Treatment of Depressed College Students," *Journal of Counseling Psychology* 28(1981): 243–49.

J. Jones, *Group Psychotherapy as Experiencing Interpersonal Perceiving and Developing of Values* (Stockholm: Almquist & Wiksell, 1977).

23. J. Donovan, J. Bennett, and C. McElroy, "The Crisis Group—An Outcome Study," *American Journal of Psychiatry,* 136(1979):906–910.

24. L. W. Hoffman and M. Hoffman, eds., *Review of Child Development Research,* vol. I (New York: Russell Sage Foundation, 1964).

L. W. Hoffman and M. Hoffman, eds., *Review of Child Development Research,* vol. II (New York: Russell Sage Foundation, 1966).

P. Chodoff, "A Critique of the Freudian Theory of Infantile Sexuality," *American Journal of Psychiatry* 123(1966):507–18.

J. Kagan, "Perspectives on Continuity," in J. Kagan and O. G. Brim, eds., *Constancy and Change in Human Development* (Cambridge, Mass.: Harvard University Press, 1980)

J. Kagan, *The Nature of the Child* (New York: Basic Books, 1984), pp. 99–111.

Chapter 3. Group Cohesiveness

1. M. Smith, G. Glass, and T. Miller, *The Benefits of Psychotherapy* (Baltimore: Johns Hopkins University Press, 1980).

A. E. Bergin and M. Lambert, "The Evaluation of Therapeutic Outcomes," in S. Garfield and A. E. Bergin, eds., *Handbook of Psychotherapy and Behavioral Change: An Empirical Analysis,* 2nd ed. (New York: John Wiley, 1978), pp. 139–83.

L. Luborsky, B. Singer, and L. Luborsky, "Comparative Studies of Psychotherapies," *Archives of General Psychiatry* 32(1975):995–1008.

J. Meltzoff and M. Kornreich, *Research in Psychotherapy,* (Chicago, Aldin: 1970).

2. Smith, Glass, and Miller, *Benefits of Psychotherapy* [1], p. 87.

3. T. Kaul and R. Bednar, "Experiential Group Research," in *Handbook for Psychotherapy and Behavior Change,* 3rd ed. (New York: John Wiley, 1985).

4. A. E. Bergin, "The Effects of Psychotherapy: Negative Results Revisited," *Journal of Counseling Psychology* 10(1963):244–50.

H. Strupp, S. Hadley, and B. Gomes-Schwartz, *Psychotherapy for Better or Worse: The Problem of Negative Effects,* (New York: Jason Aronson, 1977)

Bergin and Lambert, "Evaluation of Therapeutic Outcomes" [1], pp. 152–62.

5. D. Orlinsky and K. Howard in "The Relation of Process to Outcome in Psychotherapy," in Garfield and Bergin, *Handbook* [1], pp. 283–329.

H. Strupp, R. E. Fox, and K. Lessler, *Patients View Their Psychotherapy* (Baltimore: Johns Hopkins University Press, 1969).

P. Martin and A. Sterne, "Post-hospital Adjustment as Related to Therapists In-therapy Behavior," *Psychotherapy: Theory, Research and Practice* 13(1976):267–73.

G. Barrett-Leonard, "Dimensions of Therapist Response as Causal Factors in Therapeutic Change," *Psychological Monographs* 76 (43 whole, no. 562[1962]).

A. Gurman and A. Razin, *Effective Psychotherapy: A Handbook for Research* (New York: Pergamon Press, 1977).

M. Parloff, I. Waskow, and B. Wolfe, "Research on Therapist. Variables in Relation to Process and Outcome," in Garfield and Bergin, *Handbook* [1], pp. 233–82.

P. Buckley, et al., "Psychodynamic Variables as Predictors of Psychotherapy Outcome," *American Journal of Psychiatry* 141(6[June 1984]):742–48.

6. F. Fiedler, "Factor Analyses of Psychoanalytic, Non-Directive and Adlerian Therapeutic Relationships," *Journal of Consulting Psychology* 15(1951):32–38.

F. Fiedler, "A Comparison of Therapeutic Relationships in Psychoanalytic, Non-Directive and Adlerian Therapy," *Journal of Consulting Psychology* 14(1950):436–45.

M. Lieberman, M. Miles, and I. Yalom, *Encounter Groups: First Facts,* (New York: Basic Books, 1973).

7. Bergin and Lambert, "Evaluation of Therapeutic Outcomes," [1], p. 151.

M. J. Lambert and A. E. Bergin, "Psychotherapeutic Outcomes and Issues Related to Behavioral and Humanistic Approaches," *Cornell Journal of Social Relations* 8(1973): 47–61.

Gurman and Razin, *Effective Psychotherapy* [5].

R. Sloane, et al., *Short-Term Analytically Oriented Psychotherapy vs. Behavior Therapy,* (Cambridge, Mass.: Harvard University Press, 1975).

8. D. Cartwright and A. Zander, eds., *Group Dynamics: Research and Theory* (Evanston, Ill.: Row, Peterson, 1962), p. 74.

9. J. D. Frank, "Some Determinants, Manifestations and Effects of Cohesion in Therapy Groups," *International Journal of Group Psychotherapy* 7(1957):53–62.

10. N. Evans and P. Jarvis, "Group Cohesion: A Review and Reevaluation," *Small Group Behavior* 2(1980):359–70.

11. S. Budge, "Group Cohesiveness Reexamined," *Group* 5(1981):10–18.

12. Frank, "Some Determinants" [9].

13. L. Festinger, H. W. Riecker, and S. Schachter, *When Prophecy Fails,* (Minneapolis: University of Minnesota Press, 1956).

14. H. Dickoff and M. Lakin, "Patients' Views of Group Psychotherapy: Retrospections and Interpretations," *International Journal of Group Psychotherapy* 13(1963):61–73. Twenty-eight patients who had been in either clinic or private outpatient groups were studied. The chief limitation of this exploratory inquiry is that the group therapy experience was of exceptionally brief duration (mean number of meetings attended = 11).

15. I. Yalom, *Theory and Practice of Group Psychotherapy,* 1st ed. (New York: Basic Books, 1970).

16. R. Cabral, J. Best, and A. Paton, "Patients' and Observers' Assessments of Process and Outcome in Group Therapy," *American Journal of Psychiatry* 132(1975):1052–54.

17. F. T. Kapp, et al., "Group Participation and Self-Perceived Personality Change," *Journal of Nervous Mental Disorders,* 139(1964)255–265.

18. J. Jones, "Group Psychotherapy as Experiencing Interpersonal Perceiving and Developing of Values," Doctoral Thesis at Uppsala University, Sweden. 1977. The findings in this study and in the preceding one are tentative. The instruments to measure change

were not, as recognized by the authors, standardized for reliability or validity. Furthermore, when personality change and group cohesiveness are tested simultaneously by a self-administered questionnaire, we cannot control for the possibility that patients who are attracted to their groups will be inclined to support their stance by reporting or perceiving themselves as improved. Cognitive dissonance theory teaches us that an individual who has made a decision will misperceive, deny, and distort data that would discredit that decision.

19. I. D. Yalom, et al., "Prediction of Improvement in Group Therapy," *Archives of General Psychiatry* 17(1967):159–68. Three measures of outcome (symptoms, functioning, and relationships) were assessed both in a psychiatric interview by a team of raters and in a self-assessment scale.

20. I. Falloon, "Interpersonal Variables in Behavioral Group Therapy," *British Journal of Medical Psychology* 54(1981):133–41.

21. J. Flowers, C. Booraem, and K. Hartman, "Client Improvement on Higher and Lower Intensity Problems as a Function of Group Cohesiveness," *Psychotherapy: Theory, Research and Practice* 18(1981):246–51.

22. J. B. Clark and S. A. Culbert, "Mutually Therapeutic Perception and Self-Awareness in a T-Group," *Journal of Applied Behavioral Science* 1(1965):180–94.

23. Outcome was measured by a well-validated rating scale (designed by A. M. Walker, R. A. Rablen, and C. Rogers, "Development of a Scale to Measure Process Changes in Psychotherapy," *Journal of Clinical Psychology* 16([1960]:79–85) to measure change in one's ability to relate to others, to construe one's experience, to approach one's affective life, and to confront and cope with one's chief problem areas. Samples of each member's speech were independently rated on this scale by trained naïve judges from taped excerpts early and late in the course of the group.
Intermember relationships were measured by the Barrett-Lennard Relationship Inventory (Barrett-Lennard, "Dimensions of Therapist Response" [5] which provided a measure of how each member viewed each other member (and the therapist) in terms of "unconditional, positive regard, empathic understanding, and congruence."

24. Lieberman, Yalom, and Miles, *Encounter Groups* [6].

25. (1) A critical incident questionnaire. Each member was asked, after each meeting, to describe the most significant event of that meeting. All events pertaining to group attraction, communion, belongingness, and so on were tabulated. (2) A cohesiveness questionnaire, similar to the one described above (Yalom, et al., "Predictions of Improvement" [19]) was administered early and late during the course of the group.

26. C. Rogers, "A Theory of Therapy, Personality and Interpersonal Relationships," in S. Koch, ed., *Psychology: A Study of a Science*, vol. III (New York: McGraw-Hill, 1959), pp. 184–256.

27. K. Horney, *Neurosis and Human Growth* (New York: W. W. Norton, 1950), p. 15.

28. C. Truax, "The Process of Group Therapy: Relationships between Hypothesized Therapeutic Conditions and Intrapersonal Exploration," *Psychological Monographs* 75(5111[1961]).

29. A. M. Walker, R. A. Rablen, and C. Rogers, "Development of a Scale to Measure Process Changes in Psychotherapy," *Journal of Clinical Psychology* 16(1960):79–85.

30. C. Rogers, personal communication, April 1967.

31. A. H. Maslow, *The Farther Reaches of Human Nature* (New York: Viking Press, 1972).

32. C. Rogers, "The Process of the Basic Encounter Group," unpublished mimeograph, Western Behavioral Science Institute, La Jolla, California, 1966.

33. I. Rubin, "The Reduction of Prejudice through Laboratory Training," *Journal of Applied Behavioral Science* 3(1967):29–50.

34. D. Miller, "The Study of Social Relationships: Situation, Identity, and Social Interaction," in S. Koch, ed., *Psychology: A Study of a Science*, vol. III (New York: McGraw-Hill, 1959), pp. 639–737.

35. H. S. Sullivan, *Conceptions of Modern Psychiatry* (London: Tavistock, 1955), p. 22.

36. Miller, "Study of Social Relationships" [34], p. 696.

37. E. J. Murray, "A Content Analysis for Study in Psychotherapy," *Psychological Monographs* 70(13[1956]).

38. Yalom, et al., "Prediction of Improvement" [19].

39. Before beginning therapy, the patients completed a modified Jourard self-disclosure questionnaire (S. Jourard, "Self-Disclosure Patterns in British and American College Females," *Journal of Social Psychology* 54[1961]:315–20). Individuals who had previously disclosed much of themselves (relevant to the other group members) to close friends or to groups of individuals were destined to become popular in their groups.

S. Hurley demonstrated, in a ten-week counseling group, that popularity was correlated with self-disclosure in the group as well as prior to group therapy (S. Hurley, "Self-Disclosure in Small Counseling Groups," unpublished doctoral thesis, Michigan State University, 1967).

40. Measured by the FIRO–B questionnaire (see chapter 10).

41. Lieberman, Yalom, and Miles, *Encounter Groups* [6].

42. D. Lundgren and D. Miller, "Identity and Behavioral Change in Training Groups," *Human Relations Training News* 9(Spring 1965).

43. G. C. Homans, *The Human Group* (New York: Harcourt, Brace, 1950).

44. Yalom, et al., "Prediction of Improvement" [19].

I. D. Yalom, "A Study of Group Therapy Drop-Outs," *Archives of General Psychiatry* 14(1966):393–414.

G. Bach, *Intensive Group Therapy* (New York: Ronald Press, 1954).

Garfield and Bergin, *Handbook* [1].

45. E. Nash, et al., "Some Factors Related to Patients Remaining in Group Psychotherapy," *International Journal of Group Psychotherapy* 7(1957):264–75.

46. Yalom, "Group Therapy Drop-Outs" [43].

47. Yalom, et al., "Predictions of Improvement" [38].

I. D. Yalom and K. Rand, "Compatibility and Cohesiveness in Therapy Groups," *Archives of General Psychiatry* 13(1966):267–76.

48. P. C. Sagi, D. W. Olmstead, and F. Atalsek, "Predicting Maintenance of Membership in Small Groups," *Journal of Abnormal Social Psychology* 51(1955):308–11.

L. Libo, "Measuring Group Cohesiveness," monograph, Ann Arbor, Michigan, Institute for Social Research, 1953.

49. Sagi, Olmstead, and Atalsek, "Predicting Maintenance of Membership" [48].

50. Yalom and Rand, "Compatibility and Cohesiveness" [47].

51. Yalom, et al., "Prediction of Improvement" [38].

52. Lieberman, Yalom, and Miles, *Encounter Groups* [6].

53. I. Yalom, J. Tinklenberg, and M. Gilula, "Curative Factors in Group Therapy," unpublished study.

54. M. Sherif, et al., *Intergroup Conflict and Cooperation: The Robbers' Cave Experiment* (Norman: University of Oklahoma Book Exchange, 1961).

55. R. Bednar and C. Battersby, "The Effects of Specific Cognitive Structure on Early Group Development," *Journal of Applied Behavioral Science* 12(1976):513–22.

P. Evanson and R. Bednar, "Effects of Specific Cognitive and Behavioral Structure on Early Group Behavior and Atmosphere," *Journal of Counseling Psychology* 77(1978):-258–62.

F. Lee and R. Bednar, "Effects of Group Structure and Risk-taking Disposition on Group Behavior, Attitudes and Atmosphere," *Journal of Counseling Psychology* 24(1977):191–99.

J. Stokes, "Toward an Understanding of Cohesion in Personal Change Groups," *International Journal of Group Psychotherapy* 33(1983):449–67.

56. N. Evans and P. Jarvis, "Group Cohesion: A Review and Evaluation," *Small Group Behavior* 11(1980):357–70.

S. Budge, "Group Cohesiveness Reexamined," *Group* 5(1980):10–18.

R. Bednar and T. Kaul, "Experiential Group Research," in Garfield and Bergin, *Handbook* [1] p. 803.

57. J. Frank, "Some Values of Conflict in Therapeutic Groups," *Group Psychotherapy* 8(1955):142–51.

58. A. Pepitone and G. Reichling, "Group Cohesiveness and the Expression of Hostility," *Human Relations* 8(1955):327–37.

59. M. E. Wright, "The Influence of Frustration Upon the Social Relations of Young Children," *Character and Personality* 12(1943):111–22.

60. D. Cartwright and A. Zander, "Group Cohesiveness: Introduction," in *Group Dynamics: Research and Theory* (Evanston, Ill.: Row, Peterson, 1962), pp. 69–74.

A. Goldstein, K. Heller, and L. Sechrest, *Psychotherapy and the Psychology of Behavior Change* (New York: John Wiley, 1966).

61. Ibid.

62. Cartwright and Zander, "Group Cohesiveness" [60], p. 89.

63. K. Back, "Influence through Social Communication," *Journal of Abnormal Social Psychology* 46(1951):398–405.

64. G. Rasmussen and A. Zander, "Group Membership and Self-Evaluation," *Human Relations* 7(1954):239–51.

65. S. Seashore, "Group Cohesiveness in the Industrial Work Group," Monograph, Ann Arbor, Michigan, Institute for Social Research, 1954.

66. Rasmussen and Zander, "Group Membership and Self-Evaluation" [65].

Goldstein, Heller, and Sechrest, *Psychotherapy and the Psychology of Behavior Change* [60], p. 329.

67. R. Kirschner, R. Dies, and R. Brown, "Effects of Experiential Manipulation of Self-disclosure on Group Cohesiveness," *Journal of Consulting and Clinical Psychology* 46(1978):1171–77.

68. Schacter, "Deviation, Rejection and Communication" [61].

A. Zander and A. Havelin, "Social Comparison and Intergroup Attraction," cited in Cartwright and Zander, *Group Dynamics* [60], p. 94.

69. Goldstein, Heller, and Sechrest, *Psychotherapy and the Psychology of Behavior Change* [60].

70. S. Schachter, "Deviation, Rejection and Communication," *Journal of Abnormal Social Psychology* 46(1951):190–207.

Chapter 4. The Therapeutic Factors: An Integration

1. S. Bloch, R. Crouch, and J. Reibstein, "Therapeutic Factors in Group Psychotherapy," *Archives of General Psychiatry* 38(May 1981):519–26.

2. H. Roback, "Experimental Comparison of Outcome in Insight and Non-Insight-oriented Therapy Groups," *Journal of Consulting Psychology* 38(1972):411–17.

J. F. Lomont, et al., "Group Assertion Training and Group Insight Therapies," *Psychological Reports* 25(1969):463–70.

S. I. Abramowitz and C. V. Abramowitz, "Psychological-mindedness and Benefit from Insight-oriented Group Therapy," *Archives of General Psychiatry* 30(1974):610–15.

S. Abramowitz and C. Jackson, "Comparative Effectiveness of There-and-Then versus Here-and-Now Therapist Interpretations in Group Psychotherapy," *Journal of Counseling Psychology* 21(1974):288–94.

3. S. Freedman and J. Hurley, "Perceptions of Helpfulness and Behavior in Groups," *Group* 4(1980):51–58.

J. B. Schaffer and S. F. Dreyer, "Staff and Inpatient Perceptions of Change Mechanisms in Group Psychotherapy," *American Journal of Psychiatry* 139(1 [January 1982]):127–28.

W. M. Fawcett Hill, "Further Consideration of Therapeutic Mechanisms in Group Therapy," *Small Group Behavior* 6(4[November 1975]):421–29.

M. Rohrbaugh and B. Bartels, "Participants' Perceptions of 'Curative Factors' in Therapy and Growth Groups," *Small Group Behavior* 6(4[November 1975]):430–56.

R. Cabral and A. Paton, "Evaluation of Group Therapy: Correlations between Clients' and Observers' Assessments," *British Journal of Psychiatry* 126(1975):475–77.

T. Butler, "Level of Functioning and Length of Time in Treatment Variables Influencing Patients' Therapeutic Experience in Group Psychotherapy," *Dissertation Abstracts International* 41(7[January 1981]):2749-B.

T. Butler and A. Fuhriman, "Patient Perspective on the Curative Process: A Comparison of Day Treatment and Outpatient Psychotherapy Groups," *Small Group Behavior* 11(4[November 1980]):371–88.

A. Fuhriman and T. Butler, "Curative Factors in Group Therapy, A Review of the Recent Literature," *Small Group Behavior* 14(2[May 1983]):131–42.

J. Maxmen and N. H. Hanover, "Group Therapy as Viewed by Hospitalized Patients," *Archives of General Psychiatry* 28(March 1973):404–8.

S. Melson, et al., "Short-term Intensive Group Psychotherapy in a Multispecialty Medical Clinic," submitted for publication 1985, *International Journal of Group Psychotherapy.*

S. Bloch and J. Reibstein, "Perceptions by Patients and Therapists of Therapeutic Factors in Group Psychotherapy, *British Journal of Psychiatry* 137(1980):274–78.

J. Flowers, "The Differential Outcome Effects of Simple Advice, Alternatives and Instructions in Group Psychotherapy," *International Journal of Group Psychotherapy* 29(1979):305–15.

B. Corder, L. Whiteside, and T. Haizlip, "A Study of Curative Factors in Group Psychotherapy with Adolescents," *International Journal of Group Psychotherapy* 31(3[July 1981]):345–54.

R. Cabral, J. Best, and A. Paton, "Patients' and Observers' Assessments of Process and Outcome in Group Therapy: A Follow-up Study," *American Journal of Psychiatry* 132(10[October 1975]):1052–54.

M. Lieberman, I. Yalom, and M. Miles, *Encounter Groups: First Facts* (New York: Basic Books, 1973).

L. Long and C. Cope, "Curative Factors in a Male Felony Offender Group," *Small Group Behavior* 11(1980):389–98.

R. K. Mower (1980), cited by T. Butler and A. Fuhriman, "Level of Functioning and Length of Time in Treatment: Variables Influencing Patients' Therapeutic Experience in Group Therapy," *International Journal of Group Psychotherapy* 33(1983):484–504.

R. Marcovitz and J. Smith, "Patients' Perceptions of Curative Factors in Short-term Group Psychotherapy," *International Journal of Group Psychotherapy* 33(1983):21–37.

4. Cabral and Paton, "Evaluation of Group Therapy" [3].

Bloch and Reibstein, "Perceptions by Patients and Therapists of Therapeutic Factors" [3].

Cabral, Best, and Paton, "Patients' and Observers' Assessments of Process and Outcome" [3].

5. B. Berzon, C. Pious, and R. Parson, "The Therapeutic Event in Group Psychotherapy: A Study of Subjective Reports by Group Members," *Journal of Individual Psychology* 19(1963):204–12.

6. H. Dickoff and M. Lakin, "Patients' Views of Group Psychotherapy: Retrospections and Interpretations," *International Journal of Group Psychotherapy* 13(1963):61–73.

7. I. Yalom, J. Tinklenberg, and M. Gilula, "Curative Factors in Group Therapy," unpublished study, 1968.

8. There were four checks to ensure that our sample was a successfully treated one: (1) the therapists' evaluation; (2) length of treatment: previous research (I. D. Yalom, et al., "Prediction of Improvement in Group Therapy," *Archives of General Psychiatry* 17[1967]:159–68) in the same clinic demonstrated that the group patients who remained in therapy for that length of time had an extremely high rate of improvement; (3) the investigators' independent interview ratings of improvement along a thirteen-point scale in four areas—symptoms, functioning, interpersonal relationships, and self-concept; and (4) the patients' self-rating along the same scale.

9. The number in each of the seven piles thus approaches a normal distribution curve and facilitates statistical assessment. For further information about the Q-sort technique, see J. Block, *The Q-Sort Method in Personality Assessment and Psychiatric Research.* (Springfield, Ill.: Charles C Thomas, 1961).

10. Freedman and Hurley, "Perceptions of Helpfulness and Behavior" [3]. Rohrbaugh and Bartels, "Participants' Perceptions of 'Curative Factors' " [3]. Corder, Whiteside, and Haizlip, "A Study of Curative Factors" [3].

11. Rohrbaugh and Bartels, "Participants' Perceptions of 'Curative Factors' " [3].

12. Freedman and Hurley, "Perceptions of Helpfulness and Behavior" [3].

13. Corder, Whiteside, and Haizlip, "A Study of Curative Factors" [3].

14. These seven studies (and the four personal-growth group studies and the inpatient group studies presented in tables 4.3 and 4.4) do not use the sixty-item Q-sort but use instead an abbreviated instrument based on the Q-sort. Generally the instrument consists of twelve statements, each describing one of the therapeutic factors, which patients are asked to rank-order. Two additional studies use another method: group members are asked to describe an incident in their group experience which was personally critically important; the incident is then coded by trained raters into group categories. In the Lieberman, Yalom, and Miles encounter group study, the most important factors involved expression of a feeling (both positive and negative) to another person, attainment of insight, vicarious therapy, and responding with strong positive and/or negative feelings (Lieberman, Yalom, and Miles, *Encounter Groups* [3]). In the Bloch and Reibstein study of thirty-three outpatients, the most valued factors were self-understanding, self-disclosure (which includes some elements of catharsis and interpersonal learning on other tests), and learning from interpersonal actions (Bloch and Reibstein, "Perceptions by Patients and Therapists of Therapeutic Factors" [3]). Although the structure of the categories is different, the findings of these projects are consistent with the other studies described in tables 4.2 and 4.3.

15. Lieberman, Yalom, and Miles, *Encounter Groups* [3].

16. Freedman and Hurley, "Perceptions of Helpfulness and Behavior" [3].
Rohrbaugh and Bartel, "Participants' Perceptions of 'Curative Factors' " [3].
Corder, Whiteside, and Haizlip, "A Study of Curative Factors" [3].

17. Freedman and Hurley "Perceptions of Helpfulness and Behavior" [3].

18. A. Maslow, "The Need to Know and the Fear of Knowing," *Journal of General Psychology* 68(1963):111–25.

19. Rohrbaugh and Bartels, "Participants' Perceptions of 'Curative Factors' " [3].

20. A. Maslow, *Motivation and Personality* (New York: Harper, 1954).

21. Maslow, "The Need to Know" [19].
D. Berlyne, *Conflict, Arousal and Curiosity* (New York: McGraw-Hill, 1960).

22. Maslow, "The Need to Know" [19].

23. R. W. White, "Motivation Reconsidered: The Concept of Competence," *Psychological Review* 66(1959):297–333.

24. A. S. Dibner, "Ambiguity and Anxiety," *Journal of Abnormal Social Psychology* 56(1958):165–74.

25. L. Postman and J. S. Brunner, "Perception under Stress," *Psychological Review* 55(1948):314–23.
E. Verville, "The Effect of Emotional and Motivational Sets on the Perception of Incomplete Pictures," *Journal of General Psychology* 69(1946):133–45.

26. S. J. Korchin et al., "Experience of Perceptual Distortion as a Source of Anxiety," *Archives of Neurology and Psychiatry* 80(1958):98–113.

27. Maslow, "The Need to Know" [19].

28. D. Rosenthal, "Changes in Some Moral Values Following Psychotherapy," *Journal of Consulting Psychology* 19(1955):431–36.

29. Lieberman, Yalom, and Miles, *Encounter Groups* [3].

30. M. Leszcz, I. Yalom, and M. Norden, "The Value of Inpatient Group Psychotherapy and Therapeutic Process: Patients' Perceptions," *International Journal of Group Psychotherapy* 35(July 1985).
G. Steinfeld and J. Mabli, "Perceived Curative Factors in Group Therapy by Residents of a Therapeutic Community," *Criminal Justice and Behavior* 1(3[September 1974]):278–88.
Butler and Fuhriman, "Patient Perspective on the Curative Process" [3].
Schaffer and Dreyer, "Staff and Inpatient Perceptions of Change Mechanisms" [3].

31. E. Jones, *The Life and Work of Sigmund Freud*, vol I (New York: Basic Books, 1953), p. 40.

32. I. Yalom, *Existential Psychotherapy* (New York: Basic Books, 1980).

33. M. Heidegger, *Being and Time* (New York: Harper & Row, 1962), pp. 210–24.

34. J. P. Sartre, *Being and Nothingness*, translated by Hazel Barnes (New York: Philosophical Library, 1956), p. 633.

35. K. Jaspers, cited in J. Choron, *Death and Western Thought* (New York: Collier Books, 1963), p. 226.

36. I. Yalom and C. Greaves, "Group Therapy with the Terminally Ill," *American Journal of Psychiatry* 134(April 1977):4.   •

37. F. Nietzsche, quoted in V. Frankl, *Man's Search for Meaning* (New York: Pocket Books, 1959), p. 164.

38. D. Spiegel, J. Bloom, and I. Yalom, "Group Support for Patients with Metastatic Cancer," *Archives of General Psychiatry* 38(May 1981).
Yalom, *Existential Psychotherapy* [32], pp. 36–37.

39. R. Corsini and B. Rosenberg, "Mechanisms of Group Psychotherapy: Processes and Dynamics," *Journal of Abnormal Social Psychology* 51(1955):406–11.

40. W. F. Hill, Analysis of Interviews of Group Therapists' Papers, *Provo Papers* 1: 1(1957).

41. W. F. Hill, "Further Consideration of Therapeutic Mechanisms in Group Therapy," *Small Group Behavior* 6(4[November 1975]):421–29.

42. F. Fiedler, "A Comparison of Therapeutic Relationships in Psychoanalytic, Non-directive and Adlerian Therapy," *Journal of Consulting Psychology* 14(1950):436–45.

43. R. W. Heine, "A Comparison of Patients' Reports on Psychotherapeutic Experience with Psychoanalytic, Non-Directive and Adlerian Therapists," *American Journal of Psychotherapy* 7(1953):16–23.

44. C. Truax and R. Carkhuff, *Toward Effective Counseling and Psychotherapy* (Chicago: Aldine Press, 1967).

45. H. Strupp, R. Fox, and K. Lessler, *Patients View Their Psychotherapy* (Baltimore: Johns Hopkins University Press, 1969).

46. Lieberman, Yalom, and Miles, *Encounter Groups* [3].

47. Schaffer and Dreyer, "Staff and Inpatient Perceptions of Change Mechanisms [3].

48. Bloch and Reibstein, "Perceptions by Patients and Therapists of Therapeutic Factors" [3].

49. H. Feifel and J. Eells, "Patients and Therapists Assess the Same Psychotherapy," *Journal of Consulting Psychology* 27(1963):310–18.

50. G. Blaine and C. McArthur, "What Happened in Therapy as Seen by the Patient and His Psychiatrist," *Journal of Nervous and Mental Disorders* 127(1958):344–50.

51. I. D. Yalom and Ginny Elkin, *Every Day Gets a Little Closer: A Twice-Told Therapy* (New York: Basic Books, 1974).

52. R. Marcovitz and J. Smith, "Patients' Perceptions of Curative Factors in Short-term Group Psychotherapy," *International Journal of Group Psychotherapy* 33(1983):21–37.

53. M. Lieberman and L. Borman, *Self-Help Groups for Coping with Crisis* (San Francisco: Jossey-Bass, 1979), pp. 202–5.

54. T. Butler and A. Fuhriman, "Curative Factors in Group Therapy, A Review of the Recent Literature," *Small Group Behavior* 14(2[May 1983]):131–42.

55. I. Yalom, J. Tinklenberg, and M. Gilula, "Curative Factors in Group Therapy," unpublished study, 1968.

56. Lieberman, Yalom, and Miles, *Encounter Groups* [3].

57. Butler, "Level of Functioning and Length of Time" [3].

58. Leszcz, Yalom, and Norden, "The Value of Inpatient Group Psychotherapy and Therapeutic Process" [30].

59. Lieberman, Yalom, and Miles, *Encounter Groups* [3].

60. S. Freedman and J. Hurley, "Maslow's Needs: Individuals' Perception of Helpful Factors in Growth Groups," *Small Group Behavior* 10(1979):355–67.

Chapter 5. The Therapist: Basic Tasks

1. G. Psathas and R. Hardert, "Trainer Interventions and Normative Patterns in the T-Group," *Journal of Applied Behavioral Science* 2(1966):149–69.

2. D. Shapiro and L. Birk, "Group Therapy in Experimental Perspective," *International Journal of Group Psychotherapy* 17(1967):211–24.

3. R. C. Jacobs and D. T. Campbell, "The Perpetuation of an Arbitrary Tradition through Several Generations of a Laboratory Microculture," *Journal of Abnormal Social Psychology* 62(1961):649–58.

4. M. Sherif, "Group Influences upon the Formation of Norms and Attitudes," in E. E. Maccoby, T. M. Newcomb, and E. L. Hartley, eds., *Readings in Social Psychology* (New York: Holt, Rinehart, & Winston, 1958), pp. 219–32.

5. Shapiro and Birk, "Group Therapy in Experimental Perspective" [2].

6. J. Marmor, cited in R. Liberman, "Social Reinforcement of Group Dynamics: An Evaluative Study," presented at American Group Psychotherapy Association Convention, Chicago, January 1968.

7. R. V. Heckel, S. L. Wiggins, and H. C. Salzberg, "Conditioning against Silences in Group Therapy," *Journal of Clinical Psychology* 18(1962):216–17.

8. M. Dinoff et al., "Conditioning the Verbal Behavior of a Psychiatric Population in a Group Therapy-Like Situation," *Journal of Clinical Psychology* 16(1960):371–72.

M. A. Lieberman, "The Implications of a Total Group Phenomenon: Analysis for Patients and Therapists," *International Journal of Group Psychotherapy* 17(1967):71–81.

9. A. Bandura, "Modelling Approaches to the Modification of Phobic Disorders," presented at the Ciba Foundation Symposium: The Role of Learning in Psychotherapy, London, 1968.

A. Bandura, J. Grusec, and F. Menlove, "Vicarious Extinction of Avoidance Behavior," *Journal of Personality and Social Psychology* 5(1967):16–23.

10. A. Bandura, D. Ross, and J. Ross, "Imitation of Film Mediated Aggressive Models," *Journal of Abnormal and Social Psychology* 66(1963):3–11.

11. A. M. Schwartz and H. L. Hawkins, "Patient Models and Affect Statements in Group Therapy," paper read at American Psychological Association Meetings, Chicago, September 1965.

12. A. Goldstein et al., "The Use of Planted Patients in Group Psychotherapy," *American Journal of Psychotherapy* 21(1967):767–74.

13. I. Yalom, *Existential Psychotherapy* (New York: Basic Books, 1983), pp. 178–87.

Chapter 6. The Therapist: Working in the Here-and-Now

1. M. Miles, "On Naming the Here-and-Now," unpublished essay.

2. The Freud/Jung Letters, *The Correspondence between Sigmund Freud and C. G. Jung*, edited by William McGuire (Princeton: Princeton University Press, 1974).

3. M. Lieberman, I. Yalom, and M. Miles, *Encounter Groups: First Facts* (New York: Basic Books, 1973).

4. Milton Berger, "Nonverbal Communications in Group Psychotherapy," *International Journal of Group Psychotherapy* 8(1958):161–78.

5. I. D. Yalom and J. H. Handlon, "The Use of Multiple Therapists in the Teaching of Psychiatric Residents," *Journal of Nervous and Mental Diseases* 141(1966):684–92.

6. S. H. Foulkes and E. J. Anthony, *Group Psychotherapy: The Psychoanalytic Approach*, 2nd ed. (Baltimore: Penguin Books, 1965), p. 153.

7. E. Berne, *Games People Play* (New York: Grove Press, 1964).

8. O. Rank, *Will Therapy and Truth and Reality* (New York: Alfred A. Knopf, 1950).

R. May, *Love and Will* (New York: W. W. Norton, 1969).

S. Arieti, *The Will to Be Human* (New York: Quadrangle Books, 1972).

L. Farber, *The Ways of the Will* (New York: Basic Books, 1966).

A. Wheelis, "Will and Psychoanalysis," *Journal of Psychoanalytic Association* 4(1956):285–303.

I. Yalom, *Existential Psychotherapy* (New York: Basic Books, 1983).

9. Yalom, *Existential Psychotherapy* [8], pp. 286–350.

10. Farber, *The Ways of the Will* [8].

11. T. Aquinas, quoted in P. Edwards, ed., *The Encyclopedia of Philosophy* (New York: Macmillan/Free Press, 1967), vol. VII, p. 112.

12. J. Frank, *Persuasion and Healing* (Baltimore: Johns Hopkins University Press, 1973), p. 220.

13. E. Goffman, "The Moral Career of the Mental Patient," *Psychiatry* 22(1959):123–42.

14. C. Rycroft, *Psychoanalysis Observed* (London: Constable, 1966), p. 18.
15. Foulkes and Anthony, *Group Psychotherapy* [6], p. 29.
16. Ibid., p. 238.
17. W. R. Bion, *Experiences in Groups and Other Papers* (New York: Basic Books, 1959).
H. Ezriel, "A Psycho-analytic Approach to Group Treatment," *British Journal of Medical Psychology* 23(1950):59–74.
18. M. Klein, cited by J. Strachey, "The Nature of the Therapeutic Action of Psychoanalysis," *International Journal of Psychoanalysis* 15(1934):127–59.
19. Bion, *Experiences in Groups* [28].
20. L. Horwitz, "Group Centered Interventions in Therapy Groups," *Comprehensive Group Studies* 2(1971):311–31.
W. Bion and J. Rickman, "Intra-group Tensions in Therapy," *Lancet,* 27 November 1943.
M. Sherwood, "Bion's Experiences in Groups: A Critical Evaluation," *Human Relations* 17(1964):113–30.
Bion, *Experiences in Groups* [28].
I. Yalom, *The Theory and Practice of Group Psychotherapy,* 2nd ed. (New York: Basic Books, 1975).
21. Sherwood, "Bion's Experiences in Groups" [31].
22. Bion, *Experiences in Groups* [28].
23. Ibid.
24. Ibid.
25. R. Dies, "Leadership in Short-term Groups," in R. Dies and K. Roy Mackensie, eds., *Advances in Group Therapy* (New York: International Universities Press, 1983), pp. 27–78.
J. Caligor, "Perceptions of the Group Therapist and the Drop-out from Group," in L. R. Wolberg, M. L. Aronson, and A. R. Wolberg, eds., *Group Therapy 1977: An Overview* (New York: Stratton Intercontinental Medical Books, 1977), pp. 112–28.
26. D. Malan, "Group Psychotherapy: A Long Term Followup Study," *Archives of General Psychiatry* 33(1976):1303–15.
27. M. Nichols and T. Taylor, "Impact of Therapist Interventions on Early Sessions of Group Therapy," *Journal of Clinical Psychology* 31(1975):726–29.
28. D. S. Whitaker and M. Lieberman, *Psychotherapy through the Group Process* (New York: Atherton Press, 1964).
29. S. H. Foulkes, *Therapeutic Group Analysis* (New York: International Universities Press, 1965).
30. H. Ezriel, "A Psycho-Analytic Approach to Group Treatment," *British Journal of Medical Psychology* 23(1950):59–74.
H. Ezriel, "Notes on Psycho-Analytic Group Therapy: Interpretation and Research," *Psychiatry* 15(1952):119–26.

Chapter 7. The Therapist: Transference and Transparency

1. J. Breuer and S. Freud, "Studies on Hysteria," in S. Freud, *Standard Edition of the Complete Psychological Works of Sigmund Freud,* vol. II (London: Hogarth Press, 1955).
2. S. Freud, "Five Lectures on Psycho-analysis," in S. Freud, *Standard Edition of the Complete Psychological Works of Sigmund Freud,* vol. XI (London: Hogarth Press, 1957).
3. J. Strachey, "The Nature of the Therapeutic Action of Psychoanalysis," *International Journal of Psychoanalysis* 15(1939):127–59.
4. J. Marmor, "The Future of Psychoanalytic Therapy," *American Journal of Psychiatry* 130(November 1973):1197–1202.
5. C. A. Rycroft, *Critical Dictionary of Psychoanalysis* (New York: Basic Books, 1968).
J. Sandler, G. Dave, and A. Holder, "Basic Psychoanalytic Concepts: III Transference," *British Journal of Psychiatry* 116(1970):667–72.
6. S. Freud, *Group Psychology and the Analysis of the Ego,* in S. Freud, *Standard*

Edition of the Complete Psychological Works of Sigmund Freud, vol. XVIII (London: Hogarth Press, 1955).

7. Ibid.

8. E. Fromm, *Escape from Freedom* (New York: Holt, Rinehart & Winston, 1941), p. 21.

9. L. Tolstoy, *War and Peace* (New York: Modern Library, Random House, 1931), p. 231. Originally published, 1865–69.

10. Ibid., p. 245.

11. S. Freud, *The Future of an Illusion,* in S. Freud, *Standard Edition of the Complete Psychological Works of Sigmund Freud,* vol. XXI (London: Hogarth Press, 1961), pp. 1–56.

12. Guy Thorne, *When It Was Dark,* cited by Sigmund Freud in *Group Psychology and the Analysis of the Ego* [6].

13. I. Yalom, *Inpatient Group Psychotherapy* (New York: Basic Books, 1983).

E. Berne, "Staff Patient Conferences," *American Journal of Psychiatry* 125(1968): 286–88.

14. I. D. Yalom and J. H. Handlon, "The Use of Multiple Therapists in the Teaching of Psychiatric Residents," *Journal of Nervous and Mental Diseases* 141(1966):684–92.

15. M. J. Rioch, et al., "National Institute of Mental Health Pilot Study in Training Mental Health Counselors," *American Journal of Orthopsychiatry* 33(1963):678–89.

16. G. O. Ebersole, P. H. Leiderman, and I. D. Yalom, "Training and Non-Professional Group Therapist: A Controlled Study," *Journal of Nervous and Mental Diseases,* in press.

17. J. R. Hilgard and U. S. Moore, "Affiliative Therapy with Young Adolescents," *Journal of the American Academy of Child Psychiatry* 8(October 1969):577–605.

G. Goodman, "Companionship as Therapy: The Use of Non-Professional Talent," in J. T. Hart and T. M. Tomlinson, eds., *New Directions in Client-Centered Psychotherapy* (Boston: Houghton-Mifflin, 1968).

18. M. A. Lieberman and L. D. Borman, *Self Help Groups for Coping with Crisis* (San Francisco: Jossey-Bass, 1979).

19. S. Ferenczi quoted in M. Green, ed., *Interpersonal Analysis: The Selected Papers of Clara M. Thompson* (New York: Basic Books, 1964), p. 70.

20. S. H. Foulkes, "A Memorandum on Group Therapy," *British Military Memorandum, ADM.,* July 1945.

21. M. M. Berger, "The Function of the Leader in Developing and Maintaining a Working Therapeutic Group," unpublished mimeograph, 1967.

22. M. B. Allan, "An Investigation of Therapist and Patient Self-Help Disclosure in Outpatient Therapy Groups," *Dissertation Abstracts International* 41(03[September 1980]), no. 8021155.

23. S. Freud, "On Beginning the Treatment," in S. Freud, *Standard Edition of the Complete Psychological Works of Sigmund Freud,* vol. XII, p. 143.

24. F. Wright, P. Buirski, and N. Smith, "The Implications of Leader Transparency for the Dynamics of Short-term Process," *Group* 2(1978):210–19.

25. *Time,* 23 February 1968, p. 42.

26. A. H. Maslow, "Notes on Unstructured Groups at Lake Arrowhead," unpublished mimeograph, 1962.

27. R. Dies, "Leadership in Short-Term Groups," in R. Dies and K. Roy Mackenzie, eds., *Advances in Group Psychotherapy* (New York: International University Press, 1983), pp. 27–79.

R. Dies, "Group Therapist Transparency: A Critique of Theory and Research," *International Journal of Group Psychotherapy* 27(1977):177–200.

R. Dies and L. Cohen, "Content Considerations in Group Therapist Self-Disclosure, *International Journal of Group Psychotherapy* 76(1976):71–88.

28. S. Bellow, *Seize the Day* (New York: Viking Press, 1956).

29. M. Parloff, "Discussion of Accelerated Interaction: A Time-Limited Approach Based on the Brief Intensive Group," *International Journal of Group Psychotherapy* 28(1968):239–44.

30. Ferenczi quoted in Green, *Interpersonal Analysis* [17].

31. S. Jourard, *The Transparent Self* (Princeton: D. Van Nostrand, 1964).

F. Stoller, "Accelerated Interaction: A Time-Limited Approach Based on the Brief Intensive Group," *International Journal of Group Psychotherapy* 28(1968):220–35.

O. H. Mowrer, *The New Group Therapy* (Princeton: D. Van Nostrand, 1964).

32. S. Jourard, *The Transparent Self* [32], p. 21.
33. H. Hesse, *Magister Ludi* (New York: Frederick Unger, 1949), pp. 438–67.
34. E. O'Neill, *The Iceman Cometh* (New York: Random House, 1957).
35. H. Ibsen, *The Wild Duck* (New York: Avon Press, 1965). Originally published, 1884.
36. V. Frankl, personal communication, 1975.

Chapter 8. The Selection of Patients

1. G. Bond and M. Lieberman, "Indications for Group Psychotherapy," in C. Brady and K. Brodie, eds., *Controversy in Psychiatry* (Philadelphia: W. B. Saunders, 1978).
2. E. Nash, et al. "Some Factors Related to Patients Remaining in Group Psychotherapy," *International Journal of Group Psychotherapy* 7(1957):264–75.
J. A. Johnson, *Group Psychotherapy: A Practical Approach* (New York: McGraw-Hill, 1963).
E. Fried, "Basic Concepts in Group Therapy," in H. Kaplan and B. Sadock, eds., *Comprehensive Group Therapy* (Baltimore: William & Wilkins, 1971), pp. 50–51.
3. I. W. Graham, "Observations on Analytic Group Therapy," *International Journal of Group Psychotherapy* 9(1959):150–57.
L. Horwitz, "Indications and Contraindications for Group Psychotherapy," *Bulletin of the Menninger Clinic* 40(1971):505–7.
4. S. R. Slavson, "Criteria for Selection and Rejection of Patients for Various Kinds of Group Therapy," *International Journal of Group Psychotherapy* 5(1955):3–30.
S. Adrian, "A Systematic Approach to Selecting Group Participants," *Journal of Psychiatric Nursing* 18(2[February 1980]):37–41.
5. Nash, et al., "Some Factors" [2].
Johnson, *Group Psychotherapy* [2].
Fried, "Basic Concepts" [2].
6. Slavson, "Criteria for Selection and Rejection of Patients" [4].
R. Corsini and W. Lundin, "Group Psychotherapy in the Midwest," *Group Psychotherapy* 8(1955):316–20.
M. Rosenbaum and E. Hartley, "A Summary Review of Current Practices of Ninety-Two Group Therapists," *International Journal of Group Psychotherapy* 12(1962):194–98.
W. Friedman, "Referring Patients for Group Therapy: Some Guidelines," *Hospital and Community Psychiatry* 27(1976):121–23.
A. Frances, J. Clarkin, and J. Marachi, "Selection Criteria for Outpatient Group Psychotherapy," *Hospital and Community Psychiatry* 31(1980):245–49.
M. Woods and J. Melnick, "A Review of Group Therapy Selection Criteria," *Small Group Behavior* 10(1979):155–75.
7. J. Abrahams and L. W. McCorkle, "Group Psychotherapy at an Army Rehabilitation Center," *Diseases of the Nervous System* 8(1947):50–62.
G. Bach, *Intensive Group Therapy* (New York: Ronald Press, 1954).
A. Frances, J. Clarkin, and J. Marachi, "Selection Criteria for Outpatient Group Psychotherapy," *Hospital and Community Psychiatry* 31(1980):245–49.
Woods and Melnick, "Group Therapy Selection Criteria" [6].
8. I. D. Yalom, "Group Therapy of Incarcerated Sexual Deviants," *Journal of Nervous Mental Disorders* 132(1961):158–70.
Bond and Lieberman, "Indications for Group Psychotherapy" [1].
9. R. Kaldeck, "Group Psychotherapy with Mentally Defective Adolescents and Adults," *International Journal of Group Psychotherapy* 8(1958):185–92.
M. Scher, "Observations in an Aftercare Group," *International Journal of Group Psychotherapy* 23(1974):322–37.
E. J. Ends and C. W. Page, "Group Psychotherapy and Psychological Change," *Psychological Monograph* 73(480[1959]).
I. D. Yalom, "Group Therapy and Alcoholism," *Annals of the New York Academy of Sciences* 233(1974):85–103.
E. A. Willett, "Group Therapy in a Methadone Treatment Program," *International Journal of Addiction* 8(1973):33–34.

Bond and Lieberman, "Indications for Group Psychotherapy" [1].

10. Friedman, "Referring Patients for Group Therapy" [6].
Woods and Melnick, "Group Therapy Selection Criteria" [6].
Frances, Clarkin, and Marachi, "Selection Criteria" [6].
Horwitz, "Indications and Contraindications" [3].

11. Horwitz, "Indications and Contraindications" [3].
Friedman, "Referring Patients for Group Therapy" [6].
H. Grunebaum and W. Kates, "Whom to Refer for Group Psychotherapy," *American Journal of Psychiatry* 134(1977):130–33.

12. I. D. Yalom, "A Study of Group Therapy Dropouts," *Archives of General Psychiatry* 14(1966):393–414.

13. Nash, et al., "Some Factors" [2].

14. B. Kotkov, "The Effects of Individual Psychotherapy on Group Attendance," *International Journal of Group Psychotherapy* 5(1955):280–85.

15. S. Rosenzweig and R. Folman, "Patient and Therapist Variable Affecting Premature Termination in Group Psychotherapy," *Psychotherapy: Theory, Research and Practice* 11(1974):76–79.

16. Yalom, "Group Therapy Dropouts" [12].

17. E. Berne, "Group Attendance: Clinical and Theoretical Considerations," *International Journal of Group Psychotherapy* 5(1955):392–403.

18. Johnson, *Group Psychotherapy* [2].

19. M. Grotjahn, "Learning from Dropout Patients: A Clinical View of Patients Who Discontinued Group Psychotherapy," *International Journal of Group Psychotherapy* 22(1972):306–19.

20. L. Koran and R. Costell, "Early Termination from Group Psychotherapy," *International Journal of Group Psychotherapy* 24(1973):346–59.

21. M. Lieberman, I. Yalom, and M. Miles, *Encounter Groups: First Facts* (New York: Basic Books, 1972).

22. B. Kotkov, "Favorable Clinical Indications for Group Attendance," *International Journal of Group Psychotherapy* 8(1958):419–27.

23. B. Kotkov and A. Meadow, "Rorschach Criteria for Continuing Group Psychotherapy," *International Journal of Group Psychotherapy* 2(1952):324–31. The form-color/color-or-form ratio contributed most to this differentiation.

24. Grotjahn, "Learning from Dropout Patients" [19].

25. E. Nash, et al. "Some Factors" [2].

26. L. H. Gliedman, et al., "Incentives for Treatment Related to Remaining or Improving in Psychotherapy," *American Journal of Psychotherapy* 11(1957):589–98.
J. Frank, et al. "Why Patients Leave Psychotherapy," *Archives of Neurological Psychiatry* 77(1957):283–99.
D. Rosenthal and J. Frank, "The Fate of Psychiatric Clinic Outpatients Assigned to Psychotherapy," *Journal of Nervous and Mental Disorders* 127(1958):330–43.

27. Rosenzweig and Folman, "Patient and Therapist Variables" [15].

28. Yalom, "Group Therapy Dropouts" [12].

29. M. Horowitz, "The Recall of Interrupted Group Tasks: An Experimental Study of Individual Motivation in Relation to Group Goals," in D. Cartwright and A. Zander, eds., *Group Dynamics: Research and Theory* (New York: Row, Peterson, 1962), pp. 370–94.

30. L. Coch and J. R. French, Jr., "Overcoming Resistance to Change," in Cartwright and Zander, *Group Dynamics* [29], pp. 319–41.
E. Stotland, "Determinants of Attraction to Groups," *Journal of Social Psychology* 49(1959):71–80.

31. D. Lundgren and D. Miller, "Identity and Behavioral Changes in Training Groups," *Human Relations Training News*, Spring 1965.

32. Lieberman, Yalom, and Miles, *Encounter Groups* [21], p. 324.

33. I. D. Yalom and P. Houts, unpublished data, 1966.

34. S. Schachter, "Deviation, Rejection, and Communication," in Cartwright and Zander, *Group Dynamics* [29], pp. 260–85.

35. H. F. Leavitt, "Group Structure and Process: Some Effects of Certain Communication Patterns on Group Performance," in E. E. Maccoby, T. M. Newcomb, and E. L.

554

Hartley, eds., *Readings in Social Psychology* (New York: Holt, Rinehart & Winston, 1958), pp. 175–83.

36. J. M. Jackson, "Reference Group Processes in a Formal Organization," in Cartwright and Zander, *Group Dynamics* [29], pp. 120–40.

37. L. Festinger, S. Schachter, and K. Back, "The Operation of Group Standards," in Cartwright and Zander, *Group Dynamics* [29], pp. 241–59.

38. M. Sherif, "Group Influences upon the Formation of Norms and Attitudes," in E. Maccoby, T. Newcomb and E. Hartley, (eds.) *Readings in Social Psychology* (New York: Holt, Rinehart and Winston, 1958) p. 219–232.

39. S. E. Asch, "Interpersonal Influence: Effects of Group Pressure upon the Modification and Distortion of Judgments" in Maccoby, Newcomb, and Hartley, *Readings in Social Psychology* [35], pp. 175–83.

40. P. H. Leiderman, "Attention and Verbalization: Differentiated Responsivity of Cardiovascular and Electrodermo Systems," *Journal of Psychosomatic Research* 15(1971):-323–28.

41. Lieberman, Yalom and Miles, *Encounter Groups* [21].

42. S. Schachter, "Deviation, Rejection, and Communication" [34].

43. Yalom, "Group Therapy and Alcoholism" [9].

44. R. Harrison and B. Lubin, "Personal Style, Group Composition and Learning—Part I," *Journal of Applied Behavioral Science* 1(1965):286–94.

45. Nash, et al., "Patients Remaining in Group Psychotherapy" [2].

46. H. Grunebaum and W. Kates, "Whom to Refer for Group Psychotherapy," *American Journal of Psychiatry* 134(1977):130–33.

47. I. Yalom, et al. "Predictions of Improvement in Group Therapy," *Archives of General Psychiatry* 17(1967):159–68.

48. The forty patients studied were adult, middle-class, well educated, psychologically sophisticated outpatients who suffered from neurotic or characterologic problems. Outcome was evaluated by a team of raters who, on the basis of a structured interview, evaluated (with excellent reliability) change in symptoms, functioning, and relationships. The patients also independently rated their own outcome, using the same scale. Psychological-mindedness was measured by subscale of the California Personality Inventory and by the therapists after an initial screening interview. The therapists rated each patient on a seven-point scale after the initial interview for how well they thought he or she would do in therapy. Previous self-disclosure was measured by a modification of the Jourard Self-Disclosure Questionnaire (S. Jourard, "Self-Disclosure Patterns in British and American College Females," *Journal of Social Psychology* 54[1961]:315–20.). The patients' attraction to group therapy and their general popularity in the group were measured by a group cohesiveness questionnaire and a sociometric questionnaire.

49. Lieberman, Yalom, and Miles, *Encounter Groups* [21].

50. J. Melnick and G. Rose, "Expectancy and Risk-taking Propensity," *Small Group Behavior* 10(1979):389–401. Scales: Jackson risk-taking inventory and the Hill Interactional Matrix. Sociometric assessment: Depth of Involvement Scale (Evensen and Bednar), Moos and Humphrey Group Environment Scale.

51. A. Goldstein, "Patients' Expectancies and Non-specific Therapy as a Basis for (un)-Spontaneous Remission," *Journal of Clinical Psychology* 16(1960):399–403.

H. Friedman, "Patient-expectancy and Symptom Reduction," *Archives of General Psychiatry* 8(1963):61–67.

E. Uhlenhuth and D. Duncan, "Subjective Change with Medical Student Therapists: II. Some Determinants of Change in Psychoneurotic Outpatients," *Archives of General Psychiatry* 18(1968):532–40.

A. Goldstein and W. Shipman, "Patient Expectancies, Symptom Reduction and Aspects of the Initial Psychotherapeutic Interview," *Journal of Clinical Psychology* 17(1961):-129–33.

A. Goldstein, "Therapist and Client Expectation of Personality Change in Psychotherapy," *Journal of Counseling Psychology* 7(1960):180–84.

J. Brady, M. Reznikoff, and W. Zeller, "The Relationship of Expectation of Improvement to Actual Improvement of Hospitalized Psychiatric Patients," *Journal of Nervous and Mental Disease* 130(1960):41–44.

P. Martin and A. Sterne, "Prognostic Expectations and Treatment Outcome," *Journal of Consulting and Clinical Psychology* 43(1975):572–76.

S. Bloch, et al., "Patients' Expectations of Therapeutic Improvement and Their Outcomes," *American Journal of Psychiatry* 133(1976):1457–59.

52. J. D. Frank, "Some Determinants, Manifestations, and Effects of Cohesiveness in Therapy Groups," *International Journal of Group Psychotherapy* 7(1957):53–63.

53. G. Taylor, "Alexithymia: Concept, Measurement, and Implications for Treatment," *American Journal of Psychiatry* 141(6[June 1984]):725–52.

54. M. B. Parloff, "Therapist-Patient Relationships and Outcome of Psychotherapy," *Journal of Consulting Psychology* 25(1961):29–38.

55. R. Heslin and D. Dunphy, "Three Dimensions of Member Satisfaction in Small Groups," *Human Relations* 17(1964):99–112.

56. J. D. Frank, "Some Determinants, Manifestations, and Effects of Cohesiveness in Therapy Groups," *International Journal of Group Psychotherapy* 7(1957):53–63.

E. J. Ends and C. W. Page, "Group Psychotherapy and Psychological Changes," *Psychological Monographs* 73(480[1959]).

Chapter 9. The Composition of Therapy Groups

1. P. Ash, "The Reliability of Psychiatric Diagnosis," *Journal of Abnormal and Social Psychology* 44(1949):272–76.

A. T. Beck, et al., "Reliability of Psychiatric Diagnoses: A Study of Consistency of Clinical Judgments and Ratings," *American Journal of Psychiatry* 119(1962):351–57.

S. Bloch, et al., "The Evaluation of Outcome in Psychotherapy by Independent Judges: A New Approach," *British Journal of Psychiatry* 131(1977):410–14.

G. Mellsop, et al., "The Reliability of Axis II of DSM-III," *American Journal of Psychiatry* 139(1982):1360–61.

2. W. Piper and M. Marrache, "Selecting Suitable Patients: Pretraining for Group Therapy as a Method for Group Selection," *Small Group Behavior* 12(1981):459–74.

3. W. Hill, Hill Interactional Matrix. Los Angeles: Youth Studies Center, University of Southern California, 1965.

4. A. Camus, *The Fall* (New York: Alfred A. Knopf, 1956).

5. J. Deer and A. W. Silver, "Predicting Participation and Behavior in Group Therapy from Test Protocols," *Journal of Clinical Psychology* 18(1962):322–25.

C. Zimet, "Character Defense Preference and Group Therapy Interaction," *Archives of General Psychiatry* 3(1960):168–75.

E. F. Borgatta and A. E. Esclenbach, "Factor Analysis of Rorschach Variable and Behavior Observation," *Psychological Reports*, 3:129–136, 1955.

G. Bond and M. Lieberman, "Indications for Group Psychotherapy," in C. Brady and K. Brodie, eds., *Controversy in Psychiatry* (Philadelphia: W. B. Saunders, 1978).

6. K. Menninger, M. Mayman, and P. Pruyser, *The Vital Balance* (New York: Viking Press, 1963).

7. K. Horney, *Neurosis and Human Growth* (New York: W. W. Norton, 1950).

8. E. Fromm, *Man for Himself* (New York: Rinehart, 1947).

E. Fromm, *Escape from Freedom* (New York: Farrar & Rinehart, 1957).

9. R. Plutchik, "The Multifactor Analytic Theory of Emotion," *Journal of Psychology* 50(1960):153–71.

10. H. Kellerman, *Group Psychotherapy and Personality: Intersecting Structures* (New York: Grune & Stratton, 1979).

11. T. Leary, *Interpersonal Diagnosis of Personality* (New York: Ronald Press, 1957).

12. P. J. Aston, "Behavioral Correlates of Thematic Apperception Responses," unpublished manuscript, Tavistock Clinic, London, 1966.

13. J. Sutherland, H. S. Gill, and H. Phillipson, "Psychodiagnostic Appraisal in the Light of Recent Theoretical Developments," *British Journal of Medical Psychology* 40(1967):299–315.

14. S. Ben-Zeev, "Sociometric Choice and Patterns of Member Participation," in D.

Stock and H. A. Thelen, eds., *Emotional Dynamics and Group Culture* (New York: New York University Press, 1958), pp. 84–91.

15. K. Anchor, J. Vojtisek, and S. Berger, "Social Desirability as a Predictor of Self-disclosure in Groups," *Psychotherapy: Theory, Research and Practice* 9(1972):262–64.

16. W. F. Hill, "The Influence of Subgroups on Participation in Human Relations Training Groups," unpublished doctoral dissertation, University of Chicago, 1955.

17. S. A. Joure, et al., "Differential Change among Sensitivity Training Participants as a Function of Dogmatism," *Journal of Psychology* 80(1972):151–56.

18. R. Harrison and B. Lubin, "Personal Style, Group Composition and Learning—Part 2," *Journal of Applied Behavioral Science* 1(1965):294–301.

19. C. Y. Crews and J. Melnick, "The Use of Initial and Delayed Structure in Facilitating Group Development," *Journal of Consulting Psychology* 23(1976):92–98.

20. P. R. Kilmann and R. J. Howell, "The Effects of Structure of Marathon Group Therapy and Locus of Control on Therapeutic Outcome," *Journal of Consulting and Clinical Psychology* 42(1974):912.

21. J. Melnick and G. Rose, "Expectancy and Risk Taking Propensity: Predictors of Group Performance," *Small Group Behavior* 10(1979):389–401.

22. R. Robinson, "The Relationship of Dimension of Interpersonal Trust with Group Cohesiveness, Group Status and Immediate Outcome in Short Term Group Counseling," *Dissertation Abstracts* 40(1980):5016–B.

23. G. Jackson, L. Houvany, and N. Vidiman, "A Four Dimensional Interpretation of Risk Taking," *Research Bulletin*, no. 185, London, Canada, University of Western Ontario.

24. Melnick and Rose, "Expectancy and Risk Taking Propensity" [21].

25. W. Schutz, FIRO-B: *Interpersonal Underworld* (Palo Alto, Calif.: Science and Behavior Books, 1966).

26. A. Goldstein, K. Heller, and L. Sechrest, *Psychotherapy and the Psychology of Behavior Change* (New York: John Wiley, 1966), p. 329.

27. B. M. Bishop, "Mother-Child Interaction and the Social Behavior of Children," *Psychological Monographs* 65(11[1951]:1.)
   R. H. Moos and S. R. Clemes, "A Multivariate Study of the Patient-Therapist System," *Journal of Consulting Psychology* 31(1967):119–30.
   C. Zimet, "Character Defense Preference and Group Therapy Interaction," *Archives of General Psychiatry* 3(1960):168–75.
   G. B. Bell and R. L. French, "Consistency of Individual Leadership Position in Small Groups of Varying Membership," in A. P. Hare, E. F. Borgatta, and R. F. Bales, eds., *Small Groups* (New York: Alfred A. Knopf, 1955), pp. 275–80.

28. Moos and Clemes, "Multivariate Study" [29].

29. P. M. Fitts, "German Applied Psychology during World War II," *American Psychology* 1(1946):151–61.
   M. Mandell, "Validation of Group Oral Performance Test," *Personnel Psychology* 3(1950):179–85.
   B. M. Bass, "The Leaderless Group Discussion Technique," *Personnel Psychology* 3(1950):17–32.
   H. Fields, "The Group Interview Test: Its Strength," *Public Personnel Review* 11(1950):-139–46.

30. E. F. Borgatta and R. F. Bales, "Interaction of Individuals in Reconstituted Groups," *Sociometry* 16(1953):302–20.

31. E. F. Borgatta and R. F. Bales, "Task and Accumulation of Experience as Factors in the Interaction of Small Groups," *Sociometry* 16(1953):239–52.
   B. M. Bass, "Leadership," in *Psychology and Organizational Behavior* (New York: Harper & Row, 1960).

32. V. Cerbin, "Individual Behavior in Social Situations: Its Relation to Anxiety, Neuroticism and Group Solidarity," *Journal of Experimental Psychology* 51(1956):161–68.

33. Ibid.

34. R. B. Cattell, D. R. Saunders, and G. F. Stice, "The Dimensions of Syntality in Small Groups," *Journal of Social Psychology* 28(1948):57–78.

35. S. H. Foulkes and E. J. Anthony, *Group Psychotherapy—The Psychoanalytic Approach* (Harmondsworth, Middlesex: Penguin Books, 1957).
   G. Bach, *Intensive Group Therapy* (New York: Ronald Press, 1954).

36. A. Stone, M. Parloff, and J. Frank, "The Use of Diagnostic Groups in a Group Therapy Program," *International Journal of Group Psychotherapy* 4(1954):274–84.

37. D. Abrahams and J. Enright, "Psychiatric Intake in Groups: A Pilot Study of Procedures, Problems and Prospects," *American Journal of Psychiatry* 122(1965):170–74.

38. D. Malamud and S. Machover, *Toward Self-Understanding* (Springfield, Ill.: Charles C. Thomas, 1965).

39. Piper and Marrache, "Selecting Suitable Patients" [2].

40. Generally, the research procedure is to assign subjects to groups meeting for a predetermined number of times and to observe their behavior systematically. At this point, the researchers regroup the members into new groups according to the particular aspect of behavior under study. Since the bulk of the research has been done by nonclinicians, the attitudes and behavior are described in nonclinical, but nevertheless clinically relevant, terms. Subjects may thus be placed in groups according to whether they prefer high or low structure, or positive or negative affect, or to whether they are active or passive or high or low participators or assume or shun leadership. The trial groups may be discontinued at this point or serve as a control against which to compare the experimentally composed group.

H. Baumgartel, unpublished research report (Washington, D.C.: National Training Laboratories, 1961).

R. Harrison, "Group Composition Models for Laboratory Design," *Journal of Applied Behavioral Science* 1(1965):409–32.

41. Piper and M. Marrache, "Selecting Suitable Patients" [2].

42. H. S. Sullivan, *The Psychiatric Interview* (New York: W. W. Norton, 1954).

43. F. Powdermaker and J. Frank, *Group Psychotherapy* (Cambridge, Mass.: Harvard University Press; 1953), pp. 553–64.

44. M. Lieberman, I. Yalom, and M. Miles, *Encounter Groups: First Facts* (New York: Basic Books, 1972).

45. Bach, *Intensive Group Therapy* [35].

H. D. Mullan and M. Rosenbaum, *Group Psychotherapy* (New York: Free Press of Glencoe, 1962).

N. Locke, *Group Psychoanalysis* (New York: New York University Press, 1961).

Powdermaker and Frank, *Group Psychotherapy* [43].

A. Francis, J. Clarkin, and J. P. Morachi, "Selection Criteria for Outpatient Group Psychotherapy," *Hospital and Community Psychiatry* 31(1980):245–50.

J. Best, P. Jones, and A. Paton, "The Psychotherapeutic Value of a More Homogeneous Group Composition," *International Journal of Social Psychiatry* 27(1981):43–46.

J. Melnick and M. Woods, "Analysis of Group Composition Research and Theory for Psychotherapeutic and Growth Oriented Groups," *Journal of Applied Behavioral Science* 12(1976):493–513.

W. J. Livesley and K. Roy Mackensie, "Social Roles in Therapy Groups," in R. Dies and K. Roy Mackensie, eds., *Advances in Group Therapy* (New York: International Universities Press, 1983).

H. Kellerman, *Group Psychotherapy and Personality: Intersecting Structures* (New York: Grune & Stratton, 1979).

L. Stava and R. Bednar, "Process Outcome in Encounter Groups: The Effects of Group Composition," *Small Group Behavior* 10(1979):200–213.

46. D. Whitaker and M. Lieberman, *Psychotherapy Through the Group Process,* (New York: Atherton Press, 1964).

47. Foulkes and Anthony, *Group Psychotherapy* [35], p. 94.

48. F. K. Taylor, *The Analysis of Therapeutic Groups* (London: Oxford University Press, 1961).

49. A. S. Samuels, "The Use of Group Balance as a Therapeutic Technique," *Archives of General Psychiatry* 11(1964):411–22.

50. Bach, *Intensive Group Therapy* [35], p. 25.

51. Ibid.

J. Frank, et al. "Behavioral Patterns in Early Meetings of Therapeutic Groups," *American Journal of Psychiatry* 108(1952):771–78.

D. Rosenthal, J. Frank, and E. Nash, "The Self-Righteous Moralist in Early Meetings of Therapeutic Groups," *Psychiatry* 17(1954):215–33.

Kellerman, *Group Psychotherapy and Personality* [45].

Livesley and Mackensie, "Social Roles in Therapy Groups" [45].

A. Beck, et al., "The Participation of Leaders in the Structural Development of Therapy Groups," in R. Dies and K. Roy Mackenzie, eds., *Advances in Group Therapy* (New York:International Universities Press, 1983), pp. 137–57.

52. I. Yalom, et al., "Prediction of Improvement" [52].

I. Yalom, J. Tinklenberg, and M. Gilula, "Curative Factors in Group Therapy," unpublished study, 1968.

53. I. Yalom, et al., "Prediction of Improvement in Group Therapy," *Archives of General Psychiatry* 17(1967):159–68.

I. Yalom, et al., "Preparation of Patients for Group Therapy: A Controlled Study," *Archives of General Psychiatry* 17(1967):416–27.

A. Sklar, et al., "Time Extended Group Therapy: A Controlled Study," *Comparative Group Studies*, November 1970, pp. 373–86.

I. Yalom and K. Rand, "Compatibility and Cohesiveness in Therapy Groups," *Archives of General Psychiatry* 13(1966):267–76.

54. Harrison, "Group Composition Models for Laboratory Design" [40].

Harrison and Lubin, "Personal Style, Group Composition and Learning" [18].

55. Ben-Zeev, "Sociometric Choice and Patterns of Member Participation" [14], pp. 50–64.

56. Melnick and Woods, "Analysis of Group Composition Research and Theory" [45].

57. Harrison, "Group Composition Models for Laboratory Design" [42].

Harrison and Lubin, "Personal Style, Group Composition and Learning" [18].

R. Harrison and B. Lubin, "Personal Style, Group Composition and Learning—Part 1," *Journal of Applied Behavioral Science* 1(1965):286–94.

D. Stock, "A Survey of Research on T-Groups," in L. P. Bradford, J. R. Gibb, and K. Benne, eds., *T-Group Theory and Laboratory Method* (New York: John Wiley, 1964), pp. 401–6.

Melnick and Woods, "Analysis of Group Composition Research and Theory" [45].

Melnick and Rose, "Expectancy and Risk Taking Propensity" [21].

Observer bias is often uncontrolled; subjects are often asked to compare experimental groups with a previous group without controls for the length of time in each group or the sequence of the two experiences; in addition, the experimental groups are often very short-term, and the effects of the developmental stage of the group may have been overlooked. The most serious shortcoming is in the measurement of individual outcome. Often the measures consist of only a few questions put to the subjects, and the reliability and validity of these questions were not evaluated. The follow-up interval is, with one exception, brief; and evaluation of change usually immediately follows the group experience (always a questionable procedure since the wave of positive sentiment at the termination of a group often obviates individual objectivity.)

58. H. Baumgartel, unpublished research report (Washington, D.C.: National Training Laboratories, 1961).

I. Gradolph, "The Task Approach of Groups of Single-Type and Mixed-Type Valency Compositions," in D. Stock and H. A. Thelen, eds., *Emotional Dynamics and Group Culture* (New York: New York University Press, 1958), pp. 127–30.

T. C. Greening and H. Coffey, "Working with an 'Impersonal' T-Group," *Journal of Applied Behavioral Science* 2(1966):401–11.

59. Baumgartel, unpublished research report [58].

D. Stock and J. Luft, "The T-E-T Design," unpublished manuscript (Washington, D.C.: National Training Laboratories, 1960).

60. H. Pollack, "Change in Homogeneous and Heterogeneous Sensitivity Training Groups," unpublished doctoral dissertation, University of California at Berkeley, 1966.

61. W. B. Reddy, "Interpersonal Compatibility and Self-Actualization in Sensitivity Training," *Journal of Applied Behavioral Science* 8(1972):237.

W. B. Reddy, "On Affection, Group Composition and Self-Actualization in Sensitivity Training," *Journal of Consulting and Clinical Psychology* 38(1971):211–14.

62. Harrison, "Group Composition Models for Laboratory Design" [40].

D. Stock and W. F. Hill, "Intersubgroup Dynamics as a Factor in Group Growth," in

D. Stock and H. A. Thelen, eds., *Emotional Dynamics and Group Culture* (New York: New York University Press, 1958), pp. 50–64.

63. Harrison and Lubin, "Personal Style, Group Composition and Learning" [18].

64. Schutz, *FIRO-B: Interpersonal Underworld* [25], pp. 120–43.

65. Gradolph, "The Task Approach of Groups" [58].

66. W. Schutz, "On Group Composition," *Journal of Abnormal and Social Psychology* 62(1961):275–81.

M. A. Lieberman, "The Relationship of Group Climate to Individual Change," unpublished doctoral dissertation, University of Chicago, 1958.

Melnick and Woods, "Analysis of Group Composition Research and Theory" [45].

67. Stock and Luft, "The T-E-T Design" [59].

Melnick and Woods, "Analysis of Group Composition Research and Theory" [45].

68. T. M. Newcomb, "The Prediction of Interpersonal Attraction," *American Psychology* 11(1956):575–86.

69. J. Frank, "Some Values of Conflict in Therapeutic Groups," *Group Psychotherapy* 8(1955):142–51.

70. Lieberman, "The Relationship of Group Climate to Individual Change" [68].

Chapter 10. Creation of the Group: Place, Time, Size, Preparation

1. G. Bach, cited by F. Stroller, "Marathon Group Therapy," in G. M. Gazda, ed., *Innovations to Group Psychotherapy* (Springfield, Ill.: Charles C. Thomas, 1968).

2. R. Adler, "Reporter at Large," *The New Yorker*, 15 April 1967, pp. 55–58.

The New York Times, 20 December 1970.

J. Sohl, *The Lemon Eaters* (New York: Simon & Schuster, 1967).

3. R. MacGregor, "Multiple Impact Therapy with Families," *Family Process* 1(1962):15–29.

4. Stoller, "Marathon Group Therapy" [1].

E. Mintz, "Time-Extended Marathon Groups," *Psychotherapy, Research and Practice* 4(1967):65–70.

M. Parloff, "Discussion of F. Stoller's Paper," *International Journal of Group Psychotherapy* 18(1968):239–44.

B. Navidzadeh, "The Application of Marathon Group Psychotherapy in Outpatient Clinic Settings," paper presented at American Group Psychotherapy Association Convention, Chicago, January 1968.

S. B. Lawrence, cited in *Palo Alto Times*, 3 January 1967.

F. Stoller, "Accelerated Interaction: A Time-Limited Approach Based on the Brief Intensive Group," *International Journal of Group Psychotherapy* 18(1968):220–35.

N. G. Dinges and R. G. Weigel, "The Marathon Group: A Review of Practice and Research," *Comparative Group Studies* 2(4[November 1971]):339–458.

5. S. B. Lawrence, cited in *Palo Alto Times*, 3 January 1967.

6. Stoller, "Accelerated Interaction" [4].

7. Navidzadeh, "Marathon Group Psychotherapy in Outpatient Clinic Settings" [4].

8. G. Bach, "Marathon Group Dynamics," *Psychological Reports* 20(1967):1147–58.

9. A. W. Rachman, "Marathon Group Psychotherapy," *Journal of Group Psychoanalysis and Process* 2(1969):57–74.

10. Stoller, "Marathon Group Therapy" [1], p. 71.

11. G. Bach and F. Stoller, "The Marathon Group," cited by Dinges and Weigel, "The Marathon Group" [4].

12. R. Weigel, "The Marathon Encounter: Requiem for a Social Movement," *Small Group Behavior* 8(1977):201–22.

13. Parloff, "Discussion of F. Stoller's Paper" [4].

14. S. E. Asch, "Effects of Group Pressure upon the Modification and Distortion of Judgments," in D. Cartwright and A. Zander (eds.), *Group Dynamics: Research and Theory* (New York: Harper & Row, 1960).

15. Dinges and Weigel, "The Marathon Group" [4].

P. Kilmann and W. Sotile, "The Marathon Encounter Group: A Review of the Outcome Literature," *Psychological Bulletin* 83(1976):827–50.

16. A. D. Sklar, et al., "Time-Extended Group Therapy: A Controlled Study," *Comparative Group Studies*, November 1970, pp. 373–86.

17. The Hill Interaction Matrix method of scoring interaction was used. The middle thirty minutes of the meeting was systematically evaluated by two trained raters who were naïve about the design of the study. (The six-hour meeting itself was not analyzed, since we were interested primarily in studying its effect on the subsequent course of therapy.) (W. F. Hill, *HIM: Hill Interaction Matrix* [Los Angeles: Youth Study Center, University of Southern California, 1965].)

18. B. Jones reports similar findings in a study of three ongoing therapy groups, two of which received weekend marathons (B. Jones, "The Effect of a Marathon Experience upon Ongoing Group Therapy," *Dissertation Abstracts* [1977]:3887–B).

19. I. Yalom, et al., "The Impact of a Weekend Group Experience on Individual Therapy," *Archives of General Psychiatry* 34(1977):399–415.

20. M. Lorr, "Relation of Treatment Frequency and Duration to Psychotherapeutic Outcome," in H. Strupp and L. Luborsky, eds., *Conference on Research in Psychotherapy* (Washington, D.C.: American Psychological Association, 1962), pp. 134–41.

21. C. Fulkerson, D. Hawkins, and A. Alden, "Psychotherapy Groups of Insufficient Size," *International Journal of Group Psychotherapy* 31(1981):73–81.

22. G. F. Castore, "Number of Verbal Interrelationships as a Determinant of Group Size," *Journal of Abnormal Social Psychology* 64(1962):456–57.

23. A. Goldstein, K. Heller, and L. Sechrest, *Psychotherapy and the Psychology of Behavior Change* (New York: John Wiley, 1966), p. 341.

24. A. P. Hare, *Handbook of Small Group Research* (New York: Free Press of Glencoe, 1962), pp. 224–45.

25. A. P. Hare, "A Study of Interaction and Consensus in Different Sized Groups," *American Social Review* 17(1952):261–67.

26. L. F. Carter, et al., "The Behavior of Leaders and Other Group Members," *Journal of Abnormal Social Psychology* 46(1958):256–60.

27. S. H. Foulkes, oral communication, April 1968.

28. A. P. Goldstein, *Therapist/Patient Expectancies in Psychotherapy*, (New York: Pergamon Press, 1962).

S. Lipkin, "Clients' Feelings and Attitudes in Relation to the Outcome of Client-Centered Therapy," *Psychological Monographs* 68(374[1954]).

H. L. Lennard and A. Bernstein, *The Anatomy of Psychotherapy* (New York: Columbia University Press, 1960).

S. Bloch, et al., "Patients' Expectations of Therapeutic Improvement and Their Outcomes," *American Journal of Psychiatry* 133(1976):1457–59.

29. R. Bednar and G. F. Lawlis, "Empirical Research in Group Therapy," in A. E. Bergin and S. L. Garfield, eds., *Handbook of Psychotherapy and Behavior Change* (New York: John Wiley, 1971).

J. Mann, "Evaluation of Group Psychotherapy," in J. L. Moreno, ed., *The International Handbook of Group Psychotherapy* (New York: Philosophical Library, 1966), pp. 129–48.

A. Bergin, "The Implications of Psychotherapy Research for Therapeutic Practice," *Journal of Abnormal Psychology* 71(1966):235–46.

M. Smith, G. Glass, and T. Miller, *The Benefits of Psychotherapy* (Baltimore and London: Johns Hopkins University Press, 1980).

30. H. Martin and K. Shewmaker, "Written Instructions in Group Therapy," *Group Psychotherapy* 15(1962):24.

G. Silver, "Systematic Presentation of Pre-Therapy Information in Group Psychotherapy: Its Relationship to Attitude and Behavioral Change, *Dissertation Abstracts* (1976):4481–B.

R. Warehime, "Interactional Gestalt Therapy," *Small Group Behavior* 12(1[February 1981]):37–54.

E. Gauron and E. Rawlings, "A Procedure for Orienting New Members to Group Psychotherapy," *Small Group Behavior* 6(3[August 1975]):293–307.

T. Zarle and S. Willis, "A Pre-Group Training Technique for Encounter Group Stress," *Journal of Counseling Psychology* 22(1975):49–53.

B. Corder, et al., "Pre-Therapy Training for Adolescents in Group Psychotherapy: Contracts, Guidelines, and Pre-Therapy Preparation," *Adolescence* 15(59[Fall 1980]):-699–706.

31 R. Crandall, "The Assimilation of Newcomers into Groups," *Small Group Behavior* 9(3[August 1978]):331–36

32. Gauron and Rawlings, "Orienting New Members to Group Psychotherapy" [31].

33. L. Annis and D. Perry, "Self-disclosure in Unsupervised Groups: Effects of Video-taped Models," *Small Group Behavior* 9(1[February 1978]):102–8.

P. Pilkonis, et al., "Training Complex Social Skills for Use in a Psychotherapy Group: A Case Study," *International Journal of Group Psychotherapy* 30(1980):347–56.

E. Werth, "A Comparison of Pretraining Methods for Encounter Group Therapy," *Dissertation Abstracts* 40(1979).

T. Curran, "Increasing Motivation to Change in Group Treatment," *Small Group Behavior* 9(3[August 1978]):337–48.

M. Wogan, et al., "Influencing Interaction and Outcomes in Group Psychotherapy," *Small Group Behavior* 8(1[February 1977]):25–46.

Corder, et al., "Pre-Therapy Training for Adolescents" [31].

M. Cartwright, "Brief Reports: A Preparatory Method for Group Counseling," *Journal of Counseling Psychology* 23(1[1976]):75–77.

34. D. I. Malamud and S. Machover, *Toward Self-Understanding: Group Techniques in Self-Confrontation* (Springfield, Ill.: Charles C. Thomas, 1965).

M. D. Bettis, D. Malamud, and R. F. Malamud, "Deepening a Group's Insight into Human Relations," *Journal of Clinical Psychology* 5(1949):114–22.

W. Piper, "Pretraining for Group Psychotherapy: A Cognitive-Experiential Approach," *Archives of General Psychiatry* 36(October 1979):1250–56.

W. Piper, et al. "Preparation of Patients: A Study of Group Pretraining for Group Psychotherapy," *International Journal of Group Psychotherapy* 32(3) [July 1982]):309–25.

P. Pilkonis, et al., "Training Complex Social Skills for Use in a Psychotherapy Group: A Case Study," *International Journal of Group Psychotherapy* 30(1980):347–56.

E. Werth, "A Comparison of Pretraining Methods for Encounter Group Therapy," *Disseration Abstracts* 40(1979).

S. Budman, et al., "Experiential Pre-Group Preparation and Screening," *Group* 5(1[1981]):19–26.

W. Piper and M. Marrache, "Selecting Suitable Patients: Pretraining for Group Therapy as a Method of Patient Selection," *Small Group Behavior* 12(4[November 1981]):459–75.

Wogan, et al., "Influencing Interaction and Outcomes" [33].

35. Budman, et al., "Experiential Pre-Group Preparation and Screening" [34].

36. Piper, et al., "Preparation of Patients" [34].

37. I. D. Yalom, et al., "Preparation of Patients for Group Therapy," *Archives of General Psychiatry* 17(1967):416–27.

38. Goldstein, *Therapist/Patient Expectancies in Psychotherapy* [28].

Lipkin, "Clients' Feelings and Attitudes in Relation to Outcome" [28].

Lennard and Bernstein, *The Anatomy of Psychotherapy* [28].

39. The interaction of the groups was measured by scoring each statement during the meeting on a sixteen-cell matrix (Hill Interaction Matrix). Scoring was performed by a team of raters naïve to the experimental design. Faith in therapy was tested by post-group patient-administered questionnaires (Hill, *HIM-Hill Interaction Matrix* [17]).

40. M. Wogan et al., "Influencing Motivation to Change in Group Treatment," *Small Group Behavior* (1[February 1977]):25–46.

41. J. B. Heitler, "Clinical Impressions of an Experimental Attempt to Prepare Lower-Class Patients for Expressive Group Psychotherapy," *International Journal of Group Psychotherapy* 29(1974):308–22.

42. Werth, "A Comparison of Pretraining Methods" [33].

43. Silver, "Systematic Presentation of Pre-Therapy Information" [31].

44. Piper, et al. "Pretraining for Group Psychotherapy" [34].

45. Piper, et al., "Preparation of Patients" [34].

Annis and Perry, "Self-Disclosure in Unsupervised Groups" [33].

J. Samuel, "The Individual and Comparative Effects of a Pre-Group Preparation upon Two Different Therapy Groups," *Dissertation Abstracts International* 41(5[November 1980]):1919–B.

S. Barnett, "The Effect of Preparatory Training in Communication Skills on Group Therapy with Lower Socioeconomic Class Alcoholics," *Dissertation Abstracts International* 41(7[January 1981]):2744–B.

46. Pilkonis, et al. "Training Complex Social Skills for Use in a Psychotherapy Group" [34].

Barnett, "Preparatory Training in Communication Skills with Lower Socioeconomic Class Alcoholics" [44].

47. Pilkonis, et al. "Training Complex Social Skills for Use in a Psychotherapy Group" [34].

48. T. Zarle and S. Willis, "A Pre-group Training Technique for Encounter Group Stress," *Journal of Counseling Psychology* 22(1975):49–53.

49. T. Curran, "Increasing Motivation to Change in Group Treatment," *Small Group Behavior* 9(3[August 1978]):337–48.

50. Ibid.

51. Cartwright, "A Preparatory Method for Group Counseling" [33].

52. Werth, "A Comparison of Pretraining Methods" [31].

Piper, et al., "Preparation of Patients" [34].

53. I. Gradolph, "The Task-Approach of Groups of Single-Type and Mixed-Type Valency Compositions," in D. Stock and H. Thelen, eds., *Emotional Dynamics and Group Culture* (New York: New York University Press, 1958), pp. 127–30.

D. Stock and J. Luft, "The T-E-T Design," unpublished manuscript, Washington, D. C.: National Training Laboratories, 1960.

D. Stock and W. F. Hill, "Intersubgroup Dynamics as a Factor in Group Growth," in D. Stock and H. Thelen, *Emotional Dynamics and Group Culture* (New York: New York University Press, 1958), pp. 207–21.

54. I. L. Janis, *Psychological Stress: Psychoanalytic and Behavioral Studies of Surgical Patients* (New York: John Wiley, 1958).

H. Basowitz, et al., *Anxiety and Stress,* (New York: McGraw-Hill, 1955).

R. W. White, "Motivation Reconsidered: The Concept of Competence, *Psychological Review* 66(1959):297–333.

55. White, "Motivation Reconsidered" [54].

56. B. H. Rauer and J. Reitsema, "The Effects of Varied Clarity of Group Goal and Group Path upon the Individual and His Relation to His Group," *Human Relations* 10(1957):29–45.

D. M. Wolfe, J. D. Snock, and R. A. Rosenthal, *Report to Company Participants at 1960 University of Michigan Research Project* (Ann Arbor: Institute of Social Research, 1961).

A. R. Cohen, E. Stotland, and D. M. Wolfe, "An Experimental Investigation of Need for Cognition," *Journal of Abnormal Social Psychology* 51(1955):291–94.

A. R. Cohen, "Situational Structure, Self-Esteem and Threat-Oriented Reactions to Power," in D. Cartwright, ed., *Studies in Social Power* (Ann Arbor, Mich.: Research Center for Group Dynamics, 1959), pp. 35–52.

Goldstein, Heller, and Sechrest, *Psychotherapy and the Psychology of Behavior Change* [23], p. 405.

57. Goldstein, Heller, and Sechrest, *Psychotherapy and the Psychology of Behavior Change* [23], p. 329.

E. J. Murray, "A Content Analysis for Study in Psychotherapy," *Psychological Monographs* 70 (13 [1956]).

58. L. Horwitz, "Transference in Training Groups and Therapy Groups," *International Journal of Group Psychotherapy* 14(1964):202–13.

A. Wolf, "The Psychoanalysis of Groups," in M. Rosenbaum and M. Berger, eds., *Group Psychotherapy and Group Function* (New York: Basic Books, 1963), pp. 273–328.

59. S. Schiedlinger, "The Concept of Repression in Group Psychotherapy, paper presented at American Group Psychotherapy Association Conference, New York, January 1967.

60. E. Aronson and J. Mills, "The Effect of Severity of Initiation on Liking for a Group," *Journal of Abnormal Social Psychology* 59(1959):177–81.

Chapter 11. In the Beginning

1. S. Freud, *Group Psychology and the Analysis of the Ego* (New York: Bantam Books, 1960), p. 76. Originally published in 1921.
2. M. Ross, "Physicians Who Commit Suicide: The Deck Is Not Stacked," *Psychiatric Opinion* 12(1975):26.
3. E. Semard, cited by W. Schutz, *The Interpersonal Underworld* (Palo Alto: Science and Behavior Books, 1966), p. 170.
4. Schutz, *The Interpersonal Underworld* [3], p. 24.
K. Roy Mackensie and W. John Livesley, "A Developmental Model for Brief Group Therapy," in R. Dies and K. Roy Mackensie, eds., *Advances in Group Therapy* (New York: International University Press, 1983), pp. 101–16.
5. G. Bach, *Intensive Group Psychotherapy* (New York: Ronald Press, 1954); p. 95.
6. Bach, *Intensive Group Therapy* [5].
B. Tuckman, "Developmental Sequences in Small Groups," *Psychological Bulletin* 63(1965):384–99.
S. Parker, "Leadership Patterns in a Psychiatric Ward," *Human Relations* 11(1958):-287–301.
7. P. Slater, *Microcosm* (New York: John Wiley, 1966).
8. S. Freud, *Totem and Taboo*, in S. Freud, *Standard Edition of the Complete Psychological Works of Sigmund Freud*, vol. XIII (London: Hogarth Press, 1953).
9. S. Freud, *Group Psychology and the Analysis of the Ego*, in Freud, *Standard Edition* [8], p. 123.
10. J. Friedman and S. Gassell, "The Chorus in Sophocles' *Oedipus Tyrannus*," *Psychoanalytic Quarterly* 19(1950):213–26.
S. H. Foulkes and E. J. Anthony, *Group Psychotherapy—The Psychoanalytic Approach* (Harmondsworth, Middlesex: Penguin Books, 1957).
11. W. G. Bennis, "Patterns and Vicissitudes in T-Group Development," in L. P. Bradford, J. R. Gibb, and K. D. Benne, *T-Group Theory and Laboratory Method: Innovation in Re-education* (New York: John Wiley, 1964), pp. 248–78.
12. T. Mills, personal communication, April 1968.
13. Tuckman, "Developmental Sequences in Small Groups" [6].
14. Bennis, "Patterns and Vicissitudes in T-Group Development" [11].
H. I. Clapham and A. B. Sclare, "Group Psychotherapy with Asthmatic Patients," *International Journal of Group Psychotherapy* 8(1958):44–54.
15. F. K. Taylor, "The Therapeutic Factors of Group-Analytic Treatment," *Journal of Mental Science* 96(1950):976–97.
H. Coffey, et al., "Community Service and Social Research-Group Psychotherapy in a Church Program," *Journal of Social Issues* 6(1950):14–61.
16. Parker, "Leadership Patterns in a Psychiatric Ward" [6].
R. S. Shellow, J. L. Ward, and S. Rubenfeld, "Group Therapy and the Institutionalized Delinquent," *International Journal of Group Psychotherapy* 8(1958):265–75.
17. D. Whitaker and M. A. Lieberman, *Psychotherapy through the Group Process*, (New York: Atherton Press, 1964).
J. Mann and E. V. Semrad, "The Use of Group Therapy in Psychoses," *Journal of Social Casework* 29(1948):176–81.
M. Grotjahn, "The Process of Maturation in Group Psychotherapy and in the Group Therapist," *Psychiatry* 13(1950):63–67.
A. P. Noyes, *Modern Clinical Psychiatry*, 4th ed. (Philadelphia: W. B. Saunders, 1953), pp. 589–91.
Mackensie and Livesley, "A Developmental Model for Brief Group Therapy" [5].
18. J. Abrahams, "Group Psychotherapy: Implications for Direction and Supervision of Mentally Ill Patients," in T. Muller, ed., *Mental Health in Nursing* (Washington, D.C.: Catholic University Press, 1949), pp. 77–83.
19. B. Berkowitz, "Stages of Group Development," unpublished manuscript.
20. J. J. Thorpe and B. Smith, "Phases in Group Development in Treatment of Drug Addicts," *International Journal of Group Psychotherapy* 3(1953):66–78.

21. A. Beck and L. Peters, "The Research Evidence for Distributed Leadership in Therapy Groups," *International Journal of Group Psychotherapy* 31(1981):43–71.

22. Schutz, *The Interpersonal Underworld* [3], p. 170.

23. B. Berkowitz, "Stages of Group Development," unpublished manuscript.

24. W. Bennis, et al., "A Note on Some Problems of Measurement and Prediction in a Training Group," *Group Psychotherapy* 10(1957):328–41.

25. J. Near, "Comparison of Developmental Patterns in Groups," *Small Group Behavior* 9(1978):493–505.

K. Roy Mackensie, "The Clinical Application of a Group Climate Measure," in Dies & Mackensie, *Advances in Group Therapy* [5], pp. 159–70.

E. Babed and L. Amir, "Bennis and Shepard's Theory of Group Development," *Small Group Behavior* 9(1978):477–91.

26. Schutz, *The Interpersonal Underworld* [3], p. 170.

27. D. Hamburg, personal communication, 1968.

28. Differences in leader style plague the whole realm of group development research. Clinicians describe a developmental pattern of from four to nine discrete stages, but their observations are always based on a small number of groups generally led by different therapists. The degree to which developmental stages are a function of leader behavior remains unknown. Some researchers have attempted to circumvent the problem by studying leaderless groups, but the relevancy of such research to clinical practice remains equally unclear.

Near, "Comparison of Developmental Patterns in Groups" [25].

Beck and Peters, "The Research Evidence for Distributed Leadership" [21].

Mackensie and Livesley, "A Developmental Model for Brief Group Therapy" [5].

J. Tindall, "Time-Limited and Time-Extended Encounter Groups," *Small Group Behavior* 10(1979):402–13.

R. Cople, "The Sequential Stages of Group Development," *Small Group Behavior* 9(1978):470–76.

29. M. A. Lieberman, "The Relationship of Group Climate to Individual Change," unpublished doctoral dissertation, University of Chicago, 1958.

30. I. Yalom, "A Study of Group Therapy Dropouts," *Archives of General Psychiatry* 14(1966):393–414.

31. A. Beck describes a similar set of behavior for patients she terms "scapegoat leaders" (Beck and Peters, "The Research Evidence for Distributed Leadership" [21]).

32. A. K. Rice, *Learning for Leadership* (London: Tavistock Publications, 1965).

33. I. Yalom, et al., "Prediction of Improvement in Group Therapy: An Exploratory Study," *Archives of General Psychiatry* 17(1967):159–68.

34. L. Lothstein, "The Group Psychotherapy Dropout Phenomenon Revisited," *American Journal of Psychiatry* 135(1978):1492–95.

35. W. Stone, M. Blase, and J. Bozzuto, "Late Dropouts from Group Therapy," *American Journal of Psychotherapy* 34(1980):401–13.

36. Ibid.

37. Yalom, "A Study of Group Therapy Dropouts" [30].

38. Ibid.

39. S. H. Foulkes and E. J. Anthony, *Group Psychotherapy—The Psychoanalytic Approach* (Harmondsworth, Middlesex: Penguin Books, 1957).

40. R. Crandall, "The Assimilation of Newcomers into Groups," *Small Group Behavior* 9(1978):331–37.

41. I. Yalom, "A Study of Group Therapy Dropouts," *Archives of General Psychiatry* 14(1966):393–414.

Chapter 12. The Advanced Group

1. I. Yalom, "A Study of Group Therapy Dropouts," *Archives of General Psychiatry* 14(1966):393–414.

2. H. Lindt and M. Sherman, "Social Incognito in Analytically Oriented Group Psychotherapy," *International Journal of Group Psychotherapy* 2(1952):209–20.

3. S. Freud, *Group Psychology and the Analysis of the Ego*, in S. Freud, *Standard Edition of the Complete Psychological Works of Sigmund Freud*, vol. XVIII (London: Hogarth Press, 1955), p. 123.

I. Yalom, "Group Psychology and the Analysis of the Ego: A Review," *International Journal of Group Psychotherapy*, XXIV (1[January 1974]):67–82.

4. I. Yalom and P. Houts, unpublished data, 1965.

5. R. White and R. Lippit, "Leader Behavior and Member Reaction in Three 'Social Climates,'" in D. Cartwright and A. Zander, eds., *Group Dynamics: Research and Theory* (New York: Row, Peterson, 1962), pp. 527–53.

6. A. Wolf, "The Psychoanalysis of Groups," in M. Rosenbaum and M. Berger, eds., *Group Psychotherapy and Group Function* (New York: Basic Books, 1963), p. 320.

7. A. Camus, *The Fall* (New York: Vintage Books, 1956), p. 58.

8. Ibid., p. 68.

9. Ibid, p. 63.

10. S. H. Foulkes, *Therapeutic Group Analysis* (New York: International Universities Press, 1964), p. 81.

M. Pines, "The Contributions of S. H. Foulkes to Group Analytic Psychotherapy," in L. Wolberg, R. Aronson, and A. Wolberg, eds., *Group Therapy* (New York: Stratton Intercontinental, 1978).

M. Pines, "Psychoanalysis and Group Analysis," *International Journal of Group Psychotherapy* 33(1983):155–69.

11. J. D. Frank, "Some Values of Conflict in Therapeutic Groups," *Group Psychotherapy* 8(1955):142–51.

12. C. Rogers, "Dealing with Psychological Tensions," *Journal of Applied Behavioral Science* 1(1965):6–24.

13. Frank, "Some Values of Conflict in Therapeutic Groups" [10].

14. F. Dostoevsky, "The Double," in *Great Short Works of Fyodor Dostoevsky*, ed. R. Hingley (Harper & Row, 1968).

15. L. Horwitz, "Projective Identification in Dyads and Groups," *International Journal of Group Psychotherapy* 33(1983):254–79.

16. Ibid.

17. A. Beck, et al., "Process Analysis of Group Development," in L. S. Greenberg and W. M. Pinsoff, eds., *The Psychotherapeutic Process: A Research Handbook* (New York: Guilford Press, 1984).

S. Scheidlinger, Presidential Address "On Scapegoating in Group Psychotherapy," *International Journal of Group Psychotherapy* 32(1982):131–43.

18. H. Danesh describes a short-term (twelve sessions) therapy group with a protocol carefully structured to help patients deal with anger. Patients describe the situations in which they get angry, read prepared material on anger, choose some expressive medium to vent anger (for example, painting, drawing, clay), and use structured exercises within the group to free themselves from anger (H. Danesh, "The Angry Group," *International Journal of Group Psychotherapy*, 77[1977]:59–65).

19. E. Berne, *Games People Play*, (New York: Grove Press, 1964).

20. Frank, "Some Values of Conflict in Therapeutic Groups" [10].

21. S. A. Culbert, *The Interpersonal Process of Self-Disclosure: It Takes Two to See One* ("Explorations in Applied Behavioral Science," no. 3 [New York: Renaissance Editors, 1967]).

22. I. Yalom, et al., "Prediction of Improvement in Group Therapy: An Exploratory Study," *Archives of General Psychiatry* 17(1967):159–68.

23. S. Hurley, "Self-Disclosure in Small Counseling Groups," unpublished Ph.D. dissertation, Michigan State University, 1967.

24. M. Worthy, A. Gary, and G. Kahn, "Self-Disclosure as an Exchange Process," *Journal of Personality and Social Psychology* 13(1969):59–63.

25. P. Cozby, "Self-Disclosure, Reciprocity, and Liking," *Sociometry* 35(1972):151–60.

P. Cozby, "Self-Disclosure: A Literature Review," *Psychological Bulletin* 79(1973):73–91.

J. Allen, "Implications of Research in Self-Disclosure for Group Psychotherapy," *International Journal of Group Psychotherapy* 24(1974):306–21.

26. S. Bloch, E. Crouch, and J. Reibstein, "Therapeutic Factors in Group Psychotherapy," *Archives of General Psychiatry* 38(May 1981):519–26.

W. Query, "Self-Disclosure as a Variable in Group Psychotherapy," *International Journal of Group Psychotherapy* 14(1964):107–15.

W. Query, "An Experimental Investigation of Self-Disclosure and Its Effect Upon Some Properties of Psychotherapeutic Groups," *Dissertation Abstracts International* 31(1970):-2263.

D. Johnson and L. Ridener, "Self-Disclosure, Participation and Perceived Cohesiveness in Small Group Interaction," *Psychological Reports* 35(1974):361–63.

B. Kirsher, "The Effect of Experimental Manipulation of Self-Disclosure on Group Cohesiveness," *Dissertation Abstracts International,* 37(1976):3081–82.

27. H. Peres, "An Investigation of Non-Directive Group Therapy," *Journal of Consulting Psychology* 11(1947):159–72.

28. C. Truax and R. Carkhuff, "Client and Therapist Transparency in the Psychotherapeutic Encounter," *Journal of Consulting Psychology* 12(1965):3–9.

29. M. Lieberman, I. Yalom, and M. Miles, *Encounter Groups: First Facts* (New York: Basic Books, 1973).

30. S. Bloch and J. Reibstein, "Perceptions by Patients and Therapists of Therapeutic Factors in Group Psychotherapy," *British Journal of Psychiatry* 137(1980):274–78.

Bloch, Crouch, and Reibstein, "Therapeutic Factors in Group Psychotherapy" [26].

31. L. M. Vosen "The Relationship Between Self-Disclosure and Self-Esteem," unpublished Ph.D. dissertation, University of California at Los Angeles, 1966, cited by Culbert in *The Interpersonal Process of Self-Disclosure* [21].

32. Culbert, *The Interpersonal Process of Self-Disclosure* [21].

33. A. H. Maslow, unpublished mimeographed material, 1962. .

34. E. Goffman, *The Presentation of Self in Everyday Life* (Garden City, N.Y.: Doubleday Anchor Books, 1959).

35. M. Rickers-Ouiankina, "Social Accessibility in Three Age Groups," *Psychological Reports* 2(1956):283–94.

S. M. Jourard and P. Lasakow, "Some Factors in Self-Disclosure," *Journal of Abnormal Social Psychology* 56(1950):91–98.

D. E. Bugenthal, R. Tannenbaum, and H. Bobele, unpublished manuscript, cited by Culbert, *The Interpersonal Process of Self-Disclosure* [21].

Cozby, "Self-Disclosure: A Literature Review" [21].

36. D. Strassberg and his colleagues studied eighteen chronic schizophrenic patients for ten weeks in inpatient group therapy and concluded that high self-disclosing patients made less therapeutic progress than their counterparts who revealed less personal material (D. Strassberg, et al., "Self-Disclosure in Group Therapy with Schizophrenics," *Archives of General Psychiatry* 32(1975):1259–61.

37. A. H. Maslow, unpublished mimeographed material, 1962.

38. Scott Rutan, personal communication, 1983.

Chapter 13. Problem Patients

1. I. Yalom and P. Houts, unpublished data, 1965.

2. J. Sartre, *The Age of Reason,* Eric Sutton, trans. (New York: Alfred A. Knopf, 1952), p. 144.

3. H. Bergson, *Laughter* (Garden City, N.Y.: Doubleday, 1956).

4. M. Lieberman, I. Yalom, and M. Miles, *Encounter Groups: First Facts* (New York: Basic Books, 1973).

5. D. Lundgren and D. Miller, "Identity and Behavioral Changes in Training Groups," *Human Relations Training News,* Spring 1965.

6. R. Coyne and R. Silver, "Direct, Vicarious, and Vicarious-Process Experiences," *Small Group Behavior* 11(1980):419–29.

7. J. D. Frank, et al., "Behavioral Patterns in Early Meetings of Therapeutic Groups," *American Journal of Psychiatry* 108(1952):771–78.

8. J. D. Frank, et al., "Two Behavior Patterns in Therapeutic Groups and their Apparent Motivation," *Human Relations* 5(1952):289–317.

M. Berger and M. Rosenbaum, "Notes on Help-Rejecting Complainers," *International Journal of Group Psychotherapy* 17(1967):357–70.

S. Brody, "Syndrome of the Treatment-Rejecting Patient," *Psychoanalytic Review* 51(1964):75–84.

Correspondence from Dr. Derbolowsky, *Group Analysis* 1(1[1967]):13–16.

C. Peters and H. Grunebaum, "It Could Be Worse: Effective Group Psychotherapy with the Help-Rejecting Complainers," *International Journal of Group Psychotherapy* 27(1977):471–80.

9. M. Berger and M. Rosenbaum, "Notes on Help-Rejecting Complainers," *International Journal of Group Psychotherapy* 17(1967):357–70.

10. Frank, et al., "Behavioral Patterns in Early Meetings" [7].

11. Peters and Grunebaum, "It Could Be Worse" [8].

12. Frank et al., "Behavioral Patterns in Early Meetings" [7].

13. E. Berne, *Games People Play* (New York: Grove Press, 1964).

14. D. Rosenthal, J. Frank, and E. Nash, "The Self-Righteous Moralist in Early Meetings of Therapeutic Groups," *Psychiatry* 17(1954):215–23.

15. Ibid.

16. R. Moos and I. Yalom, "Medical Students' Attitudes toward Psychiatry and Psychiatrists" *Mental Hygiene* 50(1966):246–56.

17. L. Coch and J. R. French, "Overcoming Resistance to Change," *Human Relations* 1(1948):512–32.

18. B. B. Wassel, *Group Analysis* (New York: Citadel Press, 1966), p. 148.

19. F. Volkmar and colleagues report that a homogeneous support group of lithium-maintained bipolar patients was highly useful to the patients (F. Volkmar, et al., "Group Therapy in the Management of Manic-Depressive Illness," *American Journal of Psychotherapy,* 35([1981]:226–33).

20. American Psychiatric Association, *Diagnostic and Statistical Manual of Mental Disorders,* 3rd ed., 1980.

21. O. Kernberg, *Borderline Conditions and Pathological Narcissism* (New York: Jason Aronson Books, 1975).

22. G. Valliant and J. C. Perry, "Personality Disorders," in H. Kaplan, A. Freedman, and B. Sadock, eds., *Comprehensive Psychiatry,* 3rd ed. (Baltimore: William & Wilkins, 1980).

23. Kernberg, *Borderline Conditions* [21].

H. Kohut, *The Analysis of the Self* (New York: International Universities Press, 1971).

H. Kohut, *The Restoration of the Self* (New York: International Universities Press, 1977).

24. My thanks to Dr. Alan Sklar for his critical review of the section on the borderline patient.

25. Kernberg, *Borderline Conditions* [21].

26. American Psychiatric Association, *Diagnostic and Statistical Manual of Mental Disorders,* 3rd ed., 1980.

27. L. Horwitz, "Group Psychotherapy for Borderline and Narcissistic Patients," *The Bulletin of the Menninger Clinic* 44(1980):181–200.

N. Wong, "Clinical Considerations in Group Treatment of Narcissistic Disorders," *International Journal of Group Psychotherapy* 29(1979):325–45. These two articles (by Horwitz and Wong) are particularly lucid and thoughtful; I draw much from them in my discussion of the borderline patient.

J. Grobman, "The Borderline Patient in Group Psychotherapy: A Case Report," *International Journal of Group Psychotherapy* 30(1980):299–318.

28. M. Leszcz, I. Yalom, and M. Norden, "The Value of Inpatient Group Psychotherapy: Patients' Perceptions," *International Journal of Group Psychotherapy.* 35(July 1985).

I. Yalom, *Inpatient Group Psychotherapy* (New York: Basic Books, 1983).

N. Macaskill, "The Narcissistic Core as a Focus in the Group Therapy of the Borderline Patient," *British Journal of Medical Psychology* 53(1980):137–43.

29. M. Pines, "Group Analytic Therapy of the Borderline Patient," *Group Analysis* 11(1978):115–26.

30. Horwitz, "Group Psychotherapy for Borderline and Narcissistic Patients" [27].
31. Ibid.
32. Ibid.
Wong, "Clinical Considerations in Group Treatment of Narcissistic Disorders" [27].
N. Wong, "Combined Group and Individual Treatment of Borderline and Narcissistic Patients," *International Journal of Group Psychotherapy* 30(1980):389–403.
33. J. Kosseff, "The Unanchored Self: Clinical Vignettes of Change in Narcissistic and Borderline Patients in Groups: Introduction," *International Journal of Group Psychotherapy* 30(1980):387–88.
34. Horwitz, "Group Psychotherapy for Borderline and Narcissistic Patients" [27].

Chapter 14. The Technique of the Therapist: Specialized Formats and Procedural Aids

1. K. Porter, "Combined Individual and Group Psychotherapy: A Review of the Literature 1965–1978," *International Journal of Group Psychotherapy* 30(1980):107–14.
2. K. Porter, "Combined Individual and Group Psychotherapy: Review of the Literature 1965–1978," *International Journal of Group Psychotherapy* 30(1980):107–14.
3. J. Frank, et al., "Why Patients Leave Psychotherapy," *Archives of Neurological Psychiatry* 77(1957):283–99.
E. Nash, et al., "Some Factors Related to Patients Remaining in Group Psychotherapy," *International Journal of Group Psychotherapy* 7(1957):264–75.
4. L. Ormont, "Principles and Practice of Conjoint Psychoanalytic Treatment," *American Journal of Psychiatry* 138(1981):69–73.
5. J. S. Rutan and A. Alonzo, "Group Therapy, Individual Therapy, or Both?" *International Journal of Group Psychotherapy* 32(1982):267–82.
J. S. Rutan and W. N. Stone, *Psychodynamic Group Therapy* (Lexington, Mass.: The Collamore Press, 1984).
6. Rutan and Alonzo, "Group Therapy, Individual Therapy or Both?" [5].
7. Research studies of therapists' preferences demonstrate that between 75 percent and 90 percent prefer the co-therapy mode (I. Paulson, J. Burroughs, and C. Gelb, "Cotherapy: What Is the Crux of the Relationship?" *International Journal of Group Psychotherapy* 26(1976):213–24.
R. Dies, J. Mallet, and F. Johnson, "Openness in the Co-leader Relationship: Its Effect on Group Process and Outcome," *Small Group Behavior* 10(1979):523–46.
H. Rabin, "How Does Co-therapy Compare with Regular Group Therapy," *American Journal of Psychotherapy* 21(1967):244–55.
8. Rabin, "How Does Co-therapy Compare with Regular Group Therapy" [7].
H. Spitz and S. Kopp, "Multiple Psychotherapy," *Psychiatric Quarterly Supplement* 31(1957):295–331.
Paulson, Burroughs, and Gelb, "Cotherapy: What Is the Crux of the Relationship?" [7].
Dies, Mallet, and Johnson, "Openness in the Coleader Relationship" [7].
R. Dick, K. Lessler, and J. Whiteside, "A Developmental Framework for Cotherapy," *International Journal of Group Psychotherapy* 30(1980):273–85.
9. This split is consonant with findings by Robert Bales in some well-known research on group leadership (R. Bales, "The Equilibrium Problem in Small Groups," in T. Parsons, R. F. Bales, and E. A. Shils, eds., *Working Papers in the Theory of Action* [Glencoe, Ill.: Free Press, 1953], pp. 111–61). Bales studied laboratory task groups of college students discussing some problem in human relations. Almost invariably two types of leader (as determined by activity ratings and sociometric rankings) emerged from the membership: (1) a "task-executive" leader, the most active member who spurs the group on and who helps the members perform the primary task; and (2) a social-emotional leader who attends to the group's emotional needs and reduces tension sufficiently to allow the group to proceed.
10. Rabin, "How Does Co-therapy Compare with Regular Group Therapy" [8].
Paulson, Burroughs, and Gelb, "Cotherapy: What Is the Crux of the Relationship?" [7].
11. J. Solomon and G. Solomon, "Group Therapy with Father and Son as Cotherapists:

Some Dynamic Considerations," *International Journal of Group Psychotherapy* 13(1963):-133–40.

12. I. Yalom, J. Tinklenberg and M. Gilula, unpublished data, 1967.

13. Paulson, Burroughs, and Gelb, "Cotherapy: What Is the Crux of the Relationship?" [7].

14. E. Waugh, *Brideshead Revisited* (Boston: Little, Brown, 1945).

15. A. Wolf, "The Psychoanalysis of Groups," *American Journal of Psychotherapy* 3(1949):529–57.

16. S. R. Slavson, *A Textbook in Analytic Group Psychotherapy* (New York: International Universities Press, 1964), pp. 398–99.

J. Johnson, *Group Therapy: A Practical Approach* (New York: McGraw-Hill, 1963), pp. 56–57.

17. R. Desmond and M. Seligman, "A Review of Research on Leaderless Groups," *Small Group Behavior* 8(1977):3–24.

18. I. Yalom, J. Tinklenberg and M. Gilula, unpublished data, 1967.

19. M. Jones, *The Therapeutic Community* (New York: Basic Books, 1953).

20. D. Daniels, "Milieu Therapy of Schizophrenia," in C. P. Rosenbaum, *The Meaning of Madness* (New York: Science House, 1970).

21. M. Lieberman, D. S. Whitaker, and M. Lakin, "Groups and Dyads: Never the Twain Shall Meet," unpublished mimeograph, University of Chicago, 1967.

22. Anonymous, *Calendar of Health* (New York: League for Right Living, 1908), cited in *Journal of Applied Behavioral Science* 3(1967):101.

23. M. A. Lieberman, "Self-help Groups: Their Contribution to the Health Care System," in C. Van Dyke, L. Temoshok, and L. Zegans, eds., *Emotions in Health and Illness: Application to Clinical Practice* (San Diego, Calif.: Grune & Stratton, 1984), chap. 15, pp. 231–41.

24. Ibid.

L. Perlin and M. Lieberman, "Social Sources of Emotional Distress," in R. Simmons, ed., *Research in Community and Mental Health* (Greenwich, Conn.: JAL Press, 1979), pp. 217–48.

M. A. Lieberman, L. Borman, and associates, *Self-help Groups for Coping with Crisis* (San Francisco: Jossey-Bass, 1979).

25. B. Berzon, "Final Narrative Report: Self-directed Small Group Programs," NIMH Project RD 1728, mimeographed material, Western Behavioral Science Institute, 1968.

R. B. Morton, "The Uses of the Laboratory Method in a Psychiatric Hospital—Section A: The Patient Training Laboratory; An Adaptation of the Instrumented Training Laboratory," in E. H. Schein and W. G. Bennis, eds., *Personal and Organizational Change through Group Methods: The Laboratory Approach* (New York: John Wiley, 1965), pp. 114–51.

26. Berzon, "Final Narrative Report" [25].

27. Ibid.

28. E. G. Aiken, "Alternate Forms of a Semantic Differential for Measurement of Changes in Self-Description," *Psychological Reports* 16(1965):177–78.

29. G. Gevrin, "JOBS Project Report," Institute for Social Research, University of Michigan, 1967.

30. Berzon, "Final Narrative Report" [25].

31. M. Lieberman, I. Yalom, and M. Miles, *Encounter Groups: First Facts* (New York: Basic Books, 1973).

32. D. Zimmerman, "Some Characteristics of Dreams in Group-Analytic Psychotherapy," *International Journal of Group Psychotherapy* 17(1967):524–35.

33. M. Berger, ed. *Videotape Techniques in Psychiatric Training and Treatment*, rev. ed. (New York: Brunner/Mazel, 1978).

34. D. Miller, "The Effects of Immediate and Delayed Audio and Videotaped Feedback on Group Counseling," *Comparative Group Studies* 1(1970):19–47.

M. Robinson, "A Study of the Effects of Focused Videotaped Feedback in Group Counseling, *Comparative Group Studies* 1(1970):47–77.

35. N. Mayades and D. O'Brien, "The Use of Videotape in Group Therapy," in Berger, *Videotape Techniques* [33], pp. 216–29.

36. M. Berger, "The Use of Video Tape with Psychotherapy Groups in a Community

Mental Health Program," paper delivered at the American Group Psychotherapy Conference, Chicago, January 1968.

Berger, *Videotape Techniques* [33].

37. M. Berger, "Video Tape with Psychotherapy Groups in a Community Mental Health Program" [36].

38. I. Yalom, S. Brown, and S. Bloch, "The Written Summary as a Group Psychotherapy Technique," *Archives of General Psychiatry* 32(May 1975):605–13.

39. S. Brown and I. Yalom, "Interactional Group Therapy with Alcoholics," *Journal of Studies on Alcohol* 38(1977):426–56.

40. P. Finkelstein, B. Wenegrat, and I. Yalom, "Large Group Awareness Training," *Annual Review of Psychology* 33(1982):515–39.

41. F. Perls, *The Gestalt Approach and Eye Witness to Therapy* (Ben Lomond, Calif.: Science and Behavior Books, 1974).

F. Perls, *Gestalt Therapy Verbatim* (Moab, Utah: Real People Press, 1969).

F. Perls, *Ego, Hunger and Aggression* (New York: Vintage Books, Random House, 1969).

42. Perls, *Gestalt Approach and Eye Witness to Therapy* [41].

43. Lieberman, Yalom, and Miles, *Encounter Groups* [31].

44. J. Enright, "Awareness Training in the Mental Health Professions," in J. Fagan and I. L. Shepherd, eds., *Gestalt Therapy Now* (Palo Alto, Calif.: Science and Behavior, 1970).

45. J. Zinker, *Creative Process in Group Therapy* (New York: Vintage Books, 1978).

J. B. Enright, "Gestalt Therapy in Interactive Groups," in F. D. Stephenson, ed., *Gestalt Therapy Primer: Introductory Readings in Gestalt Therapy* (Springfield, Ill.: Charles C. Thomas, 1975).

J. S. Simkin and G. Yontef, "Gestalt Therapy," in R. Corsini, ed., *Current Psychotherapies* (Itasca, Ill.: F. E. Peacock, 1984).

R. Harman, "Recent Developments in Gestalt Group Therapy," *International Journal of Group Psychotherapy* 34(3[July 1984]):473–83.

46. Lieberman, Yalom, and Miles, *Encounter Groups* [31].

Chapter 15. The Specialized Therapy Group

1. Neither space limitations nor the rapidly growing numbers of specialized groups permit a comprehensive list and bibliography in this text. Computer literature searches are so accessible and efficient that the reader may easily obtain a bibliography of any specialized group. For each year preceding 1983, the October issue of the *International Journal of Group Psychotherapy* contains a comprehensive bibliography of the group therapy literature for the preceding year; and I have drawn my list of specialty groups from the 1978–83 bibliographies.

2. In the following discussion, I draw heavily from my book *Inpatient Group Psychotherapy* (New York: Basic Books, 1983). Space does not permit an in-depth discussion of technique, and I refer interested readers to this text.

3. My *Inpatient Group Psychotherapy* [2] is the first text devoted entirely to inpatient group therapy.

4. I. Yalom, M. Leszcz, and M. Norden, "The Value of Inpatient Group Psychotherapy: Patient's Perceptions," *International Journal of Group Psychotherapy* 35 (July 1985).

Yalom, *Inpatient Group Psychotherapy* [2], pp. 313–35.

5. Yalom, *Inpatient Group Psychotherapy* [2], pp. 11–14, 62–73.

6. Ibid., p. 330.

7. B. Rosen, et al., "Clinical Effectiveness of 'Short' versus 'Long' Psychiatric Hospitalization," *Archives of General Psychiatry* 33(1976):1316–22.

8. A. R. Alden, et al., "Group Aftercare for Chronic Schizophrenics," *Journal of Clinical Psychiatry* 40(1979):249–52.

R. M. Prince, et al., "Group Aftercare—Impact on a Statewide Program," *Diseases of the Nervous System* 77(1977):793–96.

J. L. Claghorn et al., "Group Therapy and Maintenance Therapy of Schizophrenics," *Archives of General Psychiatry* 31(1974):361–65.

T. Borowski and T. Tolwinski, "Treatment of Paranoid Schizophrenics with Chlorpromazine and Group Therapy," *Diseases of the Nervous System* 30(1969):201–2.

M. I. Herz, et al., "Individual versus Group Aftercare Treatment," *American Journal of Psychiatry* 131(1974):808–12.

C. O'Brien et al., "Group versus Individual Psychotherapy with Schizophrenics: A Controlled Outcome Study," *Archives of General Psychiatry* 27(1972):474–78.

L. Mosher and S. Smith, "Psychosocial Treatment: Individual, Group, Family and Community Support Approaches," *Schizophrenia Bulletin* 6(1980):10–41.

9. Yalom, *Inpatient Group Psychotherapy* [2], p. 34.

B. Corder, R. Corder, and A. Hendricks, "An Experimental Study of the Affects of Paired Patient Meetings on the Group Therapy Process," *International Journal of Group Psychotherapy* 21(1971):310–18.

J. Otteson, "Curative Caring: The Use of Buddy Groups with Chronic Schizophrenics," *Journal of Consulting and Clinical Psychology* 47(1979):649–51.

10. Yalom, *Inpatient Group Psychotherapy* [2], p. 134.

11. M. Leszcz, I. Yalom, and M. Norden, "The Value of Inpatient Group Psychotherapy: Patient's Perceptions," *International Journal of Group Psychotherapy* 35(July 1985).

12. D. Zlatin, "Member Satisfaction in Group Process in Structured vs. Unstructured Groups with Hospitalized Psychiatric Patients," unpublished doctoral dissertation, University of Maryland, 1975.

13. In some time-limited specialized groups, the therapists define the task in advance and have a protocol for each meeting of the entire life of the group (B. Kirkley, et al. "A Comparison of Two Group Treatments for Bulimia," *Journal of Consulting and Clinical Psychology* 53(February 1985): 43–48.

14. I. Yalom, M. Lieberman, and M. Miles, *Encounter Groups: First Facts* (New York: Basic Books, 1973).

15. Yalom, *Inpatient Group Psychotherapy* [2], pp. 275–312.

16. Leszcz, Yalom, and Norden, "The Value of Inpatient Group Psychotherapy" [10]. Yalom, *Inpatient Group Psychotherapy* [2], p. 262.

Chapter 16. Group Therapy and the Encounter Group

1. F. Donnelson, *An Introduction to Group Dynamics* (Monterey, Calif.: Brooks Cole, 1983).

A. Bellack and M. Herson, eds., *Research and Practice in Social Skills* (New York: Plenum, 1979).

2. B. Kilbourne and J. Richardson, "Psychotherapy and New Religions in a Pluralistic Society," *American Psychologist* 39(1984):237–51.

3. M. Lieberman and L. Borman, *Self-help Groups for Coping with Crisis* (San Francisco: Jossey-Bass, 1979).

4. P. Finklestein, B. Wenegrat and I. Yalom, "Large Group Awareness Training," *Annual Review of Psychology* 33(1982):515–39.

5. H. Coffey, personal communication, 1967.

A. Bavelas, personal communication, 1967.

A. Marrow, "Events Leading to the Establishment of the National Training Laboratories," *Journal of Applied Behavioral Science* 3(1967):144–50.

L. P. Bradford, "Biography of an Institution," *Journal of Applied Behavioral Science* 3(1967):127–44.

K. Benne, "History of the T-Group in the Laboratory Setting," in L. Bradford, J. Gibb, and K. Benne, eds., *T-Group Theory and Laboratory Method* (New York: John Wiley, 1964), pp. 80–135.

6. K. Benne, "History of the T-Group in the Laboratory Setting" [5].

7. E. H. Schein and W. G. Bennis, *Personal and Organizational Change through Group Methods* (New York: John Wiley, 1965), p. 41.

8. Ibid., p. 43.

9. A. Camus, cited in Schein and Bennis, *Personal and Organizational Change* [7], p. 46.

10. J. Luft, *Group Processes: An Introduction to Group Dynamics* (Palo Alto, Calif.: National Press, 1966).

11. I. R. Wechsler, F. Messarik, and R. Tannenbaum, "The Self in Process: A Sensitive Training Emphasis," in I. R. Wechsler and E. H. Schein, eds., *Issues in Training* (Washington, D.C.: National Education Association, National Training Laboratories, 1962), pp. 33–46.

12. Ibid.

13. Ibid.

14. M. Lieberman, I. Yalom, and M. Miles, *Encounter Groups: First Facts* (New York: Basic Books, 1973).

15. Four participants were judged from interview data to have left for "physical" reasons (that is, schedule conflicts) (Lieberman, Yalom, and Miles, *Encounter Groups* [14]).

16. H. I. Kaplan and B. J. Sadock, *Comprehensive Group Psychotherapy* (Baltimore: Williams & Wilkins, 1971).

M. Rosenbaum and M. Berger, eds., *Group Psychotherapy and Group Function* (New York: Basic Books, 1963).

A. L. Kadis, J. D. Krasner, and C. Winick, *A Practicum of Group Psychotherapy* (New York: Harper & Row, 1963).

H. Mullan and M. Rosenbaum, *Group Psychotherapy: Theory and Practice* (New York: Free Press of Glencoe, 1962).

17. Rosenbaum and Berger, *Group Psychotherapy and Group Function* [16].

18. E. W. Lazell, "The Group Treatment of Dementia Praecox," *Psychoanalytic Review* 8(1921):168–79.

19. L. C. Marsh, "Group Therapy and the Psychiatric Clinic," *Journal of Nervous and Mental Disorders* 32(1935):381–92.

20. L. Wender, "Current Trends in Group Psychotherapy," *American Journal of Psychotherapy* 3(1951):381–404.

21. T. Burrows, "The Group Method of Analysis," *Psychoanalytic Review* 19(1927):268–80.

22. P. Schilder, "Results and Problems of Group Psychotherapy in Severe Neurosis," *Mental Hygiene* 23(1939):87–98.

23. S. Slavson, "Group Therapy," *Mental Hygiene* 24(1940):36–49.

24. J. L. Moreno, *Who Shall Survive?* (New York: Beacon House, 1953).

25. L. Horwitz, "Training Groups for Psychiatric Residents," *International Journal of Group Psychotherapy* 17(1967):421–35.

L. Horwitz, "Transference in Training Groups and Therapy Groups," *International Journal of Group Psychotherapy* 14(1964):202–13.

S. Kaplan, "Therapy Groups and Training Groups: Similarities and Differences," *International Journal of Group Psychotherapy* 17(1967):473–504.

26. R. Morton, "The Patient Training Laboratory: An Adaptation of the Instrumented Training Laboratory," in Schein and Bennis, *Personal and Organizational Change* [8], pp. 114–152.

27. J. Simon "An Evaluation of est as an Adjunct to Group Psychotherapy in the Treatment of Severe Alcoholism, *Biosciences Communications* 135(1977):141–48.

J. Simon, "Observations on 67 Patients Who Took Erhard Seminars Training," *American Journal of Psychiatry* 135(1978):686–91.

28. I. Hendrick, "Instinct and the Ego During Infancy," *Psychoanalysis Quarterly* 11(1952):33–58.

29. D. E. Berlyne, "The Present Status of Research on Exploratory and Related Behavior," *Journal of Individual Psychology* 14(1958):121–26.

30. K. Horney, *Neurosis and Human Growth: The Struggle toward Self-Realization* (New York: W. W. Norton, 1950).

31. R. White, "Motivation Reconsidered," *Psychological Review* 66(1959):297–333.

32. H. Hartmann, "Notes on the Psychoanalytic Theory of the Ego," *Psychoanalytic Study of the Child* 5(1950):74–95.

33. A. Angyal, *Foundations for a Science of Personality* (New York: Commonwealth Fund, 1941).

34. K. Goldstein, *Human Nature in Light of Psychopathology* (Cambridge, Mass.: Harvard University Press, 1940).

35. Horney, *Neurosis and Human Growth* [30].

36. D. Bunker, "The Effect of Laboratory Education upon Individual Behavior," in Schein and Bennis, *Personal and Organizational Change* [7], pp. 257–67.

37. Lieberman, Yalom, and Miles, *Encounter Groups* [14].

38. M. Lieberman, and J. Gardner, "Institutional Alternatives to Psychotherapy: A Study of Growth Center Users," *Archives of General Psychiatry* 33(1976):157–62.

39. A. Freud and D. Burlingham, *War and Children* (New York: Medical War Books, 1943), pp. 99–104.

40. C. Argyris, "Conditions for Competence Acquisition and Therapy," *Journal of Applied Behavioral Science* 4(1968):147–79.

41. J. Frank, "Training and Therapy," in Bradford, Gibb, and Benne, *T-Group Theory and Laboratory Method* [5], p. 448.

42. Ibid., p. 449.

Chapter 17. Training the Group Therapist

1. T. Kaul and R. Bednar, "Experiential Group Research," in S. Garfield and A. Bergin, eds., *Handbook for Psychotherapy and Behavior Change,* 3rd ed. (New York: John Wiley, in press).

M. Smith, G. Glass, and T. Miller, *The Benefits of Psychotherapy* (Baltimore: The Johns Hopkins University Press, 1980).

2. Kaul and Bednar, "Experiential Group Research" [1].

I. Yalom, *Inpatient Group Psychotherapy* (New York: Basic Books, 1983), pp. 314–20.

3. E. Pinney, "Group Psychotherapy Training in Psychiatric Residency Programs," submitted for publication, 1984.

4. C. H. Ward, "Psychiatric Training in University Centers," *American Journal of Psychiatry* 111(1954):123–31.

5. C. H. Ward and K. Rickels, "Psychiatry Residency Training: Changes over a Decade," *American Journal of Psychiatry* 123(1966):45–54.

6. E. Pinney, S. Wells, and B. Fisher, "Group Therapy Training in Psychiatric Residency Programs: A National Survey," *American Journal of Psychiatry* 135(1978):1505–09.

7. Pinney, "Group Psychotherapy Training" [3].

8. B. Schwartz, "An Eclectic Group Therapy Course for Graduate Students in Professional Psychology," *Psychotherapy: Theory, Research and Practice* 18(1981):417–23.

9. Although didactic courses are one of the least effective methods of teaching, over 90 percent of residency teaching programs employ this teaching vehicle (Pinney "Group Psychotherapy Training" [9]).

S. Perls, "A Group Psychotherapy Training Model for Psychiatric Residents," unpublished monograph, University of New Mexico School of Medicine, 1980.

10. See Yalom, *Inpatient Group Psychotherapy* [2], pp. 259–73, for a full discussion of this format.

11. G. O. Ebersole, P. H. Leiderman, and I. D. Yalom, "Training the Nonprofessional Group Therapist," *Journal of Nervous and Mental Disorders* 149(1969):385.

12. L. Tauber, "Choice Point Analysis—Formulation, Strategy, Intervention and Result in Group Process Therapy and Supervision," *International Journal of Group Psychotherapy* 28(1978):163–83.

13. H. Roback, "Use of Patient Feedback to Improve the Quality of Group Therapy Training," *International Journal of Group Psychotherapy* 26(1976):243–47.

14. E. Pinney, "Group Psychotherapy Training" [3].

Perls, "A Group Psychotherapy Training Model" [9].

15. Perls, "A Group Psychotherapy Training Model" [9].

16. J. Prochaska and J. Norcross, "Contemporary Psychotherapist: A National Survey of Characteristics, Practices, Orientations and Attitudes," *Psychotherapy: Theory, Research and Practice* 20(2[1983]):161–73.

17. John Salvendy, "Group Therapy Trainees as Bona Fide Members in Patient Groups," in L. Wolberg and M. Aronson, eds., *Group and Family Therapy* (New York: Brunner/Mazel, 1983).

R. Alnoes and B. Sigrell, "Evaluation of the Outcome of Training Groups Using an Analytic Group Psychotherapy Technique," *Psychotherapy and Psychosomatics* 25(1975):268–75.

R. R. Dies, "Attitudes toward the Training of Group Psychotherapists," *Small Group Behavior* 5(1[1974]):65–79.

H. Mullan and M. Rosenbaum, *Group Psychotherapy* (New York: Free Press, 1978), pp. 115–73.

Ontario Group Psychotherapy Association Training Committee, "Trainee's Evaluation Form of Training Group Therapists," unpublished mimeographed, 1980 (available from Ontario Group Psychotherapy Affiliate, 27 Renova Drive, Etobicoke, Ontario M9C 3E8).

M. Pines, "Group Psychotherapy: Frame of Reference for Training," in W. DeMoor, W. Wijngaarden, and H. R. Wijngaarden, eds., *Psychotherapy: Research and Training* (Amsterdam: Elsevier/North Holland Biomedical Press, 1980), pp. 233–44.

J. T. Salvendy, "Group Psychotherapy Training: A Quest for Standards," *Canada Journal of Psychiatry* 25(1980):394–402.

R. Bathegay, "The Value of Analytic Self-experiencing Groups in the Training of Psychotherapists," *International Journal of Group Psychotherapy* 33(1983):199–213.

18. American Group Psychotherapy Association, 25 East 21st St., 6th floor, New York, N.Y. 10010.

19. Kaul and Bednar, "Experiential Group Research" [1].

I. Waskow and M. Parloff, eds., *Psychotherapy Change Measures* (Washington, D.C., N.I.M.H., U.S. Government Printing Office, Stock Number 1724–00397, 1975).

H. H. Strupp and S. W. Hadley "A Tripartite Model of Mental Health and Therapy Outcomes, *American Psychologist* 32(1977):187–96.

M. Smith, G. Glass, and T. Miller, *The Benefits of Psychotherapy* (Baltimore: The Johns Hopkins University Press, 1980).

A. Bergin and M. Lambert, "The Evaluation of Therapeutic Outcomes," in S. Garfield and A. Bergin, eds., *Handbook of Psychotherapy and Behavioral Change: An Empirical Analysis*, 2nd ed. (New York: John Wiley, 1978).

E. Coche, "Change Measures in Clinical Practice in Group Psychotherapy," in R. Dies and K. R. Mackenzie, eds., *Advances in Group Therapy* (New York: International Universities Press, 1983).

20. W. O. Jewell, cited by T. Volsky, et al., *The Outcomes of Counseling and Psychotherapy: Theory and Research* (Minneapolis: University of Minnesota Press, 1965), p. 154.

J. B. Chassan, *Research Design in Clinical Psychology and Psychiatry* (New York: Appleton-Century Crofts, 1967), p. 254.

21. E. Silber and J. S. Tippet, "Self-Esteem: Clinical Assessment and Validation," *Psychological Reports* 16(1965):1017–71.

22. M. B. Shapiro, "The Measurement of Clinically Relevant Variables," *Journal of Psychosomatic Research* 8(1964):245–54.

J. P. N. Phillips, "Techniques for Scaling the Symptoms of an Individual Psychiatric Patient," *Journal of Psychosomatic Research* 8(1964):255–71.

S. Kellam and J. B. Chassan "Social Context and Symptom Fluctuation," *Psychiatry* 25(1962):370–81.

P. Lewis and J. McCants, "Some Current Issues in Group Psychotherapy Research," *International Journal of Group Psychotherapy* 23(1973):268–91.

R. Weigel and J. Corazzini, "Small Group Research: Suggestions for Solving Common Methodological and Design Problems," *Small Group Behavior* 9(1978):193–220.

E. Coche, "Change Measures and Clinical Practice in Group Psychotherapy," in Dies and Mackenzie, eds. *Advances in Group Therapy* [19].

23. D. H. Malan, et al., "A Study of Psychodynamic Changes in Untreated Neurotic Patients. I: Improvements that are Questionable on Dynamic Criteria," *British Journal of Psychiatry* 114(1968):525–51.

24. S. Leacock, "Gertrude the Governess or Simple 17," *A Treasury of the Best Works of Stephen Leacock* (New York: Dodd Mead, 1954).

INDEX

Primary task *(continued)*
group development, 301; group flight from, 190; patient selection and, 228; in Tavistock approach, 194; written summaries and, 440
Primitive cultures, 180
Privacy, healthy need for, 364–65
Problem-solving groups, 285
Procedural norms, 130
Process, definition of, 137–43
Process illumination, 136, 143–45, 147–50; clinical illustrations of, 138–43, 147–48; and common group tensions, 161–63; mass group, 186–98; patient acceptance of, 170–72; and patient orientation, 168–70; of primary task versus secondary gratification, 163–66; and process recognition, 158–68; techniques of, 158–72; theoretical overview of, 172–81; and therapist's feelings, 167–68; in trainee groups, 530; *see also* Interpretations
Procrastination, 40–41
Professional interdisciplinary struggles, 460–61
Projection, 243
Projective identification, 354
Provocateurs, 312
Psathas, G., 117
Punch, 326
Psychoanalytic theory, 93–94; *see also* Freud, Sigmund
Psychological constructs, 179
Psychological testing, 256
Psychotic patients, 228, 395–402; in early stages of group, 395–97; hospitalized, *see* Acute inpatient groups; in later stages of group, 397–402; predictions of behavior of, 254; premature termination by, 232
Public esteem, 58–63
Punctuality, 314–20; *see also* Tardiness
Pure cognizance, 87, 88

Rand, K., 64, 245
Rank, Otto, 175
Rawlings, E., 294
Reactive fears, 196, 197
Reality testing: for borderline patients, 408–10; concurrent therapy and, 416; in consensual validation, 211; in corrective emotional experience, 26; and enabling solution, 197; and feedback to therapist, 219; and imitative behavior, 90; limited opportunity for, maladaptive self-disclosure and, 363; in therapeutic communities, 284; and therapist as model-setting

participant, 123; of transference neurosis, 200; and transference problems, 245
Rebellion in group development, 304–9
Reconstruction of past, 184
Recovery, Inc., 7, 13, 106, 135, 284, 427, 487
Re-entry phenomenon, 216
Referrals, inappropriate, 244
Regression: in borderline patients, 408; combatting of, in therapeutic communities, 284; fear of, 242; in inpatients, 470
Reibstein, J., 103
Reichling, P., 67n
Reinforcing techniques, 119–21
Religious fundamentalism, 238–39
Religious movements, 487
Removal of patients from group, 323–25; due to absenteeism, 316
Repetitive patterns, 171
Repression, 166
Research orientation, 533–37
Resistance, 152–53; analysis of, 451; to anxiety-laden issues, 188, 190; clinical illustration of, 153–54; to interventions, 344; and premature termination, 322; and primary task versus secondary gratification, 163, 166; to self-disclosure, 304; in tardiness and absenteeism, 314–15; of trainees to group experience, 525
Responsibility: concept of, 176; definition of, 98; fostered by leaderless meetings, 425; freedom and, 225; of group for its functioning, 125–26; preparing patients to assume, 294; and sexual relationships between members, 348–49; in therapeutic communities, 284
Restrictive solutions, 197
Retaliation, fear of, 144–45
Richard II (Shakespeare), 209
Rioch, M. J., 214
Risk-taking: in acute inpatient groups, 469, 484; cohesiveness and, 66; modeling and, 121; predictive validity of, 258; propensity for, as inclusion criterion, 246; in self-disclosure, 360–61
"Risky shift," 420
Rivalry, 354; and concurrent individual therapy, 417–18; dreams related to, 432–33; feelings of, 161, 162; transference and, 205, 207
Robber's Cave experiment, 65
Rogers, Carl, 56–57, 86, 352n, 361, 489, 496, 506
Rogers-Rablen scale, 57
Rohrbaugh, M., 86n
Role heterogeneity, 266–67
Role playing, social learning through, 16
Role switching, 470
Rorschach test, 232, 256